MY LIFE

MY LIFE

BY

RICHARD WAGNER

VOLUME ONE

Authorized Translation

WILDSIDE PRESS CLASSICS

MY LIFE BY RICHARD WAGNER

Published by Wildside Press LLC
www.wildsidebooks.com

PREFACE

THE contents of these volumes have been written down directly from my dictation, over a period of several years, by my friend and wife, who wished me to tell her the story of my life. It was the desire of both of us that these details of my life should be accessible to our family and to our sincere and trusted friends; and we decided therefore, in order to provide against a possible destruction of the one manuscript, to have a small number of copies printed at our own expense. As the value of this autobiography consists in its unadorned veracity, which, under the circumstances, is its only justification, therefore my statements had to be accompanied by precise names and dates; hence there could be no question of their publication until some time after my death, should interest in them still survive in our descendants, and on that point I intend leaving directions in my will.

If, on the other hand, we do not refuse certain intimate friends a sight of these papers now, it is that, relying on their genuine interest in the contents, we are confident that they will not pass on their knowledge to any who do not share their feelings in the matter.

RICHARD WAGNER.

CONTENTS

Part I. 1813–1842

	PAGES
CHILDHOOD AND SCHOOLDAYS	1-53
MUSICAL STUDIES	53-89
TRAVELS IN GERMANY (FIRST MARRIAGE)	89-195
PARIS: 1839-42	195-264

Part II. 1842–1850 (Dresden)

'RIENZI'	265-285
'THE FLYING DUTCHMAN'	285-321
LISZT, SPONTINI, MARSCHNER, ETC.	321-363
'TANNHÄUSER'	363-383
FRANCK, SCHUMANN, SEMPER, GUTZKOW, AUERBACH	383-393
'LOHENGRIN' (LIBRETTO)	393-397
NINTH SYMPHONY	397-403
SPOHR, GLUCK, HILLER, DEVRIENT	403-412
OFFICIAL POSITION. STUDIES IN HISTORICAL LITERATURE	412-417
'RIENZI' AT BERLIN	417-429
RELATIONS WITH THE MANAGEMENT, MOTHER'S DEATH, ETC.	429-439
GROWING SYMPATHY WITH POLITICAL EVENTS, BAKUNIN	439-472
THE MAY INSURRECTION	472-500
FLIGHT: WEIMAR, ZÜRICH, PARIS, BORDEAUX, GENEVA, ZÜRICH	500-543

CONTENTS

Part III. 1850–1861

PAGES

ZÜRICH: KARLRITTER, HANS VON BÜLOW, HERWEGH, UHLIG, WESENDONCKS, ETC 545-590

'NIBELUNGEN RING,' LISZT AT ZÜRICH, SCHOPENHAUER, COMPOSITION OF THE 'RHEINGOLD' AND 'WALKÜRE' . 590-619

LONDON (PHILHARMONIC CONCERTS) 619-636

ZÜRICH, SELISBERG, MORNEX, BRUNNEN ('TRISTAN') . . . 636-648

LISZT AND PRINCESS WITTGENSTEIN (ZÜRICH, ST. GALL) . . 648-656

THE 'ASYL' ('TRISTAN') 657-689

VENICE ('TRISTAN') 689-705

LUCERNE ('TRISTAN') 706-714

PARIS (PRODUCTION OF 'TANNHÄUSER') 714-786

Part IV. 1861–1864

WEIMAR, REICHENHALL, VIENNA 787-807

PARIS (LIBRETTO OF THE 'MEISTERSINGER') 807-811

BIEBRICH ('MEISTERSINGER') 811-844

VIENNA: REHEARSALS OF 'TRISTAN,' CONCERTS 845-851

CONCERTS AT ST. PETERSBURG AND MOSCOW 851-863

RESIDENCE AT PENZING, NEAR VIENNA 864-881

FLIGHT: ZÜRICH, STUTTGART 881-886

MESSAGE FROM THE KING 886-887

MY LIFE

MY LIFE

PART I

1813-1842

I was born at Leipzig on the 22nd of May 1813, in a room on the second floor of the 'Red and White Lion,' and two days later was baptized at St. Thomas's Church, and christened Wilhelm Richard.

My father, Friedrich Wagner, was at the time of my birth a clerk in the police service at Leipzig, and hoped to get the post of Chief Constable in that town, but he died in the October of that same year. His death was partly due to the great exertions imposed upon him by the stress of police work during the war troubles and the battle of Leipzig, and partly to the fact that he fell a victim to the nervous fever which was raging at that time. As regards his father's position in life, I learnt later that he had held a small civil appointment as toll collector at the Ranstädt Gate, but had distinguished himself from those in the same station by giving his two sons a superior education, my father, Friedrich, studying law, and the younger son, Adolph, theology.

My uncle subsequently exercised no small influence on my development; we shall meet him again at a critical turning-point in the story of my youth.

My father, whom I had lost so early, was, as I discovered afterwards, a great lover of poetry and literature in general, and possessed in particular an almost passionate affection for the drama, which was at that time much in vogue among the educated classes. My mother told me, among other things, that he took her to Lauchstädt for the first performance of the *Braut von Messina,* and that on the promenade he pointed out Schiller and Goethe to her, and reproved her warmly for never having heard of these great men. He is said to have been not altogether free from a gallant interest in actresses. My mother used to complain jokingly that she often had to keep lunch waiting for him while he was paying court to a certain famous actress of the day.[1] When she scolded him, he vowed that he had been delayed by papers that had to be attended to, and as a proof of his assertion pointed to his fingers, which were supposed to be stained with ink, but on closer inspection were found to be quite clean. His great fondness for the theatre was further shown by his choice of the actor, Ludwig Geyer, as one of his intimate friends. Although his choice of this friend was no doubt mainly due to his love for the theatre, he at the same time introduced into his family the noblest of benefactors; for this modest artist, prompted by a warm interest in the lot of his friend's large family, so unexpectedly left destitute, devoted the remainder of his life to making strenuous efforts to maintain and educate the orphans. Even when the police official was spending his evenings at the theatre, the worthy actor generally filled his place in the family circle, and it seems had frequently to appease my mother, who, rightly or wrongly, complained of the frivolity of her husband.

How deeply the homeless artist, hard pressed by life and tossed to and fro, longed to feel himself at home in a sympathetic family circle, was proved by the fact that a year after his friend's death he married his widow, and from that time forward became a most loving father to the seven children that had been left behind.

In this onerous undertaking he was favoured by an unexpected improvement in his position, for he obtained a remunerative, respectable, and permanent engagement, as a character actor, at the newly established Court Theatre in Dresden. His talent for painting, which had already helped him to earn a livelihood when forced by extreme poverty to break off his university studies, again stood him in good stead in his position at Dresden. True, he complained even more than his critics that he had been kept from a regular and systematic study of this art, yet his extraordinary aptitude, for portrait painting in particular, secured him such important commissions that he unfortunately exhausted his strength prematurely by his

[1] Madame Hartwig.

twofold exertions as painter and actor. Once, when he was invited to Munich to fulfil a temporary engagement at the Court Theatre, he received, through the distinguished recommendation of the Saxon Court, such pressing commissions from the Bavarian Court for portraits of the royal family that he thought it wise to cancel his contract altogether. He also had a turn for poetry. Besides fragments — often in very dainty verse — he wrote several comedies, one of which, *Der Bethlehemitische Kindermord*, in rhymed Alexandrines, was often performed; it was published and received the warmest praise from Goethe.

This excellent man, under whose care our family moved to Dresden when I was two years old, and by whom my mother had another daughter, Cecilia, now also took my education in hand with the greatest care and affection. He wished to adopt me altogether, and accordingly, when I was sent to my first school, he gave me his own name, so that till the age of fourteen I was known to my Dresden schoolfellows as Richard Geyer; and it was not until some years after my stepfather's death, and on my family's return to Leipzig, the home of my own kith and kin, that I resumed the name of Wagner.

The earliest recollections of my childhood are associated with my stepfather, and passed from him to the theatre. I well remember that he would have liked to see me develop a talent for painting; and his studio, with the easel and the pictures upon it, did not fail to impress me. I remember in particular that I tried, with a childish love of imitation, to copy a portrait of King Frederick Augustus of Saxony; but when this simple daubing had to give place to a serious study of drawing, I could not stand it, possibly because I was discouraged by the pedantic technique of my teacher, a cousin of mine, who was rather a bore. At one time during my early boyhood I became so weak after some childish ailment that my mother told me later she used almost to wish me dead, for it seemed as though I should never get well. However, my subsequent good health apparently astonished my parents. I afterwards learnt the noble part played by my excellent stepfather on this occasion also; he never gave way to despair, in spite of the cares and troubles of so large a family, but remained patient throughout, and never lost the hope of pulling me through safely.

My imagination at this time was deeply impressed by my acquaintance with the theatre, with which I was brought into contact, not only as a childish spectator from the mysterious stagebox, with its access to the stage, and by visits to the wardrobe with its fantastic costumes, wigs and other disguises, but also by taking a part in the performances myself. After I had been filled with fear by seeing my father play the villain's part in such tragedies as *Die Waise und der Mörder, Die beiden Galeerensklaven,* I occasionally took part in comedy. I remember that I appeared in *Der Weinberg an der Elbe,* a piece specially written to welcome the King of Saxony on his return from captivity, with music by the conductor, C. M. von Weber. In this I figured in a *tableau vivant* as an angel, sewn up in tights with wings on my back, in a graceful pose which I had laboriously practised. I also remember on this occasion being given a big iced cake, which I was assured the King had intended for me personally. Lastly, I can recall taking a child's part in which I had a few words to speak in Kotzebue's *Menschenhass und Reue,*[1] which furnished me with an excuse at school for not having learnt my lessons. I said I had too much to do, as I had to learn by heart an important part in *Den Menschen ausser der Reihe.*[2]

On the other hand, to show how seriously my father regarded my education, when I was six years old he took me to a clergyman in the country at Possendorf, near Dresden, where I was to be given a sound and healthy training with other boys of my own class. In the evening, the vicar, whose name was Wetzel, used to tell us the story of Robinson Crusoe, and discuss it with us in a highly instructive manner. I was, moreover, much impressed by a biography of Mozart which was read aloud; and the newspaper accounts and monthly reports of the events of the Greek War of Independence stirred my imagination deeply. My love for Greece, which afterwards made me turn with enthusiasm to the mythology and history of ancient Hellas, was thus the natural outcome of the intense and painful interest I took in the

[1] 'Misanthropy and Remorse.'
[2] 'The Man out of the Rank or Row.' In the German this is a simple phonetic corruption of Kotzebue's title, which might easily occur to a child who had only heard, and not read, that title. — EDITOR.

events of this period. In after years the story of the struggle of the Greeks against the Persians always revived my impressions of this modern revolt of Greece against the Turks.

One day, when I had been in this country home scarcely a year, a messenger came from town to ask the vicar to take me to my parents' house in Dresden, as my father was dying.

We did the three hours' journey on foot; and as I was very exhausted when I arrived, I scarcely understood why my mother was crying. The next day I was taken to my father's bedside; the extreme weakness with which he spoke to me, combined with all the precautions taken in the last desperate treatment of his complaint — acute hydrothorax — made the whole scene appear like a dream to me, and I think I was too frightened and surprised to cry.

In the next room my mother asked me to show her what I could play on the piano, wisely hoping to divert my father's thoughts by the sound. I played *Ueb' immer Treu' und Redlichkeit,* and my father said to her, 'Is it possible he has musical talent?'

In the early hours of the next morning my mother came into the great night nursery, and, standing by the bedside of each of us in turn, told us, with sobs, that our father was dead, and gave us each a message with his blessing. To me she said, ' He hoped to make something of you.'

In the afternoon my schoolmaster, Wetzel, came to take me back to the country. We walked the whole way to Possendorf, arriving at nightfall. On the way I asked him many questions about the stars, of which he gave me my first intelligent idea.

A week later my stepfather's brother arrived from Eisleben for the funeral. He promised, as far as he was able, to support the family, which was now once more destitute, and undertook to provide for my future education.

I took leave of my companions and of the kind-hearted clergyman, and it was for his funeral that I paid my next visit to Possendorf a few years later. I did not go to the place again till long afterwards, when I visited it on an excursion such as I often made, far into the country, at the time when I was conducting the orchestra in Dresden. I was much grieved not to find the old parsonage still there, but in its place a more pretentious modern structure, which so turned me against the locality, that thenceforward my excursions were always made in another direction.

This time my uncle brought me back to Dresden in the carriage. I found my mother and sister in the deepest mourning, and remember being received for the first time with a tenderness not usual in our family; and I noticed that the same tenderness marked our leavetaking, when, a few days later, my uncle took me with him to Eisleben.

This uncle, who was a younger brother of my stepfather, had settled there as a goldsmith, and Julius, one of my elder brothers, had already been apprenticed to him. Our old grandmother also lived with this bachelor son, and as it was evident that she could not live long, she was not informed of the death of her eldest son, which I, too, was bidden to keep to myself. The servant carefully removed the crape from my coat, telling me she would keep it until my grandmother died, which was likely to be soon.

I was now often called upon to tell her about my father, and it was no great difficulty for me to keep the secret of his death, as I had scarcely realised it myself. She lived in a dark back room looking out upon a narrow courtyard, and took a great delight in watching the robins that fluttered freely about her, and for which she always kept fresh green boughs by the stove. When some of these robins were killed by the cat, I managed to catch others for her in the neighbourhood, which pleased her very much, and, in return, she kept me tidy and clean. Her death, as had been expected, took place before long, and the crape that had been put away was now openly worn in Eisleben.

The back room, with its robins and green branches, now knew me no more, but I soon made myself at home with a soap-boiler's family, to whom the house belonged, and became popular with them on account of the stories I told them.

I was sent to a private school kept by a man called Weiss, who left an impression of gravity and dignity upon my mind.

Towards the end of the fifties I was greatly moved at reading in a musical paper the account of a concert at Eisleben, consisting of parts of *Tannhäuser,* at which my former master, who had not forgotten his young pupil, had been present.

The little old town with Luther's house, and the numberless memorials it contained of his stay there, has often, in later days, come back to me in dreams. I have always wished to revisit it and verify the clearness of my recollections, but, strange to say, it has never been my fate to do so. We lived in the market-place, where I was often entertained by strange sights, such, for instance, as performances by a troupe of acrobats, in which a man walked a rope stretched from tower to tower across the square, an achievement which long inspired me with a passion for such feats of daring. Indeed, I got so far as to walk a rope fairly easily myself with the help of a balancing-pole. I had made the rope out of cords twisted together and stretched across the courtyard, and even now I still feel a desire to gratify my acrobatic instincts. The thing that attracted me most, however, was the brass band of a Hussar regiment quartered at Eisleben. It often played a certain piece which had just come out, and which was making a great sensation, I mean the 'Huntsmen's Chorus' out of the *Freischütz,* that had been recently performed at the Opera in Berlin. My uncle and brother asked me eagerly about its composer, Weber, whom I must have seen at my parents' house in Dresden, when he was conductor of the orchestra there.

About the same time the *Jungfernkranz* was zealously played and sung by some friends who lived near us. These two pieces cured me of my weakness for the 'Ypsilanti' Waltz, which till that time I had regarded as the most wonderful of compositions.

I have recollections of frequent tussles with the town boys, who were constantly mocking at me for my 'square' cap; and I remember, too, that I was very fond of rambles of adventure among the rocky banks of the Unstrut.

My uncle's marriage late in life, and the starting of his new home, brought about a marked alteration in his relations to my family.

After a lapse of a year I was taken by him to Leipzig, and handed over for some days to the Wagners, my own father's relatives, consisting of my uncle Adolph and his sister

Friederike Wagner. This extraordinarily interesting man, whose influence afterwards became ever more stimulating to me, now for the first time brought himself and his singular environment into my life.

He and my aunt were very close friends of Jeannette Thomé, a queer old maid who shared with them a large house in the market-place, in which, if I am not mistaken, the Electoral family of Saxony had, ever since the days of Augustus the Strong, hired and furnished the two principal storeys for their own use whenever they were in Leipzig.

So far as I know, Jeannette Thomé really owned the second storey, of which she inhabited only a modest apartment looking out on the courtyard. As, however, the King merely occupied the hired rooms for a few days in the year, Jeannette and her circle generally made use of his splendid apartments, and one of these staterooms was made into a bedroom for me.

The decorations and fittings of these rooms also dated from the days of Augustus the Strong. They were luxurious with heavy silk and rich rococo furniture, all of which were much soiled with age. As a matter of fact, I was delighted by these large strange rooms, looking out upon the bustling Leipzig market-place, where I loved above all to watch the students in the crowd making their way along in their old-fashioned 'Club' attire, and filling up the whole width of the street.

There was only one portion of the decorations of the rooms that I thoroughly disliked, and this consisted of the various portraits, but particularly those of high-born dames in hooped petticoats, with youthful faces and powdered hair. These appeared to me exactly like ghosts, who, when I was alone in the room, seemed to come back to life, and filled me with the most abject fear. To sleep alone in this distant chamber, in that old-fashioned bed of state, beneath those unearthly pictures, was a constant terror to me. It is true I tried to hide my fear from my aunt when she lighted me to bed in the evening with her candle, but never a night passed in which I was not a prey to the most horrible ghostly visions, my dread of which would leave me in a bath of perspiration.

The personality of the three chief occupants of this storey was admirably adapted to materialise the ghostly impressions of the house into a reality that resembled some strange fairy-tale.

Jeannette Thomé was very small and stout; she wore a fair Titus wig, and seemed to hug to herself the consciousness of vanished beauty. My aunt, her faithful friend and guardian, who was also an old maid, was remarkable for the height and extreme leanness of her person. The oddity of her otherwise very pleasant face was increased by an exceedingly pointed chin.

My uncle Adolph had chosen as his permanent study a dark room in the courtyard. There it was that I saw him for the first time, surrounded by a great wilderness of books, and attired in an unpretentious indoor costume, the most striking feature of which was a tall, pointed felt cap, such as I had seen worn by the clown who belonged to the troupe of rope-dancers at Eisleben. A great love of independence had driven him to this strange retreat. He had been originally destined for the Church, but he soon gave that up, in order to devote himself entirely to philological studies. But as he had the greatest dislike of acting as a professor and teacher in a regular post, he soon tried to make a meagre livelihood by literary work. He had certain social gifts, and especially a fine tenor voice, and appears in his youth to have been welcome as a man of letters among a fairly wide circle of friends at Leipzig.

On a trip to Jena, during which he and a companion seem to have found their way into various musical and oratorical associations, he paid a visit to Schiller. With this object in view, he had come armed with a request from the management of the Leipzig Theatre, who wanted to secure the rights of *Wallenstein,* which was just finished. He told me later of the magic impression made upon him by Schiller, with his tall slight figure and irresistibly attractive blue eyes. His only complaint was that, owing to a well-meant trick played on him by his friend, he had been placed in a most trying position; for the latter had managed to send Schiller a small volume of Adolph Wagner's poems in advance.

The young poet was much embarrassed to hear Schiller address him in flattering terms on the subject of his poetry, but was convinced that the great man was merely encouraging him out of kindness. Afterwards he devoted himself entirely to philological studies — one of his best-known publications in that department being his *Parnasso Italiano,* which he dedicated to Goethe in an Italian poem. True, I have heard experts say that the latter was written in unusually pompous Italian; but Goethe sent him a letter full of praise, as well as a silver cup from his own household plate. The impression that I, as a boy of eight, conceived of Adolph Wagner, amid the surroundings of his own home, was that he was a peculiarly puzzling character.

I soon had to leave the influence of this environment and was brought back to my people at Dresden. Meanwhile my family, under the guidance of my bereaved mother, had been obliged to settle down as well as they could under the circumstances. My eldest brother Albert, who originally intended to study medicine, had, upon the advice of Weber, who had much admired his beautiful tenor voice, started his theatrical career in Breslau. My second sister Louisa soon followed his example, and became an actress. My eldest sister Rosalie had obtained an excellent engagement at the Dresden Court Theatre, and the younger members of the family all looked up to her; for she was now the main support of our poor sorrowing mother. My family still occupied the same comfortable home which my father had made for them. Some of the spare rooms were occasionally let to strangers, and Spohr was among those who at one time lodged with us. Thanks to her great energy, and to help received from various sources (among which the continued generosity of the Court, out of respect to the memory of my late stepfather, must not be forgotten), my mother managed so well in making both ends meet, that even my education did not suffer.

After it had been decided that my sister Clara, owing to her exceedingly beautiful voice, should also go on the stage, my mother took the greatest care to prevent me from developing any taste whatever for the theatre. She never ceased to reproach herself for having consented to the theatrical career of my eldest brother, and as my second brother showed no greater talents than those which were useful to him as a goldsmith, it was now her chief desire to see some progress made towards the fulfilment of the hopes and wishes of my stepfather, 'who hoped to make something of me.' On the completion of my eighth year I was sent to the Kreuz Grammar School in Dresden, where it was hoped I would study! There I was placed at the bottom of the lowest class, and started my education under the most unassuming auspices.

My mother noted with much interest the slightest signs I might show of a growing love and ability for my work. She herself, though not highly educated, always created a lasting impression on all who really learnt to know her, and displayed a peculiar combination of practical domestic efficiency and keen intellectual animation. She never gave one of her children any definite information concerning her antecedents. She came from Weissenfels, and admitted that her parents had been bakers [1] there. Even in regard to her maiden name she always spoke with some embarrassment, and intimated that it was 'Perthes,' though, as we afterwards ascertained, it was in reality 'Bertz.' Strange to say, she had been placed in a high-class boarding-school in Leipzig, where she had enjoyed the advantage of the care and interest of one of 'her father's influential friends,' to whom she afterwards referred as being a Weimar prince who had been very kind to her family in Weissenfels. Her education in that establishment seems to have been interrupted on account of the sudden death of this 'friend.' She became acquainted with my father at a very early age, and married him in the first bloom of her youth, he also being very young, though he already held an appointment. Her chief characteristics seem to have been a keen sense of humour and an amiable temper, so we need not suppose that it was merely a sense of duty towards the family of a departed comrade that afterwards induced the admirable Ludwig Geyer to enter into matrimony with her when she was no longer youthful, but rather that he was impelled to that step by a sincere and warm regard for the widow of his friend. A portrait of her, painted by Geyer during the lifetime of my father, gives one a very favourable impression of what she must have been. Even from the time when my recollection of her is quite distinct, she always had to wear a cap owing to some slight affection of the head, so that I have no recollection of her as

[1] According to more recent information — mill-owners.

a young and pretty mother. Her trying position at the head of a numerous family (of which I was the seventh surviving member), the difficulty of obtaining the wherewithal to rear them, and of keeping up appearances on very limited resources, did not conduce to evolve that tender sweetness and solicitude which are usually associated with motherhood. I hardly ever recollect her having fondled me. Indeed, demonstrations of affection were not common in our family, although a certain impetuous, almost passionate and boisterous manner always characterised our dealings. This being so, it naturally seemed to me quite a great event when one night I, fretful with sleepiness, looked up at her with tearful eyes as she was taking me to bed, and saw her gaze back at me proudly and fondly, and speak of me to a visitor then present with a certain amount of tenderness.

What struck me more particularly about her was the strange enthusiasm and almost pathetic manner with which she spoke of the great and of the beautiful in Art. Under this heading, however, she would never have let me suppose that she included dramatic art, but only Poetry, Music, and Painting. Consequently, she often even threatened me with her curse should I ever express a desire to go on the stage. Moreover, she was very religiously inclined. With intense fervour she would often give us long sermons about God and the divine quality in man, during which, now and again, suddenly lowering her voice in a rather funny way, she would interrupt herself in order to rebuke one of us. After the death of our stepfather she used to assemble us all round her bed every morning, when one of us would read out a hymn or a part of the Church service from the prayer-book before she took her coffee. Sometimes the choice of the part to be read was hardly appropriate, as, for instance, when my sister Clara on one occasion thoughtlessly read the 'Prayer to be said in time of War,' and delivered it with so much expression that my mother interrupted her, saying: 'Oh, stop! Good gracious me! Things are not quite so bad as that. There's no war on at present!'

In spite of our limited means we had lively and — as they appeared to my boyish imagination — even brilliant evening parties sometimes. After the death of my stepfather, who, thanks to his success as a portrait painter, in the later years of his life had raised his income to what for those days was a really decent total, many agreeable acquaintances of very good social position whom he had made during this flourishing period still remained on friendly terms with us, and would occasionally join us at our evening gatherings. Amongst those who came were the members of the Court Theatre, who at that time gave very charming and highly entertaining parties of their own, which, on my return to Dresden later on, I found had been altogether given up.

Very delightful, too, were the picnics arranged between us and our friends at some of the beautiful spots around Dresden, for these excursions were always brightened by a certain artistic spirit and general good cheer. I remember one such outing we arranged to Loschwitz, where we made a kind of gypsy camp, in which Carl Maria von Weber played his part in the character of cook. At home we also had some music. My sister Rosalie played the piano, and Clara was beginning to sing. Of the various theatrical performances we organised in those early days, often after elaborate preparation, with the view of amusing ourselves on the birthdays of our elders, I can hardly remember one, save a parody on the romantic play of *Sappho*, by Grillparzer, in which I took part as one of the singers in the crowd that preceded Phaon's triumphal car. I endeavoured to revive these memories by means of a fine puppet show, which I found among the effects of my late stepfather, and for which he himself had painted some beautiful scenery. It was my intention to surprise my people by means of a brilliant performance on this little stage. After I had very clumsily made several puppets, and had provided them with a scanty wardrobe made from cuttings of material purloined from my sisters, I started to compose a chivalric drama, in which I proposed to rehearse my puppets. When I had drafted the first scene, my sisters happened to discover the MS. and literally laughed it to scorn, and, to my great annoyance, for a long time afterwards they chaffed me by repeating one particular sentence which I had put into the mouth of the heroine, and which was — *Ich höre schon den Ritter trabsen* (' I hear his knightly footsteps falling ').

I now returned with renewed ardour to the theatre, with which, even at this time, my family was in close touch. *Der Freischütz* in particular appealed very strongly to my imagination, mainly on account of its ghostly theme. The emotions of terror and the dread of ghosts formed quite an important factor in the development of my mind. From my earliest childhood certain mysterious and uncanny things exercised an enormous influence over me. If I were left alone in a room for long, I remember that, when gazing at lifeless objects such as pieces of furniture, and concentrating my attention upon them, I would suddenly shriek out with fright, because they seemed to me alive. Even during the latest years of my boyhood, not a night passed without my waking out of some ghostly dream and uttering the most frightful shrieks, which subsided only at the sound of some human voice. The most severe rebuke or even chastisement seemed to me at those times no more than a blessed release. None of my brothers or sisters would sleep anywhere near me. They put me to sleep as far as possible away from the others, without thinking that my cries for help would only be louder and longer; but in the end they got used even to this nightly disturbance.

In connection with this childish terror, what attracted me so strongly to the theatre — by which I mean also the stage, the rooms behind the scenes, and the dressing-rooms — was not so much the desire for entertainment and amusement such as that which impels the present-day theatre-goers, but the fascinating pleasure of finding myself in an entirely different atmosphere, in a world that was purely fantastic and often gruesomely attractive. Thus to me a scene, even a wing, representing a bush, or some costume or characteristic part of it, seemed to come from another world, to be in some way as attractive as an apparition, and I felt that contact with it might serve as a lever to lift me from the dull reality of daily routine to that delightful region of spirits. Everything connected with a theatrical performance had for me the charm of mystery, it both bewitched and fascinated me, and while I was trying, with the help of a few playmates, to imitate the performance of *Der Freischütz,* and to devote myself energetically to reproducing the needful costumes and masks in my

STUDY OF MATHEMATICS AND THE CLASSICS

grotesque style of painting, the more elegant contents of my sisters' wardrobes, in the beautifying of which I had often seen the family occupied, exercised a subtle charm over my imagination; nay, my heart would beat madly at the very touch of one of their dresses.

In spite of the fact that, as I already mentioned, our family was not given to outward manifestations of affection, yet the fact that I was brought up entirely among feminine surroundings must necessarily have influenced the development of the sensitive side of my nature. Perhaps it was precisely because my immediate circle was generally rough and impetuous, that the opposite characteristics of womanhood, especially such as were connected with the imaginary world of the theatre, created a feeling of such tender longing in me.

Luckily these fantastic humours, merging from the gruesome into the mawkish, were counteracted and balanced by more serious influences undergone at school at the hands of my teachers and schoolfellows. Even there, it was chiefly the weird that aroused my keenest interest. I can hardly judge whether I had what would be called a good head for study. I think that, in general, what I really liked I was soon able to grasp without much effort, whereas I hardly exerted myself at all in the study of subjects that were uncongenial. This characteristic was most marked in regard to arithmetic and, later on, mathematics. In neither of these subjects did I ever succeed in bringing my mind seriously to bear upon the tasks that were set me. In the matter of the Classics, too, I paid only just as much attention as was absolutely necessary to enable me to get a grasp of them; for I was stimulated by the desire to reproduce them to myself dramatically. In this way Greek particularly attracted me, because the stories from Greek mythology so seized upon my fancy that I tried to imagine their heroes as speaking to me in their native tongue, so as to satisfy my longing for complete familiarity with them. In these circumstances it will be readily understood that the grammar of the language seemed to me merely a tiresome obstacle, and by no means in itself an interesting branch of knowledge.

The fact that my study of languages was never very thorough, perhaps best explains the fact that I was afterwards so ready to cease troubling about them altogether. Not until much later did this study really begin to interest me again, and that was only when I learnt to understand its physiological and philosophical side, as it was revealed to our modern Germanists by the pioneer work of Jakob Grimm. Then, when it was too late to apply myself thoroughly to a study which at last I had learned to appreciate, I regretted that this newer conception of the study of languages had not yet found acceptance in our colleges when I was younger.

Nevertheless, by my successes in philological work I managed to attract the attention of a young teacher at the Kreuz Grammar School, a Master of Arts named Sillig, who proved very helpful to me. He often permitted me to visit him and show him my work, consisting of metric translations and a few original poems, and he always seemed very pleased with my efforts in recitation. What he thought of me may best be judged perhaps from the fact that he made me, as a boy of about twelve, recite not only 'Hector's Farewell' from the *Iliad,* but even Hamlet's celebrated monologue. On one occasion, when I was in the fourth form of the school, one of my schoolfellows, a boy named Starke, suddenly fell dead, and the tragic event aroused so much sympathy, that not only did the whole school attend the funeral, but the headmaster also ordered that a poem should be written in commemoration of the ceremony, and that this poem should be published. Of the various poems submitted, among which there was one by myself, prepared very hurriedly, none seemed to the master worthy of the honour which he had promised, and he therefore announced his intention of substituting one of his own speeches in the place of our rejected attempts. Much distressed by this decision, I quickly sought out Professor Sillig, with the view of urging him to intervene on behalf of my poem. We thereupon went through it together. Its well-constructed and well-rhymed verses, written in stanzas of eight lines, determined him to revise the whole of it carefully. Much of its imagery was bombastic, and far beyond the conception of a boy of my age. I recollect that in one part I had drawn extensively from the monologue in Addison's *Cato,* spoken by Cato just before his suicide. I had met with this passage in an English grammar, and it had made a deep impression upon me. The words: 'The stars shall fade away, the sun himself grow dim with age, and nature sink in years,' which, at all events, were a direct plagiarism, made Sillig laugh — a thing at which I was a little offended. However, I felt very grateful to him, for, thanks to the care and rapidity with which he cleared my poem of these extravagances, it was eventually accepted by the headmaster, printed, and widely circulated.

The effect of this success was extraordinary, both on my schoolfellows and on my own family. My mother devoutly folded her hands in thankfulness, and in my own mind my vocation seemed quite a settled thing. It was clear, beyond the possibility of a doubt, that I was destined to be a poet. Professor Sillig wished me to compose a grand epic, and suggested as a subject 'The Battle of Parnassus,' as described by Pausanias. His reasons for this choice were based upon the legend related by Pausanias, viz., that in the second century B.C. the Muses from Parnassus aided the combined Greek armies against the destructive invasion of the Gauls by provoking a panic among the latter. I actually began my heroic poem in hexameter verse, but could not get through the first canto.

Not being far enough advanced in the language to understand the Greek tragedies thoroughly in the original, my own attempts to construct a tragedy in the Greek form were greatly influenced by the fact that quite by accident I came across August Apel's clever imitation of this style in his striking poems 'Polyïdos' and 'Aitolier.' For my theme I selected the death of Ulysses, from a fable of Hyginus, according to which the aged hero is killed by his son, the offspring of his union with Calypso. But I did not get very far with this work either, before I gave it up.

My mind became so bent upon this sort of thing, that duller studies naturally ceased to interest me. The mythology, legends, and, at last, the history of Greece alone attracted me.

I was fond of life, merry with my companions, and always ready for a joke or an adventure. Moreover, I was constantly forming friendships, almost passionate in their ardour, with one or the other of my comrades, and in choosing my associates I was mainly influenced by the extent to which my new acquaintance appealed to my eccentric imagination. At one time it would be poetising and versifying that decided my choice of a friend; at another, theatrical enterprises, while now and then it would be a longing for rambling and mischief.

Furthermore, when I reached my thirteenth year, a great change came over our family affairs. My sister Rosalie, who had become the chief support of our household, obtained an advantageous engagement at the theatre in Prague, whither mother and children removed in 1826, thus giving up the Dresden home altogether. I was left behind in Dresden, so that I might continue to attend the Kreuz Grammar School until I was ready to go up to the university. I was therefore sent to board and lodge with a family named Böhme, whose sons I had known at school, and in whose house I already felt quite at home. With my residence in this somewhat rough, poor, and not particularly well-conducted family, my years of dissipation began. I no longer enjoyed the quiet retirement necessary for work, nor the gentle, spiritual influence of my sisters' companionship. On the contrary, I was plunged into a busy, restless life, full of rough horseplay and of quarrels. Nevertheless, it was there that I began to experience the influence of the gentler sex in a manner hitherto unknown to me, as the grown-up daughters of the family and their friends often filled the scanty and narrow rooms of the house. Indeed, my first recollections of boyish love date from this period. I remember a very beautiful young girl, whose name, if I am not mistaken, was Amalie Hoffmann, coming to call at the house one Sunday. She was charmingly dressed, and her appearance as she came into the room literally struck me dumb with amazement. On other occasions I recollect pretending to be too helplessly sleepy to move, so that I might be carried up to bed by the girls, that being, as they thought, the only remedy for my condition. And I repeated this, because I found, to my surprise, that their attention under these circumstances brought me into closer and more gratifying proximity with them.

The most important event during this year of separation from my family was, however, a short visit I paid to them in Prague. In the middle of the winter my mother came to Dresden, and took me back with her to Prague for a week. Her way of travelling was quite unique. To the end of her days she preferred the more dangerous mode of travelling in a hackney carriage to the quicker journey by mail-coach, so that we spent three whole days in the bitter cold on the road from Dresden to Prague. The journey over the Bohemian mountains often seemed to be beset with the greatest dangers, but happily we survived our thrilling adventures and at last arrived in Prague, where I was suddenly plunged into entirely new surroundings.

For a long time the thought of leaving Saxony on another visit to Bohemia, and especially Prague, had had quite a romantic attraction for me. The foreign nationality, the broken German of the people, the peculiar headgear of the women, the native wines, the harp-girls and musicians, and finally, the ever present signs of Catholicism, its numerous chapels and shrines, all produced on me a strangely exhilarating impression. This was probably due to my craze for everything theatrical and spectacular, as distinguished from simple bourgeois customs. Above all, the antique splendour and beauty of the incomparable city of Prague became indelibly stamped on my fancy. Even in my own family surroundings I found attractions to which I had hitherto been a stranger. For instance, my sister Ottilie, only two years older than myself, had won the devoted friendship of a noble family, that of Count Pachta, two of whose daughters, Jenny and Auguste, who had long been famed as the leading beauties of Prague, had become fondly attached to her. To me, such people and such a connection were something quite novel and enchanting. Besides these, certain *beaux esprits* of Prague, among them W. Marsano, a strikingly handsome and charming man, were frequent visitors at our house. They often earnestly discussed the tales of Hoffmann, which at that date were comparatively new, and had created some sensation. It was now that I made my first though rather superficial acquaintance with this romantic visionary, and so received a stimulus which influenced me for many years even to the point of infatuation, and gave me very peculiar ideas of the world.

In the following spring, 1827, I repeated this journey from Dresden to Prague, but this time on foot, and accompanied by my friend Rudolf Böhme. Our tour was full of adventure. We got to within an hour of Teplitz the first night, and next day we had to get a lift in a wagon, as we had walked our feet sore; yet this only took us as far as Lowositz, as our funds had quite run out. Under a scorching sun, hungry and half-fainting, we wandered along bypaths through absolutely unknown country, until at sundown we happened to reach the main road just as an elegant travelling coach came in sight. I humbled my pride so far as to pretend I was a travelling journeyman, and begged the distinguished travellers for alms, while my friend timidly hid himself in the ditch by the roadside. Luckily we decided to seek shelter for the night in an inn, where we took counsel whether we should spend the alms just received on a supper or a bed. We decided for the supper, proposing to spend the night under the open sky. While we were refreshing ourselves, a strange-looking wayfarer entered. He wore a black velvet skull-cap, to which a metal lyre was attached like a cockade, and on his back he bore a harp. Very cheerfully he set down his instrument, made himself comfortable, and called for a good meal. He intended to stay the night, and to continue his way next day to Prague, where he lived, and whither he was returning from Hanover.

My good spirits and courage were stimulated by the jovial manners of this merry fellow, who constantly repeated his favourite motto, '*non plus ultra.*' We soon struck up an acquaintance, and in return for my confidence, the strolling player's attitude to me was one of almost touching sympathy. It was agreed that we should continue our journey together next day on foot. He lent me two twenty-kreutzer pieces (about ninepence), and allowed me to write my Prague address in his pocket-book. I was highly delighted at this personal success. My harpist grew extravagantly merry; a good deal of Czernosek wine was drunk; he sang and played on his harp like a madman, continually reiterating his '*non plus ultra,*' till at last, overcome with wine, he fell down on the straw, which had been spread out on the floor for our common bed. When the sun once more peeped in, we could not rouse him, and we had to make up our minds to set off in the freshness of the early morning without him, feeling convinced that the sturdy fellow would overtake us during the day. But it was in vain that we looked out for him on the road and during our subsequent stay in Prague. Indeed, it was not until several weeks later that the extraordinary fellow turned up at my mother's, not so much to collect payment of his loan, as to inquire about the welfare of the young friend to whom that loan had been made.

The remainder of our journey was very fatiguing, and the joy I felt when I at last beheld Prague from the summit of a hill, at about an hour's distance, simply beggars description. Approaching the suburbs, we were for the second time met by a splendid carriage, from which my sister Ottilie's two lovely friends called out to me in astonishment. They had recognised me immediately, in spite of my terribly sunburnt face, blue linen blouse, and bright red cotton cap. Overwhelmed with shame, and with my heart beating like mad, I could hardly utter a word, and hurried away to my mother's to attend at once to the restoration of my sunburnt complexion. To this task I devoted two whole days, during which I swathed my face in parsley poultices; and not till then did I seek the pleasures of society. When, on the return journey, I looked back once more on Prague from the same hilltop, I burst into tears, flung myself on the earth, and for a long time could not be induced by my astonished companion to pursue the journey. I was downcast for the rest of the way, and we arrived home in Dresden without any further adventures.

During the same year I again gratified my fancy for long excursions on foot by joining a numerous company of grammar school boys, consisting of pupils of several classes and of various ages, who had decided to spend their summer holidays in a tour to Leipzig. This journey also stands out among the memories of my youth, by reason of the strong impressions it left behind. The characteristic feature of our party was that we all aped the student, by behaving and dressing extravagantly in the most approved student fashion. After going as far as Meissen on the market-boat, our path lay off the main road.

through villages with which I was as yet unfamiliar. We spent the night in the vast barn of a village inn, and our adventures were of the wildest description. There we saw a large marionette show, with almost life-sized figures. Our entire party settled themselves in the auditorium, where their presence was a source of some anxiety to the managers, who had only reckoned on an audience of peasants. *Genovefa* was the play given. The ceaseless silly jests, and constant interpolations and jeering interruptions, in which our corps of embryo-students indulged, finally aroused the anger even of the peasants, who had come prepared to weep. I believe I was the only one of our party who was pained by these impertinences, and in spite of involuntary laughter at some of my comrades' jokes, I not only defended the play itself, but also its original, simple-minded audience. A popular catch-phrase which occurred in the piece has ever since remained stamped on my memory. 'Golo' instructs the inevitable Kaspar that, when the Count Palatine returns home, he must 'tickle him behind, so that he should feel it in front' (*hinten zu kitzeln, dass er es vorne fühle*). Kaspar conveys Golo's order verbatim to the Count, and the latter reproaches the unmasked rogue in the following terms, uttered with the greatest pathos: 'O Golo, Golo! thou hast told Kaspar to tickle me behind, so that I shall feel it in front!'

From Grimma our party rode into Leipzig in open carriages, but not until we had first carefully removed all the outward emblems of the undergraduate, lest the local students we were likely to meet might make us rue our presumption.

Since my first visit, when I was eight years old, I had only once returned to Leipzig, and then for a very brief stay, and under circumstances very similar to those of the earlier visit. I now renewed my fantastic impressions of the Thomé house, but this time, owing to my more advanced education, I looked forward to more intelligent intercourse with my uncle Adolph. An opening for this was soon provided by my joyous astonishment on learning that a bookcase in the large anteroom, containing a goodly collection of books, was my property, having been left me by my father. I went through the books with my uncle, selected at once a number of Latin authors in the handsome Zweibrück edition, along with sundry attractive looking works of poetry and *belles-lettres*, and arranged for them to be sent to Dresden. During this visit I was very much interested in the life of the students. In addition to my impressions of the theatre and of Prague, now came those of the so-called swaggering undergraduate. A great change had taken place in this class. When, as a lad of eight, I had my first glimpse of students, their long hair, their old German costume with the black velvet skull-cap and the shirt collar turned back from the bare neck, had quite taken my fancy. But since that time the old student 'associations' which affected this fashion had disappeared in the face of police prosecutions. On the other hand, the national student clubs, no less peculiar to Germans, had become conspicuous. These clubs adopted, more or less, the fashion of the day, but with some little exaggeration. Albeit, their dress was clearly distinguishable from that of other classes, owing to its picturesqueness, and especially its display of the various club-colours. The 'Comment,' that compendium of pedantic rules of conduct for the preservation of a defiant and exclusive *esprit de corps,* as opposed to the bourgeois classes, had its fantastic side, just as the most philistine peculiarities of the Germans have, if you probe them deeply enough. To me it represented the idea of emancipation from the yoke of school and family. The longing to become a student coincided unfortunately with my growing dislike for drier studies and with my ever-increasing fondness for cultivating romantic poetry. The results of this soon showed themselves in my resolute attempts to make a change.

At the time of my confirmation, at Easter, 1827, I had considerable doubt about this ceremony, and I already felt a serious falling off of my reverence for religious observances. The boy who, not many years before, had gazed with agonised sympathy on the altarpiece in the Kreuz Kirche (Church of the Holy Cross), and had yearned with ecstatic fervour to hang upon the Cross in place of the Saviour, had now so far lost his veneration for the clergyman, whose preparatory confirmation classes he attended, as to be quite ready to make fun of him, and even to join with his comrades in withholding part of his class fees, and spending the money in sweets. How matters stood with me spiritually was revealed to me, almost to my horror, at the Communion service, when I walked in procession with my fellow-communicants to the altar to the sound of organ and choir. The shudder with which I received the Bread and Wine was so ineffaceably stamped on my memory, that I never again partook of the Communion, lest I should do so with levity. To avoid this was all the easier for me, seeing that among Protestants such participation is not compulsory.

I soon, however, seized, or rather created, an opportunity of forcing a breach with the Kreuz Grammar School, and thus compelled my family to let me go to Leipzig. In self-defence against what I considered an unjust punishment with which I was threatened by the assistant headmaster, Baumgarten-Crusius, for whom I otherwise had great respect, I asked to be discharged immediately from the school on the ground of sudden summons to join my family in Leipzig. I had already left the Böhme household three months before, and now lived alone in a small garret, where I was waited on by the widow of a court plate-washer, who at every meal served up the familiar thin Saxon coffee as almost my sole nourishment. In this attic I did little else but write verses. Here, too, I formed the first outlines of that stupendous tragedy which afterwards filled my family with such consternation. The irregular habits I acquired through this premature domestic independence induced my anxious mother to consent very readily to my removal to Leipzig, the more so as a part of our scattered family had already migrated there.

My longing for Leipzig, originally aroused by the fantastic impressions I had gained there, and later by my enthusiasm for a student's life, had recently been still further stimulated. I had seen scarcely anything of my sister Louisa, at that time a girl of about twenty-two, as she had gone to the theatre of Breslau shortly after our stepfather's death. Quite recently she had been in Dresden for a few days on her way to Leipzig, having accepted an engagement at the theatre there. This meeting with my almost unknown sister, her hearty manifestations of joy at seeing me again, as well as her sprightly, merry disposition, quite won my heart. To live with her seemed an alluring prospect, especially as my mother and

Ottilie had joined her for a while. For the first time a sister had treated me with some tenderness. When at last I reached Leipzig at Christmas in the same year (1827), and there found my mother with Ottilie and Cecilia (my half-sister), I fancied myself in heaven. Great changes, however, had already taken place. Louisa was betrothed to a respected and well-to-do bookseller, Friedrich Brockhaus. This gathering together of the relatives of the penniless bride-elect did not seem to trouble her remarkably kind-hearted fiancé. But my sister may have become uneasy on the subject, for she soon gave me to understand that she was not taking it quite in good part. Her desire to secure an entrée into the higher social circles of bourgeois life naturally produced a marked change in her manner, at one time so full of fun, and of this I gradually became so keenly sensible that finally we were estranged for a time. Moreover, I unfortunately gave her good cause to reprove my conduct. After I got to Leipzig I quite gave up my studies and all regular school work, probably owing to the arbitrary and pedantic system in vogue at the school there.

In Leipzig there were two higher-class schools, one called St. Thomas's School, and the other, and the more modern, St. Nicholas's School. The latter at that time enjoyed a better reputation than the former; so there I had to go. But the council of teachers before whom I appeared for my entrance examination at the New Year (1828) thought fit to maintain the dignity of their school by placing me for a time in the upper third form, whereas at the Kreuz Grammar School in Dresden I had been in the second form. My disgust at having to lay aside my Homer — from which I had already made written translations of twelve songs — and take up the lighter Greek prose writers was indescribable. It hurt my feelings so deeply, and so influenced my behaviour, that I never made a friend of any teacher in the school. The unsympathetic treatment I met with made me all the more obstinate, and various other circumstances in my position only added to this feeling. While student life, as I saw it day by day, inspired me ever more and more with its rebellious spirit, I unexpectedly met with another cause for despising the dry monotony of school régime. I refer to the influence of my uncle, Adolph Wagner, which, though he was long unconscious of it, went a long way towards moulding the growing stripling that I then was.

The fact that my romantic tastes were not based solely on a tendency to superficial amusement was shown by my ardent attachment to this learned relative. In his manner and conversation he was certainly very attractive; the many-sidedness of his knowledge, which embraced not only philology but also philosophy and general poetic literature, rendered intercourse with him a most entertaining pastime, as all those who knew him used to admit. On the other hand, the fact that he was denied the gift of writing with equal charm, or clearness, was a singular defect which seriously lessened his influence upon the literary world, and, in fact, often made him appear ridiculous, as in a written argument he would perpetrate the most pompous and involved sentences. This weakness could not have alarmed me, because in the hazy period of my youth the more incomprehensible any literary extravagance was, the more I admired it; besides which, I had more experience of his conversation than of his writings. He also seemed to find pleasure in associating with the lad who could listen with so much heart and soul. Yet unfortunately, possibly in the fervour of his discourses, of which he was not a little proud, he forgot that their substance, as well as their form, was far above my youthful powers of comprehension. I called daily to accompany him on his constitutional walk beyond the city gates, and I shrewdly suspect that we often provoked the smiles of those passers-by who overheard the profound and often earnest discussions between us. The subjects generally ranged over everything serious or sublime throughout the whole realm of knowledge. I took the most enthusiastic interest in his copious library, and tasted eagerly of almost all branches of literature, without really grounding myself in any one of them.

My uncle was delighted to find in me a very willing listener to his recital of classic tragedies. He had made a translation of Œdipus, and, according to his intimate friend Tieck, justly flattered himself on being an excellent reader.

I remember once, when he was sitting at his desk reading out a Greek tragedy to me, it did not annoy him when I fell fast asleep, and he afterwards pretended he had not noticed it. I was also induced to spend my evenings with him, owing to the friendly and genial hospitality his wife showed me. A very great change had come over my uncle's life since my first acquaintance with him at Jeannette Thomé's. The home which he, together with his sister Friederike, had found in his friend's house seemed, as time went on, to have brought in its train duties that were irksome. As his literary work assured him a modest income, he eventually deemed it more in accordance with his dignity to make a home of his own. A friend of his, of the same age as himself, the sister of the æsthete Wendt of Leipzig, who afterwards became famous, was chosen by him to keep house for him. Without saying a word to Jeannette, instead of going for his usual afternoon walk he went to the church with his chosen bride, and got through the marriage ceremonies as quickly as possible; and it was only on his return that he informed us he was leaving, and would have his things removed that very day. He managed to meet the consternation, perhaps also the reproaches, of his elderly friend with quiet composure; and to the end of his life he continued his regular daily visits to 'Mam'selle Thomé,' who at times would coyly pretend to sulk. It was only poor Friederike who seemed obliged at times to atone for her brother's sudden unfaithfulness.

What attracted me in my uncle most strongly was his blunt contempt of the modern pedantry in State, Church, and School, to which he gave vent with some humour. Despite the great moderation of his usual views on life, he yet produced on me the effect of a thorough free-thinker. I was highly delighted by his contempt for the pedantry of the schools. Once, when I had come into serious conflict with all the teachers of the Nicolai School, and the rector of the school had approached my uncle, as the only male representative of my family, with a serious complaint about my behaviour, my uncle asked me during a stroll round the town, with a calm smile as though he were speaking to one of his own age, what I had been up to with the people at school. I explained the whole affair to him, and described the punishment to which I had been subjected, and which seemed to me unjust. He pacified me, and exhorted me to be patient, telling me to comfort myself with the Spanish proverb, *un rey no puede morir,* which he explained as meaning that the ruler of a school must of necessity always be in the right.

He could not, of course, help noticing, to his alarm, the effect upon me of this kind of conversation, which I was far too young to appreciate. Although it annoyed me one day, when I wanted to begin reading Goethe's *Faust,* to hear him say quietly that I was too young to understand it, yet, according to my thinking, his other conversations about our own great poets, and even about Shakespeare and Dante, had made me so familiar with these sublime figures that I had now for some time been secretly busy working out the great tragedy I had already conceived in Dresden. Since my trouble at school I had devoted all my energies, which ought by rights to have been exclusively directed to my school duties, to the accomplishment of this task. In this secret work I had only one confidante, my sister Ottilie, who now lived with me at my mother's. I can remember the misgivings and alarm which the first confidential communication of my great poetic enterprise aroused in my good sister; yet she affectionately suffered the tortures I sometimes inflicted on her by reciting to her in secret, but not without emotion, portions of my work as it progressed. Once, when I was reciting to her one of the most gruesome scenes, a heavy thunderstorm came on. When the lightning flashed quite close to us, and the thunder rolled, my sister felt bound to implore me to stop; but she soon found it was hopeless, and continued to endure it with touching devotion.

But a more significant storm was brewing on the horizon of my life. My neglect of school reached such a point that it could not but lead to a rupture. Whilst my dear mother had no presentiment of this, I awaited the catastrophe with longing rather than with fear.

In order to meet this crisis with dignity I at length decided to surprise my family by disclosing to them the secret of my tragedy, which was now completed. They were to be informed of this great event by my uncle. I thought I could rely upon his hearty recognition of my vocation as a great poet on account of the deep harmony between us on all other questions of life, science, and art. I therefore sent him my voluminous manuscript, with a long letter which I thought would please him immensely. In this I communicated to him first my ideas with regard to the St. Nicholas's School, and then my firm determination from that time forward not to allow any mere school pedantry to check my free development. But the event turned out very different from what I had expected. It was a great shock to them. My uncle, quite conscious that he had been indiscreet, paid a visit to my mother and brother-in-law, in order to report the misfortune that had befallen the family, reproaching himself for the fact that his influence over me had not always, perhaps, been for my good. To me he wrote a serious letter of discouragement; and to this day I cannot understand why he showed so small a sense of humour in understanding my bad behaviour. To my surprise he merely said that he reproached himself for having corrupted me by conversations unsuited to my years, but he made no attempt to explain to me good-naturedly the error of my ways.

The crime this boy of fifteen had committed was, as I said before, to have written a great tragedy, entitled *Leubald und Adelaïde*.

The manuscript of this drama has unfortunately been lost, but I can still see it clearly in my mind's eye. The handwriting was most affected, and the backward-sloping tall letters with which I had aimed at giving it an air of distinction had already been compared by one of my teachers to Persian hieroglyphics. In this composition I had constructed a drama in which I had drawn largely upon Shakespeare's *Hamlet, King Lear*, and *Macbeth*, and Goethe's *Götz von Berlichingen*. The plot was really based on a modification of *Hamlet*, the difference consisting in the fact that my hero is so completely carried away by the appearance of the ghost of his father, who has been murdered under similar circumstances, and demands vengeance, that he is driven to fearful deeds of violence; and, with a series of murders on his conscience, he eventually goes mad. Leubald, whose character is a mixture of Hamlet and Harry

Hotspur, had promised his father's ghost to wipe from the face of the earth the whole race of Roderick, as the ruthless murderer of the best of fathers was named. After having slain Roderick himself in mortal combat, and subsequently all his sons and other relations who supported him, there was only one obstacle that prevented Leubald from fulfilling the dearest wish of his heart, which was to be united in death with the shade of his father: a child of Roderick's was still alive. During the storming of his castle the murderer's daughter had been carried away into safety by a faithful suitor, whom she, however, detested. I had an irresistible impulse to call this maiden 'Adelaïde.' As even at that early age I was a great enthusiast for everything really German, I can only account for the obviously un-German name of my heroine by my infatuation for Beethoven's Adelaïde, whose tender refrain seemed to me the symbol of all loving appeals. The course of my drama was now characterised by the strange delays which took place in the accomplishment of this last murder of vengeance, the chief obstacle to which lay in the sudden passionate love which arose between Leubald and Adelaïde. I succeeded in representing the birth and avowal of this love by means of extraordinary adventures. Adelaïde was once more stolen away by a robber-knight from the lover who had been sheltering her. After Leubald had thereupon sacrificed the lover and all his relations, he hastened to the robber's castle, driven thither less by a thirst for blood than by a longing for death. For this reason he regrets his inability to storm the robber's castle forthwith, because it is well defended, and, moreover, night is fast falling; he is therefore obliged to pitch his tent. After raving for a while he sinks down for the first time exhausted, but being urged, like his prototype Hamlet, by the spirit of his father to complete his vow of vengeance, he himself suddenly falls into the power of the enemy during a night assault. In the subterranean dungeons of the castle he meets Roderick's daughter for the first time. She is a prisoner like himself, and is craftily devising flight. Under circumstances in which she produces on him the impression of a heavenly vision, she makes her appearance before him. They fall in love, and fly together into the wilderness, where they realise that they are deadly enemies. The incipient insanity which was already noticeable in Leubald breaks out more violently after this discovery, and everything that can be done to intensify it is contributed by the ghost of his father, which continually comes between the advances of the lovers. But this ghost is not the only disturber of the conciliating love of Leubald and Adelaïde. The ghost of Roderick also appears, and according to the method followed by Shakespeare in *Richard III.*, he is joined by the ghosts of all the other members of Adelaïde's family whom Leubald has slain. From the incessant importunities of these ghosts Leubald seeks to free himself by means of sorcery, and calls to his aid a rascal named Flamming. One of *Macbeth's* witches is summoned to lay the ghosts; as she is unable to do this efficiently, the furious Leubald sends her also to the devil; but with her dying breath she despatches the whole crowd of spirits who serve her to join the ghosts of those already pursuing him. Leubald, tormented beyond endurance, and now at last raving mad, turns against his beloved, who is the apparent cause of all his misery. He stabs her in his fury; then finding himself suddenly at peace, he sinks his head into her lap, and accepts her last caresses as her life-blood streams over his own dying body.

I had not omitted the smallest detail that could give this plot its proper colouring, and had drawn on all my knowledge of the tales of the old knights, and my acquaintance with *Lear* and *Macbeth,* to furnish my drama with the most vivid situations. But one of the chief characteristics of its poetical form I took from the pathetic, humorous, and powerful language of Shakespeare. The boldness of my grandiloquent and bombastic expressions roused my uncle Adolph's alarm and astonishment. He was unable to understand how I could have selected and used with inconceivable exaggeration precisely the most extravagant forms of speech to be found in *Lear* and *Götz von Berlichingen.* Nevertheless, even after everybody had deafened me with their laments over my lost time and perverted talents, I was still conscious of a wonderful secret solace in the face of the calamity that had befallen me. I knew, a fact that no one else could know, namely, that my work could only be rightly judged when set to the music which I had resolved to write for it, and which I intended to start composing immediately.

I must now explain my position with respect to music hitherto. For this purpose I must go back to my earliest attempts in the art. In my family two of my sisters were musical; the elder one, Rosalie, played the piano, without, however, displaying any marked talent. Clara was more gifted; in addition to a great deal of musical feeling, and a fine rich touch on the piano, she possessed a particularly sympathetic voice, the development of which was so premature and remarkable that, under the tuition of Mieksch, her singing master, who was famous at that time, she was apparently ready for the rôle of a prima donna as early as her sixteenth year, and made her début at Dresden in Italian opera as 'Cenerentola' in Rossini's opera of that name. Incidentally I may remark that this premature development proved injurious to Clara's voice, and was detrimental to her whole career. As I have said, music was represented in our family by these two sisters. It was chiefly owing to Clara's career that the musical conductor C. M. von Weber often came to our house. His visits were varied by those of the great male-soprano Sassaroli; and in addition to these two representatives of German and Italian music, we also had the company of Mieksch, her singing master. It was on these occasions that I as a child first heard German and Italian music discussed, and learnt that any one who wished to ingratiate himself with the Court must show a preference for Italian music, a fact which led to very practical results in our family council. Clara's talent, while her voice was still sound, was the object of competition between the representatives of Italian and German opera. I can remember quite distinctly that from the very beginning I declared myself in favour of German opera; my choice was determined by the tremendous impression made on me by the two figures of Sassaroli and Weber. The Italian male-soprano, a huge potbellied giant, horrified me with his high effeminate voice, his astonishing volubility, and his incessant screeching laughter. In spite of his boundless good-nature and amiability, particularly to my family, I took an uncanny dislike to him. On account of this dreadful person, the sound of Italian, either spoken or sung, seemed to my ears almost diabolical; and when, in consequence of my poor sister's misfortune, I heard them often talking about Italian intrigues and cabals, I conceived so strong a dislike for everything connected with this nation that even in much later years I used to feel myself carried away by an impulse of utter detestation and abhorrence.

The less frequent visits of Weber, on the other hand, seemed to have produced upon me those first sympathetic impressions which I have never since lost. In contrast to Sassaroli's repulsive figure, Weber's really refined, delicate, and intellectual appearance excited my ecstatic admiration. His narrow face and finely-cut features, his vivacious though often half-closed eyes, captivated and thrilled me; whilst even the bad limp with which he walked, and which I often noticed from our windows when the master was making his way home past our house from the fatiguing rehearsals, stamped the great musician in my imagination as an exceptional and almost superhuman being. When, as a boy of nine, my mother introduced me to him, and he asked me what I was going to be, whether I wanted perhaps to be a musician, my mother told him that, though I was indeed quite mad on *Freischütz,* yet she had as yet seen nothing in me which indicated any musical talent.

This showed correct observation on my mother's part; nothing had made so great an impression on me as the music of *Freischütz,* and I tried in every possible way to procure a repetition of the impressions I had received from it, but, strange to say, least of all by the study of music itself. Instead of this, I contented myself with hearing bits from *Freischütz* played by my sisters. Yet my passion for it gradually grew so strong that I can remember taking a particular fancy for a young man called Spiess, chiefly because he could play the overture to *Freischütz,* which I used to ask him to do whenever I met him. It was chiefly the introduction to this overture which at last led me to attempt, without ever having received any instruction on the piano, to play this piece in my own peculiar way, for, oddly enough, I was the only child in our family who had not been given music lessons. This was probably due to my mother's anxiety to keep me away from any artistic interests of this kind in case they might arouse in me a longing for the theatre.

When I was about twelve years old, however, my mother engaged a tutor for me named Humann, from whom I received regular music lessons, though only of a very mediocre description. As soon as I had acquired a very imperfect knowledge of fingering I begged to be allowed to play overtures in the form of duets, always keeping Weber as the goal of my ambition. When at length I had got so far as to be able to play the overture to *Freischütz* myself, though in a very faulty manner, I felt the object of my study had been attained, and I had no inclination to devote any further attention to perfecting my technique.

Yet I had attained this much: I was no longer dependent for music on the playing of others; from this time forth I used to try and play, albeit very imperfectly, everything I wanted to know. I also tried Mozart's *Don Juan,* but was unable to get any pleasure out of it, mainly because the Italian text in the arrangement for the piano placed the music in a frivolous light in my eyes, and much in it seemed to me trivial and unmanly. (I can remember that when my sister used to sing Zerlinen's ariette, *Batti, batti, ben Masetto,* the music repelled me, as it seemed so mawkish and effeminate.)

On the other hand, my bent for music grew stronger and stronger, and I now tried to possess myself of my favourite pieces by making my own copies. I can remember the hesitation with which my mother for the first time gave me the money to buy the scored paper on which I copied out Weber's *Lützow's Jagd,* which was the first piece of music I transcribed.

Music was still a secondary occupation with me when the news of Weber's death and the longing to learn his music to *Oberon* fanned my enthusiasm into flame again. This received fresh impetus from the afternoon concerts in the Grosser Garten at Dresden, where I often heard my favourite music played by Zillmann's Town Band, as I thought, exceedingly well. The mysterious joy I felt in hearing an orchestra play quite close to me still remains one of my most pleasant memories. The mere tuning up of the instruments put me in a state of mystic excitement; even the striking of fifths on the violin seemed to me like a greeting from the spirit world — which, I may mention incidentally, had a very real meaning for me. When I was still almost a baby, the sound of these fifths, which has always excited me, was closely associated in my mind with ghosts and spirits. I remember that even much later in life I could never pass the small palace of Prince Anthony, at the end of the Ostra Allee in Dresden, without a shudder; for it was there I had first heard the sound of a violin, a very common experience to me afterwards. It was close by me, and seemed to my ears to come from the stone figures with which this palace is adorned, some of which are provided with musical instruments. When I took up my post as musical conductor at Dresden, and had to pay my official visit to Morgenroth, the President of the Concert Committee, an elderly gentleman who lived for many years opposite that princely palace, it seemed odd to find that the player of fifths who had so strongly impressed my musical fancy as a boy was anything but a supernatural spectre. And when I saw the well-known picture in which a skeleton plays on his violin to an old man on his deathbed, the ghostly character of those very notes impressed itself with particular force upon my childish imagination. When at last, as a young man, I used to listen to the Zillmann Orchestra in the Grosser Garten almost every afternoon, one may imagine the rapturous thrill with which I drew in all the chaotic variety of sound that I heard as the orchestra tuned up: the long drawn A of the oboe, which seemed like a call from the dead to rouse the other instruments, never failed to raise all my nerves to a feverish pitch of tension, and when the swelling C in the overture to *Freischütz* told me that I had stepped, as it were with both feet, right into the magic realm of awe. Any one who had been watching me at that moment could hardly have failed to see the state I was in, and this in spite of the fact that I was such a bad performer on the piano.

Another work also exercised a great fascination over me, namely, the overture to *Fidelio* in E major, the introduction to which affected me deeply. I asked my sisters about Beethoven, and learned that the news of his death had just arrived. Obsessed as I still was by the terrible grief caused by Weber's death, this fresh loss, due to the decease of this great master of melody, who had only just entered my life, filled me with strange anguish, a feeling nearly akin to my childish dread of the ghostly fifths on the violin. It was now Beethoven's music that I longed to know more thoroughly; I came to Leipzig, and found his music to *Egmont* on the piano at my sister Louisa's. After that I tried to get hold of his sonatas. At last, at a concert at the Gewandthaus, I heard one of the master's symphonies for the first time; it was the Symphony in A major. The effect on me was indescribable. To this must be added the impression produced on me by Beethoven's features, which I saw in the lithographs that were circulated everywhere at that time, and by the fact that he was deaf, and lived a quiet secluded life. I soon conceived an image of him in my mind as a sublime and unique supernatural being, with whom none could compare. This image was associated in my brain with that of Shakespeare; in ecstatic dreams I met both of them, saw and spoke to them, and on awakening found myself bathed in tears.

It was at this time that I came across Mozart's *Requiem*, which formed the starting-point of my enthusiastic absorption in the works of that master. His second finale to *Don Juan* inspired me to include him in my spirit world.

I was now filled with a desire to compose, as I had before been to write verse. I had, however, in this case to master the technique of an entirely separate and complicated subject. This presented greater difficulties than I had met with in writing verse, which came to me fairly easily. It was these difficulties that drove me to adopt a career which bore some resemblance to that of a professional musician, whose future distinction would be to win the titles of Conductor and Writer of Opera.

I now wanted to set *Leubald und Adelaïde* to music, similar to that which Beethoven wrote to Goethe's *Egmont;* the various ghosts from the spirit world, who were each to display different characteristics, were to borrow their own distinctive colouring from appropriate musical accompaniment. In order to acquire the necessary technique of composition quickly I studied Logier's *Methode des Generalbasses*, a work which was specially recommended to me at a musical lending library as a suitable text-book from which this art might be easily mastered. I have distinct recollections that the financial difficulties with which I was continually harassed throughout my life began at this time. I borrowed Logier's book on the weekly payment system, in the fond hope of having to pay for it only during a few weeks out of the savings of my weekly pocket-money. But the weeks ran on into months, and I was still unable to compose as well as I wished. Mr. Frederick Wieck, whose daughter afterwards married Robert Schumann, was at that time the proprietor of that lending library. He kept sending me troublesome reminders of the debt I owed him; and when my bill had almost reached the price of Logier's book I had to make a clean breast of the matter to my family, who thus not only learnt of my financial difficulties in general, but also of my latest transgression into the domain of music, from which, of course, at the very most, they expected nothing better than a repetition of *Leubald und Adelaïde*.

There was great consternation at home; my mother, sister, and brother-in-law, with anxious faces, discussed how my studies should be superintended in future, to prevent my having any further opportunity for transgressing in this way. No one, however, yet knew the real state of affairs at school, and they hoped I would soon see the error of my ways in this case as I had in my former craze for poetry.

But other domestic changes were taking place which necessitated my being for some little time alone in our house at Leipzig during the summer of 1829, when I was left entirely to my own devices. It was during this period that my passion for music rose to an extraordinary degree. I had secretly been taking lessons in harmony from G. Müller, afterwards organist at Altenburg, an excellent musician belonging to the Leipzig orchestra. Although the payment of these lessons was also destined to get me into hot water at home later on, I could not even make up to my teacher for the delay in the payment of his fees by giving him the pleasure of watching me improve in my studies. His teaching and exercises soon filled me with the greatest disgust, as to my mind it all seemed so dry. For me music was a spirit, a noble and mystic monster,

and any attempt to regulate it seemed to lower it in my eyes.
I gathered much more congenial instruction about it from
Hoffmann's *Phantasiestücken* than from my Leipzig orchestra
player; and now came the time when I really lived and
breathed in Hoffmann's artistic atmosphere of ghosts and
spirits. With my head quite full of Kreissler, Krespel, and
other musical spectres from my favourite author, I imagined
that I had at last found in real life a creature who resembled
them: this ideal musician in whom for a time I fancied I had
discovered a second Kreissler was a man called Flachs. He
was a tall, exceedingly thin man, with a very narrow head and
an extraordinary way of walking, moving, and speaking, whom
I had seen at all those open-air concerts which formed my
principal source of musical education. He was always with
the members of the orchestra, speaking exceedingly quickly,
first to one and then the other; for they all knew him, and
seemed to like him. The fact that they were making fun of
him I only learned, to my great confusion, much later. I
remember having noticed this strange figure from my earliest
days in Dresden, and I gathered from the conversations which
I overheard that he was indeed well known to all Dresden
musicians. This circumstance alone was sufficient to make
me take a great interest in him; but the point about him which
attracted me more than anything was the manner in which
he listened to the various items in the programme: he used
to give peculiar, convulsive nods of his head, and blow out his
cheeks as though with sighs. All this I regarded as a sign of
spiritual ecstasy. I noticed, moreover, that he was quite alone,
that he belonged to no party, and paid no attention to anything
in the garden save the music; whereupon my identification of
this curious being with the conductor Kreissler seemed quite
natural. I was determined to make his acquaintance, and I
succeeded in doing so. Who shall describe my delight when,
on going to call on him at his rooms for the first time, I found
innumerable bundles of scores! I had as yet never seen a
score. It is true I discovered, to my regret, that he possessed
nothing either by Beethoven, Mozart, or Weber; in fact, nothing but immense quantities of works, masses, and cantatas by
composers such as Staerkel, Stamitz, Steibelt, etc., all of whom

were entirely unknown to me. Yet Flachs was able to tell me so much that was good about them that the respect which I felt for scores in general helped me to overcome my regret at not finding anything by my beloved masters. It is true I learnt later that poor Flachs had only come into the possession of these particular scores through unscrupulous dealers, who had traded on his weakness of intellect and palmed off this worthless music on him for large sums of money. At all events, they were scores, and that was quite enough for me. Flachs and I became most intimate; we were always seen going about together — I, a lanky boy of sixteen, and this weird, shaky flaxpole. The doors of my deserted home were often opened for this strange guest, who made me play my compositions to him while he ate bread and cheese. In return, he once arranged one of my airs for wind instruments, and, to my astonishment, it was actually accepted and played by the band in Kintschy's Swiss Châlet. That this man had not the smallest capacity to teach me anything never once occurred to me; I was so firmly convinced of his originality that there was no need for him to prove it further than by listening patiently to my enthusiastic outpourings. But as, in course of time, several of his own friends joined us, I could not help noticing that the worthy Flachs was regarded by them all as a half-witted fool. At first this merely pained me, but a strange incident unexpectedly occurred which converted me to the general opinion about him. Flachs was a man of some means, and had fallen into the toils of a young lady of dubious character who he believed was deeply in love with him. One day, without warning, I found his house closed to me, and discovered, to my astonishment, that jealousy was the cause. The unexpected discovery of this liaison, which was my first experience of such a case, filled me with a strange horror. My friend suddenly appeared to me even more mad than he really was. I felt so ashamed of my persistent blindness that for some time to come I never went to any of the garden concerts for fear I should meet my sham Kreissler.

By this time I had composed my first Sonata in D minor. I had also begun a pastoral play, and had worked it out in what I felt sure must be an entirely unprecedented way.

I chose Goethe's *Laune der Verliebten* as a model for the form and plot of my work. I scarcely even drafted out the libretto, however, but worked it out at the same time as the music and orchestration, so that, while I was writing out one page of the score, I had not even thought out the words for the next page. I remember distinctly that following this extraordinary method, although I had not acquired the slightest knowledge about writing for instruments, I actually worked out a fairly long passage which finally resolved itself into a scene for three female voices followed by the air for the tenor. My bent for writing for the orchestra was so strong that I procured a score of *Don Juan*, and set to work on what I then considered a very careful orchestration of a fairly long air for soprano. I also wrote a quartette in D major after I had myself sufficiently mastered the alto for the viola, my ignorance of which had caused me great difficulty only a short time before, when I was studying a quartette by Haydn.

Armed with these works, I set out in the summer on my first journey as a musician. My sister Clara, who was married to the singer Wolfram, had an engagement at the theatre at Magdeburg, whither, in characteristic fashion, I set forth upon my adventure on foot.

My short stay with my relations provided me with many experiences of musical life. It was there that I met a new freak, whose influence upon me I have never been able to forget. He was a musical conductor of the name of Kühnlein, a most extraordinary person. Already advanced in years, delicate and, unfortunately, given to drink, this man nevertheless impressed one by something striking and vigorous in his expression. His chief characteristics were an enthusiastic worship of Mozart and a passionate depreciation of Weber. He had read only one book — Goethe's *Faust* — and in this work there was not a page in which he had not underlined some passage, and made some remark in praise of Mozart or in disparagement of Weber. It was to this man that my brother-in-law confided the compositions which I had brought with me in order to learn his opinion of my abilities. One evening, as we were sitting comfortably in an inn, old Kühnlein came in, and approached us with a friendly, though serious manner.

I thought I read good news in his features, but when my brother-in-law asked him what he thought of my work, he answered quietly and calmly, 'There is not a single good note in it!' My brother-in-law, who was accustomed to Kühnlein's eccentricity, gave a loud laugh which reassured me somewhat. It was impossible to get any advice or coherent reasons for his opinion out of Kühnlein; he merely renewed his abuse of Weber and made some references to Mozart which, nevertheless, made a deep impression upon me, as Kühnlein's language was always very heated and emphatic.

On the other hand, this visit brought me a great treasure, which was responsible for leading me in a very different direction from that advised by Kühnlein. This was the score of Beethoven's great Quartette in E flat major, which had only been fairly recently published, and of which my brother-in-law had a copy made for me. Richer in experience, and in the possession of this treasure, I returned to Leipzig to the nursery of my queer musical studies. But my family had now returned with my sister Rosalie, and I could no longer keep secret from them the fact that my connection with the school had been entirely suspended, for a notice was found saying that I had not attended the school for the last six months. As a complaint addressed by the rector to my uncle about me had not received adequate attention, the school authorities had apparently made no further attempts to exercise any supervision over me, which I had indeed rendered quite impossible by absenting myself altogether.

A fresh council of war was held in the family to discuss what was to be done with me. As I laid particular stress on my bent for music, my relations thought that I ought, at any rate, to learn one instrument thoroughly. My brother-in-law, Brockhaus, proposed to send me to Hummel, at Weimar, to be trained as a pianist, but as I loudly protested that by 'music' I meant 'composing,' and not 'playing an instrument,' they gave way, and decided to let me have regular lessons in harmony from Müller, the very musician from whom I had had instruction on the sly some little while before, and who had not yet been paid. In return for this I promised faithfully to go back to work conscientiously at St. Nicholas's

School. I soon grew tired of both. I could brook no control, and this unfortunately applied to my musical instruction as well. The dry study of harmony disgusted me more and more, though I continued to conceive fantasias, sonatas, and overtures, and work them out by myself. On the other hand, I was spurred on by ambition to show what I could do at school if I liked. When the Upper School boys were set the task of writing a poem, I composed a chorus in Greek, on the recent War of Liberation. I can well imagine that this Greek poem had about as much resemblance to a real Greek oration and poetry, as the sonatas and overtures I used to compose at that time had to thoroughly professional music. My attempt was scornfully rejected as a piece of impudence. After that I have no further recollections of my school. My continued attendance was a pure sacrifice on my side, made out of consideration for my family: I did not pay the slightest attention to what was taught in the lessons, but secretly occupied myself all the while with reading any book that happened to attract me.

As my musical instruction also did me no good, I continued in my wilful process of self-education by copying out the scores of my beloved masters, and in so doing acquired a neat handwriting, which in later years has often been admired. I believe my copies of the C minor Symphony and the Ninth Symphony by Beethoven are still preserved as souvenirs.

Beethoven's Ninth Symphony became the mystical goal of all my strange thoughts and desires about music. I was first attracted to it by the opinion prevalent among musicians, not only in Leipzig but elsewhere, that this work had been written by Beethoven when he was already half mad. It was considered the *non plus ultra* of all that was fantastic and incomprehensible, and this was quite enough to rouse in me a passionate desire to study this mysterious work. At the very first glance at the score, of which I obtained possession with such difficulty, I felt irresistibly attracted by the long-sustained pure fifths with which the first phrase opens: these chords, which, as I related above, had played such a supernatural part in my childish impressions of music, seemed in this case to form the spiritual keynote of my own life. This, I thought, must surely contain the secret of all secrets, and accordingly the first thing to be done was to make the score my own by a process of laborious copying. I well remember that on one occasion the sudden appearance of the dawn made such an uncanny impression on my excited nerves that I jumped into bed with a scream as though I had seen a ghost. The symphony at that time had not yet been arranged for the piano; it had found so little favour that the publisher did not feel inclined to run the risk of producing it. I set to work at it, and actually composed a complete piano solo, which I tried to play to myself. I sent my work to Schott, the publisher of the score, at Mainz. I received in reply a letter saying ' that the publishers had not yet decided to issue the Ninth Symphony for the piano, but that they would gladly keep my laborious work,' and offered me remuneration in the shape of the score of the great *Missa Solemnis* in D, which I accepted with great pleasure.

In addition to this work I practised the violin for some time, as my harmony master very rightly considered that some knowledge of the practical working of this instrument was indispensable for any one who had the intention of composing for the orchestra. My mother, indeed, paid the violinist Sipp (who was still playing in the Leipzig orchestra in 1865) eight thalers for a violin (I do not know what became of it), with which for quite three months I must have inflicted unutterable torture upon my mother and sister by practising in my tiny little room. I got so far as to play certain Variations in F sharp by Mayseder, but only reached the second or third. After that I have no further recollections of this practising, in which my family fortunately had very good reasons of their own for not encouraging me.

But the time now arrived when my interest in the theatre again took a passionate hold upon me. A new company had been formed in my birthplace under very good auspices. The Board of Management of the Court Theatre at Dresden had taken over the management of the Leipzig theatre for three years. My sister Rosalie was a member of the company, and through her I could always gain admittance to the performances; and that which in my childhood had been merely the interest aroused by a strange spirit of curiosity now became a more deep-seated and conscious passion.

Julius Cæsar, Macbeth, Hamlet, the plays of Schiller, and to crown all, Goethe's *Faust,* excited and stirred me deeply. The Opera was giving the first performances of Marschner's *Vampir* and *Templer und Jüdin.* The Italian company arrived from Dresden, and fascinated the Leipzig audience by their consummate mastery of their art. Even I was almost carried away by the enthusiasm with which the town was overwhelmed, into forgetting the boyish impressions which Signor Sassaroli had stamped upon my mind, when another miracle — which also came to us from Dresden — suddenly gave a new direction to my artistic feelings and exercised a decisive influence over my whole life. This consisted of a special performance given by Wilhelmine Schröder-Devrient, who at that time was at the zenith of her artistic career, young, beautiful, and ardent, and whose like I have never again seen on the stage. She made her appearance in *Fidelio.*

If I look back on my life as a whole, I can find no event that produced so profound an impression upon me. Any one who can remember that wonderful woman at this period of her life must to some extent have experienced the almost satanic ardour which the intensely human art of this incomparable actress poured into his veins. After the performance I rushed to a friend's house and wrote a short note to the singer, in which I briefly told her that from that moment my life had acquired its true significance, and that if in days to come she should ever hear my name praised in the world of Art, she must remember that she had that evening made me what I then swore it was my destiny to become. This note I left at her hotel, and ran out into the night as if I were mad. In the year 1842, when I went to Dresden to make my début with *Rienzi,* I paid several visits to the kind-hearted singer, who startled me on one occasion by repeating this letter word for word. It seemed to have made an impression on her too, as she had actually kept it.

At this point I feel myself obliged to acknowledge that the great confusion which now began to prevail in my life, and particularly in my studies, was due to the inordinate effect

EFFECT OF SCHRÖDER-DEVRIENT'S ART

this artistic interpretation had upon me. I did not know where to turn, or how to set about producing something myself which might place me in direct contact with the impression I had received, while everything that could not be brought into touch with it seemed to me so shallow and meaningless that I could not possibly trouble myself with it. I should have liked to compose a work worthy of a Schröder-Devrient; but as this was quite beyond my power, in my headlong despair I let all artistic endeavour slide, and as my work was also utterly insufficient to absorb me, I flung myself recklessly into the life of the moment in the company of strangely chosen associates, and indulged in all kinds of youthful excesses.

I now entered into all the dissipations of raw manhood, the outward ugliness and inward emptiness of which make me marvel to this day. My intercourse with those of my own age had always been the result of pure chance. I cannot remember that any special inclination or attraction determined me in the choice of my young friends. While I can honestly say that I was never in a position to stand aloof out of envy from any one who was specially gifted, I can only explain my indifference in the choice of my associates by the fact that through inexperience regarding the sort of companionship that would be of advantage to me, I cared only to have some one who would accompany me in my excursions, and to whom I could pour out my feelings to my heart's content without caring what effect it might have upon him. The result of this was that after a stream of confidences to which my own excitement was the only response, I at length reached the point when I turned and looked at my friend; to my astonishment I generally found that there was no question of response at all, and as soon as I set my heart on drawing something from him in return, and urged him to confide in me, when he really had nothing to tell, the connection usually came to an end and left no trace on my life. In a certain sense my strange relationship with Flachs was typical of the great majority of my ties in after-life. Consequently, as no lasting personal bond of friendship ever found its way into my life, it is easy to understand how delight in the dissipations of student life could become

a passion of some duration, because in it individual intercourse
is entirely replaced by a common circle of acquaintances. In
the midst of rowdyism and ragging of the most foolish description I remained quite alone, and it is quite possible that
these frivolities formed a protecting hedge round my inmost
soul, which needed time to grow to its natural strength and not
be weakened by reaching maturity too soon.

My life seemed to break up in all directions; I had to leave
St. Nicholas's School at Easter 1830, as I was too deeply in disgrace with the staff of masters ever to hope for any promotion
in the University from that quarter. It was now determined
that I should study privately for six months and then go to
St. Thomas's School, where I should be in fresh surroundings
and be able to work up and qualify in a short time for the
University. My uncle Adolph, with whom I was constantly
renewing my friendship, and who also encouraged me about
my music and exercised a good influence over me in that respect, in spite of the utter degradation of my life at that time,
kept arousing in me an ever fresh desire for scientific studies.
I took private lessons in Greek from a scholar, and read
Sophocles with him. For a time I hoped this noble poet would
again inspire me to get a real hold on the language, but the
hope was vain. I had not chosen the right teacher, and,
moreover, his sitting-room in which we pursued our studies
looked out on a tanyard, the repulsive odour of which affected
my nerves so strongly that I became thoroughly disgusted
both with Sophocles and Greek. My brother-in-law, Brockhaus, who wanted to put me in the way of earning some pocket-
money, gave me the correcting of the proof-sheets of a new
edition he was bringing out of Becker's *Universal History*,
revised by Löbell. This gave me a reason for improving by
private study the superficial general instruction on every subject which is given at school, and I thus acquired the valuable
knowledge which I was destined to have in later life of most
of the branches of learning so uninterestingly taught in class.
I must not forget to mention that, to a certain extent, the attraction exercised over me by this first closer study of history
was due to the fact that it brought me in eightpence a sheet,
and I thus found myself in one of the rarest positions in my life,

actually earning money; yet I should be doing myself an injustice if I did not bear in mind the vivid impressions I now for the first time received upon turning my serious attention to those periods of history with which I had hitherto had a very superficial acquaintance. All I recollect about my school days in this connection is that I was attracted by the classical period of Greek history; Marathon, Salamis, and Thermopylae composed the canon of all that interested me in the subject. Now for the first time I made an intimate acquaintance with the Middle Ages and the French Revolution, as my work in correcting dealt precisely with the two volumes which contained these two periods. I remember in particular that the description of the Revolution filled me with sincere hatred for its heroes; unfamiliar as I was with the previous history of France, my human sympathy was horrified by the cruelty of the men of that day, and this purely human impulse remained so strong in me that I remember how even quite recently it cost me a real struggle to give any weight to the true political significance of those acts of violence.

How great, then, was my astonishment when one day the current political events of the time enabled me, as it were, to gain a personal experience of the sort of national upheavals with which I had come into distant contact in the course of my proof-correcting. The special editions of the *Leipzig Gazette* brought us the news of the July Revolution in Paris. The King of France had been driven from his throne; Lafayette, who a moment before had seemed a myth to me, was again riding through a cheering crowd in the streets of Paris; the Swiss Guards had once more been butchered in the Tuileries, and a new King knew no better way of commending himself to the populace than by declaring himself the embodiment of the Republic. Suddenly to become conscious of living at a time in which such things took place could not fail to have a startling effect on a boy of seventeen. The world as a historic phenomenon began from that day in my eyes, and naturally my sympathies were wholly on the side of the Revolution, which I regarded in the light of a heroic popular struggle crowned with victory, and free from the blemish of the terrible excesses that stained the first French Revolution. As the whole of Europe, including some of the German states, was soon plunged more or less violently into rebellion, I remained for some time in a feverish state of suspense, and now first turned my attention to the causes of these upheavals, which I regarded as struggles of the young and hopeful against the old and effete portion of mankind. Saxony also did not remain unscathed; in Dresden it came to actual fighting in the streets, which immediately produced a political change in the shape of the proclamation of the regency of the future King Frederick, and the granting of a constitution. This event filled me with such enthusiasm that I composed a political overture, the prelude of which depicted dark oppression in the midst of which a strain was at last heard under which, to make my meaning clearer, I wrote the words *Friedrich und Freiheit;* this strain was intended to develop gradually and majestically into the fullest triumph, which I hoped shortly to see successfully performed at one of the Leipzig Garden Concerts.

However, before I was able to develop my politico-musical conceptions further, disorders broke out in Leipzig itself which summoned me from the precincts of Art to take a direct share in national life. National life in Leipzig at this time meant nothing more than antagonism between the students and the police, the latter being the arch-enemy upon whom the youthful love of liberty vented itself. Some students had been arrested in a street broil who were now to be rescued. The undergraduates, who had been restless for some days, assembled one evening in the Market Place and the Clubs, mustered together, and made a ring round their leaders. The whole proceeding was marked by a certain measured solemnity, which impressed me deeply. They sang *Gaudeamus igitur,* formed up into column, and picking up from the crowd any young men who sympathised with them, marched gravely and resolutely from the Market Place to the University buildings, to open the cells and set free the students who had been arrested. My heart beat fast as I marched with them to this 'Taking of the Bastille,' but things did not turn out as we expected, for in the courtyard of the Paulinum the solemn procession was stopped by Rector Krug, who had come down to meet it with his grey head bared; his assurance that the captives had already been released at his request was greeted with a thundering cheer, and the matter seemed at an end.

But the tense expectation of a revolution had grown too great not to demand some sacrifice. A summons was suddenly spread calling us to a notorious alley in order to exercise popular justice upon a hated magistrate who, it was rumoured, had unlawfully taken under his protection a certain house of ill-fame in that quarter. When I reached the spot with the tail-end of the crowd, I found the house had been broken into and all sorts of violence had been committed. I recall with horror the intoxicating effect this unreasoning fury had upon me, and cannot deny that without the slightest personal provocation I shared, like one possessed, in the frantic onslaught of the undergraduates, who madly shattered furniture and crockery to bits. I do not believe that the ostensible motive for this outrage, which, it is true, was to be found in a fact that was a grave menace to public morality, had any weight with me whatever; on the contrary, it was the purely devilish fury of these popular outbursts that drew me, too, like a madman into their vortex.

The fact that such fits of fury are not quick to abate, but, in accordance with certain natural laws, reach their proper conclusion only after they have degenerated into frenzy, I was to learn in my own person. Scarcely did the summons ring out for us to march to another resort of the same kind than I too found myself in the tide which set towards the opposite end of the town. There the same exploits were repeated, and the most ludicrous outrages perpetrated. I cannot remember that the enjoyment of alcoholic drinks contributed to the intoxication of myself and my immediate fellows. I only know that I finally got into the state that usually succeeds a debauch, and upon waking next morning, as if from a hideous nightmare, had to convince myself that I had really taken part in the events of the previous night by a trophy I possessed in the shape of a tattered red curtain, which I had brought home as a token of my prowess. The thought that people generally, and my own family in particular, were wont to put a lenient construction upon youthful escapades was a great comfort to me; outbursts of this kind on the part of the young were regarded as righteous indignation against really serious scandals, and there was no need for me to be afraid of owning up to having taken part in such excesses.

The dangerous example, however, which had been set by the undergraduates incited the lower classes and the mob to similar excesses on the following nights, against employers and any who were obnoxious to them. The matter at once assumed a more serious complexion; property was threatened, and a conflict between rich and poor stood grinning at our doors. As there were no soldiers in the town, and the police were thoroughly disorganised, the students were called in as a protection against the lower orders. An undergraduate's hour of glory now began, such as I could only have thirsted for in my schoolboy dreams. The student became the tutelar deity of Leipzig, called on by the authorities to arm and band together in defence of property, and the same young men who two days before had yielded to a rage for destruction, now mustered in the University courtyard. The proscribed names of the students' clubs and unions were shouted by the mouths of town councillors and chief constables in order to summon curiously equipped undergraduates, who thereupon, in simple mediæval array of war, scattered throughout the town, occupied the guard-rooms at the gates, provided sentinels for the grounds of various wealthy merchants, and, as occasion demanded, took places which seemed threatened, more especially inns, under their permanent protection.

Though, unluckily, I was not yet a member of their body, I anticipated the delights of academic citizenship by half-impudent, half-obsequious solicitation of the leaders of the students whom I honoured most. I had the good fortune to recommend myself particularly to these 'cocks of the walk,' as they were styled, on account of my relationship to Brockhaus, in whose grounds the main body of these champions were encamped for some time. My brother-in-law was among those who had been seriously threatened, and it was only owing to really great presence of mind and assurance that he succeeded in saving his printing works, and especially his steam presses, which were the chief object of attack, from destruction. To protect his property against further assault, detachments of students were told off to his grounds as well; the excellent entertainment which the generous master of the house offered his jovial guardians in his pleasant summer-house enticed the pick of the students to him. My brother-in-law was for several weeks guarded day and night against possible attacks by the populace, and on this occasion, as the mediator of a flowing hospitality, I celebrated among the most famous 'bloods' of the University the true saturnalia of my scholarly ambition.

For a still longer period the guarding of the gates was entrusted to the students; the unheard-of splendour which accordingly became associated with this post drew fresh aspirants to the spot from far and near. Every day huge chartered vehicles discharged at the Halle Gate whole bands of the boldest sons of learning from Halle, Jena, Göttingen, and the remotest regions. They got down close to the guards at the gate, and for several weeks never set foot in an inn or any other dwelling; they lived at the expense of the Council, drew vouchers on the police for food and drink, and knew but one care, that the possibility of a general quieting of men's minds would make their opportune guardianship superfluous. I never missed a day on guard or a night either, alas! trying to impress on my family the urgent need for my personal endurance. Of course, the quieter and really studious spirits among us soon resigned these duties, and only the flower of the flock of undergraduates remained so staunch that it became difficult for the authorities to relieve them of their task. I held out to the very last, and succeeded in making most astonishing friends for my age. Many of the most audacious remained in Leipzig even when there was no guard duty to fulfil, and peopled the place for some time with champions of an extraordinarily desperate and dissipated type, who had been repeatedly sent down from various universities for rowdyism or debt, and who now, thanks to the exceptional circumstances of the day, found a refuge in Leipzig, where at first they had been received with open arms by the general enthusiasm of their comrades.

In the presence of all these phenomena I felt as if I were surrounded by the results of an earthquake which had upset the usual order of things. My brother-in-law, Friedrich Brockhaus, who could justly taunt the former authorities of the place with their inability to maintain peace and order, was carried away by the current of a formidable movement of opposition. He made a daring speech at the Guildhall before their worships the Town Council, which brought him popularity, and he was appointed second-in-command of the newly constituted Leipzig Municipal Guard. This body at length ousted my adored students from the guard-rooms of the town gates, and we no longer had the right of stopping travellers and inspecting their passes. On the other hand, I flattered myself that I might regard my new position as a boy citizen as equivalent to that of the French National Guard, and my brother-in-law, Brockhaus, as a Saxon Lafayette, which, at all events, succeeded in furnishing my soaring excitement with a healthy stimulant. I now began to read the papers and cultivate politics enthusiastically; however, the social intercourse of the civic world did not attract me sufficiently to make me false to my beloved academic associates. I followed them faithfully from the guard-rooms to the ordinary bars, where their splendour as men of the literary world now sought retirement.

My chief ambition was to become one of them as soon as possible. This, however, could only be accomplished by being again entered at a grammar school. St. Thomas's, whose headmaster was a feeble old man, was the place where my wishes could be most speedily attained.

I joined the school in the autumn of 1830 simply with the intention of qualifying myself for the Leaving Examination by merely nominal attendance there. The chief thing in connection with it was that I and friends of the same bent succeeded in establishing a sham students' association called the Freshman's Club. It was formed with all possible pedantry, the institution of the 'Comment' was introduced, fencing-practice and sword-bouts were held, and an inaugural meeting to which several prominent students were invited, and at which I presided as 'Vice' in white buckskin trousers and great jack-boots, gave me a foretaste of the delights awaiting me as a full-blown son of the Muses.

ST. THOMAS'S SCHOOL

The masters of St. Thomas's, however, were not quite so ready to fall in with my aspirations to studentship; at the end of the half-year they were of the opinion that I had not given a thought to their institution, and nothing could persuade them that I had earned a title to academic citizenship by any acquisition of knowledge. Some sort of decision was necessary, so I accordingly informed my family that I had made up my mind not to study for a profession at the University, but to become a musician. There was nothing to prevent me matriculating as 'Studiosus Musicae,' and, without therefore troubling myself about the pedantries of the authorities at St. Thomas's, I defiantly quitted that seat af learning from which I had derived small profit, and presented myself forthwith to the rector of the University, whose acquaintance I had made on the evening of the riot, to be enrolled as a student of music. This was accordingly done without further ado, on the payment of the usual fees.

I was in a great hurry about it, for in a week the Easter vacation would begin, and the 'men' would go down from Leipzig, when it would be impossible to be elected member of a club until the vacation was over, and to stay all those weeks at home in Leipzig without having the right to wear the coveted colours seemed to me unendurable torture. Straight from the rector's presence I ran like a wounded animal to the fencing school, to present myself for admission to the Saxon Club, showing my card of matriculation. I attained my object, I could wear the colours of the Saxonia, which was in the fashion at that time, and in great request because it numbered so many delightful members in its ranks.

The strangest fate was to befall me in this Easter vacation, during which I was really the only remaining representative of the Saxon Club in Leipzig. In the beginning this club consisted chiefly of men of good family as well as the better class elements of the student world; all of them were members of highly placed and well-to-do families in Saxony in general, and in particular from the capital, Dresden, and spent their vacation at their respective homes. There remained in Leipzig during the vacations only those wandering students who had no homes, and for whom in reality it was always or never holiday time. Among these a separate club had arisen of daring and desperate young reprobates who had found a last refuge, as I said, at Leipzig in the glorious period I have recorded. I had already made the personal acquaintance of these swashbucklers, who pleased my fancy greatly, when they were guarding the Brockhaus grounds. Although the regular duration of a university course did not exceed three years, most of these men had never left their universities for six or seven years.

I was particularly fascinated by a man called Gebhardt, who was endowed with extraordinary physical beauty and strength, and whose slim heroic figure towered head and shoulders above all his companions. When he walked down the street arm-in-arm with two of the strongest of his comrades, he used suddenly to take it into his head, by an easy movement of his arm, to lift his friends high in the air and flutter along in this way as though he had a pair of human wings. When a cab was going along the streets at a sharp trot, he would seize a spoke of the wheel with one hand and force it to pull up. Nobody ever told him that he was stupid because they were afraid of his strength, hence his limitations were scarcely noticed. His redoubtable strength, combined with a temperate disposition, lent him a majestic dignity which placed him above the level of an ordinary mortal. He had come to Leipzig from Mecklenburg in the company of a certain Degelow, who was as powerful and adroit, though by no means of such gigantic proportions, as his friend, and whose chief attraction lay in his great vivacity and animated features. He had led a wild and dissipated life in which play, drink, passionate love affairs, and constant and prompt duelling had rung the changes. Ceremonious politeness, an ironic and pedantic coldness, which testified to bold self-confidence, combined with a very hot temper, formed the chief characteristics of this personage and natures akin to his. Degelow's wildness and passion were lent a curious diabolical charm by the possession of a malicious humour which he often turned against himself, whereas towards others he exercised a certain chivalrous tenderness.

These two extraordinary men were joined by others who

possessed all the qualities essential to a reckless life, together with real and headstrong valour. One of them, named Stelzer, a regular Berserker out of the Nibelungenlied, who was nicknamed Lope, was in his twentieth term. While these men openly and consciously belonged to a world doomed to destruction, and all their actions and escapades could only be explained by the hypothesis that they all believed that inevitable ruin was imminent, I made in their company the acquaintance of a certain Schröter, who particularly attracted me by his cordial disposition, pleasant Hanoverian accent, and refined wit. He was not one of the regular young dare-devils, towards whom he adopted a calm observant attitude, while they were all fond of him and glad to see him. I made a real friend of this Schröter, although he was much older than I was. Through him I became acquainted with the works and poems of H. Heine, and from him I acquired a certain neat and saucy wit, and I was quite ready to surrender myself to his agreeable influence in the hope of improving my outward bearing. It was his company in particular that I sought every day; in the afternoon I generally met him in the Rosenthal or Kintschy's Châlet, though always in the presence of those wonderful Goths who excited at once my alarm and admiration.

They all belonged to university clubs which were on hostile terms with the one of which I was a member. What this hostility between the various clubs meant only those can judge who are familiar with the tone prevalent among them in those days. The mere sight of hostile colours sufficed to infuriate these men, who otherwise were kind and gentle, provided they had taken the slightest drop too much. At all events, as long as the old stagers were sober they would look with good-natured complacency at a slight young fellow like me in the hostile colours moving among them so amicably. Those colours I wore in my own peculiar fashion. I had made use of the brief week during which my club was still in Leipzig to become the possessor of a splendid 'Saxon' cap, richly embroidered with silver, and worn by a man called Müller, who was afterwards a prominent constable at Dresden. I had been seized with such a violent craving for this cap that I managed to buy it from him, as he wanted money to go home. In spite of this remarkable cap I was, as I have said, welcome in the den of this band of rowdies: my friend Schröter saw to that. It was only when the grog, which was the principal beverage of these wild spirits, began to work that I used to notice curious glances and overhear doubtful speeches, the significance of which was for some time hidden from me by the dizziness in which my own senses were plunged by this baneful drink.

As I was inevitably bound on this account to be mixed up in quarrels for some time to come, it afforded me a great satisfaction that my first fight, as a matter of fact, arose from an incident more creditable to me than those provocations which I had left half unnoticed. One day Degelow came up to Schröter and me in a wine-bar that we often frequented, and in quite a friendly manner confessed to us confidentially his liking for a young and very pretty actress whose talent Schröter disputed. Degelow rejoined that this was as it might be, but that, for his part, he regarded the young lady as the most respectable woman in the theatre. I at once asked him if he considered my sister's reputation was not as good. According to students' notions it was impossible for Degelow, who doubtless had not the remotest intention of being insulting, to give me any assurance further than to say that he certainly did not think my sister had an inferior reputation, but that, nevertheless, he meant to abide by his assertion concerning the young lady he had mentioned. Hereupon followed without delay the usual challenge, opening with the words, 'You're an ass,' which sounded almost ridiculous to my own ears when I said them to this seasoned swashbuckler.

I remember that Degelow too gasped with astonishment, and lightning seemed to flash from his eyes; but he controlled himself in the presence of my friend, and proceeded to observe the usual formalities of a challenge, and chose broadswords (*krumme Säbel*) as the weapons for the fight. The event made a great stir among our companions, but I saw less reason than before to abstain from my usual intercourse with them. Only I became more strict about the behaviour of the swashbucklers, and for several days no evening passed without producing a challenge between me and some formidable bully, until at last Count Solms, the only member of my club who had returned

PREPARATIONS FOR A DUEL

to Leipzig as yet, visited me as though he were an intimate friend and inquired into what had occurred. He applauded my conduct, but advised me not to wear my colours until the return of our comrades from the vacation, and to keep away from the bad company into which I had ventured. Fortunately I had not long to wait; university life soon began again, and the fencing ground was filled. The unenviable position, in which, in student phrase, I was suspended with a half-dozen of the most terrible swordsmen, earned me a glorious reputation among the 'freshmen' and 'juniors,' and even among the older 'champions' of the Saxonia.

My seconds were duly arranged, the dates for the various duels on hand settled, and by the care of my seniors the needful time was secured for me to acquire some sort of skill in fencing. The light heart with which I awaited the fate which threatened me in at least one of the impending encounters I myself could not understand at the time; on the other hand, the way in which that fate preserved me from the consequences of my rashness seems truly miraculous in my eyes to this day, and worthy of further description.

The preparations for a duel included obtaining some experience of these encounters by being present at several of them. We freshmen attained this object by what is called 'carrying duty,' that is to say, we were entrusted with the rapiers of the corps (precious weapons of honour belonging to the association), and had to take them first to the grinder and thence to the scene of encounter, a proceeding which was attended with some danger, as it had to be done surreptitiously, since duelling was forbidden by law; in return we acquired the right of assisting as spectators at the impending engagements.

When I had earned this honour, the meeting-place chosen for the duel I was to watch was the billiard-room of an inn in the Burgstrasse; the table had been moved to one side, and on it the authorised spectators took their places. Among them I stood up with a beating heart to watch the dangerous encounters between those doughty champions. I was told on this occasion of the story of one of my friends (a Jew named Levy, but known as Lippert), who on this very floor had given

so much ground before his antagonist that the door had to
be opened for him, and he fell back through it down the steps
into the street, still believing he was engaged in the duel.
When several bouts had been finished, two men came on to
the 'pitch,' Tempel, the president of the *Markomanen,* and a
certain Wohlfart, an old stager, already in his fourteenth half-
year of study, with whom I also was booked for an encounter
later on. When this was the case, a man was not allowed to
watch, in order that the weak points of the duellist might not
be betrayed to his future opponent. Wohlfart was accordingly
asked by my chiefs whether he wanted me removed; whereupon he replied with calm contempt, ' Let them leave the
little freshman there, in God's name!' Thus I became an eye-
witness of the disablement of a swordsman who nevertheless
showed himself so experienced and skilful on the occasion that
I might well have become alarmed for the issue of my future
encounter with him. His gigantic opponent cut the artery
of his right arm, which at once ended the fight; the surgeon
declared that Wohlfart would not be able to hold a sword
again for years, under which circumstances my proposed meeting with him was at once cancelled. I do not deny that this
incident cheered my soul.

Shortly afterwards the first general reunion of our club was
held at the Green Tap. These gatherings are regular hot-
beds for the production of duels. Here I brought upon myself
a new encounter with one Tischer, but learned at the same time
that I had been relieved of two of my most formidable previous
engagements of the kind by the disappearance of my opponents,
both of whom had escaped on account of debt and left no trace
behind them. The only one of whom I could hear anything
was the terrible Stelzer, surnamed Lope. This fellow had
taken advantage of the passing of Polish refugees, who had
at that time already been driven over the frontier and were
making their way through Germany to France, to disguise
himself as an ill-starred champion of freedom, and he subsequently found his way to the Foreign Legion in Algeria. On
the way home from the gathering, Degelow, whom I was to
meet in a few weeks, proposed a ' truce.' This was a device
which, if it was accepted, as it was in this case, enabled the

future combatants to entertain and talk to one another, which was otherwise most strictly forbidden. We wandered back to the town arm-in-arm; with chivalrous tenderness my interesting and formidable opponent declared that he was delighted at the prospect of crossing swords with me in a few weeks' time; that he regarded it as an honour and a pleasure, as he was fond of me and respected me for my valorous conduct. Seldom has any personal success flattered me more. We embraced, and amid protestations which, owing to a certain dignity about them, acquired a significance I can never forget, we parted. He informed me that he must first pay a visit to Jena, where he had an appointment to fight a duel. A week later the news of his death reached Leipzig; he had been mortally wounded in the duel at Jena.

I felt as if I were living in a dream, out of which I was aroused by the announcement of my encounter with Tischer. Though he was a first-rate and vigorous fighter, he had been chosen by our chiefs for my first passage of arms because he was fairly short. In spite of being unable to feel any great confidence in my hastily acquired and little practised skill in fencing, I looked forward to this my first duel with a light heart. Although it was against the rules, I never dreamed of telling the authorities that I was suffering from a slight rash which I had caught at that time, and which I was informed made wounds so dangerous that if it were reported it would postpone the meeting, in spite of the fact that I was modest enough to be prepared for wounds. I was sent for at ten in the morning, and left home smiling to think what my mother and sisters would say if in a few hours I were brought back in the alarming state I anticipated. My chief, Herr v. Schönfeld, was a pleasant, quiet sort of man, who lived on the marsh. When I reached his house, he leant out of the window with his pipe in his mouth, and greeted me with the words: 'You can go home, my lad, it is all off; Tischer is in hospital.' When I got upstairs I found several 'leading men' assembled, from whom I learned that Tischer had got very drunk the night before, and had in consequence laid himself open to the most outrageous treatment by the inhabitants of a house of ill-fame. He was terribly hurt, and had been taken by the police in the first instance to the hospital. This inevitably meant rustication, and, above all, expulsion from the academic association to which he belonged.

I cannot clearly recall the incidents that removed from Leipzig the few remaining fire-eaters to whom I had pledged myself since that fatal vacation-time; I only know that this side of my fame as a student yielded to another. We celebrated the 'freshmen's gathering,' to which all those who could manage it drove a four-in-hand in a long procession through the town. After the president of the club had profoundly moved me with his sudden and yet prolonged solemnity, I conceived the desire to be among the very last to return home from the outing. Accordingly I stayed away three days and three nights, and spent the time chiefly in gambling, a pastime which from the first night of our festivity cast its devilish snares around me. Some half-dozen of the smartest club members chanced to be together at early dawn in the Jolly Peasant, and forthwith formed the nucleus of a gambling club, which was reinforced during the day by recruits coming back from the town. Members came to see whether we were still at it, members also went away, but I with the original six held out for days and nights without faltering.

The desire that first prompted me to take part in the play was the wish to win enough for my score (two thalers): this I succeeded in doing, and thereupon I was inspired with the hope of being able to settle all the debts I had made at that time by my winnings at play. Just as I had hoped to learn composition most quickly by Logier's method, but had found myself hampered in my object for a long period by unexpected difficulties, so my plan for speedily improving my financial position was likewise doomed to disappointment. To win was not such an easy matter, and for some three months I was such a victim to the rage for gambling that no other passion was able to exercise the slightest influence over my mind.

Neither the *Fechtboden* (where the students' fights were practised), nor the beer-house, nor the actual scene of the fights, ever saw my face again. In my lamentable position I racked my brains all day to devise ways and means of getting the money wherewith to gamble at night. In vain did my poor mother try everything in her power to induce me not to come home so late at night, although she had no idea of the real nature of my debauches: after I had left the house in the afternoon I never returned till dawn the next day, and I reached my room (which was at some distance from the others) by climbing over the gate, for my mother had refused to give me a latch-key.

In despair over my ill-luck, my passion for gambling grew into a veritable mania, and I no longer felt any inclination for those things which at one time had lured me to student life. I became absolutely indifferent to the opinion of my former companions and avoided them entirely; I now lost myself in the smaller gambling dens of Leipzig, where only the very scum of the students congregated. Insensible to any feeling of self-respect, I bore even the contempt of my sister Rosalie; both she and my mother hardly ever deigning to cast a glance at the young libertine whom they only saw at rare intervals, looking deadly pale and worn out: my ever-growing despair made me at last resort to foolhardiness as the only means of forcing hostile fate to my side. It suddenly struck me that only by dint of big stakes could I make big profits. To this end I decided to make use of my mother's pension, of which I was trustee of a fairly large sum. That night I lost everything I had with me except one thaler: the excitement with which I staked that last coin on a card was an experience hitherto quite strange to my young life. As I had had nothing to eat, I was obliged repeatedly to leave the gambling table owing to sickness. With this last thaler I staked my life, for my return to my home was, of course, out of the question. Already I saw myself in the grey dawn, a prodigal son, fleeing from all I held dear, through forest and field towards the unknown. My mood of despair had gained so strong a hold upon me that, when my card won, I immediately placed all the money on a fresh stake, and repeated this experiment until I had won quite a considerable amount. From that moment my luck grew continuously. I gained such confidence that I risked the most hazardous stakes: for suddenly it dawned upon me that this was destined to be my last day with the cards. My good fortune now became so obvious that the bank thought it wise to close. Not only had I won back all the money I had lost, but I had won enough to pay off all my debts as well. My sensations during the whole of this process were of the most sacred nature: I felt as if God and His angels were standing by my side and were whispering words of warning and of consolation into my ears.

Once more I climbed over the gate of my home in the early hours of the morning, this time to sleep peacefully and soundly and to awake very late, strengthened and as though born again.

No sense of shame deterred me from telling my mother, to whom I presented her money, the whole truth about this decisive night. I voluntarily confessed my sin in having utilised her pension, sparing no detail. She folded her hands and thanked God for His mercy, and forthwith regarded me as saved, believing it impossible for me ever to commit such a crime again.

And, truth to tell, gambling had lost all fascination for me from that moment. The world, in which I had moved like one demented, suddenly seemed stripped of all interest or attraction. My rage for gambling had already made me quite indifferent to the usual student's vanities, and when I was freed from this passion also, I suddenly found myself face to face with an entirely new world.

To this world I belonged henceforth: it was the world of real and serious musical study, to which I now devoted myself heart and soul.

Even during this wild period of my life, my musical development had not been entirely at a standstill; on the contrary, it daily became plainer that music was the only direction towards which my mental tendencies had a marked bent. Only I had got quite out of the habit of musical study. Even now it seems incredible that I managed to find time in those days to finish quite a substantial amount of composition. I have but the faintest recollection of an Overture in C major ($6/8$ time), and of a Sonata in B flat major arranged as a duet; the latter pleased my sister Ottilie, who played it with me, so much that I arranged it for orchestra. But another work of this period, an Overture in B flat major, left an indelible impression on my mind on account of an incident connected with it. This composition, in fact, was the outcome of my study of Beethoven's Ninth Symphony in about the same degree as *Leubald und Adelaïde* was the result of my study of Shakespeare. I had made a special point of bringing out the mystic meaning in the orchestra, which I divided into three distinctly different and opposite elements. I wanted to make the characteristic nature of these elements clear to the score reader the moment he looked at it by a striking display of colour, and only the fact that I could not get any green ink made this picturesque idea impossible. I employed black ink for the brass instruments alone, the strings were to have red and the wind green ink. This extraordinary score I gave for perusal to Heinrich Dorn, who was at that time musical director of the Leipzig theatre. He was very young, and impressed me as being a very clever musician and a witty man of the world, whom the Leipzig public made much of.

Nevertheless, I have never been able to understand how he could have granted my request to produce this overture.

Some time afterwards I was rather inclined to believe with others, who knew how much he enjoyed a good joke, that he intended to treat himself to a little fun. At the time, however, he vowed that he thought the work interesting, and maintained that if it were only brought out as a hitherto unknown work by Beethoven, the public would receive it with respect, though without understanding.

It was the Christmas of the fateful year 1830; as usual, there would be no performance at the theatre on Christmas Eve, but instead a concert for the poor had been organised, which received but scant support. The first item on the programme was called by the exciting title 'New Overture' — nothing more! I had surreptitiously listened to the rehearsal with some misgiving. I was very much impressed by the coolness with which Dorn fenced with the apparent confusion which the members of the orchestra showed with regard to this mysterious composition. The principal theme of the Allegro was contained in four bars; after every fourth bar, however, a fifth bar had been inserted, which had nothing to do with the melody, and which was announced by a loud bang on the kettle-drum on the second beat. As this drum-beat stood out alone, the drummer, who continually thought he was making a mistake, got confused, and did not give the right sharpness to the accent as prescribed by the score. Listening from my hidden corner, and frightened at my original intention, this accidentally different rendering did not displease me. To my genuine annoyance, however, Dorn called the drummer to the front and insisted on his playing the accents with the prescribed sharpness. When, after the rehearsal, I told the musical director of my misgivings about this important fact, I could not get him to promise a milder interpretation of the fatal drum-beat; he stuck to it that the thing would sound very well as it was. In spite of this assurance my restlessness grew, and I had not the courage to introduce myself to my friends in advance as the author of the 'New Overture.'

My sister Ottilie, who had already been forced to survive the secret readings of *Leubald und Adelaïde*, was the only person willing to come with me to hear my work. It was Christmas Eve, and there was to be the usual Christmas tree, presents, etc., at my brother-in-law's, Friedrich Brockhaus, and both of us naturally wanted to be there. My sister, in particular, who lived there, had a good deal to do with the arrangements, and could only get away for a short while, and that with great difficulty; our amiable relation accordingly had the carriage ready for her so that she might get back more quickly. I made use of this opportunity to inaugurate, as it were, my entrée into the musical world in a festive manner. The carriage drew up in front of the theatre. Ottilie went into my brother-in-law's box, which forced me to try and find a seat in the pit. I had forgotten to buy a ticket, and was refused admission by the man at the door. Suddenly the tuning up of the orchestra grew louder and louder, and I thought I should have to miss the beginning of my work. In my anxiety I revealed myself to the man at the door as the composer of the 'New Overture,' and in this way succeeded in passing without a ticket. I pushed my way through to one of the first rows of the pit, and sat down in terrible anxiety.

The Overture began: after the theme of the 'black' bras-

instruments had made itself heard with great emphasis, the 'red' Allegro theme started, in which, as I have already mentioned, every fifth bar was interrupted by the drum-beat from the 'black' world. What kind of effect the 'green' theme of the wind instruments, which joined in afterwards, produced upon the listeners, and what they must have thought when 'black,' 'red,' and 'green' themes became intermingled, has always remained a mystery to me, for the fatal drum-beat, brutally hammered out, entirely deprived me of my senses, especially as this prolonged and continually recurring effect now began to rouse, not only the attention, but the merriment of the audience. I heard my neighbours calculating the return of this effect; knowing the absolute correctness of their calculation, I suffered ten thousand torments, and became almost unconscious. At last I awoke from my nightmare when the Overture, to which I had disdained to give what I considered a trite ending, came to a standstill most unexpectedly.

No phantoms like those in Hoffmann's *Tales* could have succeeded in producing the extraordinary state in which I came to my senses on noticing the astonishment of the audience at the end of the performance. I heard no exclamations of disapproval, no hissing, no remarks, not even laughter; all I saw was intense astonishment at such a strange occurrence, which impressed them, as it did me, like a horrible nightmare. The worst moment, however, came when I had to leave the pit and take my sister home. To get up and pass through the people in the pit was horrible indeed. Nothing, however, equalled the pain of coming face to face with the man at the door; the strange look he gave me haunted me ever afterwards, and for a considerable time I avoided the pit of the Leipzig theatre.

My next step was to find my sister, who had gone through the whole sad experience with infinite pity; in silence we drove home to be present at a brilliant family festivity, which contrasted with grim irony with the gloom of my bewilderment.

In spite of it all I tried to believe in myself, and thought I could find comfort in my overture to the *Braut von Messina,* which I believed to be a better work than the fatal one I had just heard. A reinstatement, however, was out of the question, for the directors of the Leipzig theatre regarded me for a long time as a very doubtful person, in spite of Dorn's friendship. It is true that I still tried my hand at sketching out compositions to Goethe's *Faust,* some of which have been preserved to this day: but soon my wild student's life resumed its sway and drowned the last remnant of serious musical study in me.

I now began to imagine that because I had become a student I ought to attend the University lectures. From Traugott Krug, who was well known to me on account of his having suppressed the student's revolt, I tried to learn the first principles of philosophy; a single lesson sufficed to make me give this up. Two or three times, however, I attended the lectures on æsthetics given by one of the younger professors, a man called Weiss. This perseverance was due to the interest which Weiss immediately aroused in me. When I made his acquaintance at my uncle Adolph's house, Weiss had just translated the metaphysics of Aristotle, and, if I am not mistaken, dedicated them in a controversial spirit to Hegel.

On this occasion I had listened to the conversation of these two men on philosophy and philosophers, which made a tremendous impression on me. I remember that Weiss was an absent-minded man, with a hasty and abrupt manner of speaking; he had an interesting and pensive expression which impressed me immensely. I recollect how, on being accused of a want of clearness in his writing and style, he justified himself by saying that the deep problems of the human mind could not in any case be solved by the mob. This maxim, which struck me as being very plausible, I at once accepted as the principle for all my future writing. I remember that my eldest brother Albert, to whom I once had to write for my mother, grew so disgusted with my letter and style that he said he thought I must be going mad.

In spite of my hopes that Weiss's lectures would do me much good, I was not capable of continuing to attend them, as my desires in those days drove me to anything but the study of æsthetics. Nevertheless, my mother's anxiety at this time on my behalf made me try to take up music again. As Müller, the teacher under whom I had studied till that time, had not been able to inspire me with a permanent love of study, it was necessary to discover whether another teacher might not be better able to induce me to do serious work.

Theodor Weinlich, who was choirmaster and musical director at St. Thomas's Church, held at that time this important and ancient post which was afterwards occupied by Schicht, and before him by no less a person than Sebastian Bach. By education he belonged to the old Italian school of music, and had studied in Bologna under Pater Martini. He had made a name for himself in this art by his vocal compositions, in which his fine manner of treating the parts was much praised. He himself told me one day that a Leipzig publisher had offered him a very substantial fee if he would write for his firm another book of vocal exercises similar to the one which had proved so profitable to his first publisher. Weinlich told him that he had not got any exercises of the kind ready at the moment, but offered him instead a new Mass, which the publisher refused with the words: 'Let him who got the meat gnaw the bones.' The modesty with which Weinlich told me this little story showed how excellent a man he was. As he was in a very bad and weak state of health when my mother introduced me to him, he at first refused to take me as a pupil. But, after having resisted all persuasions, he at last took pity on my musical education, which, as he soon discovered from a fugue which I had brought with me, was exceedingly faulty. He accordingly promised to teach me, on condition that I should give up all attempts at composing for six months, and follow his instructions implicitly. To the first part of my promise I remained faithful, thanks to the vast vortex of dissipation into which my life as a student had drawn me.

When, however, I had to occupy myself for any length of time with nothing but four-part harmony exercises in strictly rigorous style, it was not only the student in me, but also the composer of so many overtures and sonatas, that was thoroughly disgusted. Weinlich, too, had his grievances against me, and decided to give me up.

During this period I came to the crisis of my life, which led to the catastrophe of that terrible evening at the gambling den. But an even greater blow than this fearful experience awaited me when Weinlich decided not to have anything more to do with me. Deeply humiliated and miserable, I besought the gentle old man, whom I loved dearly, to forgive me, and I promised him from that moment to work with unflagging energy. One morning at seven o'clock Weinlich sent for me to begin the rough sketch for a fugue; he devoted the whole morning to me, following my work bar by bar with the greatest attention, and giving me his valuable advice. At twelve o'clock he dismissed me with the instruction to perfect and finish the sketch by filling in the remaining parts at home.

When I brought him the fugue finished, he handed me his own treatment of the same theme for comparison. This common task of fugue writing established between me and my good-natured teacher the tenderest of ties, for, from that moment, we both enjoyed the lessons. I was astonished how quickly the time flew. In eight weeks I had not only gone through a number of the most intricate fugues, but had also waded through all kinds of difficult evolutions in counterpoint, when one day, on bringing him an extremely elaborate double fugue, he took my breath away by telling me that after this there was nothing left for him to teach me.

As I was not aware of any great effort on my part, I often wondered whether I had really become a well-equipped musician. Weinlich himself did not seem to attach much importance to what he had taught me: he said, 'Probably you will never write fugues or canons; but what you have mastered is Independence: you can now stand alone and rely upon having a fine technique at your fingers' ends if you should want it.'

The principal result of his influence over me was certainly the growing love of clearness and fluency to which he had trained me. I had already had to write the above-mentioned fugue for ordinary voices; my feeling for the melodious and vocal had in this way been awakened. In order to keep me strictly under his calming and friendly influence, he had at the same time given me a sonata to write which, as a proof of my friendship for him, I had to build up on strictly harmonic and thematic lines, for which he recommended me a very early and childlike sonata by Pleyel as a model.

Those who had only recently heard my Overture must, indeed, have wondered how I ever wrote this sonata, which has been published through the indiscretion of Messrs. Breitkopf and Härtel (to reward me for my abstemiousness Weinlich induced them to publish this poor composition). From that moment he gave me a free hand. To begin with I was allowed to compose a Fantasia for the pianoforte (in F sharp minor) which I wrote in a quite informal style by treating the melody in recitative form; this gave me intense satisfaction because it won me praise from Weinlich.

Soon afterwards I wrote three overtures which all met with his entire approval. In the following winter (1831–1832) I succeeded in getting the first of them, in D minor, performed at one of the Gewandhaus concerts.

At that time a very simple and homely tone reigned supreme in this institution. The instrumental works were not conducted by what we call 'a conductor of the orchestra,' but were simply played to the audience by the *leader* of the orchestra. As soon as the singing began, Pohlenz took his place at the conductor's desk; he belonged to the type of fat and pleasant musical directors, and was a great favourite with the Leipzig public. He used to come on the platform with a very important-looking blue baton in his hand.

One of the strangest events which occurred at that time was the yearly production of the Ninth Symphony of Beethoven; after the first three movements had been played straight through like a Haydn symphony, as well as the orchestra could manage it, Pohlenz, instead of having to conduct a vocal quartette, a cantata, or an Italian aria, took his place at the desk to undertake this highly complicated instrumental work, with its particularly enigmatical and incoherent opening, one of the most difficult tasks that could possibly be found for a musical conductor. I shall never forget the impression produced upon me at the first rehearsal by the anxiously and carefully played 3/4 time, and the way in which the wild shrieks of the trumpet (with which this movement begins) resulted in the most extraordinary confusion of sound.

He had evidently chosen this tempo in order, in some way, to manage the recitative of the double basses; but it was utterly hopeless. Pohlenz was in a bath of perspiration, the recitative did not come off, and I really began to think that Beethoven must have written nonsense; the double bass player, Temmler, a faithful veteran of the orchestra, prevailed upon Pohlenz at last, in rather coarse and energetic language, to put down the baton, and in this way the recitative really proceeded properly. All the same, I felt at this time that I had come to the humble conclusion, in a way I can hardly explain, that this extraordinary work was still beyond my comprehension. For a long time I gave up brooding over this composition, and I turned my thoughts with simple longing towards a clearer and calmer musical form.

My study of counterpoint had taught me to appreciate, above all, Mozart's light and flowing treatment of the most difficult technical problems, and the last movement of his great Symphony in C major in particular served me as example for my own work. My D minor Overture, which clearly showed the influence of Beethoven's *Coriolanus* Overture, had been favourably received by the public; my mother began to have faith in me again, and I started at once on a second overture (in C major), which really ended with a ' Fugato ' that did more credit to my new model than I had ever hoped to accomplish.

This overture, also, was soon afterwards performed at a recital given by the favourite singer, Mlle. Palazzesi (of the Dresden Italian Opera). Before this I had already introduced it at a concert given by a private musical society called ' Euterpe', when I had conducted it myself.

I remember the strange impression I received from a remark that my mother made on that occasion; as a matter of fact this work, which was written in a counterpoint style, without any real passion or emotion, had produced a strange effect upon her. She gave vent to her astonishment by warmly praising the *Egmont* Overture, which was played at the same concert, maintaining that ' this kind of music was after all more fascinating than any stupid fugue.'

At this time I also wrote (as my third opus) an overture to Raupach's drama, *König Enzio,* in which again Beethoven's influence made itself even more strongly felt. My sister Rosalie succeeded in getting it performed at the theatre before the play; for the sake of prudence they did not announce it on the programme the first time. Dorn conducted it, and as the performance went off all right, and the public showed no dissatisfaction, my overture was played with my full name on the programme several times during the run of the above-mentioned drama.

After this I tried my hand at a big Symphony (in C major); in this work I showed what I had learnt by using the influence of my study of Beethoven and Mozart towards the achievement of a really pleasant and intelligible work, in which the fugue was again present at the end, while the themes of the various movements were so constructed that they could be played consecutively.

Nevertheless, the passionate and bold element of the *Sinfonia Eroica* was distinctly discernible, especially in the first movement. The slow movement, on the contrary, contained reminiscences of my former musical mysticism. A kind of repeated interrogative exclamation of the minor third merging into the fifth connected in my mind this work (which I had finished with the utmost effort at clearness) with my very earliest period of boyish sentimentality.

When, in the following year, I called on Friedrich Rochlitz, at that time the 'Nestor' of the musical æsthetes in Leipzig, and president of the Gewandhaus, I prevailed upon him to promise me a performance of my work. As he had been given my score for perusal before seeing me, he was quite astonished to find that I was a very young man, for the character of my music had prepared him to see a much older and more experienced musician. Before this performance took place many things happened which I must first mention, as they were of great importance to my life.

My short and stormy career as a student had drowned in me not only all longing for further development, but also all interest in intellectual and spiritual pursuits. Although, as I have pointed out, I had never alienated myself entirely from music, my revived interest in politics aroused my first real disgust for my senseless student's life, which soon left no deeper traces on my mind than the remembrance of a terrible nightmare.

The Polish War of Independence against Russian supremacy filled me with growing enthusiasm. The victories which the Poles obtained for a short period during May, 1831, aroused my enthusiastic admiration: it seemed to me as though the world had, by some miracle, been created anew. As a contrast to this, the news of the battle of Ostrolenka made it appear as if the end of the world had come. To my astonishment, my boon companions scoffed at me when I commented upon some of these events; the terrible lack of all fellow-feeling and comradeship amongst the students struck me very forcibly. Any kind of enthusiasm had to be smothered or turned into pedantic bravado, which showed itself in the form of affectation and indifference. To get drunk with deliberate coldbloodedness, without even a glimpse of humour, was reckoned almost as brave a feat as duelling. Not until much later did I understand the far nobler spirit which animated the lower classes in Germany in comparison with the sadly degenerate state of the University students. In those days I felt terribly indignant at the insulting remarks which I brought upon myself when I deplored the battle of Ostrolenka.

To my honour be it said, that these and similar impressions helped to make me give up my low associates. During my studies with Weinlich the only little dissipation I allowed myself was my daily evening visit to Kintschy, the confectioner in the Klostergasse, where I passionately devoured the latest newspapers. Here I found many men who held the same political views as myself, and I specially loved to listen to the eager political discussions of some of the old men who frequented the place. The literary journals, too, began to interest me; I read a great deal, but was not very particular in my choice. Nevertheless, I now began to appreciate intelligence and wit, whereas before only the grotesque and the fantastic had had any attraction for me.

My interest in the issue of the Polish war, however, remained paramount. I felt the siege and capture of Warsaw as a personal calamity. My excitement when the remains of the Polish army began to pass through Leipzig on their way to France was indescribable, and I shall never forget the impression produced upon me by the first batch of these unfortunate soldiers on the occasion of their being quartered at the Green Shield, a public-house in the Meat Market. Much as this depressed me, I was soon roused to a high pitch of enthusiasm, for in the lounge of the Leipzig Gewandhaus, where that night Beethoven's C minor Symphony was being played, a group of heroic figures, the principal leaders of the Polish revolution, excited my admiration. I felt more particularly attracted by Count Vincenz Tyszkiéwitcz, a man of exceptionally powerful physique and noble appearance, who impressed me by his dignified and aristocratic manner and his quiet self-reliance — qualities with which I had not met before. When I saw a man of such kingly bearing in a tight-fitting coat and red velvet cap, I at once realised my foolishness in ever having worshipped the ludicrously dressed up little heroes of our students' world. I was delighted to meet this gentleman again at the house of my brother-in-law, Friedrich Brockhaus, where I saw him frequently.

My brother-in-law had the greatest pity and sympathy for the Polish rebels, and was the president of a committee whose task it was to look after their interests, and for a long time he made many personal sacrifices for their cause.

The Brockhaus establishment now became tremendously attractive to me. Around Count Vincenz Tyszkiéwitcz, who remained the lodestar of this small Polish world, gathered a great many other wealthy exiles, amongst whom I chiefly remember a cavalry captain of the name of Bansemer, a man of unlimited kindness, but of a rather frivolous nature; he possessed a marvellous team of four horses which he drove at such breakneck speed as to cause great annoyance to the people of Leipzig. Another man of importance with whom I remember dining was General Bem, whose artillery had made such a gallant stand at Ostrolenka.

Many other exiles passed through this hospitable house, some of whom impressed us by their melancholy, warlike bearing, others by their refined behaviour. Vincenz Tyszkiéwitcz, however, remained my ideal of a true man, and I loved him with a profound adoration. He, too, began to be interested in me; I used to call upon him nearly every day, and was sometimes present at a sort of martial feast, from which he often withdrew in order to be able to open his heart to me about the anxieties which oppressed him. He had, in fact, received absolutely no news of the whereabouts of his wife and little son since they separated at Volhynien. Besides this, he was under the shadow of a great sorrow which drew all sympathetic natures to him. To my sister Louise he had confided the terrible calamity that had once befallen him. He had been married before, and while staying with his wife in one of his lonely castles, in the dead of night he had seen a ghostly apparition at the window of his bedroom. Hearing his name called several times, he had taken up a revolver to protect himself from possible danger, and had shot his own wife, who had had the eccentric idea of teasing him by pretending to be a ghost. I had the pleasure of sharing his joy on hearing that his family was safe. His wife joined him in Leipzig with their beautiful boy, Janusz. I felt sorry not to be able to feel the same sympathy for this lady as I did for her husband; perhaps one of the reasons of my antipathy was the obvious and conspicuous way in which she made herself up, by means of which the poor woman probably tried to hide how much her beauty had suffered through the terrible strain of the past events. She soon went back to Galicia to try and save what she could of their property, and also to provide her husband with a pass from the Austrian Government, by means of which he could follow her.

Then came the third of May. Eighteen of the Poles who were still in Leipzig met together at a festive dinner in a hotel outside the town; on this day was to be celebrated the first anniversary of the third of May, so dear to the memory of the Poles. Only the chiefs of the Leipzig Polish Committee received invitations, and as a special favour I also was asked. I shall never forget that occasion. The dinner became an orgy; throughout the evening a brass band from the town played Polish folksongs, and these were sung by the whole company, led by a Lithuanian called Zan, in a manner now triumphant and now mournful. The beautiful 'Third of May' song more particularly drew forth a positive uproar of enthusiasm. Tears and shouts of joy grew into a terrible tumult; the excited men grouped themselves on the grass swearing eternal friend-

CHOLERA IN BRÜNN

ship in the most extravagant terms, for which the word 'Oiczisna' (Fatherland) provided the principal theme, until at last night threw her veil over this wild debauch.

That evening afterwards served me as the theme for an orchestral composition (in the form of an overture) named *Polonia;* I shall recount the fate of this work later on. My friend Tyszkiéwitcz's passport now arrived, and he made up his mind to go back to Galicia *via* Brünn, although his friends considered it was very rash of him to do so. I very much wanted to see something of the world, and Tyszkiéwitcz's offer to take me with him, induced my mother to consent to my going to Vienna, a place that I had long wished to visit. I took with me the scores of my three overtures which had already been performed, and also that of my great symphony as yet unproduced, and had a grand time with my Polish patron, who took me in his luxurious travelling-coach as far as the capital of Moravia. During a short stop at Dresden the exiles of all classes gave our beloved Count a friendly farewell dinner in Pirna, at which the champagne flowed freely, while the health was drunk of the future 'Dictator of Poland.'

At last we separated at Brünn, from which place I continued my journey to Vienna by coach. During the afternoon and night, which I was obliged to spend in Brünn by myself, I went through terrible agonies from fear of the cholera which, as I unexpectedly heard, had broken out in this place. There I was all alone in a strange place, my faithful friend just departed, and on hearing of the epidemic I felt as if a malicious demon had caught me in his snare in order to annihilate me. I did not betray my terror to the people in the hotel, but when I was shown into a very lonely wing of the house and left by myself in this wilderness, I hid myself in bed with my clothes on, and lived once again through all the horrors of ghost stories as I had done in my boyhood. The cholera stood before me like a living thing; I could see and touch it; it lay in my bed and embraced me. My limbs turned to ice, I felt frozen to the very marrow. Whether I was awake or asleep I never knew; I only remember how astonished I was when, on awakening, I felt thoroughly well and healthy.

At last I arrived in Vienna, where I escaped the epidemic

which had penetrated as far as that town. It was midsummer of the year 1832. Owing to the introductions I had with me, I found myself very much at home in this lively city, in which I made a pleasant stay of six weeks. As my sojourn, however, had no really practical purpose, my mother looked upon the cost of this holiday, short as it seemed, as an unnecessary extravagance on my part. I visited the theatres, heard Strauss, made excursions, and altogether had a very good time. I am afraid I contracted a few debts as well, which I paid off later on when I was conductor of the Dresden orchestra. I had received very pleasant impressions of musical and theatrical life, and for a long time Vienna lived in my memory as the acme of that extraordinarily productive spirit peculiar to its people. I enjoyed most of all the performances at the *Theater an der Wien,* at which they were acting a grotesque fairy play called *Die Abenteuer Fortunat's zu Wasser und zu Land,* in which a cab was called on the shores of the Black Sea and which made a tremendous impression on me. About the music I was more doubtful. A young friend of mine took me with immense pride to a performance of Gluck's *Iphigenia in Tauris,* which was made doubly attractive by a first-rate cast including Wild, Stäudigl and Binder: I must confess that on the whole I was bored by this work, but I did not dare say so. My ideas of Gluck had attained gigantic proportions from my reading of Hoffmann's well-known *Phantasies;* my anticipation of this work therefore, which I had not studied yet, had led me to expect a treatment full of overpowering dramatic force. It is possible that Schröder-Devrient's acting in *Fidelio* had taught me to judge everything by her exalted standard.

With the greatest trouble I worked myself up to some kind of enthusiasm for the great scene between Orestes and the Furies. I hoped against hope that I should be able to admire the remainder of the opera. I began to understand the Viennese taste, however, when I saw how great a favourite the opera *Zampa* became with the public, both at the Kärnthner Thor and at the Josephstadt. Both theatres competed vigorously in the production of this popular work, and although the public had seemed mad about *Iphigenia,* nothing equalled their enthusiasm for *Zampa.* No sooner had they left the Josephstadt Theatre in the greatest ecstasies about *Zampa* than they proceeded to the public-house called the Sträusslein. Here they were immediately greeted by the strains of selections from *Zampa* which drove the audience to feverish excitement. I shall never forget the extraordinary playing of Johann Strauss, who put equal enthusiasm into everything he played, and very often made the audience almost frantic with delight.

At the beginning of a new waltz this demon of the Viennese musical spirit shook like a Pythian priestess on the tripod, and veritable groans of ecstasy (which, without doubt, were more due to his music than to the drinks in which the audience had indulged) raised their worship for the magic violinist to almost bewildering heights of frenzy.

The hot summer air of Vienna was absolutely impregnated with *Zampa* and Strauss. A very poor students' rehearsal at the Conservatoire, at which they performed a Mass by Cherubini, seemed to me like an alms paid begrudgingly to the study of classical music. At the same rehearsal one of the professors, to whom I was introduced, tried to make the students play my Overture in D minor (the one already performed in Leipzig). I do not know what his opinion was, nor that of the students, with regard to this attempt; I only know they soon gave it up.

On the whole I had wandered into doubtful musical bypaths; and I now withdrew from this first educational visit to a great European art centre in order to start on a cheap, but long and monotonous return journey to Bohemia, by stage-coach. My next move was a visit to the house of Count Pachta, of whom I had pleasant recollections from my boyhood days. His estate, Pravonin, was about eight miles from Prague. Received in the kindest possible way by the old gentleman and his beautiful daughters, I enjoyed his delightful hospitality until late into the autumn. A youth of nineteen, as I then was, with a fast-growing beard (for which my sisters had already prepared the young ladies by letter), the continual and close intimacy with such kind and pretty girls could hardly fail to make a strong impression on my imagination. Jenny, the elder of the two, was slim, with black hair, blue eyes, and wonderfully noble features; the younger one, Auguste, was a little smaller, and stouter, with a magnificent complexion, fair hair, and brown eyes. The natural and sisterly manner with which both girls treated me and conversed with me did not blind me to the fact that I was expected to fall in love with one or the other of them. It amused them to see how embarrassed I got in my efforts to choose between them, and consequently they teased me tremendously.

Unfortunately, I did not act judiciously with regard to the daughters of my host: in spite of their homely education, they belonged to a very aristocratic house, and consequently hesitated between the hope of marrying men of eminent position in their own sphere, and the necessity of choosing husbands amongst the higher middle classes, who could afford to keep them in comfort. The shockingly poor, almost mediæval, education of the Austrian so-called cavalier, made me rather despise the latter; the girls, too, had suffered from the same lack of proper training. I soon noticed with disgust how little they knew about things artistic, and how much value they attached to superficial things. However much I might try to interest them in those higher pursuits which had become necessary to me, they were incapable of appreciating them. I advocated a complete change from the bad library novels, which represented their only reading, from the Italian operatic arias, sung by Auguste, and, last but not least, from the horsy, insipid cavaliers, who paid their court to both Jenny and her sister in the most coarse and offensive manner. My zeal in this latter respect soon gave rise to great unpleasantness. I became hard and insulting, harangued them about the French Revolution, and begged them with fatherly admonitions 'for the love of heaven' to be content with well-educated middle-class men, and give up those impertinent suitors who could only harm their reputation. The indignation provoked by my friendly advice I often had to ward off with the harshest retorts. I never apologised, but tried by dint of real or feigned jealousy to get our friendship back on the old footing. In this way, undecided, half in love and half angry, one cold November day I said good-bye to these pretty children. I soon met the whole family again at Prague, where I made a long sojourn, without, however, staying at the Count's residence.

My stay at Prague was to be of great musical importance to me. I knew the director of the Conservatoire, Dionys Weber, who promised to bring my symphony before the public; I also spent much of my time with an actor called Moritz, to whom, as an old friend of our family, I had been recommended, and there I made the acquaintance of the young musician Kittl.

Moritz, who noticed that not a day passed but what I went to the much-feared chief of the Conservatoire upon some pressing musical business, once despatched me with an improvised parody on Schiller's *Bürgschaft:* —

> *Zu Dionys dem Direktor schlich*
> *Wagner, die Partitur im Gewande;*
> *Ihn schlugen die Schüler im Bande:*
> *'Was wolltest du mit den Noten sprich?'*
> *Entgegnet ihm finster der Wütherich:*
> *'Die Stadt vom schlechten Geschmacke befreien!*
> *Das sollst du in den Rezensionen bereuen.'* [1]

Truly I had to deal with a kind of 'Dionysius the Tyrant.' A man who did not acknowledge Beethoven's genius beyond his Second Symphony, a man who looked upon the *Eroica* as the acme of bad taste on the master's part; who praised Mozart alone, and next to him tolerated only Lindpaintner: such a man was not easy to approach, and I had to learn the art of making use of tyrants for one's own purposes. I dissimulated; I pretended to be struck by the novelty of his ideas, never contradicted him, and, to point out the similarity of our standpoints, I referred him to the end fugue in my Overture and in my Symphony (both in C major), which I had only succeeded in making what they were through having studied Mozart. My reward soon followed: Dionys set to work to study my orchestral creations with almost youthful energy.

---

[1] To Dionys, the Director, crept
Wagner, the score in his pocket;
The students arrested him forthwith:
'What do'st thou with that music, say?'
Thus asked him the angry tyrant:
'To free the town from taste too vile!
For this the critics will make thee suffer.'

The students of the Conservatoire were compelled to practise with the greatest exactitude my new symphony under his dry and terribly noisy baton. In the presence of several of my friends, amongst whom was also the dear old Count Pachta in his capacity of President of the Conservatoire Committee, we actually held a first performance of the greatest work that I had written up to that date.

During these musical successes I went on with my love-making in the attractive house of Count Pachta, under the most curious circumstances. A confectioner of the name of Hascha was my rival. He was a tall, lanky young man who, like most Bohemians, had taken up music as a hobby; he played the accompaniments to Auguste's songs, and naturally fell in love with her. Like myself, he hated the frequent visits of the cavaliers, which seemed to be quite the custom in this city; but while my displeasure expressed itself in humour, his showed itself in gloomy melancholy. This mood made him behave boorishly in public: for instance, one evening, when the chandelier was to be lighted for the reception of one of these gentlemen, he ran his head purposely against this ornament and broke it. The festive illumination was thus rendered impossible; the Countess was furious, and Hascha had to leave the house never to return.

I well remember that the first time I was conscious of any feelings of love, these manifested themselves as pangs of jealousy, which had, however, nothing to do with real love: this happened one evening when I called at the house. The Countess kept me by her side in an ante-room, while the girls, beautifully dressed and gay, flirted in the reception-room with those hateful young noblemen. All I had ever read in Hoffmann's *Tales* of certain demoniacal intrigues, which until that moment had been obscure to me, now became really tangible facts, and I left Prague with an obviously unjust and exaggerated opinion of those things and those people, through whom I had suddenly been dragged into an unknown world of elementary passions.

On the other hand I had gained by my stay at Pravonin: I had written poetry as well as musical compositions. My musical work was a setting of *Glockentöne,* a poem by the friend of my youth, Theodor Apel. I had already written an aria for soprano which had been performed the winter before at one of the theatre concerts. But my new work was decidedly the first vocal piece I had written with real inspiration; generally speaking, I suppose it owed its characteristics to the influence of Beethoven's *Liederkreis:* all the same, the impression that it has left on my mind is that it was absolutely part of myself, and pervaded by a delicate sentimentality which was brought into relief by the dreaminess of the accompaniment. My poetical efforts lay in the direction of a sketch of a tragi-operatic subject, which I finished in its entirety in Prague under the title of *Die Hochzeit* ('The Wedding'). I wrote it without anybody's knowledge, and this was no easy matter, seeing that I could not write in my chilly little hotel-room, and had therefore to go to the house of Moritz, where I generally spent my mornings. I remember how I used quickly to hide my manuscript behind the sofa as soon as I heard my host's footsteps.

An extraordinary episode was connected with the plot of this work.

Already years ago I had come across a tragic story, whilst perusing Büsching's book on chivalry, the like of which I have never since read. A lady of noble birth had been assaulted one night by a man who secretly cherished a passionate love for her, and in the struggle to defend her honour superhuman strength was given her to fling him into the courtyard below. The mystery of his death remained unexplained until the day of his solemn obsequies, when the lady herself, who attended them and was kneeling in solemn prayer, suddenly fell forward and expired. The mysterious strength of this profound and passionate story made an indelible impression upon my mind. Fascinated, moreover, by the peculiar treatment of similar phenomena in Hoffmann's *Tales,* I sketched a novel in which musical mysticism, which I still loved so deeply, played an important part. The action was supposed to take place on the estate of a rich patron of the fine arts: a young couple was going to be married, and had invited the friend of the bridegroom, an interesting but melancholy and mysterious young man, to their wedding. Intimately connected with the whole affair was a strange old organist. The mystic relations which gradually developed between the old musician, the melancholy young man and the bride, were to grow out of the unravelment of certain intricate events, in a somewhat similar manner to that of the mediæval story above related. Here was the same idea: the young man mysteriously killed, the equally strange sudden death of his friend's bride, and the old organist found dead on his bench after the playing of an impressive requiem, the last chord of which was inordinately prolonged as if it never would end.

I never finished this novel: but as I wanted to write the libretto for an opera, I took up the theme again in its original shape, and built on this (as far as the principal features went) the following dramatic plot: —

Two great houses had lived in enmity, and had at last decided to end the family feud. The aged head of one of these houses invited the son of his former enemy to the wedding of his daughter with one of his faithful partisans. The wedding feast is thus used as an opportunity for reconciling the two families. Whilst the guests are full of the suspicion and fear of treachery, their young leader falls violently in love with the bride of his newly found ally. His tragic glance deeply affects her; the festive escort accompanies her to the bridal chamber, where she is to await her beloved; leaning against her tower-window she sees the same passionate eyes fixed on her, and realises that she is face to face with a tragedy.

When he penetrates into her chamber, and embraces her with frantic passion, she pushes him backwards towards the balcony, and throws him over the parapet into the abyss, from whence his mutilated remains are dragged by his companions. They at once arm themselves against the presumed treachery, and call for vengeance; tumult and confusion fill the courtyard: the interrupted wedding feast threatens to end in a night of slaughter. The venerable head of the house at last succeeds in averting the catastrophe. Messengers are sent to bear the tidings of the mysterious calamity to the relatives of the victim: the corpse itself shall be the medium of reconciliation, for, in the presence of the different generations of the suspected family, Providence itself shall decide which of its members has been guilty of treason. During the preparations for the obsequies the bride shows signs of approaching madness; she flies from her bridegroom, refuses to be united to him, and locks herself up in her tower-chamber. Only when, at night, the gloomy though gorgeous ceremony commences, does she appear at the head of her women to be present at the burial service, the gruesome solemnity of which is interrupted by the news of the approach of hostile forces and then by the armed attack of the kinsmen of the murdered man. When the avengers of the presumed treachery penetrate into the chapel and call upon the murderer to declare himself, the horrified lord of the manor points towards his daughter who, turning away from her bridegroom, falls lifeless by the coffin of her victim. This nocturnal drama, through which ran reminiscences of *Leubald und Adelaïde* (the work of my far-off boyhood), I wrote in the darkest vein, but in a more polished and more noble style, disdaining all light-effects, and especially all operatic embellishments. Tender passages occurred here and there all the same, and Weinlich, to whom I had already shown the beginning of my work on my return to Leipzig, praised me for the clearness and good vocal quality of the introduction I had composed to the first act; this was an Adagio for a vocal septette, in which I had tried to express the reconciliation of the hostile families, together with the emotions of the wedded couple and the sinister passion of the secret lover. My principal object was, all the same, to win my sister Rosalie's approval. My poem, however, did not find favour in her eyes: she missed all that which I had purposely avoided, insisted on the ornamentation and development of the simple situation, and desired more brightness generally. 1 made up my mind in an instant: I took the manuscript, and without a suggestion of ill-temper, destroyed it there and then. This action had nothing whatever to do with wounded vanity. It was prompted merely by my desire honestly to prove to my sister how little I thought of my own work and how much I cared for her opinion. She was held in great and loving esteem by my mother and by the rest of our family, for she was their principal breadwinner: the important salary she earned as an actress constituted nearly the whole income out of which my mother had to defray the household expenses. For the sake of her profession she enjoyed many advantages at home. Her part of the house had been specially arranged so that she should have all the necessary comfort and peace for her studies; on marketing days, when the others had to put up with the simplest fare, she had to have the same dainty food as usual. But more than any of these things did her charming gravity and her refined way of speaking place her above the younger children. She was thoughtful and gentle and never joined us in our rather loud conversation. Of course, I had been the one member of the family who had caused the greatest anxieties both to my mother and to my motherly sister, and during my life as a student the strained relations between us had made a terrible impression on me. When therefore they tried to believe in me again, and once more showed some interest in my work, I was full of gratitude and happiness. The thought of getting this sister to look kindly upon my aspirations, and even to expect great things of me, had become a special stimulus to my ambition. Under these circumstances a tender and almost sentimental relationship grew up between Rosalie and myself, which in its purity and sincerity could vie with the noblest form of friendship between man and woman. This was principally due to her exceptional individuality. She had not any real talent, at least not for acting, which had often been considered stagey and unnatural. Nevertheless she was much appreciated owing to her charming appearance as well as to her pure and dignified womanliness, and I remember many tokens of esteem which she received in those days. All the same, none of these advances ever seemed to lead to the prospect of a marriage, and year by year went by without bringing her hopes of a suitable match — a fact which to me appeared quite unaccountable. From time to time I thought I noticed that Rosalie suffered from this state of affairs. I remember one evening when, believing herself to be alone, I heard her sobbing and moaning; I stole away unnoticed, but her grief made such an impression upon me that from that moment I vowed to bring some joy into her life, principally by making a name for myself. Not without reason had our stepfather Geyer given my gentle sister the nickname of 'Geistchen' (little spirit), for if her talent as an actress was not great, her imagination and her love of art and of all high and noble things were perhaps, on that account alone, all the greater. From her lips I had first heard expressions of admiration and delight concerning those subjects which became dear to me later on, and she moved amongst a circle of serious and interesting people who loved the higher things of life without this attitude ever degenerating into affectation.

On my return from my long journey I was introduced to Heinrich Laube, whom my sister had added to her list of intimate friends. It was at the time when the after-effects of the July revolution were beginning to make themselves felt amongst the younger men of intellect in Germany, and of these Laube was one of the most conspicuous. As a young man he came from Silesia to Leipzig, his principal object being to try and form connections in this publishing centre which might be of use to him in Paris, whither he was going, and from which place Börne also made a sensation amongst us by his letters. On this occasion Laube was present at a representation of a play by Ludwig Robert, *Die Macht der Verhältnisse* ('The Power of Circumstances'). This induced him to write a criticism for the Leipzig *Tageblatt,* which made such a sensation through its terse and lively style that he was at once offered, in addition to other literary work, the post of editor of *Die elegante Welt.* In our house he was looked upon as a genius; his curt and often biting manner of speaking, which seemed to exclude all attempt at poetic expression, made him appear both original and daring: his sense of justice, his sincerity and fearless bluntness made one respect his character, hardened as it had been in youth by great adversity. On me he had a very inspiring effect, and I was very much astonished to find that he thought so much of me as to write a flattering notice about my talent in his paper after hearing the first performance of my symphony.

This performance took place in the beginning of the year 1833 at the Leipzig Schneider-Herberge. It was, by the bye, in this dignified old hall that the society 'Euterpe' held its concerts! The place was dirty, narrow, and poorly lighted, and it was here that my work was introduced to the Leipzig public for the first time, and by means of an orchestra that interpreted it simply disgracefully. I can only think of that evening as a gruesome nightmare; and my astonishment was therefore all the greater at seeing the important notice which Laube wrote about the performance. Full of hope, I therefore looked forward to a performance of the same work at the Gewandhaus concert, which followed soon after, and which came off brilliantly in every way. It was well received and well spoken of in all the papers; of real malice there was not a trace — on the contrary, several notices were encouraging, and Laube, who had quickly become celebrated, confided to me that he was going to offer me a libretto for an opera, which he had first written for Meyerbeer. This staggered me somewhat, for I was not in the least prepared to pose as a poet, and my only idea was to write a real plot for an opera. As to the precise manner, however, in which such a book had to be written, I already had a very definite and instinctive notion, and I was strengthened in the certainty of my own feelings in the matter when Laube now explained the nature of his plot to me. He told me that he wanted to arrange nothing less than *Kosziusko* into a libretto for grand opera! Once again I had qualms, for I felt at once that Laube had a mistaken idea about the character of a dramatic subject. When I inquired into the real action of the play, Laube was astonished that I should expect more than the story of the Polish hero, whose life was crowded with incident; in any case, he thought there was quite sufficient action in it to describe the unhappy fate of a whole nation. Of course the usual heroine was not missing; she was a Polish girl who had a love affair with a Russian; and in this way some sentimental situations were also to be found in the plot. Without a moment's delay I assured my sister Rosalie that I would not set this story to music: she agreed with me, and begged me only to postpone my answer to Laube. My journey to Würzburg was of great help to me in this respect, for it was easier to write my decision to Laube than to announce it to him personally. He accepted the slight rebuff with good grace, but he never forgave me, either then or afterwards, for writing my own words!

When he heard what subject I had preferred to his brilliant political poem, he made no effort to conceal his contempt for my choice. I had borrowed the plot from a dramatic fairy-tale by Gozzi, La Donna Serpente, and called it Die Feen ('The Fairies'). The names of my heroes I chose from different Ossian and similar poems: my prince was called Arindal; he was loved by a fairy called Ada, who held him under her spell and kept him in fairyland, away from his realm, until his faithful friends at last found him and induced him to return, for his country was going to rack and ruin, and even its capital had fallen into the enemy's hands. The loving fairy herself sends the prince back to his country; for the oracle has decreed that she shall lay upon her lover the severest of tasks. Only by performing this task triumphantly can he make it possible for her to leave the immortal world of fairies in order to share the fate of her earthly lover, as his wife. In a moment of deepest despair about the state of his country, the fairy queen appears to him and purposely destroys his faith in her by deeds of the most cruel and inexplicable nature. Driven mad by a thousand fears, Arindal begins to imagine that all the time he has been dealing with a wicked sorceress, and tries to escape the fatal spell by pronouncing a curse upon Ada. Wild with sorrow, the unhappy fairy sinks down, and reveals their mutual fate to the lover, now lost to her for ever, and tells him that, as a punishment for having disobeyed the decree of Fate, she is doomed to be turned into stone (in Gozzi's version she becomes a serpent). Immediately afterwards it appears that all the catastrophes which the fairy had prophesied were but deceptions: victory over the enemy as well as the growing prosperity and welfare of the kingdom now follow in quick succession: Ada is taken away by the Fates, and Arindal, a raving madman, remains behind alone. The terrible sufferings of his madness do not, however, satisfy the Fates: to bring about his utter ruin they appear before the repentant man and invite him to follow them to the nether world, on the pretext of enabling him to free Ada from the spell. Through the treacherous promises of the wicked fairies Arindal's madness grows into sublime exaltation; and one of his household magicians, a faithful friend, having in the meantime equipped him with magic weapons and charms, he now follows the traitresses. The latter cannot get over their astonishment when they see how

Arindal overcomes one after the other of the monsters of the infernal regions: only when they arrive at the vault in which they show him the stone in human shape do they recover their hope of vanquishing the valiant prince, for, unless he can break the charm which binds Ada, he must share her fate and be doomed to remain a stone for ever. Arindal, who until then has been using the dagger and the shield given him by the friendly magician, now makes use of an instrument — a lyre — which he has brought with him, and the meaning of which he had not yet understood. To the sounds of this instrument he now expresses his plaintive moans, his remorse, and his overpowering longing for his enchanted queen. The stone is moved by the magic of his love: the beloved one is released. Fairyland with all its marvels opens its portals, and the mortal learns that, owing to his former inconstancy, Ada has lost the right to become his wife on earth, but that her beloved, through his great and magic power, has earned the right to live for ever by her side in fairyland.

Although I had written *Die Hochzeit* in the darkest vein, without operatic embellishments, I painted this subject with the utmost colour and variety. In contrast to the lovers out of fairyland I depicted a more ordinary couple, and I even introduced a third pair that belonged to the coarser and more comical servant world. I purposely went to no pains in the matter of the poetic diction and the verse. My idea was not to encourage my former hopes of making a name as a poet; I was now really a 'musician' and a 'composer,' and wished to write a decent opera libretto simply because I was sure that nobody else could write one for me; the reason being that such a book is something quite unique and cannot be written either by a poet or by a mere man of letters. With the intention of setting this libretto to music, I left Leipzig in January, 1833, to stay in Würzburg with my eldest brother Albert, who at the time held an appointment at the theatre. It now seemed necessary for me to begin to apply my musical knowledge to a practical purpose, and to this end my brother had promised to help me in getting some kind of post at the small Würzburg theatre. I travelled by post to Bamberg via Hof, and in Bamberg I stayed a few days in the company of a young man called Schunke, who from a player on the horn had become an actor. With the greatest interest I learned the story of Caspar Hauser, who at that time was very well known, and who (if I am not mistaken) was pointed out to me. In addition to this, I admired the peculiar costumes of the market-women, thought with much interest of Hoffmann's stay at this place, and of how it had led to the writing of his *Tales,* and resumed my journey (to Würzburg) with a man called Hauderer, and suffered miserably from the cold all the way.

My brother Albert, who was almost a new acquaintance to me, did his best to make me feel at home in his not over luxurious establishment. He was pleased to find me less mad than he had expected me to be from a certain letter with which I had succeeded in frightening him some time previously, and he really managed to procure me an exceptional occupation as choir-master at the theatre, for which I received the monthly fee of ten guilders. The remainder of the winter was devoted to the serious study of the duties required of a musical director: in a very short time I had to tackle two new grand operas, namely, Marschner's *Vampir* and Meyerbeer's *Robert der Teufel,* in both of which the chorus played a considerable part. At first I felt absolutely like a beginner, and had to start on *Camilla von Paër,* the score of which was utterly unknown to me. I still remember that I felt I was doing a thing which I had no right to undertake: I felt quite an amateur at the work. Soon, however, Marschner's score interested me sufficiently to make the labour seem worth my while. The score of *Robert* was a great disappointment to me: from the newspapers I had expected plenty of originality and novelty; I could find no trace of either in this transparent work, and an opera with a finale like that of the second act could not be named in the same breath with any of my favourite works. The only thing that impressed me was the unearthly keyed trumpet which, in the last act, represented the voice of the mother's ghost.

It was remarkable to observe the æsthetic demoralisation into which I now fell through having daily to deal with such a work. I gradually lost my dislike for this shallow and exceedingly uninteresting composition (a dislike I shared with many

German musicians) in the growing interest which I was compelled to take in its interpretation; and thus it happened that the insipidness and affectation of the commonplace melodies ceased to concern me save from the standpoint of their capability of eliciting applause or the reverse. As, moreover, my future career as musical conductor was at stake, my brother, who was very anxious on my behalf, looked favourably on this lack of classical obstinacy on my part, and thus the ground was gradually prepared for that decline in my classical taste which was destined to last some considerable time.

All the same, this did not occur before I had given some proof of my great inexperience in the lighter style of writing. My brother wanted to introduce a ' Cavatine ' from the *Piraten,* by Bellini, into the same composer's opera, *Straniera;* the score was not to be had, and he entrusted me with the instrumentation of this work. From the piano score alone I could not possibly detect the heavy and noisy instrumentation of the ritornelles and intermezzi which, musically, were so very thin; the composer of a great C major Symphony with an end fugue could only help himself out of the difficulty by the use of a few flutes and clarinets playing in thirds. At the rehearsal the ' Cavatine ' sounded so frightfully thin and shallow that my brother made me serious reproaches about the waste of copying expenses. But I had my revenge: to the tenor aria of ' Aubry ' in Marschner's *Vampir* I added an Allegro, for which I also wrote the words.

My work succeeded splendidly, and earned the praise of both the public and my brother. In a similar German style I wrote the music to my *Feen* in the course of the year 1833. My brother and his wife left Würzburg after Easter in order to avail themselves of several invitations at friends' houses; I stayed behind with the children — three little girls of tender years — which placed me in the extraordinary position of a responsible guardian, a post for which I was not in the least suited at that time of my life. My time was divided between my work and pleasure, and in consequence I neglected my charges. Amongst the friends I made there, Alexander Müller had much influence over me; he was a good musician and pianist, and I used to listen for hours to his improvisations on given themes — an accomplishment in which he so greatly excelled, that I could not fail to be impressed. With him and some other friends, amongst whom was also Valentin Hamm, I often made excursions in the neighbourhood, on which occasions the Bavarian beer and the Frankish wine were wont to fly. Valentin Hamm was a grotesque individual, who entertained us often with his excellent violin playing; he had an enormous stretch on the piano, for he could reach an interval of a twelfth. *Der Letzte Hieb*, a public beer-garden situated on a pleasant height, was a daily witness of my fits of wild and often enthusiastic boisterousness; never once during those mild summer nights did I return to my charges without having waxed enthusiastic over art and the world in general. I also remember a wicked trick which has always remained a blot in my memory. Amongst my friends was a fair and very enthusiastic Swabian called Fröhlich, with whom I had exchanged my score of the C minor Symphony for his, which he had copied out with his own hand. This very gentle, but rather irritable young man had taken such a violent dislike to one André, whose malicious face I also detested, that he declared that this person spoilt his evenings for him, merely by being in the same room with him. The unfortunate object of his hatred tried all the same to meet us whenever he could: friction ensued, but André would insist upon aggravating us. One evening Fröhlich lost patience. After some insulting retort, he tried to chase him from our table by striking him with a stick: the result was a fight in which Frölich's friends felt they must take part, though they all seemed to do so with some reluctance. A mad longing to join the fray also took possession of me. With the others I helped in knocking our poor victim about, and I even heard the sound of one terrible blow which I struck André on the head, whilst he fixed his eyes on me in bewilderment.

I relate this incident to atone for a sin which has weighed very heavily on my conscience ever since. I can compare this sad experience only with one out of my earliest boyhood days, namely the drowning of some puppies in a shallow pool behind my uncle's house in Eisleben. Even to this day I cannot think of the slow death of these poor little creatures without horror. I have never quite forgotten some of my thoughtless and reckless actions; for the sorrows of others, and in particular those of animals, have always affected me deeply to the extent of filling me with a disgust of life.

My first love affair stands out in strong contrast against these recollections. It was only natural that one of the young chorus ladies with whom I had to practise daily should know how to attract my attentions. Therese Ringelmann, the daughter of a grave-digger, thanks to her beautiful soprano voice, led me to believe that I could make a great singer of her. After I told her of this ambitious scheme, she paid much attention to her appearance, and dressed elegantly for the rehearsals, and a row of white pearls which she wound through her hair specially fascinated me. During the summer holidays I gave Therese regular lessons in singing, according to a method which has always remained a mystery to me ever since. I also called on her very often at her house, where, fortunately, I never met her unpleasant father, but always her mother and her sisters. We also met in the public gardens, but false vanity always kept me from telling my friends of our relations. I do not know whether the fault lay with her lowly birth, her lack of education, or my own doubt about the sincerity of my affections; but in any case when, in addition to the fact that I had my reasons for being jealous, they also tried to urge me to a formal engagement, this love affair came quietly to an end.

An infinitely more genuine affair was my love for Friederike Galvani, the daughter of a mechanic, who was undoubtedly of Italian origin. She was very musical, and had a lovely voice; my brother had patronised her and helped her to a début at his theatre, which test she stood brilliantly. She was rather small, but had large dark eyes and a sweet disposition. The first oboist of the orchestra, a good fellow as well as a clever musician, was thoroughly devoted to her. He was looked upon as her *fiancé,* but, owing to some incident in his past, he was not allowed to visit at her parents' house, and the marriage was not to take place for a long time yet. When the autumn of my year in Würzburg drew near, I received an invitation from friends to be present at a country wedding at a little distance from Würzburg; the oboist and his *fiancée* had also been invited. It was a jolly, though primitive affair; we drank and danced, and I even tried my hand at violin playing, but I must have forgotten it badly, for even with the second violin I could not manage to satisfy the other musicians. But my success with Friederike was all the greater; we danced like mad through the many couples of peasants until at one moment we got so excited that, losing all self-control, we embraced each other while her real lover was playing the dance music. For the first time in my life I began to feel a flattering sensation of self-respect when Friederike's *fiancé*, on seeing how we two flirted, accepted the situation with good grace, if not without some sadness. I had never had the chance of thinking that I could make a favourable impression on any young girl. I never imagined myself good-looking, neither had I ever thought it possible that I could attract the attention of pretty girls.

On the other hand, I had gradually acquired a certain self-reliance in mixing with men of my own age. Owing to the exceptional vivacity and innate susceptibility of my nature — qualities which were brought home to me in my relations with members of my circle — I gradually became conscious of a certain power of transporting or bewildering my more indolent companions.

From my poor oboist's silent self-control on becoming aware of the ardent advances of his betrothed towards me, I acquired, as I have said, the first suggestion of the fact that I might count for something, not only among men, but also among women. The Frankish wine helped to bring about a state of ever greater confusion, and under the cover of its influence I at length declared myself, quite openly, to be Friederike's lover. Ever so far into the night, in fact, when day was already breaking, we set off home together to Würzburg in an open wagon. This was the crowning triumph of my delightful adventure; for while all the others, including, in the end, the jealous oboist, slept off their debauch in the face of the dawning day, I, with my cheek against Friederike's, and listening to the warbling of the larks, watched the coming of the rising sun.

On the following day we had scarcely any idea of what had

happened. A certain sense of shame, which was not unbecoming, held us aloof from one another: and yet I easily won access to Friederike's family, and from that time forward was daily a welcome guest, when for some hours I would linger in unconcealed intimate intercourse with the same domestic circle from which the unhappy betrothed remained excluded. No word was ever mentioned of this last connection; never once did it even dawn upon Friederike to effect any change in the state of affairs, and it seemed to strike no one that I ought, so to speak, to take the *fiancé*'s place. The confiding manner in which I was received by all, and especially by the girl herself, was exactly similar to one of Nature's great processes, as, for instance, when spring steps in and winter passes silently away. Not one of them ever considered the material consequences of the change, and this is precisely the most charming and flattering feature of this first youthful love affair, which was never to degenerate into an attitude which might give rise to suspicion or concern. These relations ended only with my departure from Würzburg, which was marked by the most touching and most tearful leavetaking.

For some time, although I kept up no correspondence, the memory of this episode remained firmly imprinted on my mind. Two years later, while making a rapid journey through the old district, I once more visited Friederike: the poor child approached me utterly shamefaced. Her oboist was still her lover, and though his position rendered marriage impossible, the unfortunate young woman had become a mother. I have heard nothing more of her since.

Amid all this traffic of love I worked hard at my opera, and, thanks to the loving sympathy of my sister Rosalie, I was able to find the necessary good spirits for the task. When at the commencement of the summer my earnings as a conductor came to an end, this same sister again made it her business loyally to provide me with ample pocket-money, so that I might devote myself solely to the completion of my work, without troubling about anything or being a burden to any one. At a much later date I came across a letter of mine written to Rosalie in those days, which were full of a tender, almost adoring love for that noble creature.

When the winter was at hand my brother returned, and the theatre reopened. Truth to tell, I did not again become connected with it, but acquired a position, which was even more prominent, in the concerts of the Musical Society in which I produced my great overture in C major, my symphony, and eventually portions of my new opera as well. An amateur with a splendid voice, Mademoiselle Friedel, sang the great aria from *Ada*. In addition to this, a trio was given which, in one of its passages, had such a moving effect upon my brother, who took part in it, that, to his astonishment, as he himself admitted, he completely lost his cue on account of it.

By Christmas my work had come to an end, my score was written out complete with the most laudable neatness, and now I was to return to Leipzig for the New Year, in order to get my opera accepted by the theatre there. On the way home I visited Nuremberg, where I stayed a week with my sister Clara and with her husband, who were engaged at the theatre there. I well remember how happy and comfortable I felt during this pleasant visit to the very same relatives who a few years previously, when I had stayed with them at Magdeburg, had been upset by my resolve to adopt music as a calling. Now I had become a real musician, had written a grand opera, and had already brought out many things without coming to grief. The sense of all this was a great joy to me, while it was no less flattering to my relatives, who could not fail to see that the supposed misfortune had in the end proved to my advantage. I was in a jolly mood and quite unrestrained — a state of mind which was very largely the result not only of my brother-in-law's cheerful and sociable household, but also of the pleasant tavern life of the place. In a much more confident and elated spirit I returned to Leipzig, where I was able to lay the three huge volumes of my score before my highly delighted mother and sister.

Just then my family was the richer for the return of my brother Julius from his long wanderings. He had worked a good while in Paris as a goldsmith, and had now set up for himself in that capacity in Leipzig. He too, like the rest, was eager to hear something out of my opera, which, to be sure, was not so easy, as I entirely lacked the gift of playing anything of the sort in an easy and intelligible way. Only when I was able to work myself into a state of absolute ecstasy was it possible for me to render something with any effect. Rosalie knew that I meant it to draw a sort of declaration of love from her; but I have never felt certain whether the embrace and the sisterly kiss which were awarded me after I had sung my great aria from *Ada,* were bestowed on me from real emotion or rather out of affectionate regard. On the other hand, the zeal with which she urged my opera on the director of the theatre, Ringelhardt, the conductor and the manager was unmistakable, and she did it so effectually that she obtained their consent for its performance, and that very speedily. I was particularly interested to learn that the management immediately showed themselves eager to try to settle the matter of the costumes for my drama: but I was astonished to hear that the choice was in favour of oriental attire, whereas I had intended, by the names I had selected, to suggest a northern character for the setting. But it was precisely these names which they found unsuitable, as fairy personages are not seen in the North, but only in the East; while apart from this, the original by Gozzi, which formed the basis of the work, undoubtedly bore an oriental character. It was with the utmost indignation that I opposed the insufferable turban and caftan style of dress, and vehemently advocated the knightly garb worn in the early years of the Middle Ages. I then had to come to a thorough understanding with the conductor, Stegmayer, on the subject of my score. He was a remarkable, short, fat man, with fair curly hair, and an exceptionally jovial disposition; he was, however, very hard to bring to a point. When over our wine we always arrived at an understanding very quickly, but as soon as we sat at the piano, I had to listen to the most extraordinary objections concerning the trend of which I was for some time extremely puzzled. As the matter was much delayed by this vacillation, I put myself into closer communication with the stage manager of the opera, Hauser, who at that time was much appreciated as a singer and patron of art by the people of Leipzig.

With this man, too, I had the strangest experiences: he who had captivated the audiences of Leipzig, more especially with his impersonation of the barber and the Englishman in

Fra Diavolo, suddenly revealed himself in his own house as the most fanatical adherent of the most old-fashioned music. I listened with astonishment to the scarcely veiled contempt with which he treated even Mozart, and the only thing he seemed to regret was that we had no operas by Sebastian Bach. After he had explained to me that dramatic music had not actually been written yet, and that properly speaking Gluck alone had shown any ability for it, he proceeded to what seemed an exhaustive examination of my own opera, concerning which all I had wished to hear from him was whether it was fit to be performed. Instead of this, however, his object seemed to be to point out the failure of my purpose in every number. I sweated blood under the unparalleled torture of going through my work with this man; and I told my mother and sister of my grave depression. All these delays had already succeeded in making it impossible to perform my opera at the date originally fixed, and now it was postponed until August of the current year (1834).

An incident which I shall never forget inspired me with fresh courage. Old Bierey, an experienced and excellent musician, and in his day a successful composer, who, thanks more particularly to his long practice as a conductor at the Breslau theatre, had acquired a perfectly practical knowledge of such things, was then living at Leipzig, and was a good friend of my people. My mother and sister begged him to give his opinion about the fitness of my opera for the stage, and I duly submitted the score to him. I cannot say how deeply affected and impressed I was to see this old gentleman appear one day among my relatives, and to hear him declare with genuine enthusiasm that he simply could not understand how so young a man could have composed such a score. His remarks concerning the greatness which he had recognised in my talent were really irresistible, and positively amazed me. When asked whether he considered the work presentable and calculated to produce an effect, he declared his only regret was that he was no longer at the head of a theatre, because, had he been, he would have thought himself extremely lucky to secure such a man as myself permanently for his enterprise. At this announcement my family was overcome with joy, and their feelings were all the more justified seeing that, as they all knew, Bierey was by no means an amiable romancer, but a practical musician well seasoned by a life full of experience.

The delay was now borne with better spirits, and for a long time I was able to wait hopefully for what the future might bring. Among other things, I now began to enjoy the company of a new friend in the person of Laube, who at that time, although I had not set his *Kosziusko* to music, was at the zenith of his fame. The first portion of his novel, *Young Europe,* the form of which was epistolary, had appeared, and had a most stimulating effect on me, more particularly in conjunction with all the youthful hopefulness which at that time pulsated in my veins. Though his teaching was essentially only a repetition of that in Heinse's *Ardinghello,* the forces that then surged in young breasts were given full and eloquent expression. The guiding spirit of this tendency was followed in literary criticism, which was aimed mainly at the supposed or actual incapacity of the semi-classical occupants of our various literary thrones. Without the slightest mercy the pedants,[1] among whom Tieck for one was numbered, were treated as sheer encumbrances and hindrances to the rise of a new literature. That which led to a remarkable revulsion of my feelings with regard to those German composers who hitherto had been admired and respected, was partly the influence of these critical skirmishes, and the luring sprightliness of their tone; but mainly the impression made by a fresh visit of Schröder-Devrient to Leipzig, when her rendering of Romeo in Bellini's *Romeo and Juliet* carried every one by storm. The effect of it was not to be compared with anything that had been witnessed theretofore. To see the daring, romantic figure of the youthful lover against a background of such obviously shallow and empty music prompted one, at all events, to meditate doubtfully upon the cause of the great lack of effect in solid German music as it had been applied hitherto to the drama. Without for the moment plunging too deeply into this meditation, I allowed myself to be borne along with the current of my youthful feelings, then roused to ardour, and turned involuntarily to the task of working off all that brooding seriousness

---

[1] *Zöpfe* in the German text. — TRANSLATOR.

which in my earlier years had driven me to such pathetic mysticism.

What Pohlenz had not done by his conducting of the Ninth Symphony, what the Vienna Conservatoire, Dionys Weber, and many other clumsy performances (which had led me to regard classical music as absolutely colourless) had not fully accomplished, was achieved by the inconceivable charm of the most unclassical Italian music, thanks to the wonderful, thrilling, and entrancing impersonation of Romeo by Schröder-Devrient. What effect such powerful, and as regards their causes, incomprehensible, effects had upon my opinion was shown in the frivolous way in which I was able to contrive a short criticism of Weber's *Euryanthe* for the *Elegante Zeitung*. This opera had been performed by the Leipzig company shortly before the appearance of Schröder-Devrient: cold and colourless performers, among whom the singer in the title-rôle, appearing in the wilderness with the full sleeves which were then the pink of fashion, is still a disagreeable memory. Very laboriously, and without verve, but simply with the object of satisfying the demands of classical rules, this company did its utmost to dispel even the enthusiastic impressions of Weber's music which I had formed in my youth. I did not know what answer to make to a brother critic of Laube's, when he pointed out to me the laboured character of this operatic performance, as soon as he was able to contrast it with the entrancing effect of that Romeo evening. Here I found myself confronted with a problem, the solving of which I was just at that time disposed to take as easily as possible, and displayed my courage by discarding all prejudice, and that daringly, in the short criticism just mentioned in which I simply scoffed at *Euryanthe*. Just as I had had my season of wild oat sowing as a student, so now I boldly rushed into the same courses in the development of my artistic taste.

It was May, and beautiful spring weather, and a pleasure trip that I now undertook with a friend into the promised land of my youthful romance, Bohemia, was destined to bring the unrestrained 'Young-European' mood in me to full maturity. This friend was Theodor Apel. I had known him a long while, and had always felt particularly flattered by the fact that I had won his hearty affection; for, as the son of the gifted master of metre and imitator of Greek forms of poetry, August Apel, I felt that admiring deference for him which I had never yet been able to bestow upon the descendant of a famous man. Being well-to-do and of a good family, his friendship gave me such opportunities of coming into touch with the easy circumstances of the upper classes as were not of frequent occurrence in my station of life. While my mother, for instance, regarded my association with this highly respectable family with great satisfaction, I for my part was extremely gratified at the thought of the cordiality with which I was received in such circles.

Apel's earnest wish was to become a poet, and I took it for granted that he had all that was needed for such a calling; above all, what seemed to me so important, the complete freedom that his considerable fortune assured him by liberating him from all need of earning his living or of adopting a profession for a livelihood. Strange to say, his mother, who on the death of his distinguished father had married a Leipzig lawyer, was very anxious about the vocation he should choose, and wished her son to make a fine career in the law, as she was not at all disposed to favour his poetical gifts. And it was to her attempts to convert me to her view, in order that by my influence I might avert the calamity of a second poet in the family, in the person of the son, that I owed the specially friendly relations that obtained between herself and me. All her suggestions succeeded in doing, however, was to stimulate me, even more than my own favourable opinion of his talent could, to confirm my friend in his desire to be a poet, and thus to support him in his rebellious attitude towards his family.

He was not displeased at this. As he was also studying music and composed quite nicely, I succeeded in being on terms of the greatest intimacy with him. The fact that he had spent the very year in which I had sunk into the lowest depths of undergraduate madness, studying at Heidelberg and not at Leipzig, had kept him unsullied by any share in my strange excesses, and when we now met again at Leipzig, in the spring of 1834, the only thing that we still had in common was the æsthetic aspiration of our lives, which we now strove by way of experiment to divert into the direction of the enjoyment of life. Gladly would we have flung ourselves into lively adventures if only the conditions of our environment and of the whole middle-class world in which we lived had in any way admitted of such things. Despite all the promptings of our instincts, however, we got no further than planning this excursion to Bohemia. At all events, it was something that we made the journey not by the post, but in our own carriage, and our genuine pleasure continued to lie in the fact that at Teplitz, for instance, we daily took long drives in a fine carriage. When in the evening we had supped off trout at the Wilhelmsburg, drunk good Czernosek wine with Bilin water, and duly excited ourselves over Hoffmann, Beethoven, Shakespeare, Heinse's *Ardinghello*, and other matters, and then, with our limbs comfortably outstretched in our elegant carriage, drove back in the summer twilight to the 'King of Prussia,' where we occupied the large balcony-room on the first floor, we felt that we had spent the day like young gods, and for sheer exuberance could think of nothing better to do than to indulge in the most frightful quarrels which, especially when the windows were open, would collect numbers of alarmed listeners in the square before the inn.

One fine morning I stole away from my friend in order to take my breakfast alone at the 'Schlackenburg,' and also to seize an opportunity of jotting down the plan of a new operatic composition in my note-book. With this end in view, I had mastered the subject of Shakespeare's *Measure for Measure*, which, in accordance with my present mood, I soon transformed pretty freely into a libretto entitled *Liebesverbot*. *Young Europe* and *Ardinghello*, and the strange frame of mind into which I had fallen with regard to classical operatic music, furnished me with the keynote of my conception, which was directed more particularly against puritanical hypocrisy, and which thus tended boldly to exalt 'unrestrained sensuality.' I took care to understand the grave Shakespearean theme only in this sense. I could see only the gloomy strait-laced viceroy, his heart aflame with the most passionate love for the beautiful novice, who, while she beseeches him to pardon her brother condemned to death for illicit love, at the same time kindles the most dangerous fire in the stubborn Puritan's breast by infecting him with the lovely warmth of her human emotion.

The fact that these powerful features are so richly developed in Shakespeare's creation only in order that, in the end, they may be weighed all the more gravely in the scales of justice, was no concern of mine: all I cared about was to expose the sinfulness of hypocrisy and the unnaturalness of such cruel moral censure. Thus I completely dropped *Measure for Measure*, and made the hypocrite be brought to justice only by the avenging power of love. I transferred the theme from the fabulous city of Vienna to the capital of sunny Sicily, in which a German viceroy, indignant at the inconceivably loose morals of the people, attempts to introduce a puritanical reform, and comes miserably to grief over it. *Die Stumme von Portici* probably contributed to some extent to this theme, as did also certain memories of *Die Sizilianische Vesper*. When I remember that at last even the gentle Sicilian Bellini constituted a factor in this composition, I cannot, to be sure, help smiling at the strange medley in which the most extraordinary misunderstandings here took shape.

This remained for the present a mere draft. Studies from life destined for my work were first to be carried out on this delightful excursion to Bohemia. I led my friend in triumph to Prague, in the hope of securing the same impressions for him which had stirred me so profoundly when I was there. We met my fair friends in the city itself; for, owing to the death of old Count Pachta, material changes had taken place in the family, and the surviving daughters no longer went to Pravonin. My behaviour was full of arrogance, and by means of it I doubtless wished to vent a certain capricious lust of revenge for the feelings of bitterness with which I had taken leave of this circle some years previously. My friend was well received. The changed family circumstances forced the charming girls ever more and more imperatively to come to some decision as to their future, and a wealthy bourgeois, though not exactly in trade himself, but in possession of ample means, seemed to the anxious mother, at all events, a good adviser. Without either showing or feeling any malice in the matter, I expressed my pleasure at the sight of the strange confusion caused by Theodor's introduction into the family by the merriest and wildest jests: for my only intercourse with the ladies consisted purely of jokes and friendly chaff. They could not understand how it was that I had altered so strangely. There was no longer any of that love of wrangling, that rage for instructing, and that zeal in converting in me which formerly they had found so irritating. But at the same time not a sensible word could I be made to utter, and they who were now wanting to talk over many things seriously could get nothing out of me save the wildest tomfoolery. As on this occasion, in my character of an uncaged bird, I boldly allowed myself many a liberty against which they felt themselves powerless, my exuberant spirits were excited all the more when my friend, who was led away by my example, tried to imitate me — a thing they took in very bad part from him.

Only once was there any attempt at seriousness between us: I was sitting at the piano, and was listening to my companion, who was telling the ladies that in a conversation at the hotel I had found occasion to express myself most warmly to some one who appeared to be surprised on hearing of the domestic and industrious qualities of my lady friends. I was deeply moved when, as the outcome of my companion's remarks, I gathered what unpleasant experiences the poor things had already been through: for what seemed to me a very natural action on my part, appeared to fill them with unexpected pleasure. Jenny, for instance, came up to me and hugged me with great warmth. By general consent I was now granted the right of behaving with almost studied rudeness, and I replied even to Jenny's warm outburst only with my usual banter.

In our hotel, the 'Black Horse,' which was so famous in those days, I found the playground in which I was able to carry the mischievous spirit not exhausted at the Pachta's house to the point of recklessness. Out of the most accidental material in table and travelling guests we succeeded in gathering a company around us which allowed us, until far into the night, to lead it into the most inconceivable follies. To all this I was incited more particularly by the personality of a very timid and undersized business man from Frankfort *on the Oder*, who longed to seem of a daring disposition; and his presence stimulated me, if only owing to the remarkable chance it gave me of coming into contact with some one who was at home in Frankfort 'on the Oder.' Any one who knows how things then stood in Austria can form some idea of my recklessness when I say that I once went so far as to cause our symposium in the public room to bellow the *Marseillaise* out loud into the night. Therefore, when after this heroic exploit was over, and while I was undressing, I clambered on the outer ledges of the windows from one room to the other on the second floor, I naturally horrified those who did not know of the love of acrobatic feats which I had cultivated in my earliest boyhood.

Even if I had exposed myself without fear to such dangers, I was soon sobered down next morning by a summons from the police. When, in addition to this, I recalled the singing of the *Marseillaise*, I was filled with the gravest fears. After having been detained at the station a long time, owing to a strange misunderstanding, the upshot of it was that the inspector who was told off to examine me found that there was not sufficient time left for a serious hearing, and, to my great relief, I was allowed to go after replying to a few harmless questions concerning the intended length of my stay. Nevertheless, we thought it advisable not to yield to the temptation of playing any more pranks beneath the spread wings of the double eagle.

By means of a circuitous route into which we were led by our insatiable longing for adventures — adventures which, as a matter of fact, occurred only in our imagination, and which to all intents and purposes were but modest diversions on the road — we at length got back to Leipzig. And with this return home the really cheerful period of my life as a youth definitely closed. If, up to that time, I had not been free from serious errors and moments of passion, it was only now that care cast its first shadow across my path.

My family had anxiously awaited my return in order to inform me that the post of conductor had been offered to me by the Magdeburg Theatre Company. This company during the current summer month was performing at a watering place called Lauchstädt. The manager could not get on with an incompetent conductor that had been sent to him, and in his extremity had applied to Leipzig in the hope of getting a substitute forthwith. Stegmayer, the conductor, who had no inclination to practise my score *Feen* during the hot summer weather, as he had promised to do, promptly recommended me for the post, and in that way really managed to shake off a very troublesome tormentor. For although, on the one hand, I really desired to be able to abandon myself freely and without restraint to the torrent of adventures that constitute the artist's life, yet a longing for independence, which could be won only by my earning my own living, had been greatly strengthened in me by the state of my affairs. Albeit, I had the feeling that a solid basis for the gratification of this desire was not to be laid in Lauchstädt; nor did I find it easy to assist the plot concocted against the production of my *Feen*. I therefore determined to make a preliminary visit to the place just to see how things stood.

This little watering-place had, in the days of Goethe and Schiller, acquired a very wide reputation. Its wooden theatre had been built according to the design of the former, and the first performance of the *Braut von Messina* had been given there. But although I repeated all this to myself, the place made me feel rather doubtful. I asked for the house of the director of the theatre. He proved to be out, but a small dirty boy, his son, was told to take me to the theatre to find 'Papa.' Papa, however, met us on the way. He was an elderly man; he wore a dressing-gown, and on his head a cap. His delight at greeting me was interrupted by complaints about a serious indisposition, for which his son was to fetch him a cordial from a shop close by. Before despatching the boy on this errand he pressed a real silver penny into his hand with a certain ostentation which was obviously for my benefit. This person was Heinrich Bethmann, surviving husband of the famous actress of that name, who, having lived in the heyday of the German stage, had won the favour of the King of Prussia; and won it so lastingly, that long after her death it had continued to be extended to her spouse. He always drew a nice pension from the Prussian court, and permanently enjoyed its support without ever being able to forfeit its protection by his irregular and dissipated ways.

At the time of which I am speaking he had sunk to his lowest, owing to continued theatre management. His speech and manners revealed the sugary refinement of a bygone day, while all that he did and everything about him testified to the most shameful neglect. He took me back to his house, where he presented me to his second wife, who, crippled in one foot, lay on an extraordinary couch while an elderly bass, concerning whose excessive devotion Bethmann had already complained to me quite openly, smoked his pipe beside her. From there the director took me to his stage manager, who lived in the same house.

With the latter, who was just engaged in a consultation about the repertory with the theatre attendant, a toothless old skeleton, he left me to settle the necessary arrangements. As soon as Bethmann had gone, Schmale, the stage manager, shrugged his shoulders and smiled, assuring me that that was just the way of the director, to put everything on his back and trouble himself about nothing. There he had been sitting for over an hour, discussing with Kröge what should be put on next Sunday: it was all very well his starting *Don Juan,* but how could he get a rehearsal carried out, when the Merseburg town bandsmen, who formed the orchestra, would not come over on Saturday to rehearse?

All the time Schmale kept reaching out through the open window to a cherry tree from which he picked and persistently ate the fruit, ejecting the stones with a disagreeable noise. Now it was this last circumstance in particular which decided me; for, strange to say, I have an innate aversion from fruit. I informed the stage manager that he need not trouble at all about *Don Juan* for Sunday, since for my part, if they had reckoned on my making my first appearance at this performance, I must anyhow disappoint the director, as I had no choice but to return at once to Leipzig, where I had to put my affairs in order. This polite manner of tendering my absolute refusal to accept the appointment — a conclusion I had quickly arrived at in my own mind — forced me to practise some dissimulation, and made it necessary for me to appear as if I really had some other purpose in coming to Lauchstädt. This pretence in itself was quite unnecessary, seeing that I was quite determined never to return there again.

People offered to help me in finding a lodging, and a young actor whom I had chanced to know at Würzburg undertook to be my guide in the matter. While he was taking me to the best lodging he knew, he told me that presently he would do me the kindness of making me the housemate of the prettiest and nicest girl to be found in the place at the time. She was the junior lead of the company, Mademoiselle Minna Planer, of whom doubtless I had already heard.

As luck would have it, the promised damsel met us at the door of the house in question. Her appearance and bearing formed the most striking contrast possible to all the unpleasant impressions of the theatre which it had been my lot to receive on this fateful morning. Looking very charming and fresh, the young actress's general manner and movements were full of a certain majesty and grave assurance which lent an agreeable and captivating air of dignity to her otherwise pleasant expression. Her scrupulously clean and tidy dress completed the startling effect of the unexpected encounter. After I had been introduced to her in the hall as the new conductor, and after she had done regarding with astonishment the stranger who seemed so young for such a title, she recommended me kindly to the landlady of the house, and begged that I might be well looked after; whereupon she walked proudly and serenely across the street to her rehearsal.

I engaged a room on the spot, agreed to *Don Juan* for Sunday, regretted greatly that I had not brought my luggage with me from Leipzig, and hastened to return thither as quickly as possible in order to get back to Lauchstädt all the sooner. The die was cast. The serious side of life at once confronted me in the form of significant experiences. At Leipzig I had to take a furtive leave of Laube. At the instance of Prussia he had been warned off Saxon soil, and he half guessed at the meaning which was to be attached to this move. The time of undisguised reaction against the Liberal movement of the early 'thirties had set in: the fact that Laube was concerned in no sort of political work, but had devoted himself merely to literary activity, always aiming simply at æsthetic objects, made the action of the police quite incomprehensible to us for the time being. The disgusting ambiguity with which the Leipzig authorities answered all his questions as to the cause of his expulsion soon gave him the strongest suspicions as to what their intentions towards him actually were.

Leipzig, as the scene of his literary labours, being inestimably precious, it mattered greatly to him to keep within reach of it. My friend Apel owned a fine estate on Prussian soil, within but a few hours' distance of Leipzig, and we conceived the wish of seeing Laube hospitably harboured there. My friend, who without infringing the legal stipulations was in a position to give the persecuted man a place of refuge, immediately assented, and with great readiness, to our desire, but confessed to us next day, after having communicated with his family, that he thought he might incur some unpleasantnesses if he entertained Laube. At this the latter smiled, and in a manner I shall never forget, though I have noticed in the course of my life that the expression which I then saw in his face was one which has often flitted over my own features. He took his leave, and in a short time we heard that he had been arrested, owing to having undertaken fresh proceedings against former members of the Burschenschaft (Students' League), and had been lodged in the municipal prison at Berlin. I had thus had two experiences which weighed me down like lead, so I packed my scanty portmanteau, took leave of my mother and sister, and, with a stout heart, started on my career as a conductor.

In order to be able to look upon the little room under Minna's lodging as my new home, I was forced also to make the best of Bethmann's theatrical enterprise. As a matter of fact, a performance of *Don Juan* was given at once, for the director, who prided himself on being a connoisseur of things artistic, suggested that opera to me as one with which it would be wise for an aspiring young artist, of a good family, to make his début. Despite the fact that, apart from some of my own instrumental compositions, I had never yet conducted, and least of all in opera, the rehearsal and the performance went off fairly well. Only once or twice did discrepancies appear in the recitative of Donna Anna; yet this did not involve me in any kind of hostility, and when I took my place unabashed and calm for the production of *Lumpaci Vagabundus,* which I had practised very thoroughly, the people generally seemed to have gained full confidence in the theatre's new acquisition.

The fact that I submitted without bitterness and even with some cheerfulness to this unworthy use of my musical talent, was due less to my taste being at this period, as I called it, in its salad days, than to my intercourse with Minna Planer, who was employed in that magic trifle as the Amorous Fairy. Indeed, in the midst of this dust-cloud of frivolity and vulgarity, she always seemed very much like a fairy, the reasons of whose descent into this giddy whirl, which of a truth seemed neither to carry her away nor even to affect her, remained an absolute mystery. For while I could discover nothing in the opera singers save the familiar stage caricatures and grimaces, this fair actress differed wholly from those about her in her unaffected soberness and dainty modesty, as also in the absence of all theatrical pretence and stiltedness. There was only one young man whom I could place beside Minna on the ground of qualities like those I recognised in her. This fellow was Friedrich Schmitt, who had only just adopted the stage as a career in the hope of making a 'hit' in opera, to which, as the possessor of an excellent tenor voice, he felt himself called. He too differed from the rest of the company, especially in the earnestness which he brought to bear upon his studies and his work in general: the soulful manly pitch of his chest voice, his clear, noble enunciation and intelligent rendering of his words, have always remained as standards in my memory. Owing to the fact that he was wholly devoid of theatrical talent, and acted clumsily and awkwardly, a check was soon put to his progress, but he always remained dear to me as a clever and original man of trustworthy and upright character — my only associate.

But my dealings with my kind housemate soon became a cherished habit, while she returned the ingenuously impetuous advances of the conductor of one-and-twenty with a certain tolerant astonishment which, remote as it was from all coquetry and ulterior motives, soon made familiar and friendly intercourse possible with her. When, one evening, I returned late to my ground-floor room, by climbing through the window, for I had no latch-key, the noise of my entry brought Minna to her window just over mine. Standing on my window ledge I begged her to allow me to bid her good-night once more. She had not the slightest objection to this, but declared it must be done from the window, as she always had her door locked by the people of the house, and nobody could get in that way. She kindly facilitated the handshake by leaning far out of her window, so that I could take her hand as I stood on my ledge. When later on I had an attack of erysipelas, from which I often suffered, and with my face all swollen and frightfully distorted concealed myself from the world in my gloomy room, Minna visited me repeatedly, nursed me, and assured me that my distorted features did not matter in the least. On recovering, I paid her a visit and complained of a rash that had remained round my mouth, and which seemed so unpleasant that I apologised for showing it to her. This also she made light of. Then I inferred she would not give me a kiss, whereupon she at once gave me practical proof that she did not shrink from that either.

This was all done with a friendly serenity and composure that had something almost motherly about it, and it was free from all suggestion of frivolity or of heartlessness. In a few weeks the company had to leave Lauchstädt to proceed to Rudolstadt and fulfil a special engagement there. I was particularly anxious to make this journey, which in those days was an arduous undertaking, in Minna's company, and if only I had succeeded in getting my well-earned salary duly paid by Bethmann, nothing would have hindered the fulfilment of my wish. But in this matter I encountered exceptional difficulties, which in the course of eventful years grew in chronic fashion into the strangest of ailments. Even at Lauchstädt I had discovered that there was only one man who drew his salary in full, namely the bass Kneisel, whom I had seen smoking his pipe beside the couch of the director's lame wife. I was assured that if I cared greatly about getting some of my wages from time to time, I could obtain this favour only by paying court to Mme. Bethmann. This time I preferred once more

SYMPHONY IN E MAJOR

to appeal to my family for help, and therefore travelled to Rudolstadt through Leipzig, where, to the sad astonishment of my mother, I had to replenish my coffer with the necessary supplies. On the way to Leipzig I had travelled with Apel through his estate, he having fetched me from Lauchstädt for the purpose. His arrival was fixed in my memory by a noisy banquet which my wealthy friend gave at the hotel in my honour. It was on this occasion that I and one of the other guests succeeded in completely destroying a huge, massively built Dutch-tile stove, such as we had in our room at the inn. Next morning none of us could understand how it had happened.

It was on this journey to Rudolstadt that I first passed through Weimar, where on a rainy day I strolled with curiosity, but without emotion, towards Goethe's house. I had pictured something rather different, and thought I should experience livelier impressions from the active theatre life of Rudolstadt, to which I felt strongly attracted. In spite of the fact that I was not to be conductor myself, this post having been entrusted to the leader of the royal orchestra, who had been specially engaged for our performances, yet I was so fully occupied with rehearsals for the many operas and musical comedies required to regale the frivolous public of the principality that I found no leisure for excursions into the charming regions of this little land. In addition to these severe and ill-paid labours, two passions held me chained during the six weeks of my stay in Rudolstadt. These were, first, a longing to write the libretto of *Liebesverbot;* and secondly, my growing attachment to Minna. It is true, I sketched out a musical composition about this time, a symphony in E major, whose first movement (¾ time) I completed as a separate piece. As regards style and design, this work was suggested by Beethoven's Seventh and Eighth Symphonies, and, so far as I can remember, I should have had no need to be ashamed of it, had I been able to complete it, or keep the part I had actually finished. But I had already begun at this time to form the opinion that, to produce anything fresh and truly noteworthy in the realm of symphony, and according to Beethoven's methods, was an impossibility. Whereas opera, to which I felt inwardly drawn, though I had no real example I wished to copy, presented itself to my mind in varied and alluring shapes as a most fascinating form of art. Thus, amid manifold and passionate agitations, and in the few leisure hours which were left to me, I completed the greater part of my operatic poem, taking infinitely more pains, both as regards words and versification, than with the text of my earlier *Feen*. Moreover, I found myself possessed of incomparably greater assurance in the arrangement and partial invention of situations than when writing that earlier work.

On the other hand, I now began for the first time to experience the cares and worries of a lover's jealousy. A change, to me inexplicable, manifested itself in Minna's hitherto unaffected and gentle manner towards me. It appears that my artless solicitations for her favour, by which at that time I meant nothing serious, and in which a man of the world would merely have seen the exuberance of a youthful and easily satisfied infatuation, had given rise to certain remarks and comments upon the popular actress. I was astonished to learn, first from her reserved manner, and later from her own lips, that she felt compelled to inquire into the seriousness of my intentions, and to consider their consequences. She was at that time, as I had already discovered, on very intimate terms with a young nobleman, whose acquaintance I first made in Lauchstädt, where he used to visit her. I had already realised on that occasion that he was unfeignedly and cordially attached to her; in fact, in the circle of her friends she was regarded as engaged to Herr von O., although it was obvious that marriage was out of the question, as the young lover was quite without means, and owing to the high standing of his family it was essential that he should sacrifice himself to a marriage of convenience, both on account of his social position and of the career which he would have to adopt. During this stay at Rudolstadt Minna appears to have gathered certain information on this point which troubled and depressed her, thus rendering her more inclined to treat my impetuous attempts at courtship with cool reserve.

After mature deliberation I recognised that, in any case, *Young Europe, Ardinghello,* and *Liebesverbot* could not be produced at Rudolstadt; but it was a very different matter for the *Fee Amorosa*, with its merry theatrical mood, and an *Ehrlicher Bürger Kind* to seek a decent livelihood. Therefore, greatly discouraged, I proceeded to accentuate the more extravagant situations of my *Liebesverbot* by rioting with a few comrades in the sausage-scented atmosphere of the Rudolstadt Vogelwiese. At this time my troubles again brought me more or less into contact with the vice of gambling, although on this occasion it only cast temporary fetters about me in the very harmless form of the dice and roulette-tables out on the open market-place.

We were looking forward to the time when we should leave Rudolstadt for the half-yearly winter season at the capital, Magdeburg, mainly because I should there resume my place at the head of the orchestra, and might in any case count on a better reward for my musical efforts. But before returning to Magdeburg I had to endure a trying interval at Bernburg, where Bethmann, the director, in addition to his other undertakings, had also promised sundry theatrical performances. During our brief stay in the town I had to arrange for the presentation, with a mere fraction of the company, of several operas, which were again to be conducted by the royal conductor of the place. But in addition to these professional labours, I had to endure such a meagre, ill-provided and grievously farcical existence as was enough to disgust me, if not for ever, at any rate for the time being, with the wretched profession of a theatrical conductor. Yet I survived even this, and Magdeburg was destined to lead me eventually to the real glory of my adopted profession.

The sensation of sitting in command at the very conductor's desk from which, not many years before, the great master Kühnlein had so moved the perplexed young enthusiast by the weighty wisdom of his musical directorship, was not without its charm for me, and, indeed, I very quickly succeeded in obtaining perfect confidence in conducting an orchestra. I was soon a *persona grata* with the excellent musicians of the orchestra. Their splendid combination in spirited overtures, which, especially towards the finale, I generally took at an unheard-of speed, often earned for us all the intoxicating applause of the public. The achievements of my fiery and often exuberant zeal won me recognition from the singers, and were greeted by the audience with rapturous appreciation. As in Magdeburg, at least in those days, the art of theatrical criticism was but slightly developed, this universal satisfaction was a great encouragement, and at the end of the first three months of my Magdeburg conductorship I felt sustained by the flattering and comforting assurance that I was one of the bigwigs of opera. Under these circumstances, Schmale, the stage manager, who has been my good friend ever since, proposed a special gala performance for New Year's Day, which he felt sure would be a triumph. I was to compose the necessary music. This was very speedily done; a rousing overture, several melodramas and choruses were all greeted with enthusiasm, and brought us such ample applause that we repeated the performance with great success, although such repetitions after the actual gala day were quite contrary to usage.

With the new year (1835) there came a decisive turning-point in my life. After the rupture between Minna and myself at Rudolstadt, we had been to some extent lost to one another; but our friendship was resumed on our meeting again in Magdeburg; this time, however, it remained cool and purposely indifferent. When she first appeared in the town, a year before, her beauty had attracted considerable notice, and I now learned that she was the object of great attention from several young noblemen, and had shown herself not unmoved by the compliment implied by their visits. Although her reputation, thanks to her absolute discretion and self-respect, remained beyond reproach, my objection to her receiving such attentions grew very strong, owing possibly, in some degree, to the memory of the sorrows I had endured in Pachta's house in Prague. Although Minna assured me that the conduct of these gentlemen was much more discreet and decent than that of theatre-goers of the bourgeois class, and especially than that of certain young musical conductors, she never succeeded in soothing the bitterness and insistence with which I protested against her acceptance of such attentions. So we spent three unhappy months in ever-increasing estrangement, and at the same time, in half-frantic despair, I pretended to be fond of the most undesirable associates, and acted in every way with such blatant levity that Minna, as she told me afterwards, was filled with the deepest anxiety and solicitude concerning me. Moreover, as the ladies of the opera company were not slow to pay court to their youthful conductor, and especially as one young woman, whose reputation was not spotless, openly set her cap at me, this anxiety of Minna's seems at last to have culminated in a definite decision. I hit upon the idea of treating the *élite* of our opera company to oysters and punch in my own room on New Year's Eve. The married couples were invited, and then came the question whether Fräulein Planer would consent to take part in such a festivity. She accepted quite ingenuously, and presented herself, as neatly and becomingly dressed as ever, in my bachelor apartments, where things soon grew pretty lively. I had already warned my landlord that we were not likely to be very quiet, and reassured him as to any possible damage to his furniture. What the champagne failed to accomplish, the punch eventually succeeded in doing; all the restraints of petty conventionality, which the company usually endeavoured to observe, were cast aside, giving place to an unreserved demeanour all round, to which no one objected. And then it was that Minna's queenly dignity distinguished her from all her companions. She never lost her self-respect; and whilst no one ventured to take the slightest liberty with her, every one very clearly recognised the simple candour with which she responded to my kindly and solicitous attentions. They could not fail to see that the link existing between us was not to be compared to any ordinary *liaison,* and we had the satisfaction of seeing the flighty young lady who had so openly angled for me fall into a fit over the discovery.

From that time onward I remained permanently on the best of terms with Minna. I do not believe that she ever felt any sort of passion or genuine love for me, or, indeed, that she was capable of such a thing, and I can therefore only describe her feeling for me as one of heartfelt goodwill, and the sincerest desire for my success and prosperity, inspired as she was with the kindest sympathy, and genuine delight at, and admiration for, my talents. All this at last became part of her nature. She obviously had a very favourable opinion of my abilities, though she was surprised at the rapidity of my success. My eccentric nature, which she knew so well how to humour pleasantly by her gentleness, stimulated her to the continual exercise of the power, so flattering to her own vanity, and without ever betraying any desire or ardour herself, she never met my impetuous advances with coldness.

At the Magdeburg theatre I had already made the acquaintance of a very interesting woman called Mme. Haas. She was an actress, no longer in her first youth, and played so-called 'chaperone's parts.' This lady won my sympathy by telling me she had been friendly ever since her youth with Laube, in whose destiny she continued to take a heartfelt and cordial interest. She was clever, but far from happy, and an unprepossessing exterior, which with the lapse of years grew more uninviting, did not tend to make her any happier. She lived in meagre circumstances, with one child, and appeared to remember her better days with a bitter grief. My first visit to her was paid merely to inquire after Laube's fate, but I soon became a frequent and familiar caller. As she and Minna speedily became fast friends, we three often spent pleasant evenings talking together. But when, later on, a certain jealousy manifested itself on the part of the elder woman towards the younger, our confidential relations were more or less disturbed, for it particularly grieved me to hear Minna's talents and mental gifts criticised by the other. One evening I had promised Minna to have tea with her and Mme. Haas, but I had thoughtlessly promised to go to a whist party first. This engagement I purposely prolonged, much as it wearied me, in the deliberate hope that her companion — who had already grown irksome to me — might have left before my arrival. The only way in which I could do this was by drinking hard, so that I had the very unusual experience of rising from a sober whist party in a completely fuddled condition, into which I had imperceptibly fallen, and in which I refused to believe. This incredulity deluded me into keeping my engagement for tea, although it was so late. To my intense disgust the elder woman was still there when I arrived, and her presence at once had the effect of rousing my tipsiness to a violent outbreak; for she seemed astonished at my rowdy and unseemly behaviour, and made several remarks upon it intended for jokes, whereupon I scoffed at her in the coarsest manner, so that she immediately left the house in high dudgeon. I had still sense enough to be conscious of Minna's astonished laughter at my outrageous conduct. As soon as she realised, however, that my condition was such as to render my removal impossible without great commotion, she rapidly formed a resolution which must indeed have cost her an effort, though it was carried out with the utmost calmness and good-humour. She did all she could for me, and procured me the necessary relief, and when I sank into a heavy slumber, unhesitatingly resigned her own bed to my use. There I slept until awakened by the wonderful grey of dawn. On recognising where I was, I at once realised and grew ever more convinced of the fact that this morning's sunrise marked the starting-point of an infinitely momentous period of my life. The demon of care had at last entered into my existence.

Without any light-hearted jests, without gaiety or joking of any description, we breakfasted quietly and decorously together, and at an hour when, in view of the compromising circumstances of the previous evening, we could set out without attracting undue notice, I set off with Minna for a long walk beyond the city gates. Then we parted, and from that day forward freely and openly gratified our desires as an acknowledged pair of lovers.

The peculiar direction which my musical activities had gradually taken continued to receive ever fresh impetus, not only from the successes, but also from the disasters which about this time befell my efforts. I produced the overture to my *Feen* with very satisfactory results at a concert given by the Logengesellschaft, and thereby earned considerable applause. On the other hand, news came from Leipzig confirming the shabby action of the directors of the theatre in that place with regard to the promised presentation of this opera. But, happily for me, I had begun the music for my *Liebesverbot*, an occupation which so absorbed my thoughts that I lost all interest in the earlier work, and abstained with proud indifference from all further effort to secure its performance in Leipzig. The success of its overture alone amply repaid me for the composition of my first opera.

Meanwhile, in spite of numerous other distractions, I found time, during the brief six months of this theatrical season in Magdeburg, to complete a large portion of my new opera, besides doing other work. I ventured to introduce two duets from it at a concert given in the theatre, and their reception encouraged me to proceed hopefully with the rest of the opera.

During the second half of this season my friend Apel came to sun himself enthusiastically in the splendour of my musical directorship. He had written a drama, *Columbus*, which I recommended to our management for production. This was a peculiarly easy favour to win, as Apel volunteered to have a new scene, representing the Alhambra, painted at his own expense. Besides this, he proposed to effect many welcome improvements in the condition of the actors taking part in his play; for, owing to the continued preference displayed by the directress for Kneisel, the bass, they had all suffered very much from uncertainty about their wages. The piece itself appeared to me to contain much that was good. It described the difficulties and struggles of the great navigator before he set sail on his first voyage of discovery. The drama ended with the momentous departure of his ships from the harbour of Palos, an episode whose results are known to all the world. At my desire Apel submitted his play to my uncle Adolph, and even in his critical opinion it was remarkable for its lively and characteristic popular scenes. On the other hand, a love romance, which he had woven into the plot, struck me as unnecessary and dull. In addition to a brief chorus for some Moors who were expelled from Granada, to be sung on their departure from the familiar home country, and a short orchestral piece by way of conclusion, I also dashed off an overture for my friend's play. I sketched out the complete draft of this one evening at Minna's house, while Apel was left free to talk to her as much and as loudly as he liked. The effect this composition was calculated to produce rested on a fundamental idea which was quite simple, yet startling in its development. Unfortunately I worked it out rather hurriedly. In not very carefully chosen phrasing the orchestra was to represent the ocean, and, as far as might be, the ship upon it. A forcible, pathetically yearning and aspiring theme was the only comprehensible idea amid the swirl of enveloping sound. When the whole had been repeated, there was a sudden jump to a different theme in extreme *pianissimo,* accompanied by the swelling vibrations of the first violins, which was intended to represent a Fata Morgana. I had secured three pairs of trumpets in different keys, in order to produce this exquisite, gradually dawning and seductive theme with the utmost niceties of shade and variety of modulation. This was intended to represent the land of desire towards which the hero's eyes are turned, and whose shores seem continually to rise before him only to sink elusively beneath the waves, until at last they soar in very deed above the western horizon, the crown of all his toil and search, and stand clearly and unmistakably revealed to all the sailors, a vast continent of the future. My six trumpets were now to combine in one key, in order that the theme assigned to them might re-echo in glorious jubilation. Familiar as I was with the excellence of the Prussian regimental trumpeters, I could rely upon a startling effect, especially in this concluding passage. My overture astonished every one, and was tumultuously applauded. The play itself, however, was acted without dignity. A conceited comedian, named Ludwig Meyer, completely ruined the title part, for which he excused himself on the ground that, having to act as stage manager also, he had been unable to commit his lines to memory. Nevertheless, he managed to enrich his wardrobe with several splendid costumes at Apel's expense, wearing them, as Columbus, one after the other. At all events, Apel had lived to see a play of his own actually performed, and although this was never repeated, yet it afforded me an opportunity of increasing my personal popularity with the people of Magdeburg, as the overture was several times repeated at concerts by special request.

But the chief event of this theatrical season occurred towards its close. I induced Mme. Schröder-Devrient, who was staying in Leipzig, to come to us for a few special performances, when, on two occasions, I had the great satisfaction and stimulating experience of myself conducting the operas in which she sang, and thus entering into immediate artistic collaboration with her. She appeared as Desdemona and Romeo. In the latter rôle particularly she surpassed herself, and kindled a fresh flame in my breast. This visit brought us also into closer personal contact. So kindly disposed and sympathetic did she show herself towards me, that she even volunteered to lend me her services at a concert which I proposed to give for my own benefit, although this would necessitate her returning after a brief absence. Under circumstances so auspicious I could only expect the best possible results from my concert, and in my situation at that time its proceeds were a matter of vital importance to me. My scanty salary from the Magdeburg opera company had become altogether illusory, being paid only in small and irregular instalments, so that I could see but one way of meeting my daily expenses. These included frequent entertainment of a large circle of friends, consisting of singers and players, and the situation had become unpleasantly accentuated by no small number of debts. True, I did not know their exact amount; but reckoned that I could at least form an advantageous, if indefinite, estimate of the sum to be realized by my concert, whereby the two unknown quantities might balance each other. I therefore consoled my creditors with the tale of these fabulous receipts, which were to pay them all in full the day after the concert. I even went so far as to invite them to come and be paid at the hotel to which I had moved at the close of the season.

And, indeed, there was nothing unreasonable in my counting on the highest imaginable receipts, when supported by so great and popular a singer, who, moreover, was returning to Magdeburg on purpose for the event. I consequently acted with reckless prodigality as regards cost, launching out into all manner of musical extravagance, such as engaging an excellent and much larger orchestra, and arranging many rehearsals. Unfortunately for me, however, nobody would believe that such a famous actress, whose time was so precious, would really return again to please a little Magdeburg conductor. My pompous announcement of her appearance was almost universally regarded as a deceitful manœuvre, and people took offence at the high prices charged for seats. The result was that the hall was only very scantily filled, a fact which particularly grieved me on account of my generous patroness. Her promise I had never doubted. Punctually on the day appointed she reappeared to support me, and now had the painful and unaccustomed experience of performing before a small audience. Fortunately, she treated the matter with great good-humour (which, I learned later, was prompted by other motives, not personally concerning me). Among several pieces she sang Beethoven's *Adelaïde* most exquisitely, wherein, to my own astonishment, I accompanied her on the piano. But, alas! another and more unexpected mishap befell my concert, through our unfortunate selection of pieces. Owing to the excessive reverberation of the saloon in the Hotel ' The City of London,' the noise was unbearable. My Columbus *Overture*, with its six trumpets, had early in the evening filled the audience with terror; and now, at the end, came Beethoven's *Schlacht bei Vittoria*, for which, in enthusiastic expectation of limitless receipts, I had provided every imaginable orchestral luxury. The firing of cannon and musketry was organised with the utmost elaboration, on both the French and English sides, by means of specially constructed and costly apparatus; while trumpets and bugles had been doubled and trebled. Then began a battle, such as has seldom been more cruelly fought in a concert-room. The orchestra flung itself, so to speak, upon the scanty audience with such an overwhelming superiority of numbers that the latter speedily gave up all thought of resistance and literally took to flight. Mme. Schröder-Devrient had kindly taken a front seat, that she might hear the concert to an end. Much as she may have been inured to terrors of this kind, this was more than she could stand, even out of friendship for me. When, therefore, the English made a fresh desperate assault upon the French position, she took to flight, almost wringing her hands. Her action became the signal for a panic-stricken stampede. Every one rushed out; and Wellington's victory was finally celebrated in a confidential outburst between myself and the orchestra alone. Thus ended this wonderful musical festival. Schröder-Devrient at once departed, deeply regretting the ill-success of her well-meant effort, and kindly left me to my fate.

After seeking comfort in the arms of my sorrowing sweetheart, and attempting to nerve myself for the morrow's battle, which did not seem likely to end in a victorious symphony, I returned next morning to the hotel. I found I could only reach my rooms by running the gauntlet between long rows of men and women in double file, who had all been specially invited thither for the settlement of their respective affairs. Reserving the right to select individuals from among my visitors for separate interview, I first of all led in the second trumpeter of the orchestra, whose duty it had been to look after the cash and the music. From his account I learned that, owing to the high fees which, in my generous enthusiasm, I had promised to the orchestra, a few more shillings and sixpences would still have to come out of my own pocket to meet these charges alone. When this was settled, the position of affairs was plain. The next person I invited to come in was Mme. Gottschalk, a trustworthy Jewess, with whom I wanted to come to some arrangement respecting the present crisis. She perceived at once that more than ordinary help was required in this case, but did not doubt that I should be able to obtain it from my opulent connections in Leipzig. She undertook, therefore, to appease the other creditors with tranquillising assurances, and railed, or pretended to rail, against their indecent conduct with great vigour. Thus at last we succeeded, though not without some difficulty, in making the corridor outside my door once more passable.

The theatrical season was now over, our company on the point of dissolution, and I myself free from my appointment. But meanwhile the unhappy director of our theatre had passed from a state of chronic to one of acute bankruptcy. He paid with paper money, that is to say, with whole sheets of box-tickets for performances which he guaranteed should take place. By dint of great craft Minna managed to extract some profit even from these singular treasury-bonds. She was living at this time most frugally and economically. Moreover, as the dramatic company still continued its efforts on behalf of its members — only the opera troupe having been dissolved — she remained at the theatre. Thus, when I started out on my compulsory return to Leipzig, she saw me off with hearty good-wishes for our speedy reunion, promising to spend the next holidays in visiting her parents in Dresden, on which occasion she hoped also to look me up in Leipzig.

Thus it came about that early in May I once more went home to my own folk, in order that after this abortive first attempt at civic independence, I might finally lift the load of debt with which my efforts in Magdeburg had burdened me. An intelligent brown poodle faithfully accompanied me, and was entrusted to my family for food and entertainment as the only visible property I had acquired. Nevertheless, my mother and Rosalie succeeded in founding good hopes for my future career upon the bare fact of my being able to conduct an orchestra. To me, on the other hand, the thought of returning once more to my former life with my family was very discomfiting. My relation to Minna in particular spurred me on to resume my interrupted career as speedily as possible. The great change which had come over me in this respect was more apparent than ever when Minna spent a few days with me in Leipzig on her way home. Her familiar and genial presence proclaimed that my days of parental dependence were past and gone. We discussed the renewal of my Magdeburg engagement, and I promised her an early visit in Dresden. I obtained permission from my mother and sister to invite her one evening to tea, and in this way I introduced her to my family. Rosalie saw at once how matters stood with me, but made no further use of the discovery than to tease me about being in love. To her the affair did not appear dangerous; but to me things wore a very different aspect, for this love-lorn attachment was entirely in keeping with my independent spirit, and my ambition to win myself a place in the world of art.

My distaste for Leipzig itself was furthermore strengthened by a change which occurred there at this time in the realm of music. At the very time that I, in Magdeburg, was attempting to make my reputation as a musical conductor by thoughtless submission to the frivolous taste of the day, Mendelssohn-Bartholdy was conducting the Gewandhaus concerts, and inaugurating a momentous epoch for himself and the musical taste of Leipzig. His influence had put an end to the simple ingenuousness with which the Leipzig public had hitherto judged the productions of its sociable subscription concerts. Through the influence of my good old friend Pohlenz, who was not yet altogether laid on the shelf, I managed to produce my

Columbus Overture at a benefit concert given by the favourite young singer, Livia Gerhart. But, to my amazement, I found that the taste of the musical public in Leipzig had been given a different bent, which not even my rapturously applauded overture, with its brilliant combination of six trumpets, could influence. This experience deepened my dislike of everything approaching a classical tone, in which sentiment I found myself in complete accord with honest Pohlenz, who sighed good-naturedly over the downfall of the good old times.

Arrangements for a musical festival at Dessau, under Friedrich Schneider's conductorship, offered me a welcome chance of quitting Leipzig. For this journey, which could be performed on foot in seven hours, I had to procure a passport for eight days. This document was destined to play an important part in my life for many years to come; for on several occasions and in various European countries it was the only paper I possessed to prove my identity. In fact, owing to my evasion of military duty in Saxony, I never again succeeded in obtaining a regular pass until I was appointed musical conductor in Dresden. I derived very little artistic pleasure or benefit of any kind from this occasion; on the contrary, it gave a fresh impetus to my hatred of the classical. I heard Beethoven's Symphony in C minor conducted by a man whose physiognomy, resembling that of a drunken satyr, filled me with unconquerable disgust. In spite of an interminable row of contrabassi, with which a conductor usually coquettes at musical festivals, his performance was so expressionless and inane that I turned away in disgust as from an alarming and repulsive problem, and desisted from all attempts to explain the impassable gulf which, as I again perceived, yawned between my own vivid and imaginative conception of this work and the only living presentations of it which I had ever heard. But for the present my tormented spirits were cheered and calmed by hearing the classical Schneider's oratorio *Absalom* rendered as an absolute burlesque.

It was in Dessau that Minna had made her first début on the stage, and while there I heard her spoken of by frivolous young men in the tone usual in such circles when discussing young and beautiful actresses. My eagerness in contradicting this chatter and confounding the scandalmongers revealed to me more clearly than ever the strength of the passion which drew me to her.

I therefore returned to Leipzig without calling on my relatives, and there procured means for an immediate journey to Dresden. On the way (the journey was still performed by express coach) I met Minna, accompanied by one of her sisters, already on the way back to Magdeburg. Promptly procuring a posting ticket for the return journey to Leipzig, I actually set off thither with my dear girl; but by the time we reached the next station I had succeeded in persuading her to turn back with me to Dresden. By this time the mail-coach was far ahead of us, and we had to travel by special post-chaise. This lively bustling to and fro seemed to astonish the two girls, and put them into high spirits. The extravagance of my conduct had evidently roused them to the expectation of adventures, and it now behoved me to fulfil this expectation. Procuring from a Dresden acquaintance the necessary cash, I conducted my two lady friends through the Saxon Alps, where we spent several right merry days of innocent and youthful gaiety. Only once was this disturbed by a passing fit of jealousy on my part, for which, indeed, there was no occasion, but which fed itself in my heart on a nervous apprehension of the future, and upon the experience I had already gained of womenkind. Yet, despite this blot, our excursion still lingers in my memory as the sweetest and almost sole remembrance of unalloyed happiness in the whole of my life as a young man. One evening in particular stands out in bright relief, during which we sat together almost all night at the watering-place of Schandau in glorious summer weather. Indeed, my subsequent long and anxious connection with Minna, interwoven as it was with the most painful and bitter vicissitudes, has often appeared to me as a persistently prolonged expiation of the brief and harmless enjoyment of those few days.

After accompanying Minna to Leipzig, whence she continued her journey to Magdeburg, I presented myself to my family, but told them nothing of my Dresden excursion. I now braced my energies, as though under the stern compulsion of a strange and deep sense of duty, to the task of making such arrangements as would speedily restore me to my dear one's side. To this end a fresh engagement had to be negotiated with Director Bethmann for the coming winter season. Unable to await the conclusion of our contract in Leipzig, I availed myself of Laube's presence at the baths in Kösen, near Naumburg, to pay him a visit. Laube had only recently been discharged from the Berlin municipal gaol, after a tormenting inquisition of nearly a year's duration. On giving his parole not to leave the country until the verdict had been given, he had been permitted to retire to Kösen, from which place he, one evening, paid us a secret visit in Leipzig. I can still call his woebegone appearance to mind. He seemed hopelessly resigned, though he spoke cheerfully with regard to all his earlier dreams of better things; and owing to my own worries at that time about the critical state of my affairs, this impression still remains one of my saddest and most painful recollections. While at Kösen I showed him a good many of the verses for my *Liebesverbot,* and although he spoke coldly of my presumption in wishing to write my own libretto, I was slightly encouraged by his appreciation of my work.

Meanwhile I impatiently awaited letters from Magdeburg. Not that I had any doubt as to the renewal of my engagement; on the contrary, I had every reason to regard myself as a good acquisition for Bethmann; but I felt as though nothing which tended to bring me nearer to Minna could move fast enough. As soon as I received the necessary tidings, I hurried away to make all needful arrangements on the spot for ensuring a magnificent success in the coming Magdeburg operatic season.

Through the tireless munificence of the King of Prussia fresh and final assistance had been granted to our perennially bankrupt theatrical director. His Majesty had assigned a not inconsiderable sum to a committee consisting of substantial Magdeburg citizens, as a subsidy to be expended on the theatre under Bethmann's management. What this meant, and the respect with which I thereupon regarded the artistic conditions of Magdeburg, may be best imagined if one remembers the neglected and forlorn surroundings amid which such provincial theatres usually drag out their lives. I offered at once to undertake a long journey in search of good operatic singers. I said

BOHEMIA

I would find the means for this at my own risk, and the only guarantee I demanded from the management for eventual reimbursement was that they should assign me the proceeds of a future benefit performance. This offer was gladly accepted, and in pompous tones the director furnished me with the necessary powers, and moreover gave me his parting blessing. During this brief interval I lived once more in intimate communion with Minna — who now had her mother with her — and then took fresh leave of her for my venturesome enterprise.

But when I got to Leipzig I found it by no means easy to procure the funds, so confidently counted on when in Magdeburg, for the expenses of my projected journey. The glamour of the royal protection of Prussia for our theatrical undertaking, which I portrayed in the liveliest colours to my good brother-in-law Brockhaus, quite failed to dazzle him, and it was at the cost of great pains and humiliation that I finally got my ship of discovery under weigh.

I was naturally drawn first of all to my old wonderland of Bohemia. There I merely touched at Prague and, without visiting my lovely lady friends, I hurried forward so that I might first sample the opera company then playing for the season at Karlsbad. Impatient to discover as many talents as I could as soon as possible, so as not to exhaust my funds to no purpose, I attended a performance of *La Dame Blanche,* sincerely hoping to find the whole performance first class. But not until much later did I fully realise how wretched was the quality of all these singers. I selected one of them, a bass named Gräf, who was singing Gaveston. When in due course he made his début at Magdeburg, he provoked so much well-founded dissatisfaction, that I could not find a word to say in reply to the mockery which this acquisition brought upon me.

But the small success with which the real object of my tour was attended was counterbalanced by the pleasantness of the journey itself. The trip through Eger, over the Fichtel mountains, and the entry into Bayreuth, gloriously illuminated by the setting sun, have remained happy memories to this day.

My next goal was Nuremberg, where my sister Clara and her husband were acting, and from whom I might reckon on sound information as to the object of my search. It was particularly nice to be hospitably received in my sister's house, where I hoped to revive my somewhat exhausted means of travel. In this hope I reckoned chiefly upon the sale of a snuff-box presented to me by a friend, which I had secret reasons to suppose was made of platinum. To this I could add a gold signet-ring, given me by my friend Apel for composing the overture to his *Columbus*. The value of the snuff-box unfortunately proved to be entirely imaginary; but by pawning these two jewels, the only ones I had left, I hoped to provide myself with the bare necessaries for continuing my journey to Frankfort. It was to this place and the Rhine district that the information I had gathered led me to direct my steps. Before leaving I persuaded my sister and brother-in-law to accept engagements in Magdeburg; but I still lacked a first tenor and a soprano, whom hitherto I had altogether failed to discover.

My stay in Nuremberg was most agreeably prolonged through a renewed meeting with Schröder-Devrient, who just at that time was fulfilling a short engagement in that town. Meeting her again was like seeing the clouds disperse, which, since our last meeting, had darkened my artistic horizon.

The Nuremberg operatic company had a very limited repertoire. Besides *Fidelio* they could produce nothing save *Die Schweizerfamilie,* a fact about which this great singer complained, as this was one of her first parts sung in early youth, for which she was hardly any longer suited, and which, in addition, she had played *ad nauseam*. I also looked forward to the performance of *Die Schweizerfamilie* with misgivings, and even with anxiety, for I feared lest this tame opera and the old-fashioned sentimental part of Emmeline would weaken the great impression the public, as well as myself, had formed up to that moment of the work of this sublime artist. Imagine, therefore, how deeply moved and astonished I was, on the evening of the performance, to find that it was in this very part that I first realised the truly transcendental genius of this extraordinary woman. That anything so great as her interpretation of the character of the Swiss maiden could not be handed down to posterity as a monument for all time can only be looked upon as one of the most sublime sacrifices

EXTRAVAGANT GAIETY

demanded by dramatic art, and as one of its highest manifestations. When, therefore, such phenomena appear, we cannot hold them in too great reverence, nor look upon them as too sacred.

Apart from all these new experiences which were to become of so much value to my whole life and to my artistic development, the impressions I received at Nuremberg, though they were apparently trivial in their origin, left such indelible traces on my mind, that they revived within me later on, though in quite a different and novel form.

My brother-in-law, Wolfram, was a great favourite with the Nuremberg theatrical world; he was witty and sociable, and as such made himself much liked in theatrical circles. On this occasion I received singularly delightful proofs of the spirit of extravagant gaiety manifested on these evenings at the inn, in which I also took part. A master carpenter, named Lauermann, a little thick-set man, no longer young, of comical appearance and gifted only with the roughest dialect, was pointed out to me in one of the inns visited by our friends as one of those oddities who involuntarily contributed most to the amusement of the local wags. Lauermann, it seems, imagined himself an excellent singer, and as a result of this presumption, evinced interest only in those in whom he thought he recognised a like talent. In spite of the fact that, owing to this singular peculiarity, he became the butt of constant jest and scornful mockery, he never failed to appear every evening among his laughter-loving persecutors. So often had he been laughed at and hurt by their scorn, that it became very difficult to persuade him to give a display of his artistic skill, and this at last could only be effected by artfully devised traps, so laid as to appeal to his vanity. My arrival as an unknown stranger was utilised for a manœuvre of this kind. How poor was the opinion they held of the unfortunate mastersinger's judgment was revealed when, to my great amazement, my brother-in-law introduced me to him as the great Italian singer, Lablache. To his credit I must confess that Lauermann surveyed me for a long time with incredulous distrust, and commented with cautious suspicion on my juvenile appearance, but especially on the evidently tenor character of my voice. But the whole art of these tavern associates and their principal enjoyment consisted in leading this poor enthusiast to believe the incredible, a task on which they spared neither time nor pains.

My brother-in-law succeeded in making the carpenter believe that I, while receiving fabulous sums for my performances, wished by a singular act of dissimulation, and by visiting public inns, to withdraw from the general public; and that, moreover, when it came to a meeting between 'Lauermann' and 'Lablache,' the only real interest could be to hear Lauermann and not Lablache, seeing that the former had nothing to learn from the latter, but only Lablache from him. So singular was the conflict between incredulity, on the one hand, and keenly excited vanity on the other, that finally the poor carpenter became really attractive to me. I began to play the rôle assigned me with all the skill I could command, and after a couple of hours, which were relieved by the strangest antics, we at last gained our end. The wondrous mortal, whose flashing eyes had long been fixed on me in the greatest excitement, worked his muscles in the peculiarly fantastic fashion which we are accustomed to associate with a music-making automaton, the mechanism of which has been duly wound up: his lips quivered, his teeth gnashed, his eyes rolled convulsively, until finally there broke forth, in a hoarse oily voice, an uncommonly trivial street-ballad. Its delivery, accompanied by a regular movement of his outstretched thumbs behind the ears, and during which his fat face glowed the brightest red, was unhappily greeted with a wild burst of laughter from all present, which excited the unlucky master to the most furious wrath. With studied cruelty this wrath was greeted by those, who until then had shamelessly flattered him, with the most extravagant mockery, until the poor wretch at last absolutely foamed with rage.

As he was leaving the inn amid a hail of curses from his infamous friends, an impulse of genuine pity prompted me to follow him, that I might beg his forgiveness and seek in some way to pacify him, a task all the more difficult since he was especially bitter against me as the latest of his enemies, and the one who had so deeply deceived his eager hope of hearing the genuine Lablache. Nevertheless, I succeeded in stopping him on the threshold; and now the riotous company silently entered into an extraordinary conspiracy to induce Lauermann to sing again that very evening. How they managed this I can as little remember as I can call to mind the effect of the spirituous liquors I imbibed. In any case, I suspect that drink must eventually have been the means of subduing Lauermann, just as it also rendered my own recollections of the wonderful events of that prolonged evening at the inn extremely vague. After Lauermann had for the second time suffered the same mockery, the whole company felt itself bound to accompany the unhappy man to his home. They carried him thither in a wheelbarrow, which they found outside the house, and in this he arrived, in triumph, at his own door, in one of those marvellous narrow alleys peculiar to the old city. Frau Lauermann, who was aroused from slumber to receive her husband, enabled us, by her torrent of curses, to form some idea of the nature of their marital and domestic relations. Mockery of her husband's vocal talents was with her also a familiar theme; but to this she now added the most dreadful reproaches for the worthless scamps who, by encouraging him in this delusion, kept him from profitably following his trade, and even led him to such scenes as the present one. Thereupon the pride of the suffering mastersinger reasserted itself; for while his wife painfully assisted him to mount the stairs, he harshly denied her right to sit in judgment upon his vocal gifts, and sternly ordered her to be silent. But even now this wonderful night-adventure was by no means over. The entire swarm moved once more in the direction of the inn. Before the house, however, we found a number of fellows congregated, among them several workmen, against whom, owing to police regulations as to closing hours, the doors were shut. But the regular guests of the house, who were of our party, and who were on terms of old friendship with the host, thought that it was nevertheless permissible and possible to demand entrance. The host was troubled at having to bar his door against friends, whose voices he recognised; yet it was necessary to prevent the new arrivals from forcing a way in with them. Out of this situation a mighty confusion arose, which, what with shouting and clamour and an inexplicable growth in the number of the disputants, soon assumed a truly demoniacal character. It seemed to me as though in a few moments the whole town would break into a tumult, and I thought I should once more have to witness a revolution, the real origin of which no man could comprehend. Then suddenly I heard some one fall, and, as though by magic, the whole mass scattered in every direction. One of the regular guests, who was familiar with an ancient Nuremberg boxing trick, desiring to put an end to the interminable riot and to cut his way home through the crowd, gave one of the noisiest shouters a blow with his fist between the eyes, laying him senseless on the ground, though without seriously injuring him. And this it was that so speedily broke up the whole throng. Within little more than a minute of the most violent uproar of hundreds of human voices, my brother-in-law and I were able to stroll arm-in-arm through the moonlit streets, quietly jesting and laughing, on our way home; and then it was that, to my amazement and relief, he informed me that he was accustomed to this sort of life every evening.

At last, however, it became necessary seriously to attend to the purpose of my journey. Only in passing did I touch at Würzburg for a day. I remember nothing of the meeting with my relations and acquaintance beyond the melancholy visit to Friederike Galvani already mentioned. On reaching Frankfort I was obliged to seek at once the shelter of a decent hotel, in order to await there the result of my solicitations for subsidies from the directorate of the Magdeburg theatre. My hopes of securing the real stars of our operatic undertaking were formed with a view to a season at Wiesbaden, where, I was told, a good operatic company was on the point of dissolution. I found it extremely difficult to arrange the short journey thither; yet I managed to be present at a rehearsal of *Robert der Teufel*, in which the tenor Freimüller distinguished himself. I interviewed him at once, and found him willing to entertain my proposals for Magdeburg. We concluded the necessary agreement, and I then returned with all speed to my headquarters, the Weidenbusch Hotel in Frankfort. There I had to spend another anxious week, during which I waited in vain for the necessary travelling expenses to arrive from Magdeburg. To kill time I had recourse, among other things, to a large red pocket-book which I carried about with me in my portmanteau, and in which I entered, with exact details of dates, etc., notes for my future biography — the selfsame book which now lies before me to freshen my memory, and which I have ever since added to at various periods of my life, without leaving any gaps. Through the neglect of the Magdeburg managers my situation, which was already serious, became literally desperate, when I made an acquisition in Frankfort which gave me almost more pleasure than I was able to bear. I had been present at a production of the *Zauberflöte* under the direction of Guhr, then wonderfully renowned as 'a conductor of genius,' and was agreeably surprised at the truly excellent quality of the company. It was, of course, useless to think of luring one of the leading stars into my net; on the other hand, I saw clearly enough that the youthful Fräulein Limbach, who sang the 'first boy's' part, possessed a desirable talent. She accepted my offer of an engagement, and, indeed, seemed so anxious to be rid of her Frankfort engagement that she resolved to escape from it surreptitiously. She revealed her plans to me, and begged me to assist her in carrying them out; for, inasmuch as the directors might get wind of the affair, there was no time to lose. At all events, the young lady assumed that I had abundant credit, supplied for my official business journey by the Magdeburg theatre committee, whose praises I had so diligently sung. But already I had been compelled to pledge my scanty travelling gear in order to provide for my own departure. To this point I had persuaded the host, but now found him by no means inclined to advance me the additional funds needed for carrying off a young singer. To cloak the bad behaviour of my directors I was compelled to invent some tale of misfortune, and to leave the astonished and indignant young lady behind. Heartily ashamed of this adventure, I travelled through rain and storm via Leipzig, where I picked up my brown poodle, and reaching Magdeburg, there resumed my work as musical director on the 1st of September.

The result of my business labours gave me but little joy.

The director, it is true, proved triumphantly that he had sent five whole golden louis to my address in Frankfort, and that my tenor and the youthful lady-singer had also been provided with proper contracts, but not with the fares and advances demanded. Neither of them came; only the basso Gräf arrived with pedantic punctuality from Karlsbad, and immediately provoked the chaff of our theatrical wags. He sang at a rehearsal of the *Schweizerfamilie* with such a schoolmasterly drone that I completely lost my composure. The arrival of my excellent brother-in-law Wolfram with my sister Clara was of more advantage for musical comedy than for grand opera, and caused me considerable trouble into the bargain; for, being honest folk and used to decent living, they speedily perceived that, in spite of royal protection, the condition of the theatre was but very insecure, as was natural under so unscrupulous a management as that of Bethmann, and recognised with alarm that they had seriously compromised their family position. My courage had already begun to sink when a happy chance brought us a young woman, Mme. Pollert (*née* Zeibig), who was passing through Magdeburg with her husband, an actor, in order to fulfil a special engagement in that town; she was gifted with a beautiful voice, was a talented singer, and well suited for the chief rôles. Necessity had at last driven the directors to action, and at the eleventh hour they sent for the tenor Freimüller. But I was particularly gratified when the love which had arisen between him and young Limbach in Frankfort enabled the enterprising tenor to carry away this singer, to whom I had behaved so miserably. Both arrived radiant with joy. Along with them we engaged Mme. Pollert, who, in spite of her pretentiousness, met with favour from the public. A well-trained and musically competent baritone, Herr Krug, afterwards the conductor of a choir in Karlsruhe, had also been discovered, so that all at once I stood at the head of a really good operatic company, among which the basso Gräf could be fitted in only with great difficulty, by being kept as much as possible in the background. We succeeded quickly with a series of operatic performances which were by no means ordinary, and our repertory included everything of this nature that had ever been written for the

theatre. I was particularly pleased with the presentation of
Spohr's *Jessonda,* which was truly not without sublimity, and
raised us high in the esteem of all cultured lovers of music. I
was untiring in my endeavours to discover some means of elevating our performances above the usual level of excellence
compatible with the meagre resources of provincial theatres.
I persistently fell foul of the director Bethmann by strengthening my orchestra, which he had to pay; but, on the other hand,
I won his complete goodwill by strengthening the chorus and
the theatre music, which cost him nothing, and which lent such
splendour to our presentations that subscriptions and audiences
increased enormously. For instance, I secured the regimental
band, and also the military singers, who in the Prussian army
are admirably organised, and who assisted in our performances
in return for free passes to the gallery granted to their relatives.
Thus I managed to furnish with the utmost completeness the
specially strong orchestral accompaniment demanded by the
score of Bellini's *Norma,* and was able to dispose of a body of
male voices for the impressive unison portion of the male chorus
in the introduction of that work such as even the greatest
theatres could rarely command. In later years I was able to
assure Auber, whom I often met over an ice in Tortoni's café
in Paris, that in his *Lestocq* I had been able to render the part
of the mutinous soldiery, when seduced into conspiracy, with an
absolutely full number of voices, a fact for which he thanked
me with astonishment and delight.

Amid such circumstances of encouragement the composition
of my *Liebesverbot* made rapid strides towards completion.
I intended the presentation of this piece for the benefit
performance which had been promised me as a means of
defraying my expenses, and I worked hard in the hope of
improving my reputation, and at the same time of accomplishing something by no means less desirable, and that was the
betterment of my financial position. Even the few hours
which I could snatch from business to spend at Minna's side
were devoted with unexampled zeal to the completion of my
score. My diligence moved even Minna's mother, who looked
with some uneasiness upon our love affair. She had remained
over the summer on a visit to her daughter, and managed

the house for her. Owing to her interference a new and urgent anxiety had entered into our relations, which pressed for serious settlement. It was natural that we should begin to think of what it was all going to lead to. I must confess that the idea of marriage, especially in view of my youth, filled me with dismay, and without indeed reflecting on the matter, or seriously weighing its pros and cons, a naïve and instinctive feeling prevented me even from considering the possibility of a step which would have such serious consequences upon my whole life. Moreover, our modest circumstances were in so alarming and uncertain a state that even Minna declared that she was more anxious to see these improved than to get me to marry her. But she was also driven to think of herself, and that promptly, for trouble arose with regard to her own position in the Magdeburg theatre. There she had met with a rival in her own speciality, and as this woman's husband became chief stage manager, and consequently had supreme power, she grew to be a source of great danger. Seeing, therefore, that at this very moment Minna received advantageous offers from the managers of the Königstadt theatre in Berlin, then doing a splendid business, she seized the opportunity to break off her connection with the Magdeburg theatre, and thus plunged me, whom she did not appear to consider in the matter, into the depths of despair. I could not hinder Minna from going to Berlin to fulfil a special engagement there, although this was not in accordance with her agreement, and so she departed, leaving me behind, overcome with grief and doubt as to the meaning of her conduct. At last, mad with passion, I wrote to her urging her to return, and the better to move her and not to separate her fate from my own, I proposed to her in a strictly formal manner, and hinted at the hope of early marriage. About the same time my brother-in-law, Wolfram, having quarrelled with the director Bethmann and cancelled his contract with him, also went to the Königstadt theatre to fulfil a special engagement. My good sister Clara, who had remained behind for a while amid the somewhat unpleasant conditions of Magdeburg, soon perceived the anxious and troubled temper in which her otherwise cheerful brother was rapidly consuming himself. One day she thought it advisable to show me a letter from her husband, with news from Berlin, and especially concerning Minna, in which he earnestly deplored my passion for this girl, who was acting quite unworthily of me. As she lodged at his hotel, he was able to observe that not only the company she kept, but also her own conduct, were perfectly scandalous. The extraordinary impression which this dreadful communication made upon me decided me to abandon the reserve I had hitherto shown towards my relatives with regard to my love affairs. I wrote to my brother-in-law in Berlin, telling him how matters stood with me, and that my plans greatly depended on Minna, and further, how extremely important it was for me to learn from him the indubitable truth concerning her of whom he had sent so evil an account. From my brother-in-law, usually so dry and given to joking, I received a reply which filled my heart to overflowing again. He confessed that he had accused Minna too hastily, and regretted that he had allowed idle chatter to influence him in founding a charge, which, on investigation, had proved to be altogether groundless and unjust; he declared, moreover, that on nearer acquaintance and conversation with her he had been so fully convinced of the genuineness and uprightness of her character, that he hoped with all his heart that I might see my way to marry her. And now a storm raged in my heart. I implored Minna to return at once, and was glad to learn that, for her part, she was not inclined to renew her engagement at the Berlin theatre, as she had now acquired a more intimate knowledge of the life there, and found it too frivolous. All that remained, then, was for me to facilitate the resumption of her Magdeburg engagement. To this end, therefore, at a meeting of the theatre committee, I attacked the director and his detested stage manager with such energy, and defended Minna against the wrong done her by them both with such passion and fervour, that the other members, astonished at the frank confession of my affection, yielded to my wishes without any further ado. And now I set off by extra post in the depth of night and in dreadful winter weather to meet my returning sweetheart. I greeted her with tears of deepest joy, and led her back in triumph to her cosy Magdeburg home, already become so dear to me.

Meanwhile, as our two lives, thus severed for a while, were being drawn more and more closely together, I finished the score of my *Liebesverbot* about New Year 1836. For the development of my future plans I depended not a little upon the success of this work; and Minna herself seemed not disinclined to yield to my hopes in this respect. We had reason to be concerned as to how matters would pan out for us at the beginning of the spring, for this season is always a bad one in which to start such precarious theatrical enterprises. In spite of royal support and the participation of the theatre committee in the general management of the theatre, our worthy director's state of perennial bankruptcy suffered no alteration, and it seemed as if his theatrical undertaking could not possibly last much longer in any form. Nevertheless, with the help of the really first-rate company of singers at my disposal, the production of my opera was to mark a complete change in my unsatisfactory circumstances. With the view of recovering the travelling expenses I had incurred during the previous summer, I was entitled to a benefit performance. I naturally fixed this for the presentation of my own work, and did my utmost so that this favour granted me by the directors should prove as inexpensive to them as possible. As they would nevertheless be compelled to incur some expense in the production of the new opera, I agreed that the proceeds of the first presentation should be left to them, while I should claim only those of the second. I did not consider it altogether unsatisfactory that the time for the rehearsals was postponed until the very end of the season, for it was reasonable to suppose that our company, which was often greeted with unusual applause, would receive special attention and favour from the public during its concluding performances. Unfortunately, however, contrary to our expectations, we never reached the proper close of this season, which had been fixed for the end of April; for already in March, owing to irregularity in the payment of salaries, the most popular members of the company, having found better employment elsewhere, tendered their resignations to the management, and the director, who was unable to raise the necessary cash, was compelled to bow to the inevitable. Now, indeed, my spirits sank, for it seemed more than doubtful whether my *Liebesverbot* would ever be produced at all. I owed it entirely to the warm affection felt for me personally by all members of the opera company, that the singers consented not only to remain until the end of March, but also to undertake the toil of studying and rehearsing my opera, a task which, considering the very limited time, promised to be extremely arduous. In the event of our having to give two representations, the time at our disposal was so very short that, for all the rehearsals, we had but ten days before us. And since we were concerned not with a light comedy or farce, but with a grand opera, and one which, in spite of the trifling character of its music, contained numerous and powerful concerted passages, the undertaking might have been regarded almost as foolhardy. Nevertheless, I built my hopes upon the extraordinary exertions which the singers so willingly made in order to please me; for they studied continuously, morning, noon, and night. But seeing that, in spite of all this, it was quite impossible to attain to perfection, especially in the matter of words, in the case of every one of these harassed performers, I reckoned further on my own acquired skill as conductor to achieve the final miracle of success. The peculiar ability I possessed of helping the singers and of making them, in spite of much uncertainty, seem to flow smoothly onwards, was clearly demonstrated in our orchestral rehearsals, in which, by dint of constant prompting, loud singing with the performers and vigorous directions as to necessary action, I got the whole thing to run so easily that it seemed quite possible that the performance might be a reasonable success after all. Unfortunately, we did not consider that in front of the public all these drastic methods of moving the dramatic and musical machinery would be restricted to the movements of my baton and to my facial expression. As a matter of fact the singers, and especially the men, were so extraordinarily uncertain that from beginning to end their embarrassment crippled the effectiveness of every one of their parts. Freimüller, the tenor, whose memory was most defective, sought to patch up the lively and emotional character of his badly learned rôle of the madcap Luzio by means of routine work learned in *Fra Diavolo* and *Zampa,* and especially by the aid of an enormously thick, brightly coloured and fluttering plume of feathers. Consequently, as the directors failed to have the book of words printed in time, it was impossible to blame the public for being in doubt as to the main outlines of the story, seeing that they had only the sung words to guide them. With the exception of a few portions played by the lady singers, which were favourably received, the whole performance, which I had made to depend largely upon bold, energetic action and speech, remained but a musical shadow-play, to which the orchestra contributed its own inexplicable effusions, sometimes with exaggerated noise. As characteristic of the treatment of my tone-colour, I may mention that the band-master of a Prussian military band, who, by the bye, had been well pleased with the performance, felt it incumbent upon him to give me some well-meant hints for my future guidance, as to the manipulation of the Turkish drum. Before I relate the further history of this wonderful work of my youth, I will pause a moment briefly to describe its character, and especially its poetical elements.

Shakespeare's play, which I kept throughout in mind as the foundation of my story, was worked out in the following manner: —

An unnamed king of Sicily leaves his country, as I suggest, for a journey to Naples, and hands over to the Regent appointed — whom I simply call Friedrich, with the view of making him appear as German as possible — full authority to exercise all the royal power in order to effect a complete reform in the social habits of his capital, which had provoked the indignation of the Council. At the opening of the play we see the servants of the public authority busily employed either in shutting up or in pulling down the houses of popular amusement in a suburb of Palermo, and in carrying off the inmates, including hosts and servants, as prisoners. The populace oppose this first step, and much scuffling ensues. In the thickest of the throng the chief of the sbirri, Brighella (basso-buffo), after a preliminary roll of drums for silence, reads out the Regent's proclamation, according to which the acts just performed are declared to be directed towards establishing

a higher moral tone in the manners and customs of the people. A general outburst of scorn and a mocking chorus meets this announcement. Luzio, a young nobleman and juvenile scapegrace (tenor), seems inclined to thrust himself forward as leader of the mob, and at once finds an occasion for playing a more active part in the cause of the oppressed people on discovering his friend Claudio (also a tenor) being led away to prison. From him he learns that, in pursuance of some musty old law unearthed by Friedrich, he is to suffer the penalty of death for a certain love escapade in which he is involved. His sweetheart, union with whom had been prevented by the enmity of their parents, has borne him a child. Friedrich's puritanical zeal joins cause with the parents' hatred; he fears the worst, and sees no way of escape save through mercy, provided his sister Isabella may be able, by her entreaties, to melt the Regent's hard heart. Claudio implores his friend at once to seek out Isabella in the convent of the Sisters of St. Elizabeth, which she has recently entered as novice. There, between the quiet walls of the convent, we first meet this sister, in confidential intercourse with her friend Marianne, also a novice. Marianne reveals to her friend, from whom she has long been parted, the unhappy fate which has brought her to the place. Under vows of eternal fidelity she had been persuaded to a secret *liaison* with a man of high rank. But finally, when in extreme need she found herself not only forsaken, but threatened by her betrayer, she discovered him to be the mightiest man in the state, none other than the King's Regent himself. Isabella's indignation finds vent in impassioned words, and is only pacified by her determination to forsake a world in which so vile a crime can go unpunished.
— When now Luzio brings her tidings of her own brother's fate, her disgust at her brother's misconduct is turned at once to scorn for the villainy of the hypocritical Regent, who presumes so cruelly to punish the comparatively venial offence of her brother, which, at least, was not stained by treachery. Her violent outburst imprudently reveals her to Luzio in a seductive aspect; smitten with sudden love, he urges her to quit the convent for ever and to accept his hand. She contrives to check his boldness, but resolves at once to avail herself

of his escort to the Regent's court of justice. — Here the trial scene is prepared, and I introduce it by a burlesque hearing of several persons charged by the sbirro captain with offences against morality. The earnestness of the situation becomes more marked when the gloomy form of Friedrich strides through the inrushing and unruly crowd, commanding silence, and he himself undertakes the hearing of Claudio's case in the sternest manner possible. The implacable judge is already on the point of pronouncing sentence when Isabella enters, and requests, before them all, a private interview with the Regent. In this interview she behaves with noble moderation towards the dreaded, yet despised man before her, and appeals at first only to his mildness and mercy. His interruptions merely serve to stimulate her ardour: she speaks of her brother's offence in melting accents, and implores forgiveness for so human and by no means unpardonable a crime. Seeing the effect of her moving appeal, she continues with increasing ardour to plead with the judge's hard and unresponsive heart, which can certainly not have remained untouched by sentiments such as those which had actuated her brother, and she calls upon his memory of these to support her desperate plea for pity. At last the ice of his heart is broken. Friedrich, deeply stirred by Isabella's beauty, can no longer contain himself, and promises to grant her petition at the price of her own love. Scarcely has she become aware of the unexpected effect of her words when, filled with indignation at such incredible villainy, she cries to the people through doors and windows to come in, that she may unmask the hypocrite before the world. The crowd is already rushing tumultuously into the hall of judgment, when, by a few significant hints, Friedrich, with frantic energy, succeeds in making Isabella realise the impossibility of her plan. He would simply deny her charge, boldly pretend that his offer was merely made to test her, and would doubtless be readily believed so soon as it became only a question of rebutting a charge of lightly making love to her. Isabella, ashamed and confounded, recognises the madness of her first step, and gnashes her teeth in silent despair. While then Friedrich once more announces his stern resolve to the people, and pronounces sentence on the prisoner, it suddenly occurs to Isabella, spurred by the painful recollection of Marianne's fate, that what she has failed to procure by open means she might possibly obtain by craft. This thought suffices to dispel her sorrow, and to fill her with utmost gaiety. Turning to her sorrowing brother, her agitated friends, and the perplexed crowd, she assures them all that she is ready to provide them with the most amusing of adventures. She declares that the carnival festivities, which the Regent has just strictly forbidden, are to be celebrated this year with unusual licence; for this dreaded ruler only pretends to be so cruel, in order the more pleasantly to astonish them by himself taking a merry part in all that he has just forbidden. They all believe that she has gone mad, and Friedrich in particular reproves her incomprehensible folly with passionate severity. But a few words on her part suffice to transport the Regent himself with ecstasy; for in a whisper she promises to grant his desire, and that on the following night she will send him such a message as shall ensure his happiness. — And so ends the first act in a whirl of excitement.

We learn the nature of the heroine's hastily formed plan at the beginning of the second act, in which she visits her brother in his cell, with the object of discovering whether he is worthy of rescue. She reveals Friedrich's shameful proposal to him, and asks if he would wish to save his life at the price of his sister's dishonour. Then follow Claudio's fury and fervent declaration of his readiness to die; whereupon, bidding farewell to his sister, at least for this life, he makes her the bearer of the most tender messages to the dear girl whom he leaves behind. After this, sinking into a softer mood, the unhappy man declines from a state of melancholy to one of weakness. Isabella, who had already determined to inform him of his rescue, hesitates in dismay when she sees him fall in this way from the heights of noble enthusiasm to a muttered confession of a love of life still as strong as ever, and even to a stammering query as to whether the suggested price of his salvation is altogether impossible. Disgusted, she springs to her feet, thrusts the unworthy man from her, and declares that to the shame of his death he has further added her most hearty contempt. After having handed him over again to his gaoler, her mood once more changes swiftly to one of wanton gaiety. True, she resolves to punish the waverer by leaving him for a time in uncertainty as to his fate; but stands firm by her resolve to rid the world of the abominable seducer who dared to dictate laws to his fellow-men. She tells Marianne that she must take her place at the nocturnal rendezvous, at which Friedrich so treacherously expected to meet her (Isabella), and sends Friedrich an invitation to this meeting. In order to entangle the latter even more deeply in ruin, she stipulates that he must come disguised and masked, and fixes the rendezvous in one of those pleasure resorts which he has just suppressed. To the madcap Luzio, whom she also desires to punish for his saucy suggestion to a novice, she relates the story of Friedrich's proposal, and her pretended intention of complying, from sheer necessity, with his desires. This she does in a fashion so incomprehensively light-hearted that the otherwise frivolous man, first dumb with amazement, ultimately yields to a fit of desperate rage. He swears that, even if the noble maiden herself can endure such shame, he will himself strive by every means in his power to avert it, and would prefer to set all Palermo on fire and in tumult rather than allow such a thing to happen. And, indeed, he arranges things in such a manner that on the appointed evening all his friends and acquaintances assemble at the end of the Corso, as though for the opening of the prohibited carnival procession. At nightfall, as things are beginning to grow wild and merry, Luzio appears, and sings an extravagant carnival song, with the refrain:

> Who joins us not in frolic jest
> Shall have a dagger in his breast;

by which means he seeks to stir the crowd to bloody revolt. When a band of sbirri approaches, under Brighella's leadership, to scatter the gay throng, the mutinous project seems on the point of being accomplished. But for the present Luzio prefers to yield, and to scatter about the neighbourhood, as he must first of all win the real leader of their enterprise: for here was the spot which Isabella had mischievously revealed to him as the place of her pretended meeting with the Regent. For the latter Luzio therefore lies in wait. Recognising him in an elaborate disguise, he blocks his way, and as Friedrich violently breaks loose, is on the point of following him with shouts and drawn sword, when, on a sign from Isabella, who is hidden among some bushes, he is himself stopped and led away. Isabella then advances, rejoicing in the thought of having restored the betrayed Marianne to her faithless spouse. Believing that she holds in her hand the promised pardon for her brother, she is just on the point of abandoning all thought of further vengeance when, breaking the seal, to her intense horror she recognises by the light of a torch that the paper contains but a still more severe order of execution, which, owing to her desire not to disclose to her brother the fact of his pardon, a mere chance had now delivered into her hand, through the agency of the bribed gaoler. After a hard fight with the tempestuous passion of love, and recognising his helplessness against this enemy of his peace, Friedrich has in fact already resolved to face his ruin, even though as a criminal, yet still as a man of honour. An hour on Isabella's breast, and then — his own death by the same law whose implacable severity shall also claim Claudio's life. Isabella, perceiving in this conduct only a further proof of the hypocrite's villainy, breaks out once more into a tempest of agonised despair. Upon her cry for immediate revolt against the scoundrelly tyrant, the people collect together and form a motley and passionate crowd. Luzio, who also returns, counsels the people with stinging bitterness to pay no heed to the woman's fury; he points out that she is only tricking them, as she has already tricked him — for he still believes in her shameless infidelity. Fresh confusion; increased despair of Isabella; suddenly from the background comes the burlesque cry of Brighella for help, who, himself suffering from the pangs of jealousy, has by mistake arrested the masked Regent, and thus led to the latter's discovery. Friedrich is recognised, and Marianne, trembling on his breast, is also unmasked. Amazement, indignation! Cries of joy burst forth all round; the needful explanations are quickly given, and Friedrich sullenly demands to be set before the judgment-seat of the returning King. Claudio, released from prison by the jubilant populace, informs him that the sentence of death for crimes of love is not intended for all times; messengers arrive to announce the unexpected arrival in harbour of the King; it is resolved to march in full masked procession to meet the beloved Prince, and joyously to pay him homage, all being convinced that he will heartily rejoice to see how ill the gloomy puritanism of Germany is suited to his hot-blooded Sicily. Of him it is said:

> Your merry festals please him more
> Than gloomy laws or legal lore.

Friedrich, with his freshly affianced wife, Marianne, must lead the procession, followed by Luzio and the novice, who is for ever lost to the convent.

These spirited and, in many respects, boldly devised scenes I had clothed in suitable language and carefully written verse, which had already been noticed by Laube. The police at first took exception to the title of the work, which, had I not changed it, would have led to the complete failure of my plans for its presentation. It was the week before Easter, and the theatre was consequently forbidden to produce jolly, or at least frivolous, plays during this period. Luckily the magistrate, with whom I had to treat concerning the matter, did not show any inclination to examine the libretto himself; and when I assured him that it was modelled upon a very serious play of Shakespeare's, the authorities contented themselves merely with changing the somewhat startling title. *Die Novize von Palermo,* which was the new title, had nothing suspicious about it, and was therefore approved as correct without further scruple. I fared quite otherwise in Leipzig, where I attempted to introduce this work in the place of my *Feen,* when the latter was withdrawn. The director, Ringelhardt, whom I sought to win over to my cause by assigning the part of Marianne to his daughter, then making her début in opera, chose to reject my work on the apparently very reasonable grounds that the tendency of the theme displeased him. He assured me that, even if the Leipzig magistrates had consented to its production — a fact concerning which his high esteem for that body led him to have serious doubts — he himself, as a conscientious father, could certainly not permit his daughter to take part in it.

Strange to say, I suffered nothing from the suspicious nature of the libretto of my opera on the occasion of its production in Magdeburg; for, as I have said, thanks to the unintelligible manner in which it was produced, the story remained a complete mystery to the public. This circumstance, and the fact that no opposition had been raised on the ground of its *tendency*, made a second performance possible, and as nobody seemed to care one way or the other, no objections were raised. Feeling sure that my opera had made no impression, and had left the public completely undecided about its merits, I reckoned that, in view of this being the farewell performance of our opera company, we should have good, not to say large, takings. Consequently I did not hesitate to charge 'full' prices for admittance. I cannot rightly judge whether, up to the commencement of the overture, any people had taken their places in the auditorium; but about a quarter of an hour before the time fixed for beginning, I saw only Mme. Gottschalk and her husband, and, curiously enough, a Polish Jew in full dress, seated in the stalls. Despite this, I was still hoping for an increase in the audience, when suddenly the most incredible commotion occurred behind the scenes. Herr Pollert, the husband of my prima donna (who was acting Isabella), was assaulting Schreiber, the second tenor, a very young and handsome man taking the part of Claudio, and against whom the injured husband had for some time been nursing a secret rancour born of jealousy. It appeared that the singer's husband, who had surveyed the theatre from behind the dropscene with me, had satisfied himself as to the style of the audience, and decided that the longed-for hour was at hand when, without injuring the operatic enterprise, he could wreak vengeance on his wife's lover. Claudio was so severely used by him that the unfortunate fellow had to seek refuge in the dressing-room, his face covered with blood. Isabella was told of this, and rushed despairingly to her raging spouse, only to be so soundly cuffed by him that she went into convulsions. The confusion that ensued amongst the company soon knew no bounds: they took sides in the quarrel, and little was wanting for it to turn into a general fight, as everybody seemed to regard this unhappy evening as particularly favourable for the paying off of any old scores and supposed insults. This much was clear, that the couple suffering from the effects of Herr Pollert's conjugal resentment were unfit to appear that evening. The manager was sent before the drop-scene to inform the small and strangely assorted audience gathered in the theatre that, owing to unforeseen circumstances, the representation would not take place.

This was the end of my career as director and composer in Magdeburg, which in the beginning had seemed so full of promise and had been started at the cost of considerable sacrifice. The serenity of art now gave way completely before the stern realities of life. My position gave food for meditation, and the outlook was not a cheerful one. All the hopes that I and Minna had founded upon the success of my work had been utterly destroyed. My creditors, who had been appeased by the anticipation of the expected harvest, lost faith in my talents, and now counted solely on obtaining bodily possession of me, which they endeavoured to do by speedily instituting legal proceedings. Now that every time I came home I found a summons nailed to my door, my little dwelling in the *Breiter Weg* became unbearable; I avoided going there, especially since my brown poodle, who had hitherto enlivened this retreat, had vanished, leaving no trace. This I looked upon as a bad sign, indicating my complete downfall.

At this time Minna, with her truly comforting assurance and firmness of bearing, was a tower of strength to me and the one thing I had left to fall back upon. Always full of resource, she had first of all provided for her own future, and was on the point of signing a not unfavourable contract with the directors of the theatre at Königsberg in Prussia. It was now a question of finding me an appointment in the same place as musical conductor; this post was already filled. The Königsberg director, however, gathering from our correspondence that Minna's acceptance of the engagement depended upon the possibility of my being taken on at the same theatre, held out the prospect of an approaching vacancy, and expressed his willingness to allow it to be filled by me. On the strength of this assurance it was decided that Minna should go on to Königsberg and pave the way for my arrival there.

Ere these plans could be carried out, we had still to spend a time of dreadful and acute anxiety, which I shall never forget, within the walls of Magdeburg. It is true I made one more personal attempt in Leipzig to improve my position, on which occasion I entered into the transactions mentioned above with the director of the theatre regarding my new opera. But I soon realised that it was out of the question for me to remain in my native town, and in the disquieting proximity of my family, from which I was restlessly anxious to get away. My excitability and depression were noticed by my relations. My mother entreated me, whatever else I might decide to do, on no account to be drawn into marriage while still so young. To this I made no reply. When I took my leave, Rosalie accompanied me to the head of the stairs. I spoke of returning as soon as I had attended to certain important business matters, and wanted to wish her a hurried good-bye: she grasped my hand, and gazing into my face, exclaimed, " God alone knows when I shall see you again!' This cut me to the heart, and I felt conscience-stricken. The fact that she was expressing the presentiment she felt of her early death I only realised when, barely two years later, without having seen her again, I received the news that she had died very suddenly.

I spent a few more weeks with Minna in the strictest retirement in Magdeburg: she endeavoured to the best of her ability to relieve the embarrassment of my position. In view of our approaching separation, and the length of time we might be parted, I hardly left her side, our only relaxation being the walks we took together round the outskirts of the town. Anxious forebodings weighed upon us; the May sun which lit the sad streets of Magdeburg, as if in mockery of our forlorn condition, was one day more clouded over than I have ever seen it since, and filled me with a positive dread. On our way home from one of these walks, as we were approaching the bridge crossing the Elbe, we caught sight of a man flinging himself from it into the water beneath. We ran to the bank, called for help, and persuaded a miller, whose mill was situated on the river, to hold out a rake to the drowning man, who was being swept in his direction by the current. With indescribable anxiety we waited for the decisive moment — saw the sinking man stretch out his hands towards the rake, but he failed to grasp it, and at the same moment disappeared under the mill, never to be seen again. On the morning that I accompanied Minna to the stage-coach to bid her a most sorrowful farewell, the whole population was pouring from one of the gateways of the town towards a big field, to witness the execution of a man condemned to be put to death on the wheel ' from below.' [1] The culprit was a soldier who had murdered his sweetheart in a fit of jealousy. When, later in the day, I sat down to my last dinner at the inn, I heard the dreadful details of the Prussian mode of execution being discussed on all sides. A young magistrate, who was a great lover of music, told us about a conversation he had had with the executioner, who had been procured from Halle, and with whom he had discussed the most humane method of hastening the death of the victim; in telling us about him, he recalled the elegant dress and manners of this ill-omened person with a shudder.

These were the last impressions I carried away from the scene of my first artistic efforts and of my attempts at earning an independent livelihood. Often since then on my departure from places where I had expected to find prosperity, and to which I knew I should never return, those impressions have recurred to my mind with singular persistence. I have always had much the same feelings upon leaving any place where I had stayed in the hope of improving my position.

Thus I arrived in Berlin for the first time on the 18th May, 1836, and made acquaintance with the peculiar features of that pretentious royal capital. While my position was an uncertain one, I sought a modest shelter at the Crown Prince in the Königstrasse, where Minna had stayed a few months before. I found a friend on whom I could rely when I came across Laube again, who, while awaiting his verdict, was

---

[1] *Durch das Rad von unten.* The punishment of the wheel was usually inflicted upon murderers, incendiaries, highwaymen and church robbers. There were two methods of inflicting this: (1) 'from above downwards' (*von oben nach unten*), in which the condemned man was despatched instantly owing to his neck getting broken from the start; and (2) 'from below upwards' (*von unten nach oben*), which is the method referred to above, and in which all the limbs of the victim were broken previous to his body being actually twisted through the spokes of the wheel. — EDITOR.

busying himself with private and literary work in Berlin. He was much interested in the fate of my work *Liebesverbot,* and advised me to turn my present situation to account for the purpose of obtaining the production of this opera at the Königstadt theatre. This theatre was under the direction of one of the most curious creatures in Berlin: he was called 'Cerf,' and the title of *Commissionsrath* had been conferred upon him by the King of Prussia. To account for the favours bestowed upon him by royalty, many reasons of a not very edifying nature were circulated. Through this royal patronage he had succeeded in extending considerably the privileges already enjoyed by the suburban theatre. The decline of grand opera at the Theatre Royal had brought light opera, which was performed with great success at the Königstadt theatre, into public favour. The director, puffed up by success, openly laboured under the delusion that he was the right man in the right place, and expressed his entire agreement with those who declared that one could only expect a theatre to be successfully managed by common and uneducated men, and continued to cling to his blissful and boundless state of ignorance in the most amusing manner. Relying absolutely upon his own insight, he had assumed an entirely dictatorial attitude towards the officially appointed artists of his theatre, and allowed himself to deal with them according to his likes and dislikes. I seemed destined to be favoured by this mode of procedure: at my very first visit Cerf expressed his satisfaction with me, but wished to make use of me as a 'tenor.' He offered no objection whatever to my request for the production of my opera, but, on the contrary, promised to have it staged immediately. He seemed particularly anxious to appoint me conductor of the orchestra. As he was on the point of changing his operatic company, he foresaw that his present conductor, Gläser, the composer of *Adlershorst,* would hinder his plans by taking the part of the older singers: he was therefore anxious to have me associated with his theatre, that he might have some one to support him who was favourably disposed towards the new singers.

All this sounded so plausible, that I could scarcely be blamed for believing that the wheel of fortune had taken a favourable turn for me, and for feeling a sense of lightheartedness at the thought of such rosy prospects. I had scarcely allowed myself the few modifications in my manner of living which these improved circumstances seemed to justify, ere it was made clear to me that my hopes were built upon sand. I was filled with positive dread when I soon fully realised how nearly Cerf had come to defrauding me, merely it would seem for his own amusement. After the manner of despots, he had given his favours personally and autocratically; the withdrawal and annulment of his promises, however, he made known to me through his servants and secretaries, thus placing his strange conduct towards me in the light of the inevitable result of his dependence upon officialdom.

As Cerf wished to rid himself of me without even offering me compensation, I was obliged to try to come to some understanding regarding all that had been definitely arranged between us, and this with the very people against whom he had previously warned me and had wanted me to side with him. The conductor, stage manager, secretary, etc., had to make it clear to me that my wishes could not be satisfied, and that the director owed me no compensation whatever for the time he had made me waste while awaiting the fulfilment of his promises. This unpleasant experience has been a source of pain to me ever since.

Owing to all this my position was very much worse than it had been before. Minna wrote to me frequently from Königsberg, but she had nothing encouraging to tell me with regard to my hopes in that direction. The director of the theatre there seemed unable to come to any clear understanding with his conductor, a circumstance which I was afterwards able to understand, but which at the time appeared to me inexplicable, and made my chance of obtaining the coveted appointment seem exceedingly remote. It seemed certain, however, that the post would be vacant in the autumn, and as I was drifting about aimlessly in Berlin and refused for a moment to entertain the thought of returning to Leipzig, I snatched at this faint hope, and in imagination soared above the Berlin quicksands to the safety of the harbour on the Baltic.

I only succeeded in doing so, however, after I had struggled through difficult and serious inward conflicts to which my relations with Minna gave rise. An incomprehensible feature in the character of this otherwise apparently simple-minded woman had thrown my young heart into a turmoil. A good-natured, well-to-do tradesman of Jewish extraction, named Schwabe, who till that time had been established in Magdeburg, made friendly advances to me in Berlin, and I soon discovered that his sympathy was chiefly due to the passionate interest which he had conceived for Minna. It afterwards became clear to me that an intimacy had existed between this man and Minna, which in itself could hardly be considered as a breach of faith towards me, since it had ended in a decided repulse of my rival's courtship in my favour. But the fact of this episode having been kept so secret that I had not had the faintest idea of it before, and also the suspicion I could not avoid harbouring that Minna's comfortable circumstances were in part due to this man's friendship, filled me with gloomy misgivings. But as I have said, although I could find no real cause to complain of infidelity, I was distracted and alarmed, and was at last driven to the half-desperate resolve of regaining my balance in this respect by obtaining complete possession of Minna. It seemed to me as though my stability as a citizen as well as my professional success would be assured by a recognised union with Minna. The two years spent in the theatrical world had, in fact, kept me in a constant state of distraction, of which in my heart of hearts I was most painfully conscious. I realised vaguely that I was on the wrong path; I longed for peace and quiet, and hoped to find these most effectually by getting married, and so putting an end to the state of things that had become the source of so much anxiety to me.

It was not surprising that Laube noticed by my untidy, passionate, and wasted appearance that something unusual was amiss with me. It was only in his company, which I always found comforting, that I gained the only impressions of Berlin which compensated me in any way for my misfortunes. The most important artistic experience I had, came to me through the performance of *Ferdinand Cortez,* conducted by Spontini himself, the spirit of which astonished me more than anything I had ever heard before. Though the actual production, especially as regards the chief characters, who as a whole could not be regarded as belonging to the flower of Berlin opera, left me unmoved, and though the effect never reached a point that could be even distantly compared to that produced upon me by Schröder-Devrient, yet the exceptional precision, fire, and richly organised rendering of the whole was new to me. I gained a fresh insight into the peculiar dignity of big theatrical representations, which in their several parts could, by well-accentuated rhythm, be made to attain the highest pinnacle of art. This extraordinarily distinct impression took a drastic hold of me, and above all served to guide me in my conception of *Rienzi,* so that, speaking from an artistic point of view, Berlin may be said to have left its traces on my development.

For the present, however, my chief concern was to extricate myself from my extremely helpless position. I was determined to turn my steps to Königsberg, and communicated my decision, and the hopes founded upon it, to Laube. This excellent friend, without further inquiry, made a point of exerting his energies to free me from my present state of despair, and to help me to reach my next destination, an object which, through the assistance of several of his friends, he succeeded in accomplishing. When he said good-bye to me, Laube with sympathetic foresight warned me, should I succeed in my desired career of musical conductor, not to allow myself to be entangled in the shallowness of stage life, and advised me, after fatiguing rehearsals, instead of going to my sweetheart, to take a serious book in hand, in order that my greater gifts might not go uncultivated. I did not tell him that by taking an early and decisive step in this direction I intended to protect myself effectually against the dangers of theatrical intrigues. On the 7th of July, therefore, I started on what was at that time an extremely troublesome and fatiguing journey to the distant town of Königsberg.

It seemed to me as though I were leaving the world, as I travelled on day after day through the desert marches. Then followed a sad and humiliating impression of Königsberg, where, in one of the poorest-looking suburbs, Tragheim, near the theatre, and in a lane such as one would expect to find in a village, I found the ugly house in which Minna lodged. The friendly and quiet kindness of manner, however, which was peculiar to her, soon made me feel at home. She was popular at the theatre, and was respected by the managers and actors, a fact which seemed to augur well for her betrothed, the part I was now openly to assume.

Though as yet there seemed no distinct prospect of my getting the appointment I had come for, yet we agreed that I could hold out a little longer, and that the matter would certainly be arranged in the end. This was also the opinion of the eccentric Abraham Möller, a worthy citizen of Königsberg, who was devoted to the theatre, and who took a very friendly interest in Minna, and finally also in me. This man, who was already well advanced in life, belonged to the type of theatre lovers now probably completely extinct in Germany, but of whom so much is recorded in the history of actors of earlier times. One could not spend an hour in the company of this man, who at one time had gone in for the most reckless speculations, without having to listen to his account of the glory of the stage in former times, described in most lively terms. As a man of means he had at one time made the acquaintance of nearly all the great actors and actresses of his day, and had even known how to win their friendship. Through too great a liberality he unfortunately found himself in reduced circumstances, and was now obliged to procure the means to satisfy his craving for the theatre and his desire to protect those belonging to it by entering into all kinds of strange business transactions, in which, without running any real risk, he felt there was something to be gained. He was accordingly only able to afford the theatre a very meagre support, but one which was quite in keeping with its decrepit condition.

This strange man, of whom the theatre director, Anton Hübsch, stood to a certain extent in awe, undertook to procure me my appointment. The only circumstance against me was the fact that Louis Schubert, the famous musician whom I had known from very early times as the first violoncellist of the Magdeburg orchestra, had come to Königsberg from Riga, where the theatre had been closed for a time, and where he had left his wife, in order to fill the post of musical conductor **here** until the new theatre in Riga was opened, and he could return. The reopening of the Riga theatre, which had already been fixed for the Easter of this year, had been postponed, and he was now anxious not to leave Königsberg. Since Schubert was a thorough master in his art, and since his choosing to remain or go depended entirely on circumstances over which he had no control, the theatre director found himself in the embarrassing position of having to secure some one who would be willing to wait to enter upon his appointment till Schubert's business called him away. Consequently a young musical conductor who was anxious to remain in Königsberg at any price could but be heartily welcomed as a reserve and substitute in case of emergency. Indeed, the director declared himself willing to give me a small retaining fee till the time should arrive for my definite entrance upon my duties.

Schubert, on the contrary, was furious at my arrival; there was no longer any necessity for his speedy return to Riga, since the reopening of the theatre there had been postponed indefinitely. Moreover, he had a special interest in remaining in Königsberg, as he had conceived a passion for the prima donna there, which considerably lessened his desire to return to his wife. So at the last moment he clung to his Königsberg post with great eagerness, regarded me as his deadly enemy, and, spurred on by his instinct of self-preservation, used every means in his power to make my stay in Königsberg, and the already painful position I occupied while awaiting his departure, a veritable hell to me.

While in Magdeburg I had been on the friendliest footing with both musicians and singers, and had been shown the greatest consideration by the public, I here found I had to defend myself on all sides against the most mortifying ill-will. This hostility towards me, which soon made itself apparent, contributed in no small degree to make me feel as though in coming to Königsberg I had gone into exile. In spite of my eagerness, I realised that under the circumstances my marriage with Minna would prove a hazardous undertaking. At the beginning of August the company went to Memel for a time, to open the summer season there, and I followed Minna a few days later. We went most of the way by sea, and crossed the

HARDSHIPS

Kurische Haff in a sailing vessel in bad weather with the wind against us — one of the most melancholy crossings I have ever experienced. As we passed the thin strip of sand that divides this bay from the Baltic Sea, the castle of Runsitten, where Hoffmann laid the scene of one of his most gruesome tales (*Das Majorat*), was pointed out to me. The fact that in this desolate neighbourhood, of all places in the world, I should after so long a lapse of time be once more brought in contact with the fantastic impressions of my youth, had a singular and depressing effect on my mind. The unhappy sojourn in Memel, the lamentable rôle I played there, everything in short, contributed to make me find my only consolation in Minna, who, after all, was the cause of my having placed myself in this unpleasant position. Our friend Abraham followed us from Königsberg and did all kinds of queer things to promote my interests, and was obviously anxious to put the director and conductor at variance with each other. One day Schubert, in consequence of a dispute with Hübsch on the previous night, actually declared himself too unwell to attend a rehearsal of *Euryanthe,* in order to force the manager to summon me suddenly to take his place. In doing this my rival maliciously hoped that as I was totally unprepared to conduct this difficult opera, which was seldom played, I would expose my incapacity in a manner most welcome to his hostile intentions. Although I had never really had a score of *Euryanthe* before me, his wish was so little gratified, that he elected to get well for the representation in order to conduct it himself, which he would not have done if it had been found necessary to cancel the performance on account of my incompetence. In this wretched position, vexed in mind, exposed to the severe climate, which even on summer evenings struck me as horribly cold, and occupied merely in warding off the most painful troubles of life, my time, as far as any professional advancement was concerned, was completely lost. At last, on our return to Königsberg, and particularly under the guardianship of Möller, the question as to what was to be done was more earnestly considered. Finally, Minna and I were offered a fairly good engagement in Danzig, through the influence of my brother-in-law Wolfram and his wife, who had gone there.

Möller seized this opportunity to induce the director Hübsch, who was anxious not to lose Minna, to sign a contract including us both, and by which it was understood that under any circumstances I should be officially appointed as conductor at his theatre from the following Easter. Moreover, for our wedding, a benefit performance was promised, for which we chose *Die Stumme von Portici,* to be conducted by me in person. For, as Möller remarked, it was absolutely necessary for us to get married, and to have a due celebration of the event; there was no getting out of it. Minna made no objection, and all my past endeavours and resolutions seemed to prove that my one desire was to take anchor in the haven of matrimony. In spite of this, however, a strange conflict was going on within me at this time. I had become sufficiently intimate with Minna's life and character to realise the wide difference between our two natures as fully as the important step I was about to take necessitated; but my powers of judgment were not yet sufficiently matured.

My future wife was the child of poor parents, natives of Oederan in the Erzgebirge in Saxony. Her father was no ordinary man; he possessed enormous vitality, but in his old age showed traces of some feebleness of mind. In his young days he had been a trumpeter in Saxony, and in this capacity had taken part in a campaign against the French, and had also been present at the battle of Wagram. He afterwards became a mechanic, and took up the trade of manufacturing cards for carding wool, and as he invented an improvement in the process of their production, he is said to have made a very good business of it for some time. A rich manufacturer of Chemnitz once gave him a large order to be delivered at the end of the year: the children, whose pliable fingers had already proved serviceable in this respect, had to work hard day and night, and in return the father promised them an exceptionally happy Christmas, as he expected to get a large sum of money. When the longed-for time arrived, however, he received the announcement of his client's bankruptcy. The goods that had already been delivered were lost, and the material that remained on his hands there was no prospect of selling. The family never succeeded in recovering from the state of confusion into which this misfortune had thrown them; they went to Dresden, where the father hoped to find remunerative employment as a skilled mechanic, especially in the manufacture of pianos, of which he supplied separate parts. He also brought away with him a large quantity of the fine wire which had been destined for the manufacture of the cards, and which he hoped to be able to sell at a profit. The ten-year-old Minna was commissioned to sell separate lots of it to the milliners for making flowers. She would set out with a heavy basketful of wire, and had such a gift for persuading people to buy that she soon disposed of the whole supply to the best advantage. From this time the desire was awakened in her to be of active use to her impoverished family, and to earn her own living as soon as possible, in order not to be a burden on her parents. As she grew up and developed into a strikingly beautiful woman, she attracted the attention of men at a very early age. A certain Herr von Einsiedel fell passionately in love with her, and took advantage of the inexperienced young girl when she was off her guard. Her family was thrown into the utmost consternation, and only her mother and elder sister could be told of the terrible position in which Minna found herself. Her father, from whose anger the worst consequences were to be feared, was never informed that his barely seventeen-year-old daughter had become a mother, and under conditions that had threatened her life, had given birth to a girl. Minna, who could obtain no redress from her seducer, now felt doubly called upon to earn her own livelihood and leave her father's house. Through the influence of friends, she had been brought into contact with an amateur theatrical society: while acting in a performance given there, she attracted the notice of members of the Royal Court Theatre, and in particular drew the attention of the director of the Dessau Court Theatre, who was present, and who immediately offered her an engagement. She gladly caught at this way of escape from her trying position, as it opened up the possibility of a brilliant stage career, and of some day being able to provide amply for her family. She had not the slightest passion for the stage, and utterly devoid as she was of any levity or coquetry, she merely saw in a theatrical career the means of earning a quick, and possibly even a rich, livelihood. Without any artistic training, the theatre merely meant for her the company of actors and actresses. Whether she pleased or not seemed of importance in her eyes only in so far as it affected her realisation of a comfortable independence. To use all the means at her disposal to assure this end seemed to her as necessary as it is for a tradesman to expose his goods to the best advantage.

The friendship of the director, manager, and favourite members of the theatre she regarded as indispensable, whilst those frequenters of the theatre who, through their criticism or taste, influenced the public, and thus also had weight with the management, she recognised as beings upon whom the attainment of her most fervent desires depended. Never to make enemies of them appeared so natural and so necessary that, in order to maintain her popularity, she was prepared to sacrifice even her self-respect. She had in this way created for herself a certain peculiar code of behaviour, that on the one hand prompted her to avoid scandals, but on the other hand found excuses even for making herself conspicuous as long as she herself knew that she was doing nothing wrong. Hence arose a mixture of inconsistencies, the questionable sense of which she was incapable of grasping. It was clearly impossible for her not to lose all real sense of delicacy; she showed, however, a sense of the fitness of things, which made her have regard to what was considered proper, though she could not understand that mere appearances were a mockery when they only served to cloak the absence of a real sense of delicacy. As she was without idealism, she had no artistic feeling; neither did she possess any talent for acting, and her power of pleasing was due entirely to her charming appearance. Whether in time routine would have made her become a good actress it is impossible for me to say. The strange power she exercised over me from the very first was in no wise due to the fact that I regarded her in any way as the embodiment of my ideal; on the contrary, she attracted me by the soberness and seriousness of her character, which supplemented what I felt to be wanting in my own, and afforded me the support that in my wanderings after the ideal I knew to be necessary for me.

I had soon accustomed myself never to betray my craving

after the ideal before Minna: unable to account for this even to myself, I always made a point of avoiding the subject by passing it over with a laugh and a joke; but, on this account, it was all the more natural for me to feel qualms when fears arose in my mind as to her really possessing the qualities to which I had attributed her superiority over me. Her strange tolerance with regard to certain familiarities and even importunities on the part of patrons of the theatre, directed even against her person, hurt me considerably; and on my reproaching her for this, I was driven to despair by her assuming an injured expression as though I had insulted her. It was quite by chance that I came across Schwabe's letters, and thus gained an astonishing insight into her intimacy with that man, of which she had left me in ignorance, and allowed me to gain my first knowledge during my stay in Berlin. All my latent jealousy, all my inmost doubts concerning Minna's character, found vent in my sudden determination to leave the girl at once. There was a violent scene between us, which was typical of all our subsequent altercations. I had obviously gone too far in treating a woman who was not passionately in love with me, as if I had a real right over her; for, after all, she had merely yielded to my importunity, and in no way belonged to me. To add to my perplexity, Minna only needed to remind me that from a worldly point of view she had refused very good offers in order to give way to the impetuosity of a penniless young man, whose talent had not yet been put to any real test, and to whom she had nevertheless shown sympathy and kindness.

What she could least forgive in me was the raging vehemence with which I spoke, and by which she felt so insulted, that upon realising to what excesses I had gone, there was nothing I could do but try and pacify her by owning myself in the wrong, and begging her forgiveness. Such was the end of this and all subsequent scenes, outwardly, at least, always to her advantage. But peace was undermined for ever, and by the frequent recurrence of such quarrels, Minna's character underwent a considerable change. Just as in later times she became perplexed by what she considered my incomprehensible conception of art and its proportions, which upset her ideas about everything connected with it, so now she grew more and more confused by my greater delicacy in regard to morality, which was very different from hers, especially as in many other respects I displayed a freedom of opinion which she could neither comprehend nor approve.

A feeling of passionate resentment was accordingly roused in her otherwise tranquil disposition. It was not surprising that this resentment increased as the years went on, and manifested itself in a manner characteristic of a girl sprung from the lower middle class, in whom mere superficial polish had taken the place of any true culture. The real torment of our subsequent life together lay in the fact that, owing to her violence, I had lost the last support I had hitherto found in her exceptionally sweet disposition. At that time I was filled only with a dim foreboding of the fateful step I was taking in marrying her. Her agreeable and soothing qualities still had such a beneficial effect upon me, that with the frivolity natural to me, as well as the obstinacy with which I met all opposition, I silenced the inner voice that darkly foreboded disaster.

Since my journey to Königsberg I had broken off all communication with my family, that is to say, with my mother and Rosalie, and I told no one of the step I had decided to take. Under my old friend Möller's audacious guidance I overcame all the legal difficulties that stood in the way of our union. According to Prussian law, a man who has reached his majority no longer requires his parents' consent to his marriage: but since, according to this same provision, I was not yet of age, I had recourse to the law of Saxony, to which country I belonged by birth, and by whose regulations I had already attained my majority at the age of twenty-one. Our banns had to be published at the place where we had been living during the past year, and this formality was carried out in Magdeburg without any further objections being raised. As Minna's parents had given their consent, the only thing that still remained to be done to make everything quite in order was for us to go together to the clergyman of the parish of Tragheim. This proved a strange enough visit. It took place the morning preceding the performance to be given for our benefit, in which Minna had chosen the pantomimic rôle of Fenella; her costume was

BEFORE THE WEDDING 163

not ready yet, and there was still a great deal to be done. The rainy cold November weather made us feel out of humour, when, to add to our vexation, we were kept standing in the hall of the vicarage for an unreasonable time. Then an altercation arose between us which speedily led to such bitter vituperation that we were just on the point of separating and going each our own way, when the clergyman opened the door. Not a little embarrassed at having surprised us in the act of quarrelling, he invited us in. We were obliged to put a good face on the matter, however; and the absurdity of the situation so tickled our sense of humour that we laughed; the parson was appeased, and the wedding fixed for eleven o'clock the next morning.

Another fruitful source of irritation, which often led to the outbreak of violent quarrelling between us, was the arrangement of our future home, in the interior comfort and beauty of which I hoped to find a guarantee of happiness. The economical ideas of my bride filled me with impatience. I was determined that the inauguration of a series of prosperous years which I saw before me must be celebrated by a correspondingly comfortable home. Furniture, household utensils, and all necessaries were obtained on credit, to be paid for by instalment. There was, of course, no question of a dowry, a wedding outfit, or any of the things that are generally considered indispensable to a well-founded establishment. Our witnesses and guests were drawn from the company of actors accidentally brought together by their engagement at the Königsberg theatre. My friend Möller made us a present of a silver sugar-basin, which was supplemented by a silver cake-basket from another stage friend, a peculiar and, as far as I can remember, rather interesting young man named Ernst Castell. The benefit performance of the *Die Stumme von Portici,* which I conducted with great enthusiasm, went off well, and brought us in as large a sum as we had counted upon. After spending the rest of the day before our wedding very quietly, as we were tired out after our return from the theatre, I took up my abode for the first time in our new home. Not wishing to use the bridal bed, decorated for the occasion, I lay down on a hard sofa, without even sufficient covering on me, and froze valiantly while awaiting the happiness of the following day. I was pleasantly excited the next morning by the arrival of Minna's belongings, packed in boxes and baskets. The weather, too, had quite cleared up, and the sun was shining brightly; only our sitting-room refused to get properly warm, which for some time drew down Minna's reproaches upon my head for my supposed carelessness in not having seen to the heating arrangements. At last I dressed myself in my new suit, a dark blue frock-coat with gold buttons. The carriage drove up, and I set out to fetch my bride. The bright sky had put us all in good spirits, and in the best of humour I met Minna, who was dressed in a splendid gown chosen by me. She greeted me with sincere cordiality and pleasure shining from her eyes; and taking the fine weather as a good omen, we started off for what now seemed to us a most cheerful wedding. We enjoyed the satisfaction of seeing the church as overcrowded as if a brilliant theatrical representation were being given; it was quite a difficult matter to make our way to the altar, where a group no less worldly than the rest, consisting of our witnesses, dressed in all their theatrical finery, were assembled to receive us. There was not one real friend amongst all those present, for even our strange old friend Möller was absent, because no suitable partner had been found for him. I was not for a single moment insensible to the chilling frivolity of the congregation, who seemed to impart their tone to the whole ceremony. I listened like one in a dream to the nuptial address of the parson, who, I was afterwards told, had had a share in producing the spirit of bigotry which at this time was so prevalent in Königsberg, and which exercised such a disquieting influence on its population.

A few days later I was told that a rumour had got about the town that I had taken action against the parson for some gross insults contained in his sermon; I did not quite see what was meant, but supposed that the exaggerated report arose from a passage in his address which I in my excitement had misunderstood. The preacher, in speaking of the dark days, of which we were to expect our share, bade us look to an unknown friend, and I glanced up inquiringly for further particulars of this mysterious and influential patron who chose

AFTER THE WEDDING

so strange a way of announcing himself. Reproachfully, and with peculiar emphasis, the pastor then pronounced the name of this unknown friend: Jesus. Now I was not in any way insulted by this, as people imagined, but was simply disappointed; at the same time, I thought that such exhortations were probably usual in nuptial addresses.

But, on the whole, I was so absent-minded during this ceremony, which was double Dutch to me, that when the parson held out the closed prayer-book for us to place our wedding rings upon, Minna had to nudge me forcibly to make me follow her example.

At that moment I saw, as clearly as in a vision, my whole being divided into two cross-currents that dragged me in different directions; the upper one faced the sun and carried me onward like a dreamer, whilst the lower one held my nature captive, a prey to some inexplicable fear. The extraordinary levity with which I chased away the conviction which kept forcing itself upon me, that I was committing a twofold sin, was amply accounted for by the really genuine affection with which I looked upon the young girl whose truly exceptional character (so rare in the environment in which she had been placed) led her thus to bind herself to a young man without any means of support. It was eleven o'clock on the morning of the 24th of November, 1836, and I was twenty-three and a half.

On the way home from church, and afterwards, my good spirits rose superior to all my doubts.

Minna at once took upon herself the duty of receiving and entertaining her guests. The table was spread, and a rich feast, at which Abraham Möller, the energetic promoter of our marriage, also took part, although he had been rather put out by his exclusion from the church ceremony, made up for the coldness of the room, which for a long time refused to get warm, to the great distress of the young hostess.

Everything went off in the usual uneventful way. Nevertheless, I retained my good spirits till the next morning, when I had to present myself at the magistrate's court to meet the demands of my creditors, which had been forwarded to me from Magdeburg to Königsburg.

My friend Möller, whom I had retained for my defence, had foolishly advised me to meet my creditors' demands by pleading infancy according to the law of Prussia, at all events until actual assistance for the settlement of the claims could be obtained.

The magistrate, to whom I stated this plea as I had been advised, was astonished, being probably well aware of my marriage on the previous day, which could only have taken place on the production of documentary proof of my majority. I naturally only gained a brief respite by this manœuvre, and the troubles which beset me for a long time afterwards had their origin on the first day of my marriage.

During the period when I held no appointment at the theatre I suffered various humiliations. Nevertheless, I thought it wise to make the most of my leisure in the interests of my art, and I finished a few pieces, among which was a grand overture on *Rule Britannia*.

When I was still in Berlin I had written the overture entitled *Polonia*, which has already been mentioned in connection with the Polish festival. *Rule Britannia* was a further and deliberate step in the direction of mass effects; at the close a strong military band was to be added to the already over-full orchestra, and I intended to have the whole thing performed at the Musical Festival in Königsberg in the summer.

To these two overtures I added a supplement — an overture entitled *Napoleon*. The point to which I devoted my chief attention was the selection of the means for producing certain effects, and I carefully considered whether I should express the annihilating stroke of fate that befell the French Emperor in Russia by a beat on the tom-tom or not. I believe it was to a great extent my scruples about the introduction of this beat that prevented me from carrying out my plan just then.

On the other hand, the conclusions which I had reached regarding the ill-success of *Liebesverbot* resulted in an operatic sketch in which the demands made on the chorus and the staff of singers should be more in proportion to the known capacity of the local company, as this small theatre was the only one at my disposal.

A quaint tale from the *Arabian Nights* suggested the very

subject for a light work of this description, the title of which, if I remember rightly, was *Männerlist grösser als Frauenlist* ('Man outwits Woman').

I transplanted the story from Bagdad to a modern setting. A young goldsmith offends the pride of a young woman by placing the above motto on the sign over his shop; deeply veiled, she steps into his shop and asks him, as he displays such excellent taste in his work, to express his opinion on her own physical charms; he begins with her feet and her hands, and finally, noticing his confusion, she removes the veil from her face. The jeweller is carried away by her beauty, whereupon she complains to him that her father, who has always kept her in the strictest seclusion, describes her to all her suitors as an ugly monster, his object being, she imagines, simply to keep her dowry. The young man swears that he will not be frightened off by these foolish objections, should the father raise them against his suit. No sooner said than done. The daughter of this peculiar old gentleman is promised to the unsuspecting jeweller, and is brought to her bridegroom as soon as he has signed the contract. He then sees that the father has indeed spoken the truth, the real daughter being a perfect scarecrow. The beautiful lady returns to the bridegroom to gloat over his desperation, and promises to release him from his terrible marriage if he will remove the motto from his signboard. At this point I departed from the original, and continued as follows: The enraged jeweller is on the point of tearing down his unfortunate signboard when a curious apparition leads him to pause in the act. He sees a bear-leader in the street making his clumsy beast dance, in whom the luckless lover recognises at a glance his own father, from whom he has been parted by a hard fate.

He suppresses any sign of emotion, for in a flash a scheme occurs to him by which he can utilise this discovery to free himself from the hated marriage with the daughter of the proud old aristocrat.

He instructs the bear-leader to come that evening to the garden where the solemn betrothal is to take place in the presence of the invited guests.

He then explains to his young enemy that he wishes to leave

the signboard up for the time being, as he still hopes to prove the truth of the motto.

After the marriage contract, in which the young man arrogates to himself all kinds of fictitious titles of nobility, has been read to the assembled company (composed, say, of the *élite* of the noble immigrants at the time of the French Revolution), there is heard suddenly the pipe of the bear-leader, who enters the garden with his prancing beast. Angered by this trivial diversion, the astonished company become indignant when the bridegroom, giving free vent to his feelings, throws himself with tears of joy into the arms of the bear-leader and loudly proclaims him as his long-lost father. The consternation of the company becomes even greater, however, when the bear itself embraces the man they supposed to be of noble birth, for the beast is no less a person than his own brother in the flesh who, on the death of the real bear, had donned its skin, thus enabling the poverty-stricken pair to continue to earn their livelihood in the only way left to them. This public disclosure of the bridegroom's lowly origin at once dissolves the marriage, and the young woman, declaring herself outwitted by man, offers her hand in compensation to the released jeweller.

To this unassuming subject I gave the title of the *Glückliche Bärenfamilie,* and provided it with a dialogue which afterwards met with Holtei's highest approval.

I was about to begin the music for it in a new light French style, but the seriousness of my position, which grew more and more acute, prevented further progress in my work.

In this respect my strained relations with the conductor of the theatre were still a constant source of trouble. With neither the opportunity nor the means to defend myself, I had to submit to being maligned and rendered an object of suspicion on all sides by my rival, who remained master of the field. The object of this was to disgust me with the idea of taking up my appointment as musical conductor, for which the contract had been signed for Easter. Though I did not lose my self-confidence, I suffered keenly from the indignity and the depressing effect of this prolonged strain.

When at last, at the beginning of April, the moment arrived

for the musical conductor Schubert to resign, and for me to take over the whole charge, he had the melancholy satisfaction of knowing that not only was the standing of the opera seriously weakened by the departure of the prima donna, but that there was good reason to doubt whether the theatre could be carried on at all. This month of Lent, which was such a bad time in Germany for all similar theatrical enterprises, decimated the Königsberg audience with the rest. The director took the greatest trouble imaginable to fill up the gaps in the staff of the opera by means of engaging strangers temporarily, and by new acquisitions, and in this my personality and unflagging activity were of real service; I devoted all my energy to buoying up by word and deed the tattered ship of the theatre, in which I now had a hand for the first time.

For a long time I had to try and keep cool under the most violent treatment by a clique of students, among whom my predecessor had raised up enemies for me; and by the unerring certainty of my conducting I had to overcome the initial opposition of the orchestra, which had been set against me.

After laboriously laying the foundation of personal respect, I was now forced to realise that the business methods of the director, Hübsch, had already involved too great a sacrifice to permit the theatre to make its way against the unfavourableness of the season, and in May he admitted to me that he had come to the point of being obliged to close the theatre.

By summoning up all my eloquence, and by making suggestions which promised a happy issue, I was able to induce him to persevere; nevertheless, this was only possible by making demands on the loyalty of his company, who were asked to forego part of their salaries for a time. This aroused general bitterness on the part of the uninitiated, and I found myself in the curious position of being forced to place the director in a favourable light to those who were hard hit by these measures, while I myself and my position were affected in such a manner that my situation became daily more unendurable under the accumulation of intolerable difficulties taking their root in my past.

But though I did not even then lose courage, Minna, who as my wife was robbed of all that she had a right to expect, found this turn of fate quite unbearable. The hidden canker of our married life which, even before our marriage, had caused me the most terrible anxiety and led to violent scenes, reached its full growth under these sad conditions. The less I was able to maintain the standard of comfort due to our position by working and making the most of my talents, the more did Minna, to my insufferable shame, consider it necessary to take this burden upon herself by making the most of her personal popularity. The discovery of similar condescensions — as I used to call them — on Minna's part, had repeatedly led to revolting scenes, and only her peculiar conception of her professional position and the needs it involved had made a charitable interpretation possible.

I was absolutely unable to bring my young wife to see my point of view, or to make her realise my own wounded feelings on these occasions, while the unrestrained violence of my speech and behaviour made an understanding once and for all impossible. These scenes frequently sent my wife into convulsions of so alarming a nature that, as will easily be realised, the satisfaction of reconciling her once more was all that remained to me. Certain it was that our mutual attitude became more and more incomprehensible and inexplicable to us both.

These quarrels, which now became more frequent and more distressing, may have gone far to diminish the strength of any affection which Minna was able to give me, but I had no idea that she was only waiting for a favourable opportunity to come to a desperate decision.

To fill the place of tenor in our company, I had summoned Friedrich Schmitt to Königsberg, a friend of my first year in Magdeburg, to whom allusion has already been made. He was sincerely devoted to me, and helped me as much as possible in overcoming the dangers which threatened the prosperity of the theatre as well as my own position.

The necessity of being on friendly terms with the public made me much less reserved and cautious in making new acquaintances, especially when in his company.

A rich merchant, of the name of Dietrich, had recently constituted himself a patron of the theatre, and especially of the women. With due deference to the men with whom they were connected, he used to invite the pick of these ladies to dinner at his house, and affected, on these occasions, the well-to-do Englishman, which was the beau-ideal for German merchants, especially in the manufacturing towns of the north.

I had shown my annoyance at the acceptance of the invitation, sent to us among the rest, at first simply because his looks were repugnant to me. Minna considered this very unjust. Anyhow, I set my face decidedly against continuing our acquaintance with this man, and although Minna did not insist on receiving him, my conduct towards the intruder was the cause of angry scenes between us.

One day Friedrich Schmitt considered it his duty to inform me that this Herr Dietrich had spoken of me at a public dinner in such a manner as to lead every one to suppose that he had a suspicious intimacy with my wife. I felt obliged to suspect Minna of having, in some way unknown to me, told the fellow about my conduct towards her, as well as about our precarious position.

Accompanied by Schmitt, I called this dangerous person to account on the subject in his own home. At first this only led to the usual denials. Afterwards, however, he sent secret communications to Minna concerning the interview, thus providing her with a supposed new grievance against me in the form of my inconsiderate treatment of her.

Our relations now reached a critical stage, and on certain points we preserved silence.

At the same time — it was towards the end of May, 1837 — the business affairs of the theatre had reached the crisis above mentioned, when the management was obliged to fall back on the self-sacrificing co-operation of the staff to assure the continuance of the undertaking. As I have said before, my own position at the end of a year so disastrous to my welfare was seriously affected by this; nevertheless, there seemed to be no alternative for me but to face these difficulties patiently, and relying on the faithful Friedrich Schmitt, but ignoring Minna, I began to take the necessary steps for making my post at Königsberg secure. This, as well as the arduous part

I took in the business of the theatre, kept me so busy and so much away from home, that I was not able to pay any particular attention to Minna's silence and reserve.

On the morning of the 31st of May I took leave of Minna, expecting to be detained till late in the afternoon by rehearsals and business matters. With my entire approval she had for some time been accustomed to have her daughter Nathalie, who was supposed by every one to be her youngest sister, to stay with her.

As I was about to wish them my usual quiet good-bye, the two women rushed after me to the door and embraced me passionately, Minna as well as her daughter bursting into tears. I was alarmed, and asked the meaning of this excitement, but could get no answer from them, and I was obliged to leave them and ponder alone over their peculiar conduct, of the reason for which I had not even the faintest idea.

I arrived home late in the afternoon, worn out by my exertions and worries, dead-tired, pale and hungry, and was surprised to find the table not laid and Minna not at home, the maid telling me that she had not yet returned from her walk with Nathalie.

I waited patiently, sinking down exhausted at the work-table, which I absent-mindedly opened. To my intense astonishment it was empty. Horror-struck, I sprang up and went to the wardrobe, and realised at once that Minna had left the house; her departure had been so cunningly planned that even the maid was unaware of it.

With death in my soul I dashed out of the house to investigate the cause of Minna's disappearance.

Old Möller, by his practical sagacity, very soon found out that Dietrich, his personal enemy, had left Königsberg in the direction of Berlin by the special coach in the morning.

This horrible fact stood staring me in the face.

I had now to try and overtake the fugitives. With the lavish use of money this might have been possible, but funds were lacking, and had, in part, to be laboriously collected.

On Möller's advice I took the silver wedding presents with me in case of emergency, and after the lapse of a few terrible hours went off, also by special coach, with my distressed old friend. We hoped to overtake the ordinary mail-coach, which had started a short time before, as it was probable that Minna would also continue her journey in this, at a safe distance from Königsberg.

This proved impossible, and when next morning at break of day we arrived in Elbing, we found our money exhausted by the lavish use of the express coach, and were compelled to return; we discovered, moreover, that even by using the ordinary coach we should be obliged to pawn the sugar-basin and cake-dish.

This return journey to Königsberg rightly remains one of the saddest memories of my youth. Of course, I did not for a moment entertain the idea of remaining in the place; my one thought was how I could best get away. Hemmed in between the law-suits of my Magdeburg creditors and the Königsberg tradesmen, who had claims on me for the payment by instalment of my domestic accounts, my departure could only be carried out in secrecy. For this very reason, too, it was necessary for me to raise money, particularly for the long journey from Königsberg to Dresden, whither I determined to go in quest of my wife, and these matters detained me for two long and terrible days.

I received no news whatever from Minna; from Möller I ascertained that she had gone to Dresden, and that Dietrich had only accompanied her for a short distance on the excuse of helping her in a friendly way.

I succeeded in assuring myself that she really only wished to get away from a position that filled her with desperation, and for this purpose had accepted the assistance of a man who sympathised with her, and that she was for the present seeking rest and shelter with her parents. My first indignation at the event accordingly subsided to such an extent that I gradually acquired more sympathy for her in her despair, and began to reproach myself both for my conduct and for having brought unhappiness on her.

I became so convinced of the correctness of this view during the tedious journey to Dresden via Berlin, which I eventually undertook on the 3rd of June, that when at last I found Minna at the humble abode of her parents, I was really quite unable to express anything but repentence and heartbroken sympathy.

It was quite true that Minna thought herself badly treated by me, and declared that she had only been forced to take this desperate step by brooding over our impossible position, to which she thought me both blind and deaf. Her parents were not pleased to see me: the painfully excited condition of their daughter seemed to afford sufficient justification for her complaints against me. Whether my own sufferings, my hasty pursuit, and the heartfelt expression of my grief made any favourable impression on her, I can really hardly say, as her manner towards me was very confused and, to a certain extent, incomprehensible. Still she was impressed when I told her that there was a good prospect of my obtaining the post of musical conductor at Riga, where a new theatre was about to be opened under the most favourable conditions. I felt that I must not press for new resolutions concerning the regulation of our future relations just then, but must strive the more earnestly to lay a better foundation for them. Consequently, after spending a fearful week with my wife under the most painful conditions, I went to Berlin, there to sign my agreement with the new director of the Riga theatre. I obtained the appointment on fairly favourable terms which, I saw, would enable me to keep house in such a style that Minna could retire from the theatre altogether. By this means she would be in a position to spare me all humiliation and anxiety.

On returning to Dresden, I found that Minna was ready to lend a willing ear to my proposed plans, and I succeeded in inducing her to leave her parents' house, which was very cramped for us, and to establish herself in the country at Blasewitz, near Dresden, to await our removal to Riga. We found modest lodgings at an inn on the Elbe, in the farmyard of which I had often played as a child. Here Minna's frame of mind really seemed to be improving. She had begged me not to press her too hard, and I spared her as much as possible. After a few weeks I thought I might consider the period of uneasiness past, but was surprised to find the situation growing worse again without any apparent reason. Minna then told me of some advantageous offers she had received from different theatres, and astonished me one day by announcing her intention of taking a short pleasure trip with a girl friend and her family. As I felt obliged to avoid putting any restraint upon her, I offered no objection to the execution of this project, which entailed a week's separation, but accompanied her back to her parents myself, promising to await her return quietly at Blasewitz. A few days later her eldest sister called to ask me for the written permission required to make out a passport for my wife. This alarmed me, and I went to Dresden to ask her parents what their daughter was about. There, to my surprise, I met with a very unpleasant reception; they reproached me coarsely for my behaviour to Minna, whom they said I could not even manage to support, and when I only replied by asking for information as to the whereabouts of my wife, and about her plans for the future, I was put off with improbable statements. Tormented by the sharpest forebodings, and understanding nothing of what had occurred, I went back to the village, where I found a letter from Königsberg, from Möller, which poured light on all my misery. Herr Dietrich had gone to Dresden, and I was told the name of the hotel at which he was staying. The terrible illumination thrown by this communication upon Minna's conduct showed me in a flash what to do. I hurried into town to make the necessary inquiries at the hotel mentioned, and found that the man in question had been there, but had moved on again. He had vanished, and Minna too! I now knew enough to demand of the Fates why, at such an early age, they had sent me this terrible experience which, as it seemed to me, had poisoned my whole existence.

I sought consolation for my boundless grief in the society of my sister Ottilie and her husband, Hermann Brockhaus, an excellent fellow to whom she had been married for some years. They were then living at their pretty summer villa in the lovely Grosser Garten, near Dresden. I had looked them up at once the first time I went to Dresden, but as I had not at that time the slightest idea of how things were going to turn out, I had told them nothing, and had seen but little of them. Now I was moved to break my obstinate silence, and unfold to them the cause of my misery, with but few reservations.

For the first time I was in a position gratefully to appreciate the advantages of family intercourse, and of the direct and disinterested intimacy between blood relations. Explanations were hardly necessary, and as brother and sister we found ourselves as closely linked now as we had been when we were children. We arrived at a complete understanding without having to explain what we meant; I was unhappy, she was happy; consolation and help followed as a matter of course.

This was the sister to whom I once had read *Leubald und Adelaïde* in a thunderstorm; the sister who had listened, filled with astonishment and sympathy, to that eventful performance of my first overture on Christmas Eve, and whom I now found married to one of the kindest of men, Hermann Brockhaus, who soon earned a reputation for himself as an expert in oriental languages. He was the youngest brother of my elder brother-in-law, Friedrich Brockhaus. Their union was blessed by two children; their comfortable means favoured a life free from care, and when I made my daily pilgrimage from Blasewitz to the famous Grosser Garten, it was like stepping from a desert into paradise to enter their house (one of the popular villas), knowing that I would invariably find a welcome in this happy family circle. Not only was my spirit soothed and benefited by intercourse with my sister, but my creative instincts, which had long lain dormant, were stimulated afresh by the society of my brilliant and learned brother-in-law. It was brought home to me, without in any way hurting my feelings, that my early marriage, excusable as it may have been, was yet an error to be retrieved, and my mind regained sufficient elasticity to compose some sketches, designed this time not merely to meet the requirements of the theatre as I knew it. During the last wretched days I had spent with Minna at Blasewitz, I had read Bulwer Lytton's novel, *Rienzi;* during my convalescence in the bosom of my sympathetic family, I now worked out the scheme for a grand opera under the inspiration of this book. Though obliged for the present to return to the limitations of a small theatre, I tried from this time onwards to aim at enlarging my sphere of action. I sent my overture, *Rule Britannia,* to the Philharmonic Society in London, and tried to get into communication with Scribe in Paris about a setting for H. König's novel, *Die Hohe Braut*, which I had sketched out. Thus I spent the remainder of this summer of ever-happy memory. At the end of August I had to leave for Riga to take up my new appointment. Although I knew that my sister Rosalie had shortly before married the man of her choice, Professor Oswald Marbach of Leipzig, I avoided that city, probably with the foolish notion of sparing myself any humiliation, and went straight to Berlin, where I had to receive certain additional instructions from my future director, and also to obtain my passport. There I met a younger sister of Minna's, Amalie Planer, a singer with a pretty voice, who had joined our opera company at Magdeburg for a short time. My report of Minna quite overwhelmed this exceedingly kind-hearted girl. We went to a performance of *Fidelio* together, during which she, like myself, burst into tears and sobs. Refreshed by the sympathetic impression I had received, I went by way of Schwerin, where I was disappointed in my hopes of finding traces of Minna, to Lübeck, to wait for a merchant ship going to Riga. We had set sail for Travemünde when an unfavourable wind set in, and held up our departure for a week: I had to spend this disagreeable time in a miserable ship's tavern. Thrown on my own resources I tried, amongst other things, to read *Till Eulenspiegel,* and this popular book first gave me the idea of a real German comic opera. Long afterwards, when I was composing the words for my *Junger Siegfried,* I remember having many vivid recollections of this melancholy sojourn in Travemünde and my reading of *Till Eulenspiegel.* After a voyage of four days we at last reached port at Bolderaa. I was conscious of a peculiar thrill on coming into contact with Russian officials, whom I had instinctively detested since the days of my sympathy with the Poles as a boy. It seemed to me as if the harbour police must read enthusiasm for the Poles in my face, and would send me to Siberia on the spot, and I was the more agreeably surprised, on reaching Riga, to find myself surrounded by the familiar German element which, above all, pervaded everything connected with the theatre.

After my unfortunate experiences in connection with the

conditions of small German stages, the way in which this newly opened theatre was run had at first a calming effect on my mind. A society had been formed by a number of well-to-do theatregoers and rich business men to raise, by voluntary subscription, sufficient money to provide the sort of management they regarded as ideal with a solid foundation. The director they appointed was Karl von Holtei, a fairly popular dramatic writer, who enjoyed a certain reputation in the theatrical world. This man's ideas about the stage represented a special tendency, which was at that time on the decline. He possessed, in addition to his remarkable social gifts, an extraordinary acquaintance with all the principal people connected with the theatre during the past twenty years, and belonged to a society called *Die Liebenswürdigen Libertins* (' The Amiable Libertines '). This was a set of young would-be wits, who looked upon the stage as a playground licensed by the public for the display of their mad pranks, from which the middle class held aloof, while people of culture were steadily losing all interest in the theatre under these hopeless conditions.

Holtei's wife had in former days been a popular actress at the Königstadt theatre in Berlin, and it was here, at the time when Henriette Sontag raised it to the height of its fame, that Holtei's style had been formed. The production there of his melodrama *Leonore* (founded on Bürger's ballad) had in particular earned him a wide reputation as a writer for the stage, besides which he produced some *Liederspiele,* and among them one, entitled *Der Alte Feldherr,* became fairly popular. His invitation to Riga had been particularly welcome, as it bid fair to gratify his craving to absorb himself completely in the life of the stage; he hoped, in this out-of-the-way place, to indulge his passion without restraint. His peculiar familiarity of manner, his inexhaustible store of amusing small talk, and his airy way of doing business, gave him a remarkable hold on the tradespeople of Riga, who wished for nothing better than such entertainment as he was able to give them. They provided him liberally with all the necessary means and treated him in every respect with entire confidence. Under his auspices my own engagement had been very easily secured. Surly old pedants he would have none of, favouring young men

THE THEATRE OPENS

on the score of their youth alone. As far as I myself was concerned, it was enough for him to know that I belonged to a family which he knew and liked, and hearing, moreover, of my fervent devotion to modern Italian and French music in particular, he decided that I was the very man for him. He had the whole shoal of Bellini's, Donizetti's, Adam's, and Auber's operatic scores copied out, and I was to give the good people of Riga the benefit of them with all possible speed.

The first time I visited Holtei I met an old Leipzig acquaintance, Heinrich Dorn, my former mentor, who now held the permanent municipal appointment of choir-master at the church and music-teacher in the schools. He was pleased to find his curious pupil transformed into a practical opera conductor of independent position, and no less surprised to see the eccentric worshipper of Beethoven changed into an ardent champion of Bellini and Adam. He took me home to his summer residence, which was built, according to Riga phraseology, 'in the fields,' that is literally, on the sand. While I was giving him some account of the experiences through which I had passed, I grew conscious of the strangely deserted look of the place. Feeling frightened and homeless, my initial uneasiness gradually developed into a passionate longing to escape from all the whirl of theatrical life which had wooed me to such inhospitable regions. This uneasy mood was fast dispelling the flippancy which at Magdeburg had led to my being dragged down to the level of the most worthless stage society, and had also conduced to spoil my musical taste. It also contained the germs of a new tendency which developed during the period of my activity at Riga, brought me more and more out of touch with the theatre, thereby causing Director Holtei all the annoyance which inevitably attends disappointment.

For some time, however, I found no difficulty in making the best of a bad bargain. We were obliged to open the theatre before the company was complete. To make this possible, we gave a performance of a short comic opera by C. Blum, called *Marie, Max und Michel*. For this work I composed an additional air for a song which Holtei had written for the bass singer, Günther; it consisted of a sentimental introduction and a gay military rondo, and was very much appreciated. Later on,

I introduced another additional song into the *Schweizerfamilie*, to be sung by another bass singer, Scheibler; it was of a devotional character, and pleased not only the public, but myself, and showed signs of the upheaval which was gradually taking place in my musical development. I was entrusted with the composition of a tune for a National Hymn written by Brakel in honour of the Tsar Nicholas's birthday. I tried to give it as far as possible the right colouring for a despotic patriarchal monarch, and once again I achieved some fame, for it was sung for several successive years on that particular day. Holtei tried to persuade me to write a bright, gay comic opera, or rather a musical play, to be performed by our company just as it stood. I looked up the libretto of my *Glückliche Bärenfamilie*, and found Holtei very well disposed towards it (as I have stated elsewhere); but when I unearthed the little music which I had already composed for it, I was overcome with disgust at this way of writing; whereupon I made a present of the book to my clumsy, good-natured friend, Löbmann, my right-hand man in the orchestra, and never gave it another thought from that day to this. I managed, however, to get to work on the libretto of *Rienzi*, which I had sketched out at Blasewitz. I developed it from every point of view, on so extravagant a scale, that with this work I deliberately cut off all possibility of being tempted by circumstances to produce it anywhere but on one of the largest stages in Europe.

But while this helped to strengthen my endeavour to escape from all the petty degradations of stage life, new complications arose which affected me more and more seriously, and offered further opposition to my aims. The prima donna engaged by Holtei had failed us, and we were therefore without a singer for grand opera. Under the circumstances, Holtei joyfully agreed to my proposal to ask Amalie, Minna's sister (who was glad to accept an engagement that brought her near me), to come to Riga at once. In her answer to me from Dresden, where she was then living, she informed me of Minna's return to her parents, and of her present miserable condition owing to a severe illness. I naturally took this piece of news very coolly, for what I had heard about Minna since she left me for the last time had forced me to authorise my old friend at Königsberg to take steps to procure a divorce. It was certain that Minna had stayed for some time at a hotel in Hamburg with that ill-omened man, Herr Dietrich, and that she had spread abroad the story of our separation so unreservedly that the theatrical world in particular had discussed it in a manner that was positively insulting to me. I simply informed Amalie of this, and requested her to spare me any further news of her sister.

Hereupon Minna herself appealed to me, and wrote me a positively heartrending letter, in which she openly confessed her infidelity. She declared that she had been driven to it by despair, but that the great trouble she had thus brought upon herself having taught her a lesson, all she now wished was to return to the right path. Taking everything into account, I concluded that she had been deceived in the character of her seducer, and the knowledge of her terrible position had placed her both morally and physically in a most lamentable condition, in which, now ill and wretched, she turned to me again to acknowledge her guilt, crave my forgiveness, and assure me, in spite of all, that she had now become fully aware of her love for me. Never before had I heard such sentiments from Minna, nor was I ever to hear the same from her again, save on one touching occasion many years later, when similar outpourings moved and affected me in the same way as this particular letter had done. In reply I told her that there should never again be any mention between us of what had occurred, for which I took upon myself the chief blame; and I can pride myself on having carried out this resolution to the letter.

When her sister's engagement was satisfactorily settled, I at once invited Minna to come to Riga with her. Both gladly accepted my invitation, and arrived from Dresden at my new home on 19th October, wintry weather having already set in. With much regret I perceived that Minna's health had really suffered, and therefore did all in my power to provide her with all the domestic comforts and quiet she needed. This presented difficulties, for my modest income as a conductor was all I had at my disposal, and we were both firmly determined not to let Minna go on the stage again. On the other hand, the carrying out of this resolve, in view of the financial inconvenience it entailed, produced strange complications, the nature of which was only revealed to me later, when startling developments divulged the real moral character of the manager Holtei. For the present I had to let people think that I was jealous of my wife. I bore patiently with the general belief that I had good reasons to be so, and rejoiced meanwhile at the restoration of our peaceful married life, and especially at the sight of our humble home, which we made as comfortable as our means would allow, and in the keeping of which Minna's domestic talents came strongly to the fore. As we were still childless, and were obliged as a rule to enlist the help of a dog in order to give life to the domestic hearth, we once lighted upon the eccentric idea of trying our luck with a young wolf which was brought into the house as a tiny cub. When we found, however, that this experiment did not increase the comfort of our home life, we gave him up after he had been with us a few weeks. We fared better with sister Amalie; for she, with her good-nature and simple homely ways, did much to make up for the absence of children for a time. The two sisters, neither of whom had had any real education, often returned playfully to the ways of their childhood. When they sang children's duets, Minna, though she had had no musical training, always managed very cleverly to sing seconds, and afterwards, as we sat at our evening meal, eating Russian salad, salt salmon from the Dwina, or fresh Russian caviare, we were all three very cheerful and happy far away in our northern home.

Amalie's beautiful voice and real vocal talent at first won for her a very favourable reception with the public, a fact which did us all a great deal of good. Being, however, very short, and having no very great gift for acting, the scope of her powers was very limited, and as she was soon surpassed by more successful competitors, it was a real stroke of good luck for her that a young officer in the Russian army, then Captain, now General, Carl von Meck, fell head over ears in love with the simple girl, and married her a year later. The unfortunate part of this engagement, however, was that it caused many difficulties, and brought the first cloud over our *ménage à trois*. For, after a while, the two sisters quarrelled bitterly, and I had the very unpleasant experience of living for a whole year in the same house with two relatives who neither saw nor spoke to each other.

We spent the winter at the beginning of 1838 in a very small dingy dwelling in the old town; it was not till the spring that we moved into a pleasanter house in the more salubrious Petersburg suburb, where, in spite of the sisterly breach before referred to, we led a fairly bright and cheerful life, as we were often able to entertain many of our friends and acquaintances in a simple though pleasant fashion. In addition to members of the stage I knew a few people in the town, and we received and visited the family of Dorn, the musical director, with whom I became quite intimate. But it was the second musical director, Franz Löbmann, a very worthy though not a very gifted man, who became most faithfully attached to me. However, I did not cultivate many acquaintances in wider circles, and they grew fewer as the ruling passion of my life grew steadily stronger; so that when, later on, I left Riga, after spending nearly two years there, I departed almost as a stranger, and with as much indifference as I had left Magdeburg and Königsberg. What, however, specially embittered my departure was a series of experiences of a particularly disagreeable nature, which firmly determined me to cut myself off entirely from the necessity of mixing with any people like those I had met with in my previous attempts to create a position for myself at the theatre.

Yet it was only gradually that I became quite conscious of all this. At first, under the safe guidance of my renewed wedded happiness, which had for a time been so disturbed in its early days, I felt distinctly better than I had before in all my professional work. The fact that the material position of the theatrical undertaking was assured exercised a healthy influence on the performances. The theatre itself was cooped up in a very narrow space; there was as little room for scenic display on its tiny stage as there was accommodation for rich musical effects in the cramped orchestra. In both directions the strictest limits were imposed, yet I contrived to introduce considerable reinforcements into an orchestra which was really only calculated for a string quartette, two first and two second violins, two violas, and one 'cello. These successful exertions of mine were the first cause of the dislike Holtei evinced towards me later on. After this we were able to get good concerted music for the opera. I found the thorough study of Méhul's opera, *Joseph in Aegypten,* very stimulating. Its noble and simple style, added to the touching effect of the music, which quite carries one away, did much towards effecting a favourable change in my taste, till then warped by my connection with the theatre.

It was most gratifying to feel my former serious taste again aroused by really good dramatic performances. I specially remember a production of *King Lear,* which I followed with the greatest interest, not only at the actual performances, but at all the rehearsals as well. Yet these educative impressions tended to make me feel ever more and more dissatisfied with my work at the theatre. On the one hand, the members of the company became gradually more distasteful to me, and on the other I was growing discontented with the management. With regard to the staff of the theatre, I very soon found out the hollowness, vanity, and the impudent selfishness of this uncultured and undisciplined class of people, for I had now lost my former liking for the Bohemian life that had such an attraction for me at Magdeburg. Before long there were but a few members of our company with whom I had not quarrelled, thanks to one or the other of these drawbacks. But my saddest experience was, that in such disputes, into which in fact I was led simply by my zeal for the artistic success of the performances as a whole, not only did I receive no support from Holtei, the director, but I actually made him my enemy. He even declared publicly that our theatre had become far too respectable for his taste, and tried to convince me that good theatrical performances could not be given by a strait-laced company.

In his opinion the idea of the dignity of theatrical art was pedantic nonsense, and he thought light serio-comic vaudeville the only class of performance worth considering. Serious opera, rich musical *ensemble,* was his particular aversion, and my demands for this irritated him so that he met them only with scorn and indignant refusals. Of the strange connection between this artistic bias and his taste in the domain of morality I was also to become aware, to my horror, in due course. For the present I felt so repelled by the declaration of his artistic antipathies, as to let my dislike for the theatre as a profession steadily grow upon me. I still took pleasure in some good performances which I was able to get up, under favourable circumstances, at the larger theatre at Mitau, to where the company went for a time in the early part of the summer. Yet it was while I was there, spending most of my time reading Bulwer Lytton's novels, that I made a secret resolve to try hard to free myself from all connection with the only branch of theatrical art which had so far been open to me.

The composition of my *Rienzi,* the text of which I had finished in the early days of my sojourn in Riga, was destined to bridge me over to the glorious world for which I had longed so intensely. I had laid aside the completion of my *Glückliche Bärenfamilie,* for the simple reason that the lighter character of this piece would have thrown me more into contact with the very theatrical people I most despised. My greatest consolation now was to prepare *Rienzi* with such an utter disregard of the means which were available there for its production, that my desire to produce it would force me out of the narrow confines of this puny theatrical circle to seek a fresh connection with one of the larger theatres. It was after our return from Mitau, in the middle of the summer of 1838, that I set to work on this composition, and by so doing roused myself to a state of enthusiasm which, considering my position, was nothing less than desperate dare-devilry. All to whom I confided my plan perceived at once, on the mere mention of my subject, that I was preparing to break away from my present position, in which there could be no possibility of producing my work, and I was looked upon as light-headed and fit only for an asylum.

To all my acquaintances my procedure seemed stupid and reckless. Even the former patron of my peculiar Leipzig overture thought it impracticable and eccentric, seeing that I had again turned my back on light opera. He expressed this opinion very freely in the *Neue Zeitschrift für Musik,* in a report of a concert I had given towards the end of the previous winter, and openly ridiculed the Magdeburg *Columbus* Overture and the *Rule Britannia* Overture previously mentioned. I myself had not taken any pleasure in the performance of either of these overtures, as my predilection for cornets, strongly marked in both these overtures, again played me a sorry trick, as I had evidently expected too much of our Riga musicians, and had to endure all kinds of disappointment on the occasion of the performance. As a complete contrast to my extravagant setting of *Rienzi,* this same director, H. Dorn, had set to work to write an opera in which he had most carefully borne in mind the conditions obtaining at the Riga theatre. *Der Schöffe von Paris,* an historical operetta of the period of the siege of Paris by Joan of Arc, was practised and performed by us to the complete satisfaction of the composer. However, the success of this work gave me no reason for abandoning my project to complete my *Rienzi,* and I was secretly pleased to find that I could regard this success without a trace of envy. Though animated by no feeling of rivalry, I gradually gave up associating with the Riga artists, confining myself chiefly to the performance of the duties I had undertaken, and worked away at the two first acts of my big opera without troubling myself at all whether I should ever get so far as to see it produced.

The serious and bitter experiences I had had so early in life had done much to guide me towards that intensely earnest side of my nature that had manifested itself in my earliest youth. The effect of these bitter experiences was now to be still further emphasised by other sad impressions. Not long after Minna had rejoined me, I received from home the news of the death of my sister Rosalie. It was the first time in my life that I had experienced the passing away of one near and dear to me. The death of this sister struck me as a most cruel and significant blow of fate; it was out of love and respect for her that I had turned away so resolutely from my youthful excesses, and it was to gain her sympathy that I had devoted special thought and care to my first great works. When the passions and cares of life had come upon me and driven me away from my home, it was she who had read deep down into my sorely stricken heart, and who had bidden me that anxious farewell on my departure from Leipzig. At the time of my disappearance, when the news of my wilful marriage and of my consequent unfortunate position reached my family, it was she who, as my mother informed me later, never lost her faith in me, but who always cherished the hope that I would one day reach the full development of my capabilities and make a genuine success of my life.

Now, at the news of her death, and illuminated by the recollection of that one impressive farewell, as by a flash of lightning I saw the immense value my relations with this sister had been to me, and I did not fully realise the extent of her influence until later on, when, after my first striking successes, my mother tearfully lamented that Rosalie had not lived to witness them. It really did me good to be again in communication with my family. My mother and sisters had had news of my doings somehow or other, and I was deeply touched, in the letters which I was now receiving from them, to hear no reproaches anent my headstrong and apparently heartless behaviour, but only sympathy and heartfelt solicitude. My family had also received favourable reports about my wife's good qualities, a fact about which I was particularly glad, as I was thus spared the difficulties of defending her questionable behaviour to me, which I should have been at pains to excuse. This produced a salutary calm in my soul, which had so recently been a prey to the worst anxieties. All that had driven me with such passionate haste to an improvident and premature marriage, all that had consequently weighed on me so ruinously, now seemed set at rest, leaving peace in its stead. And although the ordinary cares of life still pressed on me for many years, often in a most vexatious and troublesome form, yet the anxieties attendant on my ardent youthful wishes were in a manner subdued and calm. From thence forward till the attainment of my professional independence, all my life's struggles could be directed entirely towards that more ideal aim which, from the time of the conception of my *Rienzi*, was to be my only guide through life.

It was only later that I first realised the real character of my life in Riga, from the utterance of one of its inhabitants, who was astonished to learn of the success of a man of whose importance, during the whole of his two years' sojourn in the small capital of Livonia, nothing had been known. Thrown entirely on my own resources, I was a stranger to every one. As I mentioned before, I kept aloof from all the theatre folk, in consequence of my increasing dislike of them, and therefore, when at the end of March, 1839, at the close of my second winter there, I was given my dismissal by the management, although this occurrence surprised me for other reasons, yet I felt fully reconciled to this compulsory change in my life. The reasons which led to this dismissal were, however, of such a nature that I could only regard it as one of the most disagreeable experiences of my life. Once, when I was lying dangerously ill, I heard of Holtei's real feelings towards me. I had caught a severe cold in the depth of winter at a theatrical rehearsal, and it at once assumed a serious character, owing to the fact that my nerves were in a state of constant irritation from the continual annoyance and vexatious worry caused by the contemptible character of the theatrical management. It was just at the time when a special performance of the opera *Norma* was to be given by our company in Mitau. Holtei insisted on my getting up from a sick-bed to make this wintry journey, and thus to expose myself to the danger of seriously increasing my cold in the icy theatre at Mitau. Typhoid fever was the consequence, and this pulled me down to such an extent that Holtei, who heard of my condition, is said to have remarked at the theatre that I should probably never conduct again, and that, to all intents and purposes, 'I was on my last legs.' It was to a splendid homœopathic physician, Dr. Prutzer, that I owed my recovery and my life. Not long after that Holtei left our theatre and Riga for ever; his occupation there, with 'the far too respectable conditions,' as he expressed it, had become intolerable to him. In addition, however, circumstances had arisen in his domestic life (which had been much affected by the death of his wife) which seemed to make him consider a complete break with Riga eminently desirable. But to my astonishment I now first became aware that I too had unconsciously been a sufferer from the troubles he had brought upon himself. When Holtei's successor in the management — Joseph Hoffmann the singer — informed me that his predecessor had made it a condition to his taking over the post that he should enter into the same engagement that Holtei had made with the conductor Dorn for the post which I had hitherto filled, and my reappointment had therefore been made an impossibility, my wife met my astonishment at this news by giving me the reason, of which for some considerable time past she had been well aware, namely, Holtei's special dislike of us both. When I was afterwards informed by Minna of what had happened — she having purposely kept it from me all this time, so as not to cause bad feeling between me and my director — a ghastly light was thrown upon the whole affair. I did indeed remember perfectly how, soon after Minna's arrival in Riga, I had been particularly pressed by Holtei not to prevent my wife's engagement at the theatre. I asked him to talk things quietly over with her, so that he might see that Minna's unwillingness rested on a mutual understanding, and not on any jealousy on my part. I had intentionally given him the time when I was engaged at the theatre on rehearsals for the necessary discussions with my wife. At the end of these meetings I had, on my return, often found Minna in a very excited condition, and at length she declared emphatically that under no circumstances would she accept the engagement offered by Holtei. I had also noticed in Minna's demeanour towards me a strange anxiety to know why I was not unwilling to allow Holtei to try to persuade her. Now that the catastrophe had occurred, I learned that Holtei had in fact used these interviews for making improper advances to my wife, the nature of which I only realised with difficulty on further acquaintance with this man's peculiarities, and after having heard of other instances of a similar nature. I then discovered that Holtei considered it an advantage to get himself talked about in connection with pretty women, in order thus to divert the attention of the public from other conduct even more disreputable. After this Minna was exceedingly indignant at Holtei, who, finding his own suit rejected, appeared as the medium for another suitor, on whose behalf he urged that he would think none the worse of her for rejecting him, a greyhaired and penniless man, but at the same time advocated the suit of Brandenburg, a very wealthy and handsome young merchant. His fierce indignation at this double repulse, his humiliation at having revealed his real nature to no purpose, seems, to judge from Minna's observations, to have been exceedingly great. I now understood too well that his frequent and profoundly contemptuous sallies against respectable actors and actresses had not been mere spirited exaggerations, but that he had probably often had to complain of being put thoroughly to shame on this account.

The fact that the playing of such criminal parts as the one he had had in view with my wife was unable to divert the ever-increasing attention of the outside world from his vicious and dissolute habits, does not seem to have escaped him; for those behind the scenes told me candidly that it was owing to the fear of very unpleasant revelations that he had suddenly decided to give up his position at Riga altogether. Even in much later years I heard about Holtei's bitter dislike of me, a dislike which showed itself, among other things, in his denunciation of *The Music of the Future*,[1] and of its tendency to jeopardise the simplicity of pure sentiment. I have previously mentioned that he displayed so much personal animosity against me during the latter part of the time we were together in Riga that he vented his hostility upon me in every possible way. Up to that time I had felt inclined to ascribe it to the divergence of our respective views on artistic points.

To my dismay I now became aware that personal considerations alone were at the bottom of all this, and I blushed to realise that by my former unreserved confidence in a man whom I thought was absolutely honest, I had based my knowledge of human nature on such very weak foundations. But still greater was my disappointment when I discovered the real character of my friend H. Dorn. During the whole time of our intercourse at Riga, he, who formerly treated me more like a good-natured elder brother, had become my most confidential friend. We saw and visited each other almost daily, very frequently in our respective homes. I kept not a single secret from him, and the performance of his *Schöffe von Paris* under my direction was as successful as if it had been under his own. Now, when I heard that my post had been given to him, I felt obliged to ask him about it, in order to learn whether there was any mistake on his part as to my intention regarding the position I had hitherto held. But from his letter in reply

---

[1] *Zukunftsmusik* is a pamphlet revealing some of Wagner's artistic aims and aspirations, written 1860–61. — EDITOR.

I could clearly see that Dorn had really made use of Holtei's dislike for me to extract from him, before his departure, an arrangement which was both binding on his successor and also in his (Dorn's) own favour. As my friend he ought to have known that he could benefit by this agreement only in the event of my resigning my appointment in Riga, because in our confidential conversations, which continued to the end, he always carefully refrained from touching on the possibility of my going away or remaining. In fact, he declared that Holtei had distinctly told him he would on no account re-engage me, as I could not get on with the singers. He added that after this one could not take it amiss if he, who had been inspired with fresh enthusiasm for the theatre by the success of his *Schöffe von Paris*, had seized and turned to his own advantage the chance offered to him. Moreover, he had gathered from my confidential communications that I was very awkwardly situated, and that, owing to my small salary having been cut down by Holtei from the very beginning, I was in a very precarious position on account of the demands of my creditors in Königsberg and Magdeburg. It appeared that these people had employed against me a lawyer, who was a friend of Dorn's, and that, consequently, he had come to the conclusion that I would not be able to remain in Riga. Therefore, even as my friend, he had felt his conscience quite clear in accepting Holtei's proposal.

In order not to leave him in the complacent enjoyment of this self-deception, I put it clearly before him that he could not be ignorant of the fact that a higher salary had been promised to me for the third year of my contract; and that, by the establishment of orchestral concerts, which had already made a favourable start, I now saw my way to getting free from those long-standing debts, having already overcome the difficulties of the removal and settling down. I also asked him how he would act if I saw it was to my own interest to retain my post, and to call on him to resign his agreement with Holtei, who, as a matter of fact, after his departure from Riga, had withdrawn his alleged reason for my dismissal. To this I received no answer, nor have I had one up to the present day; but, on the other hand, in 1865, I was astonished to see

Dorn enter my house in Munich unannounced, and when to his joy I recognised him, he stepped up to me with a gesture which clearly showed his intention of embracing me. Although I managed to evade this, yet I soon saw the difficulty of preventing him from addressing me with the familiar form of 'thou,' as the attempt to do so would have necessitated explanations that would have been a useless addition to all my worries just then; for it was the time when my *Tristan* was being produced.

Such a man was Heinrich Dorn. Although, after the failure of three operas, he had retired in disgust from the theatre to devote himself exclusively to the commercial side of music, yet the success of his opera, *Der Schöffe von Paris,* in Riga helped him back to a permanent place among the dramatic musicians of Germany. But to this position he was first dragged from obscurity, across the bridge of infidelity to his friend, and by the aid of virtue in the person of Director Holtei, thanks to a magnanimous oversight on the part of Franz Listz. The preference of King Friedrich Wilhelm IV. for church scenes contributed to secure him eventually his important position at the greatest lyric theatre in Germany, the Royal Opera of Berlin. For he was prompted far less by his devotion to the dramatic muse than by his desire to secure a good position in some important German city, when, as already hinted, through Liszt's recommendation he was appointed musical director of Cologne Cathedral. During a fête connected with the building of the cathedral he managed, as a musician, so to work upon the Prussian monarch's religious feelings, that he was appointed to the dignified post of musical conductor at the Royal Theatre, in which capacity he long continued to do honour to German dramatic music in conjunction with Wilhelm Taubert.

I must give J. Hoffmann, who from this time forward was the manager of the Riga theatre, the credit of having felt the treachery practised upon me very deeply indeed. He told me that his contract with Dorn bound him only for one year, and that the moment the twelve months had elapsed he wished to come to a fresh agreement with me. As soon as this was known, my patrons in Riga came forward with offers of teaching engagements and arrangements for sundry concerts, by way of compensating me for the year's salary which I should lose by being away from my work as a conductor. Though I was much gratified by these offers, yet, as I have already pointed out, the longing to break loose from the kind of theatrical life which I had experienced up to that time so possessed me that I resolutely seized this chance of abandoning my former vocation for an entirely new one. Not without some shrewdness, I played upon my wife's indignation at the treachery I had suffered, in order to make her fall in with my eccentric notion of going to Paris. Already in my conception of *Rienzi* I had dreamed of the most magnificent theatrical conditions, but now, without halting at any intermediate stations, my one desire was to reach the very heart of all European grand opera. While still in Magdeburg I had made H. König's romance, *Die Hohe Braut,* the subject of a grand opera in five acts, and in the most luxurious French style. After the scenic draft of this opera, which had been translated into French, was completely worked out, I sent it from Königsberg to Scribe in Paris. With this manuscript I sent a letter to the famous operatic poet, in which I suggested that he might make use of my plot, on condition that he would secure me the composition of the music for the Paris Opera House. To convince him of my ability to compose Parisian operatic music, I also sent him the score of my *Liebesverbot*. At the same time I wrote to Meyerbeer, informing him of my plans, and begging him to support me. I was not at all disheartened at receiving no reply, for I was content to know that now at last ' I was in communication with Paris.' When, therefore, I started out upon my daring journey from Riga, I seemed to have a comparatively serious object in view, and my Paris projects no longer struck me as being altogether in the air. In addition to this I now heard that my youngest sister, Cecilia, had become betrothed to a certain Eduard Avenarius, an employee of the Brockhaus book-selling firm, and that he had undertaken the management of their Paris branch. To him I applied for news of Scribe, and for an answer to the application I had made to that gentleman some years previously. Avenarius called on Scribe, and from him received an acknowledgment of the receipt of my earlier communication. Scribe also showed that he had some recollection of the subject itself; for he said that, so far as he could remember, there was a *joueuse de harpe* in the piece, who was ill-treated by her brother. The fact that this merely incidental item had alone remained in his memory led me to conclude that he had not extended his acquaintance with the piece beyond the first act, in which the item in question occurs. When, moreover, I heard that he had nothing to say in regard to my score, except that he had had portions of it played over to him by a pupil of the Conservatoire, I really could not flatter myself that he had entered into definite and conscious relations with me. And yet I had palpable evidence in a letter of his to Avenarius, which the latter forwarded to me, that Scribe had actually occupied himself with my work, and that I was indeed in communication with him, and this letter of Scribe's made such an impression upon my wife, who was by no means inclined to be sanguine, that she gradually overcame her apprehensions in regard to the Paris adventure. At last it was fixed and settled that on the expiry of my second year's contract in Riga (that is to say, in the coming summer, 1839), we should journey direct from Riga to Paris, in order that I might try my luck there as a composer of opera.

The production of my *Rienzi* now began to assume greater importance. The composition of its second act was finished before we started, and into this I wove a heroic ballet of extravagant dimensions. It was now imperative that I should speedily acquire a knowledge of French, a language which, during my classical studies at the Grammar School, I had contemptuously laid aside. As there were only four weeks in which to recover the time I had lost, I engaged an excellent French master. But as I soon realised that I could achieve but little in so short a time, I utilised the hours of the lessons in order to obtain from him, under the pretence of receiving instruction, an idiomatic translation of my *Rienzi* libretto. This I wrote with red ink on such parts of the score as were finished, so that on reaching Paris I might immediately submit my half-finished opera to French judges of art.

Everything now seemed to be carefully prepared for my

departure, and all that remained to be done was to raise the necessary funds for my undertaking. But in this respect the outlook was bad. The sale of our modest household furniture, the proceeds of a benefit concert, and my meagre savings only sufficed to satisfy the importunate demands of my creditors in Magdeburg and Königsberg. I knew that if I were to devote all my cash to this purpose, there would not be a farthing left. Some way out of the fix must be found, and this our old Königsberg friend, Abraham Möller, suggested in his usual flippant and obscure manner. Just at this critical moment he paid us a second visit to Riga. I acquainted him with the difficulties of our position, and all the obstacles which stood in the way of my resolve to go to Paris. In his habitual laconical way he counselled me to reserve all my savings for our journey, and to settle with my creditors when my Parisian successes had provided the necessary means. To help us in carrying out this plan, he offered to convey us in his carriage across the Russian frontier at top speed to an East Prussian port. We should have to cross the Russian frontier without passports, as these had been already impounded by our foreign creditors. He assured us that we should find it quite simple to carry out this very hazardous expedition, and declared that he had a friend on a Prussian estate close to the frontier who would render us very effective assistance. My eagerness to escape at any price from my previous circumstances, and to enter with all possible speed upon the wider field, in which I hoped very soon to realise my ambition, blinded me to all the unpleasantnesses which the execution of his proposal must entail. Director Hoffmann, who considered himself bound to serve me to the utmost of his ability, facilitated my departure by allowing me to leave some months before the expiration of my engagement. After continuing to conduct the operatic portion of the Mitau theatrical season through the month of June, we secretly started in a special coach hired by Möller and under his protection. The goal of our journey was Paris, but many unheard-of hardships were in store for us before we were to reach that city.

The sense of contentment involuntarily aroused by our passage through the fruitful Courland in the luxuriant month of July, and by the sweet illusion that now at last I had cut myself loose from a hateful existence, to enter upon a new and boundless path of fortune, was disturbed from its very outset by the miserable inconveniences occasioned by the presence of a huge Newfoundland dog called Robber. This beautiful creature, originally the property of a Riga merchant, had, contrary to the nature of his race, become devotedly attached to me. After I had left Riga, and during my long stay in Mitau, Robber incessantly besieged my empty house, and so touched the hearts of my landlord and the neighbours by his fidelity, that they sent the dog after me by the conductor of the coach to Mitau, where I greeted him with genuine effusion, and swore that, in spite of all difficulties, I would never part with him again. Whatever might happen, the dog must go with us to Paris. And yet, even to get him into the carriage proved almost impossible. All my endeavours to find him a place in or about the vehicle were in vain, and, to my great grief, I had to watch the huge northern beast, with his shaggy coat, gallop all day long in the blazing sun beside the carriage. At last, moved to pity by his exhaustion, and unable to bear the sight any longer, I hit upon a most ingenious plan for bringing the great animal with us into the carriage, where, in spite of its being full to overflowing, he was just able to find room.

On the evening of the second day we reached the Russo-Prussian frontier. Möller's evident anxiety as to whether we should be able to cross it safely showed us plainly that the matter was one of some danger. His good friend from the other side duly turned up with a small carriage, as arranged, and in this conveyance drove Minna, myself, and Robber through by-paths to a certain point, whence he led us on foot to a house of exceedingly suspicious exterior, where, after handing us over to a guide, he left us. There we had to wait until sundown, and had ample leisure in which to realise that we were in a smugglers' drinking den, which gradually became filled to suffocation with Polish Jews of most forbidding aspect.

At last we were summoned to follow our guide. A few hundred feet away, on the slope of a hill, lay the ditch which runs the whole length of the Russian frontier, watched continually and at very narrow intervals by Cossacks. Our chance was to utilise the few moments after the relief of the watch, during which the sentinels were elsewhere engaged. We had, therefore, to run at full speed down the hill, scramble through the ditch, and then hurry along until we were beyond the range of the soldiers' guns; for the Cossacks were bound in case of discovery to fire upon us even on the other side of the ditch. In spite of my almost passionate anxiety for Minna, I had observed with singular pleasure the intelligent behaviour of Robber, who, as though conscious of the danger, silently kept close to our side, and entirely dispelled my fear that he would give trouble during our dangerous passage. At last our trusted helpmeet reappeared, and was so delighted that he hugged us all in his arms. Then, placing us once more in his carriage, he drove us to the inn of the Prussian frontier village, where my friend Möller, positively sick with anxiety, leaped sobbing and rejoicing out of bed to greet us.

It was only now that I began to realise the danger to which I had exposed, not only myself, but also my poor Minna, and the folly of which I had been guilty through my ignorance of the terrible difficulties of secretly crossing the frontier — difficulties concerning which Möller had foolishly allowed me to remain in ignorance.

I was simply at a loss to convey to my poor exhausted wife how extremely I regretted the whole affair.

And yet the difficulties we had just overcome were but the prelude to the calamities incidental to this adventurous journey which had such a decisive influence on my life. The following day, when, with courage renewed, we drove through the rich plain of Tilsit to Arnau, near Königsberg, we decided, as the next stage of our journey, to proceed from the Prussian harbour of Pillau by sailing vessel to London. Our principal reason for this was the consideration of the dog we had with us. It was the easiest way to take him. To convey him by coach from Königsberg to Paris was out of the question, and railways were unknown. But another consideration was our budget; the whole result of my desperate efforts amounted to not quite one hundred ducats, which were to cover not only the journey to Paris, but our expenses there until I should have earned something. Therefore, after a few days' rest in the inn at Arnau, we drove to the little seaport town of Pillau, again accompanied by Möller, in one of the ordinary local conveyances, which was not much better than a wagon. In order to avoid Königsberg, we passed through the smaller villages and over bad roads. Even this short distance was not to be covered without accident. The clumsy conveyance upset in a farmyard, and Minna was so severely indisposed by the accident, owing to an internal shock, that I had to drag her — with the greatest difficulty, as she was quite helpless — to a peasant's house. The people were surly and dirty, and the night we spent there was a painful one for the poor sufferer. A delay of several days occurred before the departure of the Pillau vessel, but this was welcome as a respite to allow of Minna's recovery. Finally, as the captain was to take us without a passport, our going on board was accompanied by exceptional difficulties. We had to contrive to slip past the harbour watch to our vessel in a small boat before daybreak. Once on board, we still had the troublesome task of hauling Robber up the steep side of the vessel without attracting attention, and after that to conceal ourselves at once below deck, in order to escape the notice of officials visiting the ship before its departure. The anchor was weighed, and at last, as the land faded gradually out of sight, we thought we could breathe freely and feel at ease.

We were on board a merchant vessel of the smallest type. She was called the *Thetis;* a bust of the nymph was erected in the bows, and she carried a crew of seven men, including the captain. With good weather, such as was to be expected in summer, the journey to London was estimated to take eight days. However, before we had left the Baltic, we were delayed by a prolonged calm. I made use of the time to improve my knowledge of French by the study of a novel, *La Dernière Aldini,* by George Sand. We also derived some entertainment from associating with the crew. There was an elderly and peculiarly taciturn sailor named Koske, whom we observed carefully because Robber, who was usually so friendly, had taken an irreconcilable dislike to him. Oddly enough, this fact was to add in some degree to our troubles in the hour of danger. After seven days' sailing we were no further than

ON BOARD THE THETIS 199

Copenhagen, where, without leaving the vessel, we seized an opportunity of making our very spare diet on board more bearable by various purchases of food and drink. In good spirits we sailed past the beautiful castle of Elsinore, the sight of which brought me into immediate touch with my youthful impressions of *Hamlet*. We were sailing all unsuspecting through the Cattegat to the Skagerack, when the wind, which had at first been merely unfavourable, and had forced us to a process of weary tacking, changed on the second day to a violent storm. For twenty-four hours we had to struggle against it under disadvantages which were quite new to us. In the captain's painfully narrow cabin, in which one of us was without a proper berth, we were a prey to sea-sickness and endless alarms. Unfortunately, the brandy cask, at which the crew fortified themselves during their strenuous work, was let into a hollow under the seat on which I lay at full length. Now it happened to be Koske who came most frequently in search of the refreshment which was such a nuisance to me, and this in spite of the fact that on each occasion he had to encounter Robber in mortal combat. The dog flew at him with renewed rage each time he came climbing down the narrow steps. I was thus compelled to make efforts which, in my state of complete exhaustion from sea-sickness, rendered my condition every time more critical. At last, on 27th July, the captain was compelled by the violence of the west wind to seek a harbour on the Norwegian coast. And how relieved I was to behold that far-reaching rocky coast, towards which we were being driven at such speed! A Norwegian pilot came to meet us in a small boat, and, with experienced hand, assumed control of the *Thetis*, whereupon in a very short time I was to have one of the most marvellous and most beautiful impressions of my life. What I had taken to be a continuous line of cliffs turned out on our approach to be a series of separate rocks projecting from the sea. Having sailed past them, we perceived that we were surrounded, not only in front and at the sides, but also at our back, by these reefs, which closed in behind us so near together that they seemed to form a single chain of rocks. At the same time the hurricane was so broken by the rocks in our rear that the further we sailed through this ever-changing labyrinth of projecting rocks, the calmer the sea became, until at last the vessel's progress was perfectly smooth and quiet as we entered one of those long sea-roads running through a giant ravine — for such the Norwegian fjords appeared to me.

A feeling of indescribable content came over me when the enormous granite walls echoed the hail of the crew as they cast anchor and furled the sails. The sharp rhythm of this call clung to me like an omen of good cheer, and shaped itself presently into the theme of the seamen's song in my *Fliegender Holländer*. The idea of this opera was, even at that time, ever present in my mind, and it now took on a definite poetic and musical colour under the influence of my recent impressions. Well, our next move was to go on shore. I learned that the little fishing village at which we landed was called Sandwike, and was situated a few miles away from the much larger town of Arendal. We were allowed to put up at the hospitable house of a certain ship's captain, who was then away at sea, and here we were able to take the rest we so much needed, as the unabated violence of the wind in the open detained us there two days. On 31st July the captain insisted on leaving, despite the pilot's warning. We had been on board the *Thetis* a few hours, and were in the act of eating a lobster for the first time in our lives, when the captain and the sailors began to swear violently at the pilot, whom I could see at the helm, rigid with fear, striving to avoid a reef — barely visible above the water — towards which our ship was being driven. Great was our terror at this violent tumult, for we naturally thought ourselves in the most extreme danger. The vessel did actually receive a severe shock, which, to my vivid imagination, seemed like the splitting up of the whole ship. Fortunately, however, it transpired that only the side of our vessel had fouled the reef, and there was no immediate danger. Nevertheless, the captain deemed it necessary to steer for a harbour to have the vessel examined, and we returned to the coast and anchored at another point. The captain then offered to take us in a small boat with two sailors to Tromsond, a town of some importance situated at a few hours' distance, where he had to invite the harbour officials to examine his ship. This again proved a most attractive and impressive excursion. The view of one fjord in particular, which extended far inland, worked on my imagination like some unknown, awe-inspiring desert. This impression was intensified, during a long walk from Tromsond up to the plateau, by the terribly depressing effect of the dun moors, bare of tree or shrub, boasting only a covering of scanty moss, which stretch away to the horizon, and merge imperceptibly into the gloomy sky. It was long after dark when we returned from this trip in our little boat, and my wife was very anxious. The next morning (1st August), reassured as to the condition of the vessel, and the wind favouring us, we were able to go to sea without further hindrance.

After four days' calm sailing a strong north wind arose, which drove us at uncommon speed in the right direction. We began to think ourselves nearly at the end of our journey when, on 6th August, the wind changed, and the storm began to rage with unheard-of violence. On the 7th, a Wednesday, at half-past two in the afternoon, we thought ourselves in imminent danger of death. It was not the terrible force with which the vessel was hurled up and down, entirely at the mercy of this sea monster, which appeared now as a fathomless abyss, now as a steep mountain peak, that filled me with mortal dread; my premonition of some terrible crisis was aroused by the despondency of the crew, whose malignant glances seemed superstitiously to point to us as the cause of the threatening disaster. Ignorant of the trifling occasion for the secrecy of our journey, the thought may have occurred to them that our need of escape had arisen from suspicious or even criminal circumstances. The captain himself seemed, in his extreme distress, to regret having taken us on board; for we had evidently brought him ill-luck on this familiar passage — usually a rapid and uncomplicated one, especially in summer. At this particular moment there raged, beside the tempest on the water, a furious thunderstorm overhead, and Minna expressed the fervent wish to be struck by lightning with me rather than to sink, living, into the fearful flood. She even begged me to bind her to me, so that we might not be parted as we sank. Yet another night was spent amid these incessant terrors, which only our extreme exhaustion helped to mitigate.

The following day the storm had subsided; the wind remained unfavourable, but was mild. The captain now tried to find our bearings by means of his astronomical instruments. He complained of the sky, which had been overcast so many days, swore that he would give much for a single glimpse of the sun or the stars, and did not conceal the uneasiness he felt at not being able to indicate our whereabouts with certainty. He consoled himself, however, by following a ship which was sailing some knots ahead in the same direction, and whose movements he observed closely through the telescope. Suddenly he sprang up in great alarm, and gave a vehement order to change our course. He had seen the ship in front go aground on a sand-bank, from which, he asserted, she could not extricate herself; for he now realised that we were near the most dangerous part of the belt of sand-banks bordering the Dutch coast for a considerable distance. By dint of very skilful sailing, we were enabled to keep the opposite course towards the English coast, which we in fact sighted on the evening of 9th August, in the neighbourhood of Southwold. I felt new life come into me when I saw in the far distance the English pilots racing for our ship. As competition is free among pilots on the English coast, they come out as far as possible to meet incoming vessels, even when the risks are very great.

The winner in our case was a powerful grey-haired man, who, after much vain battling with the seething waves, which tossed his light boat away from our ship at each attempt, at last succeeded in boarding the *Thetis*. (Our poor, hardly-used boat still bore the name, although the wooden figure-head of our patron nymph had been hurled into the sea during our first storm in the Cattegat — an ill-omened incident in the eyes of the crew.) We were filled with pious gratitude when this quiet English sailor, whose hands were torn and bleeding from his repeated efforts to catch the rope thrown to him on his approach, took over the rudder. His whole personality impressed us most agreeably, and he seemed to us the absolute guarantee of a speedy deliverance from our terrible afflictions. We rejoiced too soon, however, for we still had before us the perilous passage through the sand-banks off the English coast, where, as I was assured, nearly four hundred ships are wrecked on an

ARRIVAL IN LONDON

average every year. We were fully twenty-four hours (from the evening of the 10th to the 11th of August) amid these sandbanks, fighting a westerly gale, which hindered our progress so seriously that we only reached the mouth of the Thames on the evening of the 12th of August. My wife had, up to that point, been so nervously affected by the innumerable danger signals, consisting chiefly of small guardships painted bright red and provided with bells on account of the fog, that she could not close her eyes, day or night, for the excitement of watching for them and pointing them out to the sailors. I, on the contrary, found these heralds of human proximity and deliverance so consoling that, despite Minna's reproaches, I indulged in a long refreshing sleep. Now that we were anchored in the mouth of the Thames, waiting for daybreak, I found myself in the best of spirits; I dressed, washed, and even shaved myself up on deck near the mast, while Minna and the whole exhausted crew were wrapped in deep slumber. And with deepening interest I watched the growing signs of life in this famous estuary. Our desire for a complete release from our detested confinement led us, after we had sailed a little way up, to hasten our arrival in London by going on board a passing steamer at Gravesend. As we neared the capital, our astonishment steadily increased at the number of ships of all sorts that filled the river, the houses, the streets, the famous docks, and other maritime constructions which lined the banks. When at last we reached London Bridge, this incredibly crowded centre of the greatest city in the world, and set foot on land after our terrible three weeks' voyage, a pleasurable sensation of giddiness overcame us as our legs carried us staggering through the deafening uproar. Robber seemed to be similarly affected, for he whisked round the corners like a mad thing, and threatened to get lost every other minute. But we soon sought safety in a cab, which took us, on our captain's recommendation, to the Horseshoe Tavern, near the Tower, and here we had to make our plans for the conquest of this giant metropolis.

The neighbourhood in which we found ourselves was such that we decided to leave it with all possible haste. A very friendly little hunchbacked Jew from Hamburg suggested better quarters in the West End, and I remember vividly our drive there, in one of the tiny narrow cabs then in use, the journey lasting fully an hour. They were built to carry two people, who had to sit facing each other, and we therefore had to lay our big dog crosswise from window to window. The sights we saw from our whimsical nook surpassed anything we had imagined, and we arrived at our boarding-house in Old Compton Street agreeably stimulated by the life and the overwhelming size of the great city. Although at the age of twelve I had made what I supposed to be a translation of a monologue from Shakespeare's *Romeo and Juliet*, I found my knowledge of English quite inadequate when it came to conversing with the landlady of the King's Arms. But the good dame's social condition as a sea-captain's widow led her to think she could talk French to me, and her attempts made me wonder which of us knew least of that language. And then a most disturbing incident occurred — we missed Robber, who must have run away at the door instead of following us into the house. Our distress at having lost our good dog after having brought him all the way there with such difficulty occupied us exclusively during the first two hours we spent in this new home on land. We kept constant watch at the window until, of a sudden, we joyfully recognised Robber strolling unconcernedly towards the house from a side street. Afterwards we learned that our truant had wandered as far as Oxford Street in search of adventures, and I have always considered his amazing return to a house which he had not even entered as a strong proof of the absolute certainty of the animal's instincts in the matter of memory.

We now had time to realise the tiresome after-effects of the voyage. The continuous swaying of the floor and our clumsy efforts to keep from falling we found fairly entertaining; but when we came to take our well-earned rest in the huge English double bed, and found that that too rocked up and down, it became quite unbearable. Every time we closed our eyes we sank into frightful abysses, and, springing up again, cried out for help. It seemed as if that terrible voyage would go on to the end of our lives. Added to this we felt miserably sick; for, after the atrocious food on board, we had been only too ready to partake, with less discretion than relish, of tastier fare.

We were so exhausted by all these trials that we forgot to consider what was, after all, the vital question — the probable result in hard cash. Indeed, the marvels of the great city proved so fascinating, that we started off in a cab, for all the world as if we were on a pleasure trip, to follow up a plan I had sketched on my map of London. In our wonder and delight at what we saw, we quite forgot all we had gone through. Costly as it proved, I considered our week's stay justified in view of Minna's need of rest in the first place, and secondly, the excellent opportunity it afforded me of making acquaintances in the musical world. During my last visit to Dresden I had sent *Rule Britannia*, the overture composed at Königsberg, to Sir John Smart, president of the Philharmonic Society. It is true he had never acknowledged it, but I felt it the more incumbent on me to bring him to task about it. I therefore spent some days trying to find out where he lived, wondering meanwhile in which language I should have to make myself understood, but as the result of my inquiries I discovered that Smart was not in London at all. I next persuaded myself that it would be a good thing to look up Bulwer Lytton, and to come to an understanding about the operatic performance of his novel, *Rienzi*, which I had dramatised. Having been told, on the continent, that Bulwer was a member of Parliament, I went to the House, after a few days, to inquire on the spot. My total ignorance of the English language stood me in good stead here, and I was treated with unexpected consideration; for, as none of the lower officials in that vast building could make out what I wanted, I was sent, step by step, to one high dignitary after the other, until at last I was introduced to a distinguished-looking man, who came out of a large hall as we passed, as an entirely unintelligible individual. (Minna was with me all the time; only Robber had been left behind at the King's Arms.) He asked me very civilly what I wanted, in French, and seemed favourably impressed when I inquired for the celebrated author. He was obliged to tell me, however, that he was not in London. I went on to ask whether I could not be admitted to a debate, but was told that, in consequence of the old Houses of Parliament having been burnt down, they were using temporary premises where the space was so limited that only a few favoured visitors could procure cards of admittance. But on my pressing more urgently he relented, and shortly after opened a door leading direct into the strangers' seats in the House of Lords. It seemed reasonable to conclude from this that our friend was a lord in person. I was immensely interested to see and hear the Premier, Lord Melbourne, and Brougham (who seemed to me to take a very active part in the proceedings, prompting Melbourne several times, as I thought), and the Duke of Wellington, who looked so comfortable in his grey beaver hat, with his hands diving deep into his trousers pockets, and who made his speech in so conversational a tone that I lost my feeling of excessive awe. He had a curious way, too, of accenting his points of special emphasis by shaking his whole body. I was also much interested in Lord Lyndhurst, Brougham's particular enemy, and was amazed to see Brougham go across several times to sit down coolly beside him, apparently with a view to prompting even his opponent. The matter in hand was, as I learned afterwards from the papers, the discussion of measures to be taken against the Portuguese Government to ensure the passing of the Anti-Slavery Bill. The Bishop of London, who was one of the speakers on this occasion, was the only one of these gentlemen whose voice and manner seemed to me stiff or unnatural, but possibly I was prejudiced by my dislike of parsons generally.

After this pleasing adventure I imagined I had exhausted the attractions of London for the present, for although I could not gain admittance to the Lower House, my untiring friend, whom I came across again as I went out, showed me the room where the Commons sat, explained as much as was necessary, and gave me a sight of the Speaker's woolsack, and of his mace lying hidden under the table. He also gave me such careful details of various things that I felt I knew all there was to know about the capital of Great Britain. I had not the smallest intention of going to the Italian opera, possibly because I imagined the prices to be too ruinous. We thoroughly explored all the principal streets, often tiring ourselves out; we shuddered through a ghastly London Sunday, and wound up with a train trip (our very first) to Gravesend Park, in the company of the captain of the *Thetis*. On the 20th of August we crossed over to France by steamer, arriving the same evening at Boulogne-sur-mer, where we took leave of the sea with the fervent desire never to go on it again.

We were both of us secretly convinced that we should meet with disappointments in Paris, and it was partly on that account that we decided to spend a few weeks at or near Boulogne. It was, in any case, too early in the season to find the various important people whom I proposed to see, in town; on the other hand, it seemed to me a most fortunate circumstance that Meyerbeer should happen to be at Boulogne. Also, I had the instrumentation of part of the second act of *Rienzi* to finish, and was bent on having at least half of the work ready to show on my arrival in the costly French capital. We therefore set out to find less expensive accommodation in the country round Boulogne. Beginning with the immediate neighbourhood, our search ended in our taking two practically unfurnished rooms in the detached house of a rural wine merchant's, situated on the main road to Paris at half an hour's distance from Boulogne. We next provided scanty but adequate furniture, and in bringing our wits to bear upon this matter Minna particularly distinguished herself. Besides a bed and two chairs, we dug up a table, which, after I had cleared away my *Rienzi* papers, served for our meals, which we had to prepare at our own fireside.

While we were here I made my first call on Meyerbeer. I had often read in the papers of his proverbial amiability, and bore him no ill-will for not replying to my letter. My favourable opinion was soon to be confirmed, however, by his kind reception of me. The impression he made was good in every respect, particularly as regards his appearance. The years had not yet given his features the flabby look which sooner or later mars most Jewish faces, and the fine formation of his brow round about the eyes gave him an expression of countenance that inspired confidence. He did not seem in the least inclined to depreciate my intention of trying my luck in Paris as a composer of opera; he allowed me to read him my libretto for *Rienzi*, and really listened up to the end of the third act. He kept the two acts that were complete, saying that he wished to look them over, and assured me, when I again called on him, of his whole-hearted interest in my work. Be this as it may, it annoyed me somewhat that he should again and again fall back on praising my minute handwriting, an accomplishment he considered especially Saxonian. He promised to give me letters of recommendation to Duponchel, the manager of the Opera House, and to Habeneck, the conductor. I now felt that I had good cause to extol my good fortune which, after many vicissitudes, had sent me precisely to this particular spot in France. What better fortune could have befallen me than to secure, in so short a time, the sympathetic interest of the most famous composer of French opera! Meyerbeer took me to see Moscheles, who was then in Boulogne, and also Fräulein Blahedka, a celebrated virtuoso whose name I had known for many years. I spent a few informal musical evenings at both houses, and thus came into close touch with musical celebrities, an experience quite new to me.

I had written to my future brother-in-law, Avernarius, in Paris, to ask him to find us suitable accommodations, and we started on our journey thither on 16th September in the diligence, my efforts to hoist Robber on to the top being attended by the usual difficulties.

My first impression of Paris proved disappointing in view of the great expectations I had cherished of that city; after London it seemed to me narrow and confined. I had imagined the famous boulevards to be much vaster, for instance, and was really annoyed, when the huge coach put us down in the Rue de la Juissienne, to think that I should first set foot on Parisian soil in such a wretched little alley. Neither did the Rue Richelieu, where my brother-in-law had his book-shop, seem imposing after the streets in the west end of London. As for the *chambre garnie,* which had been engaged for me in the Rue de la Tonnellerie, one of the narrow side-streets which link the Rue St. Honoré with the Marché des Innocents, I felt positively degraded at having to take up my abode there. I needed all the consolation that could be derived from an inscription, placed under a bust of Molière, which read: *maison où naquit Molière*, to raise my courage after the mean impression the house had first made upon me. The room, which had been prepared for us on the fourth floor, was small but cheerful, decently furnished, and inexpensive. From the windows we could see the frightful bustle in the market below, which became more and more alarming as we watched it, and I wondered what we were doing in such a quarter.

Shortly after this, Avenarius had to go to Leipzig to bring home his bride, my youngest sister Cecilia, after the wedding in that city. Before leaving, he gave me an introduction to his only musical acquaintance, a German holding an appointment in the music department of the *Bibliothèque Royale*, named E. G. Anders, who lost no time in looking us up in Molière's house. He was, as I soon discovered, a man of very unusual character, and, little as he was able to help me, he left an affecting and ineffaceable impression on my memory. He was a bachelor in the fifties, whose reverses had driven him to the sad necessity of earning a living in Paris entirely without assistance. He had fallen back on the extraordinary bibliographical knowledge which, especially in reference to music, it had been his hobby to acquire in the days of his prosperity. His real name he never told me, wishing to guard the secret of that, as of his misfortunes, until after his death. For the time being he told me only that he was known as Anders, was of noble descent, and had held property on the Rhine, but that he had lost everything owing to the villainous betrayal of his gullibility and good-nature. The only thing he had managed to save was his very considerable library, the size of which I was able to estimate for myself. It filled every wall of his small dwelling. Even here in Paris he soon complained of bitter enemies; for, in spite of having come furnished with an introduction to influential people, he still held the inferior position of an employee in the library. In spite of his long service there and his great learning, he had to see really ignorant men promoted over his head. I discovered afterwards that the real reason lay in his unbusinesslike methods, and the effeminacy consequent on the delicate way in which he had been nutured in early life, which made him incapable of developing the energy necessary for his work. On a miserable pittance of fifteen hundred francs a year, he led a weary existence, full of anxiety. With nothing in view but a lonely old age, and the probability of dying in a hospital, it seemed as if our society put new life into him; for though we were poverty-stricken, we looked forward boldly and hopefully to the future. My vivacity and invincible energy filled him with hopes of my success, and from this time forward he took a most tender and unselfish part in furthering my interests. Although he was a contributor to the *Gazette Musicale*, edited by Moritz Schlesinger, he had never succeeded in making his influence felt there in the slightest degree. He had none of the versatility of a journalist, and the editors entrusted him with little besides the preparation of bibliographical notes. Oddly enough, it was with this unworldly and least resourceful of men that I had to discuss my plan for the conquest of Paris, that is, of musical Paris, which is made up of all the most questionable characters imaginable. The result was practically always the same; we merely encouraged each other in the hope that some unforeseen stroke of luck would help my cause.

To assist us in these discussions Anders called in his friend and housemate Lehrs, a philologist, my acquaintance with whom was soon to develop into one of the most beautiful friendships of my life. Lehrs was the younger brother of a famous scholar at Königsberg. He had left there to come to Paris some years before, with the object of gaining an independent position by his philological work. This he preferred, in spite of the attendant difficulties, to a post as teacher with a salary which only in Germany could be considered sufficient for a scholar's wants. He soon obtained work from Didot, the bookseller, as assistant editor of a large edition of Greek classics, but the editor traded on his poverty, and was much more concerned about the success of his enterprise than about the condition of his poor collaborator. Lehrs had therefore perpetually to struggle against poverty, but he preserved an even temper, and showed himself in every way a model of disinterestedness and self-sacrifice. At first he looked upon me only as a man in need of advice, and incidentally a fellow-sufferer in Paris; for he had no knowledge of music, and had no particular interest in it. We soon became so intimate that I had him dropping in nearly every evening with Anders, Lehrs being extremely useful to his friend, whose unsteadiness in walking obliged him to use an umbrella and a walking-stick as crutches. He was also nervous in crossing crowded thoroughfares, and particularly so at night; while he always liked to make Lehrs cross my threshold in front of him to distract the attention of Robber, of whom he stood in obvious terror. Our usually good-natured dog became positively suspicious of this visitor, and soon adopted towards him the same aggressive attitude which he had shown to the sailor Koske on board the *Thetis*. The two men lived at an *hôtel garni* in Rue de Seine. They complained greatly of their landlady, who appropriated so much of their income that they were entirely in her power. Anders had for years been trying to assert his independence by leaving her, without being able to carry out his plan. We soon threw off mutually every shred of disguise as to the present state of our finances, so that, although the two households were actually separated, our common troubles gave us all the intimacy of one united family.

The various ways by which I might obtain recognition in Paris formed the chief topic of our discussions at that time. Our hopes were at first centred on Meyerbeer's promised letters of introduction. Duponchel, the director of the Opera, did actually see me at his office, where, fixing a monocle in his right eye, he read through Meyerbeer's letter without betraying the least emotion, having no doubt opened similar communications from the composer many times before. I went away, and never heard another word from him. The elderly conductor, Habeneck, on the other hand, took an interest in my work that was not merely polite, and acceded to my request to have something of mine played at one of the orchestral practises at the Conservatoire as soon as he should have leisure. I had, unfortunately, no short instrumental piece that seemed suitable except my queer *Columbus* Overture, which I considered the most effective of all that had emanated from my pen. It had been received with great applause on the occasion of its performance in the theatre at Magdeburg, with the assistance of the valiant trumpeters from the Prussian garrison. I gave

Habeneck the score and parts, and was able to report to our committee at home that I had now one enterprise on foot.

I gave up the attempt to try and see Scribe on the mere ground of our having had some correspondence, for my friends had made it clear to me, in the light of their own experience, that it was out of the question to expect this exceptionally busy author to occupy himself seriously with a young and unknown musician. Anders was able to introduce me to another acquaintance, however, a certain M. Dumersan. This grey-haired gentleman had written some hundred vaudeville pieces, and would have been glad to see one of them performed as an opera on a larger scale before his death. He had no idea of standing on his dignity as an author, and was quite willing to undertake the translation of an existing libretto into French verse. We therefore entrusted him with the writing of my *Liebesverbot,* with a view to a performance at the Théâtre de la Renaissance, as it was then called. (It was the third existing theatre for lyric drama, the performances being given in the new Salle Ventadour, which had been rebuilt after its destruction by fire.) On the understanding that it was to be a literal translation, he at once turned the three numbers of my opera, for which I hoped to secure a hearing, into neat French verse. Besides this, he asked me to compose a chorus for a vaudeville entitled *La Descente de la Courtille,* which was to be played at the Variétés during the carnival.

This was a second opening. My friends now strongly advised me to write something small in the way of songs, which I could offer to popular singers for concert purposes. Both Lehrs and Anders produced words for these. Anders brought a very innocent *Dors, mon enfant,* written by a young poet of his acquaintance; this was the first thing I composed to a French text. It was so successful that, when I had tried it over softly several times on the piano, my wife, who was in bed, called out to me that it was heavenly for sending one to sleep. I also set *L'Attente* from Hugo's *Orientales,* and Ronsard's song, *Mignonne,* to music. I have no reason to be ashamed of these small pieces, which I published subsequently as a musical supplement to *Europa* (Lewald's publication) in 1841.

I next stumbled on the idea of writing a grand bass aria with a chorus, for Lablache to introduce into his part of Orovist in Bellini's *Norma*. Lehrs had to hunt up an Italian political refugee to get the text out of him. This was done, and I produced an effective composition *à la* Bellini (which still exists among my manuscripts), and went off at once to offer it to Lablache.

The friendly Moor, who received me in the great singer's anteroom, insisted upon admitting me straight into his master's presence without announcing me. As I had anticipated some difficulty in getting near such a celebrity, I had written my request, as I thought this would be simpler than explaining verbally.

The black servant's pleasant manner made me feel very uncomfortable; I entrusted my score and letter to him to give to Lablache, without taking any notice of his kindly astonishment at my refusal of his repeated invitation to go into his master's room and have an interview, and I left the house hurriedly, intending to call for my answer in a few days. When I came back Lablache received me most kindly, and assured me that my aria was excellent, though it was impossible to introduce it into Bellini's opera after the latter had already been performed so very often. My relapse into the domain of Bellini's style, of which I had been guilty through the writing of this aria, was therefore useless to me, and I soon became convinced of the fruitlessness of my efforts in that direction. I saw that I should need personal introductions to various singers in order to ensure the production of one of my other compositions.

When Meyerbeer at last arrived in Paris, therefore, I was delighted. He was not in the least astonished at the lack of success of his letters of introduction; on the contrary, he made use of this opportunity to impress upon me how difficult it was to get on in Paris, and how necessary it was for me to look out for less pretentious work. With this object he introduced me to Maurice Schlesinger, and leaving me at the mercy of that monstrous person, went back to Germany.

At first Schlesinger did not know what to do with me; the acquaintances I made through him (of whom the chief was the violinist Panofka) led to nothing, and I therefore returned to my advisory board at home, through whose influence I had recently received an order to compose the music to the *Two Grenadiers*, by Heine, translated by a Parisian professor. I wrote this song for baritone, and was very pleased with the result; on Ander's advice I now tried to find singers for my new compositions. Mme. Pauline Viardot, on whom I first called, went through my songs with me. She was very amiable, and praised them, but did not see why *she* should sing them. I went through the same experience with a Mme. Widmann, a grand contralto, who sang my *Dors, mon enfant* with great feeling; all the same she had no further use for my composition. A certain M. Dupont, third tenor at the grand opera, tried my setting of the Ronsard poem, but declared that the language in which it was written was no longer palatable to the Paris public. M. Geraldy, a favourite concert singer and teacher, who allowed me to call and see him frequently, told me that the *Two Grenadiers* was impossible, for the simple reason that the accompaniment at the end of the song, which I had modelled upon the *Marseillaise*, could only be sung in the streets of Paris to the accompaniment of cannons and gunshots. Habeneck was the only person who fulfilled his promise to conduct my *Columbus* Overture at one of the rehearsals for the benefit of Anders and myself. As, however, there was no question of producing this work even at one of the celebrated Conservatoire concerts, I saw clearly that the old gentleman was only moved by kindness and a desire to encourage me. It could not lead to anything further, and I myself was convinced that this extremely superficial work of my young days could only give the orchestra a wrong impression of my talents. However, these rehearsals, to my surprise, made such an unexpected impression on me in other ways that they exercised a decisive influence in the crisis of my artistic development. This was due to the fact that I listened repeatedly to Beethoven's Ninth Symphony, which, by dint of untiring practice, received such a marvellous interpretation at the hands of this celebrated orchestra, that the picture I had had of it in my mind in the enthusiastic days of my youth now stood before me almost tangibly in brilliant colours, undimmed, as though it had never been effaced by the Leipzig orchestra who had slaughtered it under Pohlenz's baton. Where formerly I had only seen mystic constellations and weird shapes without meaning, I now found, flowing from innumerable sources, a stream of the most touching and heavenly melodies which delighted my heart.

The whole of that period of the deterioration of my musical tastes which dated, practically speaking, from those selfsame confusing ideas about Beethoven, and which had grown so much worse through my acquaintance with that dreadful theatre — all these wrong views now sank down as if into an abyss of shame and remorse.

This inner change had been gradually prepared by many painful experiences during the last few years. I owed the recovery of my old vigour and spirits to the deep impression the rendering of the Ninth Symphony had made on me when performed in a way I had never dreamed of. This important event in my life can only be compared to the upheaval caused within me when, as a youth of sixteen, I saw Schröder-Devrient act in *Fidelio*.

The direct result of this was my intense longing to compose something that would give me a similar feeling of satisfaction, and this desire grew in proportion to my anxiety about my unfortunate position in Paris, which made me almost despair of success.

In this mood I sketched an overture to *Faust* which, according to my original scheme, was only to form the first part of a whole *Faust* Symphony, as I had already got the 'Gretchen' idea in my head for the second movement. This is the same composition that I rewrote in several parts fifteen years later; I had forgotten all about it, and I owed its reconstruction to the advice of Liszt, who gave me many valuable hints. This composition has been performed many times under the title of *eine Faust-ouvertüre,* and has met with great appreciation. At the time of which I am speaking, I hoped that the Conservatoire orchestra would have been willing to give the work a hearing, but I was told they thought they had done enough for me, and hoped to be rid of me for some time.

Having failed everywhere, I now turned to Meyerbeer for more introductions, especially to singers. I was very much surprised when, in consequence of my request, Meyerbeer introduced me to a certain M. Gouin, a post-office official, and Meyerbeer's sole agent in Paris, whom he instructed to do his utmost for me. Meyerbeer specially wished me to know M. Anténor Joly, director of the Théâtre de la Renaissance, the musical theatre already mentioned. M. Gouin, with almost suspicious levity, promised me to produce my opera *Liebesverbot,* which now only required translation. There was a question of having a few numbers of my opera sung to the committee of the theatre at a special audience. When I suggested that some of the singers of this very theatre should undertake to sing three of the numbers which had been already translated by Dumersan, I was refused on the plea that all these artists were far too busy. But Gouin saw a way out of the difficulty; on the authority of *Maître* Meyerbeer, he won over to our cause several singers who were under an obligation to Meyerbeer: Mme. Dorus-Gras, a real primadonna of the Grand Opera, Mme. Widmann and M. Dupont (the two last-named had previously refused to help me) now promised to sing for me at this audience.

This much, then, did I achieve in six months. It was now nearly Easter of the year 1840. Encouraged by Gouin's negotiations, which seemed to spell hope, I made up my mind to move from the obscure Quartier des Innocents to a part of Paris nearer to the musical centre; and in this I was encouraged by Lehrs' foolhardy advice.

What this change meant to me, my readers will learn when they hear under what circumstances we had dragged on our existence during our stay in Paris.

Although we were living in the cheapest possible way, dining at a very small restaurant for a franc a head, it was impossible to prevent the rest of our money from melting away. Our friend Möller had given us to understand that we could ask him if we were in need, as he would put aside for us the first money that came in from any successful business transaction. There was no alternative but to apply to him for money; in the meantime we pawned all the trinkets we possessed that were of any value. As I was too shy to make inquiries about a pawnshop, I looked up the French equivalent in the dictionary in order to be able to recognise such a place when I saw it. In my little pocket dictionary I could not find any other word than 'Lombard.' On looking at a map of Paris I found, situated in the middle of an inextricable maze of streets, a very small lane called Rue des Lombards. Thither I wended my way, but my expedition was fruitless. Often, on reading by the light of the transparent lanterns the inscription 'Mont de Piété,' I became very curious to know its meaning, and on consulting my advisory board at home about this 'Mount of Piety,'[1] I was told, to my great delight, that it was precisely there that I should find salvation. To this 'Mont de Piété' we now carried all we possessed in the way of silver, namely, our wedding presents. After that followed my wife's trinkets and the rest of her former theatrical wardrobe, amongst which was a beautiful silver-embroidered blue dress with a court train, once the property of the Duchess of Dessau. Still we heard nothing from our friend Möller, and we were obliged to wait on from day to day for the sorely needed help from Königsberg, and at last, one dark day, we pledged our wedding rings. When all hope of assistance seemed vain, I heard that the pawn-tickets themselves were of some value, as they could be sold to buyers, who thereby acquired the right to redeem the pawned articles. I had to resort even to this, and thus the blue court-dress, for instance, was lost for ever. Möller never wrote again. When later on he called on me at the time of my conductorship in Dresden, he admitted that he had been embittered against me owing to humiliating and derogatory remarks we were said to have made about him after we parted, and had resolved not to have anything further to do with us. We were certain of our innocence in the matter, and very grieved at having, through pure slander, lost the chance of such assistance in our great need.

At the beginning of our pecuniary difficulties we sustained a loss which we looked upon as providential, in spite of the grief it caused us. This was our beautiful dog, which we had managed to bring across to Paris with endless difficulty. As he was a very valuable animal, and attracted much attention,

[1] This is the correct translation of the words *Berg der Frömmigkeit* used in the original. — EDITOR.

he had probably been stolen. In spite of the terrible state of the traffic in Paris, he had always found his way home in the same clever manner in which he had mastered the difficulties of the London streets. Quite at the beginning of our stay in Paris he had often gone off by himself to the gardens of the Palais Royal, where he used to meet many of his friends, and had returned safe and sound after a brilliant exhibition of swimming and retrieving before an audience of gutter children. At the Quai du Pont-neuf he generally begged us to let him bathe; there he used to draw a large crowd of spectators round him, who were so loud in their enthusiasm about the way in which he dived for and brought to land various objects of clothing, tools, etc., that the police begged us to put an end to the obstruction. One morning I let him out for a little run as usual; he never returned, and in spite of our most strenuous efforts to recover him, no trace of him was to be found. This loss seemed to many of our friends a piece of luck, for they could not understand how it was possible for us to feed such a huge animal when we ourselves had not enough to eat. About this time, the second month of our stay in Paris, my sister Louisa came over from Leipzig to join her husband, Friedrich Brockhaus, in Paris, where he had been waiting for her for some time. They intended to go to Italy together, and Louisa made use of this opportunity to buy all kinds of expensive things in Paris. I did not expect them to feel any pity for us on account of our foolish removal to Paris, and its attendant miseries, or that they should consider themselves bound to help us in any way; but although we did not try to conceal our position, we derived no benefit from the visit of our rich relations. Minna was even kind enough to help my sister with her luxurious shopping, and we were very anxious not to make them think we wanted to rouse their pity. In return my sister introduced me to an extraordinary friend of hers, who was destined to take a great interest in me. This was the young painter, Ernst Kietz, from Dresden; he was an exceptionally kind-hearted and unaffected young man, whose talent for portrait painting (in a sort of coloured pastel style) had made him such a favourite in his own town, that he had been induced by his financial successes to come to Paris for a time to finish his art studies. He had now been working in Delaroche's studio for about a year. He had a curious and almost childlike disposition, and his lack of all serious education, combined with a certain weakness of character, had made him choose a career in which he was destined, in spite of all his talent, to fail hopelessly. I had every opportunity of recognising this, as I saw a great deal of him. At the time, however, the simple-hearted devotion and kindness of this young man were very welcome both to myself and my wife, who often felt lonely, and his friendship was a real source of help in our darkest hours of adversity. He became almost a member of the family, and joined our home circle every night, providing a strange contrast to nervous old Anders and the grave-faced Lehrs. His good-nature and his quaint remarks soon made him indispensable to us; he amused us tremendously with his French, into which he would launch with the greatest confidence, although he could not put together two consecutive sentences properly, in spite of having lived in Paris for twenty years. With Delaroche he studied oil-painting, and had obviously considerable talent in this direction, although it was the very rock on which he stranded. The mixing of the colours on his palette, and especially the cleaning of his brushes, took up so much of his time that he rarely came to the actual painting. As the days were very short in midwinter, he never had time to do any work after he had finished washing his palette and brushes, and, as far as I can remember, he never completed a single portrait. Strangers to whom he had been introduced, and who had given him orders to paint their portraits, were obliged to leave Paris without seeing them even half done, and at last he even complained because some of his sitters died before their portraits were completed. His landlord, to whom he was always in debt for rent, was the only creature who succeeded in getting a portrait of his ugly person from the painter, and, as far as I know, this is the only finished portrait in existence by Kietz. On the other hand, he was very clever at making little sketches of any subject suggested by our conversation during the evening, and in these he displayed both originality and delicacy of execution. During the winter of that year he completed a good pencil portrait of me, which he touched up two years afterwards when he knew me more intimately, finishing it off as it now stands. It pleased him to sketch me in the attitude I often assumed during our evening chats when I was in a cheerful mood. No evening ever passed during which I did not succeed in shaking off the depression caused by my vain endeavours, and by the many worries I had gone through during the day, and in regaining my natural cheerfulness, and Kietz was anxious to represent me to the world as a man who, in spite of the hard times he had to face, had confidence in his success, and rose smiling above the troubles of life. Before the end of the year 1839, my youngest sister Cecilia also arrived in Paris with her husband, Edward Avenarius. It was only natural that she should feel embarrassed at the idea of meeting us in Paris in our extremely straitened circumstances, especially as her husband was not very well off. Consequently, instead of calling on them frequently, we preferred waiting until they came to see us, which, by the way, took them a long time. On the other hand, the renewal of our acquaintance with Heinrich Laube, who came over to Paris at the beginning of 1840 with his young wife, Iduna (*née* Budäus), was very cheering. She was the widow of a wealthy Leipzig doctor, and Laube had married her under very extraordinary circumstances, since we last saw him in Berlin; they intended to enjoy themselves for a few months in Paris. During the long period of his detention, while awaiting his trial, this young lady had been so touched by his misfortunes that without knowing much of him, she had shown great sympathy and interest in his case. Laube's sentence was pronounced soon after I left Berlin; it was unexpectedly light, consisting of only one year's imprisonment in the town gaol. He was allowed to undergo this term in the prison at Muskau in Silesia, where he had the advantage of being near his friend, Prince Pückler, who in his official capacity, and on account of his influence with the governor of the prison, was permitted to afford the prisoner even the consolation of personal intercourse.

The young widow resolved to marry him at the beginning of his term of imprisonment, so that she might be near him at Muskau with her loving assistance. To see my old friend under such favourable conditions was in itself a pleasure to me; I also experienced the liveliest satisfaction at finding there was no change in his former sympathetic attitude. We met frequently; our wives also became friends, and Laube was the first to approve in his kindly humorous way of our folly in moving to Paris.

In his house I made the acquaintance of Heinrich Heine, and both of them joked good-humouredly over my extraordinary position, making even me laugh. Laube felt himself compelled to talk seriously to me about my expectations of succeeding in Paris, as he saw that I treated my situation, based on such trivial hopes, with a humour that charmed him even against his better judgment. He tried to think how he could help me without prejudicing my future. With this object he wanted me to make a more or less plausible sketch of my future plans, so that on his approaching visit to our native land he might procure some help for me. I happened just at that time to have come to an exceedingly promising understanding with the management of the Théâtre de la Renaissance. I thus seemed to have obtained a footing, and I thought it safe to assert, that if I were guaranteed the means of livelihood for six months, I could not fail within that period to accomplish something. Laube promised to make this provision, and kept his word. He induced one of his wealthy friends in Leipzig, and, following this example, my well-to-do relations, to provide me for six months with the necessary resources, to be paid in monthly instalments through Avenarius.

We therefore decided, as I have said, to leave our furnished apartments and take a flat for ourselves in the Rue du Helder. My prudent, careful wife had suffered greatly on account of the careless and uncertain manner in which I had hitherto controlled our meagre resources, and in now undertaking the responsibility, she explained that she understood how to keep house more cheaply than we could do by living in furnished rooms and restaurants. Success justified the step; the serious part of the question lay in the fact that we had to start housekeeping without any furniture of our own, and everything necessary for domestic purposes had to be procured, though we had not the wherewithal to get it. In this matter Lehrs, who was well versed in the peculiarities of Parisian life, was able to advise us. In his opinion the only compensation for the experiences we had undergone hitherto would be a success equivalent to my daring. As I did not possess the resources to allow of long years of patient waiting for success in Paris, I must either count on extraordinary luck or renounce all my hopes forthwith. The longed-for success must come within a year, or I should be ruined. Therefore I must dare all, as befitted my name, for in my case he was not inclined to derive 'Wagner'[1] from *Fuhrwerk*. I was to pay my rent, twelve hundred francs, in quarterly instalments; for the furniture and fittings, he recommended me, through his landlady, to a carpenter who provided everything that was necessary for what seemed to be a reasonable sum, also to be paid by instalments, all of which appeared very simple. Lehrs maintained that I should do no good in Paris unless I showed the world that I had confidence in myself. My trial audience was impending; I felt sure of the Théâtre de la Renaissance, and Dumersan was keenly anxious to make a complete translation of my *Liebesverbot* into French. So we decided to run the risk. On 15th April, to the astonishment of the concierge of the house in the Rue du Helder, we moved with an exceedingly small amount of luggage into our comfortable new apartments.

The very first visit I received in the rooms I had taken with such high hopes was from Anders, who came with the tidings that the Théâtre de la Renaissance had just gone bankrupt, and was closed. This news, which came on me like a thunderclap, seemed to portend more than an ordinary stroke of bad luck; it revealed to me like a flash of lightning the absolute emptiness of my prospects. My friends openly expressed the opinion that Meyerbeer, in sending me from the Grand Opera to this theatre, probably knew the whole of the circumstances. I did not pursue the line of thought to which this supposition might lead, as I felt cause enough for bitterness when I wondered what I should do with the rooms in which I was so nicely installed.

As my singers had now practised the portions of *Liebes-*

[1] 'Wagner' in German means one who dares, also a Wagoner; and 'Fuhrwerk' means a carriage. — EDITOR.

PERFORMANCE BEFORE M. MONNAIE

verbot intended for the trial audience, I was anxious at least to have them performed before some persons of influence. M. Edouard Monnaie, who had been appointed temporary director of the Grand Opera after Duponchel's retirement, was the less disposed to refuse as the singers who were to take part belonged to the institution over which he presided; moreover, there was no obligation attached to his presence at the audience. I also took the trouble to call on Scribe to invite him to attend, and he accepted with the kindest alacrity. At last my three pieces were performed before these two gentlemen in the green room of the Grand Opera, and I played the piano accompaniment. They pronounced the music charming, and Scribe expressed his willingness to arrange the libretto for me as soon as the managers of the opera had decided on accepting the piece; all that M. Monnaie had to reply to this offer was that it was impossible for them to do so at present. I did not fail to realise that these were only polite expressions; but at all events I thought it very nice of them, and particularly condescending of Scribe to have got so far as to think me deserving of a little politeness.

But in my heart of hearts I felt really ashamed of having gone back again seriously to that superficial early work from which I had taken these three pieces. Of course I had only done this because I thought I should win success more rapidly in Paris by adapting myself to its frivolous taste. My aversion from this kind of taste, which had been long growing, coincided with my abandonment of all hopes of success in Paris. I was placed in an exceedingly melancholy situation by the fact that my circumstances had so shaped themselves that I dared not express this important change in my feelings to any one, especially to my poor wife. But if I continued to make the best of a bad bargain, I had no longer any illusions as to the possibility of success in Paris. Face to face with unheard-of misery, I shuddered at the smiling aspect which Paris presented in the bright sunshine of May. It was the beginning of the slack season for any sort of artistic enterprise in Paris, and from every door at which I knocked with feigned hope I was turned away with the wretchedly monotonous phrase, *Monsieur est à la campagne*.

On our long walks, when we felt ourselves absolute strangers in the midst of the gay throng, I used to romance to my wife about the South American Free States, far away from all this sinister life, where opera and music were unknown, and the foundations of a sensible livelihood could easily be secured by industry. I told Minna, who was quite in the dark as to my meaning, of a book I had just read, Zschokke's *Die Gründung von Maryland,* in which I found a very seductive account of the sensation of relief experienced by the European settlers after their former sufferings and persecutions. She, being of a more practical turn of mind, used to point out to me the necessity of procuring means for our continued existence in Paris, for which she had thought out all sorts of economies.

I, for my part, was sketching out the plan of the poem of my *Fliegender Holländer,* which I kept steadily before me as a possible means of making a début in Paris. I put together the material for a single act, influenced by the consideration that I could in this way confine it to the simple dramatic developments between the principal characters, without troubling about the tiresome operatic accessories. From a practical point of view, I thought I could rely on a better prospect for the acceptance of my proposed work if it were cast in the form of a one-act opera, such as was frequently given as a curtain raiser before a ballet at the Grand Opera. I wrote about it to Meyerbeer in Berlin, asking for his help. I also resumed the composition of *Rienzi,* to the completion of which I was now giving my constant attention.

In the meantime our position became more and more gloomy; I was soon compelled to draw in advance on the subsidies obtained by Laube, but in so doing I gradually alienated the sympathy of my brother-in-law Avenarius, to whom our stay in Paris was incomprehensible.

One morning, when we had been anxiously consulting as to the possibility of raising our first quarter's rent, a carrier appeared with a parcel addressed to me from London; I thought it was an intervention of Providence, and broke open the seal. At the same moment a receipt-book was thrust into my face for signature, in which I at once saw that I had to pay seven francs for carriage. I recognised, moreover, that the parcel contained my overture *Rule Britannia,* returned to me from the London Philharmonic Society. In my fury I told the bearer that I would not take in the parcel, whereupon he remonstrated in the liveliest fashion, as I had already opened it. It was no use; I did not possess seven francs, and I told him he should have presented the bill for the carriage before I had opened the parcel. So I made him return the only copy of my overture to Messrs. Laffitte and Gaillard's firm, to do what they liked with it, and I never cared to inquire what became of that manuscript.

Suddenly Kietz devised a way out of these troubles. He had been commissioned by an old lady of Leipzig, called Fräulein Leplay, a rich and very miserly old maid, to find a cheap lodging in Paris for her and for his stepmother, with whom she intended to travel. As our apartment, though not spacious, was larger than we actually needed, and had very quickly become a troublesome burden to us, we did not hesitate for a moment to let the larger portion of it to her for the time of her stay in Paris, which was to last about two months. In addition, my wife provided the guests with breakfast, as though they were in furnished apartments, and took a great pride in looking at the few pence she earned in this way. Although we found this amazing example of old-maidishness trying enough, the arrangement we had made helped us in some degree to tide over the anxious time, and I was able, in spite of this disorganisation of our household arrangements, to continue working in comparative peace at my *Rienzi.*

This became more difficult after Fräulein Leplay's departure, when we let one of our rooms to a German commercial traveller, who in his leisure hours zealously played the flute. His name was Brix; he was a modest, decent fellow, and had been recommended to us by Pecht the painter, whose acquaintance we had recently made. He had been introduced to us by Kietz, who studied with him in Delaroche's studio. He was the very antithesis of Kietz in every way, and obviously endowed with less talent, yet he grappled with the task of acquiring the art of oil-painting in the shortest possible time under difficult circumstances with an industry and earnestness quite out of the common. He was, moreover, well educated, and eagerly assimilated information, and was very straightforward, earnest, and trustworthy. Without attaining to the same degree of intimacy with us as our three older friends, he was, nevertheless, one of the few who continued to stand by us in our troubles, and habitually spent nearly every evening in our company.

One day I received a fresh surprising proof of Laube's continued solicitude on our behalf. The secretary of a certain Count Kuscelew called on us, and after some inquiry into our affairs, the state of which he had heard from Laube at Karlsbad, informed us in a brief and friendly way that his patron wished to be of use to us, and with that object in view desired to make my acquaintance. In fact, he proposed to engage a small light opera company in Paris, which was to follow him to his Russian estates. He was therefore looking for a musical director of sufficient experience to assist in recruiting the members in Paris. I gladly went to the hotel where the count was staying, and there found an elderly gentleman of frank and agreeable bearing, who willingly listened to my little French compositions. Being a shewd reader of human nature, he saw at a glance that I was not the man for him, and though he showed me the most polite attention, he went no further into the opera scheme. But that very day he sent me, accompanied by a friendly note, ten golden napoleons, in payment for my services. What these services were I did not know. I thereupon wrote to him, and asked for more precise details of his wishes, and begged him to commission a composition, the fee for which I presumed he had sent in advance. As I received no reply, I made more than one effort to approach him again, but in vain. From other sources I afterwards learned that the only kind of opera Count Kuscelew recognised was Adam's. As for the operatic company to be engaged to suit his taste, what he really wanted was more a small harem than a company of artists.

So far I had not been able to arrange anything with the music publisher Schlesinger. It was impossible to persuade him to publish my little French songs. In order to do something, however, towards making myself known in this direction, I decided to have my *Two Grenadiers* engraved by him at my own expense. Kietz was to lithograph a magnificent title-page for it. Schlesinger ended by charging me fifty francs for the cost of production. The story of this publication is curious from beginning to end; the work bore Schlesinger's name, and as I had defrayed all expenses, the proceeds were, of course, to be placed to my account. I had afterwards to take the publisher's word for it that not a single copy had been sold. Subsequently, when I had made a quick reputation for myself in Dresden through my *Rienzi,* Schott the publisher in Mainz, who dealt almost exclusively in works translated from the French, thought it advisable to bring out a German edition of the *Two Grenadiers.* Below the text of the French translation he had the German original by Heine printed; but as the French poem was a very free paraphrase, in quite a different metre to the original, Heine's words fitted my composition so badly that I was furious at the insult to my work, and thought it necessary to protest against Schott's publication as an entirely unauthorised reprint. Schott then threatened me with an action for libel, as he said that, according to his agreement, his edition was not a reprint (*Nachdruck*), but a reimpression (*Abdruck*). In order to be spared further annoyance, I was induced to send him an apology in deference to the distinction he had drawn, which I did not understand.

In 1848, when I made inquiries of Schlesinger's successor in Paris (M. Brandus) as to the fate of my little work, I learned from him that a new edition had been published, but he declined to entertain any question of rights on my part. Since I did not care to buy a copy with my own money, I have to this day had to do without my own property. To what extent, in later years, others profited by similar transactions relating to the publication of my works, will appear in due course.

For the moment the point was to compensate Schlesinger for the fifty francs agreed upon, and he proposed that I should do this by writing articles for his *Gazette Musicale.*

As I was not expert enough in the French language for literary purposes, my article had to be translated and half the fee had to go to the translator. However, I consoled myself by thinking I should still receive sixty francs per sheet for the work. I was soon to learn, when I presented myself to the angry publisher for payment, what was meant by a sheet. It was measured by an abominable iron instrument, on which the lines of the columns were marked off with figures; this was applied to the article, and after careful subtraction of the spaces left for the title and signature, the lines were added up. After this process had been gone through, it appeared that what I had taken for a sheet was only half a sheet.

So far so good. I began to write articles for Schlesinger's wonderful paper. The first was a long essay, *De la musique allemande,* in which I expressed with the enthusiastic exaggeration characteristic of me at that time my appreciation of the sincerity and earnestness of German music. This article led my friend Anders to remark that the state of affairs in Germany must, indeed, be splendid if the conditions were really as I described. I enjoyed what was to me the surprising satisfaction of seeing this article subsequently reproduced in Italian, in a Milan musical journal, where, to my amusement, I saw myself described as *Dottissimo Musico Tedesco,* a mistake which nowadays would be impossible. My essay attracted favourable comment, and Schlesinger asked me to write an article in praise of the arrangement made by the Russian General Lwoff of Pergolesi's *Stabat Mater,* which I did as superficially as possible. On my own impulse I then wrote an essay in a still more amiable vein called *Du métier du virtuose et de l'indépendance de la composition.*

In the meantime I was surprised in the middle of the summer by the arrival of Meyerbeer, who happened to come to Paris for a fortnight. He was very sympathetic and obliging. When I told him my idea of writing a one-act opera as a curtain raiser, and asked him to give me an introduction to M. Léon Pillet, the recently appointed manager of the Grand Opera, he at once took me to see him, and presented me to him. But alas, I had the unpleasant surprise of learning from the serious conversation which took place between those two gentlemen as to my future, that Meyerbeer thought I had better decide to compose an act for the ballet in collaboration with another musician. Of course I could not entertain such an idea for a moment. I succeeded, however, in handing over to M. Pillet my brief sketch of the subject of the *Flying Dutchman.*

Things had reached this point when Meyerbeer again left Paris, this time for a longer period of absence.

As I did not hear from M. Pillet for quite a long time, I now began to work diligently at my composition of *Rienzi*, though, to my great distress, I had often to interrupt this task in order to undertake certain pot-boiling hack-work for Schlesinger.

As my contributions to the *Gazette Musicale* proved so unremunerative, Schlesinger one day ordered me to work out a method for the *Cornet à pistons*. When I told him about my embarrassment, in not knowing how to deal with the subject, he replied by sending me five different published 'Methods' for the *Cornet à pistons*, at that time the favourite amateur instrument among the younger male population of Paris. I had merely to devise a new sixth method out of these five, as all Schlesinger wanted was to publish an edition of his own. I was racking my brains how to start, when Schlesinger, who had just obtained a new complete method, released me from the onerous task. I was, however, told to write fourteen 'Suites' for the *Cornet à pistons* — that is to say, airs out of operas arranged for this instrument. To furnish me with material for this work, Schlesinger sent me no less than sixty complete operas arranged for the piano. I looked them through for suitable airs for my 'Suites,' marked the pages in the volumes with paper strips, and arranged them into a curious-looking structure round my work-table, so that I might have the greatest possible variety of the melodious material within my reach. When I was in the midst of this work, however, to my great relief and to my poor wife's consternation, Schlesinger told me that M. Schlitz, the first cornet player in Paris, who had looked my 'Études' through, preparatory to their being engraved, had declared that I knew absolutely nothing about the instrument, and had generally adopted keys that were too high, which Parisians would never be able to use. The part of the work I had already done was, however, accepted, Schlitz having agreed to correct it, but on condition that I should share my fee with him. The remainder of the work was then taken off my hands, and the sixty pianoforte arrangements went back to the curious shop in the Rue Richelieu.

So my exchequer was again in a sorry plight. The distressing poverty of my home grew more apparent every day, and yet I was now free to give a last touch to *Rienzi*, and by the 19th of November I had completed this most voluminous of all my operas. I had decided, some time previously, to offer the first production of this work to the Court Theatre at Dresden, so that, in the event of its being a success, I might thus resume my connection with Germany. I had decided upon Dresden as I knew that there I should have in Tichatschek the most suitable tenor for the leading part. I also reckoned on my acquaintance with Schröder-Devrient, who had always been nice to me and who, though her efforts were ineffectual, had been at great pains, out of regard for my family, to get my *Feen* introduced at the Court Theatre, Dresden. In the secretary of the theatre, Hofrat Winkler (known as Theodor Hell), I also had an old friend of my family, besides which I had been introduced to the conductor, Reissiger, with whom I and my friend Apel had spent a pleasant evening on the occasion of our excursion to Bohemia in earlier days. To all these people I now addressed most respectful and eloquent appeals, wrote out an official note to the director, Herr von Lüttichau, as well as a formal petition to the King of Saxony, and had everything ready to send off.

Meantime, I had not omitted to indicate the exact *tempi* in my opera by means of a metronome. As I did not possess such a thing, I had to borrow one, and one morning I went out to restore the instrument to its owner, carrying it under my thin overcoat. The day when this occurred was one of the strangest in my life, as it showed in a really horrible way the whole misery of my position at that time. In addition to the fact that I did not know where to look for the few francs wherewith Minna was to provide for our scanty household requirements, some of the bills which, in accordance with the custom in Paris in those days, I had signed for the purpose of fitting up our apartments, had fallen due. Hoping to get help from one source or another, I first tried to get those bills prolonged by the holders. As such documents pass through many hands, I had to call on all the holders across the length and breadth of the city. That day I was to propitiate a cheesemonger who occupied a fifth-floor apartment in the Cité. I

SUDDEN REAPPEARANCE OF ROBBER 231

also intended to ask for help from Heinrich, the brother of my brother-in-law, Brockhaus, as he was then in Paris; and I was going to call at Schlesinger's to raise the money to pay for the despatch of my score that day by the usual mail service.

As I had also to deliver the metronome, I left Minna early in the morning after a sad good-bye. She knew from experience that as I was on a money-raising expedition, she would not see me back till late at night. The streets were enveloped in a dense fog, and the first thing I recognised on leaving the house was my dog Robber, who had been stolen from us a year before. At first I thought it was a ghost, but I called out to him sharply in a shrill voice. The animal seemed to recognise me, and approached me cautiously, but my sudden movement towards him with outstretched arms seemed only to revive memories of the few chastisements I had foolishly inflicted on him during the latter part of our association, and this memory prevailed over all others. He drew timidly away from me and, as I followed him with some eagerness, he ran, only to accelerate his speed when he found he was being pursued. I became more and more convinced that he had recognised me, because he always looked back anxiously when he reached a corner; but seeing that I was hunting him like a maniac, he started off again each time with renewed energy. Thus I followed him through a labyrinth of streets, hardly distinguishable in the thick mist, until I eventually lost sight of him altogether, never to see him again. It was near the church of St. Roch, and I, wet with perspiration and quite breathless, was still bearing the metronome. For a while I stood motionless, glaring into the mist, and wondered what the ghostly reappearance of the companion of my travelling adventures on this day might portend! The fact that he had fled from his old master with the terror of a wild beast filled my heart with a strange bitterness and seemed to me a horrible omen. Sadly shaken, I set out again, with trembling limbs, upon my weary errand.

Heinrich Brockhaus told me he could not help me, and I left him. I was sorely ashamed, but made a strong effort to conceal the painfulness of my situation. My other undertakings turned out equally hopeless, and after having been kept waiting for hours at Schlesinger's, listening to my employer's very trivial conversations with his callers — conversations which he seemed purposely to protract — I reappeared under the windows of my home long after dark, utterly unsuccessful. I saw Minna looking anxiously from one of the windows. Half expecting my misfortune she had, in the meantime, succeeded in borrowing a small sum of our lodger and boarder, Brix, the flute-player, whom we tolerated patiently, though at some inconvenience to ourselves, as he was a good-natured fellow. So she was able to offer me at least a comfortable meal. Further help was to come to me subsequently, though at the cost of great sacrifices on my part, owing to the success of one of Donizetti's operas, *La Favorita,* a very poor work of the Italian maestro's, but welcomed with great enthusiasm by the Parisian public, already so much degenerated. This opera, the success of which was due mainly to two lively little songs, had been acquired by Schlesinger, who had lost heavily over Halévy's last operas.

Taking advantage of my helpless situation, of which he was well aware, he rushed into our rooms one morning, beaming all over with amusing good-humour, called for pen and ink, and began to work out a calculation of the enormous fees which he had arranged for me! He put down: '*La Favorita,* complete arrangement for pianoforte, arrangement without words, for solo; ditto, for duet; complete arrangement for quartette; the same for two violins; ditto for a *Cornet à piston.* Total fee, frcs. 1100. Immediate advance in cash, frcs. 500.' I could see at a glance what an enormous amount of trouble this work would involve, but I did not hesitate a moment to undertake it.

Curiously enough, when I brought home these five hundred francs in hard shining five-franc pieces, and piled them up on the table for our edification, my sister Cecilia Avenarius happened to drop in to see us. The sight of this abundance of wealth seemed to produce a good effect on her, as she had hitherto been rather chary of coming to see us; and after that we used to see rather more of her, and were often invited to dine with them on Sundays. But I no longer cared for any amusements. I was so deeply impressed by my past experiences that I made up my mind to work through this humiliating, albeit profitable task, with untiring energy, as though it were a penance imposed on me for the expiation of my bygone sins. To save fuel, we limited ourselves to the use of the bedroom, making it serve as a drawing-room, dining-room, and study, as well as dormitory. It was only a step from my bed to my work-table; to be seated at the dining-table, all I had to do was to turn my chair round, and I left my seat altogether only late at night when I wanted to go to bed again. Every fourth day I allowed myself a short constitutional. This penitential process lasted almost all through the winter, and sowed the seeds of those gastric disorders which were to be more or less of a trouble to me for the rest of my life.

In return for the minute and almost interminable work of correcting the score of Donizetti's opera, I managed to get three hundred francs from Schlesinger, as he could not get any one else to do it. Besides this, I had to find the time to copy out the orchestra parts of my overture to *Faust,* which I was still hoping to hear at the Conservatoire; and by the way of counteracting the depression produced by this humiliating occupation, I wrote a short story, *Eine Pilgerfahrt zu Beethoven* (A Pilgrimage to Beethoven), which appeared in the *Gazette Musicale,* under the title *Une Visite à Beethoven.* Schlesinger told me candidly that this little work had created quite a sensation, and had been received with very marked approval; and, indeed, it was actually reproduced, either complete or in parts, in a good many fireside journals.

He persuaded me to write some more of the same kind; and in a sequel entitled *Das Ende eines Musikers in Paris (Un Musicien étranger à Paris)* I avenged myself for all the misfortunes I had had to endure. Schlesinger was not quite so pleased with this as with my first effort, but it received touching signs of approval from his poor assistant; while Heinrich Heine praised it by saying that 'Hoffmann would have been incapable of writing such a thing.' Even Berlioz was touched by it, and spoke of the story very favourably in one of his articles in the *Journal des Débats.* He also gave me signs of his sympathy, though only during a conversation, after the appearance of another of my musical articles entitled *Ueber die Ouvertüre* (Concerning Overtures), mainly because I had illustrated my principle by pointing to Gluck's overture to *Iphigenia in Aulis* as a model for compositions of this class.

Encouraged by these signs of sympathy, I felt anxious to become more intimately acquainted with Berlioz. I had been introduced to him some time previously at Schlesinger's office, where we used to meet occasionally. I had presented him with a copy of my *Two Grenadiers,* but could, however, never learn any more from him concerning what he really thought of it than the fact that as he could only strum a little on the guitar, he was unable to play the music of my composition to himself on the piano. During the previous winter I had often heard his grand instrumental pieces played under his own direction, and had been most favourably impressed by them. During that winter (1839-40) he conducted three performances of his new symphony, *Romeo and Juliet,* at one of which I was present.

All this, to be sure, was quite a new world to me, and I was desirous of gaining some unprejudiced knowledge of it. At first the grandeur and masterly execution of the orchestral part almost overwhelmed me. It was beyond anything I could have conceived. The fantastic daring, the sharp precision with which the boldest combinations — almost tangible in their clearness — impressed me, drove back my own ideas of the poetry of music with brutal violence into the very depths of my soul. I was simply all ears for things of which till then I had never dreamt, and which I felt I must try to realise. True, I found a great deal that was empty and shallow in his *Romeo and Juliet,* a work that lost much by its length and form of combination; and this was the more painful to me seeing that, on the other hand, I felt overpowered by many really bewitching passages which quite overcame any objections on my part.

During the same winter Berlioz produced his *Sinfonie Fantastique* and his *Harald* ('Harold en Italie'). I was also much impressed by these works; the musical genre-pictures woven into the first-named symphony were particularly pleasing, while *Harald* delighted me in almost every respect.

It was, however, the latest work of this wonderful master, his *Trauer-Symphonie für die Opfer der Juli-Revolution* (*Grande Symphonie Funèbre et Triomphale*), most skilfully composed for massed military bands during the summer of 1840 for the anniversary of the obsequies of the July heroes, and conducted by him under the column of the Place de la Bastille, which had at last thoroughly convinced me of the greatness and enterprise of this incomparable artist. But while admiring this genius, absolutely unique in his methods, I could never quite shake off a certain peculiar feeling of anxiety. His works left me with a sensation as of something strange, something with which I felt I should never be able to be familiar, and I was often puzzled at the strange fact that, though ravished by his compositions, I was at the same time repelled and even wearied by them. It was only much later that I succeeded in clearly grasping and solving this problem, which for years exercised such a painful spell over me.

It is a fact that at that time I felt almost like a little school-boy by the side of Berlioz. Consequently I was really embarrassed when Schlesinger, determined to make good use of the success of my short story, told me he was anxious to produce some of my orchestral compositions at a concert arranged by the editor of the *Gazette Musicale*. I realised that none of my available works would in any way be suitable for such an occasion. I was not quite confident as to my *Faust* Overture because of its zephyr-like ending, which I presumed could only be appreciated by an audience already familiar with my methods. When, moreover, I learned that I should have only a second-rate orchestra — the Valentino from the Casino, Rue St. Honoré — and, moreover, that there could be only one rehearsal, my only alternative lay between declining altogether, or making another trial with my *Columbus* Overture, the work composed in my early days at Magdeburg. I adopted the latter course.

When I went to fetch the score of this composition from Habeneck, who had it stored among the archives of the Conservatoire, he warned me somewhat dryly, though not without kindness, of the danger of presenting this work to the Parisian public, as, to use his own words, it was too 'vague.' One great objection was the difficulty of finding capable musicians for the six cornets required, as the music for this instrument, so skilfully played in Germany, could hardly, if ever, be satisfactorily executed in Paris. Herr Schlitz, the corrector of my 'Suites' for *Cornet à piston,* offered his assistance. I was compelled to reduce my six cornets to four, and he told me that only two of these could be relied on.

As a matter of fact, the attempts made at the rehearsal to produce those very passages on which the effect of my work chiefly depended were very discouraging. Not once were the soft high notes played but they were flat or altogether wrong. In addition to this, as I was not going to be allowed to conduct the work myself, I had to rely upon a conductor who, as I was well aware, had fully convinced himself that my composition was the most utter rubbish — an opinion that seemed to be shared by the whole orchestra. Berlioz, who was present at the rehearsal, remained silent throughout. He gave me no encouragement, though he did not dissuade me. He merely said afterwards, with a weary smile, 'that it was very difficult to get on in Paris.'

On the night of the performance (4th February 1841) the audience, which was largely composed of subscribers to the *Gazette Musicale,* and to whom, therefore, my literary successes were not unknown, seemed rather favourably disposed towards me. I was told later on that my overture, however wearisome it had been, would certainly have been applauded if those unfortunate cornet players, by continually failing to produce the effective passages, had not excited the public almost to the point of hostility; for Parisians, for the most part, care only for the skilful parts of performances, as, for instance, for the faultless production of difficult tones. I was clearly conscious of my complete failure. After this misfortune Paris no longer existed for me, and all I had to do was to go back to my miserable bedroom and resume my work of arranging Donizetti's operas.

So great was my renunciation of the world that, like a penitent, I no longer shaved, and to my wife's annoyance, for the first and only time in my life allowed my beard to grow quite long. I tried to bear everything patiently, and the only thing that threatened really to drive me to despair was a pianist in the room adjoining ours who during the livelong day practised Liszt's fantasy on *Lucia di Lammermoor*. I had to put a stop to this torture, so, to give him an idea of what he made us endure, one day I moved our own piano, which was terribly out of tune, close up to the party wall. Then Brix with his piccolo-flute played the piano-and-violin (or flute) arrangement of the *Favorita* Overture I had just completed, while I accompanied him on the piano. The effect on our neighbour, a young piano-teacher, must have been appalling. The concierge told me the next day that the poor fellow was leaving, and, after all, I felt rather sorry.

The wife of our concierge had entered into a sort of arrangement with us. At first we had occasionally availed ourselves of her services, especially in the kitchen, also for brushing clothes, cleaning boots, and so on; but even the slight outlay that this involved was eventually too heavy for us, and after having dispensed with her services, Minna had to suffer the humiliation of doing the whole work of the household, even the most menial part of it, herself. As we did not like to mention this to Brix, Minna was obliged, not only to do all the cooking and washing up, but even to clean our lodger's boots as well. What we felt most, however, was the thought of what the concierge and his wife would think of us; but we were mistaken, for they only respected us the more, though of course we could not avoid a little familiarity at times. Now and then, therefore, the man would have a chat with me on politics. When the Quadruple Alliance against France had been concluded, and the situation under Thiers' ministry was regarded as very critical, my concierge tried to reassure me one day by saying: '*Monsieur, il y a quatre hommes en Europe qui s'appellent: le roi Louis Philippe, l'empereur d'Autriche, l'empereur de Russie, le roi de Prusse; eh bien, ces quatre sont des c . . .; et nous n'aurons pas la guerre.*'

Of an evening I very seldom lacked entertainment; but the few faithful friends who came to see me had to put up with my going on scribbling music till late in the night. Once they prepared a touching surprise for me in the form of a little party which they arranged for New Year's Eve (1840). Lehrs arrived at dusk, rang the bell, and brought a leg of veal; Kietz brought some rum, sugar, and a lemon; Pecht supplied a goose; and Anders two bottles of the champagne with which he had been presented by a musical instrument-maker in return for a flattering article he had written about his pianos. Bottles from that stock were produced only on very great occasions. I soon threw the confounded *Favorita* aside, therefore, and entered enthusiastically into the fun.

We all had to assist in the preparations, to light the fire in the salon, give a hand to my wife in the kitchen, and get what was wanted from the grocer. The supper developed into a dithyrambic orgy. When the champagne was drunk, and the punch began to produce its effects, I delivered a fiery speech which so provoked the hilarity of the company that it seemed as though it would never end. I became so excited that I first mounted a chair, and then, by way of heightening the effect, at last stood on the table, thence to preach the maddest gospel of the contempt of life together with a eulogy on the South American Free States. My charmed listeners eventually broke into such fits of sobs and laughter, and were so overcome, that we had to give them all shelter for the night — their condition making it impossible for them to reach their own homes in safety. On New Year's Day (1841) I was again busy with my *Favorita*.

I remember another similar though far less boisterous feast, on the occasion of a visit paid us by the famous violinist Vieuxtemps, an old schoolfellow of Kietz's. We had the great pleasure of hearing the young virtuoso, who was then greatly fêted in Paris, play to us charmingly for a whole evening — a performance which lent my little salon an unusual touch of 'fashion.' Kietz rewarded him for his kindness by carrying him on his shoulders to his hotel close by.

We were hard hit in the early part of this year by a mistake I made owing to my ignorance of Paris customs. It seemed to us quite a matter of course that we should wait until the proper quarter-day to give notice to our landlady. So I called on the proprietress of the house, a rich young widow living in one of her own houses in the Marias quarter. She received me, but seemed much embarrassed, and said she would speak to her agent about the matter, and eventually referred me to him. The next day I was informed by letter that my notice would have been valid had it been given two days earlier. By this omission I had rendered myself liable, according to the agreement, for another year's rent. Horrified by this news, I went to see the agent himself, and after having been kept waiting for a long time — as a matter of fact they would not let me in at all — I found an elderly gentleman, apparently crippled by some very painful malady, lying motionless before me. I frankly told him my position, and begged him most earnestly to release me from my agreement, but I was merely told that the fault was mine, and not his, that I had given notice a day too late, and consequently that I must find the rent for the next year. My concierge, to whom, with some emotion, I related the story of this occurrence, tried to soothe me by saying: ' J'aurais pu vous dire cela, car voyez, monsieur, cet homme ne vaut pas l'eau qu'il boit.'

This entirely unforeseen misfortune destroyed our last hopes of getting out of our disastrous position. We consoled ourselves for awhile with the hope of finding another lodger, but the fates were once more against us. Easter came, the new term began, and our prospects were as hopeless as ever. At last our concierge recommended us to a family who were willing to take the whole of our apartment, furniture included, off our hands for a few months. We gladly accepted this offer; for, at any rate, it ensured the payment of the rent for the ensuing quarter. We thought if only we could get away from this unfortunate place we should find some way of getting rid of it altogether. We therefore decided to find a cheap summer residence for ourselves in the outskirts of Paris.

Meudon had been mentioned to us as an inexpensive summer resort, and we selected an apartment in the avenue which joins Meudon to the neighbouring village of Bellevue. We left full authority with our concierge as to our rooms in Rue du Helder, and settled down in our new temporary abode as well as we could. Old Brix, the good-natured flutist, had to stay with us again, for, owing to the fact that his usual receipts had been delayed, he would have been in great straits had we refused to give him shelter. The removal of our scanty possessions took place on the 29th of April, and was, after all, no more than a flight from the impossible into the unknown, for how we were going to live during the following summer we had not the faintest idea. Schlesinger had no work for me, and no other sources were available.

The only help we could hope for seemed to lie in journalistic work which, though rather unremunerative, had indeed given me the opportunity of making a little success. During the previous winter I had written a long article on Weber's *Freischütz* for the *Gazette Musicale*. This was intended to prepare the way for the forthcoming first performance of this opera, after recitatives from the pen of Berlioz had been added to it. The latter was apparently far from pleased at my article. In the article I could not help referring to Berlioz's absurd idea of polishing up this old-fashioned musical work by adding ingredients that spoiled its original characteristics, merely in order to give it an appearance suited to the luxurious repertoire of Opera House. The fact that the result fully justified my forecasts did not in the least tend to diminish the ill-feeling I had roused among all those concerned in the production; but I had the satisfaction of hearing that the famous George Sand had noticed my article. She commenced the introduction to a legendary story of French provincial life by repudiating certain doubts as to the ability of the French people to understand the mystic, fabulous element which, as I had shown, was displayed in such a masterly manner in *Freischütz,* and she pointed to my article as clearly explaining the characteristics of that opera.

Another journalistic opportunity arose out of my endeavours to secure the acceptance of my *Rienzi* by the Court Theatre at Dresden. Herr Winkler, the secretary of that theatre, whom I have already mentioned, regularly reported progress; but as editor of the *Abendzeitung,* a paper then rather on the wane, he seized the opportunity presented by our negotiations in order to ask me to send him frequent and gratuitous contributions. The consequence was, that whenever I wanted to know anything concerning the fate of my opera, I had to oblige him by enclosing an article for his paper. Now, as these negotiations with the Court Theatre lasted a very long time, and involved a large number of contributions from me, I often got into the most extraordinary fixes simply owing to the fact that I was now once more a prisoner in my room, and had been so for some time, and therefore knew nothing of what was going on in Paris.

I had serious reasons for thus withdrawing from the artistic and social life of Paris. My own painful experiences and my disgust at all the mockery of that kind of life, once so attractive to me and yet so alien to my education, had quickly driven me away from everything connected with it. It is true that the production of the *Huguenots*, for instance, which I then heard for the first time, dazzled me very much indeed. Its beautiful orchestral execution, and the extremely careful and effective *mise en scène*, gave me a grand idea of the great possibilities of such perfect and definite artistic means. But, strange to say, I never felt inclined to hear the same opera again. I soon became tired of the extravagant execution of the vocalists, and I often amused my friends exceedingly by imitating the latest Parisian methods and the vulgar exaggerations with which the performances teemed. Those composers, moreover, who aimed at achieving success by adopting the style which was then in vogue, could not help, either, incurring my sarcastic criticism. The last shred of esteem which I still tried to retain for the 'first lyrical theatre in the world' was at last rudely destroyed when I saw how such an empty, altogether un-French work as Donizetti's *Favorita* could secure so long and important a run at this theatre.

During the whole time of my stay in Paris I do not think I went to the opera more than four times. The cold productions at the Opéra Comique, and the degenerate quality of the music produced there, had repelled me from the start; and the same lack of enthusiasm displayed by the singers also drove me from Italian opera. The names, often very famous ones, of these artists who sang the same four operas for years could not compensate me for the complete absence of sentiment which characterised their performance, so unlike that of Schröder-Devrient, which I so thoroughly enjoyed. I clearly saw that everything was on the down grade, and yet I cherished no hope or desire to see this state of decline superseded by a period of newer and fresher life. I preferred the small theatres, where French talent was shown in its true light; and yet, as the result of my own longings, I was too intent upon finding points of relationship in them which would excite my sympathy, for it to be possible for me to realise those peculiar excellences in them which did not happen to interest me at all. Besides, from the very beginning my own troubles had proved so trying, and the consciousness of the failure of my Paris schemes had become so cruelly apparent, that, either out of indifference or annoyance, I declined all invitations to the theatres. Again and again, much to Minna's regret, I returned tickets for performances in which *Rachel* was to appear at the Théâtre Français, and, in fact, saw that famous theatre only once, when, some time later, I had to go there on business for my Dresden patron, who wanted some more articles.

I adopted the most shameful means for filling the columns of the *Abendzeitung;* I just strung together whatever I happened to hear in the evening from Anders and Lehrs. But as they had no very exciting adventures either, they simply told me all they had picked up from papers and table-talk, and this I tried to render with as much piquancy as possible in accordance with the journalistic style created by Heine, which was all the rage at the time. My one fear was lest old Hofrath Winkler should some day discover the secret of my wide knowledge of Paris. Among other things which I sent to his declining paper was a long account of the production of *Freischütz.* He was particularly interested in it, as he was the guardian of Weber's children; and when in one of his letters he assured me that he would not rest until he had got the definite assurance that *Rienzi* had been accepted, I sent him, with my most profuse thanks, the German manuscript of my 'Beethoven' story for his paper. The 1841 edition of this gazette, then published by Arnold, but now no longer in existence, contains the only print of this manuscript.

My occasional journalistic work was increased by a request from Lewald, the editor of *Europa,* a literary monthly, asking me to write something for him. This man was the first who, from time to time, had mentioned my name to the public. As he used to publish musical supplements to his elegant and rather widely read magazine, I sent him two of my compositions from Königsberg for publication. One of these was the music I had set to a melancholy poem by Scheuerlin, entitled *Der Knabe und der Tannenbaum* (a work of which even to-day I am still proud), and my beautiful *Carnevals Lied* out of *Liebesverbot*.

When I wanted to publish my little French compositions — *Dors, mon enfant*, and the music to Hugo's *Attente* and Ronsard's *Mignonne* — Lewald not only sent me a small fee — the first I had ever received for a composition — but commissioned some long articles on my Paris impressions, which he begged me to write as entertainingly as possible. For his paper I wrote *Pariser Amusements* and *Pariser Fatalitäten*, in which I gave vent in a humorous style, à la Heine, to all my disappointing experiences in Paris, and to all my contempt for the life led by its inhabitants. In the second I described the existence of a certain Hermann Pfau, a strange good-for-nothing with whom, during my early Leipzig days, I had become more intimately acquainted than was desirable. This man had been wandering about Paris like a vagrant ever since the beginning of the previous winter, and the meagre income I derived from arrangements of *La Favorita* was often partly consumed in helping this completely broken-down fellow. So it was only fair that I should get back a few francs of the money spent on him in Paris by turning his adventures to some account in Lewald's newspapers.

When I came into contact with Léon Pillet, the manager of the Opera, my literary work took yet another direction. After numerous inquiries I eventually discovered that he had taken a fancy to my draft of the *Fliegender Holländer*. He informed me of this, and asked me to sell him the plot, as he was under contract to supply various composers with subjects for operettas. I tried to explain to Pillet, both verbally and in writing, that he could hardly expect that the plot would be properly treated except by myself, as this draft was in fact my own idea, and that it had only come to his knowledge by my having submitted it to him. But it was all to no purpose. He was obliged to admit quite frankly that the expectations I had cherished as to the result of Meyerbeer's recommendation to him would not come to anything. He said there was no likelihood of my getting a commission for a composition, even of a light opera, for the next seven years, as his already existing contracts extended over that period. He asked me to be sensible, and to sell him the draft for a small amount, so that he might have the music written by an author to be selected by him; and he added that if I still wished to try my luck at the Opera House, I had better see the 'ballet-master,' as he might want some music for a certain dance. Seeing that I contemptuously refused this proposal, he left me to my own devices.

After endless and unsuccessful attempts at getting the matter settled, I at last begged Edouard Monnaie, the Commissaire for the Royal Theatres, who was not only a friend of mine, but also editor of the *Gazette Musicale,* to act as mediator. He candidly confessed that he could not understand Pillet's liking for my plot, which he also was acquainted with; but as Pillet seemed to like it — though he would probably lose it — he advised me to accept anything for it, as Monsieur Paul Faucher, a brother-in-law of Victor Hugo's, had had an offer to work out the scheme for a similar libretto. This gentleman had, moreover, declared that there was nothing new in my plot, as the story of the *Vaisseau Fantôme* was well known in France. I now saw how I stood, and, in a conversation with Pillet, at which M. Faucher was present, I said I would come to an arrangement. My plot was generously estimated by Pillet at five hundred francs, and I received that amount from the cash office at the theatre, to be subsequently deducted from the author's rights of the future poet.

Our summer residence in the Avenue de Meudon now assumed quite a definite character. These five hundred francs had to help me to work out the words and music of my *Fliegender Holländer* for Germany, while I abandoned the French *Vaisseau Fantôme* to its fate.

The state of my affairs, which was getting ever worse and worse, was slightly improved by the settlement of this matter. May and June had gone by, and during these months our troubles had grown steadily more serious. The lovely season of the year, the stimulating country air, and the sensation of freedom following upon my deliverance from the wretchedly paid musical hack-work I had had to do all the winter, wrought their beneficial effects on me, and I was inspired to write a small story entitled *Ein glücklicher Abend*. This was translated and published in French in the *Gazette Musicale*. Soon, however, our lack of funds began to make itself felt with a severity that was very discouraging. We felt this all the more keenly when my sister Cecilia and her husband, following our example, moved to a place quite close to us. Though not wealthy, they were fairly well-to-do. They came to see us every day, but we never thought it desirable to let them know how terribly hard-up we were. One day it came to a climax. Being absolutely without money, I started out, early one morning, to walk to Paris — for I had not even enough to pay the railway fare thither — and I resolved to wander about the whole day, trudging from street to street, even until late in the afternoon, in the hope of raising a five-franc piece; but my errand proved absolutely vain, and I had to walk all the way back to Meudon again, utterly penniless.

When I told Minna, who came to meet me, of my failure, she informed me in despair that Hermann Pfau, whom I have mentioned before, had also come to us in the most pitiful plight, and actually in want of food, and that she had had to give him the last of the bread delivered by the baker that morning. The only hope that now remained was that, at any rate, my lodger Brix, who by a singular fate was now our companion in misfortune, would return with some success from the expedition to Paris which he also had made that morning. At last he, too, returned bathed in perspiration and exhausted, driven home by the craving for a meal, which he had been unable to procure in the town, as ne could not find any of the acquaintances he went to see. He begged most piteously for a piece of bread. This climax to the situation at last inspired my wife with heroic resolution; for she felt it her duty to exert herself to appease at least the hunger of her menfolk. For the first time during her stay on French soil, she persuaded the baker, the butcher, and wine-merchant, by plausible arguments, to supply her with the necessaries of life without immediate cash payment, and Minna's eyes beamed when, an hour later, she was able to put before us an excellent meal, during which, as it happened, we were surprised by the Avenarius family, who were evidently relieved at finding us so well provided for.

This extreme distress was relieved for a time, at the beginning of July, by the sale of my *Vaisseau Fantôme,* which meant my final renunciation of my success in Paris. As long as the five hundred francs lasted, I had an interval of respite for carrying on my work. The first object on which I spent my money was on the hire of a piano, a thing of which I had been entirely deprived for months. My chief intention in so doing was to revive my faith in myself as a musician, as, ever since the autumn of the previous year, I had exercised my talents as a journalist and adapter of operas only. The libretto of the *Fliegender Holländer,* which I had hurriedly written during the recent period of distress, aroused considerable interest in Lehrs; he actually declared I would never write anything better, and that the *Fliegender Holländer* would be my *Don Juan;* the only thing now was to find the music for it. As towards the end of the previous winter I still entertained the hopes of being permitted to treat this subject for the French Opera, I had already finished some of the words and music of the lyric parts, and had had the libretto translated by Émile Deschamps, intending it for a trial performance, which, alas, never took place. These parts were the ballad of Senta, the song of the Norwegian sailors, and the 'Spectre Song' of the crew of the *Fliegender Holländer.* Since that time I had been so violently torn away from the music that, when the piano arrived at my rustic retreat, I did not dare to touch it for a whole day. I was terribly afraid lest I should discover that my inspiration had left me — when suddenly I was seized with the idea that I had forgotten to write out the song of the helmsman in the first act, although, as a matter of fact, I could not remember having composed it at all, as I had in reality only just written the lyrics. I succeeded, and was pleased with the result. The same thing occurred with the 'Spinner's Song,' and when I had written out these two pieces, and, on further reflection, could not help admitting that they had really only taken shape in my mind at that moment, I was quite delirious with joy at the discovery. In seven weeks the whole of the music

THE VERSATILE M. JADIN

of the *Fliegender Holländer*, except the orchestration, was finished.

Thereupon followed a general revival in our circle; my exuberant good spirits astonished every one, and my Avenarius relations in particular thought I must really be prospering, as I was such good company. I resumed my long walks in the woods of Meudon, frequently even consenting to help Minna gather mushrooms, which, unfortunately, were for her the chief charm of our woodland retreat, though it filled our landlord with terror when he saw us returning with our spoils, as he felt sure we should be poisoned if we ate them.

My destiny, which almost invariably led me into strange adventures, here once more introduced me to the most eccentric character to be found not only in the neighbourhood of Meudon, but even in Paris. This was M. Jadin, who, though he was old enough to be able to say that he remembered seeing Madame de Pompadour at Versailles, was still vigorous beyond belief. It appeared to be his aim to keep the world in a constant state of conjecture as to his real age; he made everything for himself with his own hands, including even a quantity of wigs of every shade, ranging in the most comic variety from youthful flaxen to the most venerable white, with intermediate shades of grey; these he wore alternately, as the fancy pleased him. He dabbled in everything, and I was pleased to find he had a particular fancy for painting. The fact that all the walls of his rooms were hung with the most childish caricatures of animal life, and that he had even embellished the outside of his blinds with the most ridiculous paintings, did not disconcert me in the least; on the contrary, it confirmed my belief that he did not dabble in music, until, to my horror, I discovered that the strangely discordant sounds of a harp which kept reaching my ears from some unknown region were actually proceeding from his basement, where he had two harpsichords of his own invention. He informed me that he had unfortunately neglected playing them for a long time, but that he now meant to begin practising again assiduously in order to give me pleasure. I succeeded in dissuading him from this, by assuring him that the doctor had forbidden me to listen to the harp, as it was bad for my nerves. His figure as I saw him for the last time remains impressed on my memory, like an apparition from the world of Hoffmann's fairy-tales. In the late autumn, when we were going back to Paris, he asked us to take with us on our furniture van an enormous stove-pipe, of which he promised to relieve us shortly. One very cold day Jadin actually presented himself at our new abode in Paris, in a most preposterous costume of his own manufacture, consisting of very thin light-yellow trousers, a very short pale-green dress-coat with conspicuously long tails, projecting lace shirt frills and cuffs, a very fair wig, and a hat so small that it was constantly dropping off; he wore in addition a quantity of imitation jewellery — and all this on the undisguised assumption that he could not go about in fashionable Paris dressed as simply as in the country. He had come for the stove-pipe; we asked him where the men to carry it were; in reply he simply smiled, and expressed his surprise at our helplessness; and thereupon took the enormous stove-pipe under his arm and absolutely refused to accept our help when we offered to assist him in carrying it down the stairs, though this operation, notwithstanding his vaunted skill, occupied him quite half an hour. Every one in the house assembled to witness this removal, but he was by no means disconcerted, and managed to get the pipe through the street door, and then tripped gracefully along the pavement with it, and disappeared from our sight.

For this short though eventful period, during which I was quite free to give full scope to my inmost thoughts, I indulged in the consolation of purely artistic creations. I can only say that, when it came to an end, I had made such progress that I could look forward with cheerful composure to the much longer period of trouble and distress I felt was in store for me. This, in fact, duly set in, for I had only just completed the last scene when I found that my five hundred francs were coming to an end, and what was left was not sufficient to secure me the necessary peace and freedom from worry for composing the overture; I had to postpone this until my luck should take another favourable turn, and meanwhile I was forced to engage in the struggle for a bare subsistence, making efforts of all kinds that left me neither leisure nor peace of mind. The concierge from the Rue du Helder brought us the news that the mysterious family to whom we had let our rooms had left, and that we were now once more responsible for the rent. I had to tell him that I would not under any circumstances trouble about the rooms any more, and that the landlord might recoup himself by the sale of the furniture we had left there. This was done at a very heavy loss, and the furniture, the greater part of which was still unpaid for, was sacrificed to pay the rent of a dwelling which we no longer occupied.

Under the stress of the most terrible privations I still endeavoured to secure sufficient leisure for working out the orchestration of the score of the *Fliegender Holländer*. The rough autumn weather set in at an exceptionally early date; people were all leaving their country houses for Paris, and, among them, the Avenarius family. We, however, could not dream of doing so, for we could not even raise the funds for the journey. When M. Jadin expressed his surprise at this, I pretended to be so pressed with work that I could not interrupt it, although I felt the cold that penetrated through the thin walls of the house very severely.

So I waited for help from Ernst Castel, one of my old Königsberg friends, a well-to-do young merchant, who a short time before had called on us in Meudon and treated us to a luxurious repast in Paris, promising at the same time to relieve our necessities as soon as possible by an advance, which we knew was an easy matter to him.

By way of cheering us up, Kietz came over to us one day, with a large portfolio and a pillow under his arm; he intended to amuse us by working at a large caricature representing myself and my unfortunate adventures in Paris, and the pillow was to enable him, after his labours, to get some rest on our hard couch, which he had noticed had no pillows at the head. Knowing that we had a difficulty in procuring fuel, he brought with him some bottles of rum, to 'warm' us with punch during the cold evenings; under these circumstances I read Hoffmann's *Tales* to him and my wife.

At last I had news from Königsberg, but it only opened my eyes to the fact that the gay young dog had not meant his promise seriously. We now looked forward almost with despair to the chilly mists of approaching winter, but Kietz, declaring that it was his place to find help, packed up his portfolio, placed it under his arm with the pillow, and went off to Paris. On the next day he returned with two hundred francs, that he had managed to procure by means of generous self-sacrifice. We at once set off for Paris, and took a small apartment near our friends, in the back part of No. 14 Rue Jacob. I afterwards heard that shortly after we left it was occupied by Proudhon.

We got back to town on 30th October. Our home was exceedingly small and cold, and its chilliness in particular made it very bad for our health. We furnished it scantily with the little we had saved from the wreck of the Rue du Helder, and awaited the results of my efforts towards getting my works accepted and produced in Germany. The first necessity was at all costs to secure peace and quietness for myself for the short time which I should have to devote to the overture of the *Fliegender Holländer;* I told Kietz that he would have to procure the money necessary for my household expenses until this work was finished and the full score of the opera sent off. With the aid of a pedantic uncle, who had lived in Paris a long time and who was also a painter, he succeeded in providing me with the necessary assistance, in instalments of five or ten francs at a time. During this period I often pointed with cheerful pride to my boots, which became mere travesties of footgear, as the soles eventually disappeared altogether.

As long as I was engaged on the *Dutchman*, and Kietz was looking after me, this made no difference, for I never went out: but when I had despatched my completed score to the management of the Berlin Court Theatre at the beginning of December, the bitterness of the position could no longer be disguised. It was necessary for me to buckle to and look for help myself.

What this meant in Paris I learned just about this time from the hapless fate of the worthy Lehrs. Driven by need such as I myself had had to surmount a year before at about the same time, he had been compelled on a broiling hot day in the previous summer to scour the various quarters of the city breathlessly, to get grace for bills he had accepted, and which had fallen due. He foolishly took an iced drink, which he hoped would refresh him in his distressing condition, but it immediately made him lose his voice, and from that day he was the victim of a hoarseness which with terrific rapidity ripened the seeds of consumption, doubtless latent in him, and developed that incurable disease. For months he had been growing weaker and weaker, filling us at last with the gloomiest anxiety: he alone believed the supposed chill would be cured, if he could heat his room better for a time. One day I sought him out in his lodging, where I found him in the icy-cold room, huddled up at his writing-table, and complaining of the difficulty of his work for Didot, which was all the more distressing as his employer was pressing him for advances he had made.

He declared that if he had not had the consolation in those doleful hours of knowing that I had, at any rate, got my *Dutchman* finished, and that a prospect of success was thus opened to the little circle of friends, his misery would have been hard indeed to bear. Despite my own great trouble, I begged him to share our fire and work in my room. He smiled at my courage in trying to help other especially as my quarters offered barely space enough for myself and my wife. However, one evening he came to us and silently showed me a letter he had received from Villemain, the Ministe of Education at that time, in which the latter expressed in the warmest terms his great regret at having only just learned that so distinguished a scholar, whose able and extensive collaboration in Didot's issue of the Greek classics had made him participator in a work that was the glory of the nation, should be in such bad health and straitened circumstances. Unfortunately, the amount of public money which he had at his disposal at that moment for subsidising literature only allowed of his offering him the sum of five hundred francs, which he enclosed with apologies, asking him to accept it as a recognition of his merits on the part of the French Government, and adding that it was his intention to give earnest consideration as to how he might materially improve his position.

This filled us with the utmost thankfulness on poor Lehrs' account, and we looked on the incident almost as a miracle. We could not help assuming, however, that M. Villemain had been influenced by Didot, who had been prompted by his own guilty conscience for his despicable exploitation of Lehrs, and by the prospect of thus relieving himself of the responsibility of helping him. At the same time, from similar cases within our knowledge, which were fully confirmed by my own subsequent experience, we were driven to the conclusion that such prompt and considerate sympathy on the part of a minister would have been impossible in Germany. Lehrs would now have a fire to work by, but alas! our fears as to his declining health could not be allayed. When we left Paris in the following spring, it was the certainty that we should never see our dear friend again that made our parting so painful.

In my own great distress I was again exposed to the annoyance of having to write numerous unpaid articles for the *Abendzeitung,* as my patron, Hofrath Winkler, was still unable to give me any satisfactory account of the fate of my *Rienzi* in Dresden. In these circumstances I was obliged to consider it a good thing that Halévy's latest opera was at last a success. Schlesinger came to us radiant with joy at the success of *La Reine de Chypre,* and promised me eternal bliss for the piano score and various other arrangements I had made of this newest rage in the sphere of opera. So I was again forced to pay the penalty for composing my own *Fliegender Holländer* by having to sit down and write out arrangements of Halévy's opera. Yet this task no longer weighed on me so heavily. Apart from the wellfounded hope of being at last recalled from my exile in Paris, and thus being able, as I thought, to regard this last struggle with poverty as the decisive one, the arrangement of Halévy's score was far and away a more interesting piece of hack-work than the shameful labour I had spent on Donizetti's *Favorita.*

I paid another visit, the last for a long time to come, to the Grand Opera to hear this *Reine de Chypre.* There was, indeed, much for me to smile at. My eyes were no longer shut to the extreme weakness of this class of work, and the caricature of it that was often produced by the method of rendering it. I was sincerely rejoiced to see the better side of Halévy again. I had taken a great fancy to him from the time of his *La Juive,* and had a very high opinion of his masterly talent.

At the request of Schlesinger I also willingly consented to write for his paper a long article on Halévy's latest work. In it I laid particular stress on my hope that the French school might not again allow the benefits obtained by studying the German style to be lost by relapsing into the shallowest Italian methods. On that occasion I ventured, by way of encouraging the French school, to point to the peculiar significance of Auber, and particularly to his *Stumme von Portici,* drawing attention, on the other hand, to the overloaded melodies of Rossini, which often resembled sol-fa exercises. In reading over the proof of my article I saw that this passage about Rossini had been left out, and M. Edouard Monnaie admitted to me that, in his capacity as editor of a musical paper, he had felt himself bound to suppress it. He considered that if I had any adverse criticism to pass on the composer, I could easily get it published in any other kind of paper, but not in one devoted to the interests of music, simply because such a passage could not be printed there without seeming absurd. It also annoyed him that I had spoken in such high terms of Auber, but he let it stand. I had to listen to much from that quarter which enlightened me for ever with regard to the decay of operatic music in particular, and artistic taste in general, among Frenchmen of the present day.

I also wrote a longer article on the same opera for my precious friend Winkler at Dresden, who was still hesitating about accepting my *Rienzi.* In doing so I intentionally made merry over a mishap that had befallen Lachner the conductor. Küstner, who was theatrical director at Munich at the time, with a view to giving his friend another chance, ordered a libretto to be written for him by St. Georges in Paris, so that, through his paternal care, the highest bliss which a German composer could dream of might be assured to his protégé. Well, it turned out that when Halévy's *Reine de Chypre* appeared, it treated the same subject as Lachner's presumably original work, which had been composed in the meantime. It mattered very little that the libretto was a really good one, the value of the bargain lay in the fact that it was to be glorified by Lachner's music. It appeared, however, that St. Georges had, as a matter of fact, to some extent altered the book sent to Munich, but only by the omission of several interesting features. The fury of the Munich manager was great, whereupon St. Georges declared his astonishment that the latter could have imagined he would supply a libretto intended solely for the German stage at the paltry price offered by his German customer. As I had formed my own private opinion as to procuring French librettos for operas, and as nothing in the world would have induced me to set to music even the most effective piece of writing by Scribe or St. Georges, this occurrence delighted me immensely, and in the best of spirits I let myself go on the point for the benefit of the readers of the *Abendzeitung,* who, it is to be hoped, did not include my future 'friend' Lachner.

In addition, my work on Halévy's opera (*Reine de Chypre*) brought me into closer contact with that composer, and was the means of procuring me many an enlivening talk with that peculiarly good-hearted and really unassuming man, whose talent, alas, declined all too soon. Schlesinger, in fact, was exasperated at his incorrigible laziness. Halévy, who had looked through my piano score, contemplated several changes with a view to making it easier, but he did not proceed with them: Schlesinger could not get the proof-sheets back; the publication was consequently delayed, and he feared that the popularity of the opera would be over before the work was ready for the public. He urged me to get firm hold of Halévy very early in the morning in his rooms, and compel him to set to work at the alterations in my company.

The first time I reached his house at about ten in the morning, I found him just out of bed, and he informed me that he really must have breakfast first. I accepted his invitation, and sat down with him to a somewhat luxurious meal; my conversation seemed to appeal to him, but friends came in, and at last Schlesinger among the number, who burst into a fury at not finding him at work on the proofs he regarded as so important. Halévy, however, remained quite unmoved. In the best of good tempers he merely complained of his latest success, because he had never had more peace than of late, when his operas, almost without exception, had been failures, and he had not had anything to do with them after the first production. Moreover, he feigned not to understand why this *Reine de Chypre* in particular should have been a success; he declared

HALÉVY AND SCHLESINGER

that Schlesinger had engineered it on purpose to worry him. When he spoke a few words to me in German, one of the visitors was astonished, whereupon Schlesinger said that all Jews could speak German. Thereupon Schlesinger was asked if he also was a Jew. He answered that he had been, but had become a Christian for his wife's sake. This freedom of speech was a pleasant surprise to me, because in Germany in such cases we always studiously avoided the point, as discourteous to the person referred to. But as we never got to the proof correcting, Schlesinger made me promise to give Halévy no peace until we had done them.

The secret of his indifference to success became clear to me in the course of further conversation, as I learned that he was on the point of making a wealthy marriage. At first I was inclined to think that Halévy was simply a man whose youthful talent was only stimulated to achieve one great success with the object of becoming rich; in his case, however, this was not the only reason, as he was very modest in regard to his own capacity, and had no great opinion of the works of those more fortunate composers who were writing for the French stage at that time. In him I thus, for the first time, met with the frankly expressed admission of disbelief in the value of all our modern creations in this dubious field of art. I have since come to the conclusion that this incredulity, often expressed with much less modesty, justifies the participation of all Jews in our artistic concerns. Only once did Halévy speak to me with real candour, when, on my tardy departure for Germany, he wished me the success he thought my works deserved.

In the year 1860 I saw him again. I had learned that, while the Parisian critics were giving vent to the bitterest condemnation of the concerts I was giving at that time, he had expressed his approval, and this determined me to visit him at the Palais de l'Institut, of which he had for some time been permanent secretary. He seemed particularly eager to learn from my own lips what my new theory about music really was, of which he had heard such wild rumours. For his own part, he said, he had never found anything but music in my music, but with this difference, that mine had generally seemed very good. This gave rise to a lively discussion on my part, to which he good-humouredly agreed, once more wishing me success in Paris. This time, however, he did so with less conviction than when he bade me good-bye for Germany, which I thought was because he doubted whether I could succeed in Paris. From this final visit I carried away a depressing sense of the enervation, both moral and æsthetic, which had overcome one of the last great French musicians, while, on the other hand, I could not help feeling that a tendency to a hypocritical or frankly impudent exploitation of the universal degeneracy marked all who could be designated as Halévy's successors.

Throughout this period of constant hack-work my thoughts were entirely bent on my return to Germany, which now presented itself to my mind in a wholly new and ideal light. I endeavoured in various ways to secure all that seemed most attractive about the project, or which filled my soul with longing. My intercourse with Lehrs had, on the whole, given a decided spur to my former tendency to grapple seriously with my subjects, a tendency which had been counteracted by closer contact with the theatre. This desire now furnished a basis for closer study of philosophical questions. I had been astonished at times to hear even the grave and virtuous Lehrs, openly and quite as a matter of course, give expression to grave doubts concerning our individual survival after death. He declared that in many great men this doubt, even though only tacitly held, had been the real incitement to noble deeds. The natural result of such a belief speedily dawned on me without, however, causing me any serious alarm. On the contrary, I found a fascinating stimulus in the fact that boundless regions of meditation and knowledge were thereby opened up which hitherto I had merely skimmed in light-hearted levity.

In my renewed attempts to study the Greek classics in the original, I received no encouragement from Lehrs. He dissuaded me from doing so with the well-meant consolation, that as I could only be born once, and that with music in me, I should learn to understand this branch of knowledge without the help of grammar or lexicon; whereas if Greek were to be studied with real enjoyment, it was no joke, and would not suffer being relegated to a secondary place.

On the other hand, I felt strongly drawn to gain a closer acquaintance of German history than I had secured at school. I had Raumer's *History of the Hohenstaufen* within easy reach to start upon. All the great figures in this book lived vividly before my eyes. I was particularly captivated by the personality of that gifted Emperor Frederick II., whose fortunes aroused my sympathy so keenly that I vainly sought for a fitting artistic setting for them. The fate of his son Manfred, on the other hand, provoked in me an equally well-grounded, but more easily combated, feeling of opposition.

I accordingly made a plan of a great five-act dramatic poem, which should also be perfectly adapted to a musical setting. My impulse to embellish the story with the central figure of romantic significance was prompted by the fact of Manfred's enthusiastic reception in Luceria by the Saracens, who supported him and carried him on from victory to victory till he reached his final triumph, and this, too, in spite of the fact that he had come to them betrayed on every hand, banned by the Church, and deserted by all his followers during his flight through Apulia and the Abruzzi.

Even at this time it delighted me to find in the German mind the capacity of appreciating beyond the narrow bounds of nationality all purely human qualities, in however strange a garb they might be presented. For in this I recognised how nearly akin it is to the mind of Greece. In Frederick II. I saw this quality in full flower. A fair-haired German of ancient Swabian stock, heir to the Norman realm of Sicily and Naples, who gave the Italian language its first development, and laid a basis for the evolution of knowledge and art where hitherto ecclesiastical fanaticism and feudal brutality had alone contended for power, a monarch who gathered at his court the poets and sages of eastern lands, and surrounded himself with the living products of Arabian and Persian grace and spirit — this man I beheld betrayed by the Roman clergy to the infidel foe, yet ending his crusade, to their bitter disappointment, by a pact of peace with the Sultan, from whom he obtained a grant of privileges to Christians in Palestine such as the bloodiest victory could scarcely have secured.

In this wonderful Emperor, who finally, under the ban of that same Church, struggled hopelessly and in vain against the savage bigotry of his age, I beheld the German ideal in its highest embodiment. My poem was concerned with the fate of his favourite son Manfred. On the death of an elder brother, Frederick's empire had entirely fallen to pieces, and the young Manfred was left, under papal suzerainty, in nominal possession of the throne of Apulia. We find him at Capua, in surroundings, and attended by a court, in which the spirit of his great father survives, in a state of almost effeminate degeneration. In despair of ever restoring the imperial power of the Hohenstaufen, he seeks to forget his sadness in romance and song. There now appears upon the scene a young Saracen lady, just arrived from the East, who, by appealing to the alliance between East and West concluded by Manfred's noble father, conjures the desponding son to maintain his imperial heritage. She acts the part of an inspired prophetess, and though the prince is quickly filled with love for her, she succeeds in keeping him at a respectful distance. By a skilfully contrived flight she snatches him, not only from the pursuit of rebellious Apulian nobles, but also from the papal ban which is threatening to depose him from his throne. Accompanied only by a few faithful followers, she guides him through mountain fastnesses, where one night the wearied son beholds the spirit of Frederick II. passing with feudal array through the Abruzzi, and beckoning him on to Luceria.

To this district, situated in the Papal States, Frederick had, by a peaceful compact, transplanted the remnant of his Saracen retainers, who had previously been wreaking terrible havoc in the mountains of Sicily. To the great annoyance of the Pope, he had handed the town over to them in fee-simple, thus securing for himself a band of faithful allies in the heart of an ever-treacherous and hostile country.

Fatima, as my heroine is called, has prepared, through the instrumentality of trusty friends, a reception for Manfred in this place. When the papal governor has been expelled by a revolution, he slips through the gateway into the town, is recognised by the whole population as the son of their beloved Emperor, and, amid wildest enthusiasm, is placed at their head, to lead them against the enemies of their departed benefactor. In the meantime, while Manfred is marching on from victory to victory in his reconquest of the whole kingdom of Apulia, the tragic centre of my action still continues to be the unvoiced longing of the lovelorn victor for the marvellous heroine.

She is the child of the great Emperor's love for a noble Saracen maiden. Her mother, on her deathbed, had sent her to Manfred, foretelling that she would work wonders for his glory provided she never yielded to his passion. Whether Fatima was to know that she was his sister I left undecided in framing my plot. Meanwhile she is careful to show herself to him only at critical moments, and then always in such a way as to remain unapproachable. When at last she witnesses the completion of her task in his coronation at Naples, she determines, in obedience to her vow, to slip away secretly from the newly anointed king, that she may meditate in the solitude of her distant home upon the success of her enterprise.

The Saracen Nurreddin, who had been a companion of her youth, and to whose help she had chiefly owed her success in rescuing Manfred, is to be the sole partner of her flight. To this man, who loves her with passionate ardour, she had been promised in her childhood. Before her secret departure she pays a last visit to the slumbering king. This rouses her lover's furious jealousy, as he construes her act into a proof of unfaithfulness on the part of his betrothed. The last look of farewell which Fatima casts from a distance at the young monarch, on his return from his coronation, inflames the jealous lover to wreak instant vengeance for the supposed outrage upon his honour. He strikes the prophetess to the earth, whereupon she thanks him with a smile for having delivered her from an unbearable existence. At the sight of her body Manfred realises that henceforth happiness has deserted him for ever.

This theme I had adorned with many gorgeous scenes and complicated situations, so that when I had worked it out I could regard it as a fairly suitable, interesting, and effective whole, especially when compared with other well-known subjects of a similar nature. Yet I could never rouse myself to sufficient enthusiasm over it to give my serious attention to its elaboration, especially as another theme now laid its grip upon me. This was suggested to me by a pamphlet on the 'Venusberg,' which accidentally fell into my hands.

If all that I regarded as essentially German had hitherto drawn me with ever-increasing force, and compelled me to its eager pursuit, I here found it suddenly presented to me in the simple outlines of a legend, based upon the old and well-known ballad of 'Tannhäuser.' True, its elements were already familiar to me from Tieck's version in his *Phantasus*. But his conception of the subject had flung me back into the fantastic regions created in my mind at an earlier period by Hoffmann, and I should certainly never have been tempted to extract the framework of a dramatic work from his elaborate story. The point in this popular pamphlet which had so much weight with me was that it brought 'Tannhäuser,' if only by a passing hint, into touch with 'The Minstrel's War on the Wartburg.' I had some knowledge of this also from Hoffmann's account in his *Serapionsbrüdern*. But I felt that the writer had only grasped the old legend in a distorted form, and therefore endeavoured to gain a closer acquaintance with the true aspect of this attractive story. At this juncture Lehrs brought me the annual report of the proceedings of the Königsberg German Society, in which the 'Wartburg contest' was criticised with a fair amount of detail by Lukas. Here I also found the original text. Although I could utilise but little of the real setting for my own purpose, yet the picture it gave me of Germany in the Middle Ages was so suggestive that I found I had not previously had the smallest conception of what it was like.

As a sequel to the Wartburg poem, I also found in the same copy a critical study, 'Lohengrin,' which gave in full detail the main contents of that widespread epic.

Thus a whole new world was opened to me, and though as yet I had not found the form in which I might cope with *Lohengrin*, yet this image also lived imperishably within me. When, therefore, I afterwards made a close acquaintance with the intricacies of this legend, I could visualise the figure of the hero with a distinctness equal to that of my conception of *Tannhäuser* at this time.

Under these influences my longing for a speedy return to Germany grew ever more intense, for there I hoped to earn a new home for myself where I could enjoy leisure for creative work. But it was not yet possible even to think of occupying myself with such grateful tasks. The sordid necessities of life still bound me to Paris. While thus employed, I found an opportunity of exerting myself in a way more congenial to my desires. When I was a young man at Prague, I had made the acquaintance of a Jewish musician and composer called Dessauer — a man who was not devoid of talent, who in fact achieved a certain reputation, but was chiefly known among his intimates on account of his hypochondria. This man, who was now in flourishing circumstances, was so far patronised by Schlesinger that the latter seriously proposed to help him to a commission for Grand Opera. Dessauer had come across my poem of the *Fliegender Holländer*, and now insisted that I should draft a similar plot for him, as M. Léon Pillet's *Vaisseau Fantôme* had already been given to M. Dietsch, the latter's musical conductor, to set to music. From this same conductor Dessauer obtained the promise of a like commission, and he now offered me two hundred francs to provide him with a similar plot, and one congenial to his hypochondriacal temperament.

To meet this wish I ransacked my brain for recollections of Hoffmann, and quickly decided to work up his *Bergwerke von Falun*. The moulding of this fascinating and marvellous material succeeded as admirably as I could wish. Dessauer also felt convinced that the topic was worth his while to set to music. His dismay was accordingly all the greater when Pillet rejected our plot on the ground that the staging would be too difficult, and that the second act especially would entail insurmountable obstacles for the ballet, which had to be given each time. In place of this Dessauer wished me to compose him an oratorio on 'Mary Magdalene.' As on the day that he expressed this wish he appeared to be suffering from acute melancholia, so much so that he declared he had that morning seen his own head lying beside his bed, I thought well not to refuse his request. I asked him, therefore, to give me time, and I regret to say that ever since that day I have continued to take it.

It was amid such distractions as these that this winter at length drew to an end, while my prospects of getting to Germany gradually grew more hopeful, though with a slowness that sorely tried my patience. I had kept up a continuous correspondence with Dresden respecting *Rienzi*, and in the worthy chorus-master Fischer I at last found an honest man who was favourably disposed to me. He sent me reliable and reassuring reports as to the state of my affairs.

After receiving news, early in January, 1842, of renewed delay, I at last heard that by the end of February the work would be ready for performance. I was seriously uneasy at this, as I was afraid of not being able to accomplish the journey by that date. But this news also was soon contradicted, and the honest Fischer informed me that my opera had had to be postponed till the autumn of that year. I realised fully that it would never be performed if I could not be present in person at Dresden. When eventually in March Count Redern, the director of the Theatre Royal in Berlin, told me that my *Fliegender Holländer* had been accepted for the opera there, I thought I had sufficient reason to return to Germany at all costs as soon as possible.

I had already had various experiences as to the views of German managers on this work. Relying on the plot, which had pleased the manager of the Paris Opera so much, I had sent the libretto in the first instance to my old acquaintance Ringelhardt, the director of the Leipzig theatre. But the man had cherished an undisguised aversion for me since my *Liebesverbot*. As he could not this time possibly object to any levity in my subject, he now found fault with its gloomy solemnity and refused to accept it. As I had met Councillor Küstner, at that time manager of the Munich Court Theatre, when he was making arrangements about *La Reine de Chypre* in Paris, I now sent him the text of the *Dutchman* with a similar request. He, too, returned it, with the assurance that it was not suited to German stage conditions, or to the taste of the German public. As he had ordered a French libretto for Munich, I knew what he meant. When the score was finished, I sent it to Meyerbeer in Berlin, with a letter for Count Redern, and begged him, as he had been unable to help me to anything in Paris, in spite of his desire to do so, to be kind enough to use his influence in Berlin in favour of my composition. I was genuinely astonished at the truly prompt acceptance of my work two months later, which was accompanied by very gratifying assurances from the Count, and I was delighted to see in it a proof of Meyerbeer's sincere and energetic intervention in my favour. Strange to say, on my return to Germany soon afterwards, I was destined to learn that Count Redern had long since retired from the management of the Berlin Opera House, and that Küstner of Munich had already been appointed his successor: the upshot of this was that Count Redern's consent, though very courteous, could not by any means be taken seriously, as the realisation of it depended not on him but on his successor. What the result was remains to be seen.

A circumstance that eventually facilitated my long-desired return to Germany, which was now justified by my good prospects, was the tardily awakened interest taken in my position by the wealthy members of my family. If Didot had had reasons of his own for applying to the Minister Villemain for support for Lehrs, so also Avenarius, my brother-in-law in Paris, when he heard how I was struggling against poverty, one day took it into his head to surprise me with some quite unexpected help secured by his appeal to my sister Louisa. On 26th December of the fast-waning year 1841 I went home to Minna carrying a goose under my arm, and in the beak of the bird we found a five-hundred-franc note. This note had been given me by Avenarius as the result of a request on my behalf made by my sister Louisa to a friend of hers, a wealthy merchant named Schletter. This welcome addition to our extremely straitened resources might not in itself have been sufficient to put me in an exceedingly good-humour, had I not clearly seen in it the prospect of escaping altogether from my position in Paris. As the leading German managers had now consented to the performance of two of my compositions, I thought I might seriously approach my brother-in-law, Friedrich Brockhaus, who had repulsed me the year before when I applied to him in great distress, on the ground that he 'disapproved of my profession.' This time I might be more successful in securing the wherewithal for my return. I was not mistaken, and when the time came I was supplied from this source with the necessary travelling expenses.

With these prospects, and my position thus improved, I found myself spending the second half of the winter 1841-42 in high spirits, and affording constant entertainment to the small circle of friends which my relationship to Avenarius had created around me. Minna and I frequently spent our evenings with this family and others, amongst whom I have pleasant recollections of a certain Herr Kühne, the head of a private school, and his wife. I contributed so greatly to the success of their little soirées, and was always so willing to improvise dances on the piano for them to dance to, that I soon ran the risk of enjoying an almost burdensome popularity.

At length the hour struck for my deliverance; the day came on which, as I devoutly hoped, I might turn my back on Paris for ever. It was the 7th of April, and Paris was already gay with the first luxuriant buddings of spring. In front of our windows, which all the winter had looked upon a bleak and desolate garden, the trees were burgeoning, and the birds sang. Our emotion at parting from our dear friends Anders, Lehrs, and Kietz, however, was great, almost overwhelming. The first seemed already doomed to an early death, for his health was exceedingly bad, and he was advanced in years. About Lehrs' condition, as I have already said, there could no longer be any doubt, and it was dreadful, after so short an experience as the two and a half years which I had spent in Paris, to see the ravages that want had wrought among good, noble, and sometimes even distinguished men. Kietz, for whose future I was concerned, less on grounds of health than of morals, touched our hearts once more by his boundless and almost childlike good-nature. Fancying, for instance, that I might not have enough money for the journey, he forced me, in spite of all resistance, to accept another five-franc piece, which was about all that remained of his own fortune at the moment: he also stuffed a packet of good French snuff for me into the pocket of the coach, in which we at last rumbled through the boulevards to the barriers, which we passed but were unable to see this time, because our eyes were blinded with tears.

PART II

1842-1850

THE journey from Paris to Dresden at that time took five days and nights. On the German frontier, near Forbach, we met with stormy weather and snow, a greeting which seemed inhospitable after the spring we had already enjoyed in Paris. And, indeed, as we continued our journey through our native land once more, we found much to dishearten us, and I could not help thinking that the Frenchmen who on leaving Germany breathed more freely on reaching French soil, and unbuttoned their coats, as though passing from winter into summer, were not so very foolish after all, seeing that we, for our part, were now compelled to seek protection against this conspicuous change of temperature by being very careful to put on sufficient clothing. The unkindness of the elements became perfect torture when, later on, between Frankfort and Leipzig, we were swept into the stream of visitors to the Great Easter Fair.

The pressure on the mail-coaches was so great, that for two days and a night, amid ceaseless storm, snow and rain, we were continually changing from one wretched 'substitute' to another, thus turning our journey into an adventure of almost the same type as our former voyage at sea.

One solitary flash of brightness was afforded by our view of the Wartburg, which we passed during the only sunlit hour of this journey. The sight of this mountain fastness, which, from the Fulda side, is clearly visible for a long time, affected me deeply. A neighbouring ridge further on I at once christened the Hörselberg, and as we drove through the valley, pictured to myself the scenery for the third act of my *Tannhäuser*. This scene remained so vividly in my mind, that long afterwards I was able to give Despléchin, the Parisian scene-painter, exact details when he was working out the scenery under my direction. If I had already been impressed by the significance of the fact that my first journey through the German Rhine district, so famous in legend, should have been made on my way home from Paris, it seemed an even more ominous coincidence that my first sight of Wartburg, which was so rich in historical and mythical associations, should come just at this moment. The view so warmed my heart against wind and weather, Jews and the Leipzig Fair, that in the end I arrived, on 12th April, 1842, safe and sound, with my poor, battered, half-frozen wife, in that selfsame city of Dresden which I had last seen on the occasion of my sad separation from my Minna, and my departure for my northern place of exile.

We put up at the 'Stadt Gotha' inn. The city, in which such momentous years of my childhood and boyhood had been spent, seemed cold and dead beneath the influences of the wild, gloomy weather. Indeed, everything there that could remind me of my youth seemed dead. No hospitable house received us. We found my wife's parents living in cramped and dingy lodgings in very straitened circumstances, and were obliged at once to look about for a small abode for ourselves. This we found in the Töpfergasse for twenty-one marks a month. After paying the necessary business visits in connection with *Rienzi*, and making arrangements for Minna during my brief absence, I set out on 15th April direct for Leipzig, where I saw my mother and family for the first time in six years.

During this period, which had been so eventful for my own life, my mother had undergone a great change in her domestic position through the death of Rosalie. She was living in a pleasant roomy flat near the Brockhaus family, where she was free from all those household cares to which, owing to her large family, she had devoted so many years of anxious thought. Her bustling energy, which had almost amounted to hardness, had entirely given place to a natural cheerfulness and interest in the family prosperity of her married daughters. For the blissful calm of this happy old age she was mainly indebted to the affectionate care of her son-in-law, Friedrich Brockhaus, to whom I expressed my heartfelt thanks for his goodness. She was exceedingly astonished and pleased to see me unexpectedly enter her room. Any bitterness that ever existed between us had utterly vanished, and her only complaint was that she could not put me up in her house, instead of my brother Julius, the unfortunate goldsmith, who had none of the qualities that could make him a suitable companion for her. She was full of hope for the success of my undertaking, and felt this confidence strengthened by the favourable prophecy which our dear Rosalie had made about me shortly before her sad death.

For the present, however, I only stayed a few days in Leipzig, as I had first to visit Berlin in order to make definite arrangements with Count Redern for the performance of the *Fliegender Holländer*. As I have already observed, I was here at once destined to learn that the Count was on the point of retiring from the directorship, and he accordingly referred me for all further decisions to the new director, Küstner, who had not yet arrived in Berlin. I now suddenly realised what this strange circumstance meant, and knew that, so far as the Berlin negotiations went, I might as well have remained in Paris. This impression was in the main confirmed by a visit to Meyerbeer, who, I found, regarded my coming to Berlin as over hasty. Nevertheless, he behaved in a kind and friendly manner, only regretting that he was just on the point of 'going away,' a state in which I always found him whenever I visited him again in Berlin.

Mendelssohn was also in the capital about this time, having been appointed one of the General Musical Directors to the King of Prussia. I also sought him out, having been previously introduced to him in Leipzig. He informed me that he did not believe his work would prosper in Berlin, and that he would rather go back to Leipzig. I made no inquiry about the fate of the score of my great symphony performed at Leipzig in earlier days, which I had more or less forced upon him so many years ago. On the other hand, he did not betray to me any signs of remembering that strange offering. In the midst of the lavish comforts of his home he struck me as cold, yet it was not so much that he repelled me as that I recoiled from him. I also paid a visit to Rellstab, to whom I had a letter of introduction from his trusty publisher, my brother-in-law Brockhaus. Here it was not so much smug ease that I encountered; I doubtless felt repulsed more by the fact that he showed no inclination whatever to interest himself in my affairs.

I grew very low spirited in Berlin. I could almost have wished Commissioner Cerf back again. Miserable as had been the time I had spent here years before, I had then, at any rate, met one man, who, for all the bluntness of his exterior, had treated me with true friendliness and consideration. In vain did I try to call to mind the Berlin through whose streets I had walked, with all the ardour of youth, by the side of Laube. After my acquaintance with London, and still more with Paris, this city, with its sordid spaces and pretensions to greatness, depressed me deeply, and I breathed a hope that, should no luck crown my life, it might at least be spent in Paris rather than in Berlin.

On my return from this wholly fruitless expedition, I first went to Leipzig for a few days, where, on this occasion, I stayed with my brother-in-law, Hermann Brockhaus, who was now Professor of Oriental Languages at the University. His family had been increased by the birth of two daughters, and the atmosphere of unruffled content, illuminated by mental activity and a quiet but vivid interest in all things relating to the higher aspects of life, greatly moved my homeless and vagabond soul. One evening, after my sister had seen to her children, whom she had brought up very well, and had sent them with gentle words to bed, we gathered in the large richly stocked library for our evening meal and a long confidential chat. Here I broke out into a violent fit of weeping, and it seemed as though the tender sister, who five years before had known me during the bitterest straits of my early married life in Dresden, now really understood me. At the express suggestion of my brother-in-law Hermann, my family tendered me a loan, to help me to tide over the time of waiting for the performance of my *Rienzi* in Dresden. This, they said, they regarded merely as a duty, and assured me that I need have no hesitation whatever in accepting it. It consisted of a sum of six hundred marks, which was to be paid me in monthly instalments for six months. As I had no prospect of being able to rely on any other source of income, there was every chance of Minna's talent for management being put severely to the test, if this were to carry us through; it could be done, however, and I was able to return to Dresden with a great sense of relief.

While I was staying with my relatives I played and sang them the *Fliegender Holländer* for the first time connectedly, and seemed to arouse considerable interest by my performance, for when, later on, my sister Louisa heard the opera in Dresden, she complained that much of the effect previously produced by my rendering did not come back to her. I also sought out my old friend Apel again. The poor man had gone stone blind, but he astonished me by his cheeriness and contentment, and thereby once and for all deprived me of any reason for pitying him. As he declared that he knew the blue coat I was wearing very well, though it was really a brown one, I thought it best not to argue the point, and I left Leipzig in a state of wonder at finding every one there so happy and contented.

When I reached Dresden, on 26th April, I found occasion to grapple more vigorously with my lot. Here I was enlivened by closer intercourse with the people on whom I had to rely for a successful production of *Rienzi*. It is true that the results of my interviews with Lüttichau, the general manager, and Reissiger, the musical conductor, left me cold and incredulous. Both were sincerely astonished at my arrival in Dresden; and the same might even be said of my frequent correspondent and patron, Hofrath Winkler, who also would have preferred my remaining in Paris. But, as has been my constant experience both before and since, help and encouragement have always come to me from humbler and never from the more exalted ranks of life.

So in this case, too, I met my first agreeable sensation in the overwhelmingly cordial reception I received from the old chorus-master, Wilhelm Fischer. I had had no previous acquaintance with him, yet he was the only person who had taken the trouble to read my score carefully, and had not only conceived serious hopes for the success of my opera, but had worked energetically to secure its being accepted and practised. The moment I entered his room and told him my name, he rushed to embrace me with a loud cry, and in a second I was translated to an atmosphere of hope. Besides this man, I met in the actor Ferdinand Heine and his family another sure foundation for hearty and, indeed, deep-rooted friendship. It is true that I had known him from childhood, for at that time he was one of the few young people whom my stepfather Geyer liked to see about him. In addition to a fairly decided talent for drawing, it was chiefly his pleasant social gifts that had won him an entrance into our more intimate family circle. As he was very small and slight, my stepfather nicknamed him David*chen,* and under this appellation he used to take part with great affability and good-humour in our little festivities, and above all in our friendly excursions into the neighbouring country, in which, as I mentioned in its place, even Carl Maria von Weber used to join. Belonging to the good old school, he had become a useful, if not prominent, member of the Dresden stage. He possessed all the knowledge and qualities for a good stage manager, but never succeeded in inducing the committee to give him that appointment. It was only as a designer of costumes that he found further scope for his talents, and in this capacity he was included in the consultations over the staging of *Rienzi.*

Thus it came about that he had the opportunity of busying himself with the work of a member, now grown to man's estate, of the very family with whom he had spent such pleasant days in his youth. He greeted me at once as a child of the house, and we two homeless creatures found in our memories of this long-lost home the first common basis to our friendship. We generally spent our evenings with old Fischer at Heine's, where, amid hopeful conversation, we regaled ourselves on potatoes and herrings, of which the meal chiefly consisted. Schröder-Devrient was away on a holiday; Tichatschek, who was also on the point of going away, I had just time to see, and with him I went quickly through a part of his rôle in *Rienzi.* His brisk and lively nature, his glorious voice and great musical talent, gave special weight to his encouraging assurance that he delighted in the rôle of Rienzi. Heine also told me that the mere prospect of having many new costumes, and especially

PREPARATION FOR RIENZI

new silver armour, had inspired Tichatschek with the liveliest desire to play this part, so that I might rely on him under any circumstances. Thus I could at once give closer attention to the preparations for practice, which was fixed to begin in the late summer, after the principal singers had returned from their holiday.

I had to make special efforts to pacify my friend Fischer by my readiness to abbreviate the score, which was excessively lengthy. His intentions in the matter were so honest that I gladly sat down with him to the wearisome task. I played and sang my score to the astonished man on an old grand piano in the rehearsing-room of the Court Theatre, with such frantic vigour that, although he did not mind if the instrument came to grief, he grew concerned about my chest. Finally, amid hearty laughter, he ceased to argue about cutting down passages, as precisely where he thought something might be omitted I proved to him with headlong eloquence that it was precisely here that the main point lay. He plunged with me head over heels into the vast chaos of sound, against which he could raise no objection, beyond the testimony of his watch, whose correctness I also ended by disputing. As sops I light-heartedly flung him the big pantomime and most of the ballet in the second act, whereby I reckoned we might save a whole half-hour. Thus, thank goodness, the whole monster was at last handed over to the clerks to make a fair copy of, and the rest was left for time to accomplish.

We next discussed what we should do in the summer, and I decided upon a stay of several months at Töplitz, the scene of my first youthful flights, whose fine air and baths, I hoped, would also benefit Minna's health. But before we could carry out this intention I had to pay several more visits to Leipzig to settle the fate of my *Dutchman*. On 5th May I proceeded thither to have an interview with Küstner, the new director of the Berlin Opera, who I had been told had just arrived there. He was now placed in the awkward position of being about to produce in Berlin the very opera which he had before declined in Munich, as it had been accepted by his predecessor in office. He promised me to consider what steps he would take in this predicament. In order to learn the result of

Küstner's deliberations, I determined, on 2nd June, to seek him out, and this time in Berlin itself. But at Leipzig I found a letter in which he begged me to wait patiently a little longer for his final verdict. I took advantage of being in the neighbourhood of Halle to pay a visit to my eldest brother Albert. I was very much grieved and depressed to find the poor fellow, whom I must give the credit of having the greatest perseverance and a quite remarkable talent for dramatic song, living in the unworthy and mean circumstances which the Halle Theatre offered to him and his family. The realisation of conditions into which I myself had once nearly sunk now filled me with indescribable abhorrence. Still more harrowing was it to hear my brother speak of this state in tones which showed, alas, only too plainly, the hopeless submission with which he had already resigned himself to its horrors. The only consolation I could find was the personality and childlike nature of his stepdaughter Johanna, who was then fifteen, and who sang me Spohr's *Rose, wie bist du so schön* with great expression and in a voice of an extraordinarily beautiful quality.

Then I returned to Dresden, and at last, in wonderful weather, undertook the pleasant journey to Töplitz with Minna and one of her sisters, reaching that place on 9th June, where we took up our quarters at a second-class inn, the Eiche, at Schönau. Here we were soon joined by my mother, who paid her usual yearly visit to the warm baths all the more gladly this time because she knew she would find me there. If she had before had any prejudice against Minna because of my premature marriage to her, a closer acquaintance with her domestic gifts soon changed it into respect, and she quickly learned to love the partner of my doleful days in Paris. Although my mother's vagaries demanded no small consideration, yet what particularly delighted me about her was the astonishing vivacity of her almost childlike imagination, a faculty she retained to such a degree that one morning she complained that my relation of the *Tannhäuser* legend on the previous evening had given her a whole night of pleasant but most tiring sleeplessness.

By dint of appealing letters to Schletter, a wealthy patron of art in Leipzig, I managed to do something for Kietz, who, had remained behind in misery in Paris, and also to provide Minna with medical treatment. I also succeeded to a certain extent in ameliorating my own woeful financial position. Scarcely were these tasks accomplished, when I started off in my old boyish way on a ramble of several days on foot through the Bohemian mountains, in order that I might mentally work out my plan of the 'Venusberg' amid the pleasant associations of such a trip. Here I took the fancy of engaging quarters in Aussig on the romantic Schreckenstein, where for several days I occupied the little public room, in which straw was laid down for me to sleep on at night. I found recreation in daily ascents of the Wostrai, the highest peak in the neighbourhood, and so keenly did the fantastic solitude quicken my youthful spirit, that I clambered about the ruins of the Schreckenstein the whole of one moonlit night, wrapped only in a blanket, in order myself to provide the ghost that was lacking, and delighted myself with the hope of scaring some passing wayfarer.

Here I drew up in my pocket-book the detailed plan of a three-act opera on the 'Venusberg,' and subsequently carried out the composition of this work in strict accordance with the sketch I then made.

One day, when climbing the Wostrai, I was astonished, on turning the corner of a valley, to hear a merry dance tune whistled by a goatherd perched up on a crag. I seemed immediately to stand among the chorus of pilgrims filing past the goatherd in the valley; but I could not afterwards recall the goatherd's tune, so I was obliged to help myself out of the matter in the usual way.

Enriched by these spoils, I returned to Töplitz in a wonderfully cheerful frame of mind and robust health, but on receiving the interesting news that Tichatschek and Schröder-Devrient were on the point of returning, I was impelled to set off once more for Dresden. I took this step, not so much to avoid missing any of the early rehearsals of *Rienzi,* as because I wanted to prevent the management replacing it by something else. I left Minna for a time with my mother, and reached Dresden on 18th July.

I hired a small lodging in a queer house, since pulled down, facing the Maximilian Avenue, and entered into a fairly lively intercourse with our operatic stars who had just returned. My old enthusiasm for Schröder-Devrient revived when I saw her again more frequently in opera. Strange was the effect produced upon me when I heard her for the first time in Grétry's *Blaubart,* for I could not help remembering that this was the first opera I had ever seen. I had been taken to it as a boy of five (also in Dresden), and I still retained my wondrous first impressions of it. All my earliest childish memories were revived, and I recollected how frequently and with what emphasis I had myself sung Bluebeard's song: *Ha, die Falsche! Die Thüre offen!* to the amusement of the whole house, with a paper helmet of my own making on my head. My friend Heine still remembered it well.

In other respects the operatic performances were not such as to impress me very favourably: I particularly missed the rolling sound of the fully equipped Parisian orchestra of string instruments. I also noticed that, when opening the fine new theatre, they had quite forgotten to increase the number of these instruments in proportion to the enlarged space. In this, as well as in the general equipment of the stage, which was materially deficient in many respects, I was impressed by the sense of a certain meanness about theatrical enterprise in Germany, which became most noticeable when reproductions were given, often with wretched translations of the text, of the Paris opera repertoire. If even in Paris my dissatisfaction with this treatment of opera had been great, the feeling which once drove me thither from the German theatres now returned with redoubled energy. I actually felt degraded again, and nourished within my breast a contempt so deep that for a time I could hardly endure the thought of signing a lasting contract, even with one of the most up-to-date of German opera houses, but sadly wondered what steps I could take to hold my ground between disgust and desire in this strange world.

Nothing but the sympathy inspired by communion with persons endowed with exceptional gifts enabled me to triumph over my scruples. This statement applies above all to my great ideal, Schröder-Devrient, in whose artistic triumphs it had once been my most burning desire to be associated. It is true that many years had elapsed since my first youthful impressions of her were formed. As regards her looks, the verdict which, in the following winter, was sent to Paris by Berlioz during his stay in Dresden, was so far correct that her somewhat 'maternal' stoutness was unsuited to youthful parts, especially in male attire, which, as in *Rienzi*, made too great a demand upon the imagination. Her voice, which in point of quality had never been an exceptionally good medium for song, often landed her in difficulties, and in particular she was forced, when singing, to drag the time a little all through. But her achievements were less hampered now by these material hindrances than by the fact that her repertoire consisted of a limited number of leading parts, which she had sung so frequently that a certain monotony in the conscious calculation of effect often developed into a mannerism which, from her tendency to exaggeration, was at times almost painful.

Although these defects could not escape me, yet I, more than any one, was especially qualified to overlook such minor weaknesses, and realise with enthusiasm the incomparable greatness of her performances. Indeed, it only needed the stimulus of excitement, which this actress's exceptionally eventful life still procured, fully to restore the creative power of her prime, a fact of which I was subsequently to receive striking demonstrations. But I was seriously troubled and depressed at seeing how strong was the disintegrating effect of theatrical life upon the character of this singer, who had originally been endowed with such great and noble qualities. From the very mouth through which the great actress's inspired musical utterances reached me, I was compelled to hear at other times very similar language to that in which, with but few exceptions, nearly all heroines of the stage indulge. The possession of a naturally fine voice, or even mere physical advantages, which might place her rivals on the same footing as herself in public favour, was more than she could endure; and so far was she from acquiring the dignified resignation worthy of a great artist, that her jealousy increased to a painful extent as years went on. I noticed this all the more because I had reason to suffer from it. A fact which caused me even greater trouble, however, was that she did not grasp music easily, and the study of a new part involved difficulties which meant many a painful hour for the composer who had to make her master his work. Her difficulty in learning new parts, and particularly that of Adriano in *Rienzi*, entailed disappointments for her which caused me a good deal of trouble.

If, in her case, I had to handle a great and sensitive nature very tenderly, I had, on the other hand, a very easy task with Tichatschek, with his childish limitations and superficial, but exceptionally brilliant, talents. He did not trouble to learn his parts by heart, as he was so musical that he could sing the most difficult music at sight, and thought all further study needless, whereas with most other singers the work consisted in mastering the score. Hence, if he sang through a part at rehearsals often enough to impress it on his memory, the rest, that is to say, everything pertaining to vocal art and dramatic delivery, would follow naturally. In this way he picked up any clerical errors there might be in the libretto, and that with such incorrigible pertinacity, that he uttered the wrong words with just the same expression as if they were correct. He waved aside good-humouredly any expostulations or hints as to the sense with the remark, 'Ah! that will be all right soon.' And, in fact, I very soon resigned myself and quite gave up trying to get the singer to use his intelligence in the interpretation of the part of the hero, for which I was very agreeably compensated by the light-hearted enthusiasm with which he flung himself into his congenial rôle, and the irresistible effect of his brilliant voice.

With the exception of these two actors who played the leading parts, I had only very moderate material at my disposal. But there was plenty of goodwill, and I had recourse to an ingenious device to induce Reissiger the conductor to hold frequent piano rehearsals. He had complained to me of the difficulty he had always found in securing a well-written libretto, and thought it was very sensible of me to have acquired the habit of writing my own. In his youth he had unfortunately neglected to do this for himself, and yet this was all he lacked to make a successful dramatic composer. I feel bound to confess that he possessed 'a good deal of melody'; but this, he added, did not seem sufficient to inspire the singers with the requisite enthusiasm. His experience was that Schröder-Devrient, in his *Adèle de Foix,* would render very indifferently the same final passage with which, in Bellini's *Romeo and Juliet,* she would put the audience into an ecstasy. The reason for this, he presumed, must lie in the subject-matter. I at once promised him that I would supply him with a libretto in which he would be able to introduce these and similar melodies to the greatest advantage. To this he gladly agreed, and I therefore set aside for versification, as a suitable text for Reissiger, my *Hohe Braut,* founded on König's romance, which I had once before submitted to Scribe. I promised to bring Reissiger a page of verse for every piano rehearsal, and this I faithfully did until the whole book was done. I was much surprised to learn some time later that Reissiger had had a new libretto written for him by an actor named Kriethe. This was called the *Wreck of the Medusa.* I then learned that the wife of the conductor, who was a suspicious woman, had been filled with the greatest concern at my readiness to give up a libretto to her husband. They both thought the book was good and full of striking effects, but they suspected some sort of trap in the background, to escape from which they must certainly exercise the greatest caution. The result was that I regained possession of my libretto and was able, later on, to help my old friend Kittl with it in Prague; he set it to music of his own, and entitled it *Die Franzosen vor Nizza.* I heard that it was frequently performed in Prague with great success, though I never saw it myself; and I was also told at the same time by a local critic that this text was a proof of my real aptitude as a librettist, and that it was a mistake for me to devote myself to composition. As regards my *Tannhäuser,* on the other hand, Laube used to declare it was a misfortune that I had not got an experienced dramatist to supply me with a decent text for my music.

For the time being, however, this work of versification had the desired result, and Reissiger kept steadily to the study of *Rienzi.* But what encouraged him even more than my verses was the growing interest of the singers, and above all the genuine enthusiasm of Tichatschek. This man, who had been so ready to leave the delights of the theatre piano for a shooting party, now looked upon the rehearsals of Rienzi as a genuine treat. He always attended them with radiant eyes and boisterous good-humour. I soon felt myself in a state of constant exhilaration: favourite passages were greeted with acclamation by the singers at every rehearsal, and a concerted number of the third finale, which unfortunately had afterwards to be omitted owing to its length, actually became on that occasion a source of profit to me. For Tichatschek maintained that this B minor was so lovely that something ought to be paid for it every time, and he put down a silver penny, inviting the others to do the same, to which they all responded merrily. From that day forward, whenever we came to this passage at rehearsals, the cry was raised, 'Here comes the silver penny part,' and Schröder-Devrient, as she took out her purse, remarked that these rehearsals would ruin her. This gratuity was conscientiously handed to me each time, and no one suspected that these contributions, which were given as a joke, were often a very welcome help towards defraying the cost of our daily food. For Minna had returned from Töplitz, at the beginning of August, accompanied by my mother.

We lived very frugally in chilly lodgings, hopefully awaiting the tardy day of our deliverance. The months of August and September passed, in preparation for my work, amid frequent disturbances caused by the fluctuating and scanty repertoire of a German opera house, and not until October did the combined rehearsals assume such a character as to promise the certainty of a speedy production. From the very beginning of the general rehearsals with the orchestra we all shared the conviction that the opera would, without doubt, be a great success. Finally, the full dress rehearsals produced a perfectly intoxicating effect. When we tried the first scene of the second act with the scenery complete, and the messengers of peace entered, there was a general outburst of emotion, and even Schröder-Devrient, who was bitterly prejudiced against her part, as it was not the rôle of the heroine, could only answer my questions in a voice stifled with tears. I believe the whole theatrical body, down to its humblest officials, loved me as though I were a real prodigy, and I am probably not far wrong in saying that much of this arose from sympathy and lively fellow-feeling for a young man, whose exceptional difficulties were not unknown to them, and who now suddenly stepped out of perfect obscurity into splendour. During the interval at the full dress rehearsal, while other members had dispersed to revive their jaded nerves with lunch, I remained seated on a pile of boards on the stage, in order that no one might realise that I was in the quandary of being unable to obtain similar refreshment. An invalid Italian singer, who was taking a small part in the opera, seemed to notice this, and kindly brought me a glass of wine and a piece of bread. I was sorry that I was obliged to deprive him of even his small part in the course of the year, for its loss provoked such ill-treatment from his wife, that by conjugal tyranny he was driven into the ranks of my enemies. When, after my flight from Dresden in 1849, I learned that I had been denounced to the police by this same singer for supposed complicity in the rising which took place in that town, I bethought me of this breakfast during the *Rienzi* rehearsal, and felt I was being punished for my ingratitude, for I knew I was guilty of having brought him into trouble with his wife.

The frame of mind in which I looked forward to the first performance of my work was a unique experience which I have never felt either before or since. My kind sister Clara fully shared my feelings. She had been living a wretched middle-class life at Chemnitz, which, just about this time, she had left to come and share my fate in Dresden. The poor woman, whose undoubted artistic gifts had faded so early, was laboriously dragging out a commonplace bourgeois existence as a wife and mother; but now, under the influence of my growing success, she began joyously to breathe a new life. She and I and the worthy chorus-master Fischer used to spend our evenings with the Heine family, still over potatoes and herrings, and often in a wonderfully elated frame of mind. The evening before our first performance I was able to crown our happiness by myself ladling out a bowl of punch. With mingled tears and laughter we skipped about like happy children, and then in sleep prepared ourselves for the triumphant day to which we looked forward with such confidence.

Although on the morning of 20th October, 1842 I had resolved not to disturb any of my singers by a visit, yet I happened to come across one of them, a stiff Philistine called Risse, who was playing a minor bass part in a dull but respectable way. The day was rather cool, but wonderfully bright and sunshiny, after the gloomy weather we had just been having. Without a word this curious creature saluted me and then remained standing, as though bewitched. He simply gazed into my face with wonder and rapture, in order to find out, so he at last managed to tell me in strange confusion, how a man looked who that very day was to face such an exceptional fate. I smiled and reflected that it was indeed a day of crisis, and promised him that I would soon drink a glass with him, at the Stadt Hamburg inn, of the excellent wine he had recommended to me with so much agitation.

No subsequent experience of mine can be compared with the sensations which marked the day of the first production of *Rienzi*. At all the first performances of my works in later days, I have been so absorbed by an only too well-founded anxiety as to their success, that I could neither enjoy the opera nor form any real estimate of its reception by the public. As for my subsequent experiences at the general rehearsal of *Tristan und Isolde*, this took place under such exceptional circumstances, and its effect upon me differed so fundamentally from that produced by the first performance of *Rienzi*, that no comparison can possibly be drawn between the two.

The immediate success of *Rienzi* was no doubt assured beforehand. But the emphatic way in which the audience declared their appreciation was thus far exceptional, that in cities like Dresden the spectators are never in a position to decide conclusively upon a work of importance on the first night, and consequently assume an attitude of chilling restraint towards the works of unknown authors. But this was, in the nature of things, an exceptional case, for the numerous staff of the theatre and the body of musicians had inundated the city beforehand with such glowing reports of my opera, that the whole population awaited the promised miracle in feverish expectation. I sat with Minna, my sister Clara, and the Heine family in a pit-box, and when I try to recall my condition during that evening, I can only picture it with all the paraphernalia of a dream. Of real pleasure or agitation I felt none at all: I seemed to stand quite aloof from my work; whereas the sight of the thickly crowded auditorium agitated me so much, that I was unable even to glance at the body of the audience, whose presence merely affected me like some natural phenomenon — something like a continuous downpour of rain — from which I sought shelter in the farthest corner of my box as under a protecting roof. I was quite unconscious of applause, and when at the end of the acts I was tempestuously called for, I had every time to be forcibly reminded by Heine and driven on to the stage. On the other hand, one great anxiety filled me with growing alarm: I noticed that the first two acts had taken as long as the whole of *Freischütz,* for instance. On account of its warlike calls to arms the third act begins with an exceptional uproar, and when at its close the clock pointed to ten, which meant that the performance had already lasted full four hours, I became perfectly desperate. The fact that after this act, also, I was again loudly called, I regarded merely as a final courtesy on the part of the audience, who wished to signify that they had had quite enough for one evening, and would now leave the house in a body. As we had still two acts before us, I thought it settled that we should not be able to finish the piece, and apologised for my lack of wisdom in not having previously effected the necessary curtailments. Now, thanks to my folly, I found myself in the unheard-of predicament of being unable to finish an opera, otherwise extremely well received, simply because it was absurdly long. I could only explain the undiminished zeal of the singers, and particularly of Tichatschek, who seemed to grow lustier and cheerier the longer it lasted, as an amiable trick to conceal from me the inevitable catastrophe. But my astonishment at finding the audience still there in full muster, even in the last act — towards midnight — filled me with unbounded perplexity. I could no longer trust my eyes or ears, and regarded the whole events of the evening as a nightmare. It was past midnight when, for the last time, I had to obey the thunderous calls of the audience, side by side with my trusty singers.

My feeling of desperation at the unparalleled length of my

opera was augmented by the temper of my relatives, whom I saw for a short time after the performance. Friedrich Brockhaus and his family had come over with some friends from Leipzig, and had invited us to the inn, hoping to celebrate an agreeable success over a pleasant supper, and possibly to drink my health. But on arriving, kitchen and cellar were closed, and every one was so worn out that nothing was to be heard but outcries at the unparalleled case of an opera lasting from six o'clock till past twelve. No further remarks were exchanged, and we stole away feeling quite stupefied.

About eight the next morning I put in an appearance at the clerks' office, in order that in case there should be a second performance I might arrange the necessary curtailment of the parts. If, during the previous summer, I had contested every beat with the faithful chorus-master Fischer, and proved them all to be indispensable, I was now possessed by a blind rage for striking out. There was not a single part of my score which seemed any longer necessary — what the audience had been made to swallow the previous evening now appeared but a chaos of sheer impossibilities, each and all of which might be omitted without the slightest damage or risk of being unintelligible. My one thought now was how to reduce my convolution of monstrosities to decent limits. By dint of unsparing and ruthless abbreviations handed over to the copyist, I hoped to avert a catastrophe, for I expected nothing less than that the general manager, together with the city and the theatre, would that very day give me to understand that such a thing as the performance of my *Last of the Tribunes* might perhaps be permitted once as a curiosity, but not oftener. All day long, therefore, I carefully avoided going near the theatre, so as to give time for my heroic abbreviations to do their salutary work, and for news of them to spread through the city. But at midday I looked in again upon the copyists, to assure myself that all had been duly performed as I had ordered. I then learned that Tichatschek had also been there, and, after inspecting the omissions that I had arranged, had forbidden their being carried out. Fischer, the chorus-master, also wished to speak to me about them: work was suspended, and I foresaw great confusion. I could not understand what it all meant, and feared mischief if the arduous task were delayed. At length, towards evening, I sought out Tichatschek at the theatre. Without giving him a chance to speak, I brusquely asked him why he had interrupted the copyists' work. In a half-choked voice he curtly and defiantly rejoined, ' I will have none of my part cut out — it is too heavenly.' I stared at him blankly, and then felt as though I had been suddenly bewitched: such an unheard-of testimony to my success could not but shake me out of my strange anxiety. Others joined him, Fischer radiant with delight and bubbling with laughter. Every one spoke of the enthusiastic emotion which thrilled the whole city. Next came a letter of thanks from the Commissioner acknowledging my splendid work. Nothing now remained for me but to embrace Tichatschek and Fischer, and go on my way to inform Minna and Clara how matters stood.

After a few days' rest for the actors, the second performance took place on 26th October, but with various curtailments, for which I had great difficulty in obtaining Tichatschek's consent. Although it was still of much more than average length, I heard no particular complaints, and at last adopted Tichatschek's view that, if he could stand it, so could the audience. For six performances therefore, all of which continued to receive a similar avalanche of applause, I let the matter run its course.

My opera, however, had also excited interest among the elder princesses of the royal family. They thought its exhausting length a drawback, but were nevertheless unwilling to miss any of it. Lüttichau consequently proposed that I should give the piece at full length, but half of it at a time on two successive evenings. This suited me very well, and after an interval of a few weeks we announced *Rienzi's Greatness* for the first day, and *His Fall* for the second. The first evening we gave two acts, and on the second three, and for the latter I composed a special introductory prelude. This met with the entire approval of our august patrons, and especially of the two eldest, Princesses Amalie and Augusta. The public, on the contrary, simply regarded this in the light of now being asked to pay two entrance fees for one opera, and pronounced the new arrangement a decided fraud. Its annoyance at the change was so great that it actually threatened to be fatal to the attendance, and after three performances of the divided *Rienzi* the management was obliged to go back to the old arrangement, which I willingly made possible by introducing my cuttings again.

From this time forward the piece used to fill the house to overflowing as often as it could be presented, and the permanence of its success became still more obvious when I began to realise the envy it drew upon me from many different quarters. My first experience of this was truly painful, and came from the hands of the poet, Julius Mosen, on the very day after the first performance. When I first reached Dresden in the summer I had sought him out, and, having a really high opinion of his talent, our intercourse soon became more intimate, and was the means of giving me much pleasure and instruction. He had shown me a volume of his plays, which on the whole appealed to me exceptionally. Among these was a tragedy, *Cola Rienzi*, dealing with the same subject as my opera, and in a manner partly new to me, and which I thought effective. With reference to this poem, I had begged him to take no notice of my libretto, as in the quality of its poetry it could not possibly bear comparison with his own; and it cost him little sacrifice to grant the request. It happened that just before the first performance of my *Rienzi*, he had produced in Dresden *Bernhard von Weimar*, one of his least happy pieces, the result of which had brought him little pleasure. Dramatically it was a thing with no life in it, aiming only at political harangue, and had shared the inevitable fate of all such aberrations. He had therefore awaited the appearance of my *Rienzi* with some vexation, and confessed to me his bitter chagrin at not being able to procure the acceptance of his tragedy of the same name in Dresden. This, he presumed, arose from its somewhat pronounced political tendency, which, certainly in a spoken play on a similar subject, would be more noticeable than in an opera, where from the very start no one pays any heed to the words. I had genially confirmed him in this depreciation of the subject matter in opera; and was therefore the more startled when, on finding him at my sister Louisa's the day after the first performance, he straightway overwhelmed me with a scornful outburst of irritation at my success. But he found in me a strange sense of the essential unreality in opera of such a subject as that which I had just illustrated with so much success in *Rienzi,* so that, oppressed by a secret sense of shame, I had no serious rejoinder to offer to his candidly poisonous abuse. My line of defence was not yet sufficiently clear in my own mind to be available offhand, nor was it yet backed by so obvious a product of my own peculiar genius that I could venture to quote it. Moreover, my first impulse was only one of pity for the unlucky playwright, which I felt all the more constrained to express, because his burst of fury gave me the inward satisfaction of knowing that he recognised my great success, of which I was not yet quite clear myself.

But this first performance of *Rienzi* did far more than this. It gave occasion for controversy, and made an ever-widening breach between myself and the newspaper critics. Herr Karl Bank, who for some time had been the chief musical critic in Dresden, had been known to me before at Magdeburg, where he once visited me and listened with delight to my playing of several fairly long passages from my *Liebesverbot.* When we met again in Dresden, this man could not forgive me for having been unable to procure him tickets for the first performance of *Rienzi.* The same thing happened with a certain Herr Julius Schladebach, who likewise settled in Dresden about that time as a critic. Though I was always anxious to be gracious to everybody, yet I felt just then an invincible repugnance for showing special deference to any man because he was a critic. As time went on, I carried this rule to the point of almost systematic rudeness, and was consequently all my life through the victim of unprecedented persecution from the press. As yet, however, this ill-will had not become pronounced, for at that time journalism had not begun to give itself airs in Dresden. There were so few contributions sent from there to the outside press that our artistic doings excited very little notice elsewhere, a fact which was certainly not without its disadvantages for me. Thus for the present the unpleasant side of my success scarcely affected me at all, and for a brief space I felt myself, for the first and only time in my life, so pleasantly borne along on the breath of general goodwill, that all my former troubles seemed amply requited.

For further and quite unexpected fruits of my success now appeared with astonishing rapidity, though not so much in the form of material profit, which for the present resolved itself into nine hundred marks, paid me by the General Board as an exceptional fee instead of the usual twenty golden louis. Nor did I dare to cherish the hope of selling my work advantageously to a publisher, until it had been performed in some other important towns. But fate willed it, that by the sudden death of Rastrelli, royal director of music, which occurred shortly after the first production of *Rienzi,* an office should unexpectedly become vacant, for the filling of which all eyes at once turned to me.

While the negotiations over this matter were slowly proceeding, the General Board gave proof in another direction of an almost passionate interest in my talents. They insisted that the first performance of the *Fliegender Holländer* should on no account be conceded to the Berlin opera, but reserved as an honour for Dresden. As the Berlin authorities raised no obstacle, I very gladly handed over my latest work also to the Dresden theatre. If in this I had to dispense with Tichatschek's assistance, as there was no leading tenor part in the play, I could count all the more surely on the helpful co-operation of Schröder-Devrient, to whom a worthier task was assigned in the leading female part than that which she had had in *Rienzi.* I was glad to be able thus to rely entirely upon her, as she had grown strangely out of humour with me, owing to her scanty share in the success of *Rienzi.* The completeness of my faith in her I proved with an exaggeration by no means advantageous to my own work, by simply forcing the leading male part on Wächter, a once capable, but now somewhat delicate baritone. He was in every respect wholly unsuited to the task, and only accepted it with unfeigned hesitation. On submitting my play to my adored prima donna, I was much relieved to find that its poetry made a special appeal to her. Thanks to the genuine personal interest awakened in me under very peculiar circumstances by the character and fate of this exceptional woman, our study of the part of Senta, which often brought us into close contact, became one of the most thrilling and momentously instructive periods of my life.

It is true that the great actress, especially when under the influence of her famous mother, Sophie Schröder, who was just then with her on a visit, showed undisguised vexation at my having composed so brilliant a work as *Rienzi* for Dresden without having specifically reserved the principal part for her. Yet the magnanimity of her disposition triumphed even over this selfish impulse: she loudly proclaimed me 'a genius,' and honoured me with that special confidence which, she said, none but a genius should enjoy. But when she invited me to become both the accomplice and adviser in her really dreadful love affairs, this confidence certainly began to have its risky side; nevertheless there were at first occasions on which she openly proclaimed herself before all the world as my friend, making most flattering distinctions in my favour.

First of all I had to accompany her on a trip to Leipzig, where she was giving a concert for her mother's benefit, which she thought to make particularly attractive by including in its programme two selections from *Rienzi* — the aria of Adriano and the hero's prayer (the latter sung by Tichatschek), and both under my personal conductorship. Mendelssohn, who was also on very friendly terms with her, had been enticed to this concert too, and produced his overture to *Ruy Blas*, then quite new. It was during the two busy days spent on this occasion in Leipzig that I first came into close contact with him, all my previous knowledge of him having been limited to a few rare and altogether profitless visits. At the house of my brother-in-law, Fritz Brockhaus, he and Devrient gave us a good deal of music, he playing her accompaniment to a number of Schubert's songs. I here became conscious of the peculiar unrest and excitement with which this master of music, who, though still young, had already reached the zenith of his fame and life's work, observed or rather watched me. I could see clearly that he thought but little of a success in opera, and that merely in Dresden. Doubtless I seemed in his eyes one of a class of musicians to whom he attached no value, and with whom he proposed to have no intercourse. Nevertheless my success had certain characteristic features, which gave it a more or less alarming aspect. Mendelssohn's most ardent desire for a long time past had been to write a successful opera, and it was possible he now felt annoyed that, before he had succeeded in doing so, a triumph of this nature should suddenly be thrust into his face with blunt brutality, and based upon a style of music which he might feel justified in regarding as poor. He probably found it no less exasperating that Devrient, whose gifts he acknowledged, and who was his own devoted admirer, should now so openly and loudly sound my praises. These thoughts were dimly shaping themselves in my mind, when Mendelssohn, by a very remarkable statement, drove me, almost with violence, to adopt this interpretation. On our way home together, after the joint concert rehearsal, I was talking very warmly on the subject of music. Although by no means a talkative man, he suddenly interrupted me with curiously hasty excitement by the assertion that music had but one great fault, namely, that more than any other art it stimulated not only our good, but also our evil qualities, such, for instance, as jealousy. I blushed with shame to have to apply this speech to his own feelings towards me; for I was profoundly conscious of my innocence of ever having dreamed, even in the remotest degree, of placing my own talents or performances as a musician in comparison with his. Yet, strange to say, at this very concert he showed himself in a light by no means calculated to place him beyond all possibility of comparison with myself. A rendering of his *Hebrides* Overture would have placed him so immeasurably above my two operatic airs, that all shyness at having to stand beside him would have been spared me, as the gulf between our two productions was impassable. But in his choice of the *Ruy Blas* Overture he appears to have been prompted by a desire to place himself on this occasion so close to the operatic style that its effectiveness might be reflected upon his own work. The overture was evidently calculated for a Parisian audience, and the astonishment Mendelssohn caused by appearing in such a connection was shown by Robert Schumann in his own ungainly fashion at its close. Approaching the musician in the orchestra, he blandly, and with a genial smile, expressed his admiration of the 'brilliant orchestral piece' just played.

But in the interests of veracity let me not forget that neither he nor I scored the real success of that evening. We were both wholly eclipsed by the tremendous effect produced by the grey-haired Sophie Schröder in a recitation of Bürger's *Lenore*. While the daughter had been taunted in the newspapers with unfairly employing all sorts of musical attractions to cozen a benefit concert out of the music lovers of Leipzig for a mother who never had anything to do with that art, we, who were there as her musical aiders and abettors, had to stand like so many idle conjurers, while this aged and almost toothless dame declaimed Bürger's poem with truly terrifying beauty and grandeur. This episode, like so much else that I saw during these few days, gave me abundant food for thought and meditation.

A second excursion, also undertaken with Devrient, took me in the December of that year to Berlin, where the singer had been invited to appear at a grand state concert. I for my part wanted an interview with Director Küstner about the *Fliegender Holländer*. Although I arrived at no definite result regarding my own personal business, this short visit to Berlin was memorable for my meeting with Franz Liszt, which afterwards proved of great importance. It took place under singular circumstances, which placed both him and me in a situation of peculiar embarrassment, brought about in the most wanton fashion by Devrient's exasperating caprice.

I had already told my patroness the story of my earlier meeting with Liszt. During that fateful second winter of my stay in Paris, when I had at last been driven to be grateful for Schlesinger's hack-work, I one day received word from Laube, who always bore me in mind, that F. Liszt was coming to Paris. He had mentioned and recommended me to him when he was in Germany, and advised me to lose no time in looking him up, as he was 'generous,' and would certainly find means of helping me. As soon as I heard that he had really arrived, I presented myself at the hotel to see him. It was early in the morning. On my entrance I found several strange gentlemen waiting in the drawing-room, where, after some time, we were joined by Liszt himself, pleasant and affable, and wearing his indoor coat. The conversation was carried on in French, and turned upon his experiences during his last professional journey in Hungary. As I was unable to take part, on account of the language, I listened for some time, feeling heartily bored, until at last he asked me pleasantly what he could do for me. He seemed unable to recall Laube's recommendation, and all the answer I could give was that I desired to make his acquaintance. To this he had evidently no objection, and informed me he would take care to have a ticket sent me for his great matinée, which was to take place shortly. My sole attempt to introduce an artistic theme of conversation was a question as to whether he knew Löwe's *Erlkönig* as well as Schubert's. His reply in the negative frustrated this somewhat awkward attempt, and I ended my visit by giving him my address. Thither his secretary, Belloni, presently sent me, with a few polite words, a card of admission to a concert to be given entirely by the master himself in the Salle Erard. I duly wended my way to the overcrowded hall, and beheld the platform on which the grand piano stood, closely beleaguered by the cream of Parisian female society, and witnessed their enthusiastic ovations of this virtuoso, who was at that time the wonder of the world. Moreover, I heard several of his most brilliant pieces, such as ' Variations on *Robert le Diable,*' but carried away with me no real impression beyond that of being stunned. This took place just at the time when I abandoned a path which had been contrary to my truer nature, and had led me astray, and on which I now emphatically turned my back in silent bitterness. I was therefore in no fitting mood for a just appreciation of this prodigy, who at that time was shining in the blazing light of day, but from whom I had turned my face to the night. I went to see Liszt no more.

As already mentioned, I had given Devrient a bare outline of this story, but she had noted it with particular attention, for I happened to have touched her weak point of professional jealousy. As Liszt had also been commanded by the King of Prussia to appear at the grand state concert at Berlin, it so happened that the first time they met Liszt questioned her with great interest about the success of *Rienzi*. She thereupon observed that the composer of that opera was an altogether unknown man, and proceeded with curious malice to taunt him with his apparent lack of penetration, as proved by the fact that the said composer, who now so keenly excited his interest, was the very same poor musician whom he had lately 'turned away so contemptuously' in Paris. All this she told me with an air of triumph, which distressed me very much, and I at once set to work to correct the false impression conveyed by my former account. As we were still debating this point in her room, we were startled by hearing from the next the famous bass part in the 'Revenge' air from *Donna Anna*, rapidly executed in octaves on the piano. 'That's Liszt himself,' she cried. Liszt then entered the room to fetch her for the rehearsal. To my great embarrassment she introduced me to him with malicious delight as the composer of *Rienzi*, the man whose acquaintance he now wished to make after having previously shown him the door in his glorious Paris. My solemn asseverations that my patroness — no doubt only in fun — was deliberately distorting my account of my former visit to him, apparently pacified him so far as I was concerned, and, on the other hand, he had no doubt already formed his own opinion of the impulsive singer. He certainly regretted that he could not remember my visit in Paris, but it nevertheless shocked and alarmed him to learn that any one should have had reason to complain of such treatment at his hands. The hearty sincerity of Listz's simple words to me about this misunderstanding, as contrasted with the strangely passionate raillery of the incorrigible lady, made a most pleasing and captivating impression upon me. The whole bearing of the man, and the way in which he tried to ward off the pitiless scorn of her attacks, was something new to me, and gave me a deep insight into his character, so firm in its amiability and boundless good-nature. Finally, she teased him about the Doctor's degree which had just been conferred on him by the University of Königsberg, and pretended to mistake him for a chemist. At last he stretched himself out flat on the floor, and implored her mercy, declaring himself quite defenceless against the storm of her invective. Then turning to me with a hearty assurance that he would make it his business to hear *Rienzi*, and would in any case endeavour to give me a better opinion of himself than his evil star had hitherto permitted, we parted for that occasion.

The almost naïve simplicity and naturalness of his every phrase and word, and particularly his emphatic manner, left a most profound impression upon me. No one could fail to be equally affected by these qualities, and I now realised for the first time the almost magic power exerted by Liszt over all who came in close contact with him, and saw how erroneous had been my former opinion as to its cause.

These two excursions to Leipzig and Berlin found but brief interruptions of the period devoted at home to our study of the *Fliegender Holländer*. It was therefore, of paramount importance to me to maintain Schröder-Devrient's keen interest in her part, since, in view of the weakness of the rest of the cast, I was convinced that it was from her alone I could expect any adequate interpretation of the spirit of my work.

The part of Senta was essentially suited to her, and there were just at that moment peculiar circumstances in her life which brought her naturally emotional temperament to a high pitch of tension. I was amazed when she confided to me that she was on the point of breaking off a regular *liaison* of many years' standing, to form, in passionate haste, another much less desirable one. The forsaken lover, who was tenderly devoted to her, was a young lieutenant in the Royal Guards, and the son of Müller, the ex-Minister of Education; her new choice, whose acquaintance she had formed on a recent visit to Berlin, was Herr von Münchhausen. He was a tall, slim young man, and her predilection for him was easily explained when I became more closely acquainted with her love affairs. It seemed to me that the bestowal of her confidence on me in this matter arose from her guilty conscience; she was aware that Müller, whom I liked on account of his excellent disposition, had loved her with the earnestness of a first love, and also that she was now betraying him in the most faithless way on a trivial pretext. She must have known that her new lover was entirely unworthy of her, and that his intentions were frivolous and selfish. She knew, too, that no one, and certainly none of her older friends who knew her best, would approve of her behaviour. She told me candidly that she had felt impelled to confide in me because I was a genius, and would understand the demands of her temperament. I hardly knew what to think. I was repelled alike by her passion and the circumstances attending it; but to my astonishment I had to confess that the infatuation, so repulsive to me, held this strange woman in so powerful a grasp that I could not refuse her a certain amount of pity, nay, even real sympathy.

She was pale and distraught, ate hardly anything, and her faculties were subjected to a strain so extraordinary that I thought she would not escape a serious, perhaps a fatal illness. Sleep had long since deserted her, and whenever I brought her my unlucky *Fliegender Holländer,* her looks so alarmed me that the proposed rehearsal was the last thing I thought of. But in this matter she insisted; she made me sit down at the piano, and then plunged into the study of her rôle as if it were a matter of life and death. She found the actual learning of the part very difficult, and it was only by repeated and persevering rehearsal that she mastered her task. She would sing for hours at a time with such passion that I often sprang up in terror and begged her to spare herself; then she would point smiling to her chest, and expand the muscles of her still magnificent person, to assure me that she was doing herself no harm. Her voice really acquired at that time a youthful freshness and power of endurance. I had to confess that which often astonished me: this infatuation for an insipid nobody was very much to the advantage of my Senta. Her courage under this intense strain was so great that, as time pressed, she consented to have the general rehearsal on the very day of the first performance, and a delay which would have been greatly to my disadvantage was thus avoided.

The performance took place on 2nd January, in the year 1843. Its result was extremely instructive to me, and led to the turning-point of my career. The ill-success of the performance taught me how much care and forethought were essential to secure the adequate dramatic interpretation of my latest works. I realised that I had more or less believed that my score would explain itself, and that my singers would arrive at the right interpretation of their own accord. My good old friend Wächter, who at the time of Henriette Sontag's first success was a favourite 'Barber of Seville,' had from the first discreetly thought otherwise. Unfortunately, even Schröder-Devrient only saw when the rehearsals were too far advanced how utterly incapable Wächter was of realising the horror and supreme suffering of my Mariner. His distressing corpulence, his broad fat face, the extraordinary movements of his arms and legs, which he managed to make look like mere stumps, drove my passionate Senta to despair. At one rehearsal, when in the great scene in Act ii. she comes to him in the guise of a guardian angel to bring the message of salvation, she broke off to whisper despairingly in my ear, 'How can I say it when I look into those beady eyes? Good God, Wagner, what a muddle you have made!' I consoled her as well as I could, and secretly placed my dependence on Herr von Münchhausen, who promised faithfully to sit that evening in the front row of the stalls, so that Devrient's eyes must fall on him. And the magnificent performance of my great artiste, although she stood horribly alone on the stage, did succeed in rousing enthusiasm in the second act. The first act offered the audience nothing but a dull conversation between Herr Wächter and that Herr Risse who had invited me to an excellent glass of wine on the first night of *Rienzi*, and in the third the loudest raging of the orchestra did not rouse the sea from its dead calm nor the phantom ship in its cautious rocking. The audience fell to wondering how I could have produced this crude, meagre, and gloomy work after *Rienzi*, in every act of which incident abounded, and Tichatschek shone in an endless variety of costumes.

As Schröder-Devrient soon left Dresden for a considerable time, the *Fliegender Holländer* saw only four performances, at which the diminishing audiences made it plain that I had not pleased Dresden taste with it. The management was compelled to revive *Rienzi* in order to maintain my prestige; and the triumph of this opera compared with the failure of the *Dutchman* gave me food for reflection. I had to admit, with some misgivings, that the success of my *Rienzi* was not entirely due to the cast and staging, although I was fully alive to the defects from which the *Fliegender Holländer* suffered in this respect. Although Wächter was far from realising my conception of the *Fliegender Holländer* I could not conceal from myself the fact that Tichatschek was quite as far removed from the ideal *Rienzi*. His abominable errors and deficiencies in his presentation of the part had never escaped me; he had never been able to lay aside his brilliant and heroic leading-tenor manners in order to render that gloomy demonic strain in Rienzi's temperament on which I had laid unmistakable stress at the critical points of the drama. In the fourth act, after the pronouncement of the curse, he fell on his knees in the most melancholy fashion and abandoned himself to bewailing his fate in piteous tones. When I suggested to him that *Rienzi,* though inwardly despairing, must take up an attitude of statuesque firmness before the world, he pointed out to me the great popularity which the end of this very act had won as interpreted by himself, with an intimation that he intended making no change in it.

And when I considered the real causes of the success of *Rienzi,* I found that it rested on the brilliant and extraordinarily fresh voice of the soaring, happy singer, in the refreshing effect of the chorus and the gay movement and colouring on the stage. I received a still more convincing proof of this when we divided the opera into two, and found that the second part, which was the more important from both the dramatic and the musical point of view, was noticeably less well attended than the first, for the very obvious reason, as I thought, that the ballet occurred in the first part. My brother Julius, who had come over from Leipzig for one of the performances of *Rienzi,* gave me a still more naïve testimony as to the real point of interest in the opera. I was sitting with him in an open box, in full sight of the audience, and had therefore begged him to desist from giving any applause, even if directed only to the efforts of the singers; he restrained himself all through the evening, but his enthusiasm at a certain figure of the ballet was too much for him, and he clapped loudly, to the great amusement of the audience, telling me that he could not hold himself in any longer. Curiously enough, this same ballet secured for *Rienzi,* which was otherwise received with indifference, the enduring preference of the present King of Prussia,[1] who many years afterwards ordered the revival of this opera, although it had utterly failed in arousing public interest by its merits as a drama.

I found, when I had to be present later on at a representation of the same opera at Darmstadt, that while wholesale cuts had to be made in its best parts, it had been found necessary to expand the ballets by additions and repetitions. This ballet music, which I had put together with contemptuous haste at Riga in a few days without any inspiration, seemed to me, moreover, so strikingly weak that I was thoroughly ashamed of it even in those days at Dresden, when I had found myself compelled to suppress its best feature, the tragic pantomime. Further, the resources of the ballet in Dresden did not even admit of the execution of my stage directions for the combat in the arena, nor for the very significant round dances, both admirably carried out at a later date in Berlin. I had to be content with the humiliating substitution of a long, foolish step-dance by two insignificant dancers, which was ended by a company of soldiers marching on, bearing their shields on high so as to form a roof and remind the audience of the Roman *testudo;* then the ballet-master with his assistant, in flesh-coloured tights, leaped on to the shields and turned somersaults, a proceeding which they thought was reminiscent of the gladiatorial games. It was at this point that the house was always moved to resounding applause, and I had to own that this moment marked the climax of my success.

I thus had my doubts as to the intrinsic divergence between my inner aims and my outward success; at the same time a decisive and fatal change in my fortunes was brought about by my acceptance of the conductorship at Dresden, under circumstances as perplexing in their way as those preceding my marriage. I had met the negotiations which led up to this appointment with a hesitation and a coolness by no means affected. I felt nothing but scorn for theatrical life; a scorn that was by no means lessened by a closer acquaintance with the apparently distinguished ruling body of a court theatre, the splendours of which only conceal, with arrogant ignorance, the humiliating conditions appertaining to it and to the modern

[1] William the First.

theatre in general. I saw every noble impulse stifled in those occupied with theatrical matters, and a combination of the vainest and most frivolous interests maintained by a ridiculously rigid and bureaucratic system; I was now fully convinced that the necessity of handling the business of the theatre would be the most distasteful thing I could imagine. Now that, through Rastrelli's death, the temptation to be false to my inner conviction came to me in Dresden, I explained to my old and trusted friends that I did not think I should accept the vacant post.

But everything calculated to shake human resolution combined against this decision. The prospect of securing the means of livelihood through a permanent position with a fixed salary was an irresistible attraction. I combated the temptation by reminding myself of my success as an operatic composer, which might reasonably be expected to bring in enough to supply my moderate requirements in a lodging of two rooms, where I could proceed undisturbed with fresh compositions. I was told in answer to this that my work itself would be better served by a fixed position without arduous duties, as for a whole year since the completion of the *Fliegender Holländer* I had not, under existing circumstances, found any leisure at all for composition. I still remained convinced that Rastrelli's post of musical director, in subordination to the conductor, was unworthy of me, and I declined to entertain the proposal, thus leaving the management to look elsewhere for some one to fill the vacancy.

There was therefore no further question of this particular post, but I was then informed that the death of Morlacchi had left vacant a court conductorship, and it was thought that the King would be willing to offer me the post. My wife was very much excited at this prospect, for in Germany the greatest value is laid on these court appointments, which are tenable for life, and the dazzling respectability pertaining to them is held out to German musicians as the acme of earthly happiness. The offer opened up for us in many directions the prospect of friendly relations in a society which had hitherto been outside our experience. Domestic comfort and social prestige were very alluring to the homeless wanderers who, in bygone days of misery, had often longed for the comfort and security of an assured and permanent position such as was now open to them under the august protection of the court. The influence of Caroline von Weber did much in the long-run to weaken my opposition. I was often at her house, and took great pleasure in her society, which brought back to my mind very vividly the personality of my still dearly beloved master. She begged me with really touching tenderness not to withstand this obvious command of fate, and asserted her right to ask me to settle in Dresden, to fill the place left sadly empty by her husband's death. 'Just think,' she said, 'how can I look Weber in the face again when I join him if I have to tell him that the work for which he made such devoted sacrifices in Dresden is neglected; just imagine my feelings when I see that indolent Reissiger stand in my noble Weber's place, and when I hear his operas produced more mechanically every year. If you loved Weber, you owe it to his memory to step into his place and to continue his work.' As an experienced woman of the world she also pointed out energetically and prudently the practical side of the matter, impressing on me the duty of thinking of my wife, who would, in case of my death, be sufficiently provided for if I accepted the post.

The promptings of affection, prudence and good sense, however, had less weight with me than the enthusiastic conviction, never at any period of my life entirely destroyed, that wherever fate led me, whether to Dresden or elsewhere, I should find the opportunity which would convert my dreams into reality through currents set in motion by some change in the everyday order of events. All that was needed for this was the advent of an ardent and aspiring soul who, with good luck to back him, might make up for lost time, and by his ennobling influence achieve the deliverance of art from her shameful bonds. The wonderful and rapid change which had taken place in my fortunes could not fail to encourage such a hope, and I was seduced on perceiving the marked alteration that had taken place in the whole attitude of Lüttichau, the general director, towards me. This strange individual showed me a kindliness of which no one would hitherto have thought him capable, and that he was prompted by a genuine feeling of personal benevolence towards me I could not help being absolutely convinced, even at the time of my subsequent ceaseless differences with him.

Nevertheless, the decision came as a kind of surprise. On 2nd February 1843 I was very politely invited to the director's office, and there met the general staff of the royal orchestra, in whose presence Lüttichau, through the medium of my never-to-be-forgotten friend Winkler, solemnly read out to me a royal rescript appointing me forthwith conductor to his Majesty, with a life salary of four thousand five hundred marks a year. Lüttichau followed the reading of this document by a more or less ceremonious speech, in which he assumed that I should gratefully accept the King's favour. At this polite ceremony it did not escape my notice that all possibility of future negotiations over the figure of the salary was cut off; on the other hand, a substantial exemption in my favour, the omission of the condition, enforced even on Weber in his time, of serving a year's probation under the title of mere musical director, was calculated to secure my unconditional acceptance. My new colleagues congratulated me, and Lüttichau accompanied me with the politest phrases to my own door, where I fell into the arms of my poor wife, who was giddy with delight. Therefore I fully realised that I must put the best face I could on the matter, and unless I wished to give unheard-of offence, I must even congratulate myself on my appointment as royal conductor.

A few days after taking the oath as a servant of the King in solemn session, and undergoing the ceremony of presentation to the assembled orchestra by means of an enthusiastic speech from the general director, I was summoned to an audience with his Majesty. When I saw the features of the kind, courteous, and homely monarch, I involuntarily thought of my youthful attempt at a political overture on the theme of *Friedrich und Freiheit*. Our somewhat embarrassed conversation brightened with the King's expression of his satisfaction with those two of my operas which had been performed in Dresden. He expressed with polite hesitation his feeling that if my operas left anything to be desired, it was a clearer definition of the various characters in my musical dramas. He thought the interest in the persons was overpowered by the elemental forces figuring beside them — in *Rienzi* the mob, in the *Fliegender Holländer* the sea. I thought I understood his meaning perfectly, and this proof of his sincere sympathy and original judgment pleased me very much. He also made his excuses in advance for a possible rare attendance at my operas on his part, his sole reason for this being that he had a peculiar aversion from theatre-going, as the result of one of the rules of his early training, under which he and his brother John, who had acquired a similar aversion, were for a long time compelled regularly to attend the theatre, when he, to tell the truth, would often have preferred to be left alone to follow his own pursuits independent of etiquette.

As a characteristic instance of the courtier spirit, I afterwards learned that Lüttichau, who had had to wait for me in the anteroom during this audience, had been very much put out by its long duration. In the whole course of my life I was only admitted twice more to personal intercourse and speech with the good King. The first occasion was when I presented him with the dedication copy of the pianoforte score of my *Rienzi;* and the second was after my very successful arrangement and performance of the *Iphigenia in Aulis,* by Gluck, of whose operas he was particularly fond, when he stopped me in the public promenade and congratulated me on my work.

That first audience with the King marked the zenith of my hastily adopted career at Dresden; thenceforward anxiety reasserted itself in manifold ways. I very quickly realised the difficulties of my material situation, since it soon became evident that the advantage won by new exertions and my present appointment bore no proportion to the heavy sacrifices and obligations which I incurred as soon as I entered on an independent career. The young musical director of Riga, long since forgotten, suddenly reappeared in an astonishing reincarnation as royal conductor to the King of Saxony. The first-fruits of the universal estimate of my good fortune took the shape of pressing creditors and threats of prosecution; next followed demands from the Königsberg tradesmen, from whom I had escaped from Riga by means of that horribly wretched and miserable flight. I also heard from people in the most distant parts, who thought they had some claim on me, dating even from my student, nay, my school days, until at last I cried out in my astonishment that I expected to receive a bill next from the nurse who had suckled me. All this did not amount to any very large sum, and I merely mention it because of the ill-natured rumours which, I learned years later, had been spread abroad about the extent of my debts at that time. Out of three thousand marks, borrowed at interest from Schröder-Devrient, I not only paid these debts, but also fully compensated the sacrifices which Kietz had made on my behalf, without ever expecting any return, in the days of my poverty in Paris. I was, moreover, able to be of practical use to him. But where was I to find even this sum, as my distress had hitherto been so great that I was obliged to urge Schröder-Devrient to hurry on the rehearsals of the *Fliegender Holländer* by pointing out to her the enormous importance to me of the fee for the performance? I had no allowance for the expenses of my establishment in Dresden, though it had to be suitable for my position as royal conductor, nor even for the purchase of a ridiculous and expensive court uniform, so that there would have been no possibility of my making a start at all, as I had no private means, unless I borrowed money at interest.

But no one who knew of the extraordinary success of *Rienzi* at Dresden could help believing in an immediate and remunerative rage for my operas on the German stage. My own relatives, even the prudent Ottilie, were so convinced of it that they thought I might safely count on at least doubling my salary by the receipts from my operas. At the very beginning the prospects did indeed seem bright; the score of my *Fliegender Holländer* was ordered by the Royal Theatre at Cassel and by the Riga theatre, which I had known so well in the old days, because they were anxious to perform something of mine at an early date, and had heard that this opera was on a smaller scale, and made smaller demands on the stage management, than *Rienzi*. In May, 1843 I heard good reports of the success of the performances from both those places. But this was all for the time being, and a whole year went by without the smallest inquiry for any of my scores. An attempt was made to secure me some benefit by the publication of the pianoforte score of the *Fliegender Holländer,* as I wanted to reserve *Rienzi,* after the successes it had gained, as useful capital for a more favourable opportunity; but the plan was spoilt by the opposition of Messrs. Härtel of Leipzig, who, although ready enough to publish my opera, would only do so on the condition that I abstained from asking any payment for it.

So I had, for the present, to content myself with the moral satisfaction of my successes, of which my unmistakable popularity with the Dresden public, and the respect and attention paid to me, formed part. But even in this respect my Utopian dreams were destined to be disturbed. I think that my appearance at Dresden marked the beginning of a new era in journalism and criticism, which found food for its hitherto but slightly developed vitality in its vexation at my success. The two gentlemen I have already mentioned, C. Bank and J. Schladebach, had, as I now know, first taken up their regular abode in Dresden at that time; I know that when difficulties were raised about the permanence of Bank's appointment, they were waived, owing to the testimonials and recommendation of my present colleague Reissiger. The success of my *Rienzi* had been the source of great annoyance to these gentlemen, who were now established as musical critics to the Dresden press, because I made no effort to win their favour; they were not ill-pleased, therefore, to find an opportunity of pouring out the vitriol of their hatred over the universally popular young musician who had won the sympathy of the kindly public, partly on account of the poverty and ill-luck which had hitherto been his lot. The need for any kind of human consideration had suddenly vanished with my 'unheard-of' appointment to the royal conductorship. Now 'all was well with me,' 'too well,' in fact; and envy found its congenial food; this provided a perfectly clear and comprehensible point of attack; and soon there spread through the German press, in the columns given to Dresden news, an estimate of me which has never fundamentally changed, except in one point, to this day. This single modification, which was purely temporary and confined to papers of one political colour, occurred on my first settlement as a political refugee in Switzerland, but lasted only until, through Liszt's exertions, my operas began to be produced all over Germany, in spite of my exile. The orders from two theatres, immediately after the Dresden performance, for one of my scores, were merely due to the fact that up to that time the activity of my journalistic critics was still limited. I put down the cessation of all inquiries, certainly not without due justification, mainly to the effect of the false and calumnious reports in the papers.

My old friend Laube tried, indeed, to undertake my defence in the press. On New Year's Day, 1843 he resumed the editorship of the *Zeitung für die Elegante Welt,* and asked me to provide him with a biographical notice of myself for the first number. It evidently gave him great pleasure to present me thus in triumph to the literary world, and in order to give the subject more prominence he added a supplement to that number in the shape of a lithograph reproduction of my portrait by Kietz. But after a time even he became anxious and confused in his judgment of my works, when he saw the systematic and increasingly virulent detraction, depreciation, and scorn to which they were subjected. He confessed to me later that he had never imagined such a desperate position as mine against the united forces of journalism could possibly exist, and when he heard my view of the question, he smiled and gave me his blessing, as though I were a lost soul.

Moreover, a change was observable in the attitude of those immediately connected with me in my work, and this provided very acceptable material for the journalistic campaign. I had been led, though by no ambitious impulse, to ask to be allowed to conduct the performances of my own works. I found that at every performance of *Rienzi* Reissiger became more negligent in his conducting, and that the whole production was slipping back into the old familiar, expressionless, and humdrum performance; and as my appointment was already mooted, I had asked permission to conduct the sixth performance of my work in person. I conducted without having held a single rehearsal, and without any previous experience, at the head of the Dresden orchestra. The performance went splendidly; singers and orchestra were inspired with new life, and everybody was obliged to admit that this was the finest performance of *Rienzi* that had yet been given. The rehearsing and conducting of the *Fliegender Holländer* were willingly handed over to me, because Reissiger was overwhelmed with work, in consequence of the death of the musical director, Rastrelli. In addition to this I was asked to conduct Weber's *Euryanthe*, by way of providing a direct proof of my capacity to interpret scores other than my own. Apparently everybody was pleased, and it was the tone of this performance that made Weber's widow so anxious that I should accept the Dresden conductorship; she declared that for the first time since her husband's death she had heard his work correctly interpreted, both in expression and time.

Thereupon, Reissiger, who would have preferred to have a musical director under him, but had received instead a colleague on an equal footing, felt himself aggrieved by my appointment. Though his own indolence would have inclined him to the side of peace and a good understanding with me, his ambitious wife took care to stir up his fear of me. This never led to an openly hostile attitude on his part, but I noticed certain indiscretions in the press from that time onwards, which showed me that the friendliness of my colleague, who never talked to me without first embracing me, was not of the most honourable type.

I also received a quite unexpected proof that I had attracted the bitter envy of another man whose sentiments I had no reason to suspect. This was Karl Lipinsky, a celebrated violinist in his day, who had for many years led the Dresden orchestra. He was a man of ardent temperament and original talent, but of incredible vanity, which his emotional, suspicious Polish temperament rendered dangerous. I always found him annoying, because however inspiring and instructive his playing was as to the technical execution of the violinists, he was certainly ill-fitted to be the leader of a first-class orchestra. This extraordinary person tried to justify Director Lüttichau's praise of his playing, which could always be heard above the rest of the orchestra; he came in a little before the other violins; he was a leader in a double sense, as he was always a little ahead. He acted in much the same way with regard to expression, marking his slight variations in the piano passages with fanatical precision. It was useless to talk to him about it, as nothing but the most skilful flattery had any effect on him. So I had to endure it as best I could, and to think out ways and means of diminishing its ill effects on the orchestral performances as a whole by having recourse to the most polite circumlocutions. Even so he could not endure the higher estimation in which the performances of the orchestra under my conductorship were held, because he thought that the playing of an orchestra in which he was the leader must invariably be excellent, whoever stood at the conductor's desk. Now it happened, as is always the case when a new man with fresh ideas is installed in office, that the members of the orchestra came to me with the most varied suggestions for improvements which had hitherto been neglected; and Lipinsky, who was already annoyed about this, turned a certain case of this kind to a peculiarly treacherous use. One of the oldest contrabassists had died. Lipinsky urged me to arrange that the post should not be filled in the usual way by promotion from the ranks of our own orchestra, but should be given, on his recommendation, to a distinguished and skilful contrabassist from Darmstadt named Müller. When the musician whose rights of seniority were thus threatened, appealed to me, I kept my promise to Lipinsky, explained my views about the abuses of promotion by seniority, and declared that, in accordance with my sworn oath to the King, I held it my paramount duty to consider the maintenance of the artistic interests of the institution before everything else. I then found to my great astonishment, though it was foolish of me to be surprised, that the whole of the orchestra turned upon me as one man, and when the occasion arose for a discussion between Lipinsky and myself as to his own numerous grievances, he actually accused me of having threatened, by my remarks in the contrabassist case, to undermine the well-established rights of the members of the orchestra, whose welfare it was my duty to protect. Lüttichau, who was on the point of absenting himself from Dresden for some time, was extremely uneasy, as Reissiger was away on his holiday, at leaving musical affairs in such a dangerous state of unrest. The deceit and impudence of which I had been the victim was a revelation to me, and I gathered from this experience the calm sense necessary to set the harassed director at ease by the most conclusive assurances that I understood the people with whom I had to deal, and would act accordingly. I faithfully kept my word, and never again came into collision either with Lipinsky or any other member of the orchestra. On the contrary, all the musicians were soon so firmly attached to me that I could always pride myself on their devotion.

From that day forward, however, one thing at least was certain, namely, that I should not die as conductor at Dresden. My post and my work at Dresden thenceforward became a burden, of which the occasionally excellent results of my efforts made me all the more sensible.

My position at Dresden, however, brought me one friend whose intimate relations with me long survived our artistic collaboration in Dresden. A musical director was assigned to each conductor; he had to be a musician of repute, a hard worker, adaptable, and, above all, a Catholic, for the two conductors were Protestants, a cause of much annoyance to the clergy of the Catholic cathedral, numerous positions in which had to be filled from the orchestra. August Röckel, a nephew of Hummel, who sent in his application for this position from Weimar, furnished evidence of his suitability under all these heads. He belonged to an old Bavarian family; his father was a singer, and had sung the part of Florestan at the time of the first production of Beethoven's *Fidelio,* and had himself remained on terms of close intimacy with the Master, many details about whose life have been preserved through his care. His subsequent position as a teacher of singing led him to take up theatrical management, and he introduced German opera to the Parisians with so much success, that the credit for the popularity of *Fidelio* and *Der Freischütz* with French audiences, to whom these works were quite unknown, must be awarded to his admirable enterprise, which was also responsible for Schröder-Devrient's début in Paris. August Röckel, his son, who was still a young man, by helping his father in these and similar undertakings, had gained practical experience as a musician. As his father's business had for some time even extended to England, August had won practical knowledge of all sorts by contact with many men and things, and in addition had learned

French and English. But music had remained his chosen vocation, and his great natural talent justified the highest hopes of success. He was an excellent pianist, read scores with the utmost ease, possessed an exceptionally fine ear, and had indeed every qualification for a practical musician. As a composer he was actuated, not so much by a strong impulse to create, as the desire to show what he was capable of; the success at which he aimed was to gain the reputation of a clever operatic composer rather than recognition as a distinguished musician, and he hoped to obtain his end by the production of popular works. Actuated by this modest ambition he had completed an opera, *Farinelli*, for which he had also written the libretto, with no other aspiration than that of attaining the same reputation as his brother-in-law Lortzing.

He brought this score to me, and begged me — it was his first visit before he had heard one of my operas in Dresden — to play him something from *Rienzi* and the *Fliegender Holländer*. His frank, agreeable personality induced me to try and meet his wishes as far as I could, and I am convinced that I soon made such a great and unexpectedly powerful impression on him that from that moment he determined not to bother me further with the score of his opera. It was not until we had become more intimate and had discovered mutual personal interests, that the desire of turning his work to account induced him to ask me to show my practical friendship by turning my attention to his score. I made various suggestions as to how it might be improved, but he was soon so hopelessly disgusted with his own work that he put it absolutely aside, and never again felt seriously moved to undertake a similar task. On making a closer acquaintance with my completed operas and plans for new works, he declared to me that he felt it his vocation to play the part of spectator, to be my faithful helper and the interpreter of my new ideas, and, as far as in him lay, to remove entirely, and at all events to relieve me as far as possible from, all the unpleasantnesses of my official position and of my dealings with the outside world. He wished, he said, to avoid placing himself in the ridiculous position of composing operas of his own while living on terms of close friendship with me.

Nevertheless, I tried to urge him to turn his own talent to

account, and to this end called his attention to several plots which I wished him to work out. Among these was the idea contained in a small French drama entitled *Cromwell's Daughter,* which was subsequently used as the subject for a sentimental pastoral romance, and for the elaboration of which I presented him with an exhaustive plan.

But in the end all my efforts remained fruitless, and it became evident that his productive talent was feeble. This perhaps arose partly from his extremely needy and trying domestic circumstances, which were such that the poor fellow wore himself out to support his wife and numerous growing children. Indeed, he claimed my help and sympathy in quite another fashion than by arousing my interest in his artistic development. He was unusually clear-headed, and possessed a rare capacity for teaching and educating himself in every branch of knowledge and experience; he was, moreover, so genuinely true and good-hearted that he soon became my intimate friend and comrade. He was, and continued to be, the only person who really appreciated the singular nature of my position towards the surrounding world, and with whom I could fully and sincerely discuss the cares and sorrows arising therefrom. What dreadful trials and experiences, what painful anxieties our common fate was to bring upon us, will soon be seen.

The earlier period of my establishment in Dresden brought me also another devoted and lifelong friend, though his qualities were such that he exerted a less decisive influence upon my career. This was a young physician, named Anton Pusinelli, who lived near me. He seized the occasion of a serenade sung in honour of my thirtieth birthday by the Dresden Glee Club to express to me personally his hearty and sincere attachment. We soon entered upon a quiet friendship from which we derived a mutual benefit. He became my attentive family doctor, and during my residence in Dresden, marked as it was by accumulating difficulties, he had abundant opportunities of helping me. His financial position was very good, and his ready self-sacrifice enabled him to give me substantial succour and bound me to him by many heartfelt obligations.

A further development of my association with Dresden society was provided by the kindly advances of Chamberlain von Könneritz's family. His wife, Marie von Könneritz (*née* Fink), was a friend of Countess Ida Hahn-Hahn, and expressed her appreciation of my success as a composer with great warmth, I might almost say, with enthusiasm. I was often invited to their house, and seemed likely, through this family, to be brought into touch with the higher aristocracy of Dresden. I merely succeeded in touching the fringe, however, as we really had nothing in common. True, I here made the acquaintance of Countess Rossi, the famous Sontag, by whom, to my genuine astonishment, I was most heartily greeted, and I thereby obtained the right of afterwards approaching her in Berlin with a certain degree of familiarity. The curious way in which I was disillusioned about this lady on that occasion will be related in due course. I would only mention here that, through my earlier experiences of the world, I had become fairly impervious to deception, and my desire for closer acquaintance with these circles speedily gave way to a complete hopelessness and an entire lack of ease in their sphere of life.

Although the Könneritz couple remained friendly during the whole of my prolonged sojourn in Dresden, yet the connection had not the least influence either upon my development or my position. Only once, on the occasion of a quarrel between Lüttichau and myself, the former observed that Frau von Könneritz, by her unmeasured praises, had turned my head and made me forget my position towards him. But in making this taunt he forgot that, if any woman in the higher ranks of Dresden society had exerted a real and invigorating influence upon my inward pride, that woman was his own wife, Ida von Lüttichau (*née* von Knobelsdorf).

The power which this cultured, gentle, and distinguished lady exercised over my life was of a kind I now experienced for the first time, and might have become of great importance had I been favoured with more frequent and intimate intercourse. But it was less her position as wife of the general director than her constant ill-health and my own peculiar unwillingness to appear obtrusive, that hindered our meeting, except at rare intervals. My recollections of her merge somewhat, in my memory, with those of my own sister Rosalie. I remember the tender ambition which inspired me to win the encouraging sympathy of this sensitive woman, who was painfully wasting away amid the coarsest surroundings. My earliest hope for the fulfilment of this ambition arose from her appreciation of my *Fliegender Holländer,* in spite of the fact that, following close upon *Rienzi,* it had so puzzled the Dresden public. In this way she was the first, so to speak, who swam against the tide and met me upon my new path. So deeply was I touched by this conquest that, when I afterwards published the opera, I dedicated it to her. In the account of my later years in Dresden I shall have more to record of the warm sympathy for my new development and dearest artistic aims for which I was indebted to her. But of real intercourse we had none, and the character of my Dresden life was not affected by this acquaintance, otherwise so important in itself.

On the other hand, my theatrical acquaintances thrust themselves with irresistible importunancy into the wide foreground of my life, and in fact, after my brilliant successes, I was still restricted to the same limited and familiar sphere in which I had prepared myself for these triumphs. Indeed, the only one who joined my old friends Heine and Gaffer Fischer was Tichatschek, with his strange domestic circle. Any one who lived in Dresden at that time and chanced to know the court lithographer, Fürstenau, will be astonished to hear that, without really being aware of it myself, I entered into a familiarity that was to prove a lasting one with this man who was an intimate friend of Tichatschek's. The importance of this singular connection may be judged from the fact that my complete withdrawal from him coincided exactly with the collapse of my civic position in Dresden.

My good-humoured acceptance of election to the musical committee of the Dresden Glee Club also brought me further chance acquaintances. This club consisted of a limited number of young merchants and officials, who had more taste for any kind of convivial entertainment than for music. But it was seduously kept together by a remarkable and ambitious man, Professor Löwe, who nursed it with special objects in view, for the attainment of which he felt the need of an authority such as I possessed at that time in Dresden.

Among other aims he was particularly and chiefly concerned in arranging for the transfer of Weber's remains from London to Dresden. As this project was one which interested me also, I lent him my support, though he was in reality merely following the voice of personal ambition. He furthermore desired, as head of the Glee Club — which, by the way, from the point of view of music was quite worthless — to invite all the male choral unions of Saxony to a great gala performance in Dresden. A committee was appointed for the execution of this plan, and as things soon became pretty warm, Löwe turned it into a regular revolutionary tribunal, over which, as the great day of triumph approached, he presided day and night without resting, and by his furious zeal earned from me the nickname of 'Robespierre.'

In spite of the fact that I had been placed at the head of this enterprise, I luckily managed to evade his terrorism, as I was fully occupied with a great composition promised for the festival. The task had been assigned to me of writing an important piece for male voices only, which, if possible, should occupy half an hour. I reflected that the tiresome monotony of male singing, which even the orchestra could only enliven to a slight extent, can only be endured by the introduction of dramatic themes. I therefore designed a great choral scene, selecting the apostolic Pentecost with the outpouring of the Holy Ghost as its subject. I completely avoided any real solos, but worked out the whole in such a way that it should be executed by detached choral masses according to requirement. Out of this composition arose my *Liebesmahl der Apostel* ('Love-feast of the Apostles'), which has recently been performed in various places.

As I was obliged at all costs to finish it within a limited time, I do not mind including this in the list of my uninspired compositions. But I was not displeased with it when it was done, more especially when it was played at the rehearsals given by the Dresden choral societies under my personal supervision. When, therefore, twelve hundred singers from all parts of Saxony gathered around me in the Frauenkirche, where the performance took place, I was astonished at the comparatively feeble effect produced upon my ear by this colossal human tangle of sounds. The conclusion at which I arrived was, that these enormous choral undertakings are folly, and I never again felt inclined to repeat the experiment.

It was with much difficulty that I shook myself free of the Dresden Glee Club, and I only succeeded in doing so by introducing to Professor Löwe another ambitious man in the person of Herr Ferdinand Hiller. My most glorious exploit in connection with this association was the transfer of Weber's ashes, of which I will speak later on, though it occurred at an earlier date. I will only refer now to another commissioned composition which, as royal bandmaster, I was officially commanded to produce. On the 7th of June of this year (1843) the statue of King Frederick Augustus by Rietschl was unveiled in the Dresden Zwinger [1] with all due pomp and ceremony. In honour of this event I, in collaboration with Mendelssohn, was commanded to compose a festal song, and to conduct the gala performance. I had written a simple song for male voices of modest design, whereas to Mendelssohn had been assigned the more complicated task of interweaving the National Anthem (the English 'God Save the King,' which in Saxony is called *Heil Dir im Rautenkranz*) into the male chorus he had to compose. This he had effected by an artistic work in counterpoint, so arranged that from the first eight beats of his original melody the brass instruments simultaneously played the Anglo-Saxon popular air. My simpler song seems to have sounded very well from a distance, whereas I understood that Mendelssohn's daring combination quite missed its effect, because no one could understand why the vocalists did not sing the same air as the wind instruments were playing. Nevertheless Mendelssohn, who was present, left me a written expression of thanks for the pains I had taken in the production of his composition. I also received a gold snuff-box from the grand gala committee, presumably meant as a reward for my male chorus, but the hunting scene which was engraved on the top was so badly done that I found, to

---

[1] This is the name by which the famous Dresden Art Galleries are known. — EDITOR.

my surprise, that in several places the metal was cut through.

Amid all the distractions of this new and very different mode of life, I diligently strove to concentrate and steel my soul against these influences, bearing in mind my experiences of success in the past. By May of my thirtieth year I had finished my poem *Der Venusberg* ('The Mount of Venus'), as I called *Tannhäuser* at that time. I had not yet by any means gained any real knowledge of mediæval poetry. The classical side of the poetry of the Middle Ages had so far only faintly dawned upon me, partly from my youthful recollections, and partly from the brief acquaintance I had made with it through Lehrs' instruction in Paris.

Now that I was secure in the possession of a royal appointment that would last my lifetime, the establishment of a permanent domestic hearth began to assume great importance; for I hoped it would enable me to take up my serious studies once more, and in such a way as to make them productive — an aim which my theatrical life and the miseries of my years in Paris had rendered impossible. My hope of being able to do this was strengthened by the character of my official employment, which was never very arduous, and in which I met with exceptional consideration from the general management. Though I had only held my appointment for a few months, yet I was given a holiday this first summer, which I spent in a second visit to Töplitz, a place which I had grown to like, and whither I had sent on my wife in advance.

Keenly indeed did I appreciate the change in my position since the preceding year. I could now engage four spacious and well-appointed rooms in the same house — the *Eiche* at Schönau — where I had before lived in such straitened and frugal circumstances. I invited my sister Clara to pay us a visit, and also my good mother, whose gout necessitated her taking the Töplitz baths every year. I also seized the opportunity of drinking the mineral waters, which I hoped might have a beneficial effect on the gastric troubles from which I had suffered ever since my vicissitudes in Paris. Unfortunately the attempted cure had a contrary effect, and when I complained of the painful irritation produced, I learned that my constitution was not adapted for water cures. In fact, on my morning promenade, and while drinking my water, I had been observed to race through the shady alleys of the adjacent Thurn Gardens, and it was pointed out to me that such a cure could only be properly wrought by leisurely calm and easy sauntering. It was also remarked that I usually carried about a fairly stout volume, and that, armed with this and my bottle of mineral water, I used to take rest in lonely places.

This book was J. Grimm's *German Mythology*. All who know the work can understand how the unusual wealth of its contents, gathered from every side, and meant almost exclusively for the student, would react upon me, whose mind was everywhere seeking for something definite and distinct. Formed from the scanty fragments of a perished world, of which scarcely any monuments remained recognisable and intact, I here found a heterogeneous building, which at first glance seemed but a rugged rock clothed in straggling brambles. Nothing was finished, only here and there could the slightest resemblance to an architectonic line be traced, so that I often felt tempted to relinquish the thankless task of trying to build from such materials. And yet I was enchained by a wondrous magic. The baldest legend spoke to me of its ancient home, and soon my whole imagination thrilled with images; long-lost forms for which I had sought so eagerly shaped themselves ever more and more clearly into realities that lived again. There rose up soon before my mind a whole world of figures, which revealed themselves as so strangely plastic and primitive, that, when I saw them clearly before me and heard their voices in my heart, I could not account for the almost tangible familiarity and assurance of their demeanour. The effect they produced upon the inner state of my soul I can only describe as an entire rebirth. Just as we feel a tender joy over a child's first bright smile of recognition, so now my own eyes flashed with rapture as I saw a world, revealed, as it were, by miracle, in which I had hitherto moved blindly as the babe in its mother's womb.

But the result of this reading did not at first do much to help me in my purpose of composing part of the *Tannhäuser* music. I had had a piano put in my room at the *Eiche*, and though

I smashed all its strings, nothing satisfactory would emerge. With much pain and toil I sketched the first outlines of my music for the *Venusberg,* as fortunately I already had its theme in my mind. Meanwhile I was very much troubled by excitability and rushes of blood to the brain. I imagined I was ill, and lay for whole days in bed, where I read Grimm's German legends, or tried to master the disagreeable mythology. It was quite a relief when I hit upon the happy thought of freeing myself from the torments of my condition by an excursion to Prague. Meanwhile I had already ascended Mount Millischau once with my wife, and in her company I now made the journey to Prague in an open carriage. There I stayed once more at my favourite inn, the Black Horse, met my friend Kittl, who had now grown fat and rotund, made various excursions, revelled in the curious antiquities of the old city, and learned to my joy that the two lovely friends of my youth, Jenny and Auguste Pachta, had been happily married to members of the highest aristocracy. Thereupon, having reassured myself that everything was in the best possible order, I returned to Dresden and resumed my functions as musical conductor to the King of Saxony.

We now set to work on the preparations and furnishing of a roomy and well-situated house in the Ostra Allee, with an outlook upon the Zwinger. Everything was good and substantial, as is only right for a man of thirty who is settling down at last for the whole of his life. As I had not received any subsidy towards this outlay, I had naturally to raise the money by loan. But I could look forward to a certain harvest from my operatic successes in Dresden, and what was more natural than for me to expect soon to earn more than enough? The three most valued treasures which adorned my house were a concert grand piano by Breitkopf and Härtel, which I had bought with much pride; a stately writing-desk, now in possession of Otto Kummer, the chamber-music artist; and the title-page by Cornelius for the *Nibelungen,* in a handsome Gothic frame — the only object which has remained faithful to me to the present day. But the thing which above all else made my house seem homelike and attractive was the presence of a library, which I procured in accordance with a systematic plan laid down by my proposed line of study. On the failure of my Dresden career this library passed in a curious way into the possession of Herr Heinrich Brockhaus, to whom at that time I owed fifteen hundred marks, and who took it as security for the amount. My wife knew nothing at the time of this obligation, and I never afterwards succeeded in recovering this characteristic collection from his hands. Upon its shelves old German literature was especially well represented, and also the closely related work of the German Middle Ages, including many a costly volume, as, for instance, the rare old work, *Romans des douze Paris*. Beside these stood many excellent historical works on the Middle Ages, as well as on the German people in general. At the same time I made provision for the poetical and classical literature of all times and languages. Among these were the Italian poets, Shakespeare and the French writers, of whose language I had a passable knowledge. All these I acquired in the original, hoping some day to find time to master their neglected tongues. As for the Greek and Roman classics, I had to content myself with standard German translations. Indeed, on looking once more into my Homer — whom I secured in the original Greek — I soon recognised that I should be presuming on more leisure than my conductorship was likely to leave me, if I hoped to find time for regaining my lost knowledge of that language. Moreover, I provided most thoroughly for a study of universal history, and to this end did not fail to equip myself with the most voluminous works. Thus armed, I thought I could bid defiance to all the trials which I clearly foresaw would inevitably accompany my calling and position. In hopes, therefore, of long and peaceable enjoyment of this hard-earned home, I entered into possession with the best of spirits in October of this year (1843), and though my conductor's quarters were by no means magnificent, they were stately and substantial.

The first leisure in my new home which I could snatch from the claims of my profession and my favourite studies was devoted to the composition of *Tannhäuser,* the first act of which was completed in January of the new year, 1844. I have no recollections of any importance regarding my activities in Dresden during this winter. The only memorable events were two enterprises which took me away from home, the first to Berlin early in the year, for the production of my *Fliegender Holländer*, and the other in March to Hamburg for *Rienzi*. Of these the former made the greater impression upon my mind. The manager of the Berlin theatre, Küstner, quite took me by surprise when he announced the first performance of the *Fliegender Holländer* for an early date. As the opera house had been burnt down only about a year before, and could not possibly have been rebuilt, it had not occurred to me to remind them about the production of my opera. It had been performed in Dresden with very poor scenic accessories, and knowing how important a careful and artistic execution of the difficult scenery was for my dramatic sea-scapes, I had relied implicitly on the admirable management and staging capacities of the Berlin opera house. Consequently I was very much annoyed that the Berlin manager should select my opera as a stopgap to be produced at the Comedy Theatre, which was being used as a temporary opera house. All remonstrances proved useless, for I learned that they were not merely thinking about rehearsing the work, but that it was already actually being rehearsed, and would be produced in a few days. It was obvious that this arrangement meant that my opera was to be condemned to quite a short run in their repertoire, as it was not to be expected that they would remount it when the new opera house was opened. On the other hand, they tried to appease me by saying that this first production of the *Fliegender Holländer* was to be associated with a special engagement of Schröder-Devrient, which was to begin in Berlin immediately. They naturally thought I should be delighted to see the great actress in my own work. But this only confirmed me in the suspicion that this opera was simply wanted as a makeshift for the duration of Schröder-Devrient's visit. They were evidently in a dilemma with regard to her repertoire, which consisted mainly of so-called grand operas — such as Meyerbeer's — destined exclusively for the opera house, and which were being specially reserved for the brilliant future of the new building. I therefore realised beforehand that my *Fliegender Holländer* was to be relegated to the category of conductor's operas, and would meet with the usual predestined

fate of such productions. The whole treatment meted out to
me and my works all pointed in the same direction; but in
consideration of the expected co-operation of Schröder-Devrient
I fought against these vexatious premonitions, and set out for
Berlin to do all I could for the success of my opera. I saw at
once that my presence was very necessary. I found the conductor's desk occupied by a man calling himself Conductor
Henning (or Henniger), an official who had won promotion from
the ranks of ordinary musicians by an upright observance of
the laws of seniority, but who knew precious little about conducting an orchestra at all, and about my opera had not the
faintest glimmer of an idea. I took my seat at the desk, and
conducted one full rehearsal and two performances, in neither
of which, however, did Schröder-Devrient take part. Although
I found much to complain of in the weakness of the string
instruments and the consequent mean sound of the orchestra,
yet I was well satisfied with the actors both as regards their
capacity and their zeal. The careful staging, moreover,
which under the supervision of the really gifted stage manager,
Blum, and with the co-operation of his skilful and ingenious
mechanics, was truly excellent, gave me a most pleasant
surprise.

I was now very curious to learn what effect these pleasing
and encouraging preparations would have upon the Berlin
public when the full performance took place. My experiences
on this point were very curious. Apparently the only thing
that interested the large audience was to discover my weak
points. During the first act the prevalent opinion seemed to
be that I belonged to the category of bores. Not a single hand
was moved, and I was afterwards informed that this was fortunate, as the slightest attempt at applause would have been
ascribed to a paid claque, and would have been energetically
opposed. Küstner alone assured me that the composure with
which, on the close of this act, I quitted my desk and appeared
before the curtain, had filled him with wonder, considering this
entire absence — lucky as it appears to have been — of all applause. But so long as I myself felt content with the execution,
I was not disposed to let the public apathy discourage me,
knowing, as I did, that the crucial test was in the second act.

It lay, therefore, much nearer my heart to do all I could for the success of this than to inquire into the reasons for this attitude on the part of the Berlin public. And here the ice was really broken at last. The audience seemed to abandon all idea of finding a proper niche for me, and allowed itself to be carried away into giving vent to applause, which at last grew into the most boisterous enthusiasm. At the close of the act, amid a storm of shouts, I led forward my singers on to the stage for the customary bows of thanks. As the third act was too short to be tedious, and as the scenic effects were both new and impressive, we could not help hoping that we had won a veritable triumph, especially as renewed outbursts of applause marked the end of the performance. Mendelssohn, who happened at that time to be in Berlin, with Meyerbeer, on business relating to the general musical conductorship, was present in a stage box during this performance. He followed its progress with a pale face, and afterwards came and murmured to me in a weary tone of voice, 'Well, I should think you are satisfied now!' I met him several times during my brief stay in Berlin, and also spent an evening with him listening to various pieces of chamber-music. But never did another word concerning the *Fliegender Holländer* pass his lips, beyond inquiries as to the second performance, and as to whether Devrient or some one else would appear in it. I heard, moreover, that he had responded with equal indifference to the earnest warmth of my allusions to his own music for the *Midsummer Night's Dream*, which was being frequently played at that time, and which I had heard for the first time. The only thing he discussed with any detail was the actor Gern, who was playing in *Zettel*, and who he considered was overacting his part.

A few days later came a second performance with the same cast. My experiences on this evening were even more startling than on the former. Evidently the first night had won me a few friends, who were again present, for they began to applaud after the overture. But others responded with hisses, and for the rest of the evening no one again ventured to applaud. My old friend Heine had arrived in the meantime from Dresden, sent by our own board of directors to study the scenic arrangements of the *Midsummer Night's Dream* for our theatre. He was present at this second performance, and had persuaded me to accept the invitation from one of his Berlin relatives to have supper after the performance in a wine-bar *unter den Linden*. Very weary, I followed him to a nasty and badly lighted house, where I gulped down the wine with hasty ill-humour to warm myself, and listened to the embarrassed conversation of my good-natured friend and his companion, whilst I turned over the day's papers. I now had ample leisure to read the criticisms they contained on the first performance of my *Fliegender Holländer*. A terrible spasm cut my heart as I realised the contemptible tone and unparalleled shamelessness of their raging ignorance regarding my own name and work. Our Berlin friend and host, a thorough Philistine, said that he had known how things would go in the theatre that night, after having read these criticisms in the morning. The people of Berlin, he added, wait to hear what Rellstab and his mates have to say, and then they know how to behave. The good fellow was anxious to cheer me up, and ordered one wine after another. Heine hunted up his reminiscences of our merry *Rienzi* times in Dresden, until at last the pair conducted me, staggering along in an addled condition, to my hotel.

It was already midnight. As I was being lighted by the waiter through its gloomy corridors to my room, a gentleman in black, with a pale refined face, came forward and said he would like to speak to me. He informed me that he had waited there since the close of the play, and as he was determined to see me, had stopped till now. I excused myself on the ground of being quite unfit for business, and added that, although not exactly inclined to merriment, I had, as he might perceive, somewhat foolishly drunk a little too much wine. This I said in a stammering voice; but my strange visitor seemed only the more unwilling to be repulsed. He accompanied me to my room, declaring that it was all the more imperative for him to speak with me. We seated ourselves in the cold room, by the meagre light of a single candle, and then he began to talk. In flowing and impressive language he related that he had been present at the performance that night of my *Fliegender Holländer*, and could well conceive the humour in which the evening's experiences had left me. For this very reason he felt that nothing should hinder him from speaking to me that night, and telling me that in the *Fliegender Holländer* I had produced an unrivalled masterpiece. Moreover, the acquaintance he had made with this work had awakened in him a new and unforeseen hope for the future of German art; and that it would be a great pity if I yielded to any sense of discouragement as the result of the unworthy reception accorded to it by the Berlin public. My hair began to stand on end. One of Hoffmann's fantastic creations had entered bodily into my life. I could find nothing to say, except to inquire the name of my visitor, at which he seemed surprised, as I had talked with him the day before at Mendelssohn's house. He said that my conversation and manner had created such an impression upon him there, and had filled him with such sudden regret at not having sufficiently overcome his dislike for opera in general, to be present at the first performance, that he had at once resolved not to miss the second. His name, he added, was Professor Werder. That was no use to me, I said, he must write his name down. Getting paper and ink, he did as I desired, and we parted. I flung myself unconsciously on the bed for a deep and invigorating sleep. Next morning I was fresh and well. I paid a farewell call on Schröder-Devrient, who promised me to do all she could for the *Fliegender Holländer* as soon as possible, drew my fee of a hundred ducats, and set off for home. On my way through Leipzig I utilised my ducats for the repayment of sundry advances made me by my relatives during the earlier and poverty-stricken period of my sojourn in Dresden, and then continued my journey, to recuperate among my books and meditate upon the deep impression made on me by Werder's midnight visit.

Before the end of this winter I received a genuine invitation to Hamburg for the performance of *Rienzi*. The enterprising director, Herr Cornet, through whom it came, confessed that he had many difficulties to contend against in the management of his theatre, and was in need of a great success. This, after the reception with which it had met in Dresden, he thought he could secure by the production of *Rienzi*. I accordingly betook myself thither in the month of March. The journey at that time was not an easy one, as after Hanover one had to proceed by mail-coach, and the crossing of the Elbe, which was full of floating ice, was a risky business. Owing to a great fire that had recently broken out, the town of Hamburg was in process of being rebuilt, and there were still many wide spaces encumbered with ruins. Cold weather and an ever-gloomy sky make my recollections of my somewhat prolonged sojourn in this town anything but agreeable. I was tormented to such an extent by having to rehearse with bad material, fit only for the poorest theatrical trumpery, that, worn out and exposed to constant colds, I spent most of my leisure time in the solitude of my inn chamber. My earlier experiences of ill-arranged and badly managed theatres came back to me afresh. I was particularly depressed when I realised that I had made myself an unconscious accomplice of Director Cornet's basest interests. His one aim was to create a sensation, which he thought should be of great service to me also; and not only did he put me off with a smaller fee, but even suggested that it should be paid by gradual instalments. The dignity of scenic decoration, of which he had not the smallest idea, was completely sacrificed to the most ridiculous and tawdry showiness. He imagined that pageantry was all that was really needed to secure my success. So he hunted out all the old fairy-ballet costumes from his stock, and fancied that if they only looked gay enough, and if plenty of people were bustling about on the stage, I ought to be satisfied. But the most sorry item of all was the singer he provided for the title-rôle. He was a man of the name of Wurda, an elderly, flabby and voiceless tenor, who sang Rienzi with the expression of a lover — like Elvino, for instance, in the *Somnambula*. He was so dreadful that I conceived the idea of making the Capitol tumble down in the second act, so as to bury him sooner in its ruins, a plan which would have cut out several of the processions, which were so dear to the heart of the director. I found my one ray of light in a lady singer, who delighted me with the fire with which she played the part of Adriano. This was a Mme. Fehringer, who was afterwards engaged by Liszt for the rôle of Ortrud in the production of *Lohengrin* at Weimar, but by that time her powers had greatly deteriorated. Nothing could be more depressing than my connection with this opera under such dismal circumstances. And yet there were no outward signs of failure. The manager hoped in any case to keep *Rienzi* in his repertoire until Tichatschek was able to come to Hamburg and give the people of that town a true idea of the play. This actually took place in the following summer.

My discouragement and ill-humour did not escape the notice of Herr Cornet, and discovering that I wished to present my wife with a parrot, he managed to procure a very fine bird, which he gave me as a parting gift. I carried it with me in its narrow cage on my melancholy journey home, and was touched to find that it quickly repaid my care and became very much attached to me. Minna greeted me with great joy when she saw this beautiful grey parrot, for she regarded it as a self-evident proof that I should do something in life. We already had a pretty little dog, born on the day of the first *Rienzi* rehearsal in Dresden, which, owing to its passionate devotion to myself, was much petted by all who knew me and visited my house during those years. This sociable bird, which had no vices and was an apt scholar, now formed an addition to our household; and the pair did much to brighten our dwelling in the absence of children. My wife soon taught the bird snatches of songs from *Rienzi,* with which it would good-naturedly greet me from a distance when it heard me coming up the stairs.

And thus at last my domestic hearth seemed to be established with every possible prospect of a comfortable competency.

No further excursions for the performance of any of my operas took place, for the simple reason that no such performances were given. As I saw it was quite clear that the diffusion of my works through the theatrical world would be a very slow business, I concluded that this was probably due to the fact that no adaptations of them for the piano existed. I therefore thought that I should do well to press forward such an issue at all costs, and in order to secure the expected profits, I hit upon the idea of publishing at my own expense. I accordingly made arrangements with F. Meser, the court music-dealer, who had hitherto not got beyond the publication of a valse, and signed an agreement with him for his firm to appear as the nominal publishers on the understanding that they should receive a commission of ten per cent., whilst I provided the necessary capital.

As there were two operas to be issued, including *Rienzi*, a work of exceptional bulk, it was not likely that these publications would prove very profitable unless, in addition to the usual piano selections, I also published adaptations, such as the music without words, for duet or solo. For this a fairly large capital was necessary. I also needed funds for the repayment of the loans already mentioned, and for the settlement of old debts, as well as to pay off the remaining expenses of my house-furnishing. I was therefore obliged to try and procure much larger sums. I laid my project and its motive before Schröder-Devrient, who had just returned to Dresden, at Easter, 1844, to fulfil a fresh engagement. She believed in the future of my works, recognised the peculiarity of my position, as well as the correctness of my calculations, and declared her willingness to provide the necessary capital for the publication of my operas, refusing to consider the act as one involving any sacrifice on her part. This money she proposed to get by selling out her investments in Polish state-bonds, and I was to pay the customary rate of interest. The thing was so easily done, and seemed so much a matter of course, that I at once made all needful arrangements with my Leipzig printer, and set to work on the publication of my operas.

When the amount of work delivered brought with it a demand for considerable payments on account, I approached my friend for a first advance. And here I became confronted with a new phase of that famous lady's life, which placed me in a position which proved as disastrous as it was unexpected. After having broken away from the unlucky Herr von Münchhausen some time previously, and returned, as it appeared, with penitential ardour to her former connection with my friend, Hermann Müller, it now turned out that she had found no real satisfaction in this fresh relationship. On the contrary, the star of her being, whom she had so long and ardently desired, had now at last arisen in the person of another lieutenant of the Guards. With a vehemence which made light of her treachery to her old friend, she elected this slim young man, whose moral and intellectual weaknesses were patent to every eye, as the chosen keystone of her life's love. He took the good luck that befell him so seriously, that he would brook no jesting, and at once laid hands on the fortune of his future wife, as he considered that it was disadvantageously and insecurely invested, and thought that he knew of much more profitable ways of employing it. My friend therefore explained, with much pain and evident embarrassment, that she had renounced all control over her capital, and was unable to keep her promise to me.

Owing to this I entered upon a series of entanglements and troubles which henceforth dominated my life, and plunged me into sorrows that left their dismal mark on all my subsequent enterprises. It was clear that I could not now abandon the proposed plan of publication. The only satisfactory solution of my perplexities was to be found in the execution of my project and the success which I hoped would attend it. I was compelled, therefore, to turn all my energies to the raising of the money wherewith to publish my two operas, to which in all probability *Tannhäuser* would shortly have to be added. I first applied to my friends, and in some cases had to pay exorbitant rates of interest, even for short terms. For the present these details are sufficient to prepare the reader for the catastrophe towards which I was now inevitably drifting.

The hopelessness of my position did not at first reveal itself. There seemed no reason to despair of the eventual spread of my operatic works among the theatres in Germany, though my experience of them indicated that the process would be slow. In spite of the depressing experiences in Berlin and Hamburg, there were many encouraging signs to be seen. Above all, *Rienzi* maintained its position in favour of the people of Dresden, a place which undoubtedly occupied a position of great importance, especially during the summer months, when so many strangers from all parts of the world pass through it. My opera, which was not to be heard anywhere else, was in great request, both among the Germans and other visitors, and was always received with marked approbation, which surprised me very much. Thus a performance of *Rienzi,* especially in summer, became quite a Dionysian revelry, whose effect upon me could not fail to be encouraging.

On one occasion Liszt was among the number of these visitors. As *Rienzi* did not happen to be in the repertoire when he arrived, he induced the management at his earnest request to arrange a special performance. I met him between the acts in Tichatschek's dressing-room, and was heartily encouraged and touched by his almost enthusiastic appreciation, expressed in his most emphatic manner. The kind of life to which Liszt was at that time condemned, and which bound him to a perpetual environment of distracting and exciting elements, debarred us from all more intimate and fruitful intercourse. Yet from this time onward I continued to receive constant testimonies of the profound and lasting impression I had made upon him, as well as of his sympathetic remembrance of me. From various parts of the world, wherever his triumphal progress led him, people, chiefly of the upper classes, came to Dresden for the purpose of hearing *Rienzi*. They had been so interested by Liszt's reports of my work, and by his playing of various selections from it, that they all came expecting something of unparalleled importance.

Besides these indications of Liszt's enthusiastic and friendly sympathy, other deeply touching testimonies appeared from different quarters. The startling beginning made by Werder, on the occasion of his midnight visit after the second performance of the *Fliegender Holländer* in Berlin, was shortly afterwards followed by a similarly unsolicited approach in the form of an effusive letter from an equally unknown personage, Alwine Frommann, who afterwards became my faithful friend. After my departure from Berlin she heard Schröder-Devrient twice in the *Fliegender Holländer,* and the letter in which she described the effect produced upon her by my work conveyed to me for the first time the vigorous and profound sentiments of a deep and confident recognition such as seldom falls to the lot of even the greatest master, and cannot fail to exercise a weighty influence on his mind and spirit, which long for self-confidence.

I have no very vivid recollections of my own doings during

this first year of my position as conductor in a sphere of action which gradually grew more and more familiar. For the anniversary of my appointment, and to some extent as a personal recognition, I was commissioned to procure Gluck's *Armida*. This we performed in March, 1843, with the co-operation of Schröder-Devrient, just before her temporary departure from Dresden. Great importance was attached to this production, because, at the same moment, Meyerbeer was inaugurating his general-directorship in Berlin by a performance of the same work. Indeed, it was in Berlin that the extraordinary respect entertained for such a commemoration of Gluck had its origin. I was told that Meyerbeer went to Rellstab with the score of *Armida* in order to obtain hints as to its correct interpretation.

As not long afterwards I also heard a strange story of two silver candlesticks, wherewith the famous composer was said to have enlightened the no less famous critic when showing him the score of his *Feldlager in Schlesien*, I decided to attach no great importance to the instructions he might have received, but rather to help myself by a careful handling of this difficult score, and by introducing some softness into it through modulating the variations in tone as much as possible. I had the gratification later of receiving an exceedingly warm appreciation of my rendering from Herr Eduard Devrient, a great Gluck connoisseur. After hearing this opera as presented by us, and comparing it with the Berlin performance, he heartily praised the tenderly modulated character of our rendering of certain parts, which, he said, had been given in Berlin with the coarsest bluntness. He mentioned, as a striking instance of this, a brief chorus in C major of male and female nymphs in the third act. By the introduction of a more moderate *tempo* and very soft *piano* I had tried to free this from the original coarseness with which Devrient had heard it rendered in Berlin — presumably with traditional fidelity. My most innocent device, and one which I frequently adopted, for disguising the irritating stiffness or the orchestral movement in the original, was a careful modification of the *Basso-continuo*, which was taken uninterruptedly in common time. This I felt obliged to remedy, partly by *legato* playing, and partly by *pizzicato*.

Our management were lavish in their expenditure on externals, especially decoration, and as a spectacular opera the piece drew fairly large houses, thus earning me the reputation of being a very suitable conductor for Gluck, and one who was in close sympathy with him. This result was the more conspicuous from the fact that *Iphigenia in Tauris* which is a far superior work, and in which Devrient's interpretation of the title-rôle was admirable had been performed to empty houses.

I had to live upon this reputation for a long time, as it often happened that I was compelled to give inferior performances of repertoire pieces, including Mozart's operas. The mediocrity of these was particularly disappointing to those who, after my success in *Armida*, had expected a great deal from my rendering of these pieces, and were much disappointed in consequence. Even sympathetic hearers sought to explain their disappointment on the ground that I did not appreciate Mozart and could not understand him. But they failed to realise how impossible it was for me, as a mere conductor, to exercise any real influence on such desultory performances, which were merely given as stopgaps, and often without rehearsal. Indeed, in this matter I often found myself in a false position, which, as I was powerless to remedy it, contributed not a little to render unbearable both my new office and my dependence upon the meanest motives of a paltry theatrical routine, already overweighted with the cares of business. This, in fact, became worse than I had expected, in spite of my previous knowledge of the precariousness of such a life. My colleague Reissiger, to whom from time to time I poured out my woes regarding the scant attention given by the general management to our demands for the maintenance of correct representations in the realm of opera, comforted me by saying that I, like himself, would sooner or later relinquish all these fads and submit to the inevitable fate of a conductor. Thereupon he proudly smote his stomach, and hoped that I might soon be able to boast of one as round as his own.

I received further provocation for my growing dislike of these jog-trot methods from a closer acquaintance with the spirit in which even eminent conductors undertook the reproduction of our masterpieces. During this first year Mendelssohn was invited to conduct his *St. Paul* for one of the Palm Sunday concerts in the Dresden chapel, which was famous at that time. The knowledge I thus acquired of this work, under such favourable circumstances, pleased me so much, that I made a fresh attempt to approach the composer with sincere and friendly motives; but a remarkable conversation which I had with him on the evening of this performance quickly and strangely repelled my impulse. After the oratorio Reissiger was to produce Beethoven's Eighth Symphony. I had noticed in the preceding rehearsal that Reissiger had fallen into the error of all the ordinary conductors of this work by taking the *tempo di minuetto* of the third movement at a meaningless waltz time, whereby not only does the whole piece lose its imposing character, but the trio is rendered absolutely ridiculous by the impossibility of the violoncello part being interpreted at such a speed. I had called Reissiger's attention to this defect, and he acquiesced in my opinion, promising to take the part in question at true *minuetto tempo*. I related this to Mendelssohn, when he was resting after his own performance in the box beside me, listening to the symphony. He, too, acknowledged that I was right, and thought that it ought to be played as I said. And now the third movement began. Reissiger, who, it is true, did not possess the needful power suddenly to impress so momentous a change of time upon his orchestra with success, followed the usual custom and took the *tempo di minuetto* in the same old waltz time. Just as I was about to express my anger, Mendelssohn gave me a friendly nod, as though he thought that this was what I wanted, and that I had understood the music in this way. I was so amazed by this complete absence of feeling on the part of the famous musician, that I was struck dumb, and thenceforth my own particular opinion of Mendelssohn gradually matured, an opinion which was afterwards confirmed by R. Schumann. The latter, in expressing the sincere pleasure he had felt on listening to the time at which I had taken the first movement of Beethoven's Ninth Symphony, told me that he had been compelled to hear it year after year taken by Mendelssohn at a perfectly distracting speed.

Amid my yearning anxiety to exert some influence upon the

spirit in which our noblest masterpieces were executed, I had to struggle against the profound dissatisfaction I felt with my employment on the ordinary theatre repertoire. It was not until Palm Sunday of the year 1844, just after my dispiriting expedition to Hamburg, that my desire to conduct the Pastoral Symphony was satisfied. But many faults still remained unremedied, and for the removal of these I had to adopt indirect methods which gave me much trouble. For instance, at these famous concerts the arrangement of the orchestra, the members of which were seated in a long, thin, semicircular row round the chorus of singers, was so inconceivably stupid that it required the explanation given by Reissiger to make me understand such folly. He told me that all these arrangements dated from the time of the late conductor Morlacchi, who, as an Italian composer of operas, had no true realisation of the importance of the orchestra nor of its necessities. When, therefore, I asked why they had permitted him to meddle with things he did not understand, I learned that the preference shown to this Italian, both by the court and the general management, even in opposition to Carl Maria von Weber, had always been absolute and brooked no contradiction. I was warned that, even now, we should experience great difficulty in ridding ourselves of these inherited vices, because the opinion still prevailed in the highest circles that he must have understood best what he was about.

Once more my childish memories of the eunuch Sassaroli flashed through my mind, and I remembered the warning of Weber's widow as to the significance of my succession to her husband's post of conductor in Dresden. But, in spite of all this, our performance of the Pastoral Symphony succeeded beyond expectation, and the incomparable and wonderfully stimulating enjoyment, which I was in future to derive from my intercourse with Beethoven's works, now first enabled me to realise his prolific strength. Röckel shared in this enjoyment with heartfelt sympathy; he supported me with eye and ear at every rehearsal, always stood by my side, and was at one with me both in his appreciation and his aims.

After this encouraging success I was to receive the gratification of another triumph in the summer, which, although it

OVATION FOR THE KING OF SAXONY

was of no particular moment from the musical point of view, was of great social importance. The King of Saxony, towards whom, as I have already said, I had felt warmly drawn when he was Prince Friedrich, was expected home from a long visit to England. The reports received of his stay there had greatly rejoiced my patriotic soul. While this homely monarch, who shrank from all pomp and noisy demonstration, was in England, it happened that the Tsar Nicholas arrived quite unexpectedly on a visit to the Queen. In his honour great festivities and military reviews were held, in which our King, much against his will, was obliged to participate, and he was consequently compelled to receive the enthusiastic acclamations of the English crowd, who were most demonstrative in showing their preference for him, as compared with the unpopular Tsar. This preference was also reflected in the newspapers, so that a flattering incense floated over from England to our little Saxony which filled us all with a peculiar pride in our King. While I was in this mood, which absorbed me completely, I learned that preparations were being made in Leipzig for a special welcome to the King on his return, which was to be further dignified by a musical festival in the directing of which Mendelssohn was to take part. I made inquiries as to what was going to be done in Dresden, and learned that the King did not propose to call there at all, but was going direct to his summer residence at Pillnitz.

A moment's reflection showed me that this would only further my desire of preparing a pleasant and hearty reception for his Majesty. As I was a servant of the Crown, any attempt on my part to render an act of homage in Dresden might have had the appearance of an official parade which would not be admissible. I seized the idea, therefore, of hurriedly collecting together all who could either play or sing, so that we might perform a Reception song hastily composed in honour of the event. The obstacle to my plan was that my Director Lüttichau was away at one of his country seats. To come to an understanding with my colleague Reissiger would, moreover, have involved delay, and given the enterprise the very aspect of an official ovation which I wished to avoid. As no time was to be lost, if anything worthy of the occasion was to be done —

as the King was due to arrive in a few days — I availed myself of my position as conductor of the Glee Club, and summoned all its singers and instrumentalists to my aid. In addition to these, I invited the members of our theatrical company, and also those of the orchestra, to join us. This done, I drove quickly to Pillnitz to arrange matters with the Lord Chamberlain, whom I found favourably disposed towards my project. The only leisure I could snatch for composing the verses of my song and setting them to music was during the rapid drive there and back, for by the time I reached home I had to have every thing ready for the copyist and lithographer. The agreeable sensation of rushing through the warm summer air and lovely country, coupled with the sincere affection with which I was inspired for our German Prince, and which had prompted my effort, elated me and worked me up to a high pitch of tension, in which I now formed a clear conception of the lyrical outlines of the 'Tannhäuser March,' which first saw the light of day on the occasion of this royal welcome. I soon afterwards developed this theme, and thus produced the march which became the most popular of the melodies I had hitherto composed.

On the next day it had to be tried over with a hundred and twenty instrumentalists and three hundred singers. I had taken the liberty of inviting them to meet me on the stage of the Court Theatre, where everything went off capitally. Every one was delighted, and I not the least so, when a messenger arrived from the director, who had just returned to town, requesting an immediate interview. Lüttichau was enraged beyond measure at my high-handed proceedings in this matter, of which he had been informed by our good friend Reissiger. If his baronial coronet had been on his head during this interview, it would assuredly have tumbled off. The fact that I should have conducted my negotiations in person with the court officials, and could report that my endeavours had met with extraordinarily prompt success, aroused his deepest fury, for the chief importance of his own position consisted in always representing everything which had to be obtained by these means as surrounded by the greatest obstacles, and hedged in by the strictest etiquette. I offered to cancel everything, but that only embarrassed him the more. I thereupon asked him what he wanted me to do, if the plan was still to be carried out. On this point he seemed uncertain, but thought I had shown a great lack of fellow-feeling in having not only ignored him, but Reissiger as well. I answered that I was perfectly ready to hand over my composition and the conducting of the piece to Reissiger. But he could not swallow this, as he really had an exceedingly poor opinion of Reissiger, of which I was very well aware. His real grievance was that I had arranged the whole business with the Lord Chamberlain, Herr von Reizenstein, who was his personal enemy, and he added that I could form no conception of the rudeness he had been obliged to endure from the hands of this official. This outburst of confidence made it easier for me to exhibit an almost sincere emotion, to which he responded by a shrug of the shoulders, meaning that he must resign himself to a disagreeable necessity.

But my project was even more seriously threatened by the wretched weather than by this storm with the director; for it rained all day in torrents. If it lasted, which it seemed only too likely to do, I could hardly start on the special boat at five o'clock in the morning, as proposed, with my hundreds of helpers, to give an early morning concert at Pillnitz, two hours away. I anticipated such a disaster with genuine dismay. But Röckel consoled me by saying that I could rely upon it that we should have glorious weather the next day; for I was lucky! This belief in my luck has followed me ever since, even down to my latest days; and amid the great misfortunes which have so often hampered my enterprises, I have felt as if this statement were a wicked insult to fate. But this time, at least, my friend was right; the 12th of August, 1844 was from sunrise till late at night the most perfect summer day that I can remember in my whole life. The sensation of blissful content with which I saw my light-hearted legion of gaily dressed bandsmen and singers gathering through the auspicious morning mists on board our steamer, swelled my breast with a fervent faith in my lucky star.

By my friendly impetuosity I had succeeded in overcoming Reissiger's smouldering resentment, and had persuaded him to share the honour of our undertaking by conducting the performance of my composition himself. When we arrived at the spot, everything went off splendidly. The King and royal family were visibly touched, and in the evil times that followed the Queen of Saxony spoke of this occasion, I am told, with peculiar emotion, as the fairest day of her life. After Reissiger had wielded his baton with great dignity, and I had sung with the tenors in the choir, we two conductors were summoned to the presence of the royal family. The King warmly expressed his thanks, while the Queen paid us the high compliment of saying that I composed very well and that Reissiger conducted very well. His Majesty asked us to repeat the last three stanzas only, as, owing to a painful ulcerated tooth, he could not remain much longer out of doors. I rapidly devised a combined evolution, the remarkably successful execution of which I am very proud, even to this day. I had the entire song repeated, but, in accordance with the King's wish, only one verse was sung in our original crescent formation. At the beginning of the second verse I made my four hundred undisciplined bandsmen and singers file off in a march through the garden, which, as they gradually receded, was so arranged that the final notes could only reach the royal ear as an echoing dream-song. Thanks to my unexampled activity and ever-present help, this retreat was so steadily carried out that not the slightest faltering was perceptible either in time or delivery, and the whole might have been taken for a carefully rehearsed theatrical manœuvre. On reaching the castle court we found that, by the Queen's kindly forethought, an ample breakfast had been provided for our party on the lawn, where the tables were already spread. We often saw our royal hostess herself busily supervising the attendants, or moving with excited delight about the windows and corridors of the castle. Every eye beamed rapture to my soul, as the successful author of the general happiness, and I almost felt amid the glories of that day as though the millennium had been proclaimed. After roaming in a body through the lovely grounds of the castle, and not omitting to pay a visit to the Keppgrund which had been so dear to me in my youth, we returned late at night, and in the highest spirits, to Dresden.

Next morning I was again summoned to the presence of the director. But a change had come over him during the night.

LÜTTICHAU DEEPLY AFFECTED

As I began to offer my apologies for the anxiety I had caused him, the tall thin man, with the hard dry face, seized me by the hand and addressed me with a rapturous expression, which I am sure no one else ever saw on his face. He told me to say no more about these anxieties. I was a great man, and soon no one would know anything about him, whereas I should be universally admired and loved. I was deeply moved, and wished only to express my embarrassment at so unexpected an outburst, when he kindly interrupted me and sought an escape from his own emotion in good-humoured confidences. He referred, with a smile, to the self-denial which had yielded the place of honour on so extraordinary an occasion to an undeserving man like Reissiger. When I assured him that this act had afforded me the liveliest satisfaction, and that I had myself persuaded my colleague to take the baton, he confessed that at last he began to understand me, but failed altogether to comprehend how the other could accept a position to which he had no right.

Lüttichau's altered attitude towards me was such that for some time our intercourse on matters of business assumed an almost confidential tone. But, unfortunately, in course of time things changed for the worse, so that our relationship became one of open enmity; nevertheless, a certain peculiar tenderness towards me on the part of this singular man was always clearly perceptible. Indeed, I might almost say that much of his subsequent abuse of me sounded more like the strangely perverted plaints of a love that met with no response.

For my holiday this year I went, early in September, to Fischer's vineyard, near Loschwitz, not far from the famous Findlater vineyard, where, somewhat late in the year, I rented a summer residence. Here, under the kindly and strengthening stimulus of six week of open-air life, I composed my music for the second act of *Tannhäuser*, which I completed by the 15th of October. During this period a performance of *Rienzi* was given before an audience of no ordinary importance. For this event I went up to town. Spontini, Meyerbeer, and General Lwoff, the composer of the Russian National Anthem, were seated together in a stage box. I sought no opportunity of learning the impression made by my opera upon these learned judges and magnates of the musical world. It was enough for me to have the complacent satisfaction of knowing that they had heard my oft-repeated work performed before a crowded house and amid overwhelming applause. I was delighted at the close of the opera to have my little dog Peps, which had run after me all the way from the country, brought to me; and without waiting to greet the European celebrities, I drove off with it at once to our quiet vineyard, where Minna was greatly relieved to recover her little pet, which for hours she had believed to be lost.

Here I also received a visit from Werder, the man whose friendship I had made in Berlin under such dramatic circumstances. But this time he appeared in ordinary human guise, beneath the kindly light of heaven, by which we disputed in a friendly way concerning the true worth of the *Fliegender Holländer,* my mind having somewhat turned against this work since *Tannhäuser* had got into my head. It certainly seemed odd to find myself contradicted on this point by my friend, and to receive instruction from him on the significance of my own work.

When we returned to our winter quarters I tried to avoid allowing so lengthy an interval to elapse between the composition of the second and third acts as had separated that of the first and second. In spite of many absorbing engagements I succeeded in my aim. By carefully cultivating a habit of taking solitary walks, and thanks to their soothing influence over me, I managed to finish the music of Act iii. by the 29th of December, that is to say, before the end of the year.

During this period my time was otherwise very seriously occupied by a visit paid us by Spontini with reference to a proposed presentation of his *Vestalin,* the preparation for which had just begun. The singular episodes and characteristic features of the intercourse which I thus gained with this eminent and hoary-headed master are still so vividly imprinted on my memory that they seem worthy of a place in this record.

Since, with the co-operation of Schröder-Devrient, we could, on the whole, rely upon an admirable presentation of the opera, I had inspired Lüttichau with the idea of inviting Spontini to undertake the personal superintendence of his justly famous work. He had just left Berlin for ever, after enduring great humiliation there, and such an invitation at this moment would be a well-timed proof of respect. This was accordingly sent, and as I had myself been entrusted with the conductorship of the opera, I was given the singular task of deciding this point with the master. My letter, it appears, although written in French, inspired him with a high opinion of my zeal for the enterprise, and in a gracious reply he informed me what his special wishes were regarding the arrangements to be made for his collaboration. As far as the vocalists were concerned, and seeing that a Schröder-Devrient was among the number, he frankly expressed his satisfaction. As for chorus and ballet, he took it for granted that nothing would be lacking to the dignity of the performance; and finally, as regarded the orchestra, he expected that this also would be sure to please him, as he presumed it contained the necessary complement of excellent instruments which, to use his own words, 'he hoped would furnish the performance with twelve good contrabassi' (*le tout garni de douze bonnes contre-basses*). This phrase bowled me over, for the proportion thus bluntly stated in figures gave me so logical a conception of his exalted expectations, that I hurried away at once to the director to warn him that the enterprise on which we had embarked would not, after all, prove as easy as we thought. His alarm was great, and he said that some plan must at once be devised for breaking off the engagement.

When Schröder-Devrient heard of our dilemma, knowing Spontini well, she laughed as though she would never stop at the ingenuous impudence with which we had issued our invitation. A trifling indisposition from which she then suffered provided a reasonable excuse for a delay, more or less prolonged, and this she generously placed at our disposal. Spontini had, in fact, urged us to use all possible despatch in the execution of our project, for, as he was impatiently awaited in Paris, he could spare us but little time. It fell to my lot to weave the tissue of innocent deceptions by which we hoped to divert the master from a definite acceptance of our invitation. Now we could breathe again, and duly began rehearsing. But on the very day before we proposed to hold our full-dress rehearsal at our leisure, lo and behold! about noon a carriage drove up to my door, in which, clad in a long blue coat of pilot-cloth, sat no other than the haughty master himself, whose manners resembled those of a Spanish grandee. All unattended and greatly excited, he entered my room, showed me my letters, and proved from our correspondence that the invitation had not been declined, but that he had in all points accurately complied with our wishes. Forgetting for the moment all the possible embarrassments which might arise, in my genuine delight at beholding the wonderful man before me, and hearing his work conducted by himself, I at once undertook to do everything I possibly could to meet his desires. This declaration I made with the utmost sincerity of zeal. He smiled with almost childlike kindliness on hearing me, and I at once begged him to conduct the rehearsal arranged for the morrow. He thereupon grew suddenly thoughtful, and began to weigh the numerous disadvantages of such an action on his part. So acute did his agitation become that he had the greatest difficulty in expressing himself clearly on any point, and I found it no easy matter to inquire what arrangements on our part would persuade him to undertake the morrow's rehearsal. After a moment's reflection he asked what sort of baton I was accustomed to use when conducting. With my hands I indicated the approximate length and thickness of a medium-sized wooden rod, such as our choir-attendant was in the habit of supplying, freshly covered with white paper. He sighed, and asked if I thought it possible to procure him by to-morrow a baton of black ebony, whose very respectable length and thickness he indicated by a gesture, and on each end of which a fairly large knob of ivory was to be affixed. I promised to have one prepared for the next rehearsal, which should at least be similar in appearance to what he desired, and another of the specified materials in time for the actual performance. Visibly relieved, he then passed his hand over his brow, and granted me permission to announce his consent to conduct on the following day. After once more strongly enforcing his instructions as to the baton, he went back to his hotel.

I seemed to be moving in a dream, and hastened in a whirlwind of excitement to publish the news of what had happened and was to be expected. We were fairly trapped. Schröder-Devrient offered to become our scapegoat, while I entered into precise details with the theatre carpenter concerning the baton. This turned out so far correct that it possessed the requisite length and breadth, was black in its colour, and had two large white knobs. Then came the fateful rehearsal. Spontini was evidently ill at ease on his seat in the orchestra. First of all he wished to have the oboists placed behind him. As this partial change of position just at that moment would have caused much confusion in the disposition of the orchestra, I promised to effect the alteration after the rehearsal. He said no more, and took up his baton. In a moment I understood why he attached such importance to its form and size. He held it, not as other conductors do, by the end, but gripped it about the middle with his clenched fist, waving it so as to make it evident that he wielded his baton like a field-marshal's staff, not for beating time, but for command.

Confusion arose in the very first scene, which was increased by the fact that the master's instructions, both to orchestra and singers, were rendered almost unintelligible by his confused use of the German language. This much at least we were soon able to grasp, that he was particularly anxious to disabuse us of the idea that this was a full-dress rehearsal, and to show us that he was set upon a thorough re-study of the opera from the very beginning. Great, indeed, was the despair of my good old chorus-master and stage manager, Fischer — who before had enthusiastically advocated the invitation of Spontini — when he recognised that the dislocation of our repertoire was now inevitable. This feeling swelled by degrees to open anger, in the blindness of which every fresh suggestion of Spontini's appeared but frivolous fault-finding, to which he bluntly responded in the coarsest German. After one of the choruses Spontini beckoned me to his side and whispered: ' *Mais savez-vous, vos chœurs ne chantent pas mal* '; whereupon Fischer, regarding this with suspicion, shouted out to me in a rage: ' What does the old hog want now ? ' and I had some trouble to pacify the speedily converted enthusiast.

But our most serious delay arose, during the first act,

through the evolutions of a triumphal march. With the most vociferous emphasis the master expressed intense dissatisfaction with the apathetic demeanour of our populace during the procession of vestal virgins. He was quite unaware of the fact that, in obedience to our stage manager's instructions, they had fallen on their knees upon the appearance of the priestesses; for he was so excited, and withal so terribly shortsighted, that nothing which appealed to the eye alone was perceptible to his senses. What he demanded was that the Roman army should manifest its devout respect in more drastic fashion by flinging themselves as one man to the ground, and marking this by delivering a crashing blow of their spears on their shields. Endless attempts were made, but some one always clattered either too soon or too late. Then he repeated the action himself several times with his baton on the desk, but all to no purpose; the crash was not sufficiently sharp and emphatic. This reminded me of the impression made upon me some years before in Berlin by the wonderful precision and almost alarming effect with which I had seen similar evolutions carried out in the play of *Ferdinand Cortez*, and I realized that it would require an immediate and tedious accentuation of our customary softness of action in such manœuvres before we could meet the fastidious master's requirements. At the end of the first act Spontini went on the stage himself, in order to give a detailed explanation of his reasons for wishing to defer his opera for a considerable time, so as to prepare by multitudinous rehearsals for its production in accordance with his taste. He expected to find the actors of the Dresden Court Theatre gathered there to hear him; but the company had already dispersed. Singers and stage manager had hastily scattered in every direction to give vent, each in his own fashion, to the misery of the situation. None but the workmen, lamp-cleaners, and a few of the chorus gathered in a semicircle around Spontini, in order to have a look at that remarkable man, as he held forth with wonderful effect on the requirements of true theatrical art. Turning towards the dismal scene, I gently and respectfully pointed out to Spontini the uselessness of his declamation, and promised that everything should eventually be done precisely as he desired.

Finally, I succeeded in extricating him from the undignified position in which, to my horror, he had been placed, by telling him that Herr Eduard Devrient, who had seen the *Vestalin* in Berlin, and carried every detail of the performance in his mind, should personally drill our chorus and supers into a becoming solemnity during the reception of the vestals. This pacified him, and we proceeded to settle on a plan for a series of rehearsals according to his wishes. But, in spite of all this, I was the only person to whom this strange turn of affairs was not unwelcome; for through the burlesque extravagances of Spontini, and notwithstanding his extraordinary eccentricities, which, however, I learned in time to understand, I could perceive the miraculous energy with which he pursued and attained an ideal of theatrical art such as in our days had become almost unknown.

We began, therefore, with a pianoforte rehearsal, at which the master made a point of telling the singers what he wanted. He did not tell us anything new, however, for he said little about the details of the rendering; on the other hand, he expatiated upon the general interpretation, and I noticed that in doing this, he had accustomed himself to make the most decided allowances for the great singers, especially Schröder-Devrient and Tichatschek. The only thing he did was to forbid the latter to use the word *Braut* (bride) with which Licinius had to address Julia in the German translation; this word sounded horrible in his ears, and he could not understand how anybody could set such a vulgar sound as that to music. He gave a long lecture, however, to the somewhat coarse and less talented singer who took the part of the high-priest, and explained to him how to understand and interpret this character from the dialogue (in recitative) between him and Haruspex. He told him that he must understand that the whole thing was based upon priestcraft and superstition. Pontifex must make it clear that he does not fear his antagonist at the head of the Roman army, because, should the worst come to the worst, he has his machines ready, which, if necessary, will miraculously rekindle the dead fire of Vesta. In this way, even though Julia should escape the sacrifice, the power of the priesthood would still be unassailable.

During one of the rehearsals I asked Spontini why he, who, as a rule, made such very effective use of the trombone, should have left it entirely out in the magnificent triumphal march of the first act. Very much astonished he asked: '*Est-ce que je n'ai pas de trombones?*' I showed him the printed score, and he then asked me to add the trombones to the march, so that, if possible, they might be used at the next rehearsal. He also said: '*J'ai entendu dans votre* Rienzi *un instrument, que vous appelez Basse-tuba; je ne veux pas bannir cet instrument de l'orchestre: faites m'en une partie pour la* Vestale.' It gave me great pleasure to perform this task for him with all the care and good judgment I could dispose of. When at the rehearsal he heard the effect for the first time, he threw me a really grateful glance, and so much appreciated the really simple additions I had made to his score, that a little later on he wrote me a very friendly letter from Paris in which he asked me kindly to send him the extra instrumental parts I had prepared for him. His pride would not allow him, however, to ask outright for something for which I alone had been responsible, so he wrote: '*Envoyez-moi une partition des trombones pour la marche triomphale et de la Basse-tuba telle qu'elle a été exécutée sous ma direction à Dresde.*' Apart from this, I also showed how greatly I respected him, in the eagerness with which, at his special request, I regrouped all the instruments in the orchestra. He was forced to this request more by habit than by principle, and how very important it seemed to him not to make the slightest change in his customary arrangements, was proved to me when he explained his method of conducting. He conducted the orchestra, so he said, only with his eyes: ' My left eye is the first violin, my right eye the second, and if the eye is to have power, one must not wear glasses (as so many bad conductors do), even if one is short-sighted. I,' he admitted confidentially, ' cannot see twelve inches in front of me, but all the same I can make them play as I want, merely by fixing them with my eye.' In some respects the arbitrary way in which he used to arrange his orchestra was really very irrational. From his old days in Paris he had retained the habit of placing the two oboists immediately behind him, and although this was a fad which owed its origin to a mere accident.

it was one to which he always adhered. The consequence was that these players had to avert the mouthpiece of their instruments from the audience, and our excellent oboist was so angry about this arrangement, that it was only by dint of great diplomacy that I succeeded in pacifying him.

Apart from this, Spontini's method was based upon the absolutely correct system (which even at the present time is misunderstood by some German orchestras) of spreading the string quartette over the whole orchestra. This system further consisted in preventing the brass and percussion instruments from culminating in one point (and drowning each other) by dividing them on both sides, and by placing the more delicate wind instruments at a judicious distance from each other, thus forming a chain between the violins. Even some great and celebrated orchestras of the present day still retain the custom of dividing the mass of instruments into two halves, the string and the wind instruments, an arrangement that denotes roughness and a lack of understanding of the sound of the orchestra, which ought to blend harmoniously and be well balanced.

I was very glad to have the chance of introducing this excellent improvement in Dresden, for now that Spontini himself had initiated it, it was an easy matter to get the King's command to let the alteration stand. Nothing remained after Spontini's departure but to modify and correct certain eccentricities and arbitrary features in his arrangements; and from that moment I attained a high level of success with my orchestra.

With all the peculiarities he showed at rehearsals, this exceptional man fascinated both musicians and singers to such an extent that the production attracted quite an unusual amount of attention. Very characteristic was the energy with which he insisted on exceptionally sharp rhythmic accents; through his association with the Berlin orchestra he had acquired the habit of marking the note that he wished to be brought out with the word *diese* (this), which at first was quite incomprehensible to me. The great singer Tichatschek, who had a positive genius for rhythm, was highly pleased by this; for he also had acquired the habit of compelling the chorus to great precision in very important entries, and maintained that if one only accentuated the first note properly, the rest followed as a matter of course. On the whole, therefore, a spirit of devotion to the master gradually pervaded the orchestra; the violas alone bore him a grudge for a while, and for this reason. In the accompaniment of the lugubrious cantilena of Julia at the end of the second act, he would not put up with the way in which the violas played the horribly sentimental accompaniment. Suddenly turning towards them he called in a sepulchral tone, 'Are the violas dying?' The two pale and incurably melancholy old men who held on tenaciously to their posts in the orchestra, notwithstanding their right to a pension, stared at Spontini with real fright, reading a threat in his words, and I had to explain Spontini's wish in sober language in order to call them back to life.

On the stage Herr Eduard Devrient helped very materially in bringing about wonderfully distinct *ensembles;* he also knew how to gratify a certain wish of Spontini's, which threw us all into tremendous confusion. In accordance with the cuts adopted by all the German theatres, we too ended the opera with the fiery duet, supported by the chorus, between Licinius and Julia after their rescue. The master, however, insisted on adding a lively chorus and ballet to the finale, according to the antiquated method of ending common to French *opera seria*. He was absolutely against finishing his work with a dismal churchyard episode; consequently the whole scene had to be altered. Venus was to shine resplendent in a rose bower, and the long-suffering lovers were to be wedded at her altar, amid lively dancing and singing, by rose-bedecked priests and priestesses. We performed it like this, but unluckily not with the success we had all hoped for.

In the course of the production, which was proceeding with wonderful accuracy and verve, we came across a difficulty with regard to the principal part for which none of us had been prepared. Our great Schröder-Devrient was obviously no longer of an age to give the desired effect as the youngest of the vestal virgins; she had acquired matronly contours, and her age was moreover accentuated by the extremely girlish-looking high-priestess with whom she had to act, and whose youth it was difficult to dissimulate. This was my niece, Johanna

Wagner, who, because of her marvellous voice and great talent as an actress, made every one in the audience long to see the parts of the two women reversed. Schröder-Devrient, who was well aware of this fact, tried by every effective means in her power to overcome her most difficult position; this effort, however, resulted not infrequently in great exaggeration and straining of the voice, and in one very important place her part was sadly overacted. When, after the great trio in the second act, she had to gasp the words, ' *er ist frei* ' (' he is free '), and to move away from her rescued lover towards the front of the stage, she made the mistake of speaking the words instead of singing them.

She had often proved the effect of a decisive word uttered with an exaggerated and yet careful imitation of the ordinary accents of the spoken language, by exciting the audience's wildest enthusiasm when she almost whispered the words, ' *Noch einen Schritt und du bist todt!* ' (' Just one more step and thou art dead! ') in *Fidelio*. This terrific effect, which I too had felt, was produced by the shock — like unto the blow of an executioner's axe — which I received on suddenly coming down from the ideal sphere to which music itself can exalt the most awful situations, to the naked surface of dreadful reality. This sensation was due simply to the knowledge of the utmost height of the sublime, and the memory of the impression I received led me to call that particular moment the moment of lightning; for it was as if two different worlds that meet, and yet are divided, were suddenly illumined and revealed as by a flash. Thoroughly to understand such a moment, and not to treat it wrongly, was the whole secret, and this I fully realised on that day from the absolute failure on the great singer's part to produce the right effect. The toneless, hoarse way in which she uttered the words was like throwing cold water over the audience and myself, and not one of those present could see any more in the incident than a botched theatrical effect. It is possible that the public had expected too much, for they were curious to see Spontini conduct, and the prices had been raised accordingly; it may also have been that the whole style of the work, with its antiquated French plot, seemed rather obsolete in spite of the majestic beauty of the music; or, perhaps, the very tame end left the same cold impression as Devrient's dramatic failure. In any case there was no real enthusiasm, and the only sign of approval was a rather lukewarm call for the celebrated master, who, covered with numerous decorations, made a sad impression on me as he bowed his thanks to the audience for their very moderate applause.

Nobody was less blind to the somewhat disappointing result than Spontini himself. He decided, however, to defy fate, and to this end had recourse to means which he had often employed in Berlin, in order to get packed houses for his operatic productions. Thus, he always gave Sunday performances, for experience had taught him that he could always have a full house on that day. As the next Sunday on which his *Vestalin* was to be produced was still some time ahead, his prolonged stay gave us several more chances of enjoying his interesting company. I have such a vivid recollection of the hours spent with him either at Madame Devrient's or at my house, that I shall be pleased to quote a few reminiscences.

I shall never forget a dinner at Schröder-Devrient's house at which we had a charming conversation with Spontini and his wife (a sister of the celebrated pianoforte maker, Erard). Spontini generally listened deferentially to what the others had to say, his attitude being that of a man who expected to be asked for his opinion. When he did speak in the end it was with a sort of rhetorical solemnity, in sharp and precise sentences, categorical and well accentuated, which forbade contradiction from the outset. Herr Ferdinand Hiller was among the invited guests, and he began to speak about Liszt. After some time Spontini gave his opinion in his characteristic fashion, but in a spirit which showed only too clearly, that from the heights of his Berlin throne he had not judged the affairs of the world either with impartiality or goodwill. While he was laying down the law in this style he could not brook any interruption. When, therefore, during the dessert, the general conversation became livelier, and Madame Devrient happened to laugh with her neighbour at the table in the middle of a long harangue of Spontini's, he shot an extremely angry glance at his wife. Madame Devrient apologised for her at once by saying that it was she (Madame Devrient) who had been laughing about some lines on a *bonbonnière*, whereupon Spontini retorted: '*Pourtant je suis sûr que c'est ma femme qui a suscité ce rire; je ne veux pas que l'on rie devant moi, je ne rie jamais moi, j'aime le sérieux.*' In spite of that he sometimes succeeded in being jovial. For instance, it amused him to set us all wondering at the way in which he crunched enormous lumps of sugar with his marvellous teeth. After dinner, when we drew our chairs closer together, he usually became very excited.

As far as he was capable of affection he seemed really to like me; he declared openly that he loved me, and said that he would prove this best by trying to keep me from the misfortune of proceeding in my career as a dramatic composer. He said he knew it would be difficult to convince me of the value of this friendly service, but as he felt it his sacred duty to look after my happiness in this particular line, he was prepared to stay in Dresden for another half-year, during which period he suggested that we should produce his other operas, and especially *Agnes von Hohenstaufen*, under his direction. To explain his views about the fatal mistake of trying to succeed as a dramatic composer ' after Spontini,' he began by praising me in these terms: '*Quand j'ai entendu votre* Rienzi, *j'ai dit, c'est un homme de génie, mais déjà il a plus fait qu'il ne peut faire.*' In order to show me what he meant by this paradox, he proceeded as follows: '*Après Gluck c'est moi qui ai fait la grande révolution avec la* Vestale; *j'ai introduit le* Vorhalt de la sexte' (the suspension of the sixth) '*dans l'harmonie et la grosse caisse dans l'orchestre; avec* Cortez *j'ai fait un pas de plus en avant; puis j'ai fait trois pas avec* Olympie. Nurmahal, Alcidor *et tout ce que j'ai fait dans les premiers temps à Berlin, je vous les livre, c'étaient des œuvres occasionnelles; mais depuis j'ai fait cent pas en avant avec* Agnès de Hohenstaufen, *où j'ai imaginé un emploi de l'orchestre remplaçant parfaitement l'orgue.*'

Since then he had tried his hand at a new work, *Les Athéniennes;* the Crown Prince (now King of Prussia [1]) had urged him to finish this work, and to testify to the truth of his words, he took several letters which he had received from this monarch

[1] William the First.

out of his pocket-book, and handed them to us for inspection. Not until he had insisted upon our reading them carefully through did he continue by saying that, in spite of this flattering invitation, he had given up the idea of setting this excellent subject to music, because he felt sure he could never surpass his *Agnes von Hohenstaufen,* nor invent anything new. In conclusion he said: '*Or, comment voulez-vous que quiconque puisse inventer quelque chose de nouveau, moi Spontini déclarant ne pouvoir en aucune façon surpasser mes œuvres précédentes, d'autre part etant avise que depuis la* Vestale *il n'a point été écrit une note qui ne fut volée de mes partitions.*'

To prove that this assertion was not merely talk, but that it was based on scientific investigations, he quoted his wife, who was supposed to have read with him an elaborate discussion on the subject by a celebrated member of the French academy, and he added that the essay in question had, for some mysterious reason, never been printed. In this very important and scientific treatise it was proved that without Spontini's invention of the suspension of the sixth in his *Vestalin,* the whole of modern melody would not have existed, and that any and every form of melody that had been used since had been borrowed from his compositions. I was thunderstruck, but hoped all the same to bring the inexorable master to a better frame of mind, especially in regard to certain reservations he had made. I acknowledged that the academician in question was right in many ways, but I asked him if he did not believe that if somebody brought him a dramatic poem full of an absolutely new and hitherto unknown spirit, it would not inspire him to invent new musical combinations? With a ring of compassion in his voice, he replied that my question was wholly mistaken; in what would the novelty consist? '*Dans la* Vestale *j'ai composé un sujet romain, dans* Ferdinand Cortez *un sujet espagnol-mexicain, dans* Olympie *un sujet gréco-macédonien, enfin dans* Agnès de Hohenstaufen *un sujet allemand: tout le reste ne vaut rien!*' He hoped that I was not thinking of the so-called romantic style *à la Freischütz?* With such childish stuff no serious man could have anything to do; for art was a serious thing, and *he* had exhausted serious art! And, after all, what nation could produce the composer who could surpass *him?* Surely not the Italians, whom he characterised simply as *cochons;* certainly not the French, who had only imitated the Italians; nor the Germans, who would never get beyond their childhood in music, and who, if they had ever possessed any talent, had had it all spoilt for them by the Jews ? ' *Oh, croyez-moi, il y avait de l'espoir pour l'Allemagne lorsque j'étais empereur de la musique à Berlin; mais depuis que le roi de Prusse a livré sa musique au désordre occasionné par les deux juifs errants qu'il a attirés, tout espoir est perdu.*'

Our charming hostess now thought it time to change the subject, and to divert the master's thoughts. The theatre was situated quite near to her house; she invited him to go across with our friend Heine, who was amongst the guests, and to have a look at *Antigone,* which was then being given, and which was sure to interest him on account of the antique equipment of the stage, which had been carried out according to Semper's excellent plans. At first he wanted to refuse, on the plea that he had seen all this so much better when his *Olympia* had been performed. After a while he consented; but in a very short time he returned to his original opinion, and, smiling scornfully, assured us that he had seen and heard enough to strengthen him in his verdict. Heine told us that shortly after he and Spontini had taken their seats in the almost empty amphitheatre, and as soon as the Bacchus chorus had started, Spontini had said to him: ' *C'est de la Berliner Sing-Academie, allons-nous-en.*' Through an open door a streak of light had fallen on a lonely figure behind one of the columns; Heine had recognised Mendelssohn, and concluded that he had overheard Spontini's remark.

From the master's very excited conversations we soon realised very distinctly that he intended to stay longer in Dresden, so as to get all his operas performed. It was Schröder-Devrient's idea to save Spontini, in his own interest, from the mortifying disappointment of finding all his enthusiastic hopes in regard to a second performance of *Vestalin* unfounded, and, if possible, to prevent this second performance during his stay in Dresden. She pretended to be ill, and the director requested me to inform Spontini of the fact that his production would have to be indefinitely postponed. This visit was so distasteful to me, that I was glad to make it in Röckel's company. He was also a friend of Spontini's, and his French was moreover much better than mine. As we were quite prepared for a bad reception, we were really frightened to enter. Imagine, therefore, our astonishment when we found the master, who had already been informed of the news in a letter from Devrient, in the very brightest spirits.

He told us that he had to leave immediately for Paris, and that from there he was to travel to Rome, the Holy Father having commanded him to come in order to receive the title of 'Count of San Andrea.' Then he showed us a second document, in which the King of Denmark was supposed to have raised him to the Danish nobility. This meant, however, only that the title of 'Ritter' of the 'Elephanten-Order' had been conferred upon him; and although this was indeed a high honour, in speaking about it he only mentioned the word 'Ritter' without referring to the particular order, because this seemed to him too ordinary for a person of his dignity. He was, however, childishly pleased over the affair, and felt that he had been miraculously rescued from the narrow sphere of his Dresden *Vestalin* production to find himself suddenly transported into regions of glory, from which he looked down upon the distressing 'opera' world with sublime self-content.

Meanwhile Röckel and I silently thanked the Holy Father and the King of Denmark from the bottom of our hearts. We bade an affectionate farewell to the strange master, and to cheer him I promised him seriously to think over his friendly advice with regard to my career as a composer of opera.

Later on I heard what Spontini had said about me, on hearing that I had fled from Dresden for political reasons, and had sought refuge in Switzerland. He thought that this was in consequence of my share in a plot of high treason against the King of Saxony, whom he looked upon as my benefactor, because I had been nominated conductor of the royal orchestra, and he expressed his opinion about me by ejaculating in tones of the deepest anguish: '*Quelle ingratitude!*'

From Berlioz, who was at Spontini's deathbed until the end, I heard that the master had struggled most determinedly against death, and had cried repeatedly, '*Je ne veux pas mourir, je ne veux pas mourir!*' When Berlioz tried to comfort him by saying, '*Comment pouvez-vous penser mourir vous, mon maître, qui êtes immortel!*' Spontini retorted angrily, '*Ne faites pas de mauvaises plaisanteries!*' In spite of all the extraordinary experiences I had had with him, the news of his death, which I received in Zürich, touched me very deeply. Later on I expressed my feelings towards him, and my opinion of him as an artist, in a somewhat condensed form in the *Eidgenossischen Zeitung,* and in this article the quality I extolled more particularly in him was that, unlike Meyerbeer, who was then the rage, and the very aged Rossini, he believed absolutely in himself and his art. All the same, and somewhat to my disgust, I could not but see that this belief in himself had deteriorated into a veritable superstition.

I do not remember in those days having gone deeply into my feelings about Spontini's exceedingly strange individuality, nor do I recollect having troubled to discover how far they were consistent with the high opinion I formed of him after I had got to know him more intimately. Obviously I had only seen the caricature of the man, although the tendency towards such plainly overweening self-confidence may, at all events, have manifested itself earlier in life. At the same time, one could trace in all this the influence of the decay of the musical and dramatic life of the period, which Spontini, situated as he was in Berlin, was well able to witness. The surprising fact that he saw his chief merit in unessential details showed plainly that his judgment had become childish; in my opinion this did not detract from the great value of his works, however much he might exaggerate their value. In a sense I could justify his boundless self-confidence, which was principally the outcome of the comparison between himself and the great composers who were now replacing him; for in my heart of hearts I shared the contempt which he felt for these artists, although I did not dare to say so openly. And thus it came about that, in spite of his many somewhat absurd idiosyncrasies, I learned during this meeting at Dresden to feel a deep sympathy for this man, the like of whom I was never again to meet.

My next experiences of important musical celebrities of this age were of quite a different character. Amongst the more distinguished of these was Heinrich Marschner, who, as a very young man, had been nominated musical director of the Dresden orchestra by Weber. After Weber's death he seemed to have hoped that he would take his place entirely, and it was due less to the fact that his talent was still unknown, than to his repellent manner, that he was disappointed in his expectations. His wife, however, suddenly came into some money, and this windfall enabled him to devote all his energies to his work as composer of operas, without being obliged to fill any fixed post.

During the wild days of my youth Marschner lived in Leipzig, where his operas *Der Vampir* and *Templer und Jüdin* saw their first appearance. My sister Rosalie had once taken me to him in order to hear his opinion about me. He did not treat me uncivilly, but my visit led to nothing. I was also present at the first night of his opera *Des Falkner's Braut,* which however was not a success. Then he went to Hanover. His opera *Hans Heiling,* which was originally produced in Berlin, I heard for the first time in Würzburg; it showed vacillation in its tendency, and a decrease in constructive power. After that he produced several other operas, such as *Das Schloss am Aetna* and *Der Bäbu,* which never became popular. He was always neglected by the management at Dresden, as though they bore him some grudge, and only his *Templer* was played at all often. My colleague, Reissiger, had to conduct this opera, and as in his absence I always had to take his place, it also fell to my lot on one occasion to direct a performance of this work.

This was during the time that I worked at my *Tannhäuser*. I remember that, although I had often conducted this opera before in Magdeburg, on this occasion the wild nature of the instrumentation and its lack of mastership affected me to such an extent that it literally made me ill, and as soon as he returned, therefore, I implored Reissiger at any cost to resume the leadership. On the other hand, immediately after my nomination I had started on the production of *Hans Heiling,* but merely for the sake of the artistic honour. The insufficient distribution of the parts, however, a difficulty which in those days could not be overcome, made a complete success impossible. In any case, though, the whole spirit of the work seemed to be terribly old-fashioned.

I now heard that Marschner had finished another opera called *Adolph von Nassau,* and in a criticism of this work, of the genuineness of which I was unable to judge, particular stress was laid upon the 'patriotic and noble German atmosphere' of this new creation. I did my best to make the Dresden theatre take the initiative, and to urge Lüttichau to secure this opera before it was produced elsewhere. Marschner, who did not seem to have been treated with particular consideration by the Hanoverian opera authorities, accepted the invitation with great joy, sent his score, and declared himself willing to come to Dresden for the first performance. Lüttichau, however, was not anxious to see him take his place at the head of the orchestra; while I, also, was of the opinion that the too frequent appearance of outside conductors, even if it were for the purpose of conducting their own works, would not only lead to confusion, but might also fail to be as amusing and instructive as Spontini's visit had proved to be. It was therefore decided that I should conduct the new opera myself. And how I lived to regret it!

The score arrived: to a weak plot by Karl Golmick the composer of the *Templer* had written such superficial music, that the principal effect lay in a drinking song for a quartette, in which the German Rhine and German wine played the usual stereotyped part peculiar to such male quartettes. I lost all courage; but we had to go on with it now, and all I could do was to try, by maintaining a grave bearing, to make the singers take an interest in their task; this, however, was not easy. To Tichatschek and Mitterwurzer were assigned the two principal male parts; being both eminently musical, they sang everything at first sight, and after each number looked up at me as if to say, 'What do you think of it all?' I maintained that it was good German music; they must not allow themselves to get confused. But all they did was to stare at each other in amazement, not knowing what to make of me. Nevertheless, in the end they could not stand it any longer, and when they saw that I still retained my gravity, they burst into loud laughter, in which I could not help joining.

I now had to take them into my confidence, and make them
promise to follow my lead and pretend to be serious, for it
was impossible to give up the opera at this stage. A Viennese
'colorature' singer of the latest style — Madame Spatser
Gentiluomo — who came to us from Hanover, and on whose
services Marschner greatly relied, was rather taken with her
part chiefly because it gave her the chance of showing
'brilliancy.' And, indeed, there was a finale in which my
'German master' had actually tried to steal a march on
Donizetti. The Princess had been poisoned by a golden rose,
a present from the wicked Bishop of Mainz, and had become
delirious. Adolph von Nassau, with the knights of the German
empire, swears vengeance, and, accompanied by the chorus,
pours out his feelings in a *stretta* of such incredible vulgarity
and amateurishness that Donizetti would have thrown it at
the head of any of his pupils who had dared to compose such
a thing. Marschner now arrived for the dress rehearsal;
he was very pleased, and, without compelling me to falsehood,
he gave me sufficient opportunities for exercising my powers
in the art of concealing my real thoughts. At all events I
must have succeeded fairly well, for he had every reason to
think himself considerately and kindly treated by me.

During the performance the public behaved very much as
the singers had done at the rehearsals. We had brought a
still-born child into the world. But Marschner was comforted
by the fact that his drinking quartette was encored. This was
reminiscent of one of Becker's songs: *Sie sollen ihn nicht
haben, den freien deutschen Rhein* ('They shall not have it,
our free German Rhine'). After the performance the composer was my guest at a supper party at which, I am sorry to
say, the singers, who had had enough of it, would not attend.
Herr Ferdinand Hiller had the presence of mind to insist, in
his toast to Marschner, that 'whatever one might say, all
stress must be laid on the *German* master and *German* art.'
Strangely enough, Marschner himself contradicted him by
saying that there was something wrong with German operatic
compositions, and that one ought to consider the singers and
how to write more brilliantly for their voices than he had
succeeded in doing up to the present.

Highly gifted as Marschner was, there can be no doubt that the decline of his genius was due partly to a tendency which even in the ageing master himself, as he frankly admitted, was effecting an important and most salutary change. In later years I met him once more in Paris at the time of my memorable production of *Tannhäuser*. I did not feel inclined to renew the old relations, for, to tell the truth, I wanted to spare myself the unpleasantness of witnessing the consequences of his change of views, of which we had seen the beginning in Dresden. I learned that he was in a state of almost helpless childishness, and that he was in the hands of a young and ambitious woman, who was trying to make a last attempt at conquering Paris for him. Among other puff paragraphs calculated to spread Marschner's glory, I read one which said that the Parisians must not believe that I (Wagner) was representative of German art; no — if only Marschner were given a hearing, it would be discovered that he was beyond a doubt better suited to the French taste than I could ever be. Marschner died before his wife had succeeded in establishing this point.

Ferdinand Hiller, on the other hand, who was in Dresden, behaved in a very charming and friendly manner, particularly at this time. Meyerbeer also stayed in the same town from time to time; precisely why, nobody knew. Once he had rented a little house for the summer near the Pirnaischer Schlag, and under a pretty tree in the garden of this place he had had a small piano installed, whereon, in this idyllic retreat, he worked at his *Feldlager in Schlesien*. He lived in great retirement, and I saw very little of him. Ferdinand Hiller, on the contrary, took a commanding position in the Dresden musical world in so far as this was not already monopolised by the royal orchestra and its masters, and for many years he worked hard for its success. Having a little private capital, he established himself comfortably amongst us, and was soon known as a delightful host, who kept a pleasant house, which, thanks to his wife's influence, was frequented by a numerous Polish colony. Frau Hiller was indeed an exceptional Jewish woman of Polish origin, and she was perhaps all the more exceptional seeing that she, in company with her husband, had been baptized a Protestant in Italy. Hiller began his career in Dresden with the production of his opera, *Der Traum in der Christnacht*. Since the unheard-of fact that *Rienzi* had been able to rouse the Dresden public to lasting enthusiasm, many an opera composer had felt himself drawn towards our 'Florence on the Elbe,' of which Laube once said that as soon as one entered it one felt bound to apologise because one found so many good things there which one promptly forgot the moment one departed.

The composer of *Der Traum in der Christnacht* looked upon this work as a peculiarly 'German composition.' Hiller had set to music a gruesome play by Raupach, *Der Müller und sein Kind* ('The Miller and his Child'), in which father and daughter, within but a short space of time, both die of consumption. He declared that he had conceived the dialogue and the music of this opera in what he called the 'popular style,' but this work met with the same fate as that which, according to Liszt, befell all his compositions. In spite of his undoubted musical merits, which even Rossini acknowledged, and whether he gave them in French in Paris or in Italian in Italy, it was his sad experience always to see his operas fail. In Germany he had tried the Mendelssohnian style, and had succeeded in composing an oratorio called *Die Zerstörung Jerusalems*, which luckily was not taken notice of by the moody theatre-going public, and which consequently received the unassailable reputation of being 'a solid German work.' He also took Mendelssohn's place as director of the Leipzig Gewandhaus concerts when the latter was called to Berlin in the capacity of general director. Hiller's evil fortune still pursued him, however, and he was unable to retain his position, everybody being given to understand that it was because his wife was not sufficiently acknowledged as concert prima-donna. Mendelssohn returned and made Hiller leave, and Hiller boasted of having quarrelled with him.

Dresden and the success of my *Rienzi* now weighed so much upon his mind that he naturally made another attempt to succeed as an opera composer. Owing to his great energy, and to his position as son of a rich banker (a special attraction even to the director of a court theatre), it happened that he induced them to put aside my poor friend Röckel's *Farinelli* (the production of which had been promised him) in favour of his (Hiller's) own work, *Der Traum in der Christnacht*. He was of the opinion that next to Reissiger and myself, a man of greater musical reputation than Röckel was needed. Lüttichau, however, was quite content to have Reissiger and myself as celebrities, particularly as we got on so well together, and he remained deaf to Hiller's wishes. To me *Der Traum in der Christnacht* was a great nuisance. I had to conduct it a second time, and before an empty house. Hiller now saw that he had been wrong in not taking my advice before, and in not shortening the opera by one act and altering the end, and he now fancied that he was doing me a great favour by at last declaring himself ready to act on my suggestion in the event of another performance of his opera being possible. I really managed to have it played once more. This was, however, to be the last time, and Hiller, who had read my book of *Tannhäuser,* thought that I had a great advantage over him in writing my own words. He therefore made me promise to help him with the choice and writing of a subject for his next opera.

Shortly afterwards Hiller was present at a performance of *Rienzi,* which was again given before a crowded and enthusiastic house. When, at the end of the second act, and after frantic recalls from the audience, I left the orchestra in a great state of excitement, Hiller, who was waiting for me in the passage, took the opportunity of adding to his very hasty congratulations, ' Do give my *Traum* once more! ' I promised him laughingly to do this if I had the chance, but I cannot remember whether it came off or not. While he was waiting for the creation of an entirely new plot for his next opera, Hiller devoted himself to the study of chamber music, to which his large and well-furnished room lent itself most admirably.

A beautiful and solemn event added to the seriousness of the mood in which I finished the music to *Tannhäuser* towards the end of the year, and neutralised the more superficial impressions made upon me by the stirring events above described. This was the removal of the remains of Carl Maria von Weber from London to Dresden in December, 1844. As I have already said, a committee had for years been agitating for this removal. From information given by a certain traveller, it had become known that the insignificant coffin which contained Weber's ashes had been disposed of in such a careless way in a remote corner of St. Paul's, that it was feared it might soon become impossible to identify it.

My energetic friend, Professor Löwe, whom I have already mentioned, had availed himself of this information in order to urge the Dresden Glee Club, which constituted his hobby, to take the matter in hand. The concert of male singers arranged to this end had been a fair success financially, and they now wanted to induce the theatre management to make similar efforts, when suddenly they met with serious opposition from this very quarter. The management of the Dresden theatre told the committee that the King had religious scruples with regard to disturbing the peace of the dead. However much we felt inclined to doubt the genuineness of these reasons, nothing could be done, and I was next approached on the subject, in the hope that my influential position might lend weight to my appeal. I entered into the spirit of the enterprise with great fervour. I consented to be made president; Herr Hofrat Schulz, director of the 'Antiken-Cabinet,' who was a well-known authority on artistic matters, and another gentleman, a Christian banker, were also elected members of the committee, and the movement thus received fresh life. Prospectuses were sent round, exhaustive plans were made, and numerous meetings held. Here, again, I met with opposition on the part of my chief, Lüttichau; if he could have done so, he would have forbidden me to move in the matter by making the most of the King's scruples referred to above. But he had had a warning not to pick a quarrel with me after his experience in the summer, when, contrary to his expectations, the music written by me to celebrate the King's arrival had found favour with the monarch. As his antipathy to the proceedings was not so very serious, Lüttichau must have seen that even the direct opposition of his Majesty could not have prevented the enterprise from being carried out privately, and that, on the contrary, the court would cut a sorry figure if the Royal Court Theatre (to which Weber once belonged) should assume

FUNERAL MARCH FOR WEBER

a hostile attitude. He therefore tried in a would-be friendly way to make me desist from furthering the cause, well knowing that, without me, the plan would fail. He tried to convince me that it would be wrong to pay this exaggerated honour to Weber's memory, whereas nobody thought of removing the ashes of Morlacchi from Italy, although the latter had given his services to the royal orchestra for a much longer period than Weber had done. What would be the consequence? By way of argument he said, 'Suppose Reissiger died on his journey to some watering-place — his wife would then be as much justified as was Frau von Weber (who had annoyed him quite enough already) in expecting her husband's dead body to be brought home with music and pomp.' I tried to calm him, and if I did not succeed in making him see the difference between Reissiger and Weber, I managed to make him understand that the affair must take its course, as the Berlin Court Theatre had already announced a benefit performance to support our undertaking.

Meyerbeer, to whom my committee had applied, was instrumental in bringing this about, and a performance of *Euryanthe* was actually given which yielded the handsome balance of six thousand marks. A few theatres of lesser importance now followed our lead. The Dresden Court Theatre, therefore, could not hold back any longer, and as we now had a fairly large sum at the bank, we were able to cover the expenses of the removal, as well as the cost of an appropriate vault and monument; we even had a nucleus fund for a statue of Weber, which we were to fight for later on. The elder of the two sons of the immortal master travelled to London to fetch the remains of his father. He brought them by boat down the Elbe, and finally arrived at the Dresden landing-stage, from whence they were to be conducted to German soil. This last journey of the remains was to take place at night. A solemn torchlight procession was to be formed, and I had undertaken to see to the funeral music.

I arranged this from two motives out of *Euryanthe,* using that part of the music in the overture which relates to the vision of spirits. I introduced the Cavatina from *Euryanthe* — *Hier dicht am Quell* ('Here near the source'), which I left unaltered, except that I transposed it into B flat major, and I finished the whole, as Weber finished his opera, by a return to the first sublime motive. I had orchestrated this symphonic piece, which was well suited to the purpose, for eight chosen wind instruments, and notwithstanding the volume of sound, I had not forgotten softness and delicacy of instrumentation. I substituted the gruesome *tremolo* of the violas, which appears in that part of the overture adapted by me, by twenty muffled drums, and as a whole attained to such an exceedingly impressive effect, especially to us who were full of thoughts of Weber, that, even in the theatre where we rehearsed, Schröder-Devrient, who was present, and who had been an intimate friend of Weber's, was deeply moved. I had never carried out anything more in keeping with the character of the subject; and the procession through the town was equally impressive.

As the very slow tempo, devoid of any strongly marked accents, offered numerous difficulties, I had had the stage cleared for the rehearsal, in order to command a sufficient space for the musicians, once they had thoroughly practised the piece, to walk round me in a circle playing all the while. Several of those who witnessed the procession from their windows assured me that the effect of the procession was indescribably and sublimely solemn. After we had placed the coffin in the little mortuary chapel of the Catholic cemetery in Friedrichstadt, where Madame Devrient met it with a wreath of flowers, we performed, on the following morning, the solemn ceremony of lowering it into the vault. Herr Hofrat Schulz and myself, as presidents of the committee, were allowed the honour of speaking by the graveside, and what afforded me an appropriate subject for the few, somewhat affecting, words which I had to pronounce, was the fact that, shortly before the removal of Weber's remains, the second son of the master, Alexander von Weber, had died. The poor mother had been so terribly affected by the sudden death of this youth, so full of life and health, that had we not been in the very midst of our arrangements, we should have been compelled to abandon them; for in this new loss the widow saw a judgment of God who, in her opinion, looked upon the removal of the remains as an act of sacrilege prompted by vanity. As the

AT WEBER'S GRAVESIDE

public seemed particularly disposed to hold the same view, it fell to my lot to set the nature of our undertaking in the proper light before the eyes of the world. And this I so far succeeded in doing that, to my satisfaction, I learned from all sides that my justification of our action had received the most general acceptance.

On this occasion I had a strange experience with regard to myself, when for the first time in my life I had to deliver a solemn public speech. Since then I have always spoken extemporarily; this time, however, as it was my first appearance as an orator, I had written out my speech, and carefully learned it by heart. As I was thoroughly under the influence of my subject, I felt so sure of my memory that I never thought of making any notes. Thanks to this omission, however, I made my brother Albert very unhappy. He was standing near me at the ceremony, and he told me afterwards that, in spite of being deeply moved, he felt at one moment as if he could have sworn at me for not having asked him to prompt me. It happened in this way: I began my speech in a clear and full voice, but suddenly the sound of my own words, and their particular intonation, affected me to such an extent that, carried away as I was by my own thoughts, I imagined I *saw* as well as *heard* myself before the breathless multitude. While I thus appeared objectively to myself I remained in a sort of trance, during which I seemed to be waiting for something to happen, and felt quite a different person from the man who was supposed to be standing and speaking there. It was neither nervousness nor absent-mindedness on my part; only at the end of a certain sentence there was such a long pause that those who saw me standing there must have wondered what on earth to think of me. At last my own silence and the stillness round me reminded me that I was not there to listen, but to speak. I at once resumed my discourse, and I spoke with such fluency to the very end that the celebrated actor, Emil Devrient, assured me that, apart from the solemn service, he had been deeply impressed simply from the standpoint of a dramatic orator.

The ceremony concluded with a poem written and set to music by myself, and, though it presented many difficulties for men's voices, it was splendidly rendered by some of the best opera singers. Lüttichau, who was present, was now not only convinced of the justice of the enterprise, but also strongly in favour of it. I was deeply thankful that everything had succeeded so well, and when Weber's widow, upon whom I called after the ceremony, told me how profoundly she, too, had been moved, the only cloud that still darkened my horizon was dispelled. In my youth I had learned to love music through my admiration for Weber's genius, and the news of his death was a terrible blow to me. To have, as it were, come into contact with him again and after so many years by this second funeral, was an event that stirred the very depths of my being.

From all the particulars I have given concerning my intimacy with the great masters who were my contemporaries, it is easy to see at what sources I had been able to quench my thirst for intellectual intercourse. It was not a very satisfactory outlook to turn from Weber's grave to his living successors; but I had still to find out how absolutely hopeless this was.

I spent the winter of 1844-5 partly in yielding to attractions from outside, and partly in indulging in the deepest meditation. By dint of great energy, and by getting up very early, even in winter, I succeeded in completing my score to *Tannhäuser* early in April, having, as already stated, finished the composition of it at the end of the preceding year. In writing down the orchestration I made things particularly difficult for myself by using the specially prepared paper which the printing process renders necessary, and which involved me in all kinds of trying formalities. I had each page transferred to the stone immediately, and a hundred copies printed from each, hoping to make use of these proofs for the rapid circulation of my work. Whether my hopes were to be fulfilled or not, I was at all events fifteen hundred marks out of pocket when all the expenses of the publication were paid.

In regard to this work which called for so many sacrifices, and which was so slow and difficult, more details will appear in my autobiography. At all events, when May came round I was in possession of a hundred neatly bound copies of my first

THE SCORE OF TANNHÄUSER

new work since the production of the *Fliegender Holländer,* and Hiller, to whom I showed some parts of it, formed a tolerably good impression of its value.

These plans for rapidly spreading the fame of my *Tannhäuser* were made with the hope of a success which, in view of my needy circumstances, seemed ever more and more desirable. In the course of one year since I had begun my own publication of my operas, much had been done to this end. In September of the year 1844 I had presented the King of Saxony with a special richly bound copy of the complete pianoforte arrangement of *Rienzi,* dedicated to his Majesty. The *Fliegender Holländer* had also been finished, and the pianoforte arrangement of *Rienzi* for duet, as well as some songs selected from both operas, had either been published or were about to be published. Apart from this I had had twenty-five copies made of the scores of both these operas by means of the so-called autographic transfer process, although only from the writing of the copyists. All these heavy expenses made it absolutely imperative that I should try to send my scores to the different theatres, and induce them to produce my operas, as the outlay on the piano scores had been heavy, and these could only have a sale if my works got to be known sufficiently well through the theatre.

I now sent the score of my *Rienzi* to the more important theatres, but they all returned my work to me, the Munich Court Theatre even sending it back unopened! I therefore knew what to expect, and spared myself the trouble of sending my *Dutchman.* From a speculative business point of view the situation was this: the hoped-for success of *Tannhäuser* would bring in its wake a demand for my earlier works. The worthy Meser, my agent, who was the music publisher appointed to the court, had also begun to feel a little doubtful, and saw that this was the only thing to do. I started at once on the publication of a pianoforte arrangement of *Tannhäuser,* preparing it myself while Röckel undertook the *Fliegender Holländer,* and a certain Klink did *Rienzi.*

The only thing that Meser was absolutely opposed to was the title of my new opera, which I had just named *Der Venusberg;* he maintained that, as I did not mix with the public, I had no idea what horrible jokes were made about this title. He said the students and professors of the medical school in Dresden would be the first to make fun of it, as they had a predilection for that kind of obscene joke. I was sufficiently disgusted by these details to consent to the change. To the name of my hero, Tannhäuser, I added the name of the subject of the legend which, although originally not belonging to the *Tannhäuser* myth, was thus associated with it by me, a fact which later on Simrock, the great investigator and innovator in the world of legend, whom I esteemed so highly, took very much amiss.

Tannhäuser un der Sängerkrieg auf Wartburg should henceforth be its title, and to give the work a mediæval appearance I had the words specially printed in Gothic characters upon the piano arrangement, and in this way introduced the work to the public.

The extra expenses this involved were very heavy; but I went to great pains to impress Meser with my belief in the success of my work. So deeply were we involved in this scheme, and so great were the sacrifices it had compelled us to make, that there was nothing else for it but to trust to a special turn of Fortune's wheel. As it happened, the management of the theatre shared my confidence in the success of *Tannhäuser*. I had induced Lüttichau to have the scenery for *Tannhäuser* painted by the best painters of the great opera house in Paris. I had seen their work on the Dresden stage: it belonged to the style of German scenic art which was then fashionable, and really gave the effect of first-class work.

The order for this, as well as the necessary negotiations with the Parisian painter, Despléchin, had already been settled in the preceding autumn. The management agreed to all my wishes, even to the ordering of beautiful costumes of mediæval character designed by my friend Heine. The only thing Lüttichau constantly postponed was the order for the Hall of Song on the Wartburg; he maintained that the Hall for Kaiser Karl the Great in Oberon, which had only recently been delivered by some French painters, would answer the purpose just as well. With superhuman efforts I had to convince my chief that we did not want a brilliant throne-room, but a scenic picture of a certain character such as I saw before my mind's eye, and that it could be painted only according to my directions. As in the end I became very irritable and cross, he soothed me by saying that he had no objection to having this scene painted, and that he would order it to be commenced at once, adding that he had not agreed immediately, only with the view of making my joy the greater, because, what one obtained without difficulty, one rarely appreciated. This Hall of Song was fated to cause me great trouble later on.

Thus everything was in full swing; circumstances were favourable, and seemed to cast a hopeful light upon the production of my new work at the beginning of the autumn season. Even the public was looking forward to it, and for the first time I saw my name mentioned in a friendly manner in a communication to the *Allgemeine Zeitung*. They actually spoke of the great expectations they had of my new work, the poem of which had been written ' with undoubted poetic feeling.'

Full of hope, I started in July on my holiday, which consisted of a journey to Marienbad in Bohemia, where my wife and I intended to take the cure. Again I found myself on the 'volcanic' soil of this extraordinary country, Bohemia, which always had such an inspiring effect on me. It was a marvellous summer, almost too hot, and I was therefore in high spirits. I had intended to follow the easy-going mode of life which is a necessary part of this somewhat trying treatment, and had selected my books with care, taking with me the poems of Wolfram von Eschenbach, edited by Simrock and San Marte, as well as the anonymous epic *Lohengrin*, with its lengthy introduction by Görres. With my book under my arm I hid myself in the neighbouring woods, and pitching my tent by the brook in company with *Titurel* and *Parcival*, I lost myself in Wolfram's strange, yet irresistibly charming, poem. Soon, however, a longing seized me to give expression to the inspiration generated by this poem, so that I had the greatest difficulty in overcoming my desire to give up the rest I had been prescribed while partaking of the water of Marienbad.

The result was an ever-increasing state of excitement. *Lohengrin*, the first conception of which dates from the end of my time in Paris, stood suddenly revealed before me, complete in every detail of its dramatic construction. The legend of the swan which forms such an important feature of all the many versions of this series of myths that my studies had brought to my notice, exercised a singular fascination over my imagination.

Remembering the doctor's advice, I struggled bravely against the temptation of writing down my ideas, and resorted to the most strange and energetic methods. Owing to some comments I had read in Gervinus's *History of German Literature,* both the *Meistersinger von Nürnberg* and *Hans Sachs* had acquired quite a vital charm for me. The Marker alone, and the part he takes in the Master-singing, were particularly pleasing to me, and on one of my lonely walks, without knowing anything particular about Hans Sachs and his poetic contemporaries, I thought out a humorous scene, in which the cobbler — as a popular artisan-poet — with the hammer on his last, gives the Marker a practical lesson by making him sing, thereby taking revenge on him for his conventional misdeeds. To me the force of the whole scene was concentrated in the two following points: on the one hand the Marker, with his slate covered with chalk-marks, and on the other Hans Sachs holding up the shoes covered with his chalk-marks, each intimating to the other that the singing had been a failure. To this picture, by way of concluding the second act, I added a scene consisting of a narrow, crooked little street in Nuremberg, with the people all running about in great excitement, and ultimately engaging in a street brawl. Thus, suddenly, the whole of my Meistersinger comedy took shape so vividly before me, that, inasmuch as it was a particularly cheerful subject, and not in the least likely to over-excite my nerves, I felt I must write it out in spite of the doctor's orders. I therefore proceeded to do this, and hoped it might free me from the thrall of the idea of *Lohengrin;* but I was mistaken; for no sooner had I got into my bath at noon, than I felt an overpowering desire to write out *Lohengrin,* and this longing so overcame me that I could not wait the prescribed hour for the bath, but when a few minutes elapsed, jumped out and, barely giving myself time to dress, ran home to write out what I had in my mind. I repeated this for several days until the complete sketch of *Lohengrin* was on paper.

The doctor then told me I had better give up taking the waters and baths, saying emphatically that I was quite unfit for such cures. My excitement had grown to such an extent that even my efforts to sleep as a rule ended only in nocturnal adventures. Among some interesting excursions that we made at this time, one to Eger fascinated me particularly, on account of its association with Wallenstein and of the peculiar costumes of the inhabitants.

In mid-August we travelled back to Dresden, where my friends were glad to see me in such good spirits; as for myself, I felt as if I had wings. In September, when all our singers had returned from their summer holidays, I resumed the rehearsals of *Tannhäuser* with great earnestness. We had now got so far, at least with the musical part of the performance, that the possible date of the production seemed quite close at hand. Schröder-Devrient was one of the first to realise the extraordinary difficulties which the production of *Tannhäuser* would entail. And, indeed, she saw these difficulties so clearly that, to my great discomfiture, she was able to lay them all before me. Once, when I called upon her, she read the principal passages aloud with great feeling and force, and then she asked me how I could have been so simple-minded as to have thought that so childish a creature as Tichatschek would be able to find the proper tones for Tannhäuser. I tried to bring her attention and my own to bear upon the nature of the music, which was written so clearly in order to bring out the necessary accent, that, in my opinion, the music actually spoke for him who interpreted the passage, even if he were only a musical singer and nothing more. She shook her head, saying that this would be all right in the case of an oratorio.

She now sang Elizabeth's prayer from the piano score, and asked me if I really thought that this music would answer my intentions if sung by a young and pretty voice without any soul or without that experience of life which alone could give the real expression to the interpretation. I sighed and said that, in that case, the youthfulness of the voice and of its owner must make up for what was lacking: at the same time, I asked her as a favour to see what she could do towards making my niece, Johanna, understand her part. All this, however, did not solve the Tannhäuser problem, for any effort at teaching Tichatschek would only have resulted in confusion. I was therefore obliged to rely entirely upon the energy of his voice, and on the singer's peculiarly sharp 'speaking' tone.

Devrient's anxiety about the principal parts arose partly out of concern about her own. She did not know what to do with the part of Venus; she had undertaken it for the sake of the success of the performance, for although a small part, so much depended upon its being ideally interpreted! Later on, when the work was given in Paris, I became convinced that this part had been written in too sketchy a style, and this induced me to reconstruct it by making extensive additions, and by supplying all that which I felt it lacked. For the moment, however, it looked as if no art on the part of the singer could give to this sketch anything of what it ought to represent. The only thing that might have helped towards a satisfactory impersonation of Venus would have been the artist's confidence in her own great physical attraction, and in the effect it would help to produce by appealing to the purely material sympathies of the public. The certainty that these means were no longer at her disposal paralysed this great singer, who could hide her age and matronly appearance no longer. She therefore became self-conscious, and unable to use even the usual means for gaining an effect. On one occasion, with a little smile of despair, she expressed herself incapable of playing Venus, for the very simple reason that she could not appear dressed like the goddess. 'What on earth am I to wear as Venus?' she exclaimed. 'After all, I cannot be clad in a belt alone. A nice figure of fun I should look, and you would laugh on the wrong side of your face!'

On the whole, I still built my hopes upon the general effect of the music alone, the great promise of which at the rehearsals greatly encouraged me. Hiller, who had looked through the score and had already praised it, assured me that the instrumentation could not have been carried out with greater sobriety. The characteristic and delicate sonority of the orchestra delighted me, and strengthened me in my resolve to be extremely sparing in the use of my orchestral material, in order to attain that abundance of combinations which I needed for my later works.

At the rehearsal my wife alone missed the trumpets and trombones that gave such brightness and freshness to *Rienzi*. Although I laughed at this, I could not help feeling anxious when she confided to me how great had been her disappointment when, at the theatre rehearsal, she noticed the really feeble impression made by the music of the *Sängerkrieg*. Speaking from the point of view of the public, who always want to be amused or stirred in some way or other, she had thus very rightly called attention to an exceedingly questionable side of the performance. But I saw at once that the fault lay less with the conception than with the fact that I had not controlled the production with sufficient care.

In regard to the conception of this scene I was literally on the horns of a dilemma, for I had to decide once for all whether this *Sängerkrieg* was to be a concert of arias or a competition in dramatic poetry. There are many people even nowadays, who, in spite of having witnessed a perfectly successful production of this scene, have not received the right impression of its purport. Their idea is that it belongs to the traditional operatic 'genre,' which demands that a number of vocal evolutions shall be juxtaposed or contrasted, and that these different songs are intended to amuse and interest the audience by means of their purely musical changes in rhythm and time on the principle of a concert programme, *i.e.* by various items of different styles. This was not at all my idea: my real intention was, if possible, to force the listener, for the first time in the history of opera, to take an interest in a poetical idea, by making him follow all its necessary developments. For it was only by virtue of this interest that he could be made to understand the catastrophe, which in this instance was not to be brought about by any outside influence, but must be the outcome simply of the natural spiritual processes at work. Hence the need of great moderation and breadth in the conception of the music; first, in order that according to my principle it might prove helpful rather than the reverse to the understanding of the poetical lines, and secondly, in order that the increasing rhythmic character of the melody which marks the ardent growth of passion may not be interrupted too arbitrarily by unnecessary changes in modulation and rhythm. Hence, too, the need of a very sparing use of orchestral instruments for the accompaniment, and an intentional suppression of all those purely musical effects which must be utilised, and that gradually, only when the situation becomes so intense that one almost ceases to think, and can only feel the tragic nature of the crisis. No one could deny that I had contrived to produce the proper effect of this principle the moment I played the *Sängerkrieg* on the piano. With the view of ensuring all my future successes, I was now confronted with the exceptional difficulty of making the opera singers understand how to interpret their parts precisely in the way I desired. I remembered how, through lack of experience, I had neglected properly to superintend the production of the *Fliegender Holländer,* and as I now fully realised all the disastrous consequences of this neglect, I began to think of means by which I could teach the singers my own interpretation. I have already stated that it was impossible to influence Tichatschek, for if he were made to do things he could not understand, he only became nervous and confused. He was conscious of his advantages. He knew that with his metallic voice he could sing with great musical rhythm and accuracy, while his delivery was simply perfect. But, to my great astonishment, I was soon to learn that all this did not by any means suffice; for, to my horror, at the first performance, that which had strangely escaped my notice in the rehearsals became suddenly apparent to me. At the close of the *Sängerkrieg,* when Tannhäuser (in frantic excitement, and forgetful of everybody present) has to sing his praise to Venus, and I saw Tichatschek moving towards Elizabeth and addressing his passionate outburst to her, I thought of Schröder-Devrient's warning in very much the same way as Crœsus must have thought when he cried, 'O Solon! Solon!' at the funeral pyre. In spite of the musical excellence of Tichatschek, the enormous life and melodic charm of the *Sängerkrieg* failed entirely.

On the other hand, I succeeded in calling into life an entirely new element such as probably had never been seen in opera! I had watched the young baritone Mitterwurzer with great interest in some of his parts — he was a strangely reticent man, and not at all sociably inclined, and I had noticed that his delightfully mellow voice possessed the rare quality of bringing out the inner note of the soul. To him I entrusted Wolfram, and I had every reason to be satisfied with his zeal and with the success of his studies. Therefore, if I wished my intention and method to become known, especially in regard to this difficult *Sängerkrieg*, I had to rely on him for the proper execution of my plans and everything they involved. I began by going through the opening song of this scene with him; but, after I had done my utmost to make him understand how I wanted it done, I was surprised to find how very difficult this particular rendering of the music appeared to him. He was absolutely incapable of repeating it after me, and with each renewed effort his singing became so commonplace and so mechanical that I realised clearly that he had not understood this piece to be anything more than a phrase in recitative form, which he might render with any inflections of the voice that happened to be prescribed, or which might be sung either this way or that, according to fancy, as was usual in operatic pieces. He, too, was astonished at his own want of capacity, but was so struck by the novelty and the justice of my views, that he begged me not to try any more for the present, but to leave him to find out for himself how best to become familiar with this newly revealed world. During several rehearsals he only sang in a whisper in order to get over the difficulty, but at the last rehearsal he acquitted himself so admirably of his task, and threw himself into it so heartily, that his work has remained to this day as my most conclusive reason for believing that, in spite of the unsatisfactory state of the world of opera to-day, it is possible not only to find, but also properly to train, the singer whom I should regard as indispensable for a correct interpretation of my works. It was through the impression made by Mitterwurzer that I ultimately succeeded in making the public understand the whole of my work. This man, who had utterly changed himself in bearing, look, and appearance in order to fit himself to the rôle of Wolfram, had, in thus solving the problem, not only become a thorough artist, but by his interpretation of his part had also proved himself my saviour at the very moment when my work was threatening to fail through the unsatisfactory result of the first performance.

By his side the part of Elizabeth made a sweet impression. The youthful appearance of my niece, her tall and slender form, the decidedly German cast of her features, as well as the incomparable beauty of her voice, with its expression of almost childlike innocence, helped her to gain the hearts of the audience, even though her talent was more theatrical than dramatic. She soon rose to fame by her impersonation of this part, and often in later years, when speaking about *Tannhäuser* performances in which she had appeared, people used to tell me that its success had been entirely due to her. Strange to say, in such reports people referred principally to the charm of her acting at the moment when she received the guests in the Wartburg Hall; and I used to account for this by remembering the untiring efforts with which my talented brother and I had trained her to perform this very part. And yet it was never possible to make her understand the proper interpretation of the prayer in the third act, and I felt inclined to say, ' O Solon! Solon! ' as I had done in the case of Tichatschek, when after the first performance I was obliged to make a considerable cut in this solo, a proceeding which greatly reduced its importance for ever afterwards. I heard later that Johanna, who for a short period actually had the reputation of being a great singer, had never succeeded in singing the prayer as it ought to be sung, whereas a French singer, Mademoiselle Marie Sax, achieved this in Paris to my entire satisfaction.

In the beginning of October we had so far progressed with our rehearsals that nothing stood in the way of an immediate production of *Tannhäuser* save the scenery, which was not yet complete. A few only of the scenes ordered from Paris had arrived, and even these had come very late. The Wartburg Valley was beautifully effective and perfect in every detail. The inner part of the Venusberg, however, gave me much anxiety: the painter had not understood me; he had painted clusters of trees and statues, which reminded one of Versailles, and had placed them in a wild cave; he had evidently not known how to combine the weird with the alluring. I had to insist on extensive alterations, and chiefly on the painting out of the shrubs and statues, all of which required time. The grotto had to lie half hidden in a rosy cloud, through which the Wartburg Valley had to loom in the distance; this was to be done in strict obedience to my own ideas.

The greatest misfortune, however, was to befall me in the shape of the tardy delivery of the scenery for the Hall of Song. This was due to great negligence on the part of the Paris artists; and we waited and waited until every detail of the opera had been studied and studied again *ad nauseam*. Daily I went to the railway station and examined all the packages and boxes that had arrived, but there was no Hall of Song. At last I allowed myself to be persuaded not to postpone the first performance any longer, and I decided to use the Hall of Karl the Great out of *Oberon,* originally suggested to me by Lüttichau, instead of the real thing. Considering the importance I attached to practical effect, this entailed a great sacrifice of my personal feelings. And true enough, when the curtain rose for the second act, the reappearance of this throne-room, which the public had seen so often, added considerably to the general disappointment of the audience, who had anticipated astonishing surprises in this opera.

On the 19th of October the first performance took place. In the morning of that day a very beautiful young lady was introduced to me by the leader Lipinsky. Her name was Mme. Kalergis, and she was a niece of the Russian Chancellor, Count von Nesselrode. Liszt had spoken to her about me with such enthusiasm that she had travelled all the way to Dresden especially to hear the first production of my new work. I thought I was right in regarding this flattering visit as a good omen. But although on this occasion she turned away from me, somewhat perplexed and disappointed by the very unintelligible performance and the somewhat doubtful reception with which it met, I had sufficient cause in after-years to know how deeply this remarkable and energetic woman had nevertheless been impressed.

A great contrast to this visit was one I received from a peculiar man called C. Gaillard. He was the editor of a Berlin musical paper, which had only just started, and in which I had read with great astonishment an entirely favourable and important criticism of my *Fliegender Holländer*. Although necessity had compelled me to remain indifferent to the attitude of the critics, yet this particular notice gave me much pleasure, and I had invited my unknown critic to come and hear the first production of *Tannhäuser* in Dresden.

This he did, and I was deeply touched to find that I had to deal with a young man who, in spite of being threatened by consumption, and being also exceedingly badly off, had come at my invitation, simply from a sense of duty and honour, and not with any mercenary motive. I saw from his knowledge and capacities that he would never be able to attain a position of great influence, but his kindness of heart and his extraordinarily receptive mind filled me with a feeling of profound respect for him. A few years later I was very sorry to hear that he had at last succumbed to the terrible disease from which I knew him to be suffering; for to the very end he remained faithful and devoted to me, in spite of the most trying circumstances.

Meanwhile I had renewed my acquaintance with the friend I had won through the production of the *Fliegender Holländer* in Berlin, and who for a long time I had never had an opportunity of knowing more thoroughly. The second time I met her was at Schröder-Devrient's, with whom she was already on friendly terms, and of whom she used to speak as 'one of my greatest conquests.'

She was already past her first youth, and had no beauty of feature except remarkably penetrating and expressive eyes that showed the greatness of soul with which she was gifted. She was the sister of Frommann, the bookseller of Jena, and could relate many intimate facts about Goethe, who had stayed at her brother's house when he was in that town. She had held the position of reader and companion to the Princess Augusta of Prussia, and had thus become intimately acquainted with her, and was regarded by her own association as almost a bosom friend and confidante of that great lady. Nevertheless,

ANALYSIS OF THE PRODUCTION 375

she lived in extreme poverty, and seemed proud of being able, by means of her talent as a painter of arabesques, to secure for herself some sort of independence. She always remained faithfully devoted to me, as she was one of the few who were uninfluenced by the unfavourable impression produced by the first performance of *Tannhäuser,* and promptly expressed her appreciation of my latest work with the greatest enthusiasm.

With regard to the production itself the conclusions I drew from it were as follows: the real faults in the work, which I have already mentioned incidentally, lay in the sketchy and clumsy portrayal of the part of Venus, and consequently of the whole of the introductory scene of the first act. In consequence of this defect the drama never even rose to the level of genuine warmth, still less did it attain to the heights of passion which, according to the poetic conception of the part, should so strongly work upon the feelings of the audience as to prepare them for the inevitable catastrophe in which the scene culminates, and thus lead up to the tragic *dénouement*. This great scene was a complete failure, in spite of the fact that it was entrusted to so great an actress as Schröder-Devrient, and a singer so unusually gifted as Tichatschek. The genius of Devrient might yet have struck the right note of passion in the scene had she not chanced to be acting with a singer incapable of all dramatic seriousness, and whose natural gifts only fitted him for joyous or declamatory accents, and who was totally incapable of expressing pain and suffering. It was not until Wolfram's touching song and the closing scene of this act were reached that the audience showed any signs of emotion. Tichatschek wrought such a tremendous effect in the concluding phrase by the jubilant music of his voice that, as I was afterwards informed, the end of this first act left the audience in a great state of enthusiasm. This was maintained, and even exceeded in the second act, during which Elizabeth and Wolfram made a very sympathetic impression. It was only the hero of *Tannhäuser* who continued to lose ground, and at last so completely failed to hold the audience that in the final scene he almost broke down himself in dejection, as though the failure of *Tannhäuser* were his own. The fatal defect of his performance lay in his inability to find the right expression for the theme of the great Adagio passage of the finale beginning with the words: ' To lead the sinner to salvation, the Heaven-sent messenger drew near.' The importance of this passage I have explained at length in my subsequent instructions for the production of *Tannhäuser*. Indeed, owing to Tichatschek's absolutely expressionless rendering, which made it seem terribly long and tedious, I had to omit it entirely from the second performance. As I did not wish to offend so devoted and, in his way, so deserving a man as Tichatschek, I let it be understood I had come to the conclusion that this theme was a failure. Moreover, as Tichatschek was thought to be an actor chosen by myself to take the parts of the heroes in my works, this passage, which was so immeasurably vital to the opera, continued to be omitted in all the subsequent productions of *Tannhäuser,* as though this proceeding had been approved and demanded by me. I therefore cherished no illusions about the value of the subsequent universal success of this opera on the German stage. My hero, who, in rapture as in woe, should always have asserted his feelings with boundless energy, slunk away at the end of the second act with the humble bearing of a penitent sinner, only to reappear in the third with a demeanour designed to awaken the charitable sympathy of the audience. His pronunciation of the Pope's excommunication, however, was rendered with his usual full rhetorical power, and it was refreshing to hear his voice dominating the accompanying trombones. Granted that this radical defect in the hero's acting had left the public in a doubtful and unsatisfied state of suspense regarding the meaning of the whole, yet the mistake in the execution of the final scene, arising from my own inexperience in this new field of dramatic creation, undoubtedly contributed to produce a chilling uncertainty as to the true significance of the scenic action. In my first complete version I had made Venus, on the occasion of her second attempt to recall her faithless lover, appear in a vision to Tannhäuser when he is in a frenzy of madness, and the awfulness of the situation is merely suggested by a faint roseate glow upon the distant Hörselberg. Even the definite announcement of Elizabeth's death was a sudden inspiration on the part of Wolfram. This idea I intended to convey to the listening audience solely by the sound of bells tolling in the distance, and by a faint gleam of torches to attract their eyes to the remote Wartburg. Moreover, there was a lack of precision and clearness in the appearance of the chorus of young pilgrims, whose duty it was to announce the miracle by their song alone. At that time I had given them no budding staves to carry, and had unfortunately spoiled their refrain by a tedious and unbroken monotony of accompaniment.

When at last the curtain fell, I was under the impression, not so much from the behaviour of the audience, which was friendly, as from my own inward conviction, that the failure of this work was to be attributed to the immature and unsuitable material used in its production. My depression was extreme, and a few friends who were present after the piece, among them my dear sister Clara and her husband, were equally affected. That very evening I decided to remedy the defects of the first night before the second performance. I was conscious of where the principal fault lay, but hardly dared give expression to my conviction. At the slightest attempt on my part to explain anything to Tichatschek I had to abandon it, as I realised the impossibility of success. I should only have made him so embarrassed and annoyed, that on one pretext or another he would never have sung *Tannhäuser* again. In order to ensure the repetition of my opera, therefore, I took the only course open to me by arrogating to myself all blame for the failure. I could thus make considerable curtailments, whereby, of course, the dramatic significance of the leading rôle was considerably lessened; this, however, did not interfere with the other parts of the opera, which had been favourably received. Consequently, although inwardly very humiliated, I hoped to gain some advantage for my work at the second performance, and was particularly desirous that this should take place with as little delay as possible. But Tichatschek was hoarse, and I had to possess my soul in patience for fully a week.

I can hardly describe what I suffered during that time; it seemed as if this delay would completely ruin my work. Every day that elapsed between the first and second performance left the result of the former more and more problematic, until at last it appeared to be a generally acknowledged failure. While the public as a whole expressed angry astonishment that, after the approval they had shown of my *Rienzi*, I had paid no attention to their taste in writing my new work, there were may kind and judicious friends who were utterly perplexed at its inefficiency, the principal parts of which they had been unable to understand, or thought were imperfectly sketched and finished. The critics, with unconcealed joy, attacked it as ravens attack carrion thrown out to them. Even the passions and prejudices of the day were drawn into the controversy in order, if possible, to confuse men's minds, and prejudice them against me. It was just at the time when the German-Catholic agitation, set in motion by Czersky and Ronge as a highly meritorious and liberal movement, was causing a great commotion. It was now made out that by *Tannhäuser* I had provoked a reactionary tendency, and that precisely as Meyerbeer with his *Huguenots* had glorified Protestantism, so I with my latest opera would glorify Catholicism.

The rumour that in writing *Tannhäuser* I had been bribed by the Catholic party was believed for a long time. While the effort was being made to ruin my popularity by this means, I had the questionable honour of being approached, first by letter, afterwards in person, by a certain M. Rousseau, at that time editor of the Prussian *Staatszeitung*, who wished for my friendship and help. I knew of him only in connection with a scathing criticism of my *Fliegender Holländer*. He informed me that he had been sent from Austria to further the Catholic cause in Berlin, but that he had had so many sad experiences of the fruitlessness of his efforts, that he was now returning to Vienna to continue his work in this direction undisturbed, with which work I had, by my *Tannhäuser*, proclaimed myself fully in accord.

That remarkable paper, the *Dresdener Anzeiger*, which was a local organ for the redress of slander and scandal, daily published some fresh bit of news to my prejudice. At last I noticed that these attacks were met by witty and forcible little snubs, and also that encouraging comments appeared in my favour, which for some time surprised me very much, as

I knew that only enemies and never friends interested themselves in such cases. But I learned, to my amusement, from Röckel, that he and my friend Heine had carried out this inspiriting campaign on my behalf.

The ill-feeling against me in this quarter was only troublesome because at that unfortunate period I was hindered from expressing myself through my work. Tichatschek continued hoarse, and it was said he would never sing in my opera again. I heard from Lüttichau that, scared by the failure of *Tannhäuser*, he was holding himself in readiness to countermand the order for the promised scenery for the Hall of Song, or to cancel it altogether. I was so terrified at the cowardice which was thus revealed, that I myself began to look upon *Tannhäuser* as doomed. My prospects and my whole position, when viewed in this mood, may be readily gathered from my communications, especially those referring to my negotiations for the publication of my works.

This terrible week dragged out like an endless eternity. I was afraid to look anybody in the face, but was one day obliged to go to Meser's music shop, where I met Gottfried Semper just buying a text-book of *Tannhäuser*. Only a short time before I had been very much put out in discussing this subject with him; he would listen to nothing I had to say about the Minnesängers and Pilgrims of the Middle Ages in connection with art, but gave me to understand that he despised me for my choice of such material.

While Meser assured me that no inquiry whatever had been received for the numbers of *Tannhäuser* already published, it was strange that my most energetic antagonist should be the only person who had actually bought and paid for a copy. In a peculiarly earnest and impressive manner he remarked to me that it was necessary to be thoroughly acquainted with the subject if a just opinion was to be passed on it, and that for this purpose, unfortunately, nothing but the text was available. This very meeting with Semper, strange as it may appear, was the first really encouraging sign that I can remember.

But I found my greatest consolation in those days of trouble and anxiety in Röckel, who from that time forward entered into a lifelong intimacy with me. He had, without my being aware of it, disputed, explained, quarrelled, and petitioned on my behalf, and thereby roused himself to a veritable enthusiasm for *Tannhäuser*. The evening before the second performance, which was at last to take place, we met over a glass of beer, and his bright demeanour had such a cheering effect upon me that we became very lively. After contemplating my head for some time, he swore that it was impossible to destroy me, that there was a something in me, something, probably, in my blood, as similar characteristics also appeared in my brother Albert, who was otherwise so unlike me. To speak more plainly, he called it the peculiar *heat* of my temperament; this heat, he thought, might consume others, whereas I appeared to feel at my best when it glowed most fiercely, for he had several times seen me positively ablaze. I laughed, and did not know what to make of his nonsense. Well, he said, I should soon see what he meant in *Tannhäuser*, for it was simply absurd to think the work would not live; and he was absolutely certain of its success. I thought over the matter on my way home, and came to the conclusion that if *Tannhäuser* did indeed win its way, and become really popular, incalculable possibilities might be attained.

At last the time arrived for our second performance. For this I thought I had made due preparation by lessening the importance of the principal part, and lowering my original ideals about some of the more important portions, and I hoped by accentuating certain undoubtedly attractive passages to secure a genuine appreciation of the whole. I was greatly delighted with the scenery which had at last arrived for the Hall of Song in the second act, the beautiful and imposing effect of which cheered us all, for we looked upon it as a good omen. Unfortunately I had to bear the humiliation of seeing the theatre nearly empty. This, more than anything else, sufficed to convince me what the opinion of the public really was in regard to my work. But, if the audience was scanty, the majority, at any rate, consisted of the first friends of my art, and the reception of the piece was very cordial. Mitterwurzer especially aroused the greatest enthusiasm. As for Tichatschek, my anxious friends, Röckel and Heine, thought it necessary to endeavour by every artifice to keep him in a good humour for his part. In order to give practical assistance in making the undoubted obscurity of the last scene clear, my friends had asked several young people, more especially artists, to give vent to torrents of applause at those parts which are not generally regarded by the opera-going public as provoking any demonstration. Strange to say, the outburst of applause thus provoked after the words, 'An angel flies to God's throne for thee, and will make his voice heard; Heinrich, thou art saved,' made the entire situation suddenly clear to the public. At all subsequent productions this continued to be the principal moment for the expression of sympathy on the part of the audience, although it had passed quite unnoticed on the first night. A few days later a third performance took place, but this time before a full house. Schröder-Devrient, depressed at the small share she was able to take in the success of my work, watched the progress of the opera from the small stage box; she informed me that Lüttichau had come to her with a beaming face, saying he thought we had now carried *Tannhäuser* happily through.

And this certainly proved to be the case; we often repeated it in the course of the winter, but noticed that when two performances followed close upon one another, there was not such a rush for the second, from which we concluded that I had not yet gained the approval of the great opera-going public, but only of the more cultured section of the community. Among these real friends of *Tannhäuser* there were many, as I gradually discovered, who as a rule never visited the theatre at all, and least of all the opera. This interest on the part of a totally new public continued to grow in intensity, and expressed itself in a delightful and hitherto unknown manner by a strong sympathy for the author. It was particularly painful to me, on Tichatschek's account, to respond alone to the calls of the audience after almost every act; however, I had at last to submit, as my refusal would only have exposed the vocalist to fresh humiliations, for when he appeared on the stage with his colleagues without me, the loud shouts for me were almost insulting to him. With what genuine eagerness did I wish that the contrary were the case, and that the excellence of the execution might overshadow the author. The conviction that I should never attain this with my *Tannhäuser* in Dresden guided me in all my future undertakings. But, at all events, in producing *Tannhäuser* in this city I had succeeded in making at least the cultured public acquainted with my peculiar tendencies, by stimulating their mental faculties and stripping the performance of all realistic accessories. I did not, however, succeed in making these tendencies sufficiently clear in a dramatic performance, and in such an irresistible and convincing manner as also to familiarise the uncultivated taste of the ordinary public with them when they saw them embodied on the stage.

By enlarging the circle of my acquaintances, and making interesting friends, I had a good opportunity during the winter of obtaining further information on this point in a way that was both instructive and encouraging. My acquaintance and close intimacy at this time with Dr. Hermann Franck of Breslau, who had for some time been living quietly in Dresden, was also very inspiring. He was very comfortably off, and was one of those men who, by a wide knowledge and good judgment, combined with considerable gifts as an author, won an excellent reputation for himself in a large and select circle of private friends, without, however, making any great name for himself with the public. He endeavoured to use his knowledge and abilities for the general good, and was induced by Brockhaus to edit the *Deutsche Allgemeine Zeitung* when it first started. This paper had been founded by Brockhaus some years earlier. However, after editing it for a year, Franck resigned this post, and from that time forward it was only on the very rarest occasions that he could be persuaded to touch anything connected with journalism. His curt and spirited remarks about his experiences in connection with the *Deutsche Allgemeine Zeitung* justified his disinclination to engage in any work connected with the public press. My appreciation was all the greater, therefore, when, without any persuasion on my part, he wrote a full report on *Tannhäuser* for the *Augsburger Allgemeine Zeitung*. This appeared in October or November, 1845, in a supplement to that paper, and although it contained the first account of a work which has since been so widely discussed, I regard it, after mature consideration, as the most far-reaching and exhaustive that has ever been written. By this means my name figured for the first time in the great European political paper, whose columns, in consequence of a remarkable change of front which was to the interests of the proprietors, have since been open to any one who wished to make merry at the expense of me or my work.

The point which particularly attracted me in Dr. Franck was the delicate and tactful art he displayed in his criticism and his methods of discussion. There was something distinguished about them that was not so much the outcome of rank and social position as of genuine world-wide culture.

The delicate coldness and reserve of his manner charmed rather than repelled me, as it was a characteristic I had not met with hitherto. When I found him expressing himself with some reserve in regard to persons who enjoyed a reputation to which I did not think they were always entitled, I was very pleased to see during my intercourse with him that in many ways I exercised a decisive influence over his opinion. Even at that time I did not care to let it pass unchallenged when people evaded the close analysis of the work of this or that celebrity, by referring in terms of eulogy to his 'good-nature.' I even cornered my worldly wise friend on this point, when a few years later I had the satisfaction of getting from him a very concise explanation of Meyerbeer's 'good-nature,' of which he had once spoken, and he recalled with a smile the extraordinary questions I had put to him at the time. He was, however, quite alarmed when I gave him a very lucid explanation of the disinterestedness and conspicuous altruism of Mendelssohn in the service of art, of which he had spoken enthusiastically. In a conversation about Mendelssohn he had remarked how delightful it was to find a man able to make real sacrifices in order to free himself from a false position that was of no service to art. It was assuredly a grand thing, he said, to have renounced a good salary of nine thousand marks as general musical conductor in Berlin, and to have retired to Leipzig as a simple conductor at the Gewandhaus concerts, and Mendelssohn was much to be admired on that account. Just at that time I happened to be in a position to give some correct details regarding this apparent sacrifice on the part of Mendelssohn, because when I had made a serious proposal to our general management about increasing the salaries of several of the poorer members of the orchestra, Lüttichau was requested to inform me that, according to the King's latest commands, the expenditure on the state bands was to be so restricted that for the present the poorer chamber musicians could not claim any consideration, for Herr von Falkenstein, the governor of the Leipzig district, who was a passionate admirer of Mendelssohn's, had gone so far as to influence the King to appoint the latter secret conductor, with a secret salary of six thousand marks. This sum, together with the salary of three thousand marks openly granted him by the management of the Leipzig Gewandhaus, would amply compensate him for the position he had renounced in Berlin, and he had consequently consented to migrate to Leipzig. This large grant had, for decency's sake, to be kept secret by the board administering the band funds, not only because it was detrimental to the interests of the institution, but also because it might give offence to those who were acting as conductors at a lower salary, if they knew another man had been appointed to a sinecure. From these circumstances Mendelssohn derived not only the advantage of having the grant kept a secret, but also the satisfaction of allowing his friends to applaud him as a model of self-sacrificing zeal for going to Leipzig; which they could easily do, although they knew him to be in a good financial position. When I explained this to Franck, he was astonished, and admitted it was one of the strangest cases he had ever come across in connection with undeserved fame.

We soon arrived at a mutual understanding in our views about many other artistic celebrities with whom we came in contact at that time in Dresden. This was a simple matter in the case of Ferdinand Hiller, who was regarded as the chief of the 'good-natured' ones. Regarding the more famous painters of the so-called Düsseldorf School, whom I met frequently through the medium of *Tannhäuser,* it was not quite so easy to come to a conclusion, as I was to a great extent influenced by the fame attached to their well-known names; but here again Franck startled me with opportune and conclusive reasons for disappointment. When it was a question between Bendemann and Hübner, it seemed to me that Hübner might very well be sacrificed to Bendemann. The latter, who had only just completed the frescoes for one of the reception-rooms at the royal palace, and had been rewarded by his friends with a banquet, appeared to me to have the right to be honoured as a great master. I was very much astonished, therefore, when Franck calmly pitied the King of Saxony for having had his room 'bedaubed' by Bendemann! Nevertheless, there was no denying that these people were 'good-natured.' My intercourse with them became more frequent, and at all events offered me opportunities of mixing with the more cultured artistic society, in distinction to the theatrical circles with which I had usually associated; yet I never derived from it the least enthusiasm or inspiration. The latter, however, appears to have been Hiller's main object, and that winter he organised a sort of social circle which held weekly meetings at the home of one or the other of its members in turn. Reinecke, who was both painter and poet, joined this society, together with Hübner and Bendemann, and had the bad fortune to write the new text for an opera for Hiller, the fate of which I will describe later on. Robert Schumann, the musician, who was also in Dresden at this time, and was busy working out on opera, which eventually developed into *Genovefa*, made advances to Hiller and myself. I had already known Schumann in Leipzig, and we had both entered upon our musical careers at about the same time. I had also occasionally sent small contributions to the *Neue Zeitschrift für Musik*, of which he had formerly been editor, and more recently a longer one from Paris on Rossini's *Stabat Mater*. He had been asked to conduct his *Paradies und Peri* at a concert to be given at the theatre; but his peculiar awkwardness in conducting on that occasion aroused my sympathy for the conscientious and energetic musician whose work made so strong an appeal to me, and a kindly and friendly confidence soon grew up between us. After a performance of *Tannhäuser*, at which he was present, he called on me one morning and declared himself fully and decidedly in favour of my work. The only objection he had to make was that the *stretta* of the second finale was too abrupt, a criticism which proved his keenness of perception; and I was able to show him, by the score, how I had been compelled, much against my inclination, to curtail the opera, and thereby create the position to which he had taken exception. We often met when out walking and, as far as it was possible with a person so sparing of words, we exchanged views on matters of musical interest. He was looking forward to the production, under my baton, of Beethoven's Ninth Symphony, as he had attended the performances at Leipzig, and had been very much disappointed by Mendelssohn's conducting, which had quite misunderstood the time of the first movement. Otherwise his society did not inspire me particularly, and the fact that he was too conservative to benefit by my views was soon shown, more especially in his conception of the poem of *Genovefa*. It was clear that my example had only made a very transient impression on him, only just enough, in fact, to make him think it advisable to write the text of an opera himself. He afterwards invited me to hear him read his libretto, which was a combination of the styles of Hebbel and Tieck. When, however, out of a genuine desire for the success of his work, about which I had serious misgivings, I called his attention to some grave defects in it, and suggested the necessary alterations, I realised how matters stood with this extraordinary person: he simply wanted me to be swayed by himself, but deeply resented any interference with the product of his own ideals, so that thenceforward I let matters alone.

In the following winter, our circle, thanks to the assiduity of Hiller, was considerably widened, and it now became a sort of club whose object was to meet freely every week in a room at Engel's restaurant at the Postplatz. Just about this time the famous J. Schnorr of Munich was appointed director of the museums in Dresden, and we entertained him at a banquet. I had already seen some of his large and well-executed cartoons, which made a deep impression on me, not only on account of their dimensions, but also by reason of the events they depicted from old German history, in which

AN ARTISTIC CIRCLE 387

I was at that time particularly interested. It was through Schnorr that I now became acquainted with the 'Munich School' of which he was the master. My heart overflowed when I thought what it meant for Dresden, if such giants of German art were to shake hands there. I was much struck by Schnorr's appearance and conversation, and I could not reconcile his whining pedagogic manner with his mighty cartoons; however, I thought it a great stroke of luck when he also took to frequenting Engel's restaurant on Saturdays. He was well versed in the old German legends, and I was delighted when they formed the topic of conversation. The famous sculptor, Hänel, used also to attend these meetings, and his marvellous talent inspired me with the greatest respect, although I was not an authority on his work, and could only judge of it by my own feelings. I soon saw that his bearing and manner were affected; he was very fond of expressing his opinion and judgment on questions of art, and I was not in a position to decide whether they were reliable or otherwise. In fact, it often occurred to me that I was listening to a Philistine swaggerer. It was only when my old friend Pecht, who had also settled in Dresden for a time, clearly and emphatically explained to me Hänel's standing as an artist, that I conquered all my secret doubts, and tried to find some pleasure in his works. Rietschel, who was also a member of our society, was the very antithesis of Hänel. I often found it difficult to believe that the pale delicate man, with the whining nervous way of expressing himself, was really a sculptor; but as similar peculiarities in Schnorr did not prevent me from recognising him as a marvellous painter, this helped me to make friends with Rietschel, as he was quite free from affectation, and had a warm sympathetic soul that drew me ever closer to him. I also remember hearing from him a very enthusiastic appreciation of my personality as a conductor. In spite, however, of being fellow-members of our versatile art club, we never attained a footing of real comradeship, for, after all, no one thought much of anybody else's talents. For instance, Hiller had arranged some orchestral concerts, and to commemorate them he was entertained at the usual banquet by his friends, when his services were gratefully acknowledged with due rhetorical pathos. Yet I never found, in my private intercourse with Hiller's friends, the least enthusiasm in regard to his work; on the contrary, I only noticed expressions of doubt and apprehensive shrugs.

These fêted concerts soon came to an end. At our social evenings we never discussed the works of the masters who were present; they were not even mentioned, and it was soon evident that none of the members knew what to talk about. Semper was the only man who, in his extraordinary fashion, often so enlivened our entertainments that Rietschel, inwardly sympathetic, though painfully startled, would heartily complain against the unrestrained outbursts that led not infrequently to hot discussions between Semper and myself. Strange to say, we two always seemed to start from the hypothesis that we were antagonists, for he insisted upon regarding me as the representative of mediæval Catholicism, which he often attacked with real fury. I eventually succeeded in persuading him that my studies and inclinations had always led me to German antiquity, and to the discovery of ideals in the early Teutonic myths. When we came to paganism, and I expressed my enthusiasm for the genuine heathen legends, he became quite a different being, and a deep and growing interest now began to unite us in such a way that it quite isolated us from the rest of the company. It was, however, impossible ever to settle anything without a heated argument, not only because Semper had a peculiar habit of contradicting everything flatly, but also because he knew his views were opposed to those of the entire company. His paradoxical assertions, which were apparently only intended to stir up strife, soon made me realise, beyond any doubt, that he was the only one present who was passionately in earnest about everything he said, whereas all the others were quite content to let the matter drop when convenient. A man of the latter type was Gutzkow, who was often with us; he had been summoned to Dresden by the general management of our court theatre, to act in the capacity of dramatist and adapter of plays. Several of his pieces had recently met with great success: *Zopf und Schwert, Das Urbild des Tartüffe,* and *Uriel Acosta,* shed an unexpected lustre on the latest dramatic repertoire, and it seemed as though the advent of Gutzkow would inaugurate a new era of glory for the Dresden theatre, where my operas had also been first produced. The good intentions of the management were certainly undeniable. My only regret on that occasion was that the hopes my old friend Laube entertained of being summoned to Dresden to fill that post were unrealised. He also had thrown himself enthusiastically into the work of dramatic literature. Even in Paris I had noticed the eagerness with which he used to study the technique of dramatic composition, especially that of Scribe, in the hope of acquiring the skill of that writer, without which, as he soon discovered, no poetical drama in German could be successful. He maintained that he had thoroughly mastered this style in his comedy, *Rococo*, and he cherished the conviction that he could work up any imaginable material into an effective stage play.

At the same time, he was very careful to show equal skill in the selection of his material. In my opinion this theory of his was a complete failure, as his only successful pieces were those in which popular interest was excited by catch-phrases. This interest was always more or less associated with the politics of the day, and generally involved some obvious diatribes about 'German unity' and 'German Liberalism.' As this important stimulus was first applied by way of experiment to the subscribers to our Residenz Theater, and afterwards to the German public generally, it had, as I have already said, to be worked out with the consummate skill which, presumably, could only be learned from modern French writers of comic opera.

I was very glad to see the result of this study in Laube's plays, more especially as when he visited us in Dresden, which he often did on the occasion of a new production, he admitted his indebtedness with modest candour, and was far from pretending to be a real poet. Moreover, he displayed great skill and an almost fiery zeal, not only in the preparation of his pieces, but also in their production, so that the offer of a post at Dresden, the hope of which had been held out to him, would at least, from a practical point of view, have been a benefit to the theatre. Finally, however, the choice fell on his rival

Gutzkow, in spite of his obvious unsuitability for the practical work of dramatist. It was evident that even as regards his successful plays his triumph was mainly due to his literary skill, because these effective plays were immediately followed by wearisome productions which made us realise, to our astonishment, that he himself could not have been aware of the skill he had previously displayed. It was, however, precisely these abstract qualities of the genuine man of letters which, in the eyes of many, cast over him the halo of literary greatness; and when Lüttichau, thinking more of a showy reputation than of permanent benefit to his theatre, decided to give the preference to Gutzkow, he thought his choice would give a special impetus to the cause of higher culture. To me the appointment of Gutzkow as the director of dramatic art at the theatre was peculiarly objectionable, as it was not long before I was convinced of his utter incompetence for the task, and it was probably owing to the frankness with which I expressed my opinion to Lüttichau that our subsequent estrangement was originally due. I had to complain bitterly of the want of judgment and the levity of those who so recklessly selected men to fill the posts of managers and conductors in such precious institutions of art as the German royal theatres. To obviate the failure I felt convinced must follow on this important appointment, I made a special request that Gutzkow should not be allowed to interfere in the management of the opera; he readily yielded, and thus spared himself great humiliation. This action, however, created a feeling of mistrust between us, though I was quite ready to remove this as far as possible by coming into personal contact with him whenever opportunity offered on those evenings when the artists used to gather at the club, as already described. I would gladly have made this strange man, whose head was anxiously bowed down on his breast, relax and unburden himself in his conversations with me, but I was unsuccessful, on account of his constant reserve and suspicion, and his studied aloofness. An opportunity arose for a discussion between us when he wanted the orchestra to take a melodramatic part (which they afterwards did) in a certain scene of his *Uriel Acosta*, where the hero had to recant his alleged heresy. The orchestra had to execute the soft tremolo for a given time on certain chords, but when I heard the performance it appeared to me absurd, and equally derogatory both for the music and the drama.

On one of these evenings I tried to come to an understanding with Gutzkow concerning this, and the employment of music generally as a melodramatic auxiliary to the drama, and I discussed my views on the subject in accordance with the highest principles I had conceived. He met all the chief points of my discussion with a nervous distrustful silence, but finally explained that I really went too far in the significance which I claimed for music, and that he failed to understand how music would be degraded if it were applied more sparingly to the drama, seeing that the claims of verse were often treated with much less respect when it was used as a mere accessory to operatic music. To put it practically, in fact, it would be advisable for the librettist not to be too dainty in this matter; it wasn't possible always to give the actor a brilliant exit; at the same time, however, nothing could be more painful than when the chief performer made his exit without any applause. In such cases a little distracting noise in the orchestra really supplied a happy diversion. This I actually heard Gutzkow say; moreover, I saw that he really meant it! After this I felt I had done with him.

It was not long before I had equally little to do with all the painters, musicians, and other zealots in art belonging to our society. At the same time, however, I came into closer contact with Berthold Auerbach. With great enthusiasm, Alwine Frommann had already drawn my attention to Auerbach's *Pastoral Stories*. The account she gave of these modest works (for that is how she characterised them) sounded quite attractive. She said that they had had the same refreshing effect on her circle of friends in Berlin as that produced by opening the window of a scented boudoir (to which she compared the literature they had hitherto been used to), and letting in the fresh air of the woods. After that I read the *Pastoral Stories of the Black Forest,* which had so quickly become famous, and I, too, was strongly attracted by the contents and tone of these realistic anecdotes about the life of the people in a locality which it was easy enough to identify from the vivid descriptions. As at this time Dresden seemed to be becoming ever more and more the rendezvous for the lights of our literary and artistic world, Auerbach also reconciled himself to taking up his quarters in this city; and for quite a long time lived with his friend Hiller, who thus again had a celebrity at his side of equal standing with himself. The short, sturdy Jewish peasant boy, as he was placed to represent himself to be, made a very agreeable impression. It was only later that I understood the significance of his green jacket, and above all of his green hunting-cap, which made him look exactly what the author of *Swabian Pastoral Stories* ought to look like, and this significance was anything but a naïve one. The Swiss poet, Gottfried Keller, once told me that, when Auerbach was in Zürich, and he had decided on taking him up, he (Auerbach) had drawn his attention to the best way in which to introduce one's literary effusions to the public, and to make money, and he advised him, above all things, to get a coat and cap like his own, for being, as he said, like himself, neither handsome nor well grown, it would be far better deliberately to make himself look rough and queer; so saying, he placed his cap on his head in such a way as to look a little rakish. For the time being, I perceived no real affectation in Auerbach; he had assimilated so much of the tone and ways of the people, and had done this so happily, that, in any case, one could not help asking oneself why, with these delightful qualities, he should move with such tremendous ease in spheres that seemed absolutely antagonistic. At all events, he always seemed in his true element even in those circles which really seemed most opposed to his assumed character; there he stood in his green coat, keen, sensitive, and natural, surrounded by the distinguished society that flattered him; and he loved to show letters he had received from the Grand Duke of Weimar and his answers to them, all the time looking at things from the standpoint of the Swabian peasant nature which suited him so admirably.

What especially attracted me to him was the fact that he was the first Jew I ever met with whom one could discuss Judaism with absolute freedom. He even seemed particularly desirous of removing, in his agreeable manner, all prejudice on this score; and it was really touching to hear him speak of his boyhood, and declare that he was perhaps the only German who had read Klopstock's *Messiah* all through. Having one day become absorbed in this work, which he read secretly in his cottage home, he had played the truant from school, and when he finally arrived too late at the school-house, his teacher angrily exclaimed: 'You confounded Jew-boy, where have you been? Lending money again?' Such experiences had only made him feel pensive and melancholy, but not bitter, and he had even been inspired with real compassion for the coarseness of his tormentors. These were traits in his character which drew me very strongly to him. As time went on, however, it seemed to me a serious matter that he could not get away from the atmosphere of these ideas, for I began to feel that the universe contained no other problem for him than the elucidation of the Jewish question. One day, therefore, I protested as good-naturedly and confidentially as I could, and advised him to let the whole problem of Judaism drop, as there were, after all, many other standpoints from which the world might be criticised. Strange to say, he thereupon not only lost his ingeniousness, but also fell to whining in an ecstatic fashion, which did not seem to me very genuine, and assured me that that would be an impossibility for him, as there was still so much in Judaism which needed his whole sympathy. I could not help recalling the surprising anguish which he had manifested on this occasion, when I learned, in the course of time, that he had repeatedly arranged Jewish marriages, concerning the happy result of which I heard nothing, save that he had, by this means, made quite a fortune. When, several years afterwards, I again saw him in Zürich, I observed that his appearance had unfortunately changed in a manner quite disconcerting: he looked really extraordinarily common and dirty; his former refreshing liveliness had turned into the usual Jewish restlessness, and it was easy to see that all he said was uttered as if he regretted that his words could not be turned to better account in a newspaper article.

During his time in Dresden, however, Auerbach's warm agreement with my artistic projects really did me good, even though it may have been only from his Semitic and Swabian standpoint; so did the novelty of the experience I was at that time undergoing as an artist, in meeting with ever-increasing regard and recognition among people of note, of acknowledged importance and of exceptional culture. If, after the success obtained by *Rienzi*, I still remained with the circle of the real theatrical world, the greater success following on *Tannhäuser* certainly brought me into contact with such people as I have mentioned above, who, though to be sure they considerably enlarged my ideas, at the same time impressed me very unfavourably with what was apparently the pinnacle of the artistic life of the period. At any rate, I felt neither rewarded nor, fortunately, even diverted by the acquaintances I won by the first performance of my *Tannhäuser* that winter. On the contrary, I felt an irresistible desire to withdraw into my shell and leave these gay surroundings into which, strangely enough, I had been introduced at the instigation of Hiller, whom I soon recognised as being a nonentity. I felt I must quickly compose something, as this was the only means of ridding myself of all the disturbing and painful excitement *Tannhäuser* had produced in me.

Only a few weeks after the first performances I had worked out the whole of the *Lohengrin* text. In November I had already read this poem to my intimate friends, and soon afterwards to the Hiller set. It was praised, and pronounced 'effective.' Schumann also thoroughly approved of it, although he did not understand the musical form in which I wished to carry it out, as he saw no resemblance in it to the old methods of writing individual solos for the various artists. I then had some fun in reading different parts of my work to him in the form of arias and cavatinas, after which he laughingly declared himself satisfied.

Serious reflection, however, aroused my gravest doubts as to the tragic character of the material itself, and to these doubts I had been led, in a manner both sensible and tactful, by Franck. He thought it offensive to effect Elsa's punishment through Lohengrin's departure; for although he understood that the characteristics of the legend were expressed precisely by this highly poetical feature, he was doubtful as to whether it did full justice to the demands of tragic feeling in its relation to dramatic realism. He would have preferred to see Lohengrin die before our eyes owing to Elsa's loving treachery. As, however, this did not seem feasible, he would have liked to see Lohengrin spell-bound by some powerful motive, and prevented from getting away. Although, of course, I would not agree to any of these suggestions, I went so far as to consider whether I could not do away with the cruel separation, and still retain the incident of Lohengrin's departure, which was essential. I then sought for a means of letting Elsa go away with Lohengrin, as a form of penance which would withdraw her also from the world. This seemed more promising to my talented friend. While I was still very doubtful about all this, I gave my poem to Frau von Lüttichau, so that she might peruse it, and criticise the point raised by Franck. In a little letter, in which she expressed her pleasure at my poem, she wrote briefly, but very decidedly, on the knotty question, and declared that Franck must be devoid of all poetry if he did not understand that it was exactly in the way I had chosen, and in no other, that Lohengrin must depart. I felt as if a load had fallen from my heart. In triumph I showed the letter to Franck, who, much abashed, and by way of excusing himself, opened a correspondence with Frau von Lüttichau, which certainly cannot have been lacking in interest, though I was never able to see any of it. In any case, the upshot of it was that *Lohengrin* remained as I had originally conceived it. Curiously enough, some time later, I had a similar experience with regard to the same subject, which again put me in a temporary state of uncertainty. When Adolf Stahr gravely raised the same objection to the solution of the *Lohengrin* question, I was really taken aback by the uniformity of opinion; and as, owing to some excitement, I was just then no longer in the same mood as when I composed *Lohengrin*, I was foolish enough to write a hurried letter to Stahr in which, with but a few slight reservations, I declared him to be right. I did not know that, by this, I was causing real grief to Liszt, who was now in the same position with regard to Stahr as Frau von Lüttichau had been with regard to Franck. Fortunately, however, the displeasure of my great friend at my supposed treachery to myself did not last long; for, without having got wind of the trouble I had caused him, and thanks to the torture I myself was going through, I came to the proper decision in a few days, and, as clear as daylight, I saw what madness it had been. I was therefore able to rejoice Liszt with the following laconical protest which I sent him from my Swiss resort: 'Stahr is wrong, and Lohengrin is right.'

For the present I remained occupied with the revision of my poem, for there could be no question of planning the music to it just now. That peaceful and harmonious state of mind which is so favourable to creative work, and always so necessary to me for composing, I now had to secure with the greatest difficulty, for it was one of the things I always had the hardest struggle to obtain. All the experiences connected with the performance of *Tannhäuser* having filled me with true despair as to the whole future of my artistic operations, I saw it was hopeless to think of its production being extended to other German theatres — for I had not been able to achieve this end even with the successful *Rienzi*. It was perfectly obvious, therefore, that my work would, at the utmost, be conceded a permanent place in the Dresden repertoire. As the result of all this, my pecuniary affairs, which have already been described, had got into such a serious state that a catastrophe seemed inevitable. While I was preparing to meet this in the best way I could, I tried to stupefy myself, on the one hand, by plunging into the study of history, mythology, and literature, which were becoming ever dearer and dearer to me, and on the other by working incessantly at my artistic enterprises. As regards the former, I was chiefly interested in the German Middle Ages, and tried to make myself familiar with every point relative to this period. Although I could not set about this task with philological precision, I proceeded with such earnestness that I studied the German records, published by Grimm, for instance, with the greatest interest. As I could not put the results of such studies immediately into my scenes, there were many who could not understand why, as an operatic composer, I should waste my time on such barren work. Different people remarked later on, that the personality of Lohengrin had a charm quite its own; but this was ascribed to the happy selection of the subject, and I was

specially praised for choosing it. Material from the German
Middle Ages, and later on, subjects from Scandinavian antiquity, were therefore looked forward to by many, and, in
the end, they were astonished that I gave them no adequate
result of all my labours. Perhaps it will be of help to them
if I now tell them to take the old records and such works to
their aid. I forgot at that time to call Hiller's attention to
my documents, and with great pride he seized upon a subject
out of the history of the Hohenstaufen. As, however, he had
no success with his work, he may perhaps think I was a little
artful for not having spoken to him of the old records.

Concerning my other duties, my chief undertaking for this
winter consisted in an exceptionally carefully prepared performance of Beethoven's Ninth Symphony, which took place
in the spring on Palm Sunday. This performance involved
many a struggle, besides a host of experiences which were destined to exercise a strong influence over my further development. Roughly they were as follows: the royal orchestra had
only one opportunity a year of showing their powers independently in a musical performance outside the Opera or the
church. For the benefit of the Pension Fund for their widows
and orphans, the old so-called Opera House was given up
to a big performance originally only intended for oratorios.
Ultimately, in order to make it more attractive, a symphony
was always added to the oratorio; and, as already mentioned,
I had performed on such occasions, once the Pastoral Symphony,
and later Haydn's *Creation*. The latter was a great joy to
me, and it was on this occasion that I first made its acquaintance. As we two conductors had stipulated for alternate
performances, the Symphony on Palm Sunday of the year 1846
fell to my lot. I had a great longing for the Ninth Symphony,
and I was led to the choice of this work by the fact that it
was almost unknown in Dresden. When the directors of the
orchestra, who were the trustees of the Pension Fund, and
who had to promote its increase, got to know of this, such a
fright seized them that they interviewed the general director,
Lüttichau, and begged him, by virtue of his high authority, to
dissuade me from carrying out my intention. They gave as a
reason for this request, that the Pension Fund would surely

suffer through the choice of this symphony, as the work was in
ill-repute in the place, and would certainly keep people from
going to the concert. The symphony had been performed
many years before by Reissiger at a charity concert, and, as
the conductor himself honestly admitted, had been an absolute
failure. Now it needed my whole ardour, and all the eloquence
I could command, to prevail over the doubts of our principal.
With the orchestral directors, however, there was nothing for
me to do but quarrel, as I heard that they were complaining all
over the town about my indiscretion. In order to add shame
to their trouble, I made up my mind to prepare the public in
such a way for the performance, upon which I had resolved,
and for the work itself, that at least the sensation caused would
lead to a full hall and thus, in a very favourable manner,
guarantee satisfactory returns, and contradict their belief
that the fund was menaced. Thus the Ninth Symphony had,
in every conceivable way, become for me a point of honour,
for the success of which I had to exercise all my powers to the
utmost. The committee had misgivings regarding the outlay
needed for procuring the orchestral parts, so I borrowed them
from the Leipzig Concert Society.

Imagine my feelings, however, on now seeing for the first
time since my earliest boyhood the mysterious pages of this
score, which I studied conscientiously! In those days the
sight of these same pages had filled me with the most mystic
reveries, and I had stayed up for nights together to copy them
out. Just as at the time of my uncertainty in Paris, on hearing
the rehearsal of the first three movements performed by the
incomparable orchestra of the Conservatoire, I had been
carried back through years of error and doubt to be placed in
marvellous touch with my earliest days, while all my inmost
aspirations had been fruitfully stimulated in a new direction,
so now in the same way the memory of that music was secretly
awakened in me as I again saw before my own eyes that which
in those early days had likewise been only a mysterious vision.
I had by this time experienced much which, in the depths
of my soul, drove me almost unconsciously to a process of
summing-up, to an almost despairing inquiry concerning my
fate. What I dared not acknowledge to myself was the fact

of the absolute insecurity of my existence both from the
artistic and financial point of view; for I saw that I was a
stranger to my own mode of life as well as to my profession,
and I had no prospects whatsoever. This despair, which I
tried to conceal from my friends, was now converted into
genuine exaltation, thanks entirely to the Ninth Symphony.
It is not likely that the heart of a disciple has ever been filled
with such keen rapture over the work of a master, as mine was
at the first movement of this symphony. If any one had come
upon me unexpectedly while I had the open score before me,
and had seen me convulsed with sobs and tears as I went
through the work in order to consider the best manner of
rendering it, he would certainly have asked with astonishment
if this were really fitting behaviour for the Conductor Royal of
Saxony! Fortunately, on such occasions I was spared the
visits of our orchestra directors, and their worthy conductor
Reissiger, and even those of F. Hiller, who was so versed in
classical music.

In the first place I drew up a programme, for which the
book of words for the chorus — always ordered according to
custom — furnished me with a good pretext. I did this in order
to provide a guide to the simple understanding of the work, and
thereby hoped to appeal not to the critical judgment, but
solely to the feelings, of the audience. This programme, in the
framing of which some of the chief passages in Goethe's *Faust*
were exceedingly helpful to me, was very well received, not
only on that occasion in Dresden, but later on in other places.
Besides this, I made use of the Dresden *Anzeiger,* by writing
all kinds of short and enthusiastic anonymous paragraphs,
in order to whet the public taste for a work which hitherto
had been in ill-repute in Dresden.

Not only did these purely extraneous exertions succeed in
making the receipts of that year by far exceed any that had
been taken theretofore, but the orchestra directors themselves,
during the remaining years of my stay in Dresden, made a point
of ensuring similarly large profits by repeated performances of
the celebrated symphony. Concerning the artistic side of the
performance, I aimed at making the orchestra give as expressive
a rendering as possible, and to this end made all kinds of notes,

myself, in the various parts, so as to make quite sure that their interpretation would be as clear and as coloured as could be desired. It was principally the custom which existed then of doubling the wind instruments, that led me to a most careful consideration of the advantages this system presented, for, in performances on a large scale, the following somewhat crude rule prevailed: all those passages marked *piano* were executed by a single set of instruments, while those marked *forte* were carried out by a duplicated set. As an instance of the way in which I took care to ensure an intelligible rendering by this means, I might point to a certain passage in the second movement of the symphony, where the whole of the string instruments play the principal and rhythmical figure in C major for the first time; it is written in triple octaves, which play uninterruptedly in unison and, to a certain degree, serve as an accompaniment to the second theme, which is only performed by feeble wood instruments. As *fortissimo* is indicated alike for the whole orchestra, the result in every imaginable rendering must be that the melody for the wood instruments not only completely disappears, but cannot even be heard through the strings, which, after all, are only accompanying. Now, as I never carried my piety to the extent of taking directions absolutely literally, rather than sacrifice the effect really intended by the master to the erroneous indications given, I made the strings play only moderately loudly instead of real *fortissimo,* up to the point where they alternate with the wind instruments in taking up the continuation of the new theme: thus the motive, rendered as it was as loudly as possible by a double set of wind instruments, was, I believe for the first time since the existence of the symphony, heard with real distinctness. I proceeded in this manner throughout, in order to guarantee the greatest exactitude in the dynamical effects of the orchestra. There was nothing, however difficult, which was allowed to be performed in such a way as not to arouse the feelings of the audience in a particular manner. For example, many brains had been puzzled by the *Fugato* in $\frac{6}{8}$ time which comes after the chorus, *Froh wie seine Sonnen fliegen,* in the movement of the finale marked *alla marcia.* In view of the preceding inspiring verses, which seemed to be preparing for combat and victory, I conceived this *Fugato* really as a glad but earnest war-song, and I took it at a continuously fiery tempo, and with the utmost vigour. The day following the first performance I had the satisfaction of receiving a visit from the musical director Anacker of Freiburg, who came to tell me somewhat penitently, that though until then he had been one of my antagonists, since the performance of the symphony he certainly reckoned himself among my friends. What had absolutely overwhelmed him, he said, was precisely my conception and interpretation of the *Fugato*. Furthermore, I devoted special attention to that extraordinary passage, resembling a recitative for the 'cellos and basses, which comes at the beginning of the last movement, and which had once caused my old friend Pohlenz such great humiliation in Leipzig. Thanks to the exceptional excellence of our bass players, I felt certain of attaining to absolute perfection in this passage. After twelve special rehearsals of the instruments alone concerned, I succeeded in getting them to perform in a way which sounded not only perfectly free, but which also expressed the most exquisite tenderness and the greatest energy in a thoroughly impressive manner.

From the very beginning of my undertaking I had at once recognised, that the only method of achieving overwhelming popular success with this symphony was to overcome, by some ideal means, the extraordinary difficulties presented by the choral parts. I realised that the demands made by these parts could be met only by a large and enthusiastic body of singers. It was above all necessary, then, to secure a very good and large choir; so, besides adding the somewhat feeble Dreissig 'Academy of Singing' to our usual number of members in the theatre chorus, in spite of great difficulties I also enlisted the help of the choir from the Kreuzschule, with its fine boys' voices, and the choir of the Dresden seminary, which had had much practice in church singing. In a way quite my own I now tried to get these three hundred singers, who were frequently united for rehearsals, into a state of genuine ecstasy; for instance, I succeeded in demonstrating to the basses that the celebrated passage *Seid umschlungen, Millionen,* and especially *Brüder, über'm Sternenzelt muss ein guter Vater wohnen,* could not be sung in an ordinary manner, but must, as it were, be proclaimed with the greatest rapture. In this I took the lead in a manner so elated that I really think I literally transported them to a world of emotion uttery strange to them for a while; and I did not desist till my voice, which had been heard clearly above all the others, began to be no longer distinguishable even to myself, but was drowned, so to speak, in the warm sea of sound.

It gave me particular pleasure, with Mitterwurzer's co-operation, to give a most overwhelmingly expressive rendering of the recitative for baritone: *Freunde, nicht diese Töne.* In view of its exceptional difficulties this passage might almost be considered impossible to perform, and yet he executed it in a way which showed what fruit our mutual interchange of ideas had borne. I also took care that, by means of the complete reconstruction of the hall, I should obtain good acoustic conditions for the orchestra, which I had arranged according to quite a new system of my own. As may be imagined, it was only with the greatest difficulty that the money for this could be found; however, I did not give up, and owing to a totally new construction of the platform, I was able to concentrate the whole of the orchestra towards the centre, and surround it, in amphitheatre fashion, by the throng of singers who were accommodated on seats very considerably raised. This was not only of great advantage to the powerful effect of the choir, but it also gave great precision and energy to the finely organised orchestra in the purely symphonic movements.

Even at the general rehearsal the hall was overcrowded. Reissiger was guilty of the incredible stupidity of working up the public mind against the symphony and drawing attention to Beethoven's very regrettable error. Gade, on the other hand, who came to visit us from Leipzig, where he was then conducting the Gewandhaus Concerts, assured me after the general rehearsal, that he would willingly have paid double the price of his ticket in order to hear the recitative by the basses once more; whilst Hiller considered that I had gone too far in my modification of the tempo. What he meant by this I learned subsequently when I heard him conducting intricate orchestral works; but of this I shall have more to say later on.

There was no denying that the performance was, on the whole, a success; in fact, it exceeded all our expectations, and was particularly well received by the non-musical public. Among these I remember the philologist Dr. Köchly, who came to me at the end of the evening and confessed that it was the first time he had been able to follow a symphonic work from beginning to end with intelligent interest. This experience left me with a pleasant feeling of ability and power, and strongly confirmed me in the belief, that if I only desired anything with sufficient earnestness, I was able to achieve it with irresistible and overwhelming success. I now had to consider, however, what the difficulties were, which hitherto had prevented a similarly happy production of my own new conceptions. Beethoven's Ninth Symphony, which was still such a problem to so many, and had, at all events, never attained to popularity, I had been able to make a complete success; yet, as often as it was put on the stage, my *Tannhäuser* taught me that the possibilities of its success had yet to be discovered. How was this to be done? This was and remained the secret question which influenced all my subsequent development.

I dared not, however, indulge at that time in any meditation on this point with the view of arriving at any particular results, for the real significance of my failure, of which I was inwardly convinced, stood absolutely bare before me with all its terrifying lessons. Albeit, I could no longer delay taking even the most disagreeable steps with the view of warding off the catastrophe which menaced my financial position.

I was led to this, thanks to the influence of a ridiculous omen. My agent, the purely nominal publisher of my three operas — *Rienzi*, the *Fliegender Holländer*, and *Tannhäuser* — the eccentric court music publisher, C. F. Meser, invited me one day to the café known as the 'Verderber' to discuss our money affairs. With great qualms we talked over the possible results of the Annual Easter Fair, and wondered whether they would be tolerably good or altogether bad. I gave him courage, and ordered a bottle of the best Haut-Sauterne. A venerable flask made its appearance; I filled the glasses, and we drank to the good success of the Fair; when suddenly we both yelled as though we had gone mad, while, with horror, we tried to rid our mouths of the strong Tarragon vinegar with which we had been served by mistake. 'Heavens!' cried Meser, 'nothing could be worse!' 'True enough,' I answered, 'no doubt there is much that will turn to vinegar for us.' My good-humour revealed to me in a flash that I must try some other way of saving myself than by means of the Easter Fair.

Not only was it necessary to refund the capital which had been got together by dint of ever-increasing sacrifices, in order to defray the expenses of the publication of my operas; but, owing to the fact that I had been obliged ultimately to seek aid from the usurers, the rumour of my debts had spread so far abroad, that even those friends who had helped me at the time of my arrival in Dresden were seized with anxiety on my account. At this time I met with a really sad experience at the hands of Madame Schröder-Devrient, who, as the result of her incomprehensible lack of discretion, did much to bring about my final undoing. When I first settled in Dresden, as I have already pointed out, she lent me three thousand marks, not only to help me to discharge my debts, but also to allow me to contribute to the maintenance of my old friend Kietz in Paris. Jealousy of my niece Johanna, and suspicion that I had made her (my niece) come to Dresden in order to make it easier for the general management to dispense with the services of the great artist, had awakened in this otherwise so noble-minded woman the usual feelings of animosity towards me, which are so often met with in the theatrical profession. She had now given up her engagement; she even declared openly that I had been partly instrumental in obtaining her dismissal; and abandoning all friendly regard for me, whereby she deeply wronged me in every respect, she placed the I.O.U. I had given her in the hands of an energetic lawyer, and without further ado this man sued me for the payment of the money. Thus I was forced to make a clean breast of everything to Lüttichau, and to beseech him to intervene for me, and if possible to obtain a royal advance that would enable me to clear my position, which was so seriously compromised.

My principal declared himself willing to support any request I might wish to address to the King on this matter. To this end I had to note down the amount of my debts; but as I soon discovered that the necessary sum could only be assigned to me as a loan from the Theatre Pension Fund, at an interest of five per cent., and that I should moreover have to secure the capital of the Pension Fund by a life insurance policy, which would cost me annually three per cent. of the capital borrowed, I was, for obvious reasons, tempted to leave out of my petition all those of my debts which were not of a pressing nature, and for the payment of which I thought I could count on the receipts which I might finally expect from my publishing enterprises. Nevertheless, the sacrifices I had to make in order to repay the help offered me increased to such an extent, that my salary of conductor, in itself very slender, promised to be materially diminished for some time to come. I was forced to make the most irksome efforts to gather together the necessary sum for the life insurance policy, and was therefore obliged frequently to appeal to Leipzig. In addition to this, I had to overcome the most appalling doubts in regard both to my health and to the probable length of my life, concerning which I fancied I had heard all sorts of malicious apprehensions expressed by those who had observed me but casually in the miserable condition which I was in at that time. My friend Pusinelli, as a doctor who was very intimate with me, eventually managed to give such satisfactory information concerning the state of my health, that I succeeded in insuring my life at the rate of three per cent.

The last of these painful journeys to Leipzig was, at all events, made under pleasant circumstances owing to a kind invitation from the old Maestro Louis Spohr. I was particularly pleased over this, because to me it meant nothing less than an act of reconciliation. As a matter of fact, Sophr had written to me on one occasion, and had declared that, stimulated by the success of my *Fliegender Holländer* and his own enjoyment of it, he had once more decided to take up the career of a dramatic composer, which of recent years had brought him such scant success. His last work was an opera — *Die Kreuzfahrer* — which he had sent to the Dresden theatre in the course of the preceding year in the hope, as he himself assured me, that I would urge on its production. After asking this favour, he drew my attention to the fact that in this work he had made an absolutely new departure from his earlier operas, and had kept to the most precise rhythmically dramatic declamation, which had certainly been made all the more easy for him by the 'excellent subject.' Without being actually surprised, my horror was indeed great when, after studying not only the text, but also the score, I discovered that the old maestro had been absolutely mistaken in regard to the account he had given me of his work. The custom in force at that time that the decision concerning the production of works should not, as a rule, rest with one of the conductors alone, did not tend to make me any less fearful of declaring myself emphatically in favour of this work. In addition to this, it was Reissiger, who, as he had often boasted, was an old friend of Spohr's, whose turn it was to select and produce a new work. Unfortunately, as I learned later, the general management had returned Spohr's opera to its author in such a curt manner as to offend him, and he complained bitterly of this to me. Genuinely concerned at this, I had evidently managed to calm and appease him, for the invitation mentioned above was clearly a friendly acknowledgment of my efforts. He wrote that it was very painful for him to have to touch at Dresden on his way to one of the watering-places; as, however, he had a real longing to make my acquaintance, he begged me to meet him in Leipzig, where he was going to stay for a few days.

This meeting with him did not leave me unimpressed. He was a tall, stately man, distinguished in appearance, and of a serious and calm temperament. He gave me to understand, in a touching, almost apologetic manner, that the essence of his education and of his aversion from the new tendencies in music, had its origin in the first impressions he had received on hearing, as a very young boy, Mozart's *Magic Flute,* a work which was quite new at that time, and which had a great influence on his whole life. Regarding my libretto to *Lohengrin,* which I had left behind for him to read, and the general impression which my personal acquaintance had made on him, he expressed himself with almost surprising warmth to my brother-in-law, Hermann Brockhaus, at whose house we had been invited to dine, and where, during the meal, the conversation was most animated. Besides this, we had met at real musical evenings at the conductor Hauptmann's as well as at Mendelssohn's, on which occasion I heard the master take the violin in one of his own quartettes. It was precisely in these circles that I was impressed by the touching and venerable dignity of his absolutely calm demeanour. Later on, I learned from witnesses — for whose testimony, be it said, I cannot vouch — that *Tannhäuser,* when it was performed at Cassel, had caused him so much confusion and pain that he declared he could no longer follow me, and feared that I must be on the wrong road.

In order to recover from all the hardships and cares I had gone through, I now managed to obtain a special favour from the management, in the form of a three months' leave, in which to improve my health in rustic retirement, and to get pure air to breathe while composing some new work. To this end I had chosen a peasant's house in the village of Gross-Graupen, which is half-way between Pillnitz and the border of what is known as 'Saxon Switzerland.' Frequent excursions to the Porsberg, to the adjacent Liebethaler, and to the far distant bastion helped to strengthen my unstrung nerves. While I was first planning the music to *Lohengrin,* I was disturbed incessantly by the echoes of some of the airs in Rossini's *William Tell,* which was the last opera I had had to conduct. At last I happened to hit on an effective means of stopping this annoying obtrusion: during my lonely walks I sang with great emphasis the first theme from the Ninth Symphony, which had also quite lately been revived in my memory. This succeeded! At Pirna, where one can bathe in the river, I was surprised, on one of my almost regular evening constitutionals, to hear the air from the Pilgrim's Chorus out of *Tannhäuser* whistled by some bather, who was invisible to me. This first sign of the possibility of popularising the work, which I had with such difficulty succeeded in getting performed in Dresden, made an impression on me which no similar experience later on has ever been able to surpass. Sometimes I received visits from friends in Dresden, and among them Hans von Bülow, who was then sixteen years old, came accompanied by Lipinsky. This gave me great pleasure, because I had already noticed the interest which he took in me. Generally, however, I had to rely only on my wife's company, and during my long walks I had to be satisfied with my little dog Peps. During this summer holiday, of which a great part of the time had at the beginning to be devoted to the unpleasant task of arranging my business affairs, and also to the improvement of my health, I nevertheless succeded in making a sketch of the music to the whole of the three acts of *Lohengrin,* although this cannot be said to have consisted of anything more than a very hasty outline.

With this much gained, I returned in August to Dresden, and resumed my duties as conductor, which every year seemed to become more and more burdensome to me. Moreover, I immediately plunged once more into the midst of troubles which had only just been temporarily allayed. The business of publishing my operas, on the success of which I still counted as the only means of liberating me from my difficult position, demanded ever-fresh sacrifices if the enterprise were to be made worth while. But as my income was now very much reduced, even the smallest outlays necessarily led me into ever-new and more painful complications; and I once more lost all courage.

On the other hand, I tried to strengthen myself by again working energetically at *Lohengrin.* While doing this, I proceeded in a manner that I have not since repeated. I first of all completed the third act, and in view of the criticism already mentioned of the characters and conclusion of this act, I determined to try to make it the very pivot of the whole opera. I wished to do this, if only for the sake of the musical motive appearing in the story of the Holy Grail; but in other respects the plan struck me as perfectly satisfactory.

Owing to previous suggestions on my part, Gluck's *Iphigenia in Aulis* was to be produced this winter. I felt it my duty to give more care and attention to this work, which interested me particularly on account of its subject, than I had given to the study of the *Armida.* In the first place, I was upset by the translation in which the opera with the Berlin score was presented to us. In order not to be led into false interpretations through the instrumental additions which I considered very badly applied in this score, I wrote for the original edition from Paris. When I had made a thorough revision of the translation, with a view merely to the correctness of declamation, I was spurred on by my increasing interest to revise the score itself. I tried to bring the poem as far as possible into agreement with Euripides' play of the same name, by the elimination of everything which, in deference to French taste, made the relationship between Achilles and Iphigenia one of tender love. The chief alteration of all was to cut out the inevitable marriage at the end. For the sake of the vitality of the drama I tried to join the arias and choruses, which generally followed immediately upon each other without rhyme or reason, by connecting links, prologues and epilogues. In this I did my best, by the use of Gluck's themes, to make the interpolations of a strange composer as unnoticeable as possible. In the third act alone was I obliged to give Iphigenia, as well as Artemis, whom I had myself introduced, recitatives of my own composition. Throughout the rest of the work I revised the whole instrumentation more or less thoroughly, but only with the object of making the existing version produce the effect I desired. It was not till the end of the year that I was able to finish this tremendous task, and I had to postpone the completion of the third act of *Lohengrin,* which I had already begun, until the New Year.

The first thing to claim my attention at the beginning of the year (1847) was the production of *Iphigenia*. I had to act as stage manager in this case, and was even obliged to help the scene-painters and the mechanicians over the smallest details. Owing to the fact that the scenes in this opera were generally strung together somewhat clumsily and without any apparent connection, it was necessary to recast them completely, in order so to animate the representation as to give to the dramatic action the life it lacked. A good deal of this faultiness of construction seemed to me due to the many conventional practices which were prevalent at the Paris Opera in Gluck's time. Mitterwurzer was the only actor in the whole cast who gave me any pleasure. In the rôle of Agamemnon he showed a thorough grasp of that character, and carried out my instructions and suggestions to the letter, so that he succeeded in giving a really splendid and intelligent rendering of the part. The success of the whole performance was far beyond my expectations, and even the directors were so surprised at the exceptional enthusiasm aroused by one of Gluck's operas, that for the second performance they, on their own initiative, had my name put on the programme as 'Reviser.' This at once drew the attention of the critics to this work, and for once they almost did me justice; my treatment of the overture, the only part of the opera which these gentlemen heard rendered in the usual trivial way, was the only thing that they could find fault with. I have discussed and given an accurate account of all that relates to this in a special article on 'Gluck's Overture to *Iphigenia in Aulis*,' and I only wish to add here that the musician who made such strange comments on this occasion was Ferdinand Hiller.

As in former years, the winter meetings of the various artistic elements in Dresden which Hiller had inaugurated, continued to take place; but they now assumed more the character of 'salons' in Hiller's own house, and it seemed to me intended solely for the purpose of laying the foundations for a general recognition of Hiller's artistic greatness. He had already founded, among the more wealthy patrons of art, the chief of whom was the banker Kaskel, a society for running subscription concerts. As it was impossible for the royal orchestra to be placed at his disposal for this purpose, he had to content himself with members of the town and military bands for his orchestra, and it cannot be denied that, thanks to his perseverance, he attained a praiseworthy result. As he produced many compositions which were still unknown in Dresden, especially from the domain of more modern music, I was often tempted to go to his concerts. His chief bait to the general public, however, seemed to lie in the fact that he presented unknown singers (among whom, unfortunately, Jenny Lind was not to be found) and virtuosos, one of which, Joachim, who was then very young, I became acquainted with.

Hiller's treatment of those works with which I was already well acquainted, showed what his musical power was really worth. The careless and indifferent manner in which he interpreted a Triple Concerto by Sebastian Bach positively astounded me. In the *tempo di minuetto* of the Eighth Symphony of Beethoven, I found that Hiller's rendering was even

STUDY OF GREEK ANTIQUITY

more astonishing than Reissiger's and Mendelssohn's. I promised to be present at the performance of this symphony if I could rely on his giving a correct rendering of the tempo of the third phrase, which was generally so painfully distorted. He assured me that he thoroughly agreed with me about it, and my disappointment at the performance was all the greater when I found the well-known waltz measure adopted again. When I called him to account about it he excused himself with a smile, saying that he had been seized with a fit of temporary abstraction just at the beginning of the phrase in question, which had made him forget his promise. For inaugurating these concerts, which, as a matter of fact, only lasted for two seasons, Hiller was given a banquet, which I also had much pleasure in attending.

People in these circles were surprised at that time to hear me speak, often with great animation, about Greek literature and history, but never about music. In the course of my reading, which I zealously pursued, and which drew me away from my professional activities to retirement and solitude, I was at that time impelled by my spiritual needs to turn my attention once more to a systematic study of this all-important source of culture, with the object of filling the perceptible gap between my boyhood's knowledge of the eternal elements of human culture and the neglect of this field of learning due to the life I had been obliged to lead. In order to approach the real goal of my desires — the study of Old and Middle High German — in the right frame of mind, I began again from the beginning with Greek antiquity, and was now filled with such overwhelming enthusiasm for this subject that, whenever I entered into conversation, and by hook or by crook had managed to get it round to this theme, I could only speak in terms of the strongest emotion. I occasionally met some one who seemed to listen to what I had to say; on the whole, however, people preferred to talk to me only about the theatre because, since my production of Gluck's *Iphigenia,* they thought themselves justified in thinking I was an authority on this subject. I received special recognition from a man to whom I quite rightly gave the credit of being at least as well versed as myself in the matter. This was Eduard Devrient, who had been forced at that time to resign his position as stage manager-in-chief owing to a plot against him on the part of the actors, headed by his own brother Emil. We were brought into closer sympathy by our conversations in connection with this, which led him into dissertations on the triviality and thorough hopelessness of our whole theatrical life, especially under the ruining influence of ignorant court managers, which could never be overcome.

We were also drawn together by his intelligent understanding of the part I had played in the production of *Iphigenia,* which he compared with the Berlin production of the same piece, that had been utterly condemned by him. He was for a long time the only man with whom I could discuss, seriously and in detail, the real needs of the theatre and the means by which its defects might be remedied. Owing to his longer and more specialised experience, there was much he could tell me and make clear to me; in particular he helped me successfully to overcome the idea that mere literary excellence is enough for the theatre, and confirmed my conviction that the path to true prosperity lay only with the stage itself and with the actors of the drama.

From this time forward, till I left Dresden, my intercourse with Eduard Devrient grew more and more friendly, though his dry nature and obvious limitations as an actor had attracted me but little before. His highly meritorious work, *Die Geschichte der deutschen Schauspielkunst* ('History of German Dramatic Art'), which he finished and published about that time, threw a fresh and instructive light on many problems which exercised my mind, and helped me to master them for the first time.

At last I managed once more to resume my task of composing the third act of *Lohengrin,* which had been interrupted in the middle of the Bridal Scene, and I finished it by the end of the winter. After the repetition, by special request, of the Ninth Symphony at the concert on Palm Sunday had revived me, I tried to find comfort and refreshment for the further progress of my new work by changing my abode, this time without asking permission. The old Marcolini palace, with a very large garden laid out partly in the French style, was situated in an outlying and thinly populated suburb of Dresden.

THE MARCOLINI PALACE

It had been sold to the town council, and a part of it was to be let. The sculptor, Hänel, whom I had known for a long time, and who had given me as a mark of friendship an ornament in the shape of a perfect plaster cast of one of the bas-reliefs from Beethoven's monument representing the Ninth Symphony, had taken the large rooms on the ground floor of a side-wing of this palace for his dwelling and studio. At Easter I moved into the spacious apartments above him, the rent of which was extremely low, and found that the large garden planted with glorious trees, which was placed at my disposal, and the pleasant stillness of the whole place, not only provided mental food for the weary artist, but at the same time, by lessening my expenses, improved my straitened finances. We soon settled down quite comfortably in the long row of pleasant rooms without having incurred any unnecessary expense, as Minna was very practical in her arrangements. The only real inconvenience which in the course of time I found our new home possessed, was its inordinate distance from the theatre. This was a great trial to me after fatiguing rehearsals and tiring performances, as the expense of a cab was a serious consideration. But we were favoured by an exceptionally fine summer, which put me in a happy frame of mind, and soon helped to overcome every inconvenience.

At this time I insisted with the utmost firmness on refraining from taking any further share in the management of the theatre, and I had most cogent reasons to bring forth in defence of my conduct. All my endeavours to set in order the wilful chaos which prevailed in the use of the costly artistic materials at the disposal of this royal institution were repeatedly thwarted, merely because I wished to introduce some method into the arrangements. In a carefully written pamphlet which, in addition to my other work, I had compiled during the past winter, I had drawn up a plan for the reorganisation of the orchestra, and had shown how we might increase the productive power of our artistic capital by making a more methodical use of the royal funds intended for its maintenance, and showing greater discretion regarding salaries. This increase in the productive power would raise the artistic spirit as well as improve the economic position of the members of the orchestra, for I should have liked them at the same time to form an independent concert society. In such a capacity it would have been their task to present to the people of Dresden, in the best possible way, a kind of music which they had hitherto hardly had the opportunity of enjoying at all. It would have been possible for such a union, which, as I pointed out, had so many external circumstances in its favour, to provide Dresden with a suitable concert-hall. I hear, however, that such a place is wanting to this day.

With this object in view I entered into close communication with architects and builders, and the plans were completed, according to which the scandalous buildings facing a wing of the renowned prison opposite the Ostra Allee, and consisting of a shed for the members of the theatre and a public wash-house, were to be pulled down and replaced by a beautiful building, which, besides containing a large concert-hall adapted to our requirements, would also have had other large rooms which could have been let out on hire at a profit. The practicality of these plans was disputed by no one, as even the administrators of the orchestra's widows' fund saw in them an opportunity for the safe and advantageous laying out of capital; yet they were returned to me, after long consideration on the part of the general management, with thanks and an acknowledgment of my careful work, and the curt reply that it was thought better for things to remain as they were.

All my proposals for meeting the useless waste and drain upon our artistic capital by a more methodical arrangement, met with the same success in every detail that I suggested. I had also found out by long experience that every proposal which had to be discussed and decided upon in the most tiring committee meetings, as for instance the starting of a repertoire, might at any moment be overthrown and altered for the worse by the temper of a singer or the plan of a junior business inspector. I was therefore driven to renounce my wasted efforts and, after many a stormy discussion and outspoken expression of my sentiments, I withdrew from taking any part whatever in any branch of the management, and limited myself entirely to holding rehearsals and conducting performances of the operas provided for me.

Although my relations with Lüttichau grew more and more strained on this account, for the time being it mattered little whether my conduct pleased him or not, as otherwise my position was one which commanded respect, on account of the ever-increasing popularity of *Tannhäuser* and *Rienzi,* which were presented during the summer to houses packed with distinguished visitors, and were invariably chosen for the gala performances.

By thus going my own way and refusing to be interfered with, I succeeded this summer, amid the delightful and perfect seclusion of my new home, in preserving myself in a frame of mind exceedingly favourable to the completion of my *Lohengrin*. My studies, which, as I have already mentioned, I pursued eagerly at the same time as I was working on my opera, made me feel more light-hearted than I had ever done before. For the first time I now mastered Æschylus with real feeling and understanding. Droysen's eloquent commentaries in particular helped to bring before my imagination the intoxicating effect of the production of an Athenian tragedy, so that I could see the *Oresteia* with my mind's eye, as though it were actually being performed, and its effect upon me was indescribable. Nothing, however, could equal the sublime emotion with which the *Agamemnon* trilogy inspired me, and to the last word of the *Eumenides* I lived in an atmosphere so far removed from the present day that I have never since been really able to reconcile myself with modern literature. My ideas about the whole significance of the drama and of the theatre were, without a doubt, moulded by these impressions. I worked my way through the other tragedians, and finally reached Aristophanes. When I had spent the morning industriously upon the completion of the music for *Lohengrin,* I used to creep into the depths of a thick shrubbery in my part of the garden to get shelter from the summer heat, which was becoming more intense every day. My delight in the comedies of Aristophanes was boundless, when once his *Birds* had plunged me into the full torrent of the genius of this wanton favourite of the Graces, as he used to call himself with conscious daring. Side by side with this poet I read the principal dialogues of Plato, and from the *Symposium* I gained such a deep insight into the wonderful beauty of Greek life that I felt myself more truly at home in ancient Athens than in any conditions which the modern world has to offer.

As I was following out a settled course of self-education, I did not wish to pursue my way further in the leading-strings of any literary history, and I consequently turned my attention from the historical studies, which seemed to be my own peculiar province, and in which department Droysen's history of Alexander and the Hellenistic period, as well as Niebuhr and Gibbon, were of great help to me, and fell back once more upon my old and trusty guide, Jakob Grimm, for the study of German aniquity. In my efforts to master the myths of Germany more thoroughly than had been possible in my former perusal of the *Nibelung* and the *Heldenbuch*, Mone's particularly suggestive commentary on this *Heldensage* filled me with delight, although stricter scholars regarded this work with suspicion on account of the boldness of some of its statements. By this means I was drawn irresistibly to the northern sagas; and I now tried, as far as was possible without a fluent knowledge of the Scandinavian languages, to acquaint myself with the *Edda,* as well as with the prose version which existed of a considerable portion of the *Heldensage*.

Read by the light of Mone's Commentaries, the *Wolsungasaga* had a decided influence upon my method of handling this material. My conceptions as to the inner significance of these old-world legends, which had been growing for a long time, gradually gained strength and moulded themselves with the plastic forms which inspired my later works.

All this was sinking into my mind and slowly maturing, whilst with unfeigned delight I was finishing the music of the first two acts of *Lohengrin,* which were now at last completed. I now succeeded in shutting out the past and building up for myself a new world of the future, which presented itself with ever-growing clearness to my mind as the refuge whither I might retreat from all the miseries of modern opera and theatre life. At the same time, my health and temper were settling down into a mood of almost unclouded serenity, which made me oblivious for a long time of all the worries of my position. I used to walk every day up into the neighbouring hills, which rose from the banks of the Elbe to the Plauenscher Grund. I generally went alone, except for the company of our little dog Peps, and my excursions always resulted in producing a satisfactory number of ideas. At the same time, I found I had developed a capacity, which I had never possessed before, for good-tempered intercourse with the friends and acquaintances who liked to come from time to time to the Marcolini garden to share my simple supper. My visitors used often to find me perched on a high branch of a tree, or on the neck of the Neptune which was the central figure of a large group of statuary in the middle of an old fountain, unfortunately always dry, belonging to the palmy days of the Marcolini estate. I used to enjoy walking with my friends up and down the broad footpath of the drive leading to the real palace, which had been laid especially for Napoleon in the fatal year 1813, when he had fixed his headquarters there.

By August, the last month of summer, I had completely finished the composition of *Lohengrin,* and felt that it was high time for me to have done so, as the needs of my position demanded imperatively that I should give my most serious attention to improving it, and it became a matter of supreme importance for me once more to take steps for having my operas produced in the German theatres.

Even the success of *Tannhäuser* in Dresden, which became more obvious every day, did not attract the smallest notice anywhere else. Berlin was the only place which had any influence in the theatrical world of Germany, and I ought long before to have given my undivided attention to that city. From all I had heard of the special tastes of Friedrich Wilhelm IV., I felt perfectly justified in assuming that he would feel sympathetically inclined towards my later works and conceptions if I could only manage to bring them to his notice in the right light. On this hypothesis I had already thought of dedicating *Tannhäuser* to him, and to gain permission to do so I had to apply to Count Redern, the court musical director. From him I heard that the King could only accept the dedication of works which had actually been performed in his presence, and of which he thus had a personal knowledge. As my *Tannhäuser* had been refused by the managers of the court theatre because it was considered too epic in form, the Count added that if I wished to remain firm in my resolve, there was only one way out of the difficulty, and that was to adapt my opera as far as possible to a military band, and try to bring it to the King's notice on parade. This drove me to determine upon another plan of attack on Berlin.

After this experience I saw that I must open my campaign there with the opera that had won the most decided triumph in Dresden. I therefore obtained an audience of the Queen of Saxony, the sister of the King of Prussia, and begged her to use her influence with her brother to obtain a performance in Berlin by royal command of my *Rienzi,* which was also a favourite with the court of Saxony. This manœuvre was successful, and I soon received a communication from my old friend Küstner to say that the production of *Rienzi* was fixed for a very early date at the Berlin Court Theatre, and at the same time expressing the hope that I would conduct my work in person. As a very handsome author's royalty had been paid by this theatre, at the instigation of Küstner, on the occasion of the production of his old Munich friend Lachner's opera, *Katharina von Cornaro,* I hoped to realise a very substantial improvement in my finances if only the success of *Rienzi* in this city in any degree rivalled that in Dresden. But my chief desire was to make the acquaintance of the King of Prussia, so that I might read him the text of my *Lohengrin,* and arouse his interest in my work. This from various signs I flattered myself was perfectly possible, in which case I intended to beg him to command the first performance of *Lohengrin* to be given at his court theatre.

After my strange experiences as to the way in which my success in Dresden had been kept secret from the rest of Germany, it seemed to me a matter of vital importance to make the future centre of my artistic enterprises the only place which exercised any influence on the outside world, and as such I was forced to regard Berlin. Inspired by the success of my recommendation to the Queen of Prussia, I hoped to gain access to the King himself, which I regarded as a most important step. Full of confidence, and in excellent spirits, I set out for Berlin in September, trusting to a favourable turn of

Fortune's wheel, in the first place for the rehearsals of *Rienzi,* though my interests were no longer centred in this work.

Berlin made the same impression on me as on the occasion of my former visit, when I saw it again after my long absence in Paris. Professor Werder, my friend of the *Fliegender Holländer,* had taken lodgings for me in advance in the renowned Gensdarmeplatz, but when I looked at the view from my windows every day I could not believe that I was in a city which was the very centre of Germany. Soon, however, I was completely absorbed by the cares of the task I had in hand.

I had nothing to complain of with regard to the official preparations for *Rienzi,* but I soon noticed that it was looked upon merely as a conductor's opera, that is to say, all the materials to hand were duly placed at my disposal, but the management had not the slightest intention of doing anything more for me. All the arrangements for my rehearsals were entirely upset as soon as a visit from Jenny Lind was announced, and she occupied the Royal Opera exclusively for some time.

During the delay thus caused I did all I could to attain my main object — an introduction to the King — and for this purpose made use of my former acquaintance with the court musical director, Count Redern. This gentleman received me at once with the greatest affability, invited me to dinner and a soirée, and entered into a hearty discussion with me about the steps necessary for attaining my purpose, in which he promised to do his utmost to help me. I also paid frequent visits to Sans-Souci, in order to pay my respects to the Queen and express my thanks to her. But I never got further than an interview with the ladies-in-waiting, and I was advised to put myself into communication with M. Illaire, the head of the Royal Privy Council. This gentleman seemed to be impressed by the seriousness of my request, and promised to do what he could to further my wish for a personal introduction to the King. He asked what my real object was, and I told him it was to get permission from the King to read my libretto *Lohengrin* to him. On the occasion of one of my oft-repeated visits from Berlin, he asked me whether I did not think it would be advisable to bring a recommendation of my work from Tieck. I was able to tell him that I had already had the pleasure of bringing my case to the notice of the old poet, who lived near Potsdam as a royal pensioner.

I remembered very well that Frau von Lüttichau had sent the themes *Lohengrin* and *Tannhäuser* to her old friend some years ago, when these matters were first mentioned between us. When I called upon Tieck, I was welcomed by him almost as a friend, and I found my long talks with him exceedingly valuable. Although Tieck had perhaps gained a somewhat doubtful reputation for the leniency with which he would give his recommendation for the dramatic works of those who applied to him, yet I was pleased by the genuine disgust with which he spoke of our latest dramatic literature, which was modelling itself on the style of modern French stagecraft, and his complaint at the utter lack of any true poetic feeling in it was heartfelt. He declared himself delighted with my poem of *Lohengrin*, but could not understand how all this was to be set to music without a complete change in the conventional structure of an opera, and on this score he objected to such scenes as that between Ortrud and Frederick at the beginning of the second act. I thought I had roused him to a real enthusiasm when I explained how I proposed to solve these apparent difficulties, and also described my own ideals about musical drama. But the higher I soared the sadder he grew when I had once made known to him my hope of securing the patronage of the King of Prussia for these conceptions, and the working out of my scheme for an ideal drama. He had no doubt that the King would listen to me with the greatest interest, and even seize upon my ideas with warmth, only I must not entertain the smallest hope of any practical result, unless I wished to expose myself to the bitterest disappointment. 'What can you expect from a man who to-day is enthusiastic about Gluck's *Iphigenia in Tauris*, and to-morrow mad about Donizetti's *Lucrezia Borgia?*' he said. Tieck's conversation about these and similar topics was much too entertaining and charming for me to give any serious weight to the bitterness of his views. He gladly promised to recommend my poem, more particularly to Privy Councillor Illaire, and dismissed me with hearty goodwill and his sincere though anxious blessing.

The only result of all my labours was that the desired invitation from the King still hung fire. As the rehearsals for *Rienzi,* which had been postponed on account of Jenny Lind's visit, were being carried on seriously again, I made up my mind to take no further trouble before the performance of my opera, as I thought myself, at any rate, justified in counting on the presence of the monarch on the first night, as the piece was being played at his express command, and at the same time I hoped this would conduce to the fulfilment of my main object. However, the nearer we came to the event the lower did the hopes I had built upon it sink. To play the part of the hero I had to be satisfied with a tenor who was absolutely devoid of talent, and far below the average. He was a conscientious, painstaking man, and had moreover been strongly recommended to me by my kind host, the renowned Meinhard. After I had taken infinite pains with him, and had in consequence, as so often happens, conjured up in my mind certain illusions as to what I might expect from his acting, I was obliged, when it came to the final test of the dress rehearsal, to confess my true opinion. I realised that the scenery, chorus, ballet, and minor parts were on the whole excellent, but that the chief character, around whom in this particular opera everything centred, faded into an insignificant phantom. The reception which this opera met with at the hands of the public when it was produced in October was also due to him; but in consequence of the fairly good rendering of a few brilliant passages, and more especially on account of the enthusiastic recognition of Frau Köster in the part of Adriano, it might have been concluded from all the external signs that the opera had been fairly successful. Nevertheless, I knew very well that this seeming triumph could have no real substance, as only the immaterial parts of my work could reach the eyes and ears of the audience; its essential spirit had not entered their hearts. Moreover, the Berlin reviewers in their usual way began their attacks immediately, with the view of demolishing any success my opera might have won, so that after the second performance, which I also conducted myself, I began to wonder whether my desperate labours were really worth while.

When I asked the few intimate friends I had their opinion on this point, I elicited much valuable information. Among these friends I must mention, in the first place, Hermann Franck, whom I found again. He had lately settled in Berlin, and did much to encourage me. I spent the most enjoyable part of those sad two months in his company, of which, however, I had but too little. Our conversation generally turned upon reminiscences of the old days, and on to topics which had no connection with the theatre, so that I was almost ashamed to trouble him with my complaints on this subject, especially as they concerned my worries about a work which I could not pretend was of any practical importance to the stage. He for his part soon arrived at the conclusion that it had been foolish of me to choose my *Rienzi* for this occasion, as it was an opera which appealed merely to the general public, in preference to my *Tannhäuser*, which might have educated a party in Berlin useful to my higher aims. He maintained that the very nature of this work would have aroused a fresh interest in the drama in the minds of people who, like himself, were no longer to be counted among regular theatre-goers, precisely because they had given up all hope of ever finding any nobler ideals of the stage.

The curious information as to the character of Berlin art in other respects, which Werder gave me from time to time, was most discouraging. With regard to the public, he told me once that at a performance of an unknown work, it was quite useless for me to expect a single member of the audience from the stalls to the gallery to take his seat with any better object in view than to pick as many holes as possible in the production. Although Werder did not wish to discourage me in any of my endeavours, he felt himself obliged to warn me continually not to expect anything above the average from the cultured society of Berlin. He liked to see proper respect paid to the really considerable gifts of the King; and when I asked him how he thought the latter would receive my ideas about the ennobling of opera, he answered, after having listened attentively to a long and fiery tirade on my part: 'The King would say to you, "Go and consult Stawinsky!"' This was the opera manager, a fat, smug creature who had grown rusty in following out the most jog-trot routine. In short, everything I learned was calculated to discourage me. I called on Bernhard Marx, who some years ago had shown a kindly interest in my *Fliegender Holländer,* and was courteously received by him. This man, who in his earlier writings and musical criticisms had seemed to me filled with a fire of energy, now struck me as extraordinarily limp and listless when I saw him by the side of his young wife, who was radiantly and bewitchingly beautiful. From his conversation I soon learned that he also had abandoned even the remotest hope of success for any efforts directed towards the object so dear to both our hearts, on account of the inconceivable shallowness of all the officials connected with the head authority. He told me of the extraordinary fate which had befallen a scheme he had brought to the notice of the King for founding a school of music. In a special audience the King had gone into the matter with the greatest interest, and noticed the minutest detail, so that Marx felt justified in entertaining the strongest possible hopes of success. However, all his labours and negotiations about the business, in the course of which he was driven from pillar to post, proved utterly futile, until at last he was told to have an interview with a certain general. This personage, like the King, had Marx's proposals explained to him in the minutest detail, and expressed his warmest sympathy with the undertaking. 'And there,' said Marx, at the end of this long rigmarole, ' the matter ended, and I never heard another word about it.'

One day I learned that Countess Rossi, the renowned Henriette Sontag, who was living in quiet seclusion in Berlin, had pleasant recollections of me in Dresden, and wished me to visit her. She had at this time already fallen into the unfortunate position which was so detrimental to her artistic career. She too complained bitterly of the general apathy of the influential classes in Berlin, which effectually prevented any artistic aims from being realised. It was her opinion that the King found a sort of satisfaction in knowing that the theatre was badly managed, for though he never opposed any criticisms which he received on the subject, he likewise never supported any proposal for its improvement. She expressed a wish to know something of my latest work, and I gave her my poem of

Lohengrin for perusal. On the occasion of my next morning call she told me she would send me an invitation to a musical evening which she was going to have at her house in honour of the Grand Duke of Mecklenburg-Strelitz, her elderly patron, and she also gave me back the manuscript of *Lohengrin,* with the assurance that it had appealed to her very much, and that while she was reading it she had often seen the little fairies and elves dancing about in front of her. As in the old days I had been heartily encouraged by the warm and friendly sympathy of this naturally cultured woman, I now felt as if cold water had been suddenly poured down my back. I soon took my leave, and never saw her again. Indeed, I had no particular object in doing so, as the promised invitation never came. Herr E. Kossak also sought me out, and although our acquaintance did not lead to much, I was sufficiently kindly received by him to give him my poem of *Lohengrin* to read. I went one day by appointment to see him, and found that his room had just been scrubbed with boiling water. The steam from this operation was so unbearable that it had already given him a headache, and was not less disagreeable to me. He looked into my face with an almost tender expression when he gave me back the manuscript of my poem, and assured me, in accents which admitted of no doubt of his sincerity, that he thought it 'very pretty.'

I found my casual intercourse with H. Truhn rather more entertaining. I used to treat him to a good glass of wine at Lutter and Wegener's, where I went occasionally on account of its association with Hoffmann, and he would then listen with apparently growing interest to my ideas as to the possible development of opera and the goal at which we should aim. His comments were generally witty and very much to the point, and his lively and animated ways pleased me very much. After the production of *Rienzi,* however, he too, as a critic, joined the majority of scoffers and detractors. The only person who supported me stoutly but uselessly, through thick and thin, was my old friend Gaillard. His little music-shop was not a success, his musical journal had already failed, so that he was only able to help me in small ways. Unfortunately I discovered not only that he was the author of many exceedingly dubious dramatic works, for which he wished to gain my support, but also that he was apparently in the last stages of the disease from which he was suffering, so that the little intercourse I had with him, in spite of all his fidelity and devotion, only exercised a melancholy and depressing influence upon me.

But as I had embarked upon this Berlin enterprise in contradiction to all my inmost wishes, and prompted solely by the desire of winning the success so vital to my position, I made up my mind to make a personal appeal to Rellstab.

As in the case of the *Fliegender Holländer* he had taken exception more particularly to its 'nebulousness' and 'lack of form,' I thought I might with advantage point out to him the brighter and clearer outline of *Rienzi*. He seemed to be pleased at my thinking I could get anything out of him, but told me at once of his firm conviction that any new art form was utterly impossible after Gluck, and that the only thing that the best of good luck and hard work was capable of producing was meaningless bombast. I then realised that in Berlin all hope had been abandoned. I was told that Meyerbeer was the only man who had been able in any way to master the situation.

This former patron of mine I met once more in Berlin, and he declared that he still took an interest in me. As soon as I arrived I called on him, but in the hall I found his servant busy packing up trunks, and learned that Meyerbeer was just going away. His master confirmed this assertion, and regretted that he would not be able to do anything for me, so I had to say good-bye and how-do-you-do at the same time. For some time I thought he really was away, but after a few weeks I learned to my surprise that he was still staying in Berlin without letting himself be seen by any one, and at last he made his appearance again at one of the rehearsals of *Rienzi*. What this meant I only discovered later from a rumour which was circulated among the initiated, and imparted to me by Eduard von Bülow, my young friend's father. Without having the slightest idea how it originated, I learned, about the middle of my stay in Berlin, from the conductor Taubert, that he had heard on very good authority that I was trying for a director's post at the court theatre, and had good expectations of securing the appointment in addition to special privileges. In order to remain on good terms with Taubert, as it was very necessary for me to do, I had to give him the most solemn assurances that such an idea had never even entered my head, and that I would not accept such a position if it were offered to me. On the other hand, all my endeavours to get access to the King continued to be fruitless. My chief mediator, to whom I always turned, was still Count Redern, and although my attention had been called to his staunch adherence to Meyerbeer, his extraordinary open and friendly manner always strengthened my belief in his honesty. At last the only medium that remained open to me was the fact that the King could not possibly stay away from the performance of *Rienzi*, given at his express command, and on this conviction I based all further hope of approaching him. Whereupon Count Redern informed me, with an expression of deep despair, that on the very day of the first performance the monarch would be away on a hunting party. Once more I begged him to make very effort in his power to secure the King's presence, at least at the second performance, and at length my inexhaustible patron told me that he could not make head or tail of it, but his Majesty seemed to have conceived an utter disinclination to accede to my wish; he himself had heard these hard words fall from the royal lips: 'Oh bother! have you come to me again with your *Rienzi?*'

At this second performance I had a pleasant experience. After the impressive second act the public showed signs of wishing to call me, and as I went from the orchestra to the vestibule, in order to be ready if necessary, my foot slipped on the smooth parquet, and I might have had perhaps a serious fall had I not felt my arm prasped by a strong hand. I turned, and recognised the Crown Prince of Prussia,[1] who had come out of his box, and who at once seized the opportunity of inviting me to follow him to his wife, who wished to make my acquaintance. She had only just arrived in Berlin, and told me that she had heard my opera for the first time that evening, and

---

[1] This Prince subsequently became the Emperor William the First. He was given the title of Crown Prince in 1840 on the death of his father, Frederick William III., as he was then heir-presumptive to his brother, Frederick William IV., whose marriage was without issue. — EDITOR.

SAD DEPARTURE FROM BERLIN

expressed her appreciation of it. She had, however, long ago received very favourable reports of me and my artistic aims from a common friend, Alwine Frommann. The whole tenor of this interview, at which the Prince was present, was unusually friendly and pleasant.

It was indeed my old friend Alwine who in Berlin had not only followed all my fortunes with the greatest sympathy, but had also done all in her power to give me consolation and courage to endure. Almost every evening, when the day's business made it possible, I used to visit her for an hour of recreation, and gain strength from her ennobling conversation for the struggle against the reverses of the following day. I was particularly pleased by the warm and intelligent sympathy which she and our mutual friend Werder devoted to *Lohengrin*, the object of all my labours at that time. On the arrival of her friend and patroness, the Crown Princess, which had been delayed till now, she hoped to hear something more definite as to how my affairs stood with the King, although she intimated to me that even this great lady was in deep disfavour, and could only bring her influence to bear upon the King by observing the strictest etiquette. But from this source also no news reached me till it was time for me to leave Berlin and I could postpone my departure no longer.

As I had to conduct a third performance of *Rienzi*, and there still remained a remote possibility of receiving a sudden command to Sans-Souci, I accordingly fixed on a date which would be the very latest I could wait to ascertain the fate of the projects I had nearest to heart. This period passed by, and I was forced to realise that my hopes of Berlin were wholly shattered.

I was in a very depressed state when I made up my mind to this conclusion. I can seldom remember having been so dreadfully affected by the influence of cold and wet weather and an eternally grey sky as during those last wretched weeks in Berlin, when everything that I heard, in addition to my own private anxieties, weighed upon me with a leaden weight of discouragement.

My conversations with Hermann Franck about the social and political situation had assumed a peculiarly gloomy tone, as the King of Prussia's efforts to summon a united conference had failed. I was among those who had at first been inclined to see a hopeful significance in this undertaking, but it was a shock to have all the intimate details relating to the project clearly set before me by so well informed a man as Franck. His dispassionate views on this subject, as well as on the Prussian State in particular, which was supposed to be representative of German intelligence, and was universally considered to be a model of order and good government, so completely disillusioned me and destroyed all the favourable and hopeful opinions I had formed of it, that I felt as if I had plunged into chaos, and realised the utter futility of expecting a prosperous settlement of the German question from this quarter. If in the midst of my misery in Dresden I had founded great hopes from gaining the King of Prussia's sympathy for my ideas, I could no longer close my eyes to the fearful hollowness which the state of affairs disclosed to me on every side.

In this despairing mood I felt but little emotion when, on going to say good-bye to Count Redern, he told me with a very sad face the news, which had just arrived, of Mendelssohn's death. I certainly did not realise this stroke of fate, which Redern's obvious grief first brought to my notice. At all events, he was spared more detailed and heartfelt explanation of my own affairs, which he had so much at heart.

The only thing that remained for me to do in Berlin was to try and make my material success balance my material loss. For a stay of two months, during which my wife and my sister Clara had been with me, lured on by the hope that the production of *Rienzi* in Berlin would be a brilliant success, I found my old friend, Director Küstner, by no means inclined to compensate me. From his correspondence with me he could prove up to the hilt that legally he had only expressed the desire for my co-operation in studying *Rienzi,* but had given me no positive invitation. As I was prevented by Count Redern's grief over Mendelssohn's death from going to him for help in these trivial private concerns, there was no alternative but for me to accept with a good grace Küstner's beneficence in paying me on the spot the royalties on the three performances which had already taken place. The Dresden authorities were surprised when I found myself obliged to beg an advance of income from them in order to conclude this brilliant undertaking in Berlin.

As I was travelling with my wife in the most horrible weather through the deserted country on my way home, I fell into a mood of the blackest despair, which I thought I might perhaps survive once in a lifetime but never again. Nevertheless, it amused me, as I sat silently looking out of the carriage into the grey mist, to hear my wife enter into a lively discussion with a commercial traveller who, in the course of friendly conversation, had spoken in a disparaging way about the 'new opera *Rienzi*.' My wife, with great heat and even passion, corrected various mistakes made by this hostile critic, and to her great satisfaction made him confess that he had not heard the opera himself, but had only based his opinion upon hearsay and the reviews. Whereupon my wife pointed out to him most earnestly that ' he could not possibly know whose future he might not injure by such irresponsible comment.'

These were the only cheering and consoling impressions which I carried back with me to Dresden, where I soon felt the direct results of the reverses I had suffered in Berlin in the condolences of my acquaintances. The papers had spread abroad the news that my opera had been a dismal failure. The most painful part of the whole proceeding was that I had to meet these expressions of pity with a cheerful countenance and the assurance that things were by no means so bad as had been made out, but that, on the contrary, I had had many pleasant experiences.

This unaccustomed effort placed me in a position strangely similar to that in which I found Hiller on my return to Dresden. He had given a performance of his new opera, *Conradin von Hohenstaufen,* here just about this time. He had kept the composition of this work a secret from me, and had hoped to make a decided hit with it after the three performances which took place in my absence. Both the poet and the composer thought that in this work they had combined the tendencies and effects of my *Rienzi* with those of my *Tannhäuser* in a manner peculiarly suited to the Dresden public. As he was just setting out for Düsseldorf, where he had been appointed concert-director, he commended his work with great confidence to my tender mercies, and regretted not having the power of appointing me the conductor of it. He acknowledged that he owed his great success partly to the wonderfully happy rendering of the male part of *Conradin* by my niece Johanna. She, in her turn, told me with equal confidence that without her Hiller's opera would not have had such an extraordinary triumph. I was now really anxious to see this fortunate work and its wonderful staging for myself; and this I was able to do, as a fourth performance was announced after Hiller and his family had left Dresden for good. When I entered the theatre at the beginning of the overture to take my place in the stalls, I was astonished to find all the seats, with a few scarcely noticeable exceptions, absolutely empty. At the other end of my row I saw the poet who had written the libretto, the gentle painter Reinike. We moved, naturally, towards the middle of the space and discussed the strange position in which we found ourselves. He poured out melancholy complaints to me about Hiller's musical setting to his poetry; the secret of the mistake which Hiller had made about the success of his work he did not explain, and was evidently very much upset at the conspicuous failure of the opera. It was from another quarter that I learned how it had been possible for Hiller to deceive himself in such an extraordinary way. Frau Hiller, who was of Polish origin, had managed at the frequent Polish gatherings which took place in Dresden to persuade a large contingent of her countrymen, who were keen theatregoers, to attend her husband's opera. On the first night these friends, with their usual enthusiasm, incited the public to applaud, but had themselves found so little pleasure in the work that they had stayed away from the second performance, which was otherwise badly attended, so that the opera could only be considered a failure. By commandeering all the help that could possibly be got from the Poles by way of applause, every effort was made to secure a third performance on a Sunday, when the theatre generally filled of its own accord. This object was achieved, and the Polish theatre aristocracy, with the charity that was habitual to them, fulfilled their duty towards the needy couple in whose drawing-room they had often spent such pleasant evenings.

APPLICATION FOR A HIGHER SALARY

Once more the composer was called before the curtain, and everything went off well. Hiller thereupon placed his confidence in the verdict on the third performance, according to which his opera was an undoubted success, just as had been the case with my *Tannhäuser*. The artificiality of this proceeding was, however, exposed by this fourth performance, at which I was present, and at which no one was under an obligation to the departed composer to attend. Even my niece was disgusted with it, and thought that the best singer in the world could not make a success of such a tedious opera. Whilst we were watching this miserable performance I managed to point out to the poet some weaknesses and faults that were to be found in the subject-matter. The latter reported my criticisms to Hiller, whereupon I received a warm and friendly letter from Düsseldorf, in which Hiller acknowledged the mistake he had made in rejecting my advice on this point. He gave me plainly to understand that it was not too late to alter the opera according to my suggestions; I should thus have had the inestimable benefit of having such an obviously well-intentioned, and, in its way, so significant, a work in the repertoire, but I never got so far as that.

On the other hand, I experienced the small satisfaction of hearing the news that two performances of my *Rienzi* had taken place in Berlin, for the success of which Conductor Taubert, as he informed me himself, thought he had won some credit on account of the extremely effective combinations he had arranged. In spite of this, I was absolutely convinced that I must abandon all hope of any lasting and profitable success from Berlin, and I could no longer hide from Lüttichau that, if 1 were to continue in the discharge of my duties with the necessary good spirits, I must insist on a rise of salary, as, beyond my regular income, I could not rely on any substantial success wherewith to meet my unlucky publishing transactions. My income was so small that I could not even live on it, but I asked nothing more than to be placed on an equal footing with my colleague Reissiger, a prospect which had been held out to me from the beginning.

At this juncture Lüttichau saw a favourable opportunity for making me feel my dependence on his goodwill, which could only be secured by my showing due deference to his wishes. After I had laid my case before the King, at a personal interview, and asked for the favour of the moderate increase in income which was my object, Lüttichau promised to make the report he was obliged to give of me as favourable as possible. How great was my consternation and humiliation when one day he opened our interview by telling me that his report had come back from the King. In it was set forth that I had unfortunately overestimated my talent on account of the foolish praise of various friends in a high position (among whom he counted Frau v. Könneritz), and had thus been led to consider that I had quite as good a right to success as Meyerbeer. I had thereby caused such serious offence that it might, perhaps, be considered advisable to dismiss me altogether. On the other hand, my industry and my praiseworthy performance with regard to the revision of Gluck's *Iphigenia,* which had been brought to the notice of the management, might justify my being given another chance, in which case my material condition must be given due consideration. At this point I could read no further, and stupefied by surprise I gave my patron back the paper. He tried at once to remove the obviously bad impression it had made upon me by telling me that my wish had been granted, and I could draw the nine hundred marks belonging to me at once from the bank. I took my leave in silence, and pondered over what course of action I must pursue in face of this disgrace, as it was quite out of the question for me to accept the nine hundred marks.

But in the midst of these adversities a visit of the King of Prussia to Dresden was one day announced, and at the same time by his special request a performance of *Tannhäuser* was arranged. He really did make his appearance in the theatre at this performance in the company of the royal family of Saxony, and stayed with apparent interest from beginning to end. On this occasion the King gave a curious explanation for having stayed away from the performances of *Rienzi* in Berlin, which was afterwards reported to me. He said he had denied himself the pleasure of hearing one of my operas in Berlin, because it was important to get a good impression of them, and he knew that in his own theatre they would only be badly produced. This strange event had, at any rate, the result of giving me back sufficient self-confidence to accept the nine hundred marks of which I was in such desperate need.

Lüttichau also seemed to make a point of winning back my trust to some extent, and I gathered from his calm friendliness that I must suppose this wholly uncultured man had no consciousness of the outrage he had done me. He returned to the idea of having orchestral concerts, in accordance with the suggestions I had made in my rejected report on the orchestra, and in order to induce me to arrange such musical performances in the theatre, said the initiative had come from the management and not from the orchestra itself. As soon as I discovered that the profits were to go to the orchestra I willingly entered into the plan. By a special device of my own the stage of the theatre was made into a concert-hall (afterwards considered first-class) by means of a sounding board enclosing the whole orchestra, which proved a great success. In future six performances were to take place during the winter months. This time, however, as it was the end of the year, and we only had the second half of the winter before us, subscription tickets were issued for only three concerts, and the whole available space in the theatre was filled by the public. I found the preparations for this fairly diverting, and entered upon the fateful year 1848 in a rather more reconciled and amiable frame of mind.

Early in the New Year the first of these orchestral concerts took place, and brought me much popularity on account of its unusual programme. I had discovered that if any real significance were to be given to these concerts, in distinction to those consisting of heterogeneous scraps of music of every different species under the sun, and which are so opposed to all serious artistic taste, we could only afford to give two kinds of genuine music alternately if a good effect was to be produced. Accordingly between two symphonies I placed one or two longer vocal pieces, which were not to be heard elsewhere, and these were the only items in the whole concert. After the Mozart Symphony in D major, I made all the musicians move from their places to make room for an imposing choir, which had to sing Palestrina's *Stabat Mater,* from an adaptation of the original recitative, which I had carefully revised, and Bach's Motet for eight voices: *Singet dem Herrn ein neues Lied* ('Sing unto the Lord a new song'); thereupon I let the orchestra again take its place to play Beethoven's *Sinfonia Eroica,* and with that to end the concert.

This success was very encouraging, and disclosed to me a somewhat consoling prospect of increasing my influence as musical conductor at a time when my disgust was daily growing stronger at the constant meddling with our opera repertoire, which made me lose more and more influence as compared with the wishes of my would-be prima donna niece, whom even Tichatschek supported. Immediately on my return from Berlin I had begun the orchestration of *Lohengrin,* and in all other respects had given myself up to greater resignation, which made me feel I could face my fate calmly, when I suddenly received a very disturbing piece of news.

In the beginning of February my mother's death was announced to me. I at once hastened to her funeral at Leipzig, and was filled with deep emotion and joy at the wonderfully calm and sweet expression of her face. She had passed the latter years of her life, which had before been so active and restless, in cheerful ease, and at the end in peaceful and almost childlike happiness. On her deathbed she exclaimed in humble modesty, and with a bright smile on her face: 'Oh! how beautiful! how lovely! how divine! Why do I deserve such favour?' It was a bitterly cold morning when we lowered the coffin into the grave in the churchyard, and the hard, frozen lumps of earth which we scattered on the lid, instead of the customary handful of dust, frightened me by the loud noise they made. On the way home to the house of my brother-in-law, Hermann Brockhaus, where the whole family were to gather together for an hour, Laube, of whom my mother had been very fond, was my only companion. He expressed his anxiety at my unusually exhausted appearance, and when he afterwards accompanied me to the station, we discussed the unbearable burden which seemed to us to lie like a dead weight on every noble effort made to resist the tendency of the time to sink into utter worthlessness. On my return to Dresden the realisation of my complete loneliness came over me for the first time with full consciousness, as I could not help knowing that with the loss of my mother every natural bond of union was loosened with my brothers and sisters, each of whom was taken up with his or her own family affairs. So I plunged dully and coldly into the only thing which could cheer and warm me, the working out of my *Lohengrin* and my studies of German antiquity.

Thus dawned the last days of February, which were to plunge Europe once more into revolution. I was among those who least expected a probable or even possible overthrow of the political world. My first knowledge of such things had been gained in my youth at the time of the July Revolution, and the long and peaceful reaction that followed it. Since then I had become acquainted with Paris, and from all the signs of public life which I saw there, I thought all that had occurred had been merely the preliminaries of a great revolutionary movement. I had been present at the erection of the *forts détachés* around Paris, which Louis Philippe had carried out, and been instructed about the strategic value of the various fixed sentries scattered about Paris, and I agreed with those who considered that everything was ready to make even an attempt at a rising on the part of the populace of Paris quite impossible. When, therefore, the Swiss War of Separation at the end of the previous year, and the successful Sicilian Revolution at the beginning of the New Year, turned all men's eyes in great excitement to watch the effect of these risings on Paris, I did not take the slightest interest in the hopes and fears which were aroused. News of the growing restlessness in the French capital did indeed reach us, but I disputed Röckel's belief that any significance could be attached to it. I was sitting in the conductor's desk at a rehearsal of *Martha* when, during an interval, Röckel, with the peculiar joy of being in the right, brought me the news of Louis Philippe's flight, and the proclamation of the Republic in Paris. This made a strange and almost astonishing impression on me, although at the same time the doubt as to the true significance of these events made it possible for me to smile to myself. I too caught the fever of excitement which had spread everywhere. The German March days were coming, and from all directions ever more alarming news kept coming in. Even within the narrow confines of my native Saxony serious petitions were framed, which the King withstood for a long time; even he was deceived, in a way which he was soon to acknowledge, as to the meaning of this commotion and the temper that prevailed in the country.

On the evening of one of these really anxious days, when the very air was heavy and full of thunder, we gave our third great orchestral concert, at which the King and his court were present, as on the two previous occasions. For the opening of this one I had chosen Mendelssohn's Symphony in A minor, which I had played on the occasion of his funeral. The mood of this piece, which even in the would-be joyful phrases is always tenderly melancholy, corresponded strangely with the anxiety and depression of the whole audience, which was more particularly accentuated in the demeanour of the royal family. I did not conceal from Lipinsky, the leader of the orchestra, my regret at the mistake I had made in the arrangement of that day's programme, as Beethoven's Fifth Symphony, also in a minor key, was to follow this minor symphony. With a merry twinkle in his eyes the eccentric Pole comforted me by exclaiming: 'Oh, let us play only the first two movements of the Symphony in C minor, then no one will know whether we have played Mendelssohn in the major or the minor key.' Fortunately before these two movements began, to our great surprise, a loud shout was raised by some patriotic spirit in the middle of the audience, who called out 'Long live the King!' and the cry was promptly repeated with unusual enthusiasm and energy on all sides. Lipinsky was perfectly right: the symphony, with the passionate and stormy excitement of the first theme, swelled out like a hurricane of rejoicing, and had seldom produced such an effect on the audience as on that night. This was the last of the newly inaugurated concerts that I ever conducted in Dresden.

Shortly after this the inevitable political changes took place. The King dismissed his ministry and elected a new one, consisting partly of Liberals and partly even of really enthusiastic Democrats, who at once proclaimed the well-known regulations, which are the same all over the world, for founding a thoroughly democratic constitution. I was really touched by this result, and by the heartfelt joy which was evident among the whole population, and I would have given much to have been able to gain access to the King, and convince myself of his hearty confidence in the people's love for him, which seemed to me so desirable a consummation. In the evening the town was gaily illuminated, and the King drove through the streets in an open carriage. In the greatest excitement I went out among the dense crowds and followed his movements, often running where I thought it likely that a particularly hearty shout might rejoice and reconcile the monarch's heart. My wife was quite frightened when she saw me come back late at night, tired out and very hoarse from shouting.

The events which took place in Vienna and Berlin, with their apparently momentous results, only moved me as interesting newspaper reports, and the meeting of a Frankfort parliament in the place of the dissolved *Bundestag* sounded strangely pleasant in my ears. Yet all these significant occurrences could not tear me for a single day from my regular hours of work. With immense, almost overweening satisfaction, I finished, in the last days of this eventful and historic month of March, the score of *Lohengrin* with the orchestration of the music up to the vanishing of the Knight of the Holy Grail into the remote and mystic distance.

About this time a young Englishwomen, Madame Jessie Laussot, who had married a Frenchman in Bordeaux, one day presented herself at my house in the company of Karl Ritter, who was barely eighteen years of age. This young man, who was born in Russia of German parents, was a member of one of those northern families who had settled down permanently in Dresden, on account of the pleasant artistic atmosphere of that place. I remembered that I had seen him once before not long after the first performance of *Tannhäuser,* when he asked me for my autograph for a copy of the score of that opera, which was on sale at the music-shop. I now learned that this copy really belonged to Frau Laussot, who had been present at those performances, and who was now introduced to me. Overcome with shyness, the young lady expressed her admiration in a way I had never experienced before, and at the same time told me how great was her regret at being called away by family affairs from her favourite home in Dresden with the Ritter family, who, she gave me to understand, were deeply devoted to me. It was with a strange, and in its way quite a new, sensation that I bade farewell to this young lady. This was the first time since my meeting with Alwine Frommann and Werder, when the *Fliegender Holländer* was produced, that I came across this sympathetic tone, which seemed to come like an echo from some old familiar past, but which I never heard close at hand. I invited young Ritter to come and see me whenever he liked, and to accompany me sometimes on my walks. His extraordinary shyness, however, seemed to prevent him from doing this, and I only remember seeing him very occasionally at my house. He used to turn up more often with Hans von Bülow, whom he seemed to know pretty well, and who had already entered the Leipzig University as a student of law. This well-informed and talkative young man showed his warm and hearty devotion to me more openly, and I felt bound to reciprocate his affection. He was the first person who made me realise the genuine character of the new political enthusiasm. On his hat, as well as on his father's, the black, red, and gold cockade was paraded before my eyes.

Now that I had finished my *Lohengrin,* and had leisure to study the course of events, I could no longer help myself sympathising with the ferment aroused by the birth of German ideals and the hopes attached to their realisation. My old friend Franck had already imbued me with a fairly sound political judgment, and, like many others, I had grave doubts as to whether the German parliament now assembling would serve any useful purpose. Nevertheless, the temper of the populace, of which there could be no question, although it might not have been given very obvious expression, and the belief, everywhere prevalent, that it was impossible to return to the old conditions, could not fail to exercise its influence upon me. But I wanted actions instead of words, and actions which would force our princes to break for ever with their old traditions, which were so detrimental to the cause of the German commonwealth. With this object I felt inspired to write a popular appeal in verse, calling upon the German princes and peoples to inaugurate a great crusade against Russia, as the country which had been the prime instigator of that policy in Germany which had so fatally separated the monarchs from their subjects. One of the verses ran as follows: —

> The old fight against the East
> Returns again to-day.
> The people's sword must not rust
> Who freedom wish for aye.

As I had no connection with political journals, and had learned by chance that Berthold Auerbach was on the staff of a paper in Mannheim, where the waves of revolution ran high, I sent him my poem with the request to do whatever he thought best with it, and from that day to this I have never heard or seen anything of it.

Whilst the Frankfort Parliament continued to sit on from day to day, and it seemed idle to conjecture whither this big talk by small men would lead, I was much impressed by the news which reached us from Vienna. In the May of this year an attempt at a reaction, such as had succeeded in Naples and remained indecisive in Paris, had been triumphantly nipped in the bud by the enthusiasm and energy of the Viennese people under the leadership of the students' band, who had acted with such unexpected firmness. I had arrived at the conclusion that, in matters directly concerning the people, no reliance could be placed on reason or wisdom, but only on sheer force supported by fanaticism or absolute necessity; but the course of events in Vienna, where I saw the youth of the educated classes working side by side with the labouring man, filled me with peculiar enthusiasm, to which I gave expression in another popular appeal in verse. This I sent to the *Oesterreichischen Zeitung,* where it was printed in their columns with my full signature.

In Dresden two political unions had been formed, as a result of the great changes that had taken place. The first was called the *Deutscher Verein* (German Union), whose programme aimed at 'a constitutional monarchy on the broadest democratic foundation.' The names of its principal leaders, among which, in spite of its broad democratic foundation, my friends

Eduard Devrient and Professor Rietschel had the courage openly to appear, guaranteed the safety of its objects. This union, which tried to include every element that regarded a real revolution with abhorrence, conjured into existence an opposition club which called itself the *Vaterlands-Verein* (Patriotic Union). In this the 'democratic foundation' seemed to be the chief basis, and the 'constitutional monarchy' only provided the necessary cloak.

Röckel canvassed passionately for the latter, as he seemed to have lost all confidence in the monarchy. The poor fellow was, indeed, in a very bad way. He had long ago given up all hope of rising to any position in the musical world; his directorship had become pure drudgery, and was, unfortunately, so badly paid that he could not possibly keep himself and his yearly increasing family on the income he derived from his post. He always had an unconquerable aversion from teaching, which was a fairly profitable employment in Dresden among the many wealthy visitors. So he went on from bad to worse, running miserably into debt, and for a long time saw no hope for his position as the father of a family except in emigration to America, where he thought he could secure a livelihood for himself and his dependants by manual labour, and for his practical mind by working as a farmer, from which class he had originally sprung. This, though tedious, would at least be certain. On our walks he had of late been entertaining me almost exclusively with ideas he had gleaned from reading books on farming, doctrines which he applied with zeal to the improvement of his encumbered position. This was the mood in which the Revolution of 1848 found him, and he immediately went over to the extreme socialist side, which, owing to the example set by Paris, threatened to become serious. Every one who knew him was utterly taken aback at the apparently vital change which had so suddenly taken place in him, when he declared that he had at last found his real vocation — that of an agitator.

His persuasive faculties, on which, however, he could not rely sufficiently for platform purposes, developed in private intercourse into stupefying energy. It was impossible to stop his flow of language with any objection, and those he could not draw over to his cause he cast aside for ever. In his enthusiasm about the problems which occupied his mind day and night, he sharpened his intellect into a weapon capable of demolishing every foolish objection, and suddenly stood in our midst like a preacher in the wilderness. He was at home in every department of knowledge. The *Vaterlands-Verein* had elected a committee for carrying into execution a plan for arming the populace; this included Röckel and other thoroughgoing democrats, and, in addition, certain military experts, among whom was my old friend Hermann Müller, the lieutenant of the Guards who had once been engaged to Schröder-Devrient. He and another officer named Zichlinsky were the only members of the Saxon army who joined the political movement. The part I played in the meetings of this committee, as in everything else, was dictated by artistic motives. As far as I can remember, the details of this plan, which at last became a nuisance, afforded very sound foundation for a genuine arming of the people, though it was impossible to carry it out during the political crisis.

My interest and enthusiasm about the social and political problems which were occupying the whole world increased every day, until public meetings and private intercourse, and the shallow platitudes which formed the staple eloquence of the orators of the day, proved to me the terrible shallowness of the whole movement.

If only I could rest assured that, while such senseless confusion was the order of the day, people well versed in these matters would withhold from any demonstration (which to my great regret I observed in Hermann Franck, and told him of, openly), then, on the contrary, I should feel myself compelled, as soon as the opportunity arose, to discuss the purport of such questions and problems according to my judgment. Needless to say, the newspapers played an exciting and prominent part on this occasion. Once, when I went incidentally (as I might go to see a play) to a meeting of the *Vaterlands-Verein,* when they were assembled in a public garden, they chose for the subject of their discussion, 'Republic or Monarchy?' I was astonished to hear and to read with what incredible triviality it was carried on, and how the sum-total of their explanation was, that, to be sure, a republic is best, but, at the worst, one could put up with a monarchy if it were well conducted. As the result of many heated discussions on this point, I was incited to lay bare my views on the subject in an article which I published in the *Dresdener Anzeiger*, but which I did not sign. My special aim was to turn the attention of the few who really took the matter seriously, from the external form of the government to its intrinsic value. When I had pursued and consistently discussed the utmost idealistic conclusions of all that which, to my mind, was necessary and inseparable from the perfect state and from social order, I inquired whether it would not be possible to realise all this with a king at the head, and entered so deeply into the matter as to portray the king in such a fashion, that he seemed even more anxious than any one else that his state should be organised on genuinely republican lines, in order that he might attain to the fulfilment of his own highest aims. I must own, however, that I felt bound to urge this king to assume a much more familiar attitude towards his people than the court atmosphere and the almost exclusive society of his nobles would seem to render possible. Finally, I pointed to the King of Saxony as being specially chosen by Fate to lead the way in the direction I had indicated, and to give the example to all the other German princes. Röckel considered this article a true inspiration from the Angel of Propitiation, but as he feared that it would not meet with proper recognition and appreciation in the paper, he urged me to lecture on it publicly at the next meeting of the *Vaterlands-Verein,* for he attached great importance to my discoursing on the subject personally. Quite uncertain as to whether I could really persuade myself to do this, I attended the meeting, and there, owing to the intolerable balderdash uttered by a certain barrister named Blöde and a master-furrier Klette, whom at that time Dresden venerated as a Demosthenes and a Cleon, I passionately decided to appear at this extraordinary tribunal with my paper, and to give a very spirited reading of it to about three thousand persons.

 The success I had was simply appalling. The astounded audience seemed to remember nothing of the speech of the

Orchestral Conductor Royal save the incidental attack I had made upon the court sycophants. The news of this incredible event spread like wildfire. The next day I rehearsed *Rienzi*, which was to be performed the following evening. I was congratulated on all sides upon my self-sacrificing audacity. On the day of the performance, however, I was informed by Eisolt, the attendant of the orchestra, that the plans had been changed, and he gave me to understand that thereby there hung a tale. True enough, the terrible sensation I had made became so great, that the directors feared the most unheard-of demonstrations at any performance of *Rienzi*. Then a perfect storm of derision and vituperation broke loose in the press, and I was besieged on all sides to such an extent that it was useless to think of self-defence. I had even offended the Communal Guard of Saxony, and was challenged by the commander to make a full apology. But the most inexorable enemies I made were the court officials, especially those holding a minor office, and to this day I still continue to be persecuted by them. I learned that, as far as it lay in their power, they incessantly besought the King, and finally the director, to deprive me at once of my office. On account of this I thought it necessary to write to the monarch personally, in order to explain to him that my action was to be regarded more in the light of a thoughtless indiscretion than as a culpable offence. I sent this letter to Herr von Lüttichau, begging him to deliver it to the King, and to arrange at the same time a short leave for me, so that the provoking disturbance should have a chance of dying down during my absence from Dresden. The striking kindness and goodwill which Herr von Lüttichau showed me on this occasion made no little impression upon me, and this I took no pains to conceal from him. As in the course of time, however, his ill-controlled rage at various things, and especially at a good deal that he had misunderstood in my pamphlet, broke loose, I learned that it was not from any humane motives that he had spoken in such a propitiatory manner to me, but rather by desire of the King himself. On this point I received most accurate information, and heard that when everybody, and even von Lüttichau himself, were besieging the King to visit me with punishment, the King had forbidden any further talk on the subject. After this very encouraging experience, I flattered myself that the King had understood not only my letter, but also my pamphlet, better than many others.

In order to change my mind a little, I determined for the present (it was the beginning of July) to take advantage of the short period of leave granted to me, by going to Vienna. I travelled by way of Breslau, where I looked up an old friend of my family, the musical director Mosewius, at whose house I spent an evening. We had a most lively conversation, but, unfortunately, were unable to steer clear of the stirring political questions of the day. What interested me most was his exceptionally large, or even, if I remember rightly, complete collection of Sebastian Bach's cantatas in most excellent copies. Besides this, he related, with a humour quite his own, several amusing musical anecdotes which were a pleasant memory for many a year. When Mosewius returned my visit in the course of the summer at Dresden, I played a part of the first act of *Lohengrin* on the piano for him, and the expression of his genuine astonishment at this conception was very gratifying to me. In later years, however, I found that he had spoken somewhat scoffingly about me; but I did not stop to reflect as to the truth of this information, or as to the real character of the man, for little by little I had had to accustom myself to the most inconceivable things. At Vienna the first thing I did was to call on Professor Fischhof, as I knew that he had in his keeping important manuscripts, chiefly by Beethoven, among which the original of the C minor Sonata, opus 111, I was particularly curious to see. Through this new friend, whom I found somewhat dry, I made the acquaintance of Herr Vesque von Püttlingen, who, as the composer of a most insignificant opera (*Joan of Arc*), which had been performed in Dresden, had with cautious good taste adopted only the last two syllables of Beethoven's name — *Hoven*. One day we were at his house to dinner, and I then recognised in him a former confidential official of Prince Metternich, who now, with his ribbon of black, red, and gold, followed the current of the age, apparently quite convinced. I made another interesting acquaintance in the person of Herr von Fonton, the Russian state councillor, and attaché at the Russian Embassy in

Vienna. I frequently met this man, both at Fischhof's house and on excursions into the surrounding country; and it was interesting to me for the first time to run up against a man who could so strongly profess his faith in the pessimistic standpoint that a consistent despotism guarantees the only order of things which can be tolerated. Not without interest, and certainly not without intelligence — for he boasted of having been educated at the most enlightened schools in Switzerland — he listened to my enthusiastic narration of the art ideal which I had in my mind, and which was destined to exercise a great and decided influence upon the human race. As he had to allow that the realisation of this ideal could not be effected through the strength of despotism, and as he was unable to foresee any rewards for my exertions, by the time we came to the champagne he thawed to such a degree of affable good-nature as to wish me every success. I learned later on that this man, of whose talent and energetic character I had at the time no small opinion, was last heard of as being in great distress.

Now, as I never undertook anything whatever without some serious object in view, I had made up my mind to avail myself of this visit to Vienna, in order to try in some practical manner to promote my ideas for the reform of the theatre. Vienna seemed to me specially suitable for this purpose, as at that time it had five theatres, all totally different in character, which were dragging on a miserable existence. I quickly worked out a plan, according to which these various theatres might be formed into a sort of co-operative organisation, and placed under one administration composed not only of active members, but also of all those having any literary connection with the theatre. With a view to submitting my plan to them, I then made inquiries about persons with such capacities as seemed most likely to answer my requirements. Besides Herr Friedrich Uhl, whom I had got to know at the very beginning through Fischer, and who did me very good service, I was told of a Herr Franck (the same, I presume, who later on published a big epic work called *Tannhäuser*), and a Dr. Pacher, an agent of Meyerbeer's, and a pettifogger of whose acquaintance later on I was to have no reason to be proud. The most sympathetic, and certainly the most important, of those chosen by me for the conference meeting at Fischhof's house, was undoubtedly Dr. Becher, a passionate and exceedingly cultivated man. He was the only one present who seriously followed the reading of my plan, although, of course, he by no means agreed with everything. I observed in him a certain wildness and vehemence, the impression of which returned to me very vividly some months later, when I heard of his being shot as a rebel who had participated in the October Insurrection at Vienna. For the present, then, I had to satisfy myself with having read the plan of my theatre reform to a few attentive listeners. All seemed to be convinced that the time was not opportune for putting forward such peaceable schemes of reform. On the other hand, Uhl thought it right to give me an idea of what was at present all the rage in Vienna, by taking me one evening to a political club of the most advanced tendencies. There I heard a speech by Herr Sigismund Engländer, who shortly afterwards attracted much attention in the political monthly papers; the unblushing audacity with which he and others expressed themselves that evening with regard to the most dreaded persons in public power astounded me almost as much as the poverty of the political views expressed on that occasion. By way of contrast I received a very nice impression of Herr Grillparzer, the poet, whose name was like a fable to me, associated as it was, from my earliest days, with his *Ahnfrau*. I approached him also with respect to the matter of my theatre reform. He seemed quite disposed to listen in a friendly manner to what I had to say to him; he did not, however, attempt to conceal his surprise at my direct appeals and the personal demands I made of him. He was the first playwright I had ever seen in an official uniform.

After I had paid an unsuccessful visit to Herr Bauernfeld, relative to the same business, I concluded that Vienna was of no more use for the present, and gave myself up to the exceptionally stimulating impressions produced by the public life of the motley crowd, which of late had undergone such marked changes. If the student band, which was always represented in great numbers in the streets, had already amused me with the extraordinary constancy with which its members sported the German colours, I was very highly diverted by the effect produced when at the theatres I saw even the ices served by attendants in the black, red, and gold of Austria. At the Karl Theatre, in the Leopold quarter of the town, I saw a new farce, by Nestroy, which actually introduced the character of Prince Metternich, and in which this statesman, on being asked whether he had poisoned the Duke of Reichstadt, had to make his escape behind the wings as an unmasked sinner. On the whole, the appearance of this imperial city — usually so fond of pleasure — impressed one with a feeling of youthful and powerful confidence. And this impression was revived in me when I heard of the energetic participation of the youthful members of the population, during those fateful October days, in the defence of Vienna against the troops of Prince Windischgrätz.

On the homeward journey I touched at Prague, where I found my old friend Kittl (who had grown very much more corpulent) still in the most terrible fright about the riotous events which had taken place there. He seemed to be of opinion that the revolt of the Tschech party against the Austrian Government was directed at him personally, and he thought fit to reproach himself with the terrible agitation of the time, which he believed he had specially inflamed by his composition of my operatic text of *Die Franzosen vor Nizza,* out of which a kind of revolutionary air seemed to have become very popular. To my great pleasure, on my homeward journey I had the company of Hänel the sculptor, whom I met on the steamer. There travelled with us also a Count Albert Nostitz, with whom he had just settled up his business concerning the statue of the Emperor Charles IV., and he was in the gayest mood, as the extremely insecure state of Austrian paper money had led to his being paid at a great profit to himself, in silver coin in accordance with his agreement. I was very pleased to find that, thanks to this circumstance, he was in such a confident mood, and so free from prejudice, that on arriving at Dresden he accompanied me the whole way — a very long distance — from the landing-stage at which we had left the steamer to my house, in an open carriage; and this despite the fact that he very well knew that, only a few weeks before, I had caused a really terrible stir in this very city.

As far as the public were concerned, the storm seemed quite to have died down, and I was able to resume my usual occupations and mode of life without any further trouble. I am sorry to say, however, that my old worries and anxieties started afresh; I stood in great need of money, and had not the vaguest notion whither to go in search of it. I then examined very thoroughly the answer I had received during the preceding winter to my petition for a higher salary. I had left it unread, as the modifications made in it had already disgusted me. If I had till now believed that it was Herr von Lüttichau who had brought about the increase of salary I had demanded, in the shape of a supplement which I was to receive annually — in itself a humiliating thing — I now saw to my horror that all the time there had been no mention save of one single supplement, and that there was nothing to show that this should be repeated annually. On learning this, I saw that I should now be at the hopeless disadvantage of coming too late with a remonstrance if I should attempt to make one; so there was nothing left for me but to submit to an insult which, under the circumstances, was quite unprecedented. My feelings towards Herr von Lüttichau, which shortly before had been rather warm owing to his supposed kind attitude towards me during the last disturbance, now underwent a serious change, and I soon had a new reason (actually connected with the abovementioned affair) for altering my favourable opinion of him, and for turning finally against him for good and all. He had informed me that the members of the Imperial Orchestra had sent him a deputation demanding my instant dismissal, as they thought that it affected their honour to be any longer under a conductor who had compromised himself politically to the extent which I had. He also informed me that he had not only reprimanded them very severely, but that he had also been at great pains to pacify them concerning me. All this, which Lüttichau had put in a highly favourable light, had latterly made me feel very friendly towards him. Then, however, as the result of inquiries into the matter, I heard accidentally through members of the orchestra that the facts of the case were almost exactly the reverse. What had happened was this, that the members of the Imperial Orchestra had been approached on all sides by the officials of the court, and had been not only earnestly requested to do what Lüttichau had declared they had done of their own accord, but also threatened with the displeasure of the King, and of incurring the strongest suspicion if they refused to comply. In order to protect themselves against this intrigue, and to avoid all evil consequences should they *not* take the required step, the musicians had turned to their principal, and had sent him a deputation, through which they declared that, as a corporation of artists, they did not in the least feel called upon to mix themselves up in a matter that did not concern them. Thus the halo with which my former attachment to Herr von Lüttichau had surrounded him at last disappeared for good and all, and it was chiefly my shame at having been so very much upset by his false conduct that now inspired me for ever with such bitter feelings for this man. What determined this feeling even more than the insults I had suffered, was the recognition of the fact that I was now utterly incapable of ever being able to enlist his influence in the cause of theatrical reform, which was so dear to me. It was natural that I should learn to attach ever less and less importance to the mere retention of the post of orchestral conductor on so extraordinarily inadequate and reduced a salary; and in keeping to this office, I merely bowed to what was an inevitable though purely accidental circumstance of a wretched fate. I did nothing to make the post more intolerable, but, at the same time, I moved not a finger to ensure its permanence.

The very next thing I must do was to attempt to establish my hopes of a larger income, so sadly doomed hitherto, upon a very much sounder basis. In this respect it occurred to me that I might consult my friend Liszt, and beg him to suggest a remedy for my grievous position. And lo and behold, shortly after those fateful March days, and not long before the completion of my *Lohengrin* score, to my very great delight and astonishment, the very man I wanted walked into my room. He had come from Vienna, where he had lived through the 'Barricade Days,' and he was going on to Weimar, where he intended to settle permanently. We spent an evening together at Schumann's, had a little music, and finally began a discussion on Mendelssohn and Meyerbeer, in which Liszt and Schumann differed so fundamentally that the latter, completely losing his temper, retired in a fury to his bedroom for quite a long time. This incident did indeed place us in a somewhat awkward position towards our host, but it furnished us with a most amusing topic of conversation on the way home. I have seldom seen Liszt so extravagantly cheerful as on that night, when, in spite of the cold and the fact that he was clad only in ordinary evening-dress, he accompanied first the music director Schubert, and then myself, to our respective homes. Subsequently I took advantage of a few days' holiday in August to make an excursion to Weimar, where I found Liszt permanently installed and, as is well known, enjoying a life of most intimate intercourse with the Grand Duke. Even though he was unable to help me in my affairs, except by giving me a recommendation which finally proved useless, his reception of me on this short visit was so hearty and so exceedingly stimulating, that it left me profoundly cheered and encouraged. On returning to Dresden I tried as far as possible to curtail my expenses and to live within my means; and, as every means of assistance failed me, I resorted to the expedient of sending out a circular letter addressed jointly to my remaining creditors, all of whom were really friends; and in this I told them frankly of my situation, and enjoined them to relinquish their demands for an indefinite time, till my affairs took a turn for the better, as without this I should certainly never be in a position to satisfy them. By this means they would, at all events, be in a position to oppose my general manager, whom I had every reason to suspect of evil designs, and who would have been only too glad to seize any signs of hostility towards me, on the part of my creditors, as a pretext for taking the worst steps against me. The assurance I required was given me unhesitatingly; my friend Pusinelli, and Frau Klepperbein (an old friend of my mother's), even going so far as to declare that they were prepared to give up all claim to the money they had lent me. Thus, in some measure reassured, and with my position relative to Lüttichau so far improved that I could consult my own wishes as to whether and when I should give up my post entirely, I now continued to fulfil my duties as a conductor as patiently and conscientiously as I was able, while with great zeal I also resumed my studies, which were carrying me ever further and further afield. Thus settled, I now began to watch the wonderful developments in the fate of my friend Röckel. As every day brought fresh rumours of threatened reactionary *coups d'état* and similar violent outbreaks, which Röckel thought it right to prevent, he drew up an appeal to the soldiers of the army of Saxony, in which he explained every detail of the cause for which he stood, and which he then had printed and distributed broadcast. This was too flagrant a misdeed for the public prosecutors: he was therefore immediately placed under arrest, and had to remain three days in gaol while an action for high treason was lodged against him. He was only released when the solicitor Minkwitz stood bail for the requisite three thousand marks (equal to £150). This return home to his anxious wife and children was celebrated by a little public festival, which the committee of the *Vaterlands-Verein* had arranged in his honour, and the liberated man was greeted as the champion of the people's cause. On the other hand, however, the general management of the court theatre, who had before suspended him temporarily, now gave him his final dismissal. Röckel let a full beard grow, and began the publication of a popular journal called the *Volksblatt,* of which he was sole editor. He must have counted on its success to compensate him for the loss of his salary as musical director, for he at once hired an office in the Brüdergasse for his undertaking. This paper succeeded in attracting the attention of a great many people to its editor, and showed up his talents in quite a new light. He never got involved in his style or indulged in any elaboration of words, but confined himself to matters of immediate importance and general interest; it was only after having discussed them in a calm and sober fashion, that he led up from them to further deductions of still greater interest connected with them. The individual articles were short, and never contained anything superfluous, in addition to which they were so clearly written, that they made an instructive and convincing appeal to the most uneducated mind. By always going to the root of things, instead of indulging in circumlocutions which, in politics, have caused such great confusion in the minds of the uneducated masses, he soon had a large circle of readers, both among cultivated and uncultivated people. The only drawback was that the price of the little weekly paper was too small to yield him a corresponding profit. Moreover, it was necessary to warn him that if the reactionary party should ever come into power again, it could never possibly forgive him for this newspaper. His younger brother, Edward, who was paying a visit at the time in Dresden, declared himself willing to accept a post as piano-teacher in England, which, though most uncongenial to him, would be lucrative and place him in a position to help Röckel's family, if, as seemed probable, he met his reward in prison or on the gallows. Owing to his connection with various societies, his time was so much taken up that my intercourse with him was limited to walks, which became more and more rare. On these occasions I often got lost in the most wildly speculative and profound discussions, while this wonderfully exciteable man always remained calmly reflective and clear-headed. First and foremost, he had planned a drastic social reform of the middle classes — as at present constituted — by aiming at a complete alteration of the basis of their condition. He constructed a totally new moral order of things, founded on the teaching of Proudhon and other socialists regarding the annihilation of the power of capital, by immediately productive labour, dispensing with the middleman. Little by little he converted me, by most seductive arguments, to his own views, to such an extent that I began to rebuild my hopes for the realisation of my ideal in art upon them. Thus there were two questions which concerned me very nearly: he wished to abolish matrimony, in the usual acceptation of the word, altogether. I thereupon asked him what he thought the result would be of promiscuous intercourse with women of a doubtful character. With amiable indignation he gave me to understand that we could have no idea about the purity of morals in general, and of the relations of the sexes in particular, so long as we were unable to free people completely from the yoke of the trades, guilds, and similar coercive institutions. He asked me to consider what the only motive would be which would induce a woman to surrender herself to a man, when not only the considerations of money, fortune, position, and family prejudices, but also the various influences necessarily arising from these, had disappeared. When I, in my turn, asked him whence he would obtain persons of great intellect and of artistic ability, if everybody were to be merged in the working classes, he met my objection by replying, that owing to the very fact that everybody would participate in the necessary labour according to his strength and capacity, work would cease to be a burden, and would become simply an occupation which would finally assume an entirely artistic character. He demonstrated this on the principle that, as had already been proved, a field, worked laboriously by a single peasant, was infinitely less productive than when cultivated by several persons in a scientific way. These and similar suggestions, which Röckel communicated to me with a really delightful enthusiasm, led me to further reflections, and gave birth to new plans upon which, to my mind, a possible organisation of the human race, which would correspond to my highest ideals in art, could alone be based. In reference to this, I immediately turned my thoughts to what was close at hand, and directed my attention to the theatre. The motive for this came not only from my own feelings, but also from external circumstances. In accordance with the latest democratic suffrage laws, a general election seemed imminent in Saxony; the election of extreme radicals, which had now taken place nearly everywhere else, showed us that if the movement lasted, there would be the most extraordinary changes even in the administration of the revenue. Apparently a general resolution had been passed to subject the Civil List to a strict revision; all that was deemed superfluous in the royal household was to be done away with; the theatre, as an unnecessary place of entertainment for a depraved portion of the public, was threatened with the withdrawal of the subsidy granted it from the Civil List. I now resolved, in view of the importance which I attached to the theatre, to suggest to the ministers that they should inform the members of parliament, that if the theatre in its present condition were not worth any sacrifice from the state, it would sink to still more doubtful tendencies — and might even become dangerous to public morals — if deprived of that state control which had for its aim the ideal, and, at the same time, felt itself called upon to place culture and education under its beneficial protection. It was of the highest importance to me to secure an organisation of the theatre, which would make the carrying out its loftiest ideals not only a possibility but also a certainty. Accordingly I drew up a project by which the same sum as that which was allotted from the Civil List for the support of a court theatre should be employed for the foundation and upkeep of a national theatre for the kingdom of Saxony. In showing the practical nature of the well-planned particulars of my scheme, I defined them with such great precision, that I felt assured my work would serve as a useful guide to the ministers as to how they should put this matter before parliament. The point now was to have a personal interview with one of the ministers, and it occurred to me that the best man to apply to in the matter would be Herr von der Pfordten, the Minister of Education. Although he already enjoyed the reputation of being a turncoat in politics, and was said to be struggling to efface the origin of his political promotion, which had taken place at a time of great agitation, the mere fact of his having formerly been a professor was sufficient to make me suppose that he was a man with whom I could discuss the question that I had so much at heart. I learned, however, that the real art institutions of the kingdom, such, for instance, as the Academy of Fine Arts, to whose number I so ardently desired to see the theatre added, belonged to the department of the Minister of the Interior. To this man — the worthy though not highly cultivated or artistic Herr Oberländer — I submitted my plans, not, however, without having first made myself known to Herr von der Pfordten, in order, for the reasons above stated, to command my project to him. This man, who apparently was very busy, received me in a polite and reassuring manner; but his whole bearing, indeed the very expression of his face, seemed to destroy all hopes I might ever have cherished of finding in him that understanding which I had expected. The minister Oberländer, on the other hand, earned my confidence by the straightforward earnestness with which he promised a thorough inquiry into the matter. Unfortunately, however, at the same time, he informed me with the most simple frankness, that he could entertain but very little hope of getting the King's authorisation for any unusual treatment of a question hitherto given over to routine. It must be understood that the relations of the King to his ministers were both strained and unconfidential, and that this was more especially so in the case of Oberländer, who never approached the monarch on any other business than that which the strictest discharge of his current duties rendered indispensable. He therefore thought it would be better if my plan could be brought forward, in the first place, by the Chamber of Deputies. As, in the event of the new Civil List being discussed, I was particularly anxious to avoid the question of the continuation of the court theatre being treated in the ignorant and short-sighted radical fashion, which was to be feared above all, I did not despair of making the acquaintance of some of the most influential among the new members of parliament. In this wise I found myself suddenly plunged into quite a new and strange world, and became acquainted with persons and opinions, the very existence of which until then I had not even suspected. I found it somewhat trying always to be obliged to meet these gentlemen at their beer and shrouded in the dense clouds of their tobacco smoke, and to have to discuss with them matters which, though very dear to me, must have seemed a little fantastic to their mind. After a certain Herr von Trütschler, a very handsome, energetic man, whose seriousness was almost gloomy, had listened to me calmly for some time, and had told me that he no longer knew anything about the state, but only about society, and that the latter would know, without either his or my aid, how it should act in regard to art and to the theatre, I was filled with such extraordinary feelings, half mingled with shame, that there and then I gave up, not only all my exertions, but all my hopes as well. The only reminder I ever had of the whole affair came some while after when, on meeting Herr von Lüttichau, I quickly gathered from his attitude to me that he had got wind of the episode, and that it only inspired him with fresh hostility towards me.

During my walks, which I now took absolutely alone, I thought ever more deeply — and much to the relief of my mind

— over my ideas concerning that state of human society for which the boldest hopes and efforts of the socialists and communists, then busily engaged in constructing their system, offered me but the roughest foundation. These efforts could begin to have some meaning and value for me only when they had attained to that political revolution and reconstruction which they aimed at; for it was only then that I, in my turn, could start my reforms in art.

At the same time my thoughts were busy with a drama, in which the Emperor Frederick I. (surnamed 'Barbarossa') was to be the hero. In it the model ruler was portrayed in a manner which lent him the greatest and most powerful significance. His dignified resignation at the impossibility of making his ideals prevail was intended not only to present a true transcript of the arbitrary multifariousness of the things of this world, but also to arouse sympathy for the hero. I wished to carry out this drama in popular rhyme, and in the style of the German used by our epic poets of the Middle Ages, and in this respect the poem *Alexander,* by the priest Lambert, struck me as a good example; but I never got further with this play than to sketch its outline in the broadest manner possible. The five acts were planned in the following manner: Act i. Imperial Diet in the Roncaglian fields, a demonstration of the significance of imperial power which should extend even to the investiture of water and air; Act ii. the siege and capture of Milan; Act iii. revolt of Henry the Lion and his overthrow at Ligano; Act iv. Imperial Diet in Augsburg, the humiliation and punishment of Henry the Lion; Act v. Imperial Diet and grand court assembly at Mainz; peace with the Lombards, reconciliation with the Pope, acceptance of the Cross, and the departure for the East. I lost all interest, however, in the carrying out of this dramatic scheme directly I discovered its resemblance to the subject-matter of the Nibelungen and Siegfried myths, which possessed a more powerful attraction for me. The points of similarity which I recognised between the history and the legend in question then induced me to write a treatise on the subject; and in this I was assisted by some stimulating monographs (found in the royal library), written by authors whose names have now escaped my memory, but which taught

THE NIBELUNGEN MYTH 457

me in a very attractive manner a considerable amount about the old original kingdom of Germany. Later on I published this fairly extensive essay with the title of *Die Nibelungen,* but in working it out I finally lost all inclination to elaborate the historical material for a real drama.

In direct connection with this I began to sketch a clear summary of the form which the old original Nibelungen myth had assumed in my mind in its immediate association with the mythological legend of the gods — a form which, though full of detail, was yet much condensed in its leading features. Thanks to this work, I was able to convert the chief part of the material itself into a musical drama. It was only by degrees, however, and after long hesitation that I dared to enter more deeply into my plans for this work; for the thought of the practical realisation of such a work on our stage literally appalled me. I must confess that it required all the despair which I then felt of ever having the chance of doing anything more for our theatre, to give me the necessary courage to begin upon this new work. Until that time I simply allowed myself to drift, while I meditated listlessly upon the possibility of things pursuing their course further under the existing circumstances. In regard to *Lohengrin,* I had got to that point when I hoped for nothing more than the best possible production of it at the Dresden theatre, and felt that I should have to be satisfied in all respects, and for all time, if I were able to achieve even that. I had duly announced the completion of the score to Herr von Lüttichau; but, in consideration of the unfavourable nature of my circumstances at the time, I had left it entirely to him to decide when my work should be produced.

Meanwhile the time arrived when the keeper of the Archives of the Royal Orchestra called to mind that it was just three hundred years since this royal institution had been founded, and that a jubilee would therefore have to be celebrated. To this end a great concert festival was planned, the programme of which was to be made up of the compositions of all the Saxon orchestral conductors that had lived since the institution had been founded. The whole body of musicians, with both their conductors at their head, were first to present their grateful homage to the King in Pillnitz; and on this occasion a musician was, for the first time, to be elevated to the rank of Knight of the Civil Order of Merit of Saxony. This musician was my colleague Reissiger. Until then he had been treated by the court, and by the manager himself, in the most scornful manner possible, but had, owing to his conspicuous loyalty at this critical time, especially to me, found exceptional favour in the eyes of our committees. When he appeared before the public decorated with the wonderful order, he was greeted with great jubilation by the loyal audience that filled the theatre on the evening of the festival concert. His overture to *Yelva* was also received with a perfect uproar of enthusiastic applause, such as had never fallen to his lot; whereas the finale of the first act from *Lohengrin,* which was produced as the work of the youngest conductor, was accorded only an indifferent reception. This was all the more strange as I was quite unaccustomed to such coolness in regard to my work on the part of the Dresden public. Following upon the concert, there was a festive supper, and when this was over, as all kinds of speeches were being made, I freely proclaimed to the orchestra, in a loud and decided tone, my views as to what was desirable for their perfection in the future. Hereupon Marschner, who, as a former musical conductor in Dresden, had been invited to the jubilee celebrations, expressed the opinion that I should do myself a great deal of harm by holding too good an opinion of the musicians. He said I ought just to consider how uncultivated these people were with whom I had to deal; he pointed out that they were trained simply for the one instrument they played; and asked me whether I did not think that by discoursing to them on the aspirations of art I would produce not only confusion, but even perhaps bad blood? Far more pleasant to me than these festivities is the remembrance of the quiet memorial ceremony which united us on the morning of the Jubilee Day, with the object of placing wreaths on Weber's grave. As nobody could find a word to utter, and even Marschner was able to give expression only to the very driest and most trivial of speeches about the departed master, I felt it incumbent upon me to say a few heartfelt words concerning the memorial ceremony for which we were gathered together.

This brief spell of artistic activity was speedily broken by fresh excitements, which kept pouring in upon us from the political world. The events of October in Vienna awakened our liveliest sympathy, and our walls daily blazed with red and black placards, with summonses to march on Vienna, with the curse of 'Red Monarchy,' as opposed to the hated 'Red Republic,' and with other equally startling matter. Except for those who were best informed as to the course of events — and who certainly did not swarm in our streets — these occurrences aroused great uneasiness everywhere. With the entry of Windischgrätz into Vienna, the acquittal of Fröbel and the execution of Blum, it seemed as though even Dresden were on the eve of an explosion. A vast demonstration of mourning was organised for Blum, with an endless procession through the streets. At the head marched the ministry, among whom the people were particularly glad to see Herr von der Pfordten taking a sympathetic share in the ceremony, as he had already become an object of suspicion to them. From that day gloomy forebodings of disaster grew ever more prevalent on every side. People even went so far as to say, with little attempt at circumlocution, that the execution of Blum had been an act of friendship on the part of the Archduchess Sophia to her sister, the Queen of Saxony, for during his agitation in Leipzig the man had made himself both hated and feared. Troops of Viennese fugitives, disguised as members of the student bands, began to arrive in Dresden, and made a formidable addition to its population, which from this time forth paraded the streets with ever-increasing confidence. One day, as I was on my way to the theatre to conduct a performance of *Rienzi,* the choir-master informed me that several foreign gentlemen had been asking for me. Thereupon half a dozen persons presented themselves, greeted me as a brother democrat, and begged me to procure them free entrance tickets. Among them I recognised a former dabbler in literature, a man named Häfner, a little hunchback, in a Calabrian hat cocked at a terrific angle, to whom I had been introduced by Uhl on the occasion of my visit to the Vienna political club. Great as was my embarrassment at this visit, which evidently astonished our musicians, I felt in no wise compelled to make any compromising admission, but quietly went to the booking-office, took six tickets and handed them to my strange visitors, who parted from me before all the world with much hearty shaking of hands. Whether this evening call improved my position as musical conductor in Dresden in the minds of the theatrical officials and others, may well be doubted; but, at all events, on no occasion was I so frantically called for after every act as at this particular performance of *Rienzi*.

Indeed, at this time I seemed to have won over to my side a party of almost passionate adherents among the theatre-going public, in opposition to the clique which had shown such marked coldness on the occasion of the gala concert already mentioned. It mattered not whether *Tannhäuser* or *Rienzi* were being played, I was always greeted with special applause; and although the political tendencies of this party may have given our management some cause for alarm, yet it forced them to regard me with a certain amount of awe. One day Lüttichau proposed to have my *Lohengrin* performed at an early date. I explained my reasons for not having offered it to him before, but declared myself ready to further his wishes, as I considered the opera company was now sufficiently powerful. The son of my old friend, F. Heine, had just returned from Paris, where he had been sent by the Dresden management to study scene-painting under the artists Despléchin and Dieterle. By way of testing his powers, with a view to an engagement at the Dresden Royal Theatre, the task of preparing suitable scenery for this opera was entrusted to him. He had already asked permission to do this for *Lohengrin* at the instigation of Lüttichau, who wished to call attention to my latest work. Consequently, when I gave my consent, young Heine's wish was granted.

I regarded this turn of events with no little satisfaction, believing that in the study of this particular work I should find a wholesome and effective diversion from all the excitement and confusion of recent events. My horror, therefore, was all the greater, when young Wilhelm Heine one day came to my room with the news that the scenery for *Lohengrin* had been suddenly countermanded, and instructions given him to prepare for another opera. I did not make any remark, nor ask the reason for this singular behaviour. The assurances which Lüttichau afterwards made to my wife — if they were really true — made me regret having laid the chief blame for this mortification at his door, and having thereby irrevocably alienated my sympathy from him. When she asked him about this many years later, he assured her that he had found the court vehemently hostile to me, and that his well-meant attempts to produce my work had met with insuperable obstacles.

However that may have been, the bitterness I now experienced wrought a decisive effect upon my feelings. Not only did I relinquish all hope of a reconciliation with the theatre authorities by a splendid production of my *Lohengrin,* but I determined to turn my back for ever on the theatre, and to make no further attempt to meddle with its concerns. By this act I expressed not merely my utter indifference as to whether I kept my position as musical conductor or no, but my artistic ambitions also entirely cut me off from all possibility of ever cultivating modern theatrical conditions again.

I at once proceeded to execute my long-cherished plans for *Siegfried's Tod,* which I had been half afraid of before. In this work I no longer gave a thought to the Dresden or any other court theatre in the world; my sole preoccupation was to produce something that should free me, once and for all, from this irrational subservience. As I could get nothing more from Röckel in this connection, I now corresponded exclusively with Eduard Devrient on matters connected with the theatre and dramatic art. When, on the completion of my poem, I read it to him, he listened with amazement, and at once realised the fact that such a production would be an absolute drug in the modern theatrical market, and he naturally could not agree to let it remain so. On the other hand, he tried so far to reconcile himself to my work as to try and make it less startling and more adapted for actual production. He proved the sincerity of his intentions by pointing out my error in asking too much of the public, and requiring it to supply from its own knowledge many things necessary for a right understanding of my subject-matter, at which I had only hinted in brief and scattered suggestions. He showed me, for instance, that before Siegfried and Brunhilda are displayed in a position

of bitter hostility towards each other, they ought first to have
been presented in their true and calmer relationship. I had,
in fact, opened the poem of *Siegfried's Tod* with those scenes
which now form the first act of the *Götterdämmerung*.
The details of Siegfried's relation to Brunhilda had been
merely outlined to the listeners in a lyrico-episodical dialogue
between the hero's wife, whom he had left behind in solitude,
and a crowd of Valkyries passing before her rock. To my
great joy, Devrient's hint on this point directed my thoughts
to those scenes which I afterwards worked out in the prologue
of this drama.

This and other matters of a similar nature brought me into
intimate contact with Eduard Devrient, and made our intercourse much more lively and pleasant. He often invited a
select circle of friends to attend dramatic readings at his house
in which I gladly took part, for I found, to my surprise, that
his gift for declamation, which quite forsook him on the stage,
here stood out in strong relief. It was, moreover, a consolation
to pour into a sympathetic ear my worries about my growing
unpopularity with the director. Devrient seemed particularly
anxious to prevent a definite breach; but of this there was
little hope. With the approach of winter the court had returned to town, and once more frequented the theatre, and
various signs of dissatisfaction in high quarters with my behaviour as conductor began to be manifested. On one occasion
the Queen thought that I had conducted *Norma* badly, and on
another that I 'had taken the time wrongly' in *Robert the
Devil*. As Lüttichau had to communicate these reprimands to
me, it was natural that our intercourse at such times should
hardly be of a nature to restore our mutual satisfaction with
each other.

Notwithstanding all this, it still seemed possible to prevent
matters from coming to a crisis, though everything continued
in a state of agitating uncertainty and fermentation. At all
events the forces of reaction, which were holding themselves
in readiness on every side, were not yet sufficiently certain that
the hour of their triumph had come as not to consider it advisable for the present, at least, to avoid all provocation. Consequently our management did not meddle with the musicians

of the royal orchestra, who, in obedience to the spirit of the times, had formed a union for debate and the protection of their artistic and civic interests. In this matter one of our youngest musicians, Theodor Uhlig, had been particularly active. He was a young man, still in his early twenties, and was a violinist in the orchestra. His face was strikingly mild, intelligent and noble, and he was conspicuous among his fellows on account of his great seriousness and his quiet but unusually firm character. He had particularly attracted my notice on several occasions by his quick insight and extensive knowledge of music. As I recognised in him a spirit keenly alert in every direction, and unusually eager for culture, it was not long before I chose him as my companion in my regular walks — a habit I still continued to cultivate — and on which Röckel had hitherto accompanied me. He induced me to come to a meeting of this union of the orchestral company, in order that I might form an opinion about it, and encourage and support so praiseworthy a movement. On this occasion I communicated to its members the contents of my memorandum to the director, which had been rejected a year before, and in which I had made suggestions for reforms in the band, and I also explained further intentions and plans arising therefrom. At the same time I was obliged to confess that I had lost all hope of carrying out any projects of the kind through the general management, and must therefore recommend them to take the initiative vigorously into their own hands. They acclaimed the idea with enthusiastic approval. Although, as I have said before, Lüttichau left these musicians unmolested in their more or less democratic union, yet he took care to be informed through spies of what took place at their highly treasonable gatherings. His chief instrument was a bugler named Lewy, who, much to the disgust of all his comrades in the orchestra, was in particularly high favour with the director. He consequently received precise, or rather exaggerated, accounts of my appearance there, and thought it was now high time to let me once more feel the weight of his authority. I was officially summoned to his presence, and had to listen to a long and wrathful tirade which he had been bottling up for some time about several matters. I also learned that he knew all about the plan of theatre reform which I had laid before the ministry. This knowledge he betrayed in a popular Dresden phrase, which until then I had never heard; he knew very well, he said, that in a memorandum respecting the theatre I had 'made him look ridiculous' (*ihm an den Laden gelegt*). In answer to this I did not refrain from telling him how I intended to act in retaliation, and when he threatened to report me to the King and demand my dismissal, I calmly replied that he might do as he pleased, as I was well assured that I could rely on his Majesty's justice to hear, not only his charges, but also my defence. Moreover, I added, this was the only befitting manner for me to discuss with the King the many points on which I had to complain, not only in my own interests, but also in those of the theatre and of art. This was not pleasant hearing for Lüttichau, and he asked how it was possible for him to try and co-operate with me, when I for my part had openly declared (to use his own expression) that all labour was wasted upon him (*Hopfen und Malz verloren seien*). We had at last to part with mutual shruggings of the shoulder. My conduct seemed to trouble my former patron, and he therefore enlisted the tact and moderation of Eduard Devrient in his service, and asked him to use his influence with me to facilitate some further arrangement between us. But, in spite of all his zeal, Devrient had to admit with a smile, after we had discussed his message, that nothing much could be done; and as I persisted in my refusal to meet the director again in consultation respecting the service of the theatre, he had at last to recognise that his own wisdom would have to help him out of the difficulty.

Throughout the whole period during which I was fated to fill the post of conductor at Dresden, the effects of this dislike on the part of the court and the director continued to make themselves felt in everything. The orchestral concerts, which had been organised by me in the previous winter, were this year placed under Reissiger's control, and at once sank to the usual level of ordinary concerts. Public interest quickly waned, and the undertaking could only with difficulty be kept alive. In opera I was unable to carry out the proposed revival of the *Fliegender Holländer,* for which I had found in Mitterwurzer's maturer talent an admirable and promising exponent. My niece Johanna, whom I had destined for the part of Senta, did not like the rôle, because it offered little opportunity for splendid costumes. She preferred *Zampa* and *Favorita*, partly to please her new protector, my erstwhile *Rienzi* enthusiast, Tichatschek, partly for the sake of *three brilliant costumes* which the management had to furnish for each of these parts. In fact, these two ringleaders of the Dresden opera of that day had formed an alliance of rebellion against my vigorous rule in the matter of operatic repertoire. Their opposition, to my great discomfiture, was crowned by success when they secured the production of this *Favorita* of Donizetti's, the arrangement of which I had once been obliged to undertake for Schlesinger in Paris. I had at first emphatically refused to have anything to do with this opera, although its principal part suited my niece's voice admirably, even in her father's judgment. But now that they knew of my feud with the director, and of my voluntary loss of influence, and finally of my evident disgrace, they thought the opportunity ripe for compelling me to conduct this tiresome work myself, as it happened to be my turn.

Besides this, my chief occupation at the royal theatre during this period consisted in conducting Flotow's opera *Martha,* which, although it failed to attract the public, was nevertheless produced with excessive frequency, owing to its convenient cast. On reviewing the results of my labours in Dresden — where I had now been nearly seven years — I could not help feeling humiliated when I considered the powerful and energetic impetus I knew I had given in many directions to the court theatre, and I found myself obliged to confess that, were I now to leave Dresden, not the smallest trace of my influence would remain behind. From various signs I also gathered that, if ever it should come to a trial before the King between the director and myself, even if his Majesty were in my favour, yet out of consideration for the courtier the verdict would go against me.

Nevertheless, on Palm Sunday of the new year, 1849, I received ample amends. In order to ensure liberal receipts, our orchestra had again decided to produce Beethoven's Ninth

Symphony. Every one did his utmost to make this one of our finest performances, and the public took up the matter with real enthusiasm. Michael Bakunin, unknown to the police, had been present at the public rehearsal. At its close he walked unhesitatingly up to me in the orchestra, and said in a loud voice, that if all the music that had ever been written were lost in the expected world-wide conflagration, we must pledge ourselves to rescue this symphony, even at the peril of our lives. Not many weeks after this performance it really seemed as though this world-wide conflagration would actually be kindled in the streets of Dresden, and that Bakunin, with whom I had meanwhile become more closely associated through strange and unusual circumstances, would undertake the office of chief stoker.

It was long before this date that I first made the acquaintance of this most remarkable man. For years I had come across his name in the newspapers, and always under extraordinary circumstances. He turned up in Paris at a Polish gathering, but although he was a Russian, he declared that it mattered little whether a man were a Russian or a Pole, so long as he wanted to be a free man, and that this was all that mattered. I heard afterwards, through George Herwegh, that he had renounced all his sources of income as a member of an influential Russian family, and that one day, when his entire fortune consisted of two francs, he had given them away to a beggar on the boulevard, because it was irksome to him to be bound by this possession to take any thought for the morrow. I was informed of his presence in Dresden one day by Röckel, after the latter had become a rampant republican. He had taken the Russian into his house, and invited me to come and make his acquaintance. Bakunin was at that time being persecuted by the Austrian government for his share in the events which took place in Prague in the summer of 1848, and because he was a member of the Slav Congress which had preceded them. He had consequently sought refuge in our city, as he did not wish to settle too far from the Bohemian frontier. The extraordinary sensation he had created in Prague arose from the fact that, when the Czechs sought the protection of Russia against the dreaded Germanising policy of Austria, he conjured them to defend themselves with fire and sword against those very Russians, and indeed against any other people who lived under the rule of a despotism like that of the Tsars. This superficial acquaintance with Bakunin's aims had sufficed to change the purely national prejudices of the Germans against him into sympathy. When I met him, therefore, under the humble shelter of Röckel's roof, I was immediately struck by his singular and altogether imposing personality. He was in the full bloom of manhood, anywhere between thirty and forty years of age. Everything about him was colossal, and he was full of a primitive exuberance and strength. I never gathered that he set much store by my acquaintance. Indeed, he did not seem to care for merely intellectual men; what he demanded was men of reckless energy. As I afterwards perceived, theory in this case had more weight with him than purely personal sentiment; and he talked much and expatiated freely on the matter. His general mode of discussion was the Socratic method, and he seemed quite at his ease when, stretched on his host's hard sofa, he could argue discursively with a crowd of all sorts of men on the problems of revolution. On these occasions he invariably got the best of the argument. It was impossible to triumph against his opinions, stated as they were with the utmost conviction, and overstepping in every direction even the extremest bounds of radicalism. So communicative was he, that on the very first evening of our meeting he gave me full details about the various stages of his development. He was a Russian officer of high birth, but smarting under the yoke of the narrowest martial tyranny, he had been led by a study of Rousseau's writings to escape to Germany under pretence of taking furlough. In Berlin he had flung himself into the study of philosophy with all the zest of a barbarian newly awakened to civilisation. Hegel's philosophy was the one which was the rage at that moment, and he soon became such an expert in it, that he had been able to hurl that master's most famous disciples from the saddle of their own philosophy, in a thesis couched in terms of the strictest Hegelian dialectic. After he had got philosophy off his chest, as he expressed it, he proceeded to Switzerland, where he preached communism, and thence wandered over France and Germany back to the borderland of the Slav world, from which quarter he looked for the regeneration of humanity, because the Slavs had been less enervated by civilisation. His hopes in this respect were centred in the more strongly pronounced Slav type characteristic of the Russian peasant class. In the natural detestation of the Russian serf for his cruel oppressor the nobleman, he believed he could trace a substratum of simple-minded brotherly love, and that instinct which leads animals to hate the men who hunt them. In support of this idea he cited the childish, almost demoniac delight of the Russian people in fire, a quality on which Rostopschin calculated in his strategic burning of Moscow. He argued that all that was necessary to set in motion a world-wide movement was to convince the Russian peasant, in whom the natural goodness of oppressed human nature had preserved its most childlike characteristics, that it was perfectly right and well pleasing to God for them to burn their lords' castles, with everything in and about them The least that could result from such a movement would be the destruction of all those things which, rightly considered, must appear, even to Europe's most philosophical thinkers, the real source of all the misery of the modern world. To set these destructive forces in action appeared to him the only object worthy of a sensible man's activity. (Even while he was preaching these horrible doctrines, Bakunin, noticing that my eyes troubled me, shielded them with his outstretched hand from the naked light for a full hour, in spite of my protestations.) This annihilation of all civilisation was the goal upon which his heart was set. Meanwhile it amused him to utilise every lever of political agitation he could lay hands on for the advancement of this aim, and in so doing he often found cause for ironical merriment. In his retreat he received people belonging to every shade of revolutionary thought. Nearest to him stood those of Slav nationality, because these, he thought, would be the most convenient and effective weapons he could use in the uprooting of Russian despotism. In spite of their republic and their socialism *à la* Proudhon, he thought nothing of the French, and as for the Germans, he never mentioned them to me. Democracy, republicanism, and anything else of the kind he regarded as unworthy of serious consideration.

Every objection raised by those who had the slightest wish to reconstruct what had been demolished, he met with overwhelming criticism. I well remember on one occasion that a Pole, startled by his theories, maintained that there must be an organised state to guarantee the individual in the possession of the fields he had cultivated. 'What!' he answered; 'would you carefully fence in your field to provide a livelihood for the police again!' This shut the mouth of the terrified Pole. He comforted himself by saying that the creators of the new order of things would arise of themselves, but that our sole business in the meantime was to find the power to destroy. Was any one of us so mad as to fancy that he would survive the desired destruction? We ought to imagine the whole of Europe with St. Petersburg, Paris, and London transformed into a vast rubbish-heap. How could we expect the kindlers of such a fire to retain any consciousness after so vast a devastation? He used to puzzle any who professed their readiness for self-sacrifice by telling them it was not the so-called tyrants who were so obnoxious, but the smug Philistines. As a type of these he pointed to a Protestant parson, and declared that he would not believe he had really reached the full stature of a man until he saw him commit his own parsonage, with his wife and child, to the flames.

I was all the more perplexed for a while, in the face of such dreadful ideas, by the fact that Bakunin in other respects proved a really amiable and tender-hearted man. He was fully alive to my own anxiety and despair with regard to the risk I ran of forever destroying my ideals and hopes for the future of art. It is true, he declined to receive any further instruction concerning these artistic schemes, and would not even look at my work on the Nibelungen saga. I had just then been inspired by a study of the Gospels to conceive the plan of a tragedy for the ideal stage of the future, entitled *Jesus of Nazareth*. Bakunin begged me to spare him any details; and when I sought to win him over to my project by a few verbal hints, he wished me luck, but insisted that I must at all costs make Jesus appear as a weak character. As for the music of the piece, he advised me, amid all the variations, to use only one set of phrases, namely: for the tenor, 'Off with His head!';

for the soprano, 'Hang Him!'; and for the basso continuo, 'Fire! fire!' And yet I felt more sympathetically drawn towards this prodigy of a man when I one day induced him to hear me play and sing the first scenes of my *Fliegender Holländer*. After listening with more attention than most people gave, he exclaimed, during a momentary pause, 'That is stupendously fine!' and wanted to hear more.

As his life of permanent concealment was very dull, I occasionally invited him to spend an evening with me. For supper my wife set before him finely cut slices of sausage and meat, which he at once devoured wholesale, instead of spreading them frugally on his bread in Saxon fashion. Noticing Minna's alarm at this, I was guilty of the weakness of telling him how we were accustomed to consume such viands, whereupon he reassured me with a laugh, saying that it was quite enough, only he would like to eat what was set before him in his own way. I was similarly astonished at the manner in which he drank wine from our ordinary-sized small glasses. As a matter of fact he detested wine, which only satisfied his craving for alcoholic stimulants in such paltry, prolonged, and subdivided doses; whereas a stiff glass of brandy, swallowed at a gulp, at once produced the same result, which, after all, was only temporarily attained. Above all, he scorned the sentiment which seeks to prolong enjoyment by moderation, arguing that a true man should only strive to still the cravings of nature, and that the only real pleasure in life worthy of a man was love.

These and other similar little characteristics showed clearly that in this remarkable man the purest impulses of an ideal humanity conflicted strangely with a savagery entirely inimical to all civilisation, so that my feelings during my intercourse with him fluctuated between involuntary horror and irresistible attraction. I frequently called for him to share my lonely wanderings. This he gladly did, not only for the sake of necessary bodily exercise, but also because he could do so in this part of the world without fear of meeting his pursuers. My attempts during our conversations to instruct him more fully regarding my artistic aims remained quite unavailing as long as we were unable to quit the field of mere discussion. All these things seemed to him premature. He refused to admit that out of the very needs of the evil present all laws for the future would have to be evolved, and that these, moreover, must be moulded upon quite different ideas of social culture. Seeing that he continued to urge destruction, and again destruction, I had at last to inquire how my wonderful friend proposed to set this work of destruction in operation. It then soon became clear, as I had suspected it would, and as the event soon proved, that with this man of boundless activity everything rested upon the most impossible hypotheses. Doubtless I, with my hopes of a future artistic remodelling of human society, appeared to him to be floating in the barren air; yet it soon became obvious to me that his assumptions as to the unavoidable demolition of all the institutions of culture were at least equally visionary. My first idea was that Bakunin was the centre of an international conspiracy; but his practical plans seem originally to have been restricted to a project for revolutionising Prague, where he relied merely on a union formed among a handful of students. Believing that the time had now come to strike a blow, he prepared himself one evening to go there. This proceeding was not free from danger, and he set off under the protection of a passport made out for an English merchant. First of all, however, with the view of adapting himself to the most Philistine culture, he had to submit his huge beard and bushy hair to the tender mercies of the razor and shears. As no barber was available, Röckel had to undertake the task. A small group of friends watched the operation, which had to be executed with a dull razor, causing no little pain, under which none but the victim himself remained passive. We bade farewell to Bakunin with the firm conviction that we should never see him again alive. But in a week he was back once more, as he had realised immediately what a distorted account he had received as to the state of things in Prague, where all he found ready for him was a mere handful of childish students. These admissions made him the butt of Röckel's good-humoured chaff, and after this he won the reputation among us of being a mere revolutionary, who was content with theoretical conspiracy. Very similar to his expectations from the Prague students were his presumptions with regard to the Russian people. These also afterwards proved to be entirely groundless, and based merely on gratuitous assumptions drawn from the supposed nature of things. I consequently found myself driven to explain the universal belief in the terrible dangerousness of this man by his theoretical views, as expressed here and elsewhere, and not as arising from any actual experience of his practical activity. But I was soon to become almost an eye-witness of the fact that his personal conduct was never for a moment swayed by prudence, such as one is accustomed to meet in those whose theories are not seriously meant. This was shortly to be proved in the momentous insurrection of May, 1849.

The winter of this year, up to the spring of 1849, passed in a many-sided development of my position and temper, as I have described them, that is to say, in a sort of dull agitation. My latest artistic occupation had been the five-act drama, *Jesus of Nazareth,* just mentioned. Henceforth I lingered on in a state of brooding instability, full of expectation, yet without any definite wish. I felt fully convinced that my activity in Dresden, as an artist, had come to an end, and I was only waiting for the pressure of circumstances to shake myself free. On the other hand, the whole political situation, both in Saxony and the rest of Germany, tended inevitably towards a catastrophe. Day by day this drew nearer, and I flattered myself into regarding my own personal fate as interwoven with this universal unrest. Now that the powers of reaction were everywhere more and more openly bracing themselves for conflict, the final decisive struggle seemed indeed close at hand. My feelings of partisanship were not sufficiently passionate to make me desire to take any active share in these conflicts. I was merely conscious of an impulse to give myself up recklessly to the stream of events, no matter whither it might lead.

Just at this moment, however, an entirely new influence forced itself in a most strange fashion into my fortunes, and was at first greeted by me with a smile of scepticism. Liszt wrote announcing an early production in Weimar of my *Tannhäuser* under his own conductorship — the first that had taken place outside Dresden — and he added with great modesty that this was merely a fulfilment of his own personal desire. In order to ensure success he had sent a special invitation to

Tichatschek to be his guest for the two first performances. When the latter returned he said that the production had, on the whole, been a success, which surprised me very much. I received a gold snuff-box from the Grand Duke as a keepsake, which I continued to use until the year 1864. All this was new and strange to me, and I was still inclined to regard this otherwise agreeable occurrence as a fleeting episode, due to the friendly feeling of a great artist. 'What does this mean for me?' I asked myself. 'Has it come too early or too late?' But a very cordial letter from Liszt induced me to visit Weimar for a few days later on, for a third performance of *Tannhäuser,* which was to be carried out entirely by native talent, with a view to the permanent addition of this opera to the repertoire. For this purpose I obtained leave of absence from my management for the second week in May.

Only a few days elapsed before the execution of this little plan; but they were destined to be momentous ones. On the 1st of May the Chambers were dissolved by the new Beust ministry, which the King had charged with carrying out his proposed reactionary policy. This event imposed upon me the friendly task of caring for Röckel and his family. Hitherto his position as a deputy had shielded him from the danger of criminal prosecution; but as soon as the Chambers were dissolved this protection was withdrawn, and he had to escape by flight from being arrested again. As I could do little to help him in this matter, I promised at least to provide for the continued publication of his popular *Volksblatt,* mainly because the proceeds from this would support his family. Scarcely was Röckel safely across the Bohemian frontier, while I was still toiling at great inconvenience to myself in the printer's office, in order to provide material for an issue of his paper, when the long-expected storm burst over Dresden. Emergency deputations, nightly mob demonstrations, stormy meetings of the various unions, and all the other signs that precede a swift decision in the streets, manifested themselves. On the 3rd May the demeanour of the crowds moving in our thoroughfares plainly showed that this consummation would soon be reached, as was undoubtedly desired. Each local deputation which petitioned for the recognition of the German constitution, which was the universal cry, was refused an audience by the government, and this with a peremptoriness which at last became startling. I was present one afternoon at a committee meeting of the *Vaterlands-Verein,* although merely as a representative of Röckel's *Volksblatt,* for whose continuance, both from economic as well as humane motives, I felt pledged. Here I was at once absorbed in watching the conduct and demeanour of the men whom popular favour had raised to the leadership of such unions. It was quite evident that events had passed beyond the control of these persons; more particularly were they utterly at a loss as to how to deal with that peculiar terrorism exerted by the lower classes which is always so ready to react upon the representatives of democratic theories. On every side I heard a medley of wild proposals and hesitating responses. One of the chief subjects under debate was the necessity of preparing for defence. Arms, and how to procure them, were eagerly discussed, but all in the midst of great disorder; and when at last they discovered that it was time to break up, the only impression I received was one of the wildest confusion. I left the hall with a young painter named Kaufmann, from whose hand I had previously seen a series of cartoons in the Dresden Art Exhibition, illustrating 'The History of the Mind.' One day I had seen the King of Saxony standing before one of these, representing the torture of a heretic under the Spanish Inquisition, and observed him turn away with a disapproving shake of the head from so abstruse a subject. I was on my way home, deep in conversation with this man, whose pale face and troubled look betrayed that he foresaw the disaster that was imminent, when, just as we reached the Postplatz, near the fountain erected from Semper's design, the clang of bells from the neighbouring tower of St. Ann's Church suddenly sounded the tocsin of revolt. With a terrified cry, 'Good God, it has begun!' my companion vanished from my side. He wrote to me afterwards to say that he was living as a fugitive in Berne, but I never saw his face again.

The clang of this bell, so close at hand, made a profound impression upon me also. It was a very sunny afternoon, and I at once noticed the same phenomenon which Goethe describes in his attempt to depict his own sensations during the bombardment of Valmy. The whole square looked as though it were illuminated by a dark yellow, almost brown, light, such as I had once before seen in Magdeburg during an eclipse of the sun. My most pronounced sensation beyond this was one of great, almost extravagant, satisfaction. I felt a sudden strange longing to play with something hitherto regarded as dangerous and important. My first idea, suggested probably by the vicinity of the square, was to inquire at Tichatschek's house for the gun which, as an enthusiastic Sunday sportsman, he was accustomed to use. I only found his wife at home, as he was away on a holiday tour. Her evident terror as to what was going to happen provoked me to uncontrollable laughter. I advised her to lodge her husband's gun in a place of safety, by handing it to the committee of the *Vaterlands-Verein* in return for a receipt, as it might otherwise soon be requisitioned by the mob. I have since learned that my eccentric behaviour on this occasion was afterwards reckoned against me as a serious crime. I then returned to the streets, to see whether anything beyond a ringing of bells and a yellowish eclipse of the sun might be going on in the town. I first made my way to the Old Market-place, where I noticed a group of men gathered round a vociferous orator. It was also an agreeable surprise to me to see Schröder-Devrient descending at the door of a hotel. She had just arrived from Berlin, and was keenly excited by the news which had reached her, that the populace had already been fired upon. As she had only recently seen an abortive insurrection crushed by arms in Berlin, she was indignant to find the same things happening in her 'peaceful Dresden,' as she termed it.

When she turned to me from the stolid crowd, which had complacently been listening to her passionate outpourings, she seemed relieved at finding some one to whom she could appeal to oppose these horrible proceedings with all his might. I met her on another occasion at the house of my old friend Heine, where she had taken refuge. When she noticed my indifference she again adjured me to use every possible effort to prevent the senseless, suicidal conflict. I heard afterwards that a charge of high treason on account of sedition had been brought against Schröder-Devrient by reason of her conduct in regard to this matter. She had to prove her innocence in a court of law, so as to establish beyond dispute her claim to the pension which she had been promised by contract for her many years' service in Dresden as an opera-singer.

On the 3rd of May I betook myself direct to that quarter of the town where I heard unpleasant rumours of a sanguinary conflict having taken place. I afterwards learned that the actual cause of the dispute between the civil and military power had arisen when the watch had been changed in front of the Arsenal. At that moment the mob, under a bold leader, had seized the opportunity to take forcible possession of the armoury. A display of military force was made, and the crowd was fired upon by a few cannon loaded with grape-shot. As I approached the scene of operations through the Rampische Gasse, I met a company of the Dresden Communal Guards, who, although they were quite innocent, had apparently been exposed to this fire. I noticed that one of the citizen guards, leaning heavily on the arm of a comrade, was trying to hurry along, in spite of the fact that his right leg seemed to be dragging helplessly behind him. Some of the crowd, seeing the blood on the pavement behind him, shouted 'He is bleeding.' In the midst of this excitement I suddenly became conscious of the cry raised on all sides: 'To the barricades! to the barricades!' Driven by a mechanical impulse I followed the stream of people, which moved once more in the direction of the Town Hall in the Old Market-place. Amid the terrific tumult I particularly noticed a significant group stretching right across the street, and striding along the Rosmaringasse. It reminded me, though the simile was rather exaggerated, of the crowd that had once stood at the doors of the theatre and demanded free entrance to *Rienzi;* among them was a hunchback, who at once suggested Goethe's Vansen in *Egmont,* and as the revolutionary cry rose about his ears, I saw him rub his hands together in great glee over the long-desired ecstasy of revolt which he had realised at last.

I recollect quite clearly that from that moment I was attracted by surprise and interest in the drama, without feeling any desire to join the ranks of the combatants. However, the agitation caused by my sympathy as a mere spectator increased

AT THE TOWN HALL

with every step I felt impelled to take. I was able to press right into the rooms of the town council, escaping notice in the tumultuous crowd, and it seemed to me as if the officials were guilty of collusion with the mob. I made my way unobserved into the council-chamber; what I saw there was utter disorder and confusion. When night fell I wandered slowly through the hastily made barricades, consisting chiefly of market stalls, back to my house in the distant Friedrichstrasse, and next morning I again watched these amazing proceedings with sympathetic interest.

On Thursday, 4th May, I could see that the Town Hall was gradually becoming the undoubted centre of the revolution. That section of the people who had hoped for a peaceful understanding with the monarch was thrown into the utmost consternation by the news that the King and his whole court, acting on the advice of his minister Beust, had left the palace, and had gone by ship down the Elbe to the fortress of Königstein. In these circumstances the town council saw they were no longer able to face the situation, and thereupon took part in summoning those members of the Saxon Chamber who were still in Dresden. These latter now assembled in the Town Hall to decide what steps should be taken for the protection of the state. A deputation was sent to the ministry, but returned with the report that they were nowhere to be found. At the same moment news arrived from all sides that, in accordance with a previous compact, the King of Prussia's troops would advance to occupy Dresden. A general outcry immediately arose for measures to be adopted to prevent this incursion of foreign troops.

Simultaneously with this, came the intelligence of the national uprising in Würtemberg, where the troops themselves had frustrated the intentions of the government by their declaration of fidelity to the parliament, and the ministry had been compelled against their will to acknowledge the Pan-German Constitution. The opinion of our politicians, who were assembled in consultation, was that the matter might still be settled by peaceful means, if it were possible to induce the Saxon troops to take up a similar attitude, as by this means the King would at least be placed under the wholesome necessity of offering patriotic resistance to the Prussian occupation of his country.

Everything seemed to depend on making the Saxon battalions in Dresden understand the paramount importance of their action. As this seemed to me the only hope of an honourable peace in this senseless chaos, I confess that, on this one occasion, I did allow myself to be led astray so far as to organise a demonstration which, however, proved futile.

I induced the printer of Röckel's *Volksblatt,* which was for the moment at a standstill, to employ all the type he would have used for his next number, in printing in huge characters on strips of paper the words: *Seid Ihr mit uns gegen fremde Truppen?* ('Are you on our side against the foreign troops?'). Placards bearing these words were fixed on those barricades which it was thought would be the first to be assaulted, and were intended to bring the Saxon troops to a halt if they were commanded to attack the revolutionaries. Of course no one took any notice of these placards except intending informers. On that day nothing but confused negotiations and wild excitement took place which threw no light on the situation. The Old Town of Dresden, with its barricades, was an interesting enough sight for the spectators. I looked on with amazement and disgust, but my attention was suddenly distracted by seeing Bakunin emerge from his hiding-place and wander among the barricades in a black frockcoat. But I was very much mistaken in thinking he would be pleased with what he saw; he recognised the childish inefficiency of all the measures that had been taken for defence, and declared that the only satisfaction he could feel in the state of affairs was that he need not trouble about the police, but could calmly consider the question of going elsewhere, as he found no inducement to take part in an insurrection conducted in such a slovenly fashion. While he walked about smoking his cigar, and making fun of the *naïveté* of the Dresden revolution, I watched the Communal Guards assembling under arms in front of the Town Hall at the summons of their commandant. From the ranks of its most popular corps, the Schützen-Compagnie, I was accosted by Rietschel, who was most anxious about the nature of the rising, and also by Semper. Rietschel, who seemed to think I was better informed of the facts than he was, assured me that he felt his position was a very difficult one. He said the select company to which he belonged was very democratic, and as his professorship at the Fine Arts Academy placed him in a peculiar position, he did not know how to reconcile the sentiments he shared with his company with his duty as a citizen. The word 'citizen' amused me; I glanced sharply at Semper and repeated the word 'citizen.' Semper responded with a peculiar smile, and turned away without further comment.

The next day (Friday the 5th of May), when I again took my place as a passionately interested spectator of the proceedings at the Town Hall, events took a decisive turn. The remnant of the leaders of the Saxon people there assembled thought it advisable to constitute themselves into a provisional government, as there was no Saxon government in existence with which negotiations could be conducted. Professor Köchly, who was an eloquent speaker, was chosen to proclaim the new administration. He performed this solemn ceremony from the balcony of the Town Hall, facing the faithful remnant of the Communal Guards and the not very numerous crowd. At the same time the legal existence of the Pan-German Constitution was proclaimed, and allegiance to it was sworn by the armed forces of the nation. I recollect that these proceedings did not seem to me imposing, and Bakunin's reiterated opinion about their triviality gradually became more comprehensible. Even from a technical point of view these reflections were justified when, to my great amusement and surprise, Semper, in the full uniform of a citizen guard, with a hat bedecked with the national colours, asked for me at the Town Hall, and informed me of the extremely faulty construction of the barricades in the Wild Strufergasse and the neighbouring Brüdergasse. To pacify his artistic conscience as an engineer I directed him to the office of the 'Military Commission for the Defence.' He followed my advice with conscientious satisfaction; possibly he obtained the necessary authorisation to give instructions for the building of suitable works of defence at that neglected point. After that I never saw him again in Dresden; but I presume that he carried out the strategic works entrusted to him by that committee with all the conscientiousness of a Michael Angelo or a Leonardo da Vinci.

The rest of the day passed in continuous negotiations over

the truce which, by arrangement with the Saxon troops, was to last until noon of the next day. In this business I noticed the very pronounced activity of a former college friend, Marschall von Bieberstein, a lawyer who, in his capacity as senior officer of the Dresden Communal Guard, distinguished himself by his boundless zeal amid the shouts of a mighty band of fellow-orators. On that day a certain Heinz, formerly a Greek colonel, was placed in command of the armed forces. These proceedings did not seem at all satisfactory to Bakunin, who put in an occasional appearance. While the provisional government placed all its hopes on finding a peaceful settlement of the conflict by moral persuasion, he, on the contrary, with his clear vision foresaw a well-planned military attack by the Prussians, and thought it could only be met by good strategic measures. He therefore urgently pressed for the acquisition of some experienced Polish officers who happened to be in Dresden, as the Saxon revolutionaries appeared to be absolutely lacking in military tactics. Everybody was afraid to take this course; on the other hand, great expectations were entertained from negotiations with the Frankfort States Assembly, which was on its last legs. Everything was to be done as far as possible in legal form. The time passed pleasantly enough. Elegant ladies with their cavaliers promenaded the barricaded streets during those beautiful spring evenings. It seemed to be little more than an entertaining drama. The unaccustomed aspect of things even afforded me genuine pleasure, combined with a feeling that the whole thing was not quite serious, and that a friendly proclamation from the government would put an end to it. So I strolled comfortably home through the numerous barricades at a late hour, thinking as I went of the material for a drama, *Achilleus*, with which I had been occupied for some time.

At home I found my two nieces, Clara and Ottilie Brockhaus, the daughters of my sister Louisa. They had been living for a year with a governess in Dresden, and their weekly visits and contagious good spirits delighted me. Every one was in a high state of glee about the revolution; they all heartily approved of the barricades, and felt no scruples about desiring victory for their defenders. Protected by the truce, this state

THE OPENING OF HOSTILITIES (1849) 481

of mind remained undisturbed the whole of Friday (5th May). From all parts came news which led us to believe in a universal uprising throughout Germany. Baden and the Palatinate were in the throes of a revolt on behalf of the whole of Germany. Similar rumours came in from free towns like Breslau. In Leipzig, volunteer student corps had mustered contingents for Dresden, which arrived amid the exultation of the populace. A fully equipped defence department was organised at the Town Hall, and young Heine, disappointed like myself in his hopes of the performance of *Lohengrin,* had also joined this body. Vigorous promises of support came from the Saxon Erzgebirge, as well as announcements that armed contingents were forthcoming. Every one thought, therefore, that if only the Old Town were kept well barricaded, it could safely defy the threat of foreign occupation. Early on Saturday, 6th May, it was obvious that the situation was becoming more serious. Prussian troops had marched into the New Town, and the Saxon troops, which it had not been considered advisable to use for an attack, were kept loyal to the flag. The truce expired at noon, and the troops, supported by several guns, at once opened the attack on one of the principal positions held by the people on the Neumarkt.

So far I had entertained no other conviction than that the matter would be decided in the most summary fashion as soon as it came to an actual conflict, for there was no evidence in the state of my own feelings (or, indeed, in what I was able to gather independently of them) of that passionate seriousness of purpose, without which tests as severe as this have never been successfully withstood. It was irritating to me, while I heard the sharp rattle of fire, to be unable to gather anything of what was going on, and I thought by climbing the Kreuz tower I might get a good view. Even from this elevation I could not see anything clearly, but I gathered enough to satisfy myself that after an hour of heavy firing the advance artillery of the Prussian troops had retired, and had at last been completely silenced, their withdrawal being signalled by a loud shout of jubilation from the populace. Apparently the first attack had exhausted itself; and now my interest in what was going on began to assume a more and more vivid hue. To obtain information in greater detail I hurried back to the Town Hall. I could extract nothing, however, from the boundless confusion which I met, until at last I came upon Bakunin in the midst of the main group of speakers. He was able to give me an extraordinarily accurate account of what had happened. Information had reached headquarters from a barricade in the Neumarkt where the attack was most serious, that everything had been in a state of confusion there before the onslaught of the troops; thereupon my friend Marschall von Bieberstein, together with Leo von Zichlinsky, who were officers in the citizen corps, had called up some volunteers and conducted them to the place of danger. Kreis-Amtmann Heubner of Freiberg, without a weapon to defend himself, and with bared head, jumped immediately on to the top of the barricade, which had just been abandoned by all its defenders. He was the sole member of the provisional government to remain on the spot, the leaders, Todt and Tschirner, having disappeared at the first sign of a panic. Heubner turned round to exhort the volunteers to advance, addressing them in stirring words. His success was complete, the barricade was taken again, and a fire, as unexpected as it was fierce, was directed upon the troops, which, as I myself saw, were forced to retire. Bakunin had been in close touch with this action, he had followed the volunteers, and he now explained to me that however narrow might be the political views of Heubner (he belonged to the moderate Left of the Saxon Chamber), he was a man of noble character, at whose service he had immediately placed his own life.

Bakunin had only needed this example to determine his own line of conduct; he had decided to risk his neck in the attempt and to ask no further questions. Heubner too was now bound to recognise the necessity for extreme measures, and no longer recoiled from any proposal on the part of Bakunin which was directed to this end. The military advice of experienced Polish officers was brought to bear on the commandant, whose incapacity had not been slow to reveal itself; Bakunin, who openly confessed that he understood nothing of pure strategy, never moved from the Town Hall, but remained at Heubner's side, giving advice and information in every direction with wonderful sangfroid. For the rest of the day the battle confined itself to skirmishes by sharpshooters from the various positions. I was itching to climb the Kreuz tower again, so as to get the widest possible survey over the whole field of action. In order to reach this tower from the Town Hall, one had to pass through a space which was under a cross-fire of rifle-shots from the troops posted in the royal palace. At a moment when this square was quite deserted, I yielded to my daring impulse, and crossed it on my way to the Kreuz tower at a slow pace, remembering that in such circumstances the young soldier is advised never to hurry, because by so doing he may draw the shot upon himself. On reaching this post of vantage I found several people who had gathered there, some of them driven by a curiosity like my own, others in obedience to an order from the headquarters of the revolutionaries to reconnoitre the enemy's movements. Amongst them I made the acquaintance of a schoolmaster called Berthold, a man of quiet and gentle disposition, but full of conviction and determination. I lost myself in an earnest philosophical discussion with him which extended to the widest spheres of religion. At the same time he showed a homely anxiety to protect us from the cone-shaped bullets of the Prussian sharpshooters by placing us ingeniously behind a barricade consisting of one of the straw mattresses which he had cajoled out of the warder. The Prussian sharpshooters were posted on the distant tower of the Frauenkirche, and had chosen the height occupied by us as their target. At nightfall I found it impossible to make up my mind to go home and leave my interesting place of refuge, so I persuaded the warder to send a subordinate to Friedrichstadt with a few lines to my wife, and with instructions to ask her to let me have some necessary provisions. Thus I spent one of the most extraordinary nights of my life, taking turns with Berthold to keep watch and sleep, close beneath the great bell with its terrible groaning clang, and with the accompaniment of the continuous rattle of the Prussian shot as it beat against the tower walls.

Sunday (the 7th of May) was one of the most beautiful days in the year. I was awakened by the song of a nightingale, which rose to our ears from the Schütze garden close by. A sacred calm and peacefulness lay over the town and the wide suburbs of Dresden, which were visible from my point of vantage. Towards sunrise a mist settled upon the outskirts, and suddenly through its folds we could hear the music of the *Marseillaise* making its way clearly and distinctly from the district of the Tharanderstrasse. As the sound drew nearer and nearer, the mist dispersed, and the glow of the rising sun spread a glittering light upon the weapons of a long column which was winding its way towards the town. It was impossible not to feel deeply impressed at the sight of this continuous procession. Suddenly a perception of that element which I had so long missed in the German people was borne in upon me in all its essential freshness and vital colour. The fact that until this moment I had been obliged to resign myself to its absence, had contributed not a little to the feelings by which I had been swayed. Here I beheld some thousand men from the Erzgebirge, mostly miners, well armed and organised, who had rallied to the defence of Dresden. Soon we saw them march up the Altmarkt opposite the Town Hall, and after receiving a joyful welcome, bivouac there to recover from their journey. Reinforcements continued to pour in the whole day long, and the heroic achievement of the previous day now received its reward in the shape of a universal elevation of spirits. A change seemed to have been made in the plan of attack by the Prussian troops. This could be gathered from the fact that numerous simultaneous attacks, but of a less concentrated type, were made upon various positions. The troops which had come to reinforce us brought with them four small cannon, the property of a certain Herr Thade von Burgk, whose acquaintance I had made before on the occasion of the anniversary of the founding of the Dresden Choral Society, when he had made a speech which was well intentioned but wearisome to the point of being ludicrous. The recollection of this speech returned to me with peculiar irony, now that his cannon were being fired from the barricade upon the enemy. I felt a still deeper impression, however, when, towards eleven o'clock, I saw the old Opera House, in which a few weeks ago I had conducted the last performance of the Ninth Symphony, burst into flames. As I have had occasion to mention before, the danger from fire to which this building was exposed, full as it was with wood and all kind of textile fabric, and originally built only for a temporary purpose, had always been a subject of terror and apprehension to those who visited it.

I was told that the Opera House had been set alight on strategical grounds, in order to face a dangerous attack on this exposed side, and also to protect the famous 'Semper' barricade from an overpowering surprise. From this I concluded that reasons of this kind act as far more powerful motives in the world than æsthetic considerations. For a long time men of taste had vainly cried aloud for abolition of this ugly building which was such an eyesore by the side of the elegant proportions of the Zwinger Gallery in its neighbourhood. In a few moments the Opera House (which as regards size was, it is true, an imposing edifice), together with its highly inflammable contents, was a vast sea of flames. When this reached the metal roofs of the neighbouring wings of the Zwinger, and enveloped them in wonderful bluish waves of fire, the first expression of regret made itself audible amongst the spectators. What a disaster! Some thought that the Natural History collection was in danger; others maintained that it was the Armoury, upon which a citizen soldier retorted that if such were the case, it would be a very good job if the 'stuffed noblemen' were burnt to cinders. But it appeared that a keen sense of the value of art knew how to curb the fire's lust for further dominion, and, as a matter of fact, it did but little damage in that quarter. Finally our post of observation, which until now had remained comparatively quiet, was filled itself with swarms and swarms of armed men, who had been ordered thither to defend the approach from the church to the Altmarkt, upon which an attack was feared from the side of the ill-secured Kreuzgasse. Unarmed men were now in the way; moreover, I had received a message from my wife summoning me home after the long and terrible anxiety she had suffered.

At last, after meeting with innumerable obstacles and overcoming a host of difficulties, I succeeded, by means of all sorts of circuitous routes, in reaching my remote suburb, from which I was cut off by the fortified portions of the town, and especially by a cannonade directed from the Zwinger. My lodgings were full to overflowing with excited women who had collected round Minna; among them the panic-stricken wife of Röckel, who suspected her husband of being in the very thick of the fight, as she thought that on the receipt of the news that Dresden had risen he would probably have returned. As a matter of fact, I had heard a rumour that Röckel had arrived on this very day, but as yet I had not obtained a glimpse of him. My young nieces helped once more to raise my spirits. The firing had put them into a high state of glee, which to some extent infected my wife, as soon as she was reassured as to my personal safety. All of them were furious with the sculptor Hänel, who had never ceased insisting upon the expedience of bolting the house to prevent an entry of the revolutionaries. All the women without exception were joking about his abject terror at the sight of some men armed with scythes who had appeared in the street. In this way Sunday passed like a sort of family jollification.

On the following morning (Monday, 8th May) I tried again to get information as to the state of affairs by forcing my way to the Town Hall from my house, which was cut off from the place of action. As in the course of my journey I was making my way over a barricade near St. Ann's Church, one of the Communal Guard shouted out to me, 'Hullo, conductor, your *der Freude schöner Götterfunken* [1] has indeed set fire to things. The rotten building is rased to the ground.' Obviously the man was an enthusiastic member of the audience at my last performance of the Ninth Symphony. Coming upon me so unexpectedly, this pathetic greeting filled me with a curious sense of strength and freedom. A little further on, in a lonely alley in the suburb of Plauen, I fell in with the musician Hiebendahl, the first oboist in the royal orchestra, and a man who still enjoyed a very high reputation; he was in the uniform of the Communal Guards, but carried no gun, and was chatting with a citizen in a similar costume. As soon as he saw me, he felt he must immediately make an appeal to me to use my influence against Röckel, who, accompanied by ordnance officers of the revolutionary party, was instituting a search for guns in this quarter. As soon as he realised that I was making

---

[1] These words refer to the opening of the Ninth Symphony chorus: 'Freude, Freude, Freude, schöner götterfunken Tochter aus Elysium'— (Praise her, praise oh praise Joy, the god-descended daughter of Elysium.) English version by Natalia Macfarren.—EDITOR.

sympathetic inquiries about Röckel, he drew back frightened, and said to me in tones of the deepest anxiety: ' But, conductor, have you no thought for your position, and what you may lose by exposing yourself in this fashion?' This remark had the most drastic effect upon me; I burst into a loud laugh, and told him that my position was not worth a thought one way or the other. This indeed was the expression of my real feelings, which had long been suppressed, and now broke out into almost jubilant utterance. At that moment I caught sight of Röckel, with two men of the citizen army who were carrying some guns, making his way towards me. He gave me a most friendly greeting, but turned at once to Hiebendahl and his companion and asked him why he was idling about here in uniform instead of being at his post. When Hiebendahl made the excuse that his gun had been requisitioned, Röckel cried out to him, ' You're a fine lot of fellows!' and went away laughing. He gave me a brief account as we proceeded of what had happened to him since I had lost sight of him, and thus spared me the obligation of giving him a report of his *Volksblatt*. We were interrupted by an imposing troop of well-armed young students of the gymnasium who had just entered the city and wished to have a safe conduct to their place of muster. The sight of these serried ranks of youthful figures, numbering several hundreds, who were stepping bravely to their duty, did not fail to make the most elevating impression upon me. Röckel undertook to accompany them over the barricade in safety to the mustering place in front of the Town Hall. He took the opportunity of lamenting the utter absence of true spirit which he had hitherto encountered in those in command. He had proposed, in case of extremity, to defend the most seriously threatened barricades by firing them with pitch brands; at the mere word the provisional government had fallen into a veritable state of panic. I let him go his way in order that I might enjoy the privilege of a solitary person and reach the Town Hall by a short cut, and it was not until thirteen years later that I again set eyes upon him.

In the Town Hall I learned from Bakunin that the provisional government had passed a resolution, on his advice, to abandon the position in Dresden, which had been entirely neglected from the beginning, and was consequently quite untenable for any length of time. This resolution proposd an armed retreat to the Erzgebirge, where it would be possible to concentrate the reinforcements pouring in from all sides, especially from Thuringia, in such strength, that the advantageous position could be used to inaugurate a German civil war that would sound no hesitating note at its outset. To persist in defending isolated barricaded streets in Dresden could, on the other hand, lend little but the character of an urban riot to the contest, although it was pursued with the highest courage. I must confess that this idea seemed to me magnificent and full of meaning. Up to this moment I had been moved only by a feeling of sympathy for a method of procedure entered upon at first with almost ironical incredulity, and then pursued with the vigour of surprise. Now, however, all that had before seemed incomprehensible, unfolded itself before my vision in the form of a great and hopeful solution. Without either feeling that I was in any way being compelled, or that it was my vocation to get some part or function allotted to me in these events, I now definitely abandoned all consideration for my personal situation, and determined to surrender myself to the stream of developments which flowed in the direction towards which my feelings had driven me with a delight that was full of despair. Still, I did not wish to leave my wife helpless in Dresden, and I rapidly devised a means of drawing her into the path which I had chosen, without immediately informing her of what my resolve meant. During my hasty return to Friedrichstadt I recognised that this portion of the town had been almost entirely cut off from the inner city by the occupation of the Prussian troops; I saw in my mind's eye our own suburb occupied, and the consequences of a state of military siege in their most repulsive light. It was an easy job to persuade Minna to accompany me on a visit, by way of the Tharanderstrasse, which was still free, to Chemnitz, where my married sister Clara lived. It was only a matter of a moment for her to arrange her household orders, and she promised to follow me to the next village in an hour with the parrot. I went on in advance with my little dog Peps, in order to hire a carriage in which to proceed on our journey to Chemnitz. It was a smiling spring morning when I traversed for the last time the paths I had so often trod on my lonely walks, with the knowledge that I should never wander along them again. While the larks were soaring to dizzy heights above my head, and singing in the furrows of the fields, the light and heavy artillery did not cease to thunder down the streets of Dresden. The noise of this shooting, which had continued uninterruptedly for several days, had hammered itself so indelibly upon my nerves, that it continued to re-echo for a long time in my brain; just as the motion of the ship which took me to London had made me stagger for some time afterwards. Accompanied by this terrible music, I threw my parting greeting to the towers of the city that lay behind me, and said to myself with a smile, that if, seven years ago, my entry had taken place under thoroughly obscure auspices, at all events my exit was conducted with some show of pomp and ceremony.

When at last I found myself with Minna in a one-horse carriage on the way to the Erzgebirge, we frequently met armed reinforcements on their way to Dresden. The sight of them always kindled an involuntary joy in us; even my wife could not refrain from addressing words of encouragement to the men; at present it seemed not a single barricade had been lost. On the other hand, a gloomy impression was made upon us by a company of regulars which was making its way towards Dresden in silence. We asked some of them whither they were bound; and their answer, 'To do their duty,' had been obviously impressed upon them by command. At last we reached my relations in Chemnitz. I terrified all those near and dear to me when I declared my intention to return to Dresden on the following day at the earliest possible hour, in order to ascertain how things were going there. In spite of all attempts to dissuade me, I carried out my decision, pursued by a suspicion that I should meet the armed forces of the Dresden people on the country highroad in the act of retreat. The nearer I approached the capital, the stronger became the confirmation of the rumours that, as yet, there was no thought in Dresden of surrender or withdrawal, but that, on the contrary, the contest was proving very favourable for the national party. All this appeared to me like one miracle after another. On this day, Tuesday, 9th of May, I once more forced my way in a high state of excitement over ground which had become more and more inaccessible. All the highways had to be avoided, and it was only possible to make progress through such houses as had been broken through. At last I reached the Town Hall in the Altstadt, just as night was falling. A truly terrible spectacle met my eyes, for I crossed those parts of the town in which preparations had been made for a house-to-house fight. The incessant groaning of big and small guns reduced to an uncanny murmur all the other sounds that came from armed men ceaselessly crying out to one another from barricade to barricade, and from one house to another, which they had broken through. Pitch brands burnt here and there, pale-faced figures lay prostrate around the watch-posts, half dead with fatigue, and any unarmed wayfarer forcing a path for himself was sharply challenged. Nothing, however, that I have lived through can be compared with the impression that I received on my entry into the chambers of the Town Hall. Here was a gloomy, and yet fairly compact and serious mass of people; a look of unspeakable fatigue was upon all faces; not a single voice had retained its natural tone. There was a hoarse jumble of conversation inspired by a state of the highest tension. The only familiar sight that survived was to be found in the old servants of the Town Hall in their curious antiquated uniform and three-cornered hats. These tall men, at other times an object of considerable fear, I found engaged partly in buttering pieces of bread, and cutting slices of ham and sausage, and partly in piling into baskets immense stores of provisions for the messengers sent by the defenders of the barricades for supplies. These men had turned into veritable nursing mothers of the revolution.

As I proceeded further, I came at last upon the members of the provisional government, among whom Todt and Tschirner, after their first panic-stricken flight, were once more to be found gliding to and fro, gloomy as spectres, now that they were chained to the performance of their heavy duties. Heubner alone had preserved his full energy; but he was a really piteous sight: a ghostly fire burned in his eyes which had not had a wink of sleep for seven nights. He was delighted

BAKUNIN AT THE TOWN HALL

to see me again, as he regarded my arrival as a good omen for the cause which he was defending; while on the other hand, in the rapid succession of events, he had come into contact with elements about which no conclusion could shape itself to his complete satisfaction. I found Bakunin's outlook undisturbed, and his attitude firm and quiet. He did not show the smallest change in his appearance, in spite of having had no sleep during the whole time, which I afterwards heard was a fact. With a cigar in his mouth he received me, seated on one of the mattresses which lay distributed over the floor of the Town Hall. At his side was a very young Pole (a Galician) named Haimberger, a violinist whom he had once asked me to recommend to Lipinsky, in order that he might give him lessons, as he did not want this raw and inexperienced boy, who had become passionately attached to him, to get drawn into the vortex of the present upheavals. Now that Haimberger had shouldered a gun, and presented himself for service at the barricades, however, Bakunin had greeted him none the less joyfully. He had drawn him down to sit by his side on the couch, and every time the youth shuddered with fear at the violent sound of the cannon-shot, he slapped him vigorously on the back and cried out: ' You are not in the company of your fiddle here, my friend. What a pity you did n't stay where you were! ' Bakunin then gave me a short and precise account of what had happened since I had left him on the previous morning. The retreat which had then been decided upon soon proved unadvisable, as it would have discouraged the numerous reinforcements which had already arrived on that day. Moreover, the desire for fighting had been so great, and the force of the defenders so considerable, that it had been possible to oppose the enemy's troops successfully so far. But as the latter had also got large reinforcements, they again had been able to make an effective combined attack on the strong Wildstruf barricade. The Prussian troops had avoided fighting in the streets, choosing instead the method of fighting from house to house by breaking through the walls. This had made it clear that all defence by barricades had become useless, and that the enemy would succeed slowly but surely in drawing near the Town Hall, the seat of the provisional government. Bakunin had now proposed that all the powder stores should be brought together in the lower rooms of the Town Hall, and that on the approach of the enemy it should be blown up. The town council, who were still in consultation in a back room, had remonstrated with the greatest vehemence. Bakunin, however, had insisted with great firmness on the execution of the measure, but in the end had been completely outwitted by the removal of all the powder stores. Moreover, Heubner, to whom Bakunin could refuse nothing, had been won over to the other side. It was now decided that as everything was ready, the retreat to the Erzgebirge, which had originally been intended for the previous day, should be fixed for the early morrow. Young Zichlinsky had already received orders to cover the road to Plauen so as to make it strategically safe. When I inquired after Röckel, Bakunin replied swiftly that he had not been seen since the previous evening, and that he had most likely allowed himself to be caught: he was in such a nervous state. I now gave an account of what I had observed on my way to and from Chemnitz, describing the great masses of reinforcements, amongst which was the communal guard of that place, several thousands strong. In Freiberg I had met four hundred reservists, who had come in excellent form to back the citizen army, but could not proceed further, as they were tired out by their forced march. It seemed obvious that this was a case in which the necessary energy to requisition wagons had been lacking, and that if the bounds of loyalty were transgressed in this matter, the advent of fresh forces would be considerably promoted. I was begged to make my way back at once, and convey the opinion of the provisional government to the people whose acquaintance I had made. My old friend Marschall von Bieberstein immediately proposed to accompany me. I welcomed his offer, as he was an officer of the provisional government, and was consequently more fitted than I was to communicate orders. This man, who had been almost extravagant in his enthusiasm before, was now utterly exhausted by sleeplessness, and unable to emit another word from his hoarse throat. He now made his way with me from the Town Hall to his house in the suburb of Plauen by the devious ways that had been indicated to us, in order to requisition a carriage for our purpose from a coachman he knew, and to bid farewell to his family, from whom he assumed he would in all probability have to separate himself for some time.

While we were waiting for the coachman we had tea and supper, talking the while, in a fairly calm and composed manner, with the ladies of the house. We arrived at Freiberg early the following morning, after various adventures, and I set out forthwith to find the leaders of the reservist contingent with whom I was already acquainted. Marschall advised them to requisition horses and carts in the villages wherever they could do so. When they had all set off in marching order for Dresden, and while I was feeling impelled by my passionate interest in the fate of that city to return to it once more, Marschall conceived the desire to carry his commission further afield, and for this purpose asked to be allowed to leave me. Whereupon I again turned my back on the heights of the Erzgebirge, and was travelling by special coach in the direction of Tharand, when I too was overcome with sleep, and was only awakened by violent shouts and the sound of some one holding a parley with the postillion. On opening my eyes I found, to my astonishment, that the road was filled with armed revolutionaries marching, not towards, but away from Dresden, and some of them were trying to commandeer the coach to relieve their weariness on the way back.

'What is the matter?' I cried. 'Where are you going?'

'Home,' was the reply. 'It is all over in Dresden. The provincial government is close behind us in that carriage down there.'

I shot out of the coach like a dart, leaving it at the disposal of the tired men, and hurried on, down the steeply sloping road, to meet the ill-fated party. And there I actually found them — Heubner, Bakunin, and Martin, the energetic post-office clerk, the two latter armed with muskets — in a smart hired carriage from Dresden which was coming slowly up the hill. On the box were, as I supposed, the secretaries, while as many as possible of the weary National Guard struggled for seats behind. I hastened to swing myself into the coach, and so came in for a conversation which thereupon took place between the driver, who was also the owner of the coach, and the provisional government. The man was imploring them to spare his carriage, which, he said, was very lightly sprung and quite unequal to carrying such a load; he begged that the people should be told not to seat themselves behind and in front. But Bakunin remained quite unconcerned, and elected to give me a short account of the retreat from Dresden, which had been successfully achieved without loss. He had had the trees in the newly planted Maximilian Avenue felled early in the morning to form a barricade against a possible flank attack of cavalry, and had been immensely entertained by the lamentations of the inhabitants, who during the process did nothing but bewail their *Scheene Beeme*.[1] All this time our driver's lamentations over his coach were growing more importunate. Finally he broke into loud sobs and tears, upon which Bakunin, regarding him with positive pleasure, called out: 'The tears of a Philistine are nectar for the gods.' He would not vouchsafe him a word, but Heubner and I found the scene tiresome, whereupon he asked me whether we two at least should not get out, as he could not ask it of the others. As a matter of fact, it was high time to leave the coach, as some new contingents of revolutionaries had formed up in rank and file all along the highway to salute the provisional government and receive orders. Heubner strode down the line with great dignity, acquainted the leaders with the state of affairs, and exhorted them to keep their trust in the righteousness of the cause for which so many had shed their blood. All were now to retire to Freiberg, there to await further orders.

A youngish man of serious mien now stepped forward from the ranks of the rebels to place himself under the special protection of the provisional government. He was a certain Menzdorff, a German Catholic priest whom I had had the advantage of meeting in Dresden. (It was he who, in the course of a significant conversation, had first induced me to read Feuerbach.) He had been dragged along as a prisoner and abominably treated by the Chemnitz municipal guard on this particular march, having originally been the instigator of a demonstration to force that body to take up arms and march

[1] Saxon corruption of *schöne Baume*, beautiful trees. — EDITOR.

ARRIVAL IN FREIBERG

to Dresden. He owed his freedom only to the chance meeting with other better disposed volunteer corps. We saw this Chemnitz town guard ourselves, stationed far away on a hill. They sent representatives to beseech Heubner to tell them how things stood. When they had received the information rquired, and had been told that the fight would be continued in a determined manner, they invited the provisional government to quarter at Chemnitz. As soon as they rejoined their main body we saw them wheel round and turn back.

With many similar interruptions the somewhat disorganised procession reached Freiberg. Here some friends of Heubner's came to meet him in the streets with the urgent request not to plunge their native place into the misery of desperate street-fighting by establishing the provisional government there. Heubner made no reply to this, but requested Bakunin and myself to accompany him into his house for a consultation. First we had to witness the painful meeting between Heubner and his wife; in a few words he pointed out the gravity and importance of the task assigned to him, reminding her that it was for Germany and the high destiny of his country that he was staking his life.

Breakfast was then prepared, and after the meal, during which a fairly cheerful mood prevailed, Heubner made a short speech to Bakunin, speaking quietly but firmly. 'My dear Bukanin,' he said (his previous acquaintance with Bakunin was so slight that he did not even know how to pronounce his name), 'before we decide anything further, I must ask you to state clearly whether your political aim is really the Red Republic, of which they tell me you are a partisan. Tell me frankly, so that I may know if I can rely on your friendship in the future?'

Bakunin explained briefly that he had no scheme for any political form of government, and would not risk his life for any of them. As for his own far-reaching desires and hopes, they had nothing whatever to do with the street-fighting in Dresden and all that this implied for Germany. He had looked upon the rising in Dresden as a foolish, ludicrous movement until he realised the effect of Heubner's noble and courageous example. From that moment every political consideration and aim had been put in the background by his sympathy with this heroic attitude, and he had immediately resolved to assist this excellent man with all the devotion and energy of a friend. He knew, of course, that he belonged to the so-called moderate party, of whose political future he was not able to form an opinion, as he had not profited much by his opportunities of studying the position of the various parties in Germany.

Heubner declared himself satisfied by this reply, and proceeded to ask Bakunin's opinion of the present state of things — whether it would not be conscientious and reasonable to dismiss the men and give up a struggle which might be considered hopeless. In reply Bakunin insisted, with his usual calm assurance, that whoever else threw up the sponge, Heubner must certainly not do so. He had been the first member of the provisional government, and it was he who had given the call to arms. The call had been obeyed, and hundreds of lives had been sacrificed; to scatter the people again would look as if these sacrifices had been made to idle folly. Even if they were the only two left, they still ought not to forsake their posts. If they went under their lives might be forfeit, but their honour must remain unsullied, so that a similar appeal in the future might not drive every one to despair.

This was quite enough for Heubner. He at once made out a summons for the election of a representative assembly for Saxony, to be held at Chemnitz. He thought that, with the assistance of the populace and of the numerous insurgent bands who were arriving from all quarters, he would be able to hold the town as the headquarters of a provisional government until the general situation in Germany had become more settled. In the midst of these discussions, Stephan Born walked into the room to report that he had brought the armed bands right into Freiberg, in good order and without any losses. This young man was a compositor who had contributed greatly to Heubner's peace of mind during the last three days in Dresden by taking over the chief command. His simplicity of manner made a very encouraging impression on us, particularly when we heard his report. When, however, Heubner asked whether he would undertake to defend Freiberg against the troops which might be expected to attack at any moment, he declared that this was an experienced officer's job, and that he himself was no soldier

AT THE TOWN HALL AT FREIBERG

and knew nothing of strategy. Under these circumstances it seemed better, if only to gain time, to fall back on the more thickly populated town of Chemnitz. The first thing to be done, however, was to see that the revolutionaries, who were assembled in large numbers at Freiberg, were properly cared for, and Born went off immediately to make preliminary arrangements. Heubner also took leave of us, and went to refresh his tired brain by an hour's sleep. I was left alone on the sofa with Bakunin, who soon fell towards me, overcome by irresistible drowsiness, and dropped the terrific weight of his head on to my shoulder. As I saw that he would not wake if I shook off this burden, I pushed him aside with some difficulty, and took leave both of the sleeper and of Heubner's house; for I wished to see for myself, as I had done for many days past, what course these extraordinary events were taking. I therefore went to the Town Hall, where I found the townspeople entertaining to the best of their ability a blustering horde of excited revolutionaries both within and without the walls. To my surprise, I found Heubner there in the full swing of work. I thought he was asleep at home, but the idea of leaving the people even for an hour without a counsellor had driven away all thought of rest. He had lost no time in superintending the organisation of a sort of commandant's office, and was again occupied with drafting and signing documents in the midst of the uproar that raged on all sides. It was not long before Bakunin too put in an appearance, principally in search of a good officer — who was not, however, forthcoming. The commandant of a large contingent from the Vogtland, an oldish man, raised Bakunin's hopes by the impassioned energy of his speeches, and he would have had him appointed commandant-general on the spot. But it seemed as if any real decision were impossible in that frenzy and confusion, and as the only hope of mastering it seemed to be in reaching Chemnitz, Heubner gave the order to march on towards that town as soon as every one had had food. Once this was settled, I told my friends I should go on in advance of their column to Chemnitz, where I should find them again next day; for I longed to be quit of this chaos. I actually caught the coach, the departure of which was fixed for that time, and obtained a seat in it. But the revolutionaries were just marching off on the same road, and we were told that we must wait until they had passed to avoid being caught in the whirlpool. This meant considerable delay, and for a long while I watched the peculiar bearing of the patriots as they marched out. I noticed in particular a Vogtland regiment, whose marching step was fairly orthodox, following the beat of a drummer who tried to vary the monotony of his instrument in an artistic manner by hitting the wooden frame alternately with the drumhead. The unpleasant rattling tone thus produced reminded me in ghostly fashion of the rattling of the skeletons' bones in the dance round the gallows by night which Berlioz had brought home to my imagination with such terrible realism in his performance of the last movement of his *Sinfonie Fantastique* in Paris.

Suddenly the desire seized me to look up the friends I had left behind, and travel to Chemnitz in their company if possible. I found they had quitted the Town Hall, and on reaching Heubner's house I was told that he was asleep. I therefore went back to the coach, which, however, was still putting off its departure, as the road was blocked with troops. I walked nervously up and down for some time, then, losing faith in the journey by coach, I went back again to Heubner's house to offer myself definitely as a travelling companion. But Heubner and Bakunin had already left home, and I could find no traces of them. In desperation I returned once more to the coach, and found it by this time really ready to start. After various delays and adventures it brought me late at night to Chemnitz, where I got out and betook myself to the nearest inn. At five o'clock the next morning I got up (after a few hours' sleep) and set out to find my brother-in-law Wolfram's house, which was about a quarter of an hour's walk from the town. On the way I asked a sentinel of the town guard whether he knew anything about the arrival of the provisional government.

'Provisional government?' was the reply. 'Why, it's all up with that.' I did not understand him, nor was I able to learn anything about the state of things when I first reached the house of my relatives, for my brother-in-law had been sent into the town as special constable. It was only on his return home, late in the afternoon, that I heard what had taken place in one hotel at Chemnitz while I had been resting in another inn. Heubner, Bakunin, and the man called Martin, whom I have mentioned already, had, it seemed, arrived before me in a hackney-coach at the gates of Chemnitz. On being asked for their names Heubner had announced himself in a tone of authority, and had bidden the town councillors come to him at a certain hotel. They had no sooner reached the hotel than they all three collapsed from excessive fatigue. Suddenly the police broke into the room and arrested them in the name of the local government, upon which they only begged to have a few hours' quiet sleep, pointing out that flight was out of the question in their present condition. I heard further that they had been removed to Altenburg under a strong military escort. My brother-in-law was obliged to confess that the Chemnitz municipal guard, which had been forced to start for Dresden much against its will, and had resolved at the very outset to place itself at the disposal of the royal forces on arriving there, had deceived Heubner by inviting him to Chemnitz, and had lured him into the trap. They had reached Chemnitz long before Heubner, and had taken over the guard at the gates with the object of seeing him arrive and of preparing for his arrest at once. My brother-in-law had been very anxious about me too, as he had been told in furious tones by the leaders of the town guard that I had been seen in close association with the revolutionaries. He thought it a wonderful intervention of Providence that I had not arrived at Chemnitz with them and gone to the same inn, in which case their fate would certainly have been mine. The recollection of my escape from almost certain death in duels with the most experienced swordsmen in my student days flashed across me like a flash of lightning. This last terrible experience made such an impression on me that I was incapable of breathing a word in connection with what had happened. My brother-in-law, in response to urgent appeals — from my wife in particular, who was much concerned for my personal safety — undertook to convey me to Altenburg in his carriage by night. From there I continued my journey by coach to Weimar, where I had originally planned to spend my holidays, little thinking that I should arrive by such devious ways.

The dreamy unreality of my state of mind at this time is best explained by the apparent seriousness with which, on meeting Liszt again, I at once began to discuss what seemed to be the sole topic of any real interest to him in connection with me — the forthcoming revival of *Tannhäuser* at Weimar. I found it very difficult to confess to this friend that I had not left Dresden in the regulation way for a conductor of the royal opera. To tell the truth, I had a very hazy conception of the relation in which I stood to the law of my country (in the narrow sense). Had I done anything criminal in the eye of the law or not? I found it impossible to come to any conclusion about it. Meanwhile, alarming news of the terrible conditions in Dresden continued to pour into Weimar. Genast, the stage manager, in particular, aroused great excitement by spreading the report that Röckel, who was well known at Weimar, had been guilty of arson. Liszt must soon have gathered from my conversation, in which I did not take the trouble to dissimulate, that I too was suspiciously connected with these terrible events, though my attitude with regard to them misled him for some time. For I was not by any means prepared to proclaim myself a combatant in the recent fights, and that for reasons quite other than would have seemed valid in the eyes of the law. My friend was therefore encouraged in his delusion by the unpremeditated effect of my attitude. When we met at the house of Princess Caroline of Wittgenstein, to whom I had been introduced the year before when she paid her flying visit to Dresden, we were able to hold stimulating conversations on all sorts of artistic topics. One afternoon, for instance, a lively discussion sprang up from a description I had given of a tragedy to be entitled *Jesus of Nazareth*. Liszt maintained a discreet silence after I had finished, whereas the Princess protested vigorously against my proposal to bring such a subject on to the stage. From the lukewarm attempt I made to support the paradoxical theories I had put forward, I realised the state of my mind at that time. Although it was not very evident to onlookers, I had been, and still was, shaken to the very depths of my being by my recent experiences.

SOJOURN WITH LISZT

In due course an orchestral rehearsal of *Tannhäuser* took place, which in various ways stimulated the artist in me afresh. Liszt's conducting, though mainly concerned with the musical rather than the dramatic side, filled me for the first time with the flattering warmth of emotion roused by the consciousness of being understood by another mind in full sympathy with my own. At the same time I was able, in spite of my dreamy condition, to observe critically the standard of capacity exhibited by the singers and their chorus-master. After the rehearsal I, together with the musical director, Stöhr, and Götze the singer, accepted Liszt's invitation to a simple dinner, at a different inn from the one where he lived. I thus had occasion to take alarm at a trait in his character which was entirely new to me. After being stirred up to a certain pitch of excitement his mood became positively alarming, and he almost gnashed his teeth in a passion of fury directed against a certain section of society which had also aroused my deepest indignation. I was strongly affected by this strange experience with this wonderful man, but I was unable to see the association of ideas which had led to his terrible outburst. I was therefore left in a state of amazement, while Liszt had to recover during the night from a violent attack of nerves which his excitement had produced. Another surprise was in store for me the next morning, when I found my friend fully equipped for a journey to Karlsruhe—the circumstances which made it necessary being absolutely incomprehensible to me. Liszt invited Director Stöhr and myself to accompany him as far as Eisenach. On our way there we were stopped by Beaulieu, the Lord Chamberlain, who wished to know whether I was prepared to be received by the Grand Duchess of Weimar, a sister of the Emperor Nicolas, at Eisenach castle. As my excuse on the score of unsuitable travelling costume was not admitted, Liszt accepted in my name, and I really met with a surprisingly kind reception that evening from the Grand Duchess, who chatted with me in the friendliest way, and introduced me to her chamberlain with all due ceremony. Liszt maintained afterwards that his noble patroness had been informed that I should be wanted by the authorities in Dresden within the next few days, and had therefore hastened to make my personal acquaintance at once, knowing that it would compromise her too heavily later on.

Liszt continued his journey from Eisenach, leaving me to be entertained and looked after by Stöhr and the musical director Kühmstedt, a diligent and skilful master of counterpoint with whom I paid my first visit to the Wartburg, which had not then been restored. I was filled with strange musings as to my fate when I visited this castle. Here I was actually on the point of entering, for the first time, the building which was so full of meaning for me; here, too, I had to tell myself that the days of my further sojourn in Germany were numbered. And in fact the news from Dresden, when we returned to Weimar the next day, was serious indeed. Liszt, on his return on the third day, found a letter from my wife, who had not dared to write direct to me. She reported that the police had searched my house in Dresden, to which she had returned, and that she had, moreover, been warned on no account to allow me to return to that city, as a warrant had been taken out against me, and I was shortly to be served with a writ and arrested. Liszt, who was now solely concerned for my personal safety, called in a friend who had some experience of law, to consider what should be done to rescue me from the danger that threatened me. Von Watzdorf, the minister whom I had already visited, had been of opinion that I should, if required, submit quietly to being taken to Dresden, and that the journey would be made in a respectable private carriage. On the other hand, reports which had reached us of the brutal way in which the Prussian troops in Dresden had gone to work in applying the state of siege were of so alarming a nature that Liszt and his friends in council urged my speedy departure from Weimar, where it would be impossible to protect me. But I insisted on taking leave of my wife, whose anxiety was great, before leaving Germany, and begged to be allowed to stay a little longer at least in the neighbourhood of Weimar. This was taken into consideration, and Professor Siebert suggested my taking temporary shelter with a friendly steward at the village of Magdala, which was three hours distant. I drove there the following morning to introduce myself to this kind steward and protector as Professor Werder from Berlin, who, with a letter of recommendation from Professor Siebert, had come to turn his financial studies to practical account in helping to administer these estates. Here in rural seclusion I spent three days, entertainment of a peculiar nature being provided by the meeting of a popular assembly, which consisted of the remainder of the contingent of revolutionaries which had marched off towards Dresden and had now returned in disorder. I listened with curious feelings, amounting almost to contempt, to the speeches on this occasion, which were of every kind and description. On the second day of my stay my host's wife came back from Weimar (where it was market-day) full of a curious tale: the composer of an opera which was being performed there on that very day had been obliged to leave Weimar suddenly because the warrant for his arrest had arrived from Dresden. My host, who had been let into my secret by Professor Seibert, asked playfully what his name was. As his wife did not seem to know, he came to her assistance with the suggestion that perhaps it was Röckel whose name was familiar at Weimar.

'Yes,' she said, 'Röckel, that was his name, quite right.'

My host laughed loudly, and said that he would not be so stupid as to let them catch him, in spite of his opera.

At last, on 22nd May, my birthday, Minna actually arrived at Magdala. She had hastened to Weimar on receiving my letter, and had proceeded from there according to instructions, bent on persuading me at all costs to flee the country immediately and for good. No attempt to raise her to the level of my own mood was successful; she persisted in regarding me as an ill advised, inconsiderate person who had plunged both himself and her into the most terrible situation. It had been arranged that I should meet her the next evening in the house of Professor Wolff at Jena to take a last farewell. She was to go by way of Weimar, while I took the footpath from Magdala. I started accordingly on my walk of about six hours, and came over the plateau into the little university town (which now received me hospitably for the first time) at sunset. I found my wife again at the house of Professor Wolff, who, thanks to Liszt, was already my friend, and with the addition of a certain

Professor Widmann another conference was held on the subject of my further escape. A writ was actually out against me for being strongly suspected of participation in the Dresden rising, and I could not under any circumstances depend on a safe refuge in any of the German federal states. Liszt insisted on my going to Paris, where I could find a new field for my work, while Widmann advised me not to go by the direct route through Frankfort and Baden, as the rising was still in full swing there, and the police would certainly exercise praiseworthy vigilance over incoming travellers with suspicious-looking passports. The way through Bavaria would be the safest, as all was quiet there again; I could then make for Switzerland, and the journey to Paris from there could be engineered without any danger. As I needed a passport for the journey, Professor Widmann offered me his own, which had been issued at Tübingen and had not been brought up to date. My wife was quite in despair, and the parting from her caused me real pain. I set off in the mail-coach and travelled, without further hindrance, through many towns (amongst them Rudolstadt, a place full of memories for me) to the Bavarian frontier. From there I continued my journey by mail-coach straight to Lindau. At the gates I, together with the other passengers, was asked for my passport. I passed the night in a state of strange, feverish excitement, which lasted until the departure of the steamer on Lake Constance early in the morning. My mind was full of the Swabian dialect, as spoken by Professor Widmann, with whose passport I was travelling. I pictured to myself my dealings with the Bavarian police should I have to converse with them in accordance with the above-mentioned irregularities in that document. A prey to feverish unrest, I spent the whole night trying to perfect myself in the Swabian dialect, but, as I was amused to find, without the smallest success. I had braced myself to meet the crucial moment early the next morning, when the policeman came into my room and, not knowing to whom the passports belonged, gave me three at random to choose from. With joy in my heart I seized my own, and dismissed the dreaded messenger in the most friendly way. Once on board the steamer I realised with true satisfaction that I had now stepped on to Swiss territory. It was a lovely spring morning; across the broad lake I could gaze at the Alpine landscape as it spread itself before my eyes. When I stepped on to Republican soil at Rorschach, I employed the first moments in writing a few lines home to tell of my safe arrival in Switzerland and my deliverance from all danger. The coach drive through the pleasant country of St. Gall to Zürich cheered me up wonderfully, and when I drove down from Oberstrass into Zürich that evening, the last day in May, at six o'clock, and saw for the first time the Glarner Alps that encircle the lake gleaming in the sunset, I at once resolved, though without being fully conscious of it, to avoid everything that could prevent my settling here.

I had been the more willing to accept my friends' suggestion to take the Swiss route to Paris, as I knew I should find an old acquaintance, Alexander Müller, at Zürich. I hoped with his help to obtain a passport to France, as I was anxious not to arrive there as a political refugee. I had been on very friendly terms with Müller once upon a time at Würzburg. He had been settled at Zürich for a long time as a teacher of music; this I learned from a pupil of his, Wilhelm Baumgartner, who had called on me in Dresden some years back to bring me a greeting from this old friend. On that occasion I entrusted the pupil with a copy of the score of *Tannhäuser* for his master, by way of remembrance, and this kind attention had not fallen on barren soil: Müller and Baumgartner, whom I visited forthwith, introduced me at once to Jacob Sulzer and Franz Hagenbuch, two cantonal secretaries who were the most likely, among all their good friends, to compass the immediate fulfilment of my desire. These two people, who had been joined by a few intimates, received me with such respectful curiosity and sympathy that I felt at home with them at once. The great assurance and moderation with which they commented on the persecutions which had overtaken me, as seen from their usual simple republican standpoint, opened to me a conception of civil life which seemed to lift me to an entirely new sphere. I felt so safe and protected here, whereas in my own country I had, without quite realising it, come to be considered a criminal owing to the peculiar connection between my disgust at the public attitude towards art and the general political disturbances. To prepossess the two secretaries entirely in my favour (one of them, Sulzer, had enjoyed an excellent classical education), my friends arranged a meeting one evening at which I was to read my poem on the *Death of Siegfried*. I am prepared to swear that I never had more attentive listeners, among men, than on that evening. The immediate effect of my success was the drawing up of a fully valid federal passport for the poor German under warrant of arrest, armed with which I started gaily on my journey to Paris after quite a short stay at Zürich. From Strassburg, where I was enthralled by the fascination of the world-famous minster, I travelled towards Paris by what was then the best means of locomotion, the so-called *malle-poste*. I remember a remarkable phenomenon in connection with this conveyance. Till then the noise of the cannonade and musketry in the fighting at Dresden had been persistently re-echoing in my ears, especially in a half-waking condition; now the humming of the wheels, as we rolled rapidly along the highroad, cast such a spell upon me that for the whole of the journey I seemed to hear the melody of *Freude, schöner Götterfunken* [1] from the Ninth Symphony being played, as it were, on deep bass instruments.

From the time of my entering Switzerland till my arrival in Paris my spirits, which had sunk into a dreamlike apathy, rose gradually to a level of freedom and comfort that I had never enjoyed before. I felt like a bird in the air whose destiny is not to founder in a morass; but soon after my arrival in Paris, in the first week of June, a very palpable reaction set in. I had had an introduction from Liszt to his former secretary Belloni, who felt it his duty, in loyalty to the instructions received, to put me into communication with a literary man, a certain Gustave Vaisse, with the object of being commissioned to write an opera libretto for production in Paris. I did not, however, make the personal acquaintance of Vaisse. The idea did not please me, and I found sufficient excuse for warding off the negotiations by saying I was afraid of the epidemic of cholera which was said to be raging in the city. I was staying in the Rue Notre Dame de Lorette for the sake of being near Belloni. Through this street funeral processions, announced by the muffled drum

[1] See note on page 486.

beats of the National Guard, passed practically every hour. Though the heat was stifling, I was strictly forbidden to touch water, and was advised to exercise the greatest precaution with regard to diet in every respect. Besides this weight of uneasiness on my spirits, the whole outward aspect of Paris, as it then appeared, had the most depressing effect on me. The motto, *liberté, égalité, fraternité,* was still to be seen on all the public buildings and other establishments, but, on the other hand, I was alarmed at seeing the first *garçons caissiers* making their way from the bank with their long money-sacks over their shoulders and their large portfolios in their hands. I had never met them so frequently as now, just when the old capitalist régime, after its triumphant struggle against the once dreaded socialist propaganda, was exerting itself vigorously to regain the public confidence by its almost insulting pomp. I had gone, as it were, mechanically into Schlesinger's music-shop, where a successor was now installed — a much more pronounced type of Jew named Brandus, of a very dirty appearance. The only person there to give me a friendly welcome was the old clerk, Monsieur Henri. After I had talked to him in loud tones for some time, as the shop was apparently empty, he at length asked me with some embarrassment whether I had not seen my master (*votre maître*) Meyerbeer.

'Is Monsieur Meyerbeer here?' I asked.

'Certainly,' was the even more embarrassed reply; 'quite near, over there behind the desk.'

And, sure enough, as I walked across to the desk Meyerbeer came out, covered with confusion. He smiled and made some excuse about pressing proof-sheets. He had been hiding there quietly for over ten minutes since first hearing my voice. I had had enough after my strange encounter with this apparition. It recalled so many things affecting myself which reflected suspicion on the man, in particular the significance of his behaviour towards me in Berlin on the last occasion. However, as I had now nothing more to do with him, I greeted him with a certain easy gaiety induced by the regret I felt at seeing his manifest confusion on becoming cognisant of my arrival in Paris. He took it for granted that I should again seek my fortune there, and seemed much surprised when I assured him, on the contrary, that the idea of having any work there was odious to me.

'But Liszt published such a brilliant article about you in the *Journal des Débats*,' he said.

'Ah,' I replied, 'it really had not occurred to me that the enthusiastic devotion of a friend should be regarded as a mutual speculation.'

'But the article made a sensation. It is incredible that you should not seek to make any profit out of it.'

This offensive meddlesomeness roused me to protest to Meyerbeer with some violence that I was concerned with anything rather than with the production of artistic work, particularly just at that time when the course of events seemed to indicate that the whole world was undergoing a reaction.

'But what do you expect to get out of the revolution?' he replied. 'Are you going to write scores for the barricades?'

Whereupon I assured him that I was not thinking of writing any scores at all. We parted, obviously without having arrived at a mutual understanding.

In the street I was also stopped by Moritz Schlesinger, who, being equally under the influence of Liszt's brilliant article, evidently considered me a perfect prodigy. He too thought I must be counting on making a hit in Paris, and was sure that I had a very good chance of doing so.

'Will you undertake my business?' I asked him. 'I have no money. Do you really think the performance of an opera by an unknown composer can be anything but a matter of money?'

'You are quite right,' said Moritz, and left me on the spot.

I turned from these disagreeable encounters in the plague-stricken capital of the world to inquire the fate of my Dresden companions, for some of those with whom I was intimate had also reached Paris, when I called on Despléchins, who had painted the scenery for *Tannhäuser*. I found Semper there, who had, like myself, been deposited in this city. We met again with no little pleasure, although we could not help smiling at our grotesque situation. Semper had retired from the battle when the famous barricade, which he in his capacity of architect kept under close observation, had been surrounded. (He thought it impossible for it to be captured.) All the same, he considered that he had exposed himself quite sufficiently to make it unsafe for him to stay after the Prussians had announced a state of siege and were occupying Dresden. He considered himself lucky as a native of Holstein to be dependent, not on the German, but on the Danish government for a passport, as this had helped him to reach Paris without difficulty. When I expressed my real and heartfelt regret at the turn of affairs which had torn him from a professional undertaking on which he had just started — the completion of the Dresden Museum — he refused to take it too seriously, saying it had given him a great deal of worry. In spite of our trying situation, it was with Semper that I spent the only bright hours of my stay in Paris. We were soon joined by another refugee, young Heine, who had once wished to paint my *Lohengrin* scenery. He had no qualms about his future, for his master Despléchins was willing to give him employment. I alone felt I had been pitched quite aimlessly into Paris. I had a passionate desire to leave this cholera-laden atmosphere, and Belloni offered me an opportunity which I promptly and joyfully seized. He invited me to follow himself and his family to a country place near La Ferté-sous-Jouarre, where I could be refreshed by pure air and absolute quiet, and wait for a change for the better in my position. I made the short journey to Rueil after another week in Paris, and took for the time being a poor lodging (one room, built with recesses) in the house of Monsieur Raphaël, a wine merchant, close by the village *mairie* where the Belloni family were staying. Here I waited further developments. During the period when all news from Germany ceased I tried to occupy myself as far as possible with reading. After going through Proudhon's writings, and in particular his *De la propriété,* in such a manner as to glean comfort for my situation in curiously divers ways, I entertained myself for a considerable time with Lamartine's *Histoire des Girondins,* a most alluring and attractive work. One day Belloni brought me news of the unfortunate rising in Paris, which had been attempted on the 13th June by the Republicans under Ledru-Rollin against the provisional government, which was then in the full tide of reaction. Great as was the indignation with which the news was received by my host and the mayor of the place (a relative of his, at whose table we ate our modest daily meal), it made, on the whole, little impression on me, as my attention was still fixed in great agitation on the events which were taking place on the Rhine, and particularly on the grand-duchy of Baden, which had been made forfeit to a provisional government. When, however, the news reached me from this quarter also that the Prussians had succeeded in subduing a movement which had not at first seemed hopeless, I felt extraordinarily downcast.

I was compelled to consider my position carefully, and the necessity of conquering my difficulties helped to allay the excitement to which I was a prey. The letters from my Weimar friends, as well as those from my wife, now brought me completely to my senses. The former expressed themselves very curtly about my behaviour with regard to recent events. The opinion was, that for the moment there would be nothing for me to do, and especially not in Dresden, or at the grand-ducal court, 'as one could not very well knock at battered doors'; '*on ne frappe pas à des portes enfoncées*' (Princess von Wittgenstein to Belloni).

I did not know what to reply, for I had never dreamt of expecting anything to come from their intervening on my behalf in that quarter; consequently I was quite satisfied that they sent me temporarily financial assistance. With this money I made up my mind to leave for Zürich and ask Alex Müller to give me shelter for a while, as his house was sufficiently large to accommodate a guest. My saddest moment came when, after a long silence, I at last received a letter from my wife. She wrote that she could not dream of living with me again; that after I had so unscrupulously thrown away a connection and position, the like of which would never again present itself to me, no woman could reasonably be expected to take any further interest in my future enterprises.

I fully appreciated my wife's unfortunate position; I could in no way assist her, except by advising her to sell our Dresden furniture, and by making an appeal on her behalf to my relatives in Leipzig.

Until then I had been able to think more lightly of the

misery of her position, simply because I had imagined her to be more deeply in sympathy with what agitated me. Often during the recent extraordinary events I had even believed that she understood my feelings. Now, however, she had disillusioned me on this point: she could see in me no more than what the public saw, and the one redeeming point of her severe judgment was that she excused my behaviour on the score that I was reckless. After I had begged Liszt to do what he could for my wife, I soon began to regard her unexpected behaviour with more equanimity. In reply to her announcement that she would not write to me again for the present, I said that I had also resolved to spare her all further anxiety about my very doubtful fate, by ceasing from communicating with her. I surveyed the panorama of our long years of association critically in my mind's eye, beginning with that first stormy year of our married life, that had been so full of sorrow. Our youthful days of worry and care in Paris had undoubtedly been of benefit to us both. The courage and patience with which she had faced our difficulties, while I on my part had tried to end them by dint of hard work, had linked us together with bonds of iron. Minna was rewarded for all these privations by Dresden successes, and more especially by the highly enviable position I had held there. Her position as wife of the conductor (Frau Kapellmeisterin) had brought her the fulfilment of her dearest wishes, and all those things which conspired to make my work in this official post so intolerable to me, were to her no more than so many threats directed against her smug content. The course I had adopted with regard to *Tannhäuser* had already made her doubtful of my success at the theatres, and had robbed her of all courage and confidence in our future. The more I deviated from the path which she regarded as the only profitable one, due partly to the change of my views (which I grew ever less willing to communicate to her), and partly to the modification in my attitude towards the stage, the more she retreated from that position of close fellowship with me which she had enjoyed in former years, and which she thought herself justified in connecting in some way with my successes.

She looked upon my conduct with regard to the Dresden catastrophe as the outcome of this deviation from the right path, and attributed it to the influence of unscrupulous persons (particularly the unfortunate Röckel), who were supposed to have dragged me with them to ruin, by appealing to my vanity. Deeper than all these disagreements, however, which, after all, were concerned only with external circumstances, was the consciousness of our fundamental incompatibility, which to me had become ever more and more apparent since the day of our reconciliation. From the very beginning we had had scenes of the most violent description; never once after these frequent quarrels had she admitted herself in the wrong or tried to be friends again.

The necessity of speedily restoring our domestic peace, as well as my conviction (confirmed by every one of her extravagant outbursts) that, in view of the great disparity of our characters and especially of our educations, it devolved upon me to prevent such scenes by observing great caution in my behaviour, always led me to take the entire blame for what had happend upon myself, and to mollify Minna by showing her that I was sorry. Unfortunately, and to my intense grief, I was forced to recognise that by acting in this way I lost all my power over her affections, and especially over her character. Now we stood in a position in which I could not possibly resort to the same means of reconciliation, for it would have meant my being inconsistent in all my views and actions. And then I found myself confronted by such hardness in the woman whom I had spoilt by my leniency, that it was out of the question to expect her to acknowledge the injustice done to myself. Suffice it to say that the wreck of my married life had contributed not inconsiderably to the ruin of my position in Dresden, and to the careless manner in which I treated it, for instead of finding help, strength, and consolation at home, I found my wife unwittingly conspiring against me, in league with all the other hostile circumstances which then beset me. After I had got over the first shock of her heartless behaviour, I was absolutely clear about this. I remember that I did not suffer any great sorrow, but that on the contrary, with the conviction of being now quite helpless, an almost exalted calm came over me when I realised that up to the present my life had been built on a foundation of sand and nothing more. At all events, the fact that I stood absolutely alone did much towards restoring my peace of mind, and in my distress I now found strength and comfort even in the fact of my dire poverty. At last assistance arrived from Weimar. I accepted it eagerly, and it was the means of extricating me from my present useless life and stranded hopes.

My next move was to find a place of refuge — one, however, which had but little attraction for me, seeing that in it there was not the slightest hope of my being able to make any further headway in the paths along which I had hitherto progressed. This refuge was Zürich, a town devoid of all art in the public sense, and where for the first time I met simple-hearted people who knew nothing about me as a musician, but who, as it appeared, felt drawn towards me by the power of my personality alone. I arrived at Müller's house and asked him to let me have a room, at the same time giving him what remained of my capital, namely twenty francs. I quickly discovered that my old friend was embarrassed by my perfectly open confidence in him, and that he was at his wit's end to know what to do with me. I soon gave up the large room containing a grand piano, which he had allotted to me on the impulse of the moment, and retired to a modest little bedroom. The meals were my great trial, not because I was fastidious, but because I could not digest them. Outside my friend's house, on the contrary, I enjoyed what, considering the habits of the locality, was the most luxurious reception. The same young men who had been so kind to me on my first journey through Zürich again showed themselves anxious to be continually in my company, and this was especially the case with one young fellow called Jakob Sulzer. He had to be thirty years of age before he was entitled to become a member of the Zürich government, and he therefore still had several years to wait. In spite of his youth, however, the impression he made on all those with whom he came in contact was that of a man of riper years, whose character was formed. When I was asked long afterwards whether I had ever met a man who, morally speaking, was the beau-ideal of real character and uprightness, I could, on reflection, think of none other than this newly gained friend, Jakob Sulzer.

He owed his early appointment as permanent Cantonal Secretary (*Staatsschreiber*), one of the most excellent government posts in the canton of Zürich, to the recently returned liberal party, led by Alfred Escher. As this party could not employ the more experienced members of the older conservative side in the public offices, their policy was to choose exceptionally gifted young men for these positions. Sulzer showed extraordinary promise, and their choice accordingly soon lighted on him. He had only just returned from the Berlin and Bonn universities with the intention of establishing himself as professor of philology at the university in his native town, when he was made a member of the new government. To fit himself for his post he had to stay in Geneva for six months to perfect himself in the French language, which he had neglected during his philological studies. He was quick-witted and industrious, as well as independent and firm, and he never allowed himself to be swayed by any party tactics. Consequently he rose very rapidly to high positions in the government, to which he rendered valuable and important services, first as Minister of Finance, a post he held for many years, and later with particular distinction as member of the School Federation. His unexpected acquaintance with me seemed to place him in a sort of dilemma; from the philological and classical studies which he had entered upon of his own choice, he suddenly found himself torn away in the most bewildering manner by this unexpected summons from the government. It almost seemed as if his meeting with me had made him regret having accepted the appointment. As he was a person of great culture, my poem, *Siegfried's Death,* naturally revealed to him my knowledge of German antiquity. He had also studied this subject, but with greater philological accuracy than I could possibly have aspired to. When, later on, he became acquainted with my manner of writing music, this peculiarly serious and reserved man became so thoroughly interested in my sphere of art, so far removed from his own field of labour, that, as he himself confessed, he felt it his duty to fight against these disturbing influences by being intentionally brusque and curt with me. In the beginning of my stay in Zürich, however, he delighted in being led some distance astray in the realms of art. The old-fashioned official residence of the first Cantonal Secretary was often the scene of unique gatherings, composed of people such as I would be sure to attract. It might even be said that these social functions occurred rather more frequently than was advisable for the reputation of a civil servant of this little philistine state. What attracted the musician Baumgartner more particularly to these meetings was the product of Sulzer's vineyards in Winterthur, to which our hosts treated his guests with the greatest liberality. When in my moods of mad exuberance I gave vent in dithyrambic effusions to my most extreme views on art and life, my listeners often responded in a manner which, more often than not, I was perfectly right in ascribing to the effects of the wine rather than to the power of my enthusiasm. Once when Professor Ettmüller, the Germanist and Edda scholar, had been invited to listen to a reading of my *Siegfried* and had been led home in a state of melancholy enthusiasm, there was a regular outburst of wanton spirits among those who had remained behind. I conceived the absurd idea of lifting all the doors of the state official's house off their hinges.

Herr Hagenbuch, another servant of the state, seeing what exertion this cost me, offered me the help of his gigantic physique, and with comparative ease we succeeded in removing every single door, and laying it aside, a proceeding at which Sulzer merely smiled good-naturedly. The next day, however, when we made inquiries, he told us that the replacing of those doors (which must have been a terrible strain on his delicate constitution) had taken him the whole night, as he had made up his mind to keep the knowledge of our orgies from the sergeant, who always arrived at a very early hour in the morning.

The extraordinary birdlike freedom of my existence had the effect of exciting me more and more. I was often frightened at the excessive outbursts of exaltation to which I was prone — no matter whom I was with — and which led me to indulge in the most extraordinary paradoxes in my conversation. Soon after I had settled in Zürich I began to write down my various ideas about things at which I had arrived through my private and artistic experiences, as well as through the influence of the political unrest of the day. As I had no choice but to try, to

the best of my ability, to earn something by my pen, I thought
of sending a series of articles to a great French journal such as
the *National,* which in those days was still extant. In these
articles I meant to propound my ideas (in my revolutionary
way) on the subject of modern art in its relation to society.
I sent six of them to an elderly friend of mine, Albert Franck,
requesting him to have them translated into French and to get
them published. This Franck was the brother of the better-
known Hermann Franck, now the head of the Franco-German
bookselling firm, which had originally belonged to my brother-
in-law, Avenarius. He sent me back my work with the very
natural remark that it was out of the question to expect the
Parisian public to understand or appreciate my articles, especially at such a critical moment.

I headed the manuscript *Kunst und Revolution* ('Art and
Revolution') and sent it to Otto Wigand in Leipzig, who
actually undertook to publish it in the form of a pamphlet, and
sent me five louis d'or for it. This unexpected success induced
me to continue to exploit my literary gifts. I looked among my
papers for the essay I had written the year before as the outcome of my historical studies of the 'Nibelungen' legend; I
gave it the title of *Die Nibelungen Weltgeschichte aus der
Sage,* and again tried my luck by sending it to Wigand.
The sensational title of *Kunst und Revolution,* as well as the
notoriety the 'royal conductor' had gained as a political
refugee, had made the radical publisher hope that the scandal
that would arise on the publication of my articles would re-
dound to his benefit! I soon discovered that he was on the
point of issuing a second edition of *Kunst und Revolution,* without, however, informing me of the fact. He also took over my
new pamphlet for another five louis d'or. This was the first
time I had earned money by means of published work, and I
now began to believe that I had reached that point when I
should be able to get the better of my misfortunes. I thought
it over, and decided to give public lectures in Zürich on subjects
related to my writings during the coming winter, hoping in
that free and haphazard fashion to keep body and soul together
for a little while, although I had no fixed appointment and did
not intend to work at music.

It seemed necessary for me to resort to these means, as I did not know how otherwise to keep myself alive. Shortly after my arrival in Zürich I had witnessed the coming of the fragments of the Baden army, dispersed over Swiss territory, and accompanied by fugitive volunteers, and this had made a painful and uncanny impression upon me. The news of the surrender near Villagos by Görgey paralysed the last hopes as to the issue of the great European struggle for liberty, which so far had been left quite undecided. With some misgiving and anxiety I now turned my eyes from all these occurrences in the outside world inwards to my own soul.

I was accustomed to patronise the *café littéraire,* where I took my coffee after my heavy mid-day meal, in a smoky atmosphere surrounded by a merry and joking throng of men playing dominoes and 'fast.' One day I stared at its common wall-paper representing antique subjects, which in some inexplicable way recalled a certain water-colour by Genelli to my mind, portraying 'The education of Dionysos by the Muses.' I had seen it at the house of my brother-in-law Brockhaus in my young days, and it had made a deep impression on me at the time. At this same place I conceived the first ideas of my *Kunstwerk der Zukunft* ('The Art-Work of the Future'), and it seemed a significant omen to me to be roused one day out of one of my post-prandial dreams by the news that Schröder-Devrient was staying in Zürich. I immediately got up with the intention of calling on her at the neighbouring hotel, 'Zum Schwerte,' but to my great dismay heard that she had just left by steamer. I never saw her again, and long afterwards only heard of her painful death from my wife, who in later years became fairly intimate with her in Dresden.

After I had spent two remarkable summer months in this wild and extraordinary fashion, I at last received reassuring news of Minna, who had remained in Dresden. Although her manner of taking leave of me had been both harsh and wounding, I could not bring myself to believe I had completely parted from her. In a letter I wrote to one of her relations, and which I presumed they would forward, I made sympathetic inquiries about her, while I had already done all that lay in my power.

through repeated appeals to Liszt, to ensure her being well cared for. I now received a direct reply, which, in addition to the fact that it testified to the vigour and activity with which she had fought her difficulties, at the same time showed me that she earnestly desired to be reunited with me. It was almost in terms of contempt that she expressed her grave doubts as to the possibility of my being able to make a living in Zürich, but she added that, inasmuch as she was my wife, she wished to give me another chance. She also seemed to take it for granted that I intended making Zürich only our temporary home, and that I would do my utmost to promote my career as a composer of opera in Paris. Whereupon she announced her intention of arriving at Rorschach in Switzerland on a certain date in September of that year, in the company of the little dog Peps, the parrot Papo, and her so-called sister Nathalie. After having engaged two rooms for our new home, I now prepared to set out on foot for St. Gall and Rorschach through the lovely and celebrated Toggenburg and Appenzell, and felt very touched after all when the peculiar family, which consisted half of pet animals, landed at the harbour of Rorschach. I must honestly confess that the little dog and the bird made me very happy. My wife at once threw cold water on my emotions, however, by declaring that in the event of my behaving badly again she was ready to return to Dresden any moment, and that she had numerous friends there, who would be glad to protect and succour her if she were forced to carry out her threat. Be this as it may, one look at her convinced me how greatly she had aged in this short time, and how much I ought to pity her, and this feeling succeeded in banishing all bitterness from my heart.

I did my utmost to give her confidence and to make her believe that our present misfortunes were but momentary. This was no easy task, as she would constantly compare the diminutive aspect of the town of Zürich with the more noble majesty of Dresden, and seemed to feel bitterly humiliated. The friends whom I introduced to her found no favour in her eyes. She looked upon the Cantonal Secretary, Sulzer, as a 'mere town clerk who would not be of any importance in Germany'; and the wife of my host Müller absolutely disgusted her when, in answer to Minna's complaints about my terrible position, she replied that my greatness lay in the very fact of my having faced it. Then again Minna appeased me by telling me of the expected arrival of some of my Dresden belongings, which she thought would be indispensable to our new home.

The property of which she spoke consisted of a Breitkopf and Härtel grand-piano that looked better than it sounded, and of the 'title-page' of the *Nibelungen* by Cornelius in a Gothic frame that used to hang over my desk in Dresden.

With this nucleus of household effects we now decided to take small lodgings in the so-called ' hinteren Escherhäusern ' in the Zeltweg. With great cleverness Minna had succeeded in selling the Dresden furniture to advantage, and out of the proceeds of this sale she had brought three hundred marks with her to Zürich to help towards setting up our new home. She told me that she had saved my small but very select library for me by giving it into the safe custody of the publisher, Heinrich Brockhaus (brother of my sister's husband and member of the Saxon Diet), who had insisted upon looking after it. Great, therefore, was her dismay when, upon asking this kind friend to send her the books, he replied that he was holding them as security for a debt of fifteen hundred marks which I had contracted with him during my days of trouble in Dresden, and that he intended to keep them until that sum was returned. As even after the lapse of many years I found it impossible to refund this money, these books, collected for my own special wants, were lost to me for ever.

Thanks more particularly to my friend Sulzer, the Cantonal Secretary, whom my wife at first despised so much on account of his title which she misunderstood, and who, although he was far from well-off himself, thought it only natural that he should help me, however moderately, out of my difficulties, we soon succeeded in making our little place look so cosy that my simple Zürich friends felt quite at home in it. My wife, with all her undeniable talents, here found ample scope in which to distinguish herself, and I remember how ingeniously she made a little what-not out of the box in which she had kindly brought my music and manuscript to Zürich.

But it was soon time to think of how to earn enough money to provide for us all. My idea of giving public lectures was treated with contempt by my wife, who looked upon it as an insult to her pride. She could acquiesce only in one plan, that suggested by Liszt, namely, that I should write an opera for Paris. To satisfy her, and in view of the fact that I could see no chance of a remunerative occupation close at hand, I actually reopened a correspondence on this matter with my great friend and his secretary Belloni in Paris. In the meantime I could not be idle, so I accepted an invitation from the Zürich musical society to conduct a classical composition at one of their concerts, and to this end I worked with their very poor orchestra at Beethoven's Symphony in A major. Although the result was successful, and I received five napoleons for my trouble, it made my wife very unhappy, for she could not forget the excellent orchestra, and the much more appreciative public, which a short time before in Dresden would have seconded and rewarded similar efforts on my part. Her one and only ideal for me was that, by hook or by crook, and with a total disregard of all artistic scruples, I should make a brilliant reputation for myself in Paris. While we were both absolutely at a loss to discover whence we should obtain the necessary funds for our journey to Paris and our sojourn there, I again plunged into my philosophical study of art, as being the only sphere still left open to me.

Harrassed by the cares of a terrible struggle for existence, I wrote the whole of *Das Kunstwerk der Zukunft* in the chilly atmosphere of a sunless little room on the ground floor during the months of November and December of that year. Minna had no objection to this occupation when I told her of the success of my first pamphlet, and the hope I had of receiving even better pay for this more extensive work.

Thus for a while I enjoyed comparative peace, although in my heart a spirit of unrest had begun to reign, thanks to my growing acquaintance with Feuerbach's works. I had always had an inclination to fathom the depths of philosophy, just as I had been led by the mystic influence of Beethoven's Ninth Symphony to search the deepest recesses of music. My first efforts at satisfying this longing had failed. None of the Leipzig professors had succeeded in fascinating me with their lectures on fundamental philosophy and logic. I had procured Schelling's work, *Transcendental Idealism,* recommended to me by Gustav Schlesinger, a friend of Laube's, but it was in vain that I racked my brains to try and make something out of the first pages, and I always returned to my Ninth Symphony.

During the latter part of my stay in Dresden I had returned to these old studies, the longing for which suddenly revived within me, and to these I added the deeper historical studies which had always fascinated me. As an introduction to philosophy I now chose Hegel's *Philosophy of History.* A good deal of this impressed me deeply, and it now seemed as if I should ultimately penetrate into the Holy of Holies along this path. The more incomprehensible many of his speculative conclusions appeared, the more I felt myself desirous of probing the question of the 'Absolute' and everything connected therewith to the core. For I so admired Hegel's powerful mind that it seemed to me he was the very keystone of all philosophical thought.

The revolution intervened; the practical tendencies of a social reconstruction distracted my attention, and as I have already stated, it was a German Catholic priest and political agitator (formerly a divinity student named Menzdorff, who used to wear a Calabrian hat)[1] who drew my attention to 'the only real philosopher of modern times,' Ludwig Feuerbach. My new Zürich friend, the piano teacher, Wilhelm Baumgartner, made me a present of Feuerbach's book on *Tod und Unsterblichkeit* ('Death and Immortality'). The well-known and stirring lyrical style of the author greatly fascinated me as a layman. The intricate questions which he propounds in this book as if they were being discussed for the first time by him, and which he treats in a charmingly exhaustive manner, had often occupied my mind since the very first days of my acquaintance with Lehrs in Paris, just as they occupy the mind of every imaginative and serious man. With me, however, this was not lasting, and I had contented myself with the poetic suggestions on these important subjects which appear here and there in the works of our great poets.

[1] A broad-rimmed, tall, white felt hat, tapering to a point, originally worn by the inhabitants of Calabria, and in 1848 a sign of Republicanism. — EDITOR.

The frankness with which Feuerbach explains his views on these interesting questions, in the more mature parts of his book, pleased me as much by their tragic as by their social-radical tendencies. It seemed right that the only true immortality should be that of sublime deeds and great works of art. It was more difficult to sustain any interest in *Das Wesen des Christenthums* (' The Essence of Christianity ') by the same author, for it was impossible whilst reading this work not to become conscious, however involuntarily, of the prolix and unskilful manner in which he dilates on the simple and fundamental idea, namely, religion explained from a purely subjective and psychological point of view. Nevertheless, from that day onward I always regarded Feuerbach as the ideal exponent of the radical release of the individual from the thraldom of accepted notions, founded on the belief in authority. The initiated will therefore not wonder that I dedicated my *Kunstwerk der Zukunft* to Feuerbach and addressed its preface to him.

My friend Sulzer, a thorough disciple of Hegel, was very sorry to see me so interested in Feuerbach, whom he did not even recognise as a philosopher at all. He said that the best thing that Feuerbach had done for me was that he had been the means of awakening my ideas, although he himself had none. But what had really induced me to attach so much importance to Feuerbach was the conclusion by means of which he had seceded from his master Hegel, to wit, that the best philosophy was to have no philosophy — a theory which greatly simplified what I had formerly considered a very terrifying study — and secondly, that only that was real which could be ascertained by the senses.

The fact that he proclaimed what we call 'spirit' to be an æsthetic perception of our senses, together with his statement concerning the futility of philosophy—these were the two things in him which rendered me such useful assistance in my conceptions of an all-embracing work of art, of a perfect drama which should appeal to the simplest and most purely human emotions at the very moment when it approached its fulfilment as *Kunstwerk der Zukunft*. It must have been this which Sulzer had in his mind when he spoke deprecatingly of Feuerbach's influence over me. At all events, after a while I certainly could not return to his works, and I remember that his newly published book, *Uber das Wesen der Religion* ('Lectures on the Essence of Religion'), scared me to such an extent by the dullness of its title alone, that when Herwegh opened it for my benefit, I closed it with a bang under his very nose.

At that time I was working with great enthusiasm upon the draft of a connected essay, and was delighted one day to receive a visit from the novelist and Tieckian scholar, Eduard von Bülow (the father of my young friend Bülow), who was passing through Zürich. In my tiny little room I read him my chapter on poetry, and could not help noticing that he was greatly startled at my ideas on literary drama and on the advent of the new Shakespeare. I thought this all the more reason why Wigand the publisher should accept my new revolutionary book, and expected him to pay me a fee which would be in proportion to the greater size of the work. I asked for twenty lous d'or, and this sum he agreed to pay me.

The prospect of receiving this amount induced me to carry out the plan, which need had forced upon me, of travelling to Paris and of trying my luck there as a composer of opera. This plan had very serious drawbacks; not only did I hate the idea, but I knew that I was doing an injustice to myself by believing in the success of my enterprise, for I felt that I could never seriously throw myself into it heart and soul. Everything, however, combined to make me try the experiment, and it was Liszt in particular who, confident of this being my only way to fame, insisted upon my reopening the negotiations into which Belloni and I had entered during the previous summer. To show with what earnestness I tried to consider the chances of carrying out my plan, I drafted out the plot of the opera, which the French poet would only have to put into verse, because I never for a moment fancied that it would be possible for him to think out and write a libretto for which I would only need to compose the music. I chose for my subject the legend of *Wieland der Schmied,* upon which I commented with some stress at the end of my recently finished *Kunstwerk der Zukunft,* and the version of which by Simrock, taken from the Wilkyna legend, had greatly attracted me.

I sketched out the complete scenario with precise indication of the dialogue for three acts, and with a heavy heart decided to hand it over to my Parisian author to be worked out. Liszt thought he saw a means of making my music known through his relations with Seghers, the musical director of a society then known as the 'Concerts de St. Cécile.' In January of the following year the *Tannhäuser* Overture was to be given under his baton, and it therefore seemed advisable that I should reach Paris some time before this event. This undertaking, which appeared to be so difficult owing to my complete lack of funds, was at last facilitated in a manner quite unexpected.

I had written home for help, and had appealed to all the old friends I could think of, but in vain. By the family of my brother Albert in particular, whose daughter had recently entered upon a brilliant theatrical career, I was treated in much the same way as one treats an invalid by whom one dreads to become infected. In contrast to their harshness I was deeply touched by the devotion of the Ritter family, who had remained in Dresden; for, apart from my acquaintance with young Karl, I scarcely knew these people at all. Through the kindness of my old friend Heine, who had been informed of my position, Frau Julie Ritter, the venerable mother of the family, had thought it her duty to place, through a business friend, the sum of fifteen hundred marks at my disposal. At about the same time I received a letter from Mme. Laussot, who had called upon me in Dresden the year before, and who now in the most affecting terms assured me of her continued sympathy.

These were the first signs of that new phase in my life upon which I entered from this day forth, and in which I accustomed myself to look upon the outward circumstances of my existence as being merely subservient to my will. And by this means I was able to escape from the hampering narrowness of my home life.

For the moment the proffered financial assistance was very distasteful to me, for it seemed to forbid my raising any further objections to the realisation of the detested Paris schemes. When, however, on the strength of this favourable change in my affairs, I suggested to my wife that we might, after all, content ourselves with remaining in Zürich, she flew into the most violent passion over my weakness and lack of spirit, and

DEPARTURE FOR PARIS

declared that if I did not make up my mind to achieve something in Paris, she would lose all faith in me. She said, moreover, that she absolutely refused to be a witness of my misery and grief as a wretched literary man and insignificant conductor of local concerts in Zürich.

We had entered upon the year 1850; I had decided to go to Paris, if only for the sake of peace, but had to postpone my journey on account of ill-health. The reaction following upon the terrible excitement of recent times had not failed to have its effect on my overwrought nerves, and a state of complete exhaustion had followed. The continual colds, in spite of which I had been obliged to work in my very unhealthy room, had at last given rise to alarming symptoms. A certain weakness of the chest became apparent, and this the doctor (a political refugee) undertook to cure by the application of pitch plasters. As the result of this treatment and the irritating effect it had upon my nerves, I lost my voice completely for a while; whereupon I was told that I must go away for a change. On going out to buy my ticket for the journey, I felt so weak and broke out into such terrible perspiration that I hastened to return to my wife in order to consult her as to the advisability, in the circumstances, of abandoning the idea of the expedition altogether. She, however, maintained (and perhaps rightly) not only that my condition was not dangerous, but that it was to a large extent due to imagination, and that, once in the right place, I would soon recover.

An inexpressible feeling of bitterness stimulated my nerves as in anger and despair I quickly left the house to buy the confounded ticket for the journey, and in the beginning of February I actually started on the road to Paris. I was filled with the most extraordinary feelings, but the spark of hope which was then kindled in my breast certainly had nothing whatever to do with the belief that had been imposed upon me from without, that I was to make a success in Paris as a composer of operas.

I was particularly anxious to find quiet rooms, for peace had now become my first necessity, no matter where I happened to be staying. The cabman who drove me from street to street through the most isolated quarters, and whom I at last accused of keeping always to the most animated parts of the city, finally protested in despair that one did not come to Paris to live in a convent. At last it occurred to me to look for what I wanted in one of the *cités* through which no vehicle seemed to drive, and I decided to engage rooms in the Cité de Provence.

True to the plans which had been forced upon me, I at once called on Herr Seghers about the performance of the *Tannhäuser* Overture.

It turned out that in spite of my late arrival I had missed nothing, for they were still racking their brains as to how to procure the necessary orchestral parts.

I therefore had to write to Liszt, asking him to order the copies, and had to wait for their arrival. Belloni was not in town, things were therefore at a standstill, and I had plenty of time to think over the object of my visit to Paris, while an unceasing accompaniment was poured out to my meditations by the barrel-organs which infest the *cités* of Paris.

I had much difficulty in convincing an agent of the government, from whom I received a visit soon after my arrival, that my presence in Paris was due to artistic reasons, and not to my doubtful position as a political refugee.

Fortunately he was impressed by the score, which I showed him, as well as by Liszt's article on the *Tannhäuser* Overture, written the year before in the *Journal des Débats,* and he left me, politely inviting me to continue my avocations peacefully and industriously, as the police had no intention of disturbing me.

I also looked up my older Parisian acquaintances. At the hospitable house of Despléchins I met Semper, who was trying to make his position as tolerable as possible by writing some inferior artistic work. He had left his family in Dresden, from which town we soon received the most alarming news. The prisons were gradually filling there with the unfortunate victims of the recent Saxon movement. Of Röckel, Bakunin, and Heubner, all we could hear was that they had been charged with high treason, and that they were awaiting the death sentence.

In view of the tidings which continually arrived concerning the cruelty and brutality with which the soldiers treated the prisoners, we could not help considering our own lot a very happy one.

My intercourse with Semper, whom I saw frequently, was generally enlivened by a gaiety which was occasionally of rather a risky nature; he was determined to rejoin his family in London, where the prospect of various appointments was open to him. My latest attempts at writing, and the thoughts expressed in my work, interested him greatly, and gave rise to animated conversations in which we were joined by Kietz, who was at first amusing, but evidently boring Semper considerably. I found the former in the identical position in which I had left him many years ago: he had made no headway with his painting, and would have been glad if the revolution had taken a more decided turn, so that, under cover of the general confusion, he might have escaped from his embarrassing position with his landlord. He made at this time quite a good pastel portrait of me in his very best and earliest style. While I was sitting I unfortunately spoke to him about my *Das Kunstwerk der Zukunft,* and thereby laid the foundation for him of troubles that lasted many years, as he tried to instil my new ideas into the Parisian bourgeoisie at whose tables he had hitherto been a welcome guest. Notwithstanding, he remained as of old a good, obliging, true-hearted fellow, and even Semper could not help putting up with him cheerfully. I also looked up my friend Anders. It was a difficult matter to find him at any hour of the day, since out of sleeping hours he was closeted in the library, where he could receive no one, and afterwards retired to the reading-room to spend his hours of rest, and generally went to dine with certain bourgeois families where he gave music lessons. He had aged considerably, but I was glad to find him, comparatively speaking, in better health than the state in which I had last seen him had allowed me to hope, as when I left Paris before he had seemed to be in a decline. Curiously enough, a broken leg had been the means of improving his health, the treatment necessary for it having taken him to a hydro, where his condition had much improved. His one idea was to see me achieve a great success in Paris, and he wished to secure a seat in advance for the first performance of my opera, which he took for granted was to appear, and kept repeating that it would be so very trying for him to occupy a place in any part of the theatre where there would be likely to be a crush. He could not see the use of my present literary work; in spite of this I was again engaged on it exclusively, as I soon ascertained there was no likelihood of my overture to *Tannhäuser* being produced. Liszt had shown the greatest zeal in obtaining and forwarding the orchestral parts; but Herr Seghers informed me that as far as his own orchestra was concerned, he found himself in a republican democracy where each instrument had an equal right to voice its opinion, and it had been unanimously decided that for the remainder of the winter season, which was now drawing to a close, my overture could be dispensed with. I gathered enough from this turn of affairs to realise how precarious my position was.

It is true, the result of my writings was hardly less discouraging. A copy of the Wigand edition of my *Kunstwerk der Zukunft* was forwarded to me full of horrible misprints, and instead of the expected remuneration of twenty louis d'or, my publisher explained that for the present he could only pay me half this sum, as, owing to the fact that at first the sale of the *Kunst und Revolution* had been very rapid, he had been led to attach too high a commercial value to my writings, a mistake he had speedily discovered when he found there was no demand for *Die Nibelungen*.

On the other hand, I received an offer of remunerative work from Adolph Kolatschek, who was also a fugitive, and was just going to bring out a German monthly journal as the organ of the progressive party. In response to this invitation I wrote a long essay on *Kunst und Klima* ('Art and Climate'), in which I supplemented the ideas I had already touched upon in my *Kunstwerk der Zukunft*. Besides this I had, since my arrival in Paris, worked out a more complete sketch of *Wieland der Schmied*. It is true that this work had no longer any value, and I wondered with apprehension what I could write home to my wife, now that the last precious remittance had been so aimlessly sacrificed. The thought of returning to Zürich was as distasteful to me as the prospect of remaining any longer in Paris. My feelings with regard to the latter alternative were intensified by the impression made upon me by Meyerbeer's opera *The Prophet,* which had just been produced and which I had not heard before. Rearing itself on the ruins of the hopes for new and more noble endeavour which had animated the better works of the past year — the only result of the negotiations of the provisional French republic for the encouragement of art — I saw this work of Meyerbeer's break upon the world like the dawn heralding this day of disgraceful desolation. I was so sickened by this performance, that though I was unfortunately placed in the centre of the stalls and would willingly have avoided the disturbance necessarily occasioned by one of the audience moving during the middle of an act, even this consideration did not deter me from getting up and leaving the house. When the famous mother of the prophet finally gives vent to her grief in the well-known series of ridiculous roulades, I was filled with rage and despair at the thought that I should be called upon to listen to such a thing, and never again did I pay the slightest heed to this opera.

But what was I to do next? Just as the South American republics had attracted me during my first miserable sojourn in Paris, so now my longing was directed towards the East, where I could live my life in a manner worthy of a human being far away from this modern world. While I was in this frame of mind I was called upon to answer another inquiry as to my state of health from Mme. Laussot in Bordeaux. It turned out that my answer prompted her to send me a kind and pressing invitation to go and stay at her house, at least for a short time, to rest and forget my troubles. In any circumstances an excursion to more southerly regions, which I had not yet seen, and a visit to people who, though utter strangers, showed such friendly interest in me, could not fail to prove attractive and flattering. I accepted, settled my affairs in Paris, and went by coach via Orléans, Tours, and Angoulême, down the Gironde to the unknown town, where I was received with great courtesy and cordiality by the young wine merchant Eugène Laussot, and presented to my sympathetic young friend, his wife. A closer acquaintance with the family, in which Mrs. Taylor, Mme. Laussot's mother, was now also included, led to a clearer understanding of the character of the sympathy bestowed upon me in such a cordial and unexpected manner by people hitherto unknown to me. Jessie, as the young wife was called at home, had, during a somewhat lengthy stay in Dresden, become very intimate with the Ritter family, and I had no reason to doubt the assurance given me, that the Laussots' interest in me and my work was principally owing to this intimacy. After my flight from Dresden, as soon as the news of my difficulties had reached the Ritters, a correspondence had been carried on between Dresden and Bordeaux with a view to ascertaining how best to assist me. Jessie attributed the whole idea to Frau Julie Ritter who, while not being well enough off herself to make me a sufficient allowance, was endeavouring to come to an understanding with Jessie's mother, the well-to-do widow of an English lawyer, whose income entirely supported the young couple in Bordeaux. This plan had so far succeeded, that shortly after my arrival in Bordeaux Mrs. Taylor informed me that the two families had combined, and that it had been decided to ask me to accept the help of three thousand francs a year until the return of better days. My one object now was to enlighten my benefactors as to the exact conditions under which I should be accepting such assistance. I could no longer reckon upon achieving any success as a composer of opera either in Paris or elsewhere; what line I should take up instead I did not know; but, at all events, I was determined to keep myself free from the disgrace which would reflect upon my whole life if I used such means as this offer presented to secure success. I feel sure I am not wrong in believing that Jessie was the only one who understood me, and though I only experienced kindness from the rest of the family, I soon discovered the gulf by which she, as well as myself, was separated from her mother and husband. While the husband, who was a handsome young man, was away the greater part of the day attending to his business, and the mother's deafness excluded her to a great extent from our conversations, we soon discovered by a rapid exchange of ideas that we shared the same opinions on many important matters, and this led to a great feeling of friendship between us. Jessie, who was at that time about twenty-two, bore little resemblance to her mother, and no doubt took after her father, of whom I heard most flattering accounts. A large and varied collection of books

left by this man to his daughter showed his tastes, for besides
carrying on his lucrative profession as a lawyer, he had devoted
himself to the study of literature and science. From him
Jessie had also learned German as a child, and she spoke that
language with great fluency. She had been brought up on
Grimm's fairy-tales, and was, moreover, thoroughly acquainted
with German poetry, as well as with that of England and
France, and her knowledge of them was as thorough as the most
advanced education could demand. French literature did not
appeal to her much. Her quick powers of comprehension were
astonishing. Everything which I touched upon she immediately
grasped and assimilated. It was the same with music: she
read at sight with the greatest facility, and was an accomplished
player. During her stay in Dresden she had been told that I
was still in search of the pianist who could play Beethoven's
great Sonata in B flat major, and she now astonished me by
her finished rendering of this most difficult piece. The emotion
aroused in me by finding such an exceptionally developed talent
suddenly changed to anxiety when I heard her sing. Her
sharp, shrill voice, in which there was strength but no real
depth of feeling, so shocked me that I could not refrain from
begging her to desist from singing in future. With regard to
the execution of the sonata, she listened eagerly to my instructions as to how it should be interpreted, though I could not
feel that she would succeed in rendering it according to my
ideas. I read her my latest essays, and she seemed to understand even the most extraordinary descriptions perfectly. My
poem on *Siegfried's Tod* moved her deeply, but she preferred
my sketch of *Wieland der Schmied*. She admitted afterwards
that she would prefer to imagine herself filling the rôle of
Wieland's worthy bride than to find herself in the position and
forced to endure the fate of Gutrune in *Siegfried*. It followed
inevitably that the presence of the other members of the family
proved embarrassing when we wanted to talk over and discuss
these various subjects. If we felt somewhat troubled at having
to confess to ourselves that Mrs. Taylor would certainly never
be able to understand why I was being offered assistance, I was
still more disconcerted at realising after a time the complete
want of harmony between the young couple, particularly from

an intellectual point of view. The fact that Laussot had for some time been well aware of his wife's dislike for him was plainly shown when he one day so far forgot himself as to complain loudly and bitterly that she would not even love a child of his if she had one, and that he therefore thought it fortunate that she was not a mother. Astonished and saddened, I suddenly gazed into an abyss which was hidden here, as is often the case, under the appearance of a tolerably happy married life. About this time, and just as my visit, which had already lasted three weeks, was drawing to a close, I received a letter from my wife that could not have had a more unfortunate effect on my state of mind. She was, on the whole, pleased at my having found new friends, but at the same time explained that if I did not immediately return to Paris, and there endeavour to secure the production of my overture with the results anticipated, she would not know what to think of me, and would certainly fail to understand me if I returned to Zürich without having effected my purpose. At the same time my depression was intensified in a terrible way by a notice in the papers announcing that Röckel, Bakunin, and Heubner had been sentenced to death, and that the date of their execution was fixed. I wrote a short but stirring letter of farewell to the two first, and as I saw no possibility of having it conveyed to the prisoners, who were confined in the fortress of Königstein, I decided to send it to Frau von Lüttichau, to be forwarded to them by her, because I thought she was the only person in whose power it might lie to do this for me, while at the same time she had sufficient generosity and independence of mind to enable her to respect and carry out my wishes, in spite of any possible difference of opinion she might entertain. I was told some time afterwards that Lüttichau had got hold of the letter and thrown it into the fire. For the time being this painful impression helped me to the determination to break with every one and everything, to lose all desire to learn more of life or of art, and, even at the risk of having to endure the greatest privations, to trust to chance and put myself beyond the reach of everybody. The small income settled upon me by my friends I wished to divide between myself and my wife, and with my half go to Greece or Asia

Minor, and there, Heaven alone knew how, seek to forget and
be forgotten. I communicated this plan to the only confidante
I had left to me, chiefly in order that she might be able to
enlighten my benefactors as to how I intended disposing of
the income they had offered me. She seemed pleased with the
idea, and the resolve to abandon herself to the same fate seemed
to her also, in her resentment against her position, to be quite
an easy matter. She expressed as much by hints and a word
dropped here and there. Without clearly realising what it
would lead to, and without coming to any understanding with
her, I left Bordeaux towards the end of April, more excited
than soothed in spirit, and filled with regret and anxiety. I
returned to Paris, for the time being, stunned and full of uncertainty as to what to do next. Feeling very unwell, exhausted,
and at the same time excited from want of sleep, I reached my
destination and put up at the Hôtel Valois, where I remained
a week, struggling to gain my self-control and to face my
strange position. Even if I had wished to resume the plans
which had been instrumental in bringing me to Paris, I soon
convinced myself that little or nothing could be done. I was
filled with distress and anger at being called upon to waste
my energies in a direction contrary to my tastes, merely to
satisfy the unreasonable demands made upon me. I was at
length obliged to answer my wife's last pressing communication, and wrote her a long and detailed letter in which I
kindly, but at the same time frankly, retraced the whole of our
life together, and explained that I was fully determined to set
her free from any immediate participation in my fate, as I felt
quite incapable of so arranging it so as to meet with her
approval. I promised her the half of whatever means I should
have at my disposal now or in the future, and told her she must
accept this arrangement with a good grace, because the occasion
had now arisen to take that step of parting from me which,
on our first meeting again in Switzerland, she had declared
herself ready to do. I ended my letter without bidding her
a final farewell. I thereupon wrote to Bordeaux immediately
to inform Jessie of the step I had taken, though my means did
not as yet allow of my forming any definite plan which I
could communicate to her for my complete flight from the

world. In return she announced that she was determined to do likewise, and asked for my protection, under which she intended to place herself when once she had set herself free. Much alarmed, I did all in my power to make her realise that it was one thing for a man, placed in such a desperate situation as myself, to cut himself adrift in the face of insurmountable difficulties, but quite another matter for a young woman, at least to all outward appearances, happily settled, to decide to break up her home, for reasons which probably no one except myself would be in a position to understand. Regarding the unconventionality of her resolve in the eyes of the world, she assured me that it would be carried out as quietly as possible, and that for the present she merely thought of arranging to visit her friends the Ritters in Dresden. I felt so upset by all this that I yielded to my craving for retirement, and sought it at no great distance from Paris. Towards the middle of April I went to Montmorency, of which I had heard many agreeable accounts, and there sought a modest hiding-place. With great difficulty I dragged myself to the outskirts of the little town, where the country still bore a wintry aspect, and turned into the little strip of garden belonging to a wine merchant, which was filled with visitors only on Sundays, and there refreshed myself with some bread and cheese and a bottle of wine. A crowd of hens surrounded me, and I kept throwing them pieces of bread, and was touched by the self-sacrificing abstemiousness with which the cock gave all to his wives though I aimed particularly at him. They became bolder and bolder, and finally flew on to the table and attacked my provisions; the cock flew after them, and noticing that everything was topsy-turvy, pounced upon the cheese with the eagerness of a craving long unsatisfied. When I found myself being driven from the table by this chaos of fluttering wings, I was filled with a gaiety to which I had long been a stranger. I laughed heartily, and looked round for the signboard of the inn. I thereby discovered that my host rejoiced in the name of Homo. This seemed a hint from Fate, and I felt I must seek shelter here at all costs. An extraordinarily small and narrow bedroom was shown me, which I immediately engaged. Besides the bed it held a rough table and two cane-bottomed chairs. I arranged one of these as a washhand-stand, and on the table I placed some books, writing materials, and the score of *Lohengrin,* and almost heaved a sigh of content in spite of my extremely cramped accommodation. Though the weather remained uncertain and the woods with their leafless trees did not seem to offer the prospect of very enticing walks, I still felt that here there was a possibility of my being forgotten, and being also in my turn allowed to forget the events that had lately filled me with such desperate anxiety. My old artistic instinct awoke again. I looked over my *Lohengrin* score, and quickly decided to send it to Liszt and leave it to him to bring it out as best he could. Now that I had got rid of this score also, I felt as free as a bird and as careless as Diogenes about what might befall me. I even invited Kietz to come and stay with me and share the pleasures of my retreat. He did actually come, as he had done during my stay in Meudon; but he found me even more modestly installed than I had been there. He was quite prepared to take pot-luck, however, and cheerfully slept on an improvised bed, promising to keep the world in touch with me upon his return to Paris. I was suddenly startled from my state of complacency by the news that my wife had come to Paris to look me up. I had an hour's painful struggle with myself to settle the course I should pursue, and decided not to allow the step I had taken in regard to her to be looked upon as an ill-considered and excusable vagary. I left Montmorency and betook myself to Paris, summoned Kietz to my hotel, and instructed him to tell my wife, who had already been trying to gain admittance to him, that he knew nothing more of me except that I had left Paris. The poor fellow, who felt as much pity for Minna as for me, was so utterly bewildered on this occasion, that he declared that he felt as though he were the axis upon which all the misery in the world turned. But he apparently realised the significance and importance of my decision, as it was necessary he should, and acquitted himself in this delicate matter with intelligence and good feeling. That night I left Paris by train for Clermont-Tonnerre, from whence I travelled on to Geneva, there to await news from Frau Ritter in Dresden. My exhaustion was such that, even had I possessed the necessary means, I could not as yet have contemplated undergoing the fatigue of a long journey. By way of gaining time for further developments I retired to Villeneuve, at the other end of the Lake of Geneva, where I put up at the Hôtel Byron, which was quite empty at the time. Here I learned that Karl Ritter had arrived in Zürich, as he said he would, with the intention of paying me a visit. Impressing upon him the necessity for the strictest secrecy, I invited him to join me at the Lake of Geneva, and in the second week in May we met at the Hôtel Byron. The characteristic which pleased me in him was his absolute devotion, his quick comprehension of my position and the necessity of my resolutions, as well as his readiness to submit without question to all my arrangements, even where he himself was concerned. He was full of my latest literary efforts, told me what an impression they had made on his acquaintances, and thereby induced me to spend the few days of rest I was enjoying in preparing my poem of *Siegfried's Tod* for publication.

I wrote a short preface dedicating this poem to my friends as a relic of the time when I had hoped to devote myself entirely to art, and especially to the composition of music. I sent this manuscript to Herr Wigand in Leipzig, who returned it to me after some time with the remark, that if I insisted on its being printed in Latin characters he would not be able to sell a single copy of it. Later on I discovered that he deliberately refused to pay me the ten louis d'or due to me for *Das Kunstwerk der Zukunft,* which I had directed him to send to my wife. Disappointing as all this was, I was nevertheless unable to engage in any further work, as only a few days after Karl's arrival the realities of life made themselves felt in an unexpected manner, most upsetting to my tranquillity of mind. I received a wildly excited letter from Mme. Laussot to tell me that she had not been able to resist telling her mother of her intentions, that in so doing she had immediately aroused the suspicion that I was to blame, and in consequence of this her disclosure had been communicated to M. Laussot, who vowed he would search everywhere for me in order to put a bullet through my body. The situation was clear enough, and I decided to go to Bordeaux immediately in order to come to an understanding with my opponent. I at once wrote fully to M. Eugène, endeavouring to make him see matters in their true light, but at the same time declared myself incapable of understanding how a man could bring himself to keep a woman with him by force, when she no longer wished to remain. I ended by informing him that I should reach Bordeaux at the same time as my letter, and immediately upon my arrival there would let him know at what hotel to find me; also that I would not tell his wife of the step I was taking, and that he could consequently act without restraint. I did not conceal from him, what indeed was the fact, that I was undertaking this journey under great difficulties, as under the circumstances I considered it impossible to wait to have my passport endorsed by the French envoy. At the same time I wrote a few lines to Mme. Laussot, exhorting her to be calm and self-possessed, but, true to my purpose, refrained from even hinting at any movement on my part. (When, years afterwards, I told Liszt this story, he declared I had acted very stupidly in not telling Mme. Laussot of my intentions.) I took leave of Karl the same day, in order to set out next morning from Geneva on my tedious journey across France. But I was so exhausted by all this that I could not help thinking I was going to die. That same night I wrote to Frau Ritter in Dresden, to this effect, giving her a short account of the incredible difficulties I had been drawn into. As a matter of fact, I suffered great inconvenience at the French frontier on account of my passport; I was made to give my exact place of destination, and it was only upon my assuring them that pressing family affairs required my immediate presence, that the authorities showed exceptional leniency and allowed me to proceed.

I travelled by Lyons through Auvergne by stage-coach for three days and two nights, till at length I reached Bordeaux. It was the middle of May, and as I surveyed the town from a height at early dawn I saw it lit up by a fire that had broken out. I alighted at the Hôtel Quatre Sœurs, and at once sent a note to M. Laussot, informing him that I held myself at his disposal and would remain in all day to receive him. It was nine o'clock in the morning when I sent him this message. I waited in vain for an answer, till at last, late in the afternoon, I received a summons from the police-station to present myself immediately. There I was first of all asked whether my passport was in order. I acknowledged the difficulty I found myself in with regard to it, and explained that family matters had necessitated my placing myself in this position.

I was thereupon informed that precisely this family matter, which had no doubt brought me there, was the cause of their having to deny me the permission to remain in Bordeaux any longer. In answer to my question, they did not conceal the fact that these proceedings against me were being carried out at the express wish of the family concerned. This extraordinary revelation immediately restored my good-humour. I asked the police inspector whether, after such a trying journey, I might not be allowed a couple of days' rest before returning; this request he readily granted, and told me that in any case there could be no chance of my meeting the family in question, as they had left Bordeaux at mid-day. I used these two days to recover from my fatigue, and also wrote a letter to Jessie, in which I told her exactly what had taken place, without concealing my contempt at the behaviour of her husband, who could expose his wife's honour by a denunciation to the police. I also added that our friendship could certainly not continue until she had released herself from so humiliating a position. The next thing was to get this letter safely delivered. The information furnished me by the police officials was not sufficient to enlighten me as to what had exactly taken place in the Laussot family, whether they had left home for some length of time or merely for a day, so I simply made up my mind to go to their house. I rang the bell and the door sprang open; without meeting any one I walked up to the first-floor flat, the door of which stood open, and went from room to room till I reached Jessie's boudoir, where I placed my letter in her work-basket and returned the way I had come. I received no reply, and set out upon my return journey as soon as the term of rest granted me had expired. The fine May weather had a cheering effect upon me, and the clear water, as well as the agreeable name of the Dordogne, along whose banks the post-chaise travelled for some distance, gave me great pleasure.

I was also entertained by the conversation of two fellow-travellers, a priest and an officer, about the necessity of putting an end to the French Republic. The priest showed himself much more humane and broad-minded than his military interlocutor, who could only repeat the one refrain, '*Il faut en finir.*' I now had a look at Lyons, and in a walk round the town tried to recall the scenes in Lamartine's *Histoire des Girondins*, where he so vividly describes the siege and surrender of the town during the period of the Convention Nationale. At last I arrived at Geneva, and returned to the Byron hotel, where Karl Ritter was awaiting me. During my absence he had heard from his family, who wrote very kindly concerning me. His mother had at once reassured him as to my condition, and pointed out that with people suffering from nervous disorders the idea of approaching death was a frequent symptom, and that there was consequently no occasion to feel anxious about me. She also announced her intention of coming to visit us in Villeneuve with her daughter Emilie in a few days' time. This news made me take heart again; this devoted family, so solicitous for my welfare, seemed sent by Providence to lead me, as I so longed to be led, to a new life. Both ladies arrived in time to celebrate my thirty-seventh birthday on the twenty-second of May. The mother, Frau Julie, particularly made a deep impression upon me. I had only met her once before in Dresden, when Karl had invited me to be present at the performance of a quartette of his own composition, given at his mother's house. On this occasion the respect and devotion shown me by each member of the family had delighted me. The mother had hardly spoken to me, but when I was leaving she was moved to tears as she thanked me for my visit. I was unable to understand her emotion at the time, but now when I reminded her of it she was surprised, and explained that she had felt so touched at my unexpected kindness to her son.

She and her daughter remained with us about a week. We sought diversion in excursions to the beautiful Valais, but did not succeed in dispelling Frau Ritter's sadness of heart, caused by the knowledge of recent events of which she had now been informed, as well as by her anxiety at the course my life was taking. As I afterwards learned, it had cost the nervous, delicate woman a great effort to undertake this journey, and when I urged her to leave her house to come and settle in

Switzerland with her family, so that we might all be united, she at last pointed out to me that in proposing what seemed to her such an eccentric undertaking, I was counting upon a strength and energy she no longer possessed. For the present she commended her son, whom she wished to leave with me, to my care, and gave me the necessary means to keep us both for the time being. Regarding the state of her fortune, she told me that her income was limited, and now that it was impossible to accept any help from the Laussots, she did not know how she would be able to come to my assistance sufficiently to assure my independence. Deeply moved, we took leave of this venerable woman at the end of a week, and she returned to Dresden with her daughter, and I never saw her again.

Still bent upon discovering a means of disappearing from the world, I thought of choosing a wild mountain spot where I could retire with Karl. For this purpose we sought the lonely Visper Thal in the canton Valais, and not without difficulty made our way along the impracticable roads to Zermatt. There, at the foot of the colossal and beautiful Matterhorn, we could indeed consider ourselves cut off from the outer world. I tried to make things as comfortable as I could in this primitive wilderness, but discovered only too soon that Karl could not reconcile himself to his surroundings. Even on the second day he owned that he thought it horrid, and suggested that it would be more pleasant in the neighbourhood of one of the lakes. We studied the map of Switzerland, and chose Thun for our next destination. Unfortunately I again found myself reduced to a state of extreme nervous fatigue, in which the slightest effort produced a profuse and weakening perspiration. Only by the greatest strength of will was I able to make my way out of the valley; but at last we reached Thun, and with renewed courage engaged a couple of modest but cheerful rooms looking out on to the road, and proposed to wait and see how we should like it. In spite of the reserve which still betrayed his shyness of character, I found conversation with my young friend always pleasant and enlivening. I now realised the pitch of fluent and overflowing vivacity to which the young man could attain, particularly at night before retiring to rest, when he would squat down beside my bed, and in the agreeable, pure dialect of the German Baltic provinces, give free expression to whatever had excited his interest. I was exceedingly cheered during these days by the perusal of the *Odyssey,* which I had not read for so long and which had fallen into my hands by chance. Homer's long-suffering hero, always homesick yet condemned to perpetual wandering, and always valiantly overcoming all difficulties, was strangely sympathetic to me. Suddenly the peaceful state I had scarcely yet entered upon was disturbed by a letter which Karl received from Mme. Laussot. He did not know whether he ought to show it to me, as he thought Jessie had gone mad. I tore it out of his hand, and found she had written to say that she felt obliged to let my friend know that she had been sufficiently enlightened about me to make her drop my acquaintance entirely. I afterwards discovered, chiefly through the help of Frau Ritter, that in consequence of my letter and my arrival in Bordeaux, M. Laussot, together with Mrs. Taylor, had immediately taken Jessie to the country, intending to remain there until the news was received of my departure, to accelerate which he had applied to the police authorities. While they were away, and without telling her of my letter and my journey, they had obtained a promise from the young woman to remain quiet for a year, give up her visit to Dresden, and, above all, to drop all correspondence with me; since, under these conditions, she was promised her entire freedom at the end of that time, she had thought it better to give her word. Not content with this, however, the two conspirators had immediately set about calumniating me on all sides, and finally to Mme. Laussot herself, saying that I was the initiator of this plan of elopement. Mrs. Taylor had written to my wife complaining of my intention to commit adultery, at the same time expressing her pity for her and offering her support; the unfortunate Minna, who now thought she had found a hitherto unsuspected reason for my resolve to remain separated from her, wrote back complaining of me to Mrs. Taylor. The meaning of an innocent remark I had once made had been strangely misinterpreted, and matters were now aggravated by making it appear as though I had intentionally lied. In the course of playful conversation Jessie had once told me that she belonged to no recognised form of religion, her father having been a member of a certain sect which did not baptise either according to the Protestant or the Roman Catholic ritual; whereupon I had comforted her by assuring her that I had come in contact with much more questionable sects, as shortly after my marriage in Königsberg I had learned that it had been solemnised by a hypocrite. God alone knows in what form this had been repeated to the worthy British matron, but, at all events, she told my wife that I had said I was 'not legally married to her.' In any case, my wife's answer to this had no doubt furnished further material with which to poison Jessie's mind against me, and this letter to my young friend was the result. I must admit that, seen by this light, the circumstance at which I felt most indignant was the way my wife had been treated, and while I was perfectly indifferent as to what the rest of the party thought of me, I immediately accepted Karl's offer to go to Zürich and see her, so as to give her the explanation necessary to her peace of mind. While awaiting his return, I received a letter from Liszt, telling me of the deep impression made upon him by my *Lohengrin* score, which had caused him to make up his mind as to the future in store for me. He at the same time announced that, as I had given him the permission to do so, he intended doing all in his power to bring about the production of my opera at the forthcoming Herder festival in Weimar. About this time I also heard from Frau Ritter, who, in consequence of events of which she was well aware, thought herself called upon to beg me not to take the matter too much to heart. At this moment Karl also returned from Zürich, and spoke with great warmth of my wife's attitude. Not having found me in Paris, she had pulled herself together with remarkable energy, and in pursuance of an earlier wish of mine, had rented a house on the lake of Zürich, installed herself comfortably, and remained there in the hope of at last hearing from me again. Besides this, he had much to tell me of Sulzer's good sense and friendliness, the latter having stood by, my wife and shown her great sympathy. In the midst of his narrative Karl suddenly exclaimed, 'Ah! these could be called sensible people; but with such a mad Englishwoman nothing could be done.' To all this I said not a word, but finally with a smile asked him whether he would like to go over to Zürich? He sprang up exclaiming, 'Yes, and as soon as possible.' 'You shall have your way,' said I; 'let us pack. I can see no sense in anything either here or there.' Without breathing another syllable about all that had happened, we left the next day for Zürich.

www.ingramcontent.com/pod-product-compliance
Lightning Source LLC
Chambersburg PA
CBHW020727160426
43192CB00006B/134

GHOSTS OF LONDON

By
ELLIOTT O'DONNELL
Author of 'Rooms of Mystery,' 'Women Bluebeards'
'Great Thames Mysteries,' 'Famous Curses'
etc.

CONTENTS

CHAPTER	PAGE
I. THE TOWER OF LONDON AND BETHLEHEM ASYLUM	1
II. ST. JAMES'S PALACE, THE GREEN PARK AND ST. JAMES'S PARK	13
III. BERKELEY SQUARE AND RED LION SQUARE	26
IV. BLOOMSBURY	40
V. BLOOMSBURY (CONTINUED) AND WESTMINSTER	52
VI. LINCOLN'S INN, THE TEMPLE, GREYFRIARS, CHARTERHOUSE, ST. BARTHOLOMEW'S THE GREAT, AND NEWGATE	69
VII. HYDE PARK	84
VIII. BLACKFRIARS AND HIGHBURY	102
IX. HOLLAND HOUSE, LONDON BRIDGES AND CHICK LANE	116
X. BIRD HAUNTINGS AND BLACKHEATH GHOSTS	133
XI. SPRING-HEELED JACK AND THE BROMPTON ROAD	145
XII. HAYMARKET THEATRE, HAM HOUSE AND CRANFORD HOUSE	156
XIII. CLUB HAUNTINGS AND SOME STRANGE HAPPENINGS IN SOHO AND BLOOMSBURY	165
XIV. THE THAMES AND KILBURN	176
XV. HIGHGATE, HAMPSTEAD AND SOUTH KENSINGTON	187
XVI. BARNES COMMON, BETHNAL GREEN AND ST. ANNE'S CHURCHYARD	198

CONTENTS

CHAPTER	PAGE
XVII. ST. PAUL'S AND CRIPPLEGATE	209
XVIII. THE COCK LANE GHOST	221
XIX. STOCKWELL, WANDSWORTH COMMON, CHELSEA AND GHOSTLY CLOCKS	233
XX. ENFIELD CHASE, SOUTH MIMMS, CHESHUNT, ETC.	248
ADDENDUM	267
INDEX	279

CHAPTER I

THE TOWER OF LONDON AND BETHLEHEM ASYLUM

IF tragedy be the most prolific source of ghosts, and my investigations have led me to believe that it is, surely no place should be more haunted than the Tower of London. For many years, more particularly in the Middle Ages, it was almost daily the scene of someone's unhappy death, for not only were executions, authorized by royal warrant, carried out there, but within its walls murders were secretly committed and accompanied, in most instances, by cruelties of a nature too ghastly and revolting to be told.

That its weird and gloomy precincts have been haunted in the past there is little doubt (this opinion is not founded only on the theory of cause and effect, but on certain records), and should certain rumours recently circulated have any foundation in fact, it would seem that similar hauntings may be experienced there at the present time. Perhaps the best authenticated story of a Tower ghost was that published in *Notes and Queries* for 1860 by Mr. Edmund Lenthal Swifte, Keeper of the Crown Jewels from 1814 to 1852. According to this story, late one Saturday night in October, 1817, Mr. and Mrs. Swifte, their son and Mrs. Swifte's sister, were seated at supper in the sitting-room of the Jewel House, which had recently been modernized. The doors, three in number, were all closed; the dark and heavy window curtains were drawn close, and the only light in the room came from two tall wax candles on the table. Mr. Swifte sat at one end of the table, his son sat beside him on his right hand, Mrs. Swifte faced the chimney piece, and her sister sat opposite her. Midnight had just struck, and Mrs. Swifte was about to take a sip of wine, when she looked up and immediately cried out, " Good God! What is that?" Upon following his wife's gaze, Mr. Swifte saw a cylindrical-shaped object like a glass tube, hovering, in mid-air, between the table and the ceiling. It was about the thickness of his arm and contained a thick fluid, part of which was white and part light-blue. As he stared at it, the white and blue intermingled and then separated, and kept on doing so for about two minutes, during which time no one spoke. Then the thing began to move very slowly, passing directly in front of Mr. Swifte's sister-in-law, his son and himself. On reaching Mrs. Swifte, it paused for a moment, and then very slowly and deliberately stationed itself immediately above her right shoulder. The moment this happened Mrs. Swifte crouched down, and putting both hands on her right shoulder shrieked out, " Oh, Christ! It has seized me."

Mad with anger and fright at the thing's attack on his wife, Mr. Swifte picked up a chair, and swinging it round his head aimed a terrific blow at the cylindrical object. The chair, however, passed right through the thing, encountering no resistance till it struck the wall ; and at the same time, apparently, or a few seconds later, upon this point Mr. Swifte is not very clear, the cylindrical object vanished. What may seem strange to some people is that only Mr. and Mrs.

Swifte saw the cylindrical object, the two present besides, saw nothing. To those, however, who, like myself, have had experience with ghostly phenomena, there is nothing very extraordinary in this circumstance, since it not infrequently happens that while some of the people present in a room or elsewhere see a ghostly form, the rest of those present do not, the reason being, so I believe, that ghosts have the power of appearing exclusively to those to whom they wish to appear; in other words, they have the power of rendering themselves visible to some and invisible to others, at one and the same time. Sceptics declare that the phenomena Mr. and Mrs. Swifte saw must have been due either to trickery or to some natural and physical agency, not necessarily in the room, but operating, may be, from a distance, but Mr. Swifte left no stone unturned to prove definitely that such could not have been the case. He was not a spiritualist, nor did he claim to be "psychic," therefore he was in a position to examine what had happened with an open and unbiassed mind, and after much deliberation and careful analysis he came to the conclusion that the phenomenon he and his wife had witnessed could not be satisfactorily explained in accordance with any known physical laws. This, apparently, was the only ghostly phenomenon he himself had experienced during his long term of office at the Tower, but we have his authority for another strange occurrence that took place there.

At about twelve o'clock one night in January, 1816, a sentry pacing the paved yard in front of the Jewel House saw a dark object coming up the flight of stone steps under the building. The steps being in semi-darkness he could form no definite idea as to the identity of this object, which was not a human being, he thought, but some queer kind of animal. However, as he stared at it, with increasing wonder and alarm, a moonbeam falling directly on it proved it to be an enormous bear, that was rapidly advancing towards him, with a horrible glitter in its eyes. For a moment or so he was too paralysed to stir, but on realizing that the creature, unless it were stopped, would soon have him in its clutches, he struck at it furiously with his bayonet. To his unmitigated horror, the bayonet passed right through the bear without encountering any hindrance and stuck in the wall beyond, whilst the bear, obviously unharmed, came on. This was the climax: with a wild shriek of terror, he fell to the ground in a fit.

"When, on the morrow, I saw the unfortunate sentinel in the main guardroom," Mr. Swifte writes, "his fellow sentinel was with him and testified to having seen him at his post, just before the alarm, awake and alert, and to have spoken to him. Moreover, I then heard the man tell his own story. I saw him once again on the following day, but changed beyond recognition; in another day or two the brave and steady soldier, who could have mounted a breach and led a forlorn hope with unshaken nerves, *died*, the victim of a shadow."

Surprise has been expressed that any man should die from the effect of having seen a ghost, but there is no reason for supposing this case to be unique. Those who are acquainted with ghost-lore will know of cases of a more or less similar nature. When I asked the late Mr. W. T. Stead for the address of a certain badly haunted house in Barnet, he refused to give it to me, declaring that the ghost was dangerous; several people who had seen it having suffered so great a shock from the encounter that death had ensued. I admit this statement seemed to me at the time to be incredible, but I have no doubt now that Mr. Stead was right, for my own subsequent experiences with ghostly phenomena have forced me to the conclusion that a certain percentage of sudden deaths from heart failure are primarily due to some horrifying manifestation from the darker side of the Unknown. Nor do such calamities always happen to people known to have led wicked and dissolute lives: they happen sometimes to the most exemplary. Very probably the phantom seen by the sentry in the Tower was that of one of the bears that used to be kept there for the cruel purpose of baiting, for tragedy in the lives of animals has the same result psychically as it has in the lives of humans; a fact, I would add, which renders the frequency of animal ghosts not at all surprising.

Another Tower haunting is that of Anne Boleyn;[1] her phantom has not only been seen on the Tower Hill: it has appeared, at least on one occasion, in the Tower chapel. According to an authentic account of her appearance in the Tower chapel, it seems that, at midnight, a certain Captain, who was on duty at the Tower, set off on his rounds, with one of the sentries. When they came to the chapel, the Captain was surprised to see that it was lighted up.

"What's the meaning of that?" he remarked to the sentry. "Surely it's too late an hour for any service."

[1] Vide *Ghostly Visitors*, by "Spectre Stricken."

"Yes, sir," the sentry responded. "There ain't no service, but I've often seen that light and stranger things too. So have the other night sentries, and I'm blessed if we can hexplain them. They beat us, they do."

"It's certainly very odd," the Captain said, and he stared, rubbed his eyes, and stared again. The light was still there, however; it was no hallucination. "Fetch a ladder," he said; and when the ladder arrived, he placed it against the chapel wall, and mounting it peered through one of the windows.

What he saw thrilled him through and through. Nothing could have been more amazing. The whole interior of the chapel was illuminated with a bluish-white light, emanating seemingly from nowhere, and coming down the centre aisle was a procession of stately men and women, clad in the court costume of Henry VIII's time. The men for the most part were extremely handsome, and the women strikingly beautiful, but at their head walked a lady more beautiful than any of them. Jewels sparkled in her hair and on her snow-white neck and arms, and the Captain, who had but lately seen and admired a portrait of Anne Boleyn, instantly recognized in the leader of the procession that unhappy lady. They advanced in absolute silence, with heads held erect and eyes that looked neither to the right nor left, but always straight ahead of them.

Presently the light, which, as I have said, seemed to emanate from nowhere, became concentrated on the leader of the procession, and the Captain, who was very susceptible to the charms of the other sex, marvelled at the beauty of her slim white fingers, which were conspicuously adorned with rings of the costliest description. On arriving at the bottom of the centre aisle, the procession made a detour of the chapel by way of the side aisles, and after perambulating thus several times, it suddenly vanished, the light disappearing with it and leaving the interior of the building in utter darkness.

It was then, and not until then, when he could no longer see the figures and marvel at their magnificence and beauty, that the Captain first began to realize that the actors in the spectacle he had witnessed were not living human beings at all, but mere phantoms. He never saw the phenomenon again, though, doubtless, he often wished he might do so.

The council-chamber, one of the state-rooms in the Tower, where tradition affirms Guy Fawkes was examined and probably racked, is said to be haunted. I can find no authentic record of any ghost having been seen there, although there are plenty of rumours to that effect. When I visited the Tower many years ago, for the first time, an official I closely questioned as to the alleged hauntings told me there was a story current concerning this particular room. It was to this effect.

A soldier on duty at the Tower, passing the council-chamber at night, heard dreadful groans proceeding from it. Thinking someone must be ill, he was about to rap, when the door abruptly opened and a huge figure, well over six feet in height, came out. In build it was like a man, but its nude body was entirely covered with reddish-brown hair, which gave it the appearance of an ape. Its face, which was clean shaven and pallid, might have been that of a middle-aged man, but the expression on it was hardly human and devilish to a degree. Without apparently noticing the soldier, who, realizing that what he saw was nothing belonging to this world, was, in consequence, petrified with horror, the thing walked along the passage, till it came to a flight of stairs, down which it vanished. The soldier thereupon regained his equanimity to some extent, but was thankful enough when his vigil for that night ended and he was able to rejoin his comrades. Unfortunately, the identity of this phantom cannot be satisfactorily established. But for the fact that the soldier who saw it was quite sure that it had the face of a man, one might have supposed it to have been the ghost of an ape whose bones had been discovered shortly before in an unoccupied turret of the Tower; no other theory was formulated, and consequently its identity remains unproven.

I cannot, of course, guarantee the truth of this story; I can only say it was told me with every appearance of sincerity. I admit that many of the noises heard in the Tower at night and attributed to ghosts may well be caused by rats that come, in shoals, from the Thames, with the tide; but, obviously, rats must be ruled out in the case of things seen, and if the things seen can only be accounted for by the superphysical, why may not the things heard be so accounted for too?

Another building, no less famous in its way than the Tower, that at one time, at least, possessed a ghost, was the Hospital of the Star of Bethlehem, London's first lunatic asylum. We have all, I imagine, heard of Bedlam, and many of us, no doubt, have friends whom we think ought to be there, but it is not all of us who know that this very significant name owes its origin

THE TOWER AND BETHLEHEM ASYLUM 9

to the Hospital of the Star of Bethlehem, of which latter word Bedlam is a contraction.

As far back as 1246, Simon Fitz-Mary, a London Sheriff, founded a priory on the site of the present Liverpool Street Station (it is interesting to remember that where we now see railway trains and crowds of eager, hustling travellers, ascetic monks and pious nuns used once to tell their beads, sprinkle holy water and chant their prayers), which priory, some centuries later, was converted into the Hospital of the Star of Bethlehem for insane people. The method of dealing with maniacs in those days differed very much from that employed in our day, for then mad people were generally regarded as obsessed by evil spirits, and in order to get rid of the latter, when exorcism failed, recourse was had to the stick.

Thus the poor unfortunate wretches who, through no fault of their own, were insane, were often subjected to the most severe chastisement, and even in more enlightened times, when such a superstition no longer existed, lunatics frequently received very brutal treatment at the hands of their keepers. It follows, therefore, that tragedies in lunatic asylums in those days were not uncommon, and probably they were far more common than was ever dreamed of by the public, despite the fact that its suspicions must have been aroused by works such as *Valentine Vox*, which was a more or less successful attempt at exposure. Happily, however, this kind of cruelty in asylums has long since ceased, and we are only reminded of it by occasional rumours of ghostly happenings in certain of the older institutions.

To return to the priory. It was given by Henry VIII

to the City of London, who, after due consideration, converted it into the aforesaid Hospital of the Star of Bethlehem. In 1675 it was moved from Bishopsgate to Moorfields, whence, after various changes, it found its way in 1812 to the junction of the Lambeth and Kennington roads, where it remained till its final removal into the country. It was not until the end of the eighteenth century that it achieved notoriety through its now world-famous ghost.

In 1780, a young and handsome Indian came to London, and took lodgings in the house of a merchant on Fish Street Hill, close to London Bridge. Now the merchant at that time happened to have in his employ a very plain and shy maid-servant, called Rebecca, who loved poetry—especially romantic poetry—and often, when in bed, used to lie awake thinking of what she had read, and repeating aloud to herself certain lines she had memorized. Hence, it may be deduced that she was both imaginative and impressionable, the sort of girl who might easily fall in love, and fall deeply. This she did, the moment she saw the young Indian lodger, and henceforth, instead of repeating lines of poetry in bed at night, she would lie awake repeating his name and conjuring up his image. Then, one day, to her unspeakable consternation, she learned he was leaving. So reserved was Rebecca and so successful in her habitual self-restraint, that the Indian had not the slightest suspicion she was in love with him. Indeed, he scarcely thought of her at all. She inspired no sentiment whatever in him. She was just the domestic—very unattractive—and nothing more. This she did not know. Indeed, she believed rather the reverse, for she had magnified his casual, non-significant and ordinary glances into those of ill-concealed, latent love, and tender admiration.

To her bitter disappointment, not a word of regret did he utter when she brought him his breakfast that last, much-dreaded morning. He just ate it hurriedly and in silence. She followed him to the door, with some of his luggage, still hoping. And then the thunderbolt. With a careless nod of his head and a still more careless good-bye, he thrust something into her cold and not unshapely palm. It was a sovereign! The other inmates of the house and the neighbours wondered infinitely, when they saw Rebecca running after the chaise, which bore away her adored one, screaming and holding out the sovereign, which, in his innocent generosity, he had given her as a tip. The money in lieu of the love she had been so eagerly hoping for turned her brain, and she was, henceforth, a hopeless lunatic.

She then became an inmate of Bedlam, that is to say, the Hospital of the Star of Bethlehem, where she remained till she died, the fatal sovereign continually in her grasp. When she died, she was still clutching it, and the sight of it in her dead fingers so aroused the cupidity of a keeper, that, biding his opportunity, he stole it. So she was buried without it. Hence the haunting. Shortly after her death strange noises were heard in the asylum at night, footsteps and the opening and shutting of doors, some of which were locked on the inside. And more. Sometimes in the daytime, and sometimes at night, the ghost of Rebecca was seen, a lean figure, with ghastly white cheeks and wild eyes, gliding about corridors, rooms and staircases, always hunting, with never-abating feverishness, for her precious, purloined sovereign.

When the asylum shifted its quarters to its last London home, Rebecca's ghost went with it and stayed there, periodically manifesting itself, according to report, to patients and officials alike, right up to the time of its removal into the country in September, 1924.

Whether the haunting is still going on, I am unable to say with any degree of authority. I can only surmise that it does, from certain rumours that have reached me.

CHAPTER II

ST. JAMES'S PALACE, THE GREEN PARK AND ST. JAMES'S PARK

WITHOUT wishing in any degree to alarm the august inhabitants of St. James's Palace, one cannot help saying that, owing to incidents that have occurred there, according to history and tradition, in the past, it would not be at all surprising to find that it harboured ghosts galore, and that denizens of another world foregathered there in large numbers.

Many centuries ago, exactly how many it is impossible to say, according to the historian Stowe, there stood on the site the Palace now occupies a religious institution, dedicated to St. James the Less, Bishop of Jerusalem. Whence, we suppose, the Palace, now a royal residence, derives its name. The institution, presumably, was nothing more or less than a hospital, its inmates consisting of fourteen sisters, maidens, that were lepers, living " chastely and honestly in divine service," and certain citizens of London, with the generosity that is so frequently a characteristic of the business men of our great metropolis, subscribed liberally in money and lands to its upkeep.

Some idea of its age may be deduced from the fact that it was rebuilt by Berkynge, Abbot of Westminster, in the reign of Henry III. The privilege of an annual fair (to be held on the eve of St. James and the six following days) was granted to it by Edward I, who decreed that all the profits therefrom should be handed over to the hospital, the custody of which was subsequently granted to Eton College by Henry VI.

It then continued, in a more or less flourishing state, till Henry VIII, in his pretended zeal for a reformed religion, ordained the dissolution of the monasteries. Coveting the ground the hospital stood on, he classed it with the monasteries, on the plea that it was founded on a religious basis, and, when it was pulled down, he erected on its site a mansion for his own private use and pleasure.

Standing amid a fairyland of flowers, and bordered by woods which Henry took good care should be well stocked with game, it was an ideal country residence, and with a cock-pit and a tilting-yard added, left nothing in the way of sport to be desired. The tilting-yard occupied the space now known as Horse Guards' Parade.

Doubtless Henry had many an orgy in his new abode, and there is no doubt, also, that it witnessed more than one outrageous act of cruelty, for kings in those days, especially kings of the temperament and character of this Tudor monarch, made short work of those who had the misfortune to incur their displeasure. Hence, the not infrequent discovery in royal demesnes of cunningly concealed human bones.

It was here, within this Palace, that hapless Charles I spent his last night on earth, a fact that might well have given rise to a haunting, if acute emotions be, as I firmly believe them not infrequently to be, the forerunners of ghostly happenings.

It was not, however, until the reign of the second Charles that we find an actual case of haunting in the royal Palace recorded.

ST. JAMES'S PALACE AND PARK

Among the numerous mistresses of the Merry Monarch was the Duchesse de Mazarine, who, according to tradition, was as fair as she was frail. That she was so in very truth, I myself believe, because there is little doubt that Charles was an unerring connoisseur of feminine beauty, and had an almost uncanny *flair* for detecting latent passion and a tendency to frailty in the other sex. The Duchess's greatest woman friend was Madame de Beauclair, mistress of the Duke of York, also, according to tradition, more than ordinarily beautiful, and between these two women there existed a depth of attachment that was rarely to be met with in a royal court of olden days. After the burning of Whitehall, both ladies were awarded very handsome apartments in the Stable Yard of St. James's Palace.

After a while, Charles and James discovering younger beauties, paid little heed to the Duchess and Madame de Beauclair; however, the neglected ones found consolation in each other's company, and, in their solitude, began to think seriously of the problem of another life. They then made a compact that whichever of them should pass away first should return, if it were possible to do so, and inform the survivor of how she was faring in the other world. This compact was continually discussed, both women being very much in earnest, and the Duchess happening to be suddenly taken very ill, Madame de Beauclair reminded her of it; whereupon the Duchess assured Madame de Beauclair that she might depend on the pledge she, the Duchess, had so often given. An hour after this conversation, which was carried on in the presence of several other people, the Duchess died.

Some years later, the author of and authority for this story [1] paid a visit to Madame de Beauclair, and their conversation turning on the problem of another world, Madame de Beauclair expressed her disbelief in one with considerable emphasis, declaring that she had sufficient reason for so doing in the failure of her friend, the Duchess, to fulfil their compact.

"Did she still exist, no matter where," Madame de Beauclair remarked, "she would most certainly have found some means of communicating with me. That she has not done so convinces me that she no longer exists and that there is no after life."

Some months later, the lady who tells this story was visiting one of Madame de Beauclair's friends, and was about to begin a game of cards with her, when a servant entered the room with a message from Madame de Beauclair. The message was to the effect that if her friend wanted to see her again in this world, she must go to her at once. However, upon learning that Madame de Beauclair was apparently well, her friend, who was suffering from a cold herself, declined to go, whereupon a second and more urgent request was received by her, accompanied by a casket containing Madame de Beauclair's watch, chain, and various articles of jewellery. The recipient of the message and request then went, and her visitor went with her. On arriving at Madame de Beauclair's, they were ushered into her presence and found her seemingly well, though extremely agitated. She had sent for them, she said, because she was quite certain her days were numbered. She had, at last, received a visit from her deceased friend, the Duchess of Mazarine.

[1] *Accredited Ghost Stories*, by T. M. Jarvis, published 1823.

"I perceived not how she entered," Madame de Beauclair went on, "but turning my eyes towards yonder corner of the room, I saw her stand in the same form and habit she was accustomed to appear in when living; fain would I have spoken, but had not the power of utterance. She took a little circlet round the chamber, seeming rather to swim than walk, then stopped by the side of that Indian chest and, looking at me with her usual sweetness, said, 'Beauclair, between the hours of twelve and one this night you will be with me.'"

Madame de Beauclair added that directly she opened her mouth, to ask her friend's phantasm a question about the other world, it vanished.

Madame de Beauclair, having nothing further to relate—it was then close on midnight—her two visitors were trying to comfort her, when, suddenly, a change came over her face—hitherto she had appeared to be in perfectly normal health—and she cried, " Oh, I am sick at heart." Mrs. Ward, her confidential maid, who was in the room all the time, at once gave her a restorative, but it had no effect. She grew rapidly worse, and in about half an hour she died, at the very hour the phantom had prophesied.

Rumour asserts that the ghosts of the Duchess and Madame de Beauclair have been seen in the Palace, from time to time, but of these rumoured appearances there does not seem to be any authentic record.

So much has been written about Charles II's love intrigues, and he has been credited with so many, that one would suppose him to be the only king in civilized times who had had concubines, but, as a matter of fact, both George I and George II kept mistresses in

B

St. James's Palace, and much scandal was caused by them.

Among the most notorious were the Duchess of Kendal, the German mistress of George I, Mrs. Brett, one of his English mistresses, and Mrs. Howard (afterwards the Countess of Suffolk), the mistress of George II. Their " goings on " might well have given rise to hauntings, for there is little doubt they were past mistresses in vices of all kinds, particularly those that appealed most to the very animal Georges. The Stuarts, one and all, no matter how profligate—and some of them, perhaps, could not have been more so—still retained certain of the gentleman, but the same could not be said with regard to the earliest of our Hanoverian monarchs.

One night Mr. Howard, missing his pretty wife from his home, made inquiries as to her whereabouts and learned that she had gone, clandestinely, to St. James's Palace. He, therefore, hurried thither in a fury, and forcing his way past every obstruction, he shouted for his wife, demanding that she should come to him at once. He had almost succeeded in finding his adored one, who was, as he feared, lying in the arms of her royal lover, when the latter, relinquishing his love-making for the moment, appeared upon the scene and ordered that the indignant husband should be thrust into the street and his eviction accompanied by the promise of a pension of £1,200 a year.

About the year 1810 a tragedy, that might well account for some of the ghostly happenings, real or imaginary, in the Palace, took place.

The Duke of Cumberland, who resided in the Palace at that date, had an Italian valet named Sellis, who, for

ST. JAMES'S PALACE AND PARK 19

some reason or another, bore him a grudge. According to his own version of the affair, the Duke awoke one night, to hear someone in the room. It was Sellis, armed with a knife, and a terrible struggle ensued. The Duke, however, being powerful and active, succeeded in overcoming the Italian, who, upon being allowed to retire to his room, immediately cut his throat, from fear of the consequence of his attempt to assassinate his royal master. There was, of necessity, an inquest, and, there being no evidence to show Sellis was insane, a simple verdict of *felo de se* was returned.

There can be little real doubt that the Duke's story was true, but unfortunately he was the least popular of an unpopular family, and horrible insinuations in reference to this tragedy were consequently levelled against him, mostly, of course, by the lower classes, who are always ready and eager to snatch at any opportunity of attacking the upper classes. A tradition that the Duke murdered his valet because his valet " knew too much," and that the valet's ghost, in consequence, periodically haunts the Palace, still apparently survives, for, according to rumour, the ghost of a man, in old-world clothes, with white face and dark, gleaming eyes, may still sometimes be seen at night in a certain part of the Palace—the part where the tragedy is said to have been enacted.

The Duke, who was thus, in my opinion, unwarrantably maligned, remained in England till 1837, when he went to Hanover, to assume the kingship of that country. He never returned to London, at least not in the material body.

Some few years prior to the Sellis mystery, as it was termed, a great sensation was caused in the West End by the appearance of a ghost in St. James's Park. It seems that some twenty or so years previously, that is to say in or about 1784, a sergeant in the Guards cut off his wife's head and threw her body into the canal, that then ran through the Park. What he did with her head is not known, nor is it known what subsequently happened to him, whether, for instance, he was apprehended and punished, or whether he managed to elude conviction and escape punishment. With regard to the haunting in 1804, sentries on duty in the Park at night declared they saw a headless woman there, and that she walked past them, greatly, of course, to their alarm, and then disappeared. The matter was much talked about, naturally, by the soldiers in the guard-room, and sentries went to their various posts in the Park, shivering and shaking. The weather, seemingly, mattered not; the headless phantom came on fine nights when the Park was bathed in moonlight and the great, silent trees stood out even more clearly than in the daytime, and it came on dark, stormy nights, when the wind blew and howled among the trees and the rain fell in sheer torrents. Heat and cold, too, had no effect on it; its nightly appearance could be counted on. A soldier pacing to and fro, apprehensively watching the black shadows of the solemn oaks and elms, would suddenly see a figure emerge from behind some tree and glide noiselessly towards him. He did not challenge it; he shut his eyes and kept them shut till it had passed. Why, because it was headless, the headless phantom of the murdered wife. The many stories told of it by affrighted sentries coming to the ears of the authorities, an official inquiry was made; and several

ST. JAMES'S PALACE AND PARK 21

depositions of men on oath were taken before Sir Richard Ford, one of the magistrates of Westminster. Here is one : [1]

"I do solemnly declare that when guard at Recruit House (now Wellington Barracks) on or about the 3rd inst., about half-past one in the morning, I perceived the figure of a woman, without a head, rise from the earth, at a distance of about two feet before me. I was so alarmed at the circumstance that I had not the power to speak to it, which was my wish to have done. But I distinctly observed that the figure was dressed in a red striped gown, with red spots between each stripe, and that part of the dress and figure appeared to me to be enveloped in a cloud. In about the space of two minutes, whilst my eyes were fixed on the object, it vanished from my sight. I was perfectly sober and collected at the time, and being in great trepidation, called to the next sentinel, who met me half-way, and to whom I communicated the strange sight I had seen."

Signed by George Jones, of Lieut.-Colonel Taylor's Company of Coldstream Guards. Westminster, Jan. 15, 1804.

The headless woman was not, however, the only source of trouble to the soldiers. Strange, uncanny sounds were frequently heard, not only in the Park itself, but in certain of the buildings adjoining the Park. With regard to them, too, depositions of soldiers on sentry duty were taken. This is one :

"I do hereby declare that, whilst on guard behind the Armoury House (to the best of my recollection about three weeks ago), I heard at twelve o'clock a

[1] *The Story of the London Parks*, by Jacob Larwood.

tremendous noise, which proceeded from the windows of an uninhabited house near to the spot where I was on duty. At the same time I heard a voice cry out, 'Bring me a light! Bring me a light!' The last word was uttered in so feeble and so changeable a tone of voice that I concluded some person was ill, and consequently offered them my assistance. I could, however, obtain no answer to my proposal, although I repeated it several times, and as often heard the voice use the same terms.

"I endeavoured to see the person who called out, but in vain. On a sudden the violent noise was renewed, which appeared to me to resemble sashes of windows lifted hastily up and down, but that they were moved in quick succession and in different parts of the house, nearly at the same time, so it seems to me impossible that one person could accomplish the whole business.

"I heard several of my regiment say they have heard similar noises and proceedings, but I have never heard the calls accounted for."

Signed, Richard Donkin, 12th Company of Coldstream Guards, Whitehall, Jan. 17, 1804.

Although both cases, that is to say, that of the headless woman and the noises in the house, were thoroughly investigated, no explanation on physical grounds was forthcoming. Both affairs remained mysteries, soluble, so it seemed, only on the hypothesis of the superphysical. The finding, in 1795, during digging operations on the Parade, of a skeleton, sex not determined, but thought to be that of a woman, gave rise to speculations regarding other sounds and sights believed to be ghostly.

St. James's Park, indeed, as may be said of all the old London parks, has witnessed many tragedies, and I know, from experience, they are all at times badly haunted. One of the more recent ghosts in St. James's and the Green Park, not counting the headless woman phantom, that is still alleged to manifest itself periodically; is that of a man in evening clothes, said to be the earth-bound spirit of an individual who either shot or poisoned himself on a bench or seat in the Green Park, probably, thirty or more years ago. Some time before the Great War I had a first-hand account of this ghost from a man who declared he had seen it.

"I was walking along the broad walk that runs parallel with Piccadilly, one wet afternoon in July," he told me, "when a tall, grey-haired man, in evening clothes, caught me up and walked on ahead of me. That anyone should choose to take a walk on such a night—for, although the rain could not be described as heavy, it was distinctly wetting, and therefore, to most people, discomforting—bareheaded, and without overcoat or mackintosh, struck me as somewhat remarkable, and, my curiosity roused, I observed him more closely, perhaps, than I should have done otherwise. I noticed that although my steps produced a slight crunching sound on the moist soil, his made no noise whatever, despite the fact that he was wearing dancing pumps, another idiosyncrasy. He continued walking ahead of me till we came to a spot where several paths intersected, and I was wondering which path he would select, when, to my amazement, he suddenly began to grow fainter and fainter until, finally, he vanished altogether, and I found myself staring into space. Realizing, then, that what I had seen was a ghost, I felt, if not actually frightened, rather scared."

There is a hillock in the Green Park, and on it a clump of trees. Some years ago, a member of the now defunct International Club for Psychic Research, in Regent Street, who is now defunct himself, used to confide in me his adoration for a certain tree in this clump. He wrote sonnets to it, made love to it, serenaded it with his favourite instrument, the flute. He was, I am convinced, deeply enamoured of it, and if half the things he told me about it were true, it must have been a very wonderful tree indeed.

He said it used to sigh and murmur when he spoke to it, but he could never interpret what it said, because it seemed to be speaking in a foreign tongue and its voice sounded so far away.

Of course, there are haunted trees in the Green Park as well as in Hyde Park, trees that harbour phantoms that have once inhabited material human bodies, and phantoms with little resemblance to anything either human or animal. I have met people who, with seeming perfect sincerity, have declared they have encountered these various kinds of tree spirits, and I believe that some of the trees that harbour phantoms exercise a peculiarly evil and harmful influence.

However, according to my friend of the International Club, there was nothing ghostly or baleful about the tree he loved. It was associated with something superphysical, it is true, but it was to fairyland rather than to ghostland that that superphysical belonged.

Of course, many people may, and undoubtedly will,

say that this man who made love to a tree was mad, and eccentric to a degree he undoubtedly was; but it must not be forgotten that in the south and west of Ireland, in Oregon, and in certain other countries, there are trees said to be obsessed or haunted at times both by ghosts and by fairies.

CHAPTER III

BERKELEY SQUARE AND RED LION SQUARE

No alleged haunting caused greater interest and sensation in the seventies and eighties of the last century than that of No. — Berkeley Square.

When I first visited London, as a schoolboy, in the early nineties, I soon found my way to Berkeley Square, and although No. — was no longer a prominent topic of conversation, it having long since lost its excessive notoriety, I was, nevertheless, thrilled when I caught a glimpse of it. Then few people questioned the truth of its once having been really haunted, the stories told about it were generally accepted as facts, and not, as what many people now consider them, fabrications. There is still much diversity of opinion as to the origin of the reports of the hauntings.

Some think they arose from the fact that the house was for some time occupied by a very eccentric hypochondriac, who shut himself up there and saw no one, inhabiting one room only and letting the other rooms go to wrack and ruin. Sometimes he wandered around them at night, a lighted candle in his hand, and this, it was surmised, led his neighbours and people passing by to believe that the premises were haunted. Moreover, as the recluse was tall and haggard, the fitful light from the candle, accentuating his pallor, made him appear eerie and spectre-like;

and thus it may have been that the report got about that the house was haunted by a very terrible-looking apparition. Other sceptics with regard to the super-physical were of the opinion that the story of the hauntings was merely an invention on the part of some caretaker, who wanted to prevent people, by scaring them, from buying or renting the house, in order that he (or she) might go on living there.

Allusion to this house was made by well-known contemporary authors, and might be found both in books and articles. Lord Lyttleton, for instance, writing of it in *Notes and Queries*,[1] said, " It is quite true that there is a house in Berkeley Square said to be haunted, and long unoccupied on that account. There are strange stories about it, into which this deponent cannot enter "; and the author of an interesting article on ghostly happenings in the now defunct *Mayfair*,[2] a society magazine, writes, " The house in Berkeley Square contains at least one room of which the atmosphere is supernaturally fatal to body and mind alike. A girl saw, heard and felt such horror in it that she went mad, and never recovered sanity enough to tell how or why.[3]

" A gentleman, a disbeliever in ghosts, dared to sleep in it, and was found a corpse in the middle of the floor, after frantically ringing for help in vain. Rumours suggest other cases of the same kind, all ending in death, madness, or both, as the result of sleeping, or trying to sleep, in that room. The very party walls of the house, when touched, are found saturated with electric horror. It is uninhabited, save

[1] November, 1872.   [2] May 10, 1879.
[3] See Addendum.

by an elderly man and woman, who act as caretakers; but even these have no access to the room. That is kept locked, the key being in the hands of a mysterious and seemingly nameless person, who comes to the house once every six months, locks up the elderly people in the basement, and then unlocks the room and occupies himself in it for hours."

Bulwer-Lytton introduces the house into at least one of his stories. Whether it was really haunted or not I cannot say. As I remarked before, its notoriety was much on the wane the first time I saw it, and I have never crossed its threshold.

During a nocturnal vigil in a haunted house, near Bristol, the late Lord Curzon of Kedleston assured me No. — Berkeley Square never was haunted. He said the stories relating to it were pure inventions, and I understood him to say, too, that the house had, at one time, belonged to a relative of his, who, in consequence of the sinister rumours about it, had caused it to be demolished and rebuilt.

The original building may, or may not, I think, have harboured beings from another world, but whether it did or not, the present house—renumbered, I am told—is absolutely free from any such phenomena.

One of the most widely-known and hair-raising versions of the hauntings of the old house is this:

One night, in the seventies of the last century, two sailors found themselves stranded in London. Having spent all their pay in riotous living they were now penniless, and since they knew no one, they were both friendless and homeless too. It was a none too pleasant situation, they told themselves, especially on a night in mid-winter. After wandering about disconsolately for some hours, they strolled into Berkeley Square. Then, one of them seeing " To be sold or let " at No. —, was seized with an inspiration.

" I say, Bill," he remarked to his mate, " why not get in there? It will be better at any rate than sleeping out-of-doors."

Bill agreed, and after a look round to see no policeman was about, they descended into the area of the house and examined the doors and windows. The latter were strongly barred, but a few mighty shoves —they were both hefty men—against a door eventually forced it open. They groped their way in the pitch dark till they bumped up against a staircase. One of them then struck a match—he had not done so before, for fear of being seen from the street—and they took stock of their surroundings.

They were in a stone passage, at the foot of the staircase leading to the first floor.

" Better upstairs," Bill commented, " it smells damp down 'ere."

" 'Ouses that 'ave stayed empty a while always do smell damp," Mick, the other sailor, responded. " Suppose we look around 'ere for some wood or summat to light a fire with, and then make for one of the back rooms upstairs?"

Bill agreed. Being handy men they soon obtained wood, by the simple process of breaking up several of the kitchen dresser drawers and removing some of the skirting boards. Some loose wallpaper likewise came in useful. Armed thus with requisites, they made their way, as lightly as possible, upstairs, and after a hasty survey of several rooms, finally decided on a back one on the second floor.

Endowed with that something which usually characterizes sailors, particularly British sailors, and enables them to overcome the most stupendous difficulties, it did not take Bill and Mick long to make a fire in the small, rusty grate, despite the dampness of the long-disused chimney. What with the ruddy flames, crackling wood and steadily-increasing heat the spirits of the tired tars soon revived, and though they were hungry, a few sips of rum satisfied them tolerably well and made them feel fairly comfortable inside.

"Better than the streets or park, eh, Bill?" Mick observed, extracting a plug of tobacco from his pocket and wedging it with a grimy thumb in his pipe.

Bill gave a grunt, taken by his companion for acquiescence, and puffed away in silence.

"Funny," he ejaculated, after some minutes, "why some 'ouses won't let and stand hempty for so long. I wonder what's the matter with this one."

"Why should anything be the matter with it?" Mick rejoined. "There's more 'ouses than people what can afford to take 'em, that's usually the trouble."

"Maybe," Bill grunted, "and maybe not. I 'ave 'eard that 'ouses where murders or suicides 'ave occurred in lie idle for years. Sooperstition, I reckon."

"That's about it," Mick said. "Surprising 'ow sleepy a fire makes one."

After this both men relapsed into silence, then, after a while, came the sound of heavy, steady breathing; they were both asleep, fast asleep.

Bill was the first to wake. A noise somewhere in the house disturbed him. He sat up shivering; the fire had burned very low and the air felt chilly. Fortunately they had laid in a good stock of wood, and in a few minutes there was once again a cheery glow. It was pitch dark outside, not the vestige of a moon, and a wind, blowing from the east or north-east, howled and moaned fitfully down the chimney and round the house-tops.

Bill took another sip of rum and was about to spread himself out on the floor again, when he heard another sound somewhere in the house. It was like the banging of a door, and seemed to proceed from the basement.

"It must be that blamed door we got in at," he said to himself, "yet I thought I made it secure enough. It's the cursed wind. Well, let it bang! I'm damned if I'm going down there in the cold and dark to fasten it."

His fidgeting about woke Mick.

"What's up, Bill?" he muttered. "Be the Roosians boarding us?"

(The great war with Russia scare was then at its height, and also the popularity of that old-fashioned music-hall ditty, "We don't want to fight, but by Jingo if we do," which was played by every barrel-organ in London.)

"No, you blamed fool," Bill snapped. "It's the b—— door we got in by banging."

"Better go down and shut it, then," Mick observed, "or some bobby will see it and nab us 'ere."

"I'm damned if I'm going down," Bill growled. "What, leave this 'ere fire and light and wander down them stairs in the dark? ... not me."

"Nor me," Mick said. ... "So let the coppers come, dozens of 'em, for all I care. They can't say much to us for taking shelter on a night like this."

"And demolishing the kitchen dressers and skirting boards," Bill chuckled. "It will cost the nobs that take this 'ouse a quid or two to replace 'em."

"Hell!" Mick grunted. "What's a quid or two to nobs." He was about to add something decidedly uncomplimentary to the wealthy classes, when another noise, outside the room, cut him short. It was a footstep, to be followed immediately by another, and yet another.

"Did you 'ear that?" he whispered. "Someone's below."

Both men sat up, all attentive now, and listened. Footsteps were coming up the staircase, and there was something about them that puzzled the two sailors. They were soft and cautious, and gave the listeners the impression they were either muffled, or produced by someone without shoes or boots, in socks or just bare feet. Every now and then they halted, as if the person, whoever he was, were listening. Then they came on again. And periodically the staircase creaked. Neither man spoke, but involuntarily they edged nearer to one another and shivered. By and by the footsteps came on to the landing and paused again. The sailors held their breaths and listened fearfully. Then, suddenly, Bill sneezed. Amid the stillness of the house it sounded like a miniature explosion. Mick opened his mouth to curse, but the words froze in his throat. There was something about those halting footsteps outside that thrilled all speech and action out of him. He had never experienced the like of them before. He sat quite still, staring at the door, and Bill did the same.

After a very brief interval, the steps began again,

and, to Bill and Mick's consternation, they came towards the room they were in—soft, stealthy steps, more like those of some great animal than of a human being. Outside the room door they halted, and again Bill and Mick got the impression someone or something was there listening very intently. Then, in the flickering uncertain light from the fire, they saw the door handle slowly begin to turn; inch by inch it opened, wider and wider, and presently they saw a shape—a thing so fantastic and indescribably horrible that they sprang to their feet in a paroxysm of terror. As it entered, creeping furtively towards Mick, Bill darted past it through the doorway out on to the landing. He heard Mick scream, but he was too obsessed with terror to think of going to his assistance.

With one hand clutching the banisters, he got down the staircase somehow and out in the street. Then he broke down, and a policeman found him, some time later, lying on the pavement in a swoon. On hearing his tale, the policeman, accompanied by several other members of the force, entered No. — and eventually discovered Mick lying in the back yard. He had, apparently, jumped from the window of the room in which he and Bill had slept, and broken his neck.

The policemen being, or pretending to be, sceptics where the superphysical was concerned, scoffed at Bill's story and marched him off to the police station. What happened to him subsequently the narrators of this story do not say, for with his capture by the police their narrative ends.

A house in Jones Street, close to Berkeley House, is haunted by some influence that tempts people to drink. I gathered from a former servant that nothing

c

ghostly is seen there, but that people staying in the house for any length of time, no matter how abstemious they may have been before, invariably become obsessed with a mania for drink. The house has, in fact, seen a whole series of drunkard tenants.

Then there is the strangling ghost of Piccadilly. Much has been written about this case, but no two accounts of it would seem to tally. The version I heard, when the haunting was first spoken about, is this :

A lady, living in a flat over a shop in Piccadilly, one night awoke with a start, to see her bedroom door open and a tall woman, with a very evil face, enter. The woman came up to the bed, and seizing the lady by her throat, with cold, bony fingers, commenced strangling her. Eventually the lady lost consciousness. When she came to, she was alone in the room. Hardly able to decide whether her experience was real or simply a nightmare, she decided to spend another night in the same room, taking care, however, this time to lock her door before getting into bed.

She awoke with a start, at about the same hour as on the previous night, to hear the door open again, despite the fact she had locked it, and see the same dreadful woman come stealthily towards her. Once again did the cold, bony fingers grip her neck, and once again did she undergo all the sensations of slow strangulation, finally losing consciousness.

On recovering this time, she was convinced the room was haunted, and on the morrow she vacated it. It was thus, I was told, that the flat acquired the reputation for being ghost-ridden. There were vague rumours current that some woman had been found dead in her bed, in the flat, under circumstances that suggested foul play; and as either her servant or a hospital nurse who was attending her was suspected, there existed, it was thought by some, an obvious explanation of the haunting.

Hearing the flat was to be let and that no one would stay in it for long, I went to see it, hoping to obtain permission to spend a night there. However, on my asking the landlord if it were true that the flat was haunted, he was very wroth.

"It's a pure fabrication," he said, "on the part of a lady whom I had to eject for being backward with her rent. She made up this story out of spite."

And thus my investigation ended. For some years after this the flat remained empty, but as it is now let, and there is no complaint, so I understand, of a haunting from the present tenant, I conclude that the ghost has either turned over a new leaf and given up its strangling habits altogether, or is away on holiday.

A no less harrowing haunting was experienced at one time in a house in St. James's Street. Like No. — Berkeley Square, this particular house in St. James's Street long stood empty. Tenants complained of eerie footsteps perambulating the stairs and passages at night, of rappings and bangings, sighing and diabolical laughter. Forms were seen, too; figures with white evil faces used to open the door of a certain room, no matter whether the door was locked or not, and frighten the inmates by peering at them in bed; and, worse still, every now and then, an invisible something would enter this room, accompanied by a ghastly smell. This was the most terrible of all the phenomena. As in the case of the Berkeley Square house, innumerable stories regarding this house were in circulation. Some seem to be fairly authentic, while the authenticity of others is dubious.

One of these stories, quoted by Mr. Ingram,[1] and therefore, perhaps, to be taken as more or less authentic, is as follows:

During the course of repairs being done to the house, the builder responsible for them, in the temporary absence of his men, went to see how far the work had proceeded, and was ascending one of the staircases, when he heard footsteps just behind him. He looked round. No one was there. He went on, and the same thing happened. He heard footsteps behind him, just as if someone was following him. Still no one to be seen. Somewhat mystified, but thinking that the sounds, possibly, were due to the acoustic properties of the house, he went into a room where a fire was burning cheerily in the hearth, and dragging a chair across the floor towards it, banged it down purposely with considerable violence, and then seated himself in it. To his amazement, all these actions were imitated by some invisible presence. When he heard the presence slam down a chair close to his and then seat itself on it, his fortitude gave way, and he ran out of the room and house in a panic.

My reference in the foregoing case to footsteps—by the way, footsteps are very common phenomena in hauntings—reminds me of an experience I once had in a haunted house in Red Lion Square. It was during the early stages of the Great War. In order to be near the Postal Censorship Headquarters in Kingsway we, my wife and I, shared a maisonnette with an actress friend of ours in one of the quaint old houses in Red

[1] *Haunted Houses and Family Traditions of Great Britain*, by J. H. Ingram.

Lion Square. The maisonnette was on the third and fourth floors of the house, the ground floor, first and second floors being let as offices; the basement was occupied by a caretaker and his family. During our stay there, nothing of a ghostly nature happened, as far as I know, till one day when I was left in our quarters alone, my wife and our friend and her maid having all gone into the country for a few days.

It was on a Saturday afternoon, and I was in my bedroom resting, when I heard heavy, ponderous footsteps slowly ascending the staircase. They came right up to the landing immediately beneath me (I was on the top floor), and halted. Thinking it was the postman, though he generally left the letters on the ground floor, or a tradesman, I went out on to the landing and looked over the banisters, which commanded a full view of the staircase. No one was to be seen. While I was still standing there, looking and wondering, the footsteps began to descend the stairs. I then started off in pursuit, and kept just behind them, all the way down to the ground floor and hall door, which I saw opened by some invisible agency and then shut. When this happened, I realized that the footsteps could only have been due to some denizen from the other world.

The impression I got when I followed them down the stairs, only a step or two behind, was that they were produced by some very old person, and this conception received some confirmation, as I will show later on. I did not hear the steps again, but on my mentioning the incident to our actress friend, on her return, she said she and other people had often experienced them, and it was well known in the Square that the house bore the reputation of being haunted.

My wife descending the staircase one evening, to post a letter, heard a heavy object fall, with a loud thud, just behind her. It sounded like a human body. She was so startled that she ran down the rest of the stairs as fast as she could, and dared not reascend the staircase alone. When she did so, some minutes later, with our friend, who had returned from the theatre, nothing was found that could in any way account for the noise.

I questioned the caretaker and his family about the house, and the eldest daughter told me she had on several occasions seen an old man, with a long, white beard, on the staircase and also peeping at her through various doorways. He always vanished, in an inexplicable fashion, if she spoke or attempted to approach him.

There were rumours of some tragedy having happened in the house many years previously, but I have not been able to find any authentic record regarding the same.

Two or three years after we left the house, the late Duke of Newcastle, who was interested in Psychical Research, though greatly opposed to what is popularly termed "Spiritualism," asked me to try to obtain permission from the occupiers of the maisonnette we had vacated, to hold a nocturnal vigil there.

The occupants proved to be two ladies, and they refused me permission, on the grounds that the landlord of the house, being greatly annoyed at the rumours he had heard of its being haunted, had threatened anyone encouraging or spreading such rumours with an action for slander of title. After a little persuasion, however, I prevailed upon them to admit that they had often heard ghostly footsteps and other sounds on the staircase and landings, and that on one occasion a friend of theirs had seen the ghost. They were having a small party one evening, and footsteps being heard ascending the staircase, one of the guests, a young man, went out on to the landing to see who was there. It was an old man with a white beard. He was then in the act of descending the stairs, and on the guest asking him if he wanted to see anyone, he replied, " Oh, it's all right," and went on. Something unusual about the old man induced the guest to follow him right down into the hall and to within a few feet of the front door, where he suddenly and inexplicably disappeared. The youthful guest then realized that he had seen a ghost.

It has been suggested that the old man was not a phantom of the dead at all, but a phantom or projection of some person alive at the time, possibly a former occupant of the house, who continually thought of it, picturing it in his mind so vividly that on certain occasions, when conditions were favourable, projection had taken place; that is to say, his immaterial self or ego had detached itself from his material body and actually visited the spot he was visualizing.

Such an explanation may appear wild and improbable to many people, but it would seem to be the most, if not the only, feasible explanation in some well-known instances of hauntings. Whether it is the true explanation of the haunting in this particular house in Red Lion Square I cannot say, but I incline to the belief that it is not, and that the phenomena there are due to an altogether different cause.

CHAPTER IV

BLOOMSBURY

THE house in which I experienced ghostly footsteps is not the only house in Red Lion Square that is said to be haunted. Close to it is another house bearing a similarly unenviable reputation. It is believed that a girl was murdered on the staircase, and that the ghost alleged to be seen on the staircase and in certain of the rooms is hers. It is said, also, that a ghostly re-enaction of the tragedy, in which this girl played so unfortunate a rôle, takes place periodically: sounds of footsteps, sighing and groaning being heard in various parts of the house and on the stairs, and a scuffle, which always terminates in an ominous thud on the hall floor beneath. I believe many efforts have been made to lay the ghost, but as, I understand, the phenomena are still experienced, it is obvious that all such efforts have proved futile.

There is a rumour in the neighbourhood that the ghost of Oliver Cromwell occasionally parades up and down the Square garden at night, usually on very stormy nights. Some historians assert that soon after the Restoration, the bodies of Oliver Cromwell, Ireton and Bradshaw were disinterred at Westminster Abbey and dragged thence on sledges to Tyburn, where they were hung on gallows till sunset. They were then cut down, and decapitated. The trunks were thrown into a hole at the foot of the gallows, while the heads were fixed on poles on the roof of Westminster Hall.

There are various traditions as to what subsequently became of the latter. Before being hanged at Tyburn, the bodies, according to one tradition, were taken to the Red Lion Inn at Holborn. Now some writers think the word Tyburn was not only applied to the spot at the north end of the Park, a spot that was situated in what was then styled Tyburn Lane, but that it was applied to any place in London where executions were of more or less frequent occurrence.

One such spot, about the time of the Restoration, occupied a prominent position in St. Giles's parish, close to where the thoroughfare now called Tottenham Court Road terminates; and another was so close to the site of Red Lion Square that one might, not unreasonably, conclude that it occupied the space that later became the Square garden, a conclusion which is borne out by the fact that for many years an obelisk, bearing the inscription, "OBTUSUM OBTUSIORIS INGENII MONUMENTUM. QUID ME RESPICIS, VIATOR? VADE", stood in the said garden.[1] Mr. Jesse, and the other writers referred to, were of the opinion that this inscription bore some cryptic reference to the bones of the three renegades that were interred in the garden, the obelisk being erected to mark the spot where they lie.

Granted the site of the Square garden was the Tyburn which witnessed the revolting exhibition of the mouldering remains, this theory that the remains were buried in the ground over which the obelisk was subsequently erected is extremely probable.

[1] *Vide* p. 546, vol. iv, *Old and New London*.

It certainly gained the credence of many people, who declared that the ghosts alleged to haunt the Square, more particularly the Square garden, were those of Cromwell, Ireton and Bradshaw. A story that was current in the immediate neighbourhood, during the Great War, came to my knowledge thus :

I was returning to my quarters in the Square, late one night, when I found a crowd of people, mostly foreigners, talking excitedly, just outside the Square garden. Thinking they were discussing the air raid which had taken place a few days before in that district, I halted, but the remark I was about to make on the damage it had done in Red Lion Street died upon my lips, as I caught the word ghosts, and I at once asked a swarthy-looking Italian, who might have been an organ-grinder or ice-cream vendor, what it referred to.

"Why," he said, in quite good English, "two women declare they have seen the ghosts that are supposed to haunt the Square," and he grinned.

"It is no laughing matter," a woman who was standing close to us exclaimed, angrily. "We did see them. Other people have seen them too."

"What were they like?" I inquired.

"Three men, wearing long black cloaks and hats with old-fashioned high crowns and very wide brims," the woman replied. "My friend and I were passing the garden, just about where we are standing now, when we saw them suddenly cross the road in front of us. They were walking abreast, and passed right through the iron railings into the garden."

"How could they?" someone asked, incredulously.

"Well, they did," the woman responded. "You

can ask my friend. We both saw them. They went through the railings, as if there were no railings there, and suddenly disappeared."

"That's right," her friend, the other woman, said, joining us. "Directly they had passed into the garden we lost sight of them. They vanished."

"There's nothing to laugh at," an old man remarked to a boy who was giggling. "I believe every word these ladies have said, for I've seen one or two equally queer things myself, though not here."

I asked him to tell me what they were, but he would not. He informed me, however, that the two women were by no means the only people who had had experiences of that sort in the Square, and he himself knew people who had seen the three men in the old-fashioned hats and cloaks.

"But that was years ago," he added, "about 1870. These three ghosts, or phantoms, or whatever else you may like to term them, only appear, it seems, either before or during some great war."

That was all the information I could extract, and as the crowd was now dispersing, I came away with the rest.

A house in Great James Street is haunted by ghostly noises, such as footsteps and creakings, and the phantom of a man who periodically visits a flat in it. A tenant of this particular flat told me of his experiences with this ghost.

One night he heard someone moving about in the sitting-room; footsteps then came into the bedroom, which communicates with the sitting-room by means of folding doors, and cautiously approached his bed. After a brief pause, during which he found himself wholly incapable of action, hands groped their way surreptitiously over the bed-clothes towards his throat. The spell that had hitherto bound him was then fortunately broken, and he was able to dive under the bed-clothes, just in time to evade the hands that were about to clutch hold of him.

After an interval, which seemed a lifetime, the hands were removed, and the steps slowly retreated to the sitting-room, and thence on to the landing outside. Then and not till then did he sum up the courage to emerge from under the bed-clothes.

Once, he told me, a friend of his who was staying with him, returning home one night before him, found a strange man in the sitting-room. He was in evening dress, and had a white handkerchief bound round his face in such a manner that only his forehead was visible. However, although apparently blindfolded, the intruder, directly my friend's friend entered the sitting-room, passed through the folding doors into the bedroom beyond. My friend's friend immediately followed him, but the room was empty. He had disappeared, and disappeared most inexplicably, because there was no mode of exit from the room other than through the folding doors and a window, which was closed at the bottom, and was, besides, a great height from the ground, the flat being on the third floor.

This, I believe, is the only occasion on which a ghost has been seen during my friend's tenancy.

At my friend's wish, I went to the flat one evening, during his temporary absence, for the purpose of investigation. I was accompanied by a friend from Ceylon and an estate agent, whom I got to know through consulting him at his office about buying a house, and who struck me as being singularly level-headed and rational. The three of us sat in the dark, or rather without any artificial light, on the staircase.

For a long time nothing happened, and we were beginning to think we had drawn a blank, when, quite suddenly, footsteps came running up the stairs towards us. The moonlight, pouring in a brilliant white stream through a window on the staircase, lighted up the whole of the flight immediately facing us, and yet, though the footsteps now were close to us, we could see no one. When they reached the stair immediately below the one I was standing on they halted, and I was conscious of being scrutinized intently by some presence, which, although invisible, was intensely real.

The estate agent, now being badly scared, switched on the light, whereupon my uncanny sensation ceased, and the presence in front of me ceased, so to say, with it. We came away soon afterwards, my friends having had quite enough of it for one night.

In Cartwright Gardens, not far from Great James Street, there are at least two houses reputed to be haunted. Years ago, Cartwright Gardens was known as Burton Crescent. It is said to have changed its name in consequence of two murders that gained it a very unenviable notoriety. The first occurred in the winter of 1878. A lodger returning to No. 4 Burton Crescent, late one day in December of that year, found his landlady, Mrs. Samuels, lying on the kitchen floor in a pool of blood. Her head had been beaten in by repeated blows.

Mary Donovan, a charwoman who had worked for

Mrs. Samuels, was arrested on the charge of murdering her, but acquitted by Mr. Flowers, the magistrate before whom she was brought, on the grounds that there was not sufficient evidence to warrant him committing her for trial.

His speech in court seemed strangely contradictory.

" I am of the opinion, however," he said, " that the evidence against you, although there are many facts in it which would point you out as having committed that offence (*i.e.* the murder of Mrs. Samuels), is not such as to justify me in placing you on your trial."

One wonders why, if there were so many facts pointing to her having killed Mrs. Samuels, he did not commit her for trial. A good deal of dissatisfaction was expressed at his verdict, and such undesirable publicity did the house acquire on account of the murder and alleged subsequent haunting that its number was finally changed.

Six years later the Crescent again came into notoriety through another crime, also destined to remain an unsolved mystery. Anne Yeats, a pretty girl of the unfortunate class, was found one day in March, 1884, in a back room on the first floor of No. 12 Burton Crescent, strangled. The crime, which in several respects resembled the Great Coram Street murder of 1872, was never brought home to anyone. As in the case of the Samuels mystery, the house gained such an unenviable reputation, not only on account of the murder, but also on account of the ghostly manifestations that, according to rumour, were subsequently experienced there, that its number was changed ; and soon afterwards Burton Crescent was rechristened Cartwright Gardens. For many years now it has enjoyed complete immunity—at least so far as is generally known—from any unpleasant happenings.

I have alluded to the Great Coram Street murder. Few crimes created a more painful sensation. The story of it, in brief, was this.

On Christmas morning, 1872, Harriet Buswell, a pretty ballet girl of loose character, was found in a back room on the second floor of No. 12 Great Coram Street (twelve would seem to be a sinister number, it has figured in several very horrible crimes) with her throat cut.

A strange man was seen to enter the room with her late on Christmas Eve, and the police arrested Dr. Gottfried Hessel, believing him to be that individual. He was proved, however, not to have left his hotel that night, and he was consequently acquitted. The real murderer was never brought to justice, and the crime is still one of the many unsolved London mysteries. So great a notoriety did Great Coram Street acquire on account of it, that its name was forthwith altered to Coram Street, while all the houses in it were renumbered. For years, however, the house in which the murder was believed to have taken place was reputed haunted, and a back room in it, on the second floor, so rumour asserted, was kept locked, because of the unearthly sounds that were heard at night proceeding from it.

One of the best authenticated cases of a phantom of the living occurred in the British Museum in the year 1888.[1] On Thursday, 12th April of that year, Dr. W. Wynn Westcott, the well-known coroner, made an appointment to meet the Rev. T. W. Lemon

---

[1] *Twenty Years of Psychical Research*, by Ed. T. Bennett.

and Mr. A. B. in the Reading Room of the British Museum the following morning, at a quarter to eleven. When Friday morning came, however, Dr. Westcott was laid up in bed with a feverish catarrh and unable, in consequence, to keep his appointment.

Just about the time he should have been there, Ryan, one of the umbrella attendants, who knew him well by sight, saw him walk past and enter the Reading Room. Some minutes later, Mrs. Salmon, a friend of the doctor's, saw him walking about the Reading Room, as if inquiring for someone, and then take his customary seat. She was so sure it was the doctor, that, on Mr. A. B. asking her if she had seen him, she said, Yes, and told Mr. A. B. where to find him. He went to the seat she mentioned, but no doctor was there. Indeed, at that hour he was, as I have said, in bed at home, suffering from a severe catarrh.

Granted that it was not someone very like him Mrs. Salmon and Ryan had seen, who or what was it? Dr. Westcott was, naturally, thinking very earnestly of his assignation and deploring his friend's disappointment at his inability to keep it. Hence, is it not feasible to suppose, that, the conditions being favourable, projection had taken place ; that is to say that the doctor's immaterial self or ego, detaching itself from his material body, had actually visited the spot he was mentally visualizing? What Mrs. Salmon and Ryan had seen was, consequently, a phantom of the living.

Mrs. Salmon's testimony to the incident in the Museum is as follows :

" Mr. A. B. asked me if I had seen Dr. Westcott. I said, ' Yes, about five minutes ago ; and he is sitting where he usually sits.' Mr. A. B. went to the seat,

and came and told me Dr. Westcott was not there. I said, 'Oh, he must be; it's only a few minutes since I saw him sit down.' I went myself. He was not to be seen. I went to the man who takes the umbrellas and said, 'Have you seen Dr. Westcott?' 'Yes,' he said, 'he went into the room about five minutes ago.' This is exactly what took place. ELLEN SALMON."
January 24th, 1898.

This testimony was subsequently published.

The case is not, perhaps, more credible than one which happened in Newquay, Cornwall, oddly enough in August of the same year. I sent an account of it to the Society for Psychical Research, and the account, verbatim, was published in their *Journal* in the autumn of 1899.

In brief, what happened was this: A young boy at the time, I was spending my holidays in Newquay. The house in which I, together with my family, stayed, was a moderately-sized apartment house. There were no other lodgers, but we had a friend staying with us, a Miss D—— from Birmingham.

One morning, she and my eldest sister went out to do some shopping in the town. About half an hour later my two other sisters, my old nurse and myself were in the hall. I was on the staircase leading into it. Suddenly Miss D—— appeared on the staircase, just above where I was standing. Down she came, passing so close to me—it was a narrow staircase—that I felt her dress brush against me, into the hall. Without looking at my sisters and my nurse, who were staring at her in astonishment, as they had seen her go out shortly before, she entered the sitting-room, closing the door behind her. My sisters and I at once opened it. The room was empty, save for the furniture, and there was no trace of Miss D—— anywhere.

At the time we had all four seen her, or what we all took to be her, she and my eldest sister were in the town shopping. Presumably, what we had seen was her projection.[1]

To quote another haunting connected with the British Museum. Everyone knows of the unlucky mummy case there, but it is not everyone who has heard of Katebit. Katebit was, so I understand, in her lifetime a priestess of the College of Amen (Amun) ra, which was founded at Thebes, during the eighteenth dynasty of the new empire, in honour of the god Amun; and she was, presumably, deemed of sufficient importance to have her body mummified, and, thus preserved, deposited in some Egyptian catacomb. Some British Goth taking her thence brought her to England, and she now resides (*N.B.* not rests) in the Oriental Department of the British Museum. I say resides instead of rests, because, if there be any truth in certain rumours, she is very far from resting. Every now and then ladies testify to seeing her head move, and some go so far as to suggest she walks at night.

Some time ago I asked an official on duty in the Oriental Department if he had ever seen or heard anything uncanny there, but he would not commit himself.

"Some people say they have," he persisted, and that is all I could get out of him.

On one occasion I had rather a strange experience there myself. I was looking at Katebit, wondering what she was like in her lifetime, when I heard a slight

---

[1] She is still living. She subsequently married and has a son at Eton.

cough immediately behind me. I turned round, but could see no one near me. After a little while I heard another cough, rather too near me to be pleasant, but again, on turning round, I could see no one. This I thought very strange. However, I should, in all probability, have attributed it to some peculiarity of the acoustic properties of the Museum, but for the fact that, as I was descending the staircase into the entrance hall, I again heard the cough, this time almost in my ear. Its origin seemed perfectly plain to me then, and I have not visited the Oriental Department of this Museum since.

CHAPTER V

BLOOMSBURY (CONTINUED) AND WESTMINSTER

QUITE one of the most remarkable psychic phenomena connected with Bloomsbury, or, indeed, with any part of London, are " The Brothers' Footsteps." Fortunately, several authentic accounts of them are still on record. The following is an extract from an article in *Notes and Queries* by Dr. E. F. Rimbault:

" The fields behind Montagu House were, from about the year 1680, until towards the end of the last century, the scenes of robbery, murder and every species of depravity and wickedness of which the heart can think. They appear to have been originally called the 'Long Fields,' and afterwards (about Strype's time) the Southampton Fields. These fields remained waste and useless with the exception of some nursery grounds near the new road to the north, and a piece of ground enclosed for the Toxophilite Society towards the north-west, near the back of Gower Street. The remainder was the resort of depraved wretches, whose amusements consisted chiefly in fighting pitched battles and other disorderly sports, especially on Sundays. Tradition had given to the superstition of that period a legendary story, of the period of the Duke of Monmouth's Rebellion, of two brothers, who fought in this field so ferociously as to destroy each other; ever since when their footsteps, formed from the vengeful struggle, were said to remain, with the indentations produced by their advancing and receding; nor could any grass or vegetable ever be produced where these footsteps were thus displayed. This extraordinary area was said to be at the extreme termination of the north-east end of Upper Montagu Street.... The latest account of these footsteps, previous to their being built over, with which I am acquainted, is the following, which I have extracted from one of Joseph Moser's Commonplace Books:

"'June 16, 1800. Went into the fields at the back of Montagu House, and there saw, for the last time, the "forty footsteps," the building material all there ready to cover them from the sight of man. I counted more than forty, but they might be the footprints of the workmen.'

"This extract is valuable, as it establishes the period of the final obliteration of the footsteps, and also confirms the legend that forty was the original number."

Another account of them appeared in the *Arminian Magazine* for 1781. It runs thus: "I think it would be worth your while to take a view of those wonderful marks of the Lord's hatred to duelling called 'The Brothers' Steps.' They are in the fields, about a third of a mile northward from Montagu House, and the awful tradition concerning them is this:—Two brothers quarrelled about a worthless woman, and, according to the fashions of those days, fought with a sword and pistol. The prints of their feet are about the depth of three metres, and nothing will vegetate, so much as to disfigure them. The number is only eighty-three, but probably some are at present filled up, for I think they were formerly more in the centre, where each unhappy combatant wounded the other to death, and a bank, on which the first who fell died, retains the form of his agonizing couch, by the curse of barrenness, while grass flourishes all about it.

"Mr. George Hall, who was the Librarian of Lincoln's Inn, first showed me these steps twenty-eight years ago, when I think they were not quite so deep as now. He remembered them about thirty years, and the man who first showed them him about thirty years more; which goes back to the year 1692; but I suppose they originated in King Charles II's reign. My mother well remembered their being ploughed up, and corn sown to deface them, about fifty years ago. But all was labour in vain; for the prints returned in a while to their pristine form, as probably will those that are now filled up."

This article bears the signature J. W., and commenting on it the Editor of the magazine says, "This account appeared to me so very extraordinary that I knew not what to think of it. I knew Mr. W. to be a person of good understanding and real piety; but still I wanted more witnesses; till a while ago, being at Mr. Cary's, in Copt-hall Buildings, I occasionally mentioned 'The Brothers' Footsteps,' and asked the company if they had heard anything of them. 'Sir,' said Mr. Cary, 'sixteen years ago I saw and counted them myself.' Another added, 'And I saw them four years ago.' I could then no longer doubt but they had been, and a week or two after I went with Mr. Cary and another person to seek them. We sought for nearly half an hour in vain, we could find no steps at all within a quarter of a mile, no, nor half a mile of Montagu House. We were almost out of hope, when an honest man, who was at work, directed us to the next ground, adjoining to a pond. There we found what we sought, about three-quarters of a mile north of Montagu House and five hundred yards east of Tottenham Court Road. The steps answer Mr. W.'s description. They are of the size of a large human foot, about three inches deep, and lie nearly from north-east to south-west. We counted only seventy-six; but we were not exact in counting. The place where one or both brothers are supposed to have fallen is still bare of grass. The labourer also showed us the bank where (the tradition is) the wretched woman sat to see the combat.

"What should we say of these things? Why to atheists, or infidels of any kind, I would not say one word about them. For 'if they hear not Moses and the prophets' they will not regard anything of this kind. But to men of candour, who believe the Bible to be of God, I would say, Is not this an astonishing instance, held forth to all the inhabitants of London, of the justice and power of God? Does not the curse He has denounced upon this ground bear some resemblance to that of Our Lord on the barren fig-tree? I see no reason nor pretence for any rational man to doubt the truth of the story, since it has been confirmed by these open visible tokens for more than a hundred years successively."

Jane and Anna Maria Porter weaved a novel round the tradition of this famous field. According to their story, the two brothers fought on different sides of the Duke of Monmouth's ill-fated Rebellion, and in the duel, which was fought in Southampton Fields, both were killed. Apropos of this novel and the mysterious footsteps, the following article appeared in the *Book for a Rainy Day*:

" Of these steps there are many traditionary stories; the one generally believed is that two brothers were in love with a lady, who would not declare a preference for either, but coolly sat upon a bank, to witness the termination of a duel, which proved fatal to both. The bank, it is said, on which she sat, and the footmarks of the brothers, when pacing the ground, never produced grass again. The fact is," the somewhat sceptical writer of the article remarks, " that these steps were so often trodden that it was impossible for the grass to grow. I have frequently passed over them; they were in a field on the site of Mr. Martin's Chapel, or very nearly so, and not on the spot as communicated to Miss Porter, who has written an entertaining novel on the subject."

To continue. If rumour can be credited, in addition to these notorious footprints, Southampton Fields can point to other ghostly happenings, for in them, on Hallow E'en and other particularly uncanny nights of the year, when youths and maidens used to foregather there, to work the spells peculiar to the occasion, some alarming phantom would frequently appear, scaring the rash experimenters almost out of their senses. In my opinion, some of the strange happenings that take place in the British Museum and certain of the houses in the immediate neighbourhood are due to tragedies that occurred in these long since vanished fields. My reference to the Museum in the above case of haunting reminds me of another haunting by a phantom. My authority is the late Mr. Robert Dale Owen.[1]

In the summer of 1857, a certain Colonel, whom I shall designate A——, his wife and infant child were residing in a house facing Woolwich Common, when one night Mrs. A——, after she had retired to bed and apparently been sound asleep, suddenly became conscious of standing by her bedside, looking at her material body, which was lying next to that of her sleeping husband. Her first idea was that she was dead, and as she looked at her face, which appeared waxy and quite colourless compared with the ruddy, healthy countenance of her husband, her idea became a conviction. She had obviously passed away in her sleep and was now a disembodied spirit. For a few moments she experienced a sensation of relief that her death had been painless, but when she thought of her family and friends, and how terribly shocked and grieved they would be at her so sudden and unexpected demise, she was overwhelmed with sorrow. While she was thus occupied, she suddenly felt herself borne by some irresistible force towards the wall of the room, and she was momentarily expecting a collision with it, when, to her astonishment and relief, she passed right through it into the open air beyond. In front of her and directly in her path was a great tree. This she also passed through, as if it were nothing material. Still impelled forward by a power she was utterly unable to control or resist, she soon found herself on the far side of Woolwich Common, close to the main entrance of the Repository. In front of the building was a sentry, but though she passed close to him, he appar-

---

[1] See *Footfalls on the Boundary of Another World*, by Robert Dale Owen.

ently did not see her. A little way on, and she passed another sentry, with the same result. Then she heard a clock strike three, and immediately afterwards found herself in the bedroom of Mrs. M——, a friend of hers, who lived at Greenwich. She was conscious of commencing a conversation with her about something, what she could not afterwards recollect, when everything suddenly became a blank, and she knew no more till she found herself in bed at home. It was then morning and the sun was pouring cheerily into the room. With the recollection of what she had gone through still fresh in her mind, she exclaimed, " So I am not dead, after all." Her husband, who was preparing to get up, asked her what she meant, and she immediately told him her experience. He was much impressed and asked her not to say a word about it for the present to Mrs. M——, who had been invited to stay with them, and would be arriving in a few days' time. Two days later, Mrs. M—— came and was walking in the garden with them, when the conversation turned, as it so often does when ladies are present, on dress. " My new bonnet is trimmed with violet," Mrs. A—— observed. " I like the colour so much I shall always choose it for my bonnets in future."

" I guessed it was your favourite colour," Mrs. M—— replied, " because you were dressed entirely in violet when you paid me a visit the night before last."

" Paid you a visit the night before last ? " Mrs. A—— ejaculated. " Are you sure I did ? "

" Yes, quite sure," Mrs. M—— said. " You appeared to me at about three o'clock ; and we talked together for some minutes. Have you no recollection of it ? "

Deeply interested, Mrs. A—— then narrated her experience to Mrs. M——, and all three (Colonel and Mrs. A—— and Mrs. M——) agreed that it must have been brought about by some superphysical agency.

In my own opinion it is merely another indication that phenomena can be produced by the living mind, and that all phenomena are not necessarily due to, or associated with, those who have passed over. Very possibly Mrs. A——, while apparently asleep, or in an actual dream state, was thinking very intently of her friend Mrs. M——, and the right measure of concentration being acquired and other conditions, at present unknown to us, being favourable, projection had taken place. Thus what Mrs. M—— had seen and spoken to was nothing more or less than the phantasm or ghost of her living friend. I believe that many so-called hauntings are thus attributable to the living. In conclusion, Mr. Dale Owen depended on no hearsay evidence for this story. It was told him by Colonel A—— and confirmed, some days later, by Mrs. M——.

An experience that once happened to a lady in the Argyll Rooms,[1] London, might either have been due to a phantasm of the living, to a phantasm of the dead, or to some unknown power associated with the superphysical world.

For the sake of those who know little of old London, the Argyll Rooms were at the corner of Little Argyll Street, a turning out of Oxford Street, only a step or two from Oxford Circus. They were founded by Colonel Greville, a well-known " man about town " during the Regency, and speedily became a rival to the fashionable Pantheon and Almack's. Everyone with

[1] See *Footfalls on the Boundary of Another World*.

any pretension at all to being in Society visited these three centres of the Smart Set during the season. It was here the eccentric Lady Margaret Crawford gave a ball to her enemies, or those she deemed such; and here, some years later, the famous contralto, Velluti, gave a concert to a packed house.

The psychic incident I have referred to as having taken place in the Argyll Rooms is this:

One evening, a year or two before the rooms were destroyed by fire, a certain Miss M—— went to a concert there with a party of friends. During the performance, she became so agitated and looked so ill, that her friends thought it advisable to take her home. For some time she refused to say what was the matter with her, but at last, on being pressed, she declared she had had a very terrible experience. At the concert she had suddenly become conscious of a naked body lying on the floor at her feet. The face was partly covered with a cloak, but, despite this, she recognized the features as those of her friend Sir J—— Y——. Her friends tried to pacify her, assuring her it was only imagination, but they tried in vain. She was positive Sir J—— Y—— had been the victim of some fatal accident, and that what she had seen was his wraith. Her surmises proved to be correct, for, on the following day, she received the news of Sir J—— Y——'s death. He had been drowned in the Southampton river through the overturning of his boat, at the very time she had seen what she believed to be his wraith. Moreover, it was ascertained that those who found his body had covered it with a cloak, leaving the face partially exposed.

Basil N. Hill, an elderly actor, whom I used to meet

occasionally in the old Lounge in Maiden Lane, once had a curious experience in the Royal Aquarium, which is a mere name to the present generation, who probably place it in the same category as Almack's and the Argyll Rooms. In my youth it was a very live place, a place where one could go in the afternoon or evening and be sure of an interesting entertainment. There was always something on, a play, or pantomime, or concert in the Imperial Theatre, which joined its western extremity, and numerous side-shows in other parts of the building. Its decease, which, I believe, was due to certain kill-joys, who prefer to see evil in almost every kind of amusement, was deplored by thousands, and has left a gap in London which has never been adequately filled.

To return, however, to Basil Hill. One day, when very down and out, he wandered on to the Thames Embankment, with the thought of suicide uppermost in his mind. Hence, he was peering over the wall into the murky, moonlit water beneath, when someone touched him on the shoulder. It was a brother actor named Bert (I don't know his surname, for Hill never mentioned it to me), equally down and out. He, too, had wandered on to the Embankment, with the same object in view.

While they were talking the matter over, wondering whether death by drowning was very painful and if the Powers on the Other Side—provided there was another side—would punish them for taking their own lives, a policeman, who had been standing a little way off, watching them for some time, came up to them and said, "Here's a bob for you, boys. It's all I can afford. Better that, however, than the river," and he slipped a shilling into Basil Hill's hand.

"How did you know we were thinking of jumping in?" Hill asked him.

"By your appearance," the constable replied. "Anyone like me, who is used to the Embankment, can always tell a real down and out. There are plenty of sham ones, but you two have the genuine desperate look, which usually means the river. Since I have been on this beat I've seen several suicides, and saved probably a score or more from jumping in. Get a bit of grub and something warm to drink with that money, and, maybe, your luck will turn in the morning."

Much touched at the policeman's kindness, both men promised to do as he suggested. On their way to a coffee stall to get some food, they agreed to meet on Waterloo Bridge the following evening, at midnight, and jump into the river together, if they had had no luck. After devouring some sandwiches and coffee with considerable avidity, neither of them having tasted food for many hours, they parted company, renewing their pledge to meet one another, on the aforesaid bridge, in twenty-four hours' time. What remained of the night Hill spent under the Covent Garden arches.

He was wandering in the direction of Poverty Corner in the morning, when he ran into another actor friend, who happened to have just got a part in a touring company.

"They're still looking for someone to play a parson's part, Basil," he said, "and you're just the man for it. Come along to the rehearsal room at eleven sharp and I'll introduce you, but get a shave and tidy up first."

With the good nature that is so characteristic of actors who have been through it themselves, he lent

Hill half a sovereign, and Hill, taking his advice, made himself look a little more presentable, and got the part. His friend offered him a bed, and he was having a merry time of it that evening, till he suddenly remembered his promise to Bert. Telling his friend he had an urgent appointment but would soon be back, he hurried, as fast as he could, to Waterloo Bridge.

When he arrived there, it was a quarter past twelve, and being a wet night the bridge was deserted. He waited there for some time, and finally concluding something had prevented Bert from coming, perhaps he, too, had had a stroke of luck, or had met with an accident, he came away.

The following evening he went to the Aquarium, to meet another friend he had run into on his way to the eleven o'clock rehearsal that morning. He was walking about, waiting for him, when, to his astonishment, he suddenly saw Bert, standing in an entrance to one of the side-shows, looking fixedly at him. He walked towards him, with the intention of asking him how he came to be there and what had happened to him the previous night, and was within a few paces of him, when he, suddenly and very mysteriously, disappeared. A few minutes later, and Hill again saw Bert, this time in another part of the hall; and, as before, Bert was gazing fixedly at him. Then, as their eyes met, Bert beckoned to him. Determined that he should not elude him again, Hill made for Bert at once, and was close to him, when, again, to his utter amazement, Bert disappeared.

Much puzzled, Hill was wondering whether he was the victim of a hallucination or an illusion of some kind or another, when the friend he had come to meet arrived, and for the next hour or two he thought no more of the incident.

As he was leaving the building with his friend, Bert passed him by in the street, and, turning round, again looked at him with the same strange fixed expression.

" Excuse me a minute," Hill remarked to his friend, " but I must speak to that fellow." He hurried after him and had almost overtaken him, when, for the third time, Bert disappeared. There was no crowd now with which he might possibly have mingled, or doorway through which he might possibly have slipped, and thus have escaped detection, there was just the pavement, deserted on account of the heavy rain. Hill had seen him on the pavement one moment, and the next moment he had seen nothing. Bert had inexplicably and unquestionably vanished.

A feeling of intense eeriness now came over Hill, and when he rejoined his friend, he was shaking all over, so much so that his friend asked him if he had seen a ghost, to which he replied huskily :

" Yes, it undoubtedly was a ghost."

The following morning he went to a Free Library and scanned the papers. One of the first headlines that caught his eye was—" Man's body found in the Thames," and under it he read that the body of the man who had been seen to jump from Waterloo Bridge, at midnight, on Monday—it was at that hour and night he had arranged to meet Bert—had been found on the mud, at low water, and subsequently identified as that of an out-of-work actor.

I had the story direct from Basil Hill, on whom the ghastly incident and tragedy left a very deep impression.

It seems that prior to the building of the Royal Aquarium there stood, close to its site, some very old buildings, one of which, an apartment house, had probably been in existence for at least four hundred years. My authority,[1] whom, for convenience, I will call Mr. B——, had been lodging in this old apartment house for about three months, when he had the following experience.

One night, having been to the theatre, it was late when he retired to bed. His room, which was long and narrow, and gloomy, even on the brightest days, was oak panelled throughout. Though he had not, so far, experienced anything unpleasant in it, he had been conscious of a something rather ominous and depressing in its atmosphere. On this particular night he had barely extinguished the light and got into bed, when he saw a strange sight. A young man, clad in the picturesque dress of the days of Charles II, emerged from the panelled wall opposite him. His doublet, embroidered with gold lace, his full, loose breeches, richly bedizened with bunches of gaily-coloured ribbons, and russet boots with broad ornamented tops, his handsome travelling cloak that reached from his shoulders to his heels and hung in folds over his left arm, and black feathered hat worn jauntily over long glossy curls, that fell about his neck and shoulders, plainly showed him to be someone of rank and distinction. Apart from the pallor of his cheeks, which, contrasting as it did with the blackness of his hair, was ghastly in the extreme, his expression and general appearance was singularly mild and pleasing.

[1] *News from the Invisible World.* Edited by T. Charley.

Mr. B—— does not explain how, after he had extinguished the light, he was able to note all these details, but, presumably, either the room was illuminated by moonlight, or, as is so often the case in haunting, the ghost emitted a light of its own.

As Mr. B—— was gazing at it, spellbound, it raised its hat with its right hand, and displayed a terrible wound in the centre of its forehead. It then made signs and gesticulations, as if desirous of warning Mr. B—— against some impending danger, and walking towards him, with a curious gliding motion, fixed its dark piercing eyes on him for fully a minute, after which it slowly retired to the wall, where it stood for several minutes, as if praying, and then sank into the floor, and disappeared.

As may be imagined, Mr. B—— did not sleep much, that night, and in the morning, greatly to his landlord's apparent astonishment, he asked for his bill, paid it and quitted the premises for good.

Some days later, he met the landlord in Hyde Park, and pressed him into confessing that the house, particularly the room he, Mr. B——, had occupied, was well known to be haunted by the ghost of a young Cavalier, who was reputed to have been murdered there in the reign of Charles II. During the time he, the landlord, had rented the house, nine people had refused to remain in the room, on account of the strange things they had heard and seen in it.

Several ghosts are said to haunt various houses in the Buckingham Palace Road. Unlike the majority of their ilk, one of them performs such really useful

BLOOMSBURY AND WESTMINSTER

actions as lighting the fire,[1] sweeping the carpets, dusting the furniture, and putting on the kettle; and it is so considerate of people's feelings and averse from giving them a shock, that it invariably remains invisible.

Another ghost in the same road is not so kindly disposed. A Miss Stanhope, who had once occupied a flat in the house, told me that she had often heard sounds in the kitchen, as if someone was there, moving about the fire-irons and cleaning the range, but she never saw anything alarming till one morning, upon going into the kitchen unusually early, she was surprised to see a strange maid kneeling on the floor, in front of the range, apparently intent on cleaning it. She was wearing one of the little flat lace caps servants used to wear many years ago and a pink calico dress. Thinking that her daily woman was ill and had sent someone in her place, Miss Stanhope exclaimed, "Who are you, why are you here?" whereupon the girl turned round, and Miss Stanhope saw her face for the first time. It was ghastly white and the large dark eyes had such a mad glitter in them that Miss Stanhope sprang back in alarm. The girl then got up and, with a horrible grin, crept towards Miss Stanhope, who shrieked with terror. Fortunately at this juncture there was the sound of a key being inserted in the front door of the flat, and, upon Miss Stanhope's woman entering, the strange girl turned round and ran into the back kitchen, closing the door behind her. Miss Stanhope, who was nearly dead with fright, explained what had happened, and begged her woman to fetch a policeman. Her woman, however, being

[1] See *Ghostly Visitors*, by "Spectre Stricken," p. 58.

both physically strong and strong-minded, marched to the back kitchen door, opened it and looked inside. No one was there, and there was no way out, save through a skylight, twelve feet from the floor.

Rather than risk a second encounter with this most unpleasant ghost, Miss Stanhope forthwith left the flat.

CHAPTER VI

LINCOLN'S INN, THE TEMPLE, GREYFRIARS, CHARTERHOUSE, ST. BARTHOLOMEW'S THE GREAT, AND NEWGATE

BOTH Lincoln's Inn and the Temple have their ghosts. According to tradition, the former was at one time visited by the most alarming and ill-omened spectre.

About the end of the seventeenth century, Robert Perceval, second son of the Right Honourable Sir John Perceval, had chambers in the Inn. He was reading for the law, but, apparently, spent much of the time he should have given to his studies in riotous and unprofitable pursuits. One night, when, yielding to a fit of industry, he did happen to be at his books, he was diverted from them by the sound of a clock, somewhere in the building, very sonorously striking the hour of midnight, and, upon looking round, he saw, to his amazement and no little alarm, a tall figure standing in front of the door. It was enveloped from head to foot in a long flowing black garment, which gave it a curiously uncanny appearance. Wondering who it could be, but supposing it to be some friend or acquaintance of his who had come in noiselessly, with the intention of frightening him, young Perceval rose from his chair and said rather angrily, for he resented the intrusion, " Who are you ? " There was no reply, only a silence that had something very disturbing as well as disconcerting about it. Then the figure gave a hollow, mocking laugh. Convinced now that it was some acquaintance enjoying a joke at his expense, Perceval snatched up his sword from a chair, near at hand, and rushing at the stranger thrust at him with it. The sword, apparently, passed through the stranger without encountering any resistance, and when Perceval withdrew it, it was clean. There was not even a spot of blood on it.

Meanwhile, the stranger stood like a statue, absolutely silent and motionless.

Greatly puzzled, but determined to solve the mystery, Perceval made a sudden snatch at the stranger's garment and tore it from him. Then he reeled back in horror, for the figure confronting him was an exact counterpart of himself, dead, with ghastly wounds on his head and breast. The sight so shocked him that he swooned. On recovering and looking round the room fearfully, he again saw the phantom. It was standing silent and motionless, in the same spot, but, as he looked at it, it turned slowly round and noiselessly left the room.

Believing its visit to him to be a warning, Perceval became a reformed character for some time, sticking to his work and shunning his usual gay and dissolute companions. However, as time went on and nothing happened, he came to the conclusion that there was no significance attached to his strange experience, and growing reckless, he again plunged, even deeper than formerly, into the fast life of the city. His indulgence in all kinds of excesses culminated in a quarrel with Beau Fielding, then at the zenith of his notoriety, and various other libertines, certain of whom evinced the

LINCOLN'S INN AND NEWGATE 71

greatest hostility to him; and as he was making for a tavern in the Strand, one day, he felt, instinctively, he was being followed. Hence, he turned round sharply, and, on doing so, saw a sinister-looking man close at his heels, obviously intent on waylaying him. Upon his asking the man who he was and why he was following him, he was rudely told that he was not being followed and that he had better mind his own business. Unconvinced and apprehensive, as he did not like the appearance of the man at all, he crossed the road and tried to elude him. It was in vain, however; the man still followed him, and presently another, equally forbidding-looking ruffian, joined him! Though a rip, Perceval was no coward, and coming to a sudden halt he drew his sword and faced his pursuers. A fight ensued. Thanks to his excellent swordsmanship, Perceval put the ruffians to flight, but was, himself, wounded in the leg. The sight of the blood trickling down his clothes reminded him ominously of the phantom that had visited him in Lincoln's Inn, and he staggered back to his quarters faint and depressed. He told certain of his friends he was doomed. And he was right, for that night a watchman groping his way near the maypole in the Strand stumbled over his dead body.

Few, if any, knew how he met his death; he may have been murdered, but no one was apprehended, and the matter remains a mystery to this day.

According to tradition, Perceval's rooms in Lincoln's Inn were subsequently haunted by divers alarming phenomena, including a figure, smeared with blood and closely resembling him; and, if there is any truth in rumour, these disturbances and manifestations are still, periodically, repeated.

Several hauntings are attributed to the Temple, but I can hear of none that has been experienced there lately. Tradition somewhat vaguely affirms that during the seventeenth century a duel took place in certain chambers of the Temple. It does not tell us even vaguely what the duel was about, but it asserts unequivocally that one of the combatants was killed, and that ever since this tragedy the room in which it occurred has been haunted, a ghostly re-enaction of the duel taking place there at certain times and seasons.

A tragedy that might well account for certain other ghostly happenings, said to occur occasionally in the Temple, was the butchery there of Mrs. Dunscomb, her companion and her maid.

In February, 1732, an old lady, Mrs. Lydia Dunscomb, with her elderly companion, Miss Elizabeth Harrison, and maid, Anne Price, a girl of about seventeen years of age, occupied rooms in Tanfield Court, a mere passage which once existed at the east side of the Temple. On Thursday, 2nd February, 1732, a certain Mrs. Frances Rhymer, whom Mrs. Dunscomb had made her executrix, went to Mrs. Dunscomb's to tea and to talk business with her. After tea Mrs. Dunscomb asked Mrs. Rhymer to open her cash-box and give her a guinea from it, as she had a small debt to pay. Mrs. Rhymer complied, and noticed the box contained a silver tankard, a number of loose sovereigns and a bag containing more. Altogether a considerable sum.

The following day Mrs. Oliphant, a laundress, had

occasion to call on Mrs. Dunscomb, and, on arriving, found her seated in her parlour with Mrs. Love, an old friend, and Elizabeth Harrison. However, despite congenial company, both Mrs. Dunscomb and Elizabeth seemed curiously depressed, and the latter remarked to Mrs. Oliphant that Mrs. Dunscomb had a presentiment she was going to die shortly and wanted her, Elizabeth Harrison, to die with her. This was said in the presence of Sarah Malcolm, a singularly handsome young charwoman, whom Mrs. Dunscomb employed, and Mrs. Oliphant noticed that, as it was said, Sarah Malcolm's face underwent a sudden change, and that, subsequently, she kept on glancing furtively at a large black box, on a cabinet, in one corner of the room, namely, Mrs. Dunscomb's cash-box.

At nine o'clock on Sunday morning Mrs. Love went to Mrs. Dunscomb's rooms and knocked on the outside door. No one came. She knocked again, louder; and, no one coming, she knocked yet again, louder still, and kept on knocking. Then she fetched Mrs. Oliphant, and they both knocked. Still no one came, and the silence that ensued had in it something so scaring that the two women decided to go for a locksmith to open the door, and were about to do so, when Sarah Malcolm joined them.

At their suggestion Sarah Malcolm then set off to fetch the locksmith, but soon returned, saying the locksmith was not at home. This was upsetting, but Mrs. Oliphant, having recovered from her scare, climbed into the house through one of the windows. Presently, the two women, waiting outside, heard a piercing scream, followed by a sudden stampede, and, almost simultaneously, the front door was flung open by Mrs. Oliphant, who, with a face aflame with excitement, cried out, " Gracious God! Oh, gracious God! They're all murdered!"[1]

What she said proved to be correct. Mrs. Dunscomb and Elizabeth Harrison had been strangled, a cord having been tied with terrible ferocity round their respective necks, while Anne Price, the maid, with her throat cut, was also lying on the floor, dead. Blood and signs of a desperate struggle were in evidence everywhere, and the black box containing the tankard and sovereigns had been rifled. The missing tankard being found in the chambers of a Mr. Kerrol, for whom Sarah Malcolm worked, wrapped up in bloodstained garments belonging to her, roused suspicion against her. She was searched, and twenty-three guineas and various articles of jewellery and clothes belonging to Mrs. Dunscomb were found on her. She was charged with both murders and arrested. When she was lodged in Newgate, fifty-three more guineas were found cunningly concealed in her hair, which was neatly plaited, and very long and beautiful.

She confessed to a share in the robbery, but denied any participation in the murders, which she attributed to two of her young male acquaintances, named Alexander, and a girl named Mary Tracey. Fortunately for these three they were able to prove their innocence, and Sarah Malcolm, alone, was tried. She was found guilty and hanged in Fleet Street, opposite Mitre Court, on the 7th of March, 1733.

At her execution the crowd was so immense, for the murders created an almost unparalleled sensation,

[1] *The Modern Newgate Calendar.* Published by Milner & Co., Ltd., 1868.

that one spectator, a woman—as usual there were more women at this show than men—was able to cross the street on the shoulders of those assembled there. She did this amid roars of laughter and much cheering.

For her execution Sarah Malcolm wore a black dress, and her cheeks and lips contrasting with it were so bright a red that they looked as if they were painted. She held herself erect, and walked almost jauntily to the scaffold, although, on arriving there, she fainted, and was a long time coming round. She died, according to some accounts, penitent, and was buried in the churchyard of St. Sepulchre's, where no criminal had been permitted burial for at least 150 years. It is said that this privilege was accorded her on account of her beauty, but whether this was so or not, such notoriety did she acquire, on account of her crimes and looks, that, two days before her execution, Hogarth obtained special permission to paint her. She wore scarlet, a very significant colour for her, when she sat to him, and if his portrait of her be a true one, she did not belie her reputation, though for perfect beauty her lips would appear to be rather too thin and her face, as a whole, rather too suggestive of cruelty and hardness. Horace Walpole, who was seemingly greatly fascinated by her, bought the sketch for £5, and, later, an imperfect impression of it, priced originally at sixpence, was sold to the Duke of Roxburghe for £8 5s., whilst a copy of her alleged confession fetched twenty pounds. Before her burial her body was exhibited at an undertaker's on Snow Hill, and, to see it, thousands of people willingly paid a small fee.

One person, believed by many to be her employer, Mr. Kerrol, was unable to control his emotion, and on seeing the body, he bent down and kissed it. Nor did her notoriety end with her burial, for some time after she was laid to rest, or rather to supposed rest, in St. Sepulchre's Churchyard, her skeleton was, in my opinion, very wrongly, disinterred and transferred to the Botanic Garden, Cambridge, where, in all probability, it is still to be seen.

This in itself would be sufficient to cause hauntings, and certain of the periodical outbursts of hauntings in the Temple, supposed by some to be associated with this young and beautiful murderess, might well be attributed to it.

In 1573 Peter Burchet, a half-crazy fanatic of the Middle Temple, while undergoing imprisonment in the Tower of London, for heretical opinions—he was first arrested for seriously wounding Sir John Hawkins of naval fame in mistake for Sir Christopher Hatton—murdered one of his keepers. For this crime he was hanged in the Strand, close to the spot where he had wounded Sir John Hawkins. This, also, is a tragedy that might well account for some one or other of the Temple's alleged periodical hauntings.

And yet another possible cause of hauntings may lie in the fact that, in 1685, John Ayliff, a barrister of the Inner Temple, was hanged for high treason, opposite the Temple Gate. So much for the Temple.

If any churchyard in London ought to be haunted, it is that of Greyfriars, for here, side by side, lie the remains of people who met with violent deaths and certain infamous wretches who richly deserved hanging, but who escaped punishment through their titles and influence. The list of those interred here include Isabella, the cruel, beautiful wife of Edward II ; John

Hastings, Earl of Pembroke, who was accidentally killed in a tournament at Woodstock Park, Christmas, 1389; Mortimer, Queen Isabella's paramour, who was hanged at Tyburn, for usurping too much power and for participation in the murder of Edward II (a murder which was, undoubtedly, planned and arranged by the Queen), and whose body, before being interred, had hung in chains for at least two days; Sir Robert Tresilian, Chief Justice of England, and Sir Nicholas Brembre, Lord Mayor of London, both temporary favourites of Richard II, and as great villains as it was possible to find in London. They were hanged at Tyburn, and everyone said they richly deserved their fate; but if all the wealthy Londoners who merit the same fate to-day were hanged, what a scarcity of gallows there would be! The list is not ended. Here, too, in this gloomy, out-of-the-way cemetery lie the severed remains of that Mortimer (Sir John), who, for no other crime than that he was believed to be a menace to the throne, on account of his genealogy, was hung, drawn and quartered at Tyburn by his enemies in 1423; whilst nearby lies all that is left of Thomas Burdet, who, for finding fault with Edward IV for wantonly killing a white buck, was barbarously tortured and executed; and all that is left of pretty Alice Hungerford, who tiring of her husband, murdered him, and had the bad luck to be found out, tried and executed. She was hanged at Tyburn in 1523.

Out of such a bunch small wonder is it that the churchyard has the reputation for being, at times, very badly haunted. Despite the alleged fact that naughty Isabella was buried with the heart of her husband laid, at her request, on her breast, her spirit could not find rest.[1] Periodically, according to report, it still hovers about the churchyard, a figure in white, with lean and haggard features and eyes glowing with diabolical hate. At least such was the description of it given me in the summer of 1898, by one who claimed intimate association with the Greyfriars and old Christ's Hospital. He told me that Greyfriars burial ground has also been haunted by strange noises and lights, supposed to owe their origin to Sir Robert Tresilian having dabbled in the Black Art. Tradition affirms that Sir Robert always carried about with him, on his person, certain images used in ceremonial witchcraft and sorcery, which were believed to act as a charm, and that these, together with a tiny bust of the devil, were found on him and removed before he was taken to be hanged at Tyburn. After his burial tradition declares the spot where he was interred was the scene of, for a while, all kinds of gruesome and alarming phenomena, and periodically, so my informant assured me, the phenomena occur now, as do hauntings by the ghost of Alice Hungerford.

In one of the cloisters of the old Christ's Hospital, adjoining the burial ground, is [2] an impression in the stone, not unlike a human foot. This is traditionally said to have been caused by the ghost of an erstwhile beadle's wife, stamping with tremendous force and energy, when addressed by some living human being in a disrespectful fashion.

This allusion to schools and their adjacent buildings reminds me that a ghost is said to haunt the head-

---

[1] See *Old and New London*, by Walter Thornbury, vol. ii. page 365.

[2] This refers to the time when the old Christ's Hospital was a school. Whether the stone remains now that the school has gone I have been unable to ascertain.

quarters of the Brothers of the old Charterhouse. Up and down the main staircase in this ancient edifice wanders, with noiseless tread, the headless phantom of a man in the dress of a bygone period. It is believed by some to be the ghost of the ill-fated Duke of Norfolk who, in 1565, bought the Charterhouse, and resided in it till 1569, when he was committed to the Tower for implication in the conspiracy to place Mary, Queen of Scots, on the throne. After his release in 1570 he was again committed to the Tower for further acts of high treason, and eventually executed in 1572, when his estates, including the Charterhouse, were confiscated by the Crown.

It was after his death that the Charterhouse, more particularly the main staircase, was declared to be haunted by his apparition, which, they say, still appears there, although very occasionally.

From the old Charterhouse to St. Bartholomew's in Smithfield is no great distance, and both have at least one feature in common, namely, the reputation of being ghost-ridden. As regards St. Bartholomew's it is not, perhaps, to be wondered at, considering the terrible scenes that were enacted under its very shadow in the days of the religious persecutions of the sixteenth century.

The spot generally used for the burnings is believed to have been exactly opposite the main entrance to the church, the victim being tied to the stake in such a manner that his face looked to the east, and to the great church door, on the threshold of which stood the prior of St. Bartholomew.

When excavating on this site for a new sewer in 1849, the workmen laid bare a number of unhewn stones, blackened with fire, ashes, charred human bones and strong oak posts, likewise charred, to one of which was fastened a staple and ring.

No reasonable person could doubt the significance of these discoveries ; they prove, more emphatically than any document or words, the hideous cruelties that were enacted in England during those hectic days, when no one's life was safe if he held any views at all upon the subject of religion.

When I was visiting the church, some years ago, I was informed by someone who was then associated with St. Bartholomew's that ghostly groans and voices were not infrequently heard at night, close to the spot where the excavations had taken place. I was also told that people have, from time to time, complained of being followed by ghostly, shuffling footsteps in one of the ambulatories of the church.

According to my informant, about forty or fifty years previously the tomb of a certain prior or knight was broken into by thieves and his bones, with various articles found in the tomb, were scattered about the church. They were all speedily put back, with the exception of a shin bone and leather bridle ; the bridle was eventually recovered, but whether the shin bone was as well, my informant could not say. Anyhow, the disturbance of these remains was supposed by some to be the cause of the ghostly, shuffling footsteps.

My same informant stated that there was a tradition to the effect that years ago a lady had seen a ghostly shape suddenly emerge from a doorway and come towards her. It was so horrible that she swooned, and never recovered from the shock. One of the clergy belonging to the church is also said to have seen it about the same time.

I asked my informant whether he himself had ever seen or heard anything ghostly in the church, and he said yes, but it was only on my promising most seriously that I would not disclose his identity that I eventually persuaded him to tell me his experiences.

He was, he said, in the church alone, one winter morning at an early hour, the church consequently being dark, when, suddenly, through the gloom loomed a figure, approaching him from one of the ambulatories. As it drew near he perceived it was a woman in a white dress, and on her drawing nearer still to him, he recognized his daughter, whom he knew to be then abroad. As he looked at her in awe and wonder, she gradually grew fainter and fainter, until, finally, she vanished altogether.

He subsequently learned that at the time he had seen what he believed to be her phantom she was seriously ill in her far-away home. I am not quite sure whether he said she eventually recovered, but I am under the impression that he did, in which case I presume that what he saw was her projection or immaterial ego.

She had been a very constant attendant at the church when she had lived with her parents in London, hence very possibly she had been thinking intently of being in the church and had thus, quite unconsciously perhaps, projected herself (her spirit self) there; the conditions for projection happening at that moment to be right.

He also told me he, too, had occasionally heard in

the same ambulatory ghostly footsteps that followed him about, without, however, frightening him.

For my own part, I must say that as I wandered about the church in the waning daylight, I certainly thought I saw a figure, seemingly coming from nowhere, suddenly cross the aisle in front of me, and vanish. Whence it came and whither it went I do not know. It was gone very quickly without making the slightest sound, and it left me, if not actually unnerved, so shaken that I moved rather hurriedly towards the nearest door, and made my exit.

The following is a story I have told before, but it will, I think, bear repeating. It relates to old Newgate; when I say old Newgate, I mean the Newgate that was demolished some thirty or so years ago and was generally termed old. As a matter of fact, it was of no great antiquity, having been built in 1770, from plans by the younger Dance. In 1780 it was partly destroyed during the Gordon Riots, but rebuilt two years later, since when, up to the time of its demolition, portions of it periodically underwent renovating and reconstructing.

The last night of its existence, that is to say the night prior to the commencement of its demolition, only two people slept in it, an official and his wife. I interviewed them both, some years ago, in Brixton, and they told me of the strange experience they had during their last night in old Newgate.

"We were sitting in the kitchen," the official began, "having just had our supper, when suddenly we heard the bell from the condemned cell ringing. The bell was in the corridor, and could only be rung by someone within the cell pulling the lever, and as we knew we were alone in the building we were not a little surprised and startled. However, armed with a lamp, off we went to fathom the mystery, or at least to see if we could do so. As we went the bell kept on ringing, and on our entering the corridor out of which the condemned cell led, we could see the bell swinging violently to and fro. As we drew close to the cell, it stopped, and all was quite still. We opened the cell door. No one was there, nor anything that could in any way account for the ringing, and we have often asked ourselves the question, who or what caused it? That is the only ghostly experience we had in Newgate during the many years we were there."

CHAPTER VII

HYDE PARK

IF we agree that tragedy is the principal cause of hauntings, instead of being surprised, we should expect to find Hyde Park badly haunted, for few, if any, of the public places in London have witnessed so many sad and terrible deaths.

Perhaps one of the most extraordinary stories of a queer happening in Hyde Park was that told me one evening, some years ago, by a Mr. Montero, at the International Club for Psychical Research, in Regent Street. This is what he said : " I am a native of the Argentine, and have been in England rather more than three years. One evening, during my first summer here, I wandered into the Park by the Marble Arch entrance, and turned down the path running parallel with the Bayswater Road. When I was about half-way between the Marble Arch and Lancaster Gate, I crossed the road on to the grass and took a seat under an elm tree, with wide-spreading branches, occupying rather an isolated position, that is to say with no other tree or seat very near it. After I had been sitting there for ten minutes or so, a tall, elderly man, who looked like a fellow-countryman, came up to me and said, ' If I were you, sir, I would not sit under that tree.' I asked him why, and he told me the following story, which he prefaced with an allusion to my comment on his nationality.

"'You are right,' he said, 'I come from the Argentine; my name is Hervada, and my home is in Buenos Aires. I am in England on business. A few nights ago I paid my first visit to the Park and sat just where you are sitting. There were a good many people about, principally couples obviously courting, but a heavy downpour of rain cleared them all off and I found myself, so far as I could see, quite alone.' Here he paused, glanced apprehensively around in a manner that impressed me as being very odd, and then went on. 'The storm did not last long, and soon after it had ceased I fell asleep and dreamed. I fancied I had gone home and was visiting my son-in-law, and with him watching my grandchildren at play in the nursery. Suddenly, with the abruptness that is so characteristic of dreams, I was back again sitting just where you are. A brilliant moon and myriads of scintillating stars enabled me to see all around me, as clearly as if it had been day. I thought I was feeling for my matchbox, to light a cigar, when two hideous, brown, bare and knotted arms suddenly clutched me round the waist and a strange hoarse voice said, " José Montero, your time has come. You will remain here and join the others, there is a place reserved for you in the rear, as you will soon see." The voice had barely said this, when a procession of shadowy figures seemed to rise from the grass and advance towards me, through the moonlight. They were of both sexes and, judging from their dress, they represented many periods in history.

"'Every variety of costume was included in this procession: stomachers, farthingales, ruffles, widebrimmed cavalier hats with long drooping feathers, full-bottomed wigs, apple-blossom sacques, cherry-coloured petticoats of quilted satin, high-heeled shoes, perukes, three-cornered hats and knee breeches, and even cloth caps and bowlers. On the shadowy figures came, walking two abreast, slowly, and with an absolutely silent tread, their faces a ghastly white in the moonbeams, and full of the most abject terror. When the last two were on a line with my chair, the voice from the tree bade me fall in.

"'For mercy's sake, let me go,' I pleaded; and I prayed a million times more earnestly than I ever prayed before.

"'"If you promise to return at this hour a year hence, I will let you go," the voice said, and without a moment's hesitation, I promised. With that everything faded away and my mind became a complete blank. When next I was cognizant of anything, I found myself still sitting in my seat, with one of the Park keepers in front of me, asking for a penny.' Here the narrator of the story paused again, then, after glancing apprehensively around, as before, he went on: 'I made inquiries about the tree, and several of the out-at-elbows who frequent the Park at night told me that nothing would persuade any of them to go near it because of its evil reputation. They (those to whom I spoke) had never seen anything themselves, they said, but they knew those who had, and knew for a fact that more than one person had been found lying dead under its branches. "We all call it," they added, "'the devil tree.'"

"'You will doubtless laugh at me, but I am convinced that this seeming dream was no dream, that I am in the power of something satanical, having pledged myself to it.'"

"I told him not to worry, that I was sure it was only a nightmare, but he adhered to his conviction that the tree was haunted by an evil spirit, and that he was doomed to die on the date the voice had specified. Before we separated he gave me his card, and asked me to dine with him one evening at the Trocadero. I did so, and we met several times again before he finally left for South America. One evening, some months after his departure, I visited Hyde Park again, entering by the Marble Arch and wandering, as on the previous occasion, down the side path in the direction of Lancaster Gate. When I was about halfway to Lancaster Gate a man crossed the path in front of me from the direction of the Bayswater Road and looked me straight in the face. It was still quite light, and, to my astonishment, I recognized Mr. Hervada. Without saying a word he crossed the road on to the grass. Yielding to an impulse I followed him. He made straight for the 'devil tree,' turned round, looked intently at me with an awful expression of terror in his eyes, and suddenly vanished. On my return home I looked in my memorandum book and found it was the anniversary of my first encounter with Mr. Hervada, the night the voice in his dream, if dream it really was, had specified. Some weeks later, a friend in common, a man that Mr. José Hervada and I both knew slightly, handed me a newspaper cutting. It was from an American paper, and it referred to the death of Mr. José Hervada. Glancing nervously through it, I discovered that Mr. Hervada's death had occurred suddenly in his own home, on the night I saw him vanish in the Park, under the 'devil tree.'"

Before the Great War, when the police regulations were not enforced as strictly as they are now, I used to spend whole nights in the Park, fraternizing with the flotsam and jetsam of humanity that knew no other home than the Park, and no other shelter from the rain and snow, and from them I heard innumerable accounts of weird happenings, seemingly inexplicable, save on the basis of what, at present, we believe to be the superphysical. Many of these stories centred round a certain tree, for instance, the following, told me one summer evening by a down-and-out, whom I sat beside on one of the benches skirting the path that runs parallel with the Bayswater Road.

"I was strolling across the grass, close to here, one night," said my informant, who had once been in the Church, at least so he said; and possibly it is true, because the Church, like every other vocation, has its black sheep and ne'er-do-wells, "when I suddenly became conscious of someone in front of me, and upon raising my head—I had been walking with head bent in deep thought—I saw a woman a few yards ahead of me. She was going along in the same direction as I was, and the moonlight was so strong on her that I could see every item of her dress. It was a shabby 'turnout,' a grey worsted shawl, a rusty black skirt, very bedraggled and frayed, an old battered bonnet, and a pair of boots, with splits in the backs of them, through which I could see her bare skin. She looked so poor and solitary that a wave of pity went through me, and I hastened my steps to give her the wherewithal for a night's lodging. Fast as I walked, however, the distance between us invariably remained the same, although she never seemed to make any alteration in her pace. We continued in this fashion, she moving along automatically, her head bent, and her bare heels glistening in the moonbeams, and I pounding away, straining every muscle in my legs to catch her up, until we came to a spot where several paths met.

"I then perceived, some little distance off, to my right, a huge, solitary tree with very curiously-shaped branches, one of which, in particular, riveted my attention. It stretched out from the trunk, at a height of six or seven feet from the ground, like a great arm, and it terminated in what looked exactly like fingers, long bony fingers, slightly curved, as if about to clutch hold of one. The woman ahead of me now turned sharply and made straight towards it. She was entirely in the open, the ground on either side of her being quite bare, and, as I gazed, I perceived a certain indistinctness, a something shadowy about her that I had not noticed before. Again I hastened my steps, in an attempt to overtake her, and again the distance between us remained the same; but the moment she came under the shadow of the tree she turned round. As she did so, one soft brilliant ray of light fell on her face, and made every feature in it stand out with frightful clearness. I say frightful clearness, because the thing that looked at me was not living, it was dead —long, long dead. I got 'the wind up' so badly that I ran out of the Park into the Bayswater Road, and spent the rest of the night wandering about the streets. Anywhere was preferable to the Park, with its gloom, and silence, and grim sepulchral trees. By the following evening, however, I had pulled myself sufficiently together to come here again. I looked everywhere, going over the same ground, for the tree, but could not find it. At last, after making fruitless inquiries of several men who had been here for years, I asked a very old man, who I was told must know every inch of the Park, if he could direct me to the tree I wanted to find, and he, at least, was able to throw some light on the matter. He took me to a broad open space, which I seemed to recognize, and pointing to a certain spot, said, ' That's where the tree you are looking for stood, about twenty years ago. I remember it very well, it had a branch exactly like a human arm and hand, and it fascinated people, fascinated them so much that they used to like to sleep under it, and quite a number who tried to do so were found dead in the morning. One or two, I believe, hanged themselves on its branches. It was cut down eventually, partly, I understood, because of these suicides, and partly because it was said that queer things had been seen and heard in its vicinity at night.'

"That is what the old fellow told me, and I believe it was true." It was thus the down-and-out ended his story. With regard to suicides in the Park, however, I think the spot most favoured by them is the Serpentine. Among those who drowned themselves there in the past was Harriet Westbrook Shelley, the unhappy wife of the poet Shelley. This sad event took place in 1816, and rumour has it that her ghost, as well as numerous other ghosts, haunts the Serpentine at night. I cannot find any authentic accounts of hauntings of this particular locality in the Park, but several stories of such hauntings have been told me, amongst others, the following.

Two ladies, taking a walk in the Park, paused on

the banks of the Serpentine and stood looking around. It was a none too pleasant autumn afternoon, as the wind was blowing from the east, and there were, consequently, few people about. Suddenly one of the ladies, looking at the water just in front of them, exclaimed, "I wonder what is causing those ripples?"

"A fish, of course," the other lady replied; "there are fish here, no doubt, though one doesn't hear of anyone catching them."

However, she had barely finished speaking, when a hand appeared above the surface of the water. It was a white, slim hand, evidently a woman's, and the long fingers were clutching the air convulsively, like those of a drowning person. On one of them, the middle finger, was a plain gold ring, that flashed and sparkled in the waning daylight. The two ladies stared at it in horror, too shocked to stir or utter a sound. After, possibly, a minute, it slowly sank out of sight, a few ripples marking the spot where it had disappeared.

"Whatever was it?" the one lady ejaculated, looking at her friend with a blanched face.

"God alone knows," her friend replied, shivering, "but let us get away from here as fast as possible."

And they almost ran out of the Park. I heard this story in a London Club.

In my chapter dealing with hauntings in St. James's Park, I purposely omitted allusion to Rosamond's Pond, now non-existent, since it was originally connected with Hyde Park by a small stream, the pond being actually constructed, I believe, as a receptacle for the waters of this stream. There seems to be some doubt as to its exact date, but it probably existed as far back as the sixteenth or seventeenth century. St. James's Park itself, as I have already stated, was originally a marshy field belonging to the Hospital for Lepers, which Henry VIII seized and converted into a residence for himself, this residence forming the foundation of what is now known as St. James's Palace. Rosamond's Pond was situated, I believe, in the south-west corner of St. James's Park, in the vicinity of Birdcage Walk, and, according to all accounts of it, there were few, if any, more picturesque and, at the same time, melancholy-looking pieces of water in the whole of London. Tall trees, with fantastically-fashioned branches, lined, at intervals, its irregular shores, which were covered in places with weeds and a variety of other dank and dismal vegetation. In its palmiest days it was a favourite trysting spot for ladies and gallants, who used to meet there at night and pledge eternal love to one another in the pale moonlight.

"*This the blest lover shall for Venus' sake,
And send up vows from Rosamond's Lake.*"

So Pope wrote of it in his *Rape of the Lock*. After it was forsaken by "the upper ten," who deserted it directly it became frequented by the non-fashionable element, it gradually passed into disrepute, until in its latter stages it was chiefly visited by footpads and bad characters of all kinds.

It had a fatal fascination for broken hearts, more particularly those of the feminine sex, and witnessed more suicides of the "unfortunate" class than any other spot in London. Small wonder is it, therefore, that long after its "filling up," which took place in 1770, its site was reputed to be very badly haunted.

To revert to Hyde Park. Some of the ghostly happenings said to take place in Hyde Park would seem to owe their origin to fatal duels. What was known as the Ring was the favourite spot for the more fashionable duels, but the less fashionable folk settled their disputes in various other places.

The Ring, which occupied high ground about 150 yards to the north of the east end of the Serpentine, was an open circular area, anchored by rails, round which, at intervals, stood very ancient trees of various species. A few of these trees are said to be still standing. As late as 1835 the Ring was traceable, though it had long since ceased to be the rendezvous for duellists and fashionable society. One of the most sanguinary encounters at the Ring was between Lord Mohun and the Duke of Hamilton, their seconds, Major Macartney and Colonel Hamilton, also fighting. Both the Duke and Lord Mohun perished on the spot.

According to some accounts of the tragedy, Lord Mohun deliberately stabbed the Duke to death, after the latter had been seriously wounded and was helpless; according to other accounts, it was Major Macartney who stabbed the Duke; while according to yet other accounts, it was a servant of Lord Mohun who committed the cruel and dastardly deed. However, be that as it may, Major Macartney was subsequently tried for the murder of the Duke and found guilty of manslaughter only. The Duke appears to have borne a pretty good reputation; at all events there were people, Dean Swift among them, who seem to have mourned his death; but Mohun is generally described as a thorough profligate and blackguard, feared by many and beloved by none. His widow's only regret, when his corpse was brought to the house, was that the blood from it dripped on the carpet and stained the bed-clothes.

Another fatal high-life duel in the Park was between Lieut.-Colonel Thomas and Colonel Gordon. It was fought in 1780, and resulted in the death of the former.

Seventeen years later, Colonel Fitzgerald was killed by Colonel King in pretty well the same spot. Very possibly some of their ghosts still haunt the scene of the tragedies. One of the rag-and-tatters brigade who used to frequent the Park in pre-war days, and who seemed too uneducated to have made himself acquainted with its long past history, told me that, when sleeping under the trees, he had, on several occasions, heard the clash of steel, just as if two men were fighting one another with swords.

" There was awful groaning, too," he said, " but it sounded rather 'ollow and far away."

The opinion of the writer is that what this tramp heard were the sounds made by the ghostly re-enactions of certain of the duels once fought, with fatal results, in the more remote parts of the Park. The Park has witnessed many cold-blooded murders, too, stabbings, and shootings, and deeds of violence of every sort, the majority of which, perhaps, are mysteries that have never been solved.

One such occurred in 1857; it created considerable interest. Some people were approaching the Serpentine one day with a Newfoundland dog, when the latter suddenly dashed on ahead and plunging in the water swam towards a dark object, some little distance away, which it seized and brought to shore. It was the dead body of a child, and a glance was sufficient to reveal the fact that it had met with foul play. The murderer was never brought to book, and, as a consequence of rumoured ghostly happenings on the banks of the Serpentine, subsequent to the discovery of the body, the spot was deserted after dusk for some weeks. That certain localities tempt people to commit homicidal acts is never more proven than in the case of Hyde Park and St. James's Park.

If the deeds were confined to the immediate vicinity of the water in these parks, one might think it was the fascination still water has for people of certain temperaments, but homicidal deeds have been very common in parts of the Park where there is no water. I am of the opinion that the key to the mystery lies in a combination of the Unknown, in superphysical forces that are attracted by still water and by certain trees, and which, in their turn, attract and influence people of certain temperaments. It is not merely the appearance of the still water glimmering in the golden sunshine or cold moonbeams that inspires a person with a sudden impulse to drown themselves or someone else, it is a power, a force lurking near the water that, magnet-like, attracts some people to its shore and there fills them with homicidal thoughts. The same applies to trees. In certain parts of countries where the natives are brought very much in touch with nature in its more primitive state, there still prevails belief in trees haunted by what in Greece are termed Stichios, or spirits for which certain trees have a peculiar fascination. It is not always trees belonging to a peculiar species that are stichmonious, because, for example, some banyan trees are haunted and others are not; it is trees possessing a certain personality, a mysterious something, at present undiagnosable, that attracts and magnetizes denizens of the other world or worlds.

I have already quoted several instances of the power such trees possess over some people, and here is one more. Again my authority is one of the fraternity of the road, and this being so, I would remark that tramps are not imaginative as a rule, and that it is not at all likely that a tramp would take the trouble to make up a story without any object.

To proceed, I was told by this tramp that a woman they called " All Button Mary," because she had so many buttons on her jacket, slept under an elm one evening, and in the morning said she intended drowning herself, as a voice from the tree had kept on whispering to her all night, telling her what a fine place the other world was, and that she must get there as quickly as possible. She did drown herself, because, later on in the day, she was found in the Serpentine.

" If that was the only case one might say it was insanity," the tramp remarked, " but it ain't. Two women, contrary to my advice, slept under the tree one night, and before morning they were fighting one another so viciously that one was badly hurt."

The elm, when stichmonious, would usually seem to be haunted by a grotesque type of spirit that affects people of certain temperaments in a very unpleasant way. If it does not tempt them to suicide or murder, it generates in them vicious desires and strange manias.

HYDE PARK

Women appear to come under its influence more than men.

The oak, of which there are many in the Park and there were still more in bygone days, has always been regarded as very closely associated with the Unknown. It was the Druids' favourite tree, and witches often held their Sabbats under its gnarled and knotted branches. Very possibly some of the oaks and elms that surrounded the Ring in the Park were stichmonious, and this might well account for the dastardly deeds that in so many cases accompanied the duels that were fought in their vicinity. I can find no mention either of beeches or birches near the Ring; though both species of trees are or were to be found in other parts of the Park. The stichmonious beech influence, which is stronger over women of certain temperaments than over men, is very far-reaching, and when it is stichmonious the beech resembles the octopus, not only in appearance, but in other respects too. It gets a wide and firm grip over its victims, which is not easy to shake off.

Within a few yards of a house I know in the North of England there is a huge beech tree; and the first time I approached it I was conscious of a curious influence exuding from it. I felt at once that it was stichmonious, and that the spirit haunting it was of the type beech trees so often attract. I am now certain of it, having known the house close to which the tree stands for some years. One tenant of the house was a foreign lady who developed an art, possibly hitherto latent in her, of acquiring husbands with money, getting most of it from them, and then contriving a divorce.

G

One of her husbands died very suddenly. I was chatting with him at eleven o'clock a.m. on the day he died, and he then appeared to be quite fit and well. Some hours later, he was dead, either shot or poisoned; and the verdict was suicide. Within a very few months another husband (her fourth) appeared upon the scene, and as soon as she grew tired of him, which she did very quickly, she gave him the alternative of a good lathering with a horse-whip or a few chops with a keen-edged hatchet. Preferring neither, he barricaded himself in his bedroom, till she had somewhat quietened down, and then fled from the house, thankful to escape with a whole skin.

She appeared to be quite impartial in her dealings with the sexes; for when she was not making unmistakable advances to some moneyed or strikingly handsome man, her attentions were turned to some subtly attractive member of her own sex. And this lady's passion thus impartially bestowed was all due, I believe, to that beautiful, wide-spreading, stichmonious beech tree, which stood in her garden, almost within hand-reach of her bedroom window.

After she left the house, it was taken by a titled lady, who soon showed that, with regard to the male sex, she had the same striking tendencies as her predecessor. After one husband had gone rather abruptly "west," she secured a second, by inveigling him into an affair, which led to his wife getting an almost immediate divorce. This second husband, a wealthy cotton spinner, was very much older than Lady ——, and he died most opportunely, she, at the time, having just met a man to whom she had taken a violent fancy. This man is now her husband, and, if the saying I once heard, when I was working on a ranch in the wilds of America, namely, " Sleep an hour under shadow of an old beech tree, and parted from your husband soon you'll be," be true, it is extremely fortunate for him that they have vacated the house overshadowed by the stichmonious beech tree and are now living, I believe, in a spot that is absolutely free from any such malign influence.

The silver birch, in my experience, possesses, when apparently stichmonious, a strong attraction for both sexes; it inspires in them the most ardent passion not only for those of the opposite sex, but for itself. In a previous chapter, I have referred to a member of the old International Club for Psychical Research who fell madly in love with a silver birch tree in the Green Park. Supposing it to have been stichmonious, the nymph haunting it must have possessed a fairy beauty that had the power to charm humans almost to distraction. I myself have felt the fascination of such trees in Hyde Park and other places, though I have never gone to the extremity of serenading them or of composing love sonnets for their edification.

I conclude this chapter with a tree story narrated to me in Hyde Park one evening many years ago.

It concerns Black Sally, a tramp, of partly gipsy origin and of rather more than middle age. Her usual beat was the West of England, between Bristol and Penzance, but occasionally she extended it and came to London. She was tall and slim, the rude members of the fraternity called her scraggy, and that she had once been handsome was self-evident, as she still showed signs of more than ordinary good looks. She owed her nickname of " Black Sally " to the fact that her face was never clean, to be more precise, to the fact that it was always dirty. It was her boast that she had not washed it for ten years, not, indeed, since the eventful night when she and her husband parted. He turned her out of doors, having found someone he liked better; and thus it was that she became a wanderer on the broad highway, with all interest in life gone, and with it all desire to wash and be cleanly. She had a constant dread that one day she and her husband would meet again, and that he would murder her. She often used to harrow the feelings of tramps in the Park, at night, with her fear and apprehension of what he would do to her.

Like many others of the fraternity, she had a real love for trees; they were, she said, her best and truest friends, and there was one tree in particular in Hyde Park that seemed to attract her more than any of the others. It was an old elm, a tree that everyone else avoided and would never sleep under, as they believed it was haunted by something very evil. Knowing its reputation, Black Sally, it seems, resisted her desire to sleep under it for some time; but so great, apparently, was her fascination that one night she succumbed to her desire, with the result that in the early hours of the morning she was found lying at the foot of her beloved tree, cold, stiff and dead.

At that period such finds were by no means uncommon, they invoked little excitement or comment among the officials of the Park and the general public, and the finding of Black Sally's body proved no exception to the rule. There being no visible marks of violence on her body, it was said by those in authority that death was due to natural causes. Some of the tramp fraternity, however, were of a different opinion. They had seen a dark, sinister-looking man, a complete stranger to them, loitering in the neighbourhood of the elm with the evil reputation, and remembering Black Sally's horror of her husband, with regard to her death they could not help coming to a conclusion of their own.

The tramp who told me this story assured me that for several nights after this tragedy had taken place, sighings and moanings were heard coming from the spot where Black Sally's body had been found, and that at night a footprint swimming in what looked like blood was always to be seen there, the blood vanishing suddenly and mysteriously with the coming of the sun. My informant took me to the tree, styled he said by him and his mates of the road "Black Sally's tree," and pointed to the ground under it. The night being light, a great silvery moon overhead, I was able to discern with considerable distinctness a mark, certainly not unlike the imprint of a human foot, a long narrow human foot, but it was dry. I commented on this, and my informant remarked, "The blood has not been there lately, only just the footprint, but those who knew Sally declare it to be hers."

As we moved away from the tree, I heard a sort of shuddering groan coming from it. I swung round; no one was there, only Black Sally's tree, its slightly nodding branches darkly outlined on the moonlit soil.

CHAPTER VIII

BLACKFRIARS AND HIGHBURY

Most people know, perhaps, that within the last century there have been several epidemics of murder in this country (in the thirties, forties and sixties, for example, there was an epidemic of poisoning by women, who, as a rule, chose their husbands for their victims), but probably not everyone knows that periodically London has experienced epidemics of haunting.

As we have seen, there was something approaching one in the parks about the beginning of last century, and there was another, covering a much wider area, in 1871 and 1872. Regarding the latter epidemic, it began thus.

There were two or three houses in Stamford Street, at the corner of Hatfield Street, that had stood empty for more than forty years. Twenty-five years previously they were owned by an eccentric old solicitor named Read, who was reputed to be very rich. He lived in a house close to them, and owing to his never trying to let them and allowing no one to enter them, save his wife and daughter, many people supposed that there must be a mystery of some sort connected with them. Some thought that the mystery was a crime committed in one of them, whilst others thought that Mr. Read had hidden some of his money in them, and these beliefs grew when, upon Mr. Read's death, it was rumoured that he had left instructions in his will that his widow should continue to keep the houses tenantless. Anyway, Mrs. Read did keep the houses tenantless, and, at her death, her only child, a daughter named Angela, followed suit. It was during Miss Angela Read's ownership of the houses that reports of their being haunted first got into circulation.[1]

People passing by them at night saw lights moving about in them, and occasionally white faces pressed against the window panes. Sceptics were of the opinion that the forlorn and desolate appearance of the houses, which were overrun with rats, may, in the first place, have suggested the idea that they were haunted, this idea gaining colour when lights were seen moving about inside them; albeit, according to these same sceptics, the lights were merely lanterns carried by Miss Read and her old servant, who, in accordance with the will of old Mr. Read, visited the houses every night, and possibly, whilst doing so, tried to find the treasure the eccentric old man was supposed to have secreted.

This, of course, may have been true. Other people, however, maintained that the lights and faces seen at the windows were superphysical, and that it was owing to these hauntings that the houses had so long stood empty. So great a notoriety did the houses acquire, that the street was crowded every night with people eager to see the alleged ghosts.

When Miss Read died she bequeathed the houses to the Consumption Hospital at Brompton, and in 1874 they were demolished. Before this event took place, however, rumour spread that certain empty

[1] See *Penny Illustrated Paper*, Dec. 1871; and *Old and New London*, vol. vi.

houses in Blackfriars, Snowhill, Newington and other parts of London also harboured ghosts.

With regard to one of these houses in Blackfriars, I heard a strange story from Mrs. M., who, in 1898, was staying in Upper Norwood. Her story was as follows :

"In the summer of 1870 my husband and I, being on the lookout for a cheap house, as our funds, at the time, were very low, went to an Estate Agent in the S.E. district. He had a large number of 'empties' on his list, but one close to the Blackfriars Road struck us as absurdly cheap, considering its accommodation. It was a twelve-roomed house, not including the basement, which the Agent told us consisted of a large kitchen and other domestic offices. The street where it stood had at one time been fairly fashionable, but of late years, like many other streets, it had deteriorated and become little better than a slum.

"'If you can put up with the people,' the Agent said, 'you might, perhaps, stick the house, but remember I have warned you.'

"My husband shrugged his shoulders—they were very broad ones.

"'Beggars can't always be choosers,' he remarked, 'and if the house is in anything like repair, we must put up with our neighbours. I presume they won't actually molest us?'

"'I don't think they will knock you on the head, if that is what you mean,' the Agent laughed. 'Still, some of them look pretty tough customers. However, you might as well take the keys and have a look.'

"Being extremely busy just then he could not spare

anyone to show us over the house, so we decided to go there alone.

"The Agent did not exaggerate when he said the street was little better than a slum. It swarmed with dirty children, playing all manner of games on the pavements, and women in bedraggled dresses, who stood on doorsteps, shouting at one another over dilapidated palings. The house of which we had the key was a corner house. Its exterior, blackened with the smoke and dirt of ages, presented a sombre, forbidding appearance, which was rendered still more unprepossessing by its general state of decay. Grass flourished in the interstices of the high, steep steps, which were broken and unsafe to tread on; the rusty iron palings surrounding the house had become loosened in their stone settings, and several of the windows on the ground floor and in the basement were cracked and broken.

"When we opened the front door, long since devoid of paint, a gaunt-looking cat, with lantern-like eyes, scurried past us into the street, and hideous cockroaches, with long sprawling legs, either darted hither and thither on the grimy hall floor, or stood still, as if transfixed with astonishment or terror, waving their long antennae. We were, furthermore, greeted with that damp, musty smell, peculiar to houses that have been long shut up.

"Once, no doubt, the house had been inhabited by well-to-do, if not actually rich, people, and marks of former splendour remained in the oak panelling of the hall and staircase. Cobwebs, however, festooned the walls and finely-moulded ceilings, whilst over all hung a sense of oppressiveness and utter desolation.

"'We can never live here,' I remarked to my husband, as we viewed, one after another, the large, bare reception rooms, oak-panelled throughout and furnished with the large Dutch tiled fireplaces that came over with the tulips in the days of William and Mary. 'I should be terrified at being here alone.'

"'We should have to let out some of the rooms,' my husband replied. 'I rather like the place, it is so quaint and old-world.'

"He had not, however, then seen the basement. It was the largest and gloomiest basement I have ever been in. A large, stone-flagged, cheerless kitchen, with a large and even more cheerless scullery beyond, both dank, and dark, and horribly suggestive of all kinds of horrors.

"We got out of it as quickly as possible, and were thinking of leaving the house, without viewing the upper part of it, when we heard what sounded like the plaintive notes of a spinet proceeding from one of the rooms. Impelled by curiosity, we ascended the stairs in the direction of the sounds, which, apparently, came from a room on the second floor. However, upon reaching the second floor landing, we heard a door on the landing above us open. The music then abruptly ceased, there were sounds of a struggle, a piercing scream, a heavy thud, and a noise like someone being choked to death. We were too taken aback at first to do anything but stare at one another in speechless horror.

"My husband, who was first to recover," Mrs. M. went on, " ran towards the stairs and was about to go up, when a woman came running down. She was tall and thin, and very pale; she had red hair and a hatchet-shaped face, and was wearing a quaintly-fashioned black dress, with a white kerchief folded round her shoulders and across her bosom, and the kind of mob cap that was in vogue among servants about eighty or a hundred years ago. In one hand she held a piece of cord. There was something so strangely sinister and startling about her that my husband shrank aside to let her pass. Upon reaching the head of the stairs, leading to the ground floor, she paused, and turning round and leering horribly, shook her bony hand menacingly at us. Then she ran swiftly down the stairs.

"Directly she disappeared," my informant added, " my husband seemed to recover the use of his limbs, and was about to tear after her, when a loud chuckling laugh prevented him. We both stood still to listen, but after that there was absolute silence. Though we were both horribly frightened, we forced ourselves to go upstairs, fully expecting to find evidences of some dreadful tragedy, but there was nothing. We went into every room, but they were all absolutely empty. No sign anywhere of a spinet or body. Just bare, dusty, oak floors and panelling.

" Convinced now that what we had heard and seen was something supernatural, we hastily left the premises, and returning to the Agent, informed him of what had occurred. He listened to us with great interest and, on our pressing him, admitted that it was not the first time people who had visited or stayed in the house had complained to him of similar happenings.

" 'There is a tradition in the neighbourhood,' he said, ' that a murder was committed in it many years ago, but whether the tradition is in accordance with fact or not, there is, undoubtedly, something queer about the place, and, in strict confidence, you are well out of it.'"

The haunting thus described by Mrs. M. reminds me of one in an old square in Highbury. By referring to my notebook I find that it was told me in the summer of 1900 by a septuagenarian artist named Stock.

The house that figures in his story has long since been pulled down. It bore the ill-omened number 13, and for years had in its tiny front garden a large board with "To be Sold or Let" in large lettering on it. Mr. Stock took it, furnished, about the year 1849, employing as his housekeeper a Mrs. Brown, who had been strongly recommended by the landlord. She undertook to "run" the establishment for him, with the aid of a charwoman to do the very rough work. Mr. Stock did not work in the house; he shared a studio, not far away, with a brother-artist.

I have called the place in which the house was situated a square, because that is what the authorities who name streets in London styled it. In reality, it was just a narrow oblong enclosure, where a score or so of melancholy trees cast their shadows on a wilderness of tall grass and rank weeds, and all the houses around it seemed to have acquired an air of chronic damp and gloom.

It was not a cheerful spot. The sun rarely seemed to discover it, and at the date I am referring to, almost every other house in it was empty. It had one great attraction for Mr. Stock, however: it was a cheap locality, and the rent he paid was small, ridiculously small.

The first night of his stay in the house he arrived about ten o'clock, and being tired after a long day's work, he asked Mrs. Brown, who was well acquainted with the geography of the place, to show him to his room at once. She went upstairs with him. It was rather a winding staircase, and his room was on the second floor. On the way to it he had to pass a window, a little above the first landing, just where the stairs took a sharp curve.

Curious to see on what the window looked, he tried to peer out of it, but the inky darkness without merely revealed the reflection of his own face and, oddly enough, the reflection of two other faces. One was that of Mrs. Brown, and the second face, close beside hers, seemed to be that of a very repulsive-looking man, at least that was Mr. Stock's first impression; but he concluded afterwards there must have been some curious flaw in the glass, and that both reflections were those of Mrs. Brown, who was certainly far from good-looking, though not actually hideous.

He found his room quite comfortable, and being very tired he slept right through the night, without waking, till it was time to get up.

The following day found him again at work in his studio, but he left off early, and after dining at the restaurant he usually patronized in Soho, he went home, and got there in time, so he told himself, to do a little reading before turning into bed.

Retiring to his room, he ensconced himself in front of the fire with a bundle of magazines. He had not calculated on the effects of the fire, however, which made him so drowsy that before very long he was fast asleep. He awoke, with a start, to find that the fire had burned very low, and that the room, in consequence, was in almost total darkness. Indeed, he feared at first that there was not sufficient vitality in the embers to light a candle, and that he would be unable, having no matches, to see how to undress and get into bed. A few skilful touches with the poker, however, soon dispelled this idea and produced a bright, cheerful flame.

He rose from his stooping posture, intending to get a spill or paper lighter from the mantelshelf, for the purpose of lighting his candle. As he did so, his glance fell on his own face in the mirror in front of him, and what he saw reflected in it caused him to stare in astonishment.

Standing at the farther end of the room, facing the door, was an elderly woman, a woman he had never seen before. That she had not been in the room a few minutes previously he could swear, for he had looked all round the room, and, in spite of the dimness of the light, seen well enough that he was alone and that the door was closed. It was closed now, but how could she have opened and closed it without his hearing, unless she had done so during the brief moment he had spent poking the fire, which seemed to him an utter impossibility?

What was very odd, too, was that she did not trouble either to speak to him or even to glance in his direction. She simply stood still, her face turned towards the door, as if listening. That she was someone belonging to the house seemed evident too, since she was wearing a kind of négligé gown of white cambric, with deep frills down the front and at the wrists. Who could she be, he wondered? Some friend of Mrs.

Brown, who had mistaken the room? Just at that moment the fire shot up into a brilliant flame, throwing a lurid light on her face and making it most startlingly clear.

Never in his life had Mr. Stock seen such a face before, and never, he told me, would he wish to see one like it again. The woman, as I have said, was elderly; she might have been sixty or she might have been more, for her hair was grizzled and her general appearance suggested feebleness. Her face, too, was lined, but it was her expression that riveted Mr. Stock's attention and appalled him. It was an expression of hopeless, utter despair and ghastly, speechless horror, blended together and concentrated in the effort of listening, and so intense was this effort of listening that it appeared to absorb every nerve and fibre in her body. She was listening to something outside the room, away on the landing or stairs, to something which from her starting eyeballs and the quivering muscles of her lower jaw, seemed to be drawing nearer and nearer. Then, suddenly, the door began to open, slowly, very slowly, and, as it did so, the woman shrank back, nearer and nearer to the wall, the horror in her face growing more and more fixed.

Suddenly the fire flame died down and the room was plunged in darkness. A few moments later, and another spurt of flame revealed to Mr. Stock that the woman was gone. The room was once again empty and the door closed. Yet there had been no sound, not even the lightest footfall. The house was wrapped in unbroken silence.

The following morning Mr. Stock tackled Mrs. Brown on the subject, and asked her who the elderly lady was who had paid him a visit the evening before.

"You've been dreaming, sir," Mrs. Brown responded, "there wasn't anyone in the house but you and me."

"Did you leave the hall door open by mistake?" Mr. Stock suggested gently.

"Leave the 'all door open?" Mrs. Brown said, with great indignation. "Why, I'd never think of doing such a thing. The hidea of it! It was shut and locked directly it grew dark."

"An elderly woman in a loose kind of dress of white cambric was in my room at about ten o'clock last night," Mr. Stock persisted.

"Then all I can say," Mrs. Brown responded, "is that you must 'ave let 'er in yourself, or been dreaming. It was a dream, I expect; gentlemen as studies art or as works in studios often 'as queer dreams. You can 'ear 'em mumbling to themselves at night."

"It was no dream," Mr. Stock said stolidly. And there the matter for the time ended.

About a fortnight after this conversation Mr. Stock came home late one night from the theatre. There was no light in the hall or upon the stairs, except from the candle he carried. After putting that ready for him on a chair, Mrs. Brown had turned out the gas. Mr. Stock went upstairs on tiptoe. When he came to the curve and the window to which I have already referred, the latter, as on the first night he spent in the house, attracted his attention, and gazing at it, he saw himself reflected in it at full length, but, to his amazement, he also perceived reflected in it the head and shoulders of a man, who, apparently, was coming

BLACKFRIARS AND HIGHBURY

up the stairs behind him. Turning sharply round, Mr. Stock then saw creeping slowly, with stealthy, noiseless footsteps, up the stairs a hunchbacked man in his shirt sleeves. The man, being below him on the staircase, with his head slightly bent, at first Mr. Stock could see only a mass of coarse, shaggy red hair, not quite long enough to conceal a pair of large, crinkly, misshapen ears; but as the hunchback came on round the curve into full view, his face became clearly discernible. Indeed, some strange light other than the flickering candle flame seemed focussed on it. It was the same dreadfully repulsive face Mr. Stock had seen reflected in the window on the night of his arrival. A low, retreating forehead; misshapen nose, that looked as if it had been broken in a fight; loose, sensual lips; brutal, wolfish jaws; light eyes, illuminated with an expression of deadly, sinister determination. It was the face of some terrible beast of prey rather than that of a human being. In one hairy hand he held an ordinary table-knife, the blade of which, worn to a point like a dagger, had evidently been recently sharpened; and stair by stair, with a snake-like crawling movement, he drew nearer to Mr. Stock, who, spellbound, shrank back close to the staircase wall. The man, however, did not appear to notice him, but passing him by crawled silently up the stairs towards his bedroom. Compelled by some power inside himself, which he could not resist, Mr. Stock mechanically followed the crawling figure. When the latter arrived at Mr. Stock's door, he paused for a few moments and looked at the knife with a grin of hideous exultation. Then, gripping the handle of the door with his coarse, bony fingers, he slowly turned it.

H

The room within was full of moonlight, which poured in a broad stream through the open window, and right in its path stood the same woman Mr. Stock had seen before, the elderly woman in the loose morning gown of white cambric.

The cause of that look of awful fear in her protruding eyes was now only too apparent, it was the hunchback, whose face shone with evil joy as he beheld her terror. What the end of the drama was, one can only surmise, for just as the hunchback entered the room and advanced with devilish slowness on his shrieking victim, a gust of wind blew the door to with a loud bang; and upon Mr. Stock throwing it open (the banging of it had broken the spell that had hitherto bound him), instead of seeing something terrible, as he fully expected he would see, he found the room just as usual, with no sign anywhere either of the woman in the cambric dress or of the dreadful hunchback. However, not daring to remain in it, he spent the night in the drawing-room, with the gas fully turned on.

A few days later he vacated the house, thus choosing, despite the desperate state of his exchequer, to sacrifice a year's rent, rather than remain in it. But what was the explanation of the mystery?

What was the dark secret of the house so strangely shadowed forth to him, a really quite matter-of-fact young man, who had never, before entering the house, seen a ghost or believed such a thing existed? Mrs. Brown either would not or could not give him any information. She persisted he had been dreaming, and that there was nothing wrong with the house. She had never seen or heard anything, and she had lived in it for several years as caretaker.

The mystery has never been fully explained; the secret, perhaps in a more materially real sense than is at present apparent, remaining hidden in the dreary walls of the place, until they were eventually pulled down. All that Mr. Stock could discover, after minute inquiries among neighbours and shopkeepers in the vicinity, was that no one of late years, excepting Mrs. Brown, had ever stayed long in the house; but that years ago, before the present landlord bought it, the house had been occupied by an old woman and her son, a very ill-favoured hunchback, who were supposed to have gone away somewhat hastily. At any rate no one saw them go, but a year or so afterwards the son returned alone, saying his mother had died abroad.

He remained in the house some months and then disappeared. No one knew whither he went, and no one cared. It was after that that the house was so often to let and was never occupied for any length of time, till Mrs. Brown came there as a caretaker. For some odd reason the strange happenings in the house did not seem to affect her. She stayed on till the end of Mr. Stock's year. The house was then sold again, with the same result: no one would live in it.

CHAPTER IX

HOLLAND HOUSE, LONDON BRIDGES AND CHICK LANE

HOLLAND HOUSE, originally the manor house of Abbots, Kensington, was built in 1607 for Sir Walter Cope, and possesses at least one ghost, that is to say if there is any truth in rumour and tradition. The ghost, which is thought to be that of the first Lord Holland, usually emerges, at the stroke of midnight, from behind a secret door in the " gilt room," and gliding noiselessly through that apartment visits other parts of the building.

It inspires all who see it with the greatest terror, owing to the fact that it is headless. Its body terminates in a mere protuberance of neck; it carries its grinning head under one arm.

Henry Rich, the first Earl of Holland, inherited the house on the death of his father-in-law, the aforesaid Sir Walter Cope. A certain unluckiness would seem to have been associated with the gilt room, for the Earl had it decorated with great splendour for a ball, to be given on the occasion of Prince Charles's marriage with Henrietta Maria of France, and although the marriage came off, the ball did not, which so greatly disappointed the Earl, that it is thought by some to account for the haunting; a theory that is rather strengthened by the fact that the ghost of the Earl, according to the tradition, is to be seen most often in the gilt room, the room round which his disappointment centred and in which, during his lifetime, he took such a very pardonable pride.

The headless condition of the ghost may be explained by the fact that Lord Holland was executed in 1649 for his unsuccessful attempt to restore Charles I to the throne. Apart from this haunting, Holland House was formerly visited by at least one other ghost.

My authority is John Aubrey,[1] who narrates the following interesting incident in connection with Lady Diana Rich, daughter of the Earl of Holland.

"The beautiful Lady Diana Rich," he says, " daughter to the Earl of Holland, as she was walking in her father's garden at Kensington, to take the fresh air before dinner, about eleven o'clock, being then very well, met with her own apparition, habit and everything, as in a looking-glass. Almost a month later, she died of the smallpox, and it is said that her sister, the Lady Isabella Thynne, saw the likeness of herself also, before she died. This account I had from a person of honour."

Aubrey believed in certain houses possessing a something about them that entailed catastrophe and ill-luck on those who inhabited them.

" 'Tis certain," he says, " that there are some houses unlucky to their inhabitants, which the revered and pious Dr. Napier could acknowledge."

"The Fleece Tavern, in Covent Garden (in York Street)," he continues, " was very unfortunate for homicides, there have been several killed there in my time. It is now (1692) a private house." In a footnote he informs us that one of the homicides was

[1] *Miscellanies*, by John Aubrey, F.R.S.

"Clifton, the master of the house, who hanged himself, having perjured himself." Still continuing, he says: "A handsome brick house on the south side of Clerkenwell Church-yard had been so unlucky for at least 40 years, that it was seldom tenanted; and at last nobody would venture to take it. Also a handsome house in Holborn, that looked towards the fields, the tenants of it did not prosper, several, about six. At the sign of —— over against Northumberland House, near Charing Cross, died the Lady Baynton (eldest daughter of Sir John Danvers of Dansey). Some years after, in the same house, died my Lady Hobbey (her sister) of the smallpox, and about 20 years after, died their nephew, Henry Danvers, Esq., of the smallpox, aged 21, wanting two weeks. He was nephew and heir to the Right Honourable Henry Danvers, Earl of Danby."

What Aubrey says about unlucky houses suggests what I have already said in this volume, that attached to certain places, trees, commons, pools and other spots is a sinister influence, which I am inclined to believe is superphysical, that prompts people to commit all kinds of crime and vicious acts.

I have referred especially to the Serpentine, the Ring, and Rosamond's Pond in connection with this hypothesis. I may now add to that list Waterloo Bridge, Westminster Bridge and the Monument. Dealing with the last-named first, some attribute the fascination the Monument possessed for suicides to its height—its altitude from the pavement is 202 feet—others to its quietude. For my own part, I am inclined to think that whereas both these peculiarities might prove an inducement to some would-be

HOLLAND HOUSE AND CHICK LANE 119

suicides, there is, nevertheless, a something in addition at the Monument, something lurking in the atmosphere there, indefinable, undiagnosable, detectable only by certain very susceptible temperaments, that suggests throwing oneself over. I have felt it on Clifton Suspension Bridge, which has witnessed many suicides since its erection about sixty-five years ago; on the St. Vincent Rocks near by, and late at night, when few have been about, on several of the London bridges. The epidemic at the Monument began with William Green, a weaver, in 1750. That financial trouble had nothing to do with his leap to death was suggested by the finding of eighteen guineas in the pocket of his coat after the fatal plunge. Some years later, the body of Thomas Craddock, a baker, was found at the base of the Monument.

It was stated officially that in leaning over the rails to look at an eagle in a cage, he had overbalanced and fallen into the street beneath, but there were many who queried this. In 1810 Lyon Levi, a diamond merchant, took the fatal leap. It was suggested in the papers that financial losses were responsible for the deed, but, if he had premeditated suicide, why that weary ascent to the summit of the Monument? Why not poison or the river?

In 1839 Margaret Meyer, daughter of a bed-ridden baker of Hemming's Row, St. Martin's-in-the-Fields, threw herself over. The next year a boy named Hawes followed suit; and two years later Jane Cooper, a servant girl from Hoxton, destroyed herself in like manner. Those who were present on this occasion witnessed something very terrible and extraordinary. Jane, when the watchman's back was turned, scrambled on to the iron railing on the top of the Monument, and tucking her clothes about her, took a headlong dive. She struck, with great force, a griffin on the base of the Monument and, rebounding, shot over a cart, that was passing at the moment, into the road beyond.

After this the City authorities caged in the top of the Monument, and there have been no suicides from it since.

Waterloo Bridge and Westminster Bridge, in past years, have figured almost equally at coroners' inquests. The total number of tragedies that have taken place on them will never be known. Those that are known make up a sum that is truly appalling. Murders, so far as statistics show, have been much less frequent on these bridges than suicides.

The most sensational occurrence on Waterloo Bridge was undoubtedly what the contemporary Press styled the Great Thames Mystery of 1857.[1] The story has been so often told that it is needless here to say more than that, for years after the said tragedy, all kinds of rumours regarding ghostly happenings on the bridge were in circulation.

Of Westminster Bridge a strange tale has been told in reference to the Jack the Ripper crimes. It was said they terminated with the suicide of a man who was seen to leap from Westminster Bridge on the stroke of midnight, December 31, 1888. This man, so it was asserted, was a member of the medical profession, who had been suspected for some time by the police. When he realized the net was closing round him and arrest would probably take place very shortly, he took the fatal leap. Whether there is any truth in this story I cannot say, but I do know that

[1] *Great Thames Mysteries*, by the author of this work.

when I was lodging in York Road, Lambeth, about ten years later, I met several people, during my nocturnal rambles, who assured me Westminster Bridge was haunted by the ghost of a man who was, periodically, seen jumping from it, as Big Ben sounded midnight.

A strange tale of a ghost on Blackfriars Bridge was told me about this time by a postman who, like myself, was lodging in York Road. He said that when crossing the bridge, very early one autumn morning, he only noticed two people on it. One was a policeman some little distance off, and the other, only a few yards away from him, a tall woman, apparently in mourning, as she was dressed all in black. Suddenly the woman commenced climbing on to the wall of the bridge. Feeling sure she was about to commit suicide, the postman ran towards her, to try and prevent her, but was too late, for she had disappeared. However, off came his coat, and he was about to jump into the river, to try to save her, when the policeman, who, as he must have seen what had just taken place, appeared to be somewhat callous, stopped him.

"Put on your coat again," he said, catching him by the arm. "It is of no use your jumping in. What you saw was no living person, it was a ghost. If you had been on the bridge at this hour yesterday morning, you would have seen the same thing, and, in all probability, it will happen again to-morrow."

The postman, who was very disbelieving regarding the superphysical, thought the policeman was trying to deceive him, and told him so.

"Well, you come here to-morrow morning and see for yourself," was the reply.

The postman said he would, and he was as good as his word. The same hour, the following morning, found him again on the bridge, and the very same thing occurred. A tall woman, all in black (she was the very same woman, he could swear, whom he had seen commit suicide on the previous night), ran to the side of the bridge, as he approached, and climbing on to the parapet, disappeared.

"Well," the same policeman, who was standing by, observed, "didn't I tell you so? I've seen her do the same thing, at the same hour, for seven consecutive mornings. I'm told it won't happen again (it's what they call periodical haunting) for a good many years, and I'm truly thankful for that, as it's a bit trying to one's nerves."

The postman agreed, and went on his way thoughtfully.

Whilst I am still dealing with ghosts in the neighbourhood of the City, reference must be made to an authentic case of haunting that occurred in St. Swithin's Lane in the fifties of the last century. It was at Number 15, a very old house, then inhabited by a family named Simpson.[1] Nothing unusual seems to have happened till after the family had been in the house for some time. Then, one day, two of the children, a girl and a boy, while on the top landing, saw a very short, elderly lady come from the direction of the staircase and enter one of the bedrooms. Wondering who she could be, they followed her immediately, but she had disappeared. There was no one in the room. Soon afterwards, the girl, on

---

[1] The case was sent to the Society for Psychical Research, and was recorded in their organ about forty-five years ago.

coming out of the drawing-room, saw the same old lady standing at the foot of the staircase, and a few minutes later she saw her for the third time walking across the landing on the second floor. There does not appear to have been anything very alarming about the ghost, for neither of the children was at all frightened. They were merely curious, as the old lady was a complete stranger to them, and they marvelled at her presence and the manner in which she kept disappearing and reappearing in different parts of the house.

On another occasion, when the children were playing in the nursery, the old lady suddenly appeared in the doorway, smiling at them. It being light, they were able to note details in her appearance. She was wearing a shabby black dress, and rather a large bonnet, with a good deal of velvet on it. When she moved away, they all followed her to one of the bedrooms, where they suddenly lost sight of her. They asked the servants who she was, and the servants, who had probably been told what to say, informed them it was a lady who had come to see their mother.

One night Mrs. Simpson was sitting in one of the rooms alone, waiting for her husband. Hearing a noise outside on the landing, she went to ascertain the cause, and saw, to her surprise and, we suppose, fear, although she does not say so, a man's face peering down at her from over the balustrade of the staircase. Summoning the servants she caused a thorough search of the house to be made at once, but without finding any trace of the man. Either again that night, or some nights later, she saw the same man on the staircase. As he was shrouded in gloom she could not see his face distinctly, but merely received the impression it was very white. He disappeared inexplicably, while she was looking at him.

Mr. Simpson was the next to see "something." He was in his office one morning—his office was on the ground floor of the house—when he suddenly saw, standing in front of him, the little old lady he had heard so much about. He recognized her from the description given him by the children. She was very pale, and had a gentle expression. She wore a dark bonnet with strings tied under her chin, and had her hands clasped together in front of her. After regarding him earnestly for some time, she moved away with a curious gliding motion and abruptly disappeared.

These would appear to be the only occasions on which the family actually saw any phenomena in the house, but they often heard strange, unaccountable noises. Occasionally there would be sounds of very mournful singing in a recess of one of the bedrooms, while on other occasions they heard moaning and sighing in the dark, cavernous cellars under the house. No satisfactory explanation of the disturbances was ever forthcoming.

The house was eventually pulled down, but whether on account of the haunting I cannot say. The case, which, as I have said, is strictly authentic, affords an excellent example of a not infrequent kind of haunting, where ghosts appear without any apparent specific purpose. It is quite a mistake to suppose that only houses that have witnessed tragedies are haunted, for I know thoroughly well-attested cases of ghostly happenings in houses that have never witnessed any violent death, the phantasms seen being those of

HOLLAND HOUSE AND CHICK LANE

people known to have passed away quite peacefully. It may have been so in the case of the old lady seen at No. 15 St. Swithin's Lane; and although the sighing and moaning certainly suggest trouble of some kind, that trouble may have had nothing to do with the female phantom, for the simple reason that hauntings are often complex, the same house harbouring phenomena that are, apparently, quite independent of one another. St. Swithin's Lane is very old; and besides, close to it is Watling Street, which is the oldest thoroughfare in London, being part of the Roman Road leading from Dover to London and thence on to South Wales. It is more than likely, therefore, that many tragedies have taken place in this locality in ages past, and the ghostly sounds heard at No. 15 St. Swithin's Lane may have originated in one or other of these tragedies that were enacted probably on, or close to, the site of the house, and they may or may not have been connected with the phantasms, respectively, of the old lady and the man on the stairs. Also, there may well have been some ghastly crime committed in those cavernous cellars in the house in St. Swithin's Lane, which time has failed to bring to light, and which will henceforth, now that the building has been demolished, remain in obscurity for ever.

A ghost that created a very widespread sensation at the time is associated with Chick Lane, afterwards known as West Street.

Chick Lane came into great notoriety in or about the year 1758 through the murder of Anne Naylor, an apprentice of Mrs. Sarah Metyard, a milliner in Bruton Street, Hanover Square. Mrs. Metyard, assisted by her daughter, Sarah Morgan Metyard, a very pretty, delicate-looking girl, and five young apprentices, had a flourishing business, her clientèle being ladies living in the locality.

Anne Naylor, being of a sickly constitution, was not able to do so much as the other girls, and she, therefore, incurred the animosity of Mrs. Metyard and her daughter. Not content with scolding and half-starving her, they constantly beat and pinched her. Indeed, so cruelly did they treat her that, in despair, she one day ran out of the house, and would have succeeded in getting away had not a milkman, be it to his eternal discredit, stopped her and handed her over to Sarah Morgan, who was pursuing her, and who, having thus captured her, dragged her back to the shop, and subsequently locked her in a garret. There she was kept for several weeks, her daily food consisting, merely, of a small piece of dry bread and a glass of water.

Seeing an opportunity she again tried to run away, but was caught in the act by her young mistress, who took hold of her by the neck, dragged her, screaming, upstairs and flung her into the same garret. The old woman, now, announcing that she must be taught a lesson, threw her on to the bed and held her down, while Sarah Morgan, after pinching and pummelling her all over, beat her unmercifully with a hearth brush. This done, they put her in a back room, and fixing a cord round her waist, they tied her hands behind her, and fastened her to the handle of the door, so as to prevent her sitting or lying down; and in order that her fellow-apprentices might be intimidated, they were ordered to work in the adjoining apartment, with strict injunctions not to afford Anne any relief.

Thus tied up, and without food of any kind, the unfortunate Anne Naylor remained for two or three days and nights. She was then liberated and told to go to bed in the garret. So great was her exhaustion that she could only just crawl to it.

The following day she was too feeble to speak, and Sarah Morgan, after pinching, kicking and slapping her, tied her again to the door. In this position she eventually died.

The other apprentices noticing that she did not move told Sarah Morgan, who said, " If she does not move soon, I'll make her." She then took off one of her shoes, and with its high heel beat Anne Naylor ferociously on the head. This treatment failing, as also did vindictive pinches and slaps, she grew alarmed and called her mother. Mrs. Metyard, realizing that Anne was dead, freed her body from the cords that were supporting it, and telling her daughter to assist her, they carried the corpse between them to the garret. They then pretended that Anne had had a fit, but had recovered and was locked in the garret, lest she should run away.

To give colour to this story, they made a great show of taking a tray with a plate of meat on it to the garret, for Anne's dinner.

As, however, they could not keep up this subterfuge indefinitely, they put Anne's body in a box, and leaving the door of the garret and the street door open, they told the other apprentices Anne had run away.

Anne's sister, who was one of the apprentices, seeing Anne's shoes and her various articles of clothing in the garret, became suspicious and informed a lodger in the house that she believed Anne was dead.

Whether the lodger told the Metyards what the girl said is not clear, but, at any rate, they got to know of it somehow, and seizing Anne's hapless sister, when the other apprentices were not present, they dragged her to some remote part of the house, and barbarously murdered her. How, is not known for certain, nor was it ever definitely ascertained what they did with the body. Anne's body they kept in the house till the stench became unbearable; then they cut it up. "The fire tells no tales," Mrs. Metyard exclaimed, as she threw one of Anne's hands into the flames. She had intended getting rid of the whole of the body in the same fashion, but the hand made such an unpleasant odour burning, that she decided to resort to some other device for the disposal of the rest of the remains. Finally, she and her daughter conveyed them to Chick Lane, a locality notorious as a haunt for bad characters of all kinds, where it was their intention to throw them into the gulley-hole, a kind of common sewer there, but being, for some reason, unable to accomplish this, they very foolishly left them in the mud and water that had collected, forming a shallow pool before the sewer gate.

Here they were found at midnight by the watchman, who told the night constable, who, in his turn, informed one of the Overseers of the Parish. The last named at once had the remains collected and taken to the watch-house, where they were examined by Mr. Umfreville, coroner for the district. He considered they were merely parts of a corpse taken from some churchyard, for the purpose of anatomy, and declined to summon a jury. And there, for the time being, the affair ended.

It was only by pure accident the truth concerning the remains ever came to light. For some time after the finding of them in Chick Lane, reports that the place was haunted by a white-robed figure got in circulation. People passing through the lane at night declared they saw a figure in white gliding mysteriously to and fro, near the gulley-hole, and the ill-reputation of the spot, consequently, increased very considerably.

The house in Bruton Street, where the murders had taken place, also got the reputation for being haunted, a similar figure being seen there.

Two years after the murders, and while these uncanny happenings were said to be taking place, a Mr. Rooker came to lodge with the Metyards, and had frequent opportunities for observing how badly Mrs. Metyard now treated Sarah Morgan. Had the latter been an unattractive girl, probably he would not have interfered, but as she was quite remarkably pretty, he persuaded her to accompany him, nominally as his servant, to a house he took in Hill Street. Mrs. Metyard, who was furious at Sarah Morgan leaving her, went to Mr. Rooker's house daily, and was so abusive both to him and her daughter that, hoping to be rid of her, Mr. Rooker moved to a little estate, bequeathed to him by a relative, at Ealing. Sarah Morgan accompanied him again, no longer, however, even nominally his servant, but his mistress, in which capacity there is little doubt she had been for some time. Dressed in very smart clothes, with a profusion of jewellery, Sarah Morgan, probably, had few equals, as regards appearance, either in Ealing or London, and all might have gone well, for some time at least, had it not been for her mother. This woman, who appears to have been remarkably well preserved and active, despite her years—she is generally described as old [1]—finding out where Sarah Morgan was living, went to Ealing and behaved in the same outrageous fashion as she had done in Hill Street.

On the 9th of June, 1768, being admitted into the house, she beat Sarah Morgan in a terrible manner, and during the struggle that ensued, many expressions were uttered by both women that caused Mr. Rooker great uneasiness. Mrs. Metyard called him "an old perfumed tea-dog," whereupon Sarah Morgan retorted by saying, "Remember, mother, you are the perfumer; you are the Chick Lane Ghost."

This reference to a haunting which many connected with the discovery of the unidentified remains near the gulley-hole, aroused Mr. Rooker's suspicions, and after Mrs. Metyard had gone, he asked Sarah Morgan to explain what she meant.

She hesitated, and it was not until he continually pressed her that she eventually burst into tears and confessed her participation in the murders of the two apprentices, begging him never to divulge a secret that so materially affected both her mother and herself. Mr. Rooker, imagining that Sarah Morgan had only performed her share in the crimes under compulsion and by the direction of her mother, and that, in consequence, she was not amenable to the law, acquainted the Overseers of the Parish of Tottenham with what Sarah Morgan had told him. As a result, Mrs. Metyard was arrested, and the evidence against her being conclusive, she was finally committed for trial. Some circumstances, however, coming out that helped to

[1] *Chronicles of Crime*. Edited by Camden Pelham. Illustrated by "Phiz."

incriminate Sarah Morgan as well, she also was arrested and with her mother conveyed to Newgate, to await her final trial.

When arraigned upon the indictment of wilful murder preferred against them at the Old Bailey Sessions, the two Metyards bitterly upbraided one another with the part each had taken in the murder, and if any evidence of their guilt had been lacking, what they said on this occasion would have been enough to secure their conviction.

They were found guilty and sentenced to be hanged. Sarah Morgan Metyard at once pleaded pregnancy, but a jury of matrons pronouncing this to be false, her execution was not deferred.

Mother and daughter were executed together at Tyburn on the 19th of July, 1768. Mrs. Metyard utterly collapsed on the way to Tyburn, and had to be carried from the cart to the scaffold. All efforts to restore her to consciousness failing, she was launched to eternity, while in a state of insensibility.

Sarah Morgan was in almost the same plight, but more sympathy was expressed for her, no doubt on account of her personal charm, which, as I have said, was very great. Many wondered how so fragile and absolutely lovely a girl could have behaved with such terrible cruelty to members of her own sex, mere children, too.

Both her body and that of Mrs. Metyard were afterwards dissected at Surgeons' Hall. Their execution, however, did not diminish, in any measure, the ill-reputation of Chick Lane, which still continued to be a place of dread after dusk, on account of the alleged ghostly happenings near the gulley-hole.

The house in Bruton Street, too, where the murders actually occurred, was for many years reputed to be haunted, and weird happenings are even now said to occur periodically in a certain building in this same thoroughfare, but whether or no it is the one formerly inhabited by the Metyards is not known for certain.

CHAPTER X

BIRD HAUNTINGS AND BLACKHEATH GHOSTS

More than one house in London has, at one time or another, been reported haunted by a phantom bird; but no bird ghost I have heard of combines such a blending of the material and immaterial, the real and the unreal, as that described by Mr. H. Spicer.[1] His story is as follows:

One night, during the early part of last century, Captain Morgan and a friend, arriving in London *en route* for the Continent, very late, looked for rooms and found some in a large eighteenth-century apartment house. In the centre of the Captain's room stood a huge four-poster bed, furnished with hangings of a sumptuous but somewhat heavy material. It suggested " the solid respectability and comfort " associated with one's ideas of the wealthy citizens of the time of Queen Anne and the first George.

The Captain, being tired, lost no time in getting into bed, and was speedily asleep. He was soon, however, awakened by a noise like the flapping of wings, and a sensation of extreme coldness. He sat up and saw, just in front of him, "an immense black bird, with outstretched wings, and red eyes flashing as if with fire." It made vicious pecks at him, which he had great difficulty in parrying. Snatching up a pillow he hit at it, but it always got out of his way,

---
[1] See *Strange Things Among Us*, by H. Spicer.

and he never once succeeded in touching it. After thus battling with it ineffectually for several minutes, he grew irritated, and jumping out of bed made a dash at it. The bird backed, still flapping and pecking, into one corner of the room, where it settled on the embroidered seat of a sofa. The moonlight shining full into the room enabled Captain Morgan to see it very distinctly, and it appeared to him to be very frightened. Thinking now that it could be easily caught, the Captain moved stealthily towards it, and then made a sudden grab at it. To his amazement, however, his fingers, instead of closing on anything material, merely clutched air. The bird had abruptly and inexplicably vanished.

He lit a lamp and searched everywhere for it, but not a trace of it could he discover. The next night, without making any allusion to what had happened, he asked his friend to change rooms with him, inventing some excuse for so doing. His friend good-naturedly complied, but came down to breakfast the following morning with a weary expression on his face. He said " he had had to contend for possession of the chamber with the most extraordinary and perplexing object he had ever encountered, to all appearance a huge blackbird, which constantly eluded his grasp, and ultimately disappeared, leaving no clue to its mode of exit." This mystery was never explained.

Mr. B., an eminent counsel known to Mr. Spicer, had a peculiar habit of suddenly twitching or tossing his head. Everyone commented on it, but few were aware of the reason. It was this: Every now and then, Mr. B. was conscious of a raven sitting on his left shoulder.

When I was giving a " talk " at St. Ives, some years

ago, a lady in the audience told of a somewhat similar instance in a West End shop.

A gentleman and lady were visiting the shop one day, when they saw, to their astonishment, one of the lady superintendents parading about with a speckled bird, belonging to a species they did not recognize, on her shoulder. Going up to her, the lady said, " Whatever kind of a bird is this on your shoulder ? " whereupon the superintendent turned ghastly white and fainted.

It subsequently transpired that whenever a member of the superintendent's family was about to die, a strange-looking bird would be seen hovering near the doomed individual.

This instance proved no exception to the rule, for the superintendent, although in apparently perfect health at the time, developed ptomaine poisoning the next day, and died within a week.

A well-known case of bird haunting that excited much attention at the time occurred at the Church of West Drayton, near Uxbridge.[1] About 1749 a rumour got into circulation that the three large vaults under West Drayton Church were haunted. In one the family of Paget were interred, and in the other the even more ancient family of De Burgh. People passing by the church at night, more especially on a Friday night, declared that they heard knockings coming from the vaults. No very satisfactory explanation of them was ever given, but as, so it was said, the remains of a murderer, who had committed suicide, and the remains of his victim were buried together in one of the vaults, many believed that the knockings

[1] See *Glimpses in the Twilight*, by the Rev. F. G. Lee, D.D.

were thus accounted for; the supposition being, of course, that the spirits of the murderer and murdered could not agree, *i.e.* were unwilling that their bodies should lie side by side, and were demonstrating in consequence.

Others, however, had a different tale to tell. They said that one night some people living close to the church heard dreadful screams coming from it. Consequently, they hurried off to ascertain the cause, and finding, on their arrival at the church, that the screams proceeded from one of the vaults, they peered into it through the ventilation grating. They then saw, just inside the vault, an enormous raven that pecked at them furiously, and all the while it did so the screaming continued.

This story of the raven was confirmed by other people, including the wife of the Parish Clerk and her daughter, who testified to seeing it in the church itself.

One evening, a youth went to the local bell-ringers, who had emphatically denied that the bird was a phantom at all, and told them that it was flying about in the chancel; whereupon four of them, taking sticks and a lantern, ran to the church to try to catch it. On reaching the church they saw the bird, which was just as the youth described it, an enormous black bird, and it was fluttering about the chancel. They at once gave chase, and on one of the men striking it with a stick, it fell down screaming, apparently badly hurt. Believing that it was at last cornered, the man who had struck it was about to pick it up, when, to the amazement of them all, it was found that the bird had vanished.

After that it was often to be seen either perched on the communion rails of the sanctuary, or flying about in one or other of the vaults. Whenever, however, anyone attempted to catch it, it always mysteriously disappeared.

The villagers, especially those who, so to say, belonged to the place, firmly believed the tradition accounting for the bird, *i.e.* that it was " the restless and miserable spirit of a murderer who had committed suicide and who, through family influence, instead of being put into a pit or hole, with a stake through his body, at the cross-road by Harmondsworth, as was the sentence by law, had been buried in consecrated ground, on the north side of the churchyard."

Mrs. de Burgh, wife of Mr. R. L. de Burgh, a former Vicar of West Drayton, informed Dr. Lee, in 1883, that, some years previously, she had often heard sounds in Drayton Church like the fluttering of some very large bird, and that these strange sounds always appeared to come from the chancel; and, as late as 1869, two ladies, going into the church one Saturday afternoon, to put some flowers on the communion-table, saw a huge black bird sitting on one of the pews. The haunting would thus seem to be confirmed. Whether it still continues I am unable to ascertain.

Ealing, to my knowledge, possesses several houses reputed to be haunted, one, at least, by a thoroughly up-to-date ghost. In a house, not far from the Broadway, a lady who spent most of her evenings at London night clubs, dancing, recently died. The night after her funeral, sounds of syncopated music and dancing were heard proceeding from the room in which she breathed her last, and these sounds are rumoured to have been heard there, periodically, ever since.

Ghostly music apparently does not affect all animals in the same way, for whereas this lady's cat—a large tabby—always runs upstairs directly the sounds commence and sits on the door-mat outside the room, apparently listening, with the greatest eagerness, to the music and dancing, a dog in the same house at once begins to bark and howl and manifest symptoms of terror and aversion.

Another house in Ealing is said to be haunted by a very beautiful hand, obviously that of a woman, for the fingers are long and tapering and the nails almond-shaped and highly manicured. It emerges from a wall in a certain room, but as its appearance is invariably the forerunner of a death in the family occupying the house, it is a very much dreaded phenomenon, and, consequently, very, very rarely mentioned.

In Ealing, as in many other suburbs of London, are the sites of several old cross-roads, where formerly suicides were buried and murderers hanged, and it is not at all unlikely that some of the present-day hauntings in Ealing houses may owe their origin to this fact.

One very well known case of haunted cross-roads near old Ealing village is narrated by Mr. Spicer.[1] According to him, not many years prior to his narration of the story, a very beautiful girl, daughter of a farmer, lived with her parents in the village of Ealing near London. She was engaged to a young man, also a farmer, but finding out something about him that convinced her he would not make her a good husband, she broke off her engagement to him, just before the

[1] See *Strange Things Among Us.*

date fixed for their marriage. Soon after this she disappeared, and, despite vigorous searching by the police and her friends, not a trace of her could be found.

Two or three years later, Mr. M——, who had known the missing girl, was returning home to Ealing one night from a party. When he came to the cross-roads, close to the village, he suddenly saw a girl walking in front of him. As she was distinctly attractive, being tall, slender, and prettily dressed, he determined to overtake her, which he did, and, I am bound to relate, shocking though it be, was about to put his arm round her waist, when she turned round and looked at him, reproachfully. He then saw, to his amazement, that she was the missing girl. Hardly, however, had he recognized her, before she abruptly and unaccountably vanished. Horrified beyond measure, he ran the rest of the way home and told his parents what had happened. The latter, feeling certain then that the girl had met with foul play, made a thorough search in the immediate vicinity of the cross-roads, and ultimately found her remains. She had, undoubtedly, been murdered. Suspicion attaching itself to the young farmer, he was eventually arrested and charged with the crime. What subsequently happened to him Mr. Spicer does not say. Possibly the haunting continued, as hauntings so often do, even after the murderer has been caught and duly punished; and houses built on the site of those cross-roads may still be subjected, at times, to visitations by the phantoms of that pretty murdered girl and her cruel, worthless assassin.

Like Ealing, Blackheath can point to several houses

and places that are said to be haunted. With regard to the latter, Shooter's Hill had a reputation second to none, not only for ghosts, but for all manner of unsavoury happenings. For many years it was the happy hunting-ground of highwaymen, footpads and undesirables of all kinds, and therefore it has figured in the writings of various authors, notably in those of Pepys, Philipott, and, at a later date, Dickens.

"Shooter's Hill was so called," Philipott[1] informs us, "for the thieving there practised, where travellers in early times were so infested with depredations and bloody mischiefs, that order was taken in the sixth year of Richard II for the enlarging of the highway, according to the statute made in the time of King Edward I, so that they venture still to rob here by prescription." In spite of the efforts made in Richard II's time to improve the highway over the hill, and, according to Hasted, the making, at some distance from the old road, in 1733, of a new one "of easier ascent and of great width," the spot still continued to retain its evil character.

Pepys, writing of it in his *Diary*, tells us what it was like in his time. Under the date of 11th April, 1661, he says, describing his journey from Dartford to London, "Mrs. Annie and I rode under the man that hangs from Shooter's Hill, and a filthy sight it was to see how his flesh is shrunk on his bones." In those days, and for long afterwards, it was the custom to hang criminals on the gibbets that were to be seen at intervals on Shooter's Hill; and it was, alas, in those days, a rare thing to see a gibbet upon which no criminal was hanging.

[1] See *Survey of Kent* (published 1659).

BLACKHEATH GHOSTS

According to Dickens,[1] even at the end of the eighteenth century, Shooter's Hill was still the occasional haunt of gentlemen of the road, and much dreaded by travellers on that account.

Later, after these pests ceased to frequent the highroads, Shooter's Hill and the adjoining locality became the scene of many a grim and mysterious tragedy, which affords still another example of the theory I have already propounded that certain localities have a something about them that may be physical or superphysical, or a blending of both, which attracts people of a peculiar temperament and impels them to commit acts of violence and crime.

In January, 1844, the skeleton of a woman was unearthed by a labourer thirty yards from the highroad leading to Shooter's Hill.[2] A terrible fracture on the back of the skull clearly indicated that the woman had met with foul play, and that she had not been dead very long was suggested by the fact that much beautifully-braided golden hair was still adhering to the skull. The beautifully-braided hair, however, proved no clue to her identity, and as, apparently, there was no clue to it, the remains were properly interred, and the mystery relating to her soon forgotten. Prior to the finding of the remains, it was said that people passing by the spot where they were found, at night, had heard unaccountable noises and occasionally had seen the phantom of a woman in a white dress, gliding about the ground. She was always spoken of as the White Lady, and when I was resident in St. John's Park, Blackheath, in 1898, I met

[1] See *A Tale of Two Cities.*
[2] *Annual Register,* 1844.

several people who remembered hearing about the appearances of this ghost.

One of these people was a Mr. Johnson, a man of independent means, then living or staying in Lewisham. When a boy, he told me, he remembered the following incident being frequently narrated by his father, usually when they had friends. To be brief, Mr. Johnson, Senior, on his way home one night, was descending Shooter's Hill, which at that time was still a very lonely and deserted locality after dusk, when he heard a cry, expressive of such awful terror and despair that he at once came to a halt. While he stood still listening, it was repeated, and it seemed to come from a spot close at hand. He called out, but there was no reply, only a death-like silence. Then, after an interval of a minute or so, the cry was repeated, and a woman, in a white dress, rose from the ground, some little way ahead of him. The moonlight being, so it seemed, focussed on her, he was able to see her very distinctly, and thinking she was ill and wanted assistance, he ran towards her. To his intense surprise, however, when he was within a few yards of her, she vanished. There was absolutely nothing in sight to afford cover, so that she could not possibly have hidden, and there was no hole in the ground into which she could have dropped. Mr. Johnson, greatly wondering, resumed his journey, but had not proceeded many paces when he heard the same cry again, this time very close to him. Although by no means a timid man, he was now thoroughly frightened, being convinced that what he had heard and seen was nothing earthly, and fearing that, if he delayed, he might see it again, he ran the rest of the way home.

BLACKHEATH GHOSTS

Mr. Johnson had not heard of the haunting prior to his experience, and he was, of course, vastly interested when he learned that the phantom he had seen had been seen by others, and was popularly supposed to be the ghost of the girl with the golden hair, whose remains had been unearthed there only a short time previously. He never, his son added, passed the place again at night-time, alone.

About twenty-seven years later, the neighbourhood of Shooter's Hill once again came into very unpleasant notoriety. The district of Kidbrooke, which lies immediately between Blackheath and Shooter's Hill, was then far more thinly populated than it is now, and one of the loneliest thoroughfares in it was Kidbrooke Lane.

At twenty to seven p.m. on 25th April, 1871, a pretty servant-maid named Jane Maria Clousen said a laughing good-bye to a girl friend in Kidbrooke, and was never seen by her again, alive. Some hours later, she was found in Kidbrooke Lane, unconscious, having obviously been struck on the head with a hammer that was lying by her side. She died shortly afterwards, without regaining consciousness. The suspicion of the police falling at once on a young man named Pook, whose father had formerly employed Jane Clousen as servant, they arrested him.

A Mr. Lazell declared, on oath, that he saw Pook in Jane's company at ten to seven p.m. on the evening of the murder, close to the spot where she was afterwards found. Dr. Letherby, who examined Pook's clothes, testified to there being blood on his trousers, and the police produced evidence to show that Pook bought a hammer, shortly before the murder, at the shop of a Mr. Thomas. All of which testimony seemed, to many minds, convincing; but as Pook was able to produce an alibi to show he could not have been in Kidbrooke Lane at the time the murder was believed to have taken place, he was acquitted; and no one else being arrested, the crime was consigned to the category of unsolved mysteries.

In certain respects it resembled that of 1844. In each case the victim was a girl; the skulls of both were battered in, and the spots, respectively, where the bodies were found were very lonely. They were not far apart, and each acquired the reputation for being haunted. As in the case of Shooter's Hill, Kidbrooke Lane, subsequent to the murder, was said to be haunted nightly by cries, and groans, and the apparition of the murdered girl. Such stories, indeed, got into circulation that the lane, for some long time, was shunned by nearly everyone after dark.

The crime was recalled in August, 1898, when Mrs. Tylor, a lone widow, was likewise battered to death in her house in Kidbrooke Park Road. As in the other two cases, no one was convicted of this crime, and consequently it remains a mystery.

These three murders, all taking place in the same neighbourhood and committed in very much the same manner, support my theory that in certain localities there may be an influence or power that impels certain people, more often the very young, to crime.

CHAPTER XI

SPRING-HEELED JACK AND THE BROMPTON ROAD

PERIODICALLY there crops up in various parts of the country a mysterious being known as Spring-heeled Jack. Sometimes this being has been proved to be a human, someone dressed up, either simply to frighten people by jumping over walls and hedges, a feat he was able to accomplish by the aid of very strong springs attached to the soles of his boots; or, else, to rob and injure as well as to frighten them; whilst, at other times, the identity and nature of the being have remained a profound mystery, many believing him to be superphysical.

Apparently, there is no authentic record of a Spring-heeled Jack prior to February, 1838, when a Spring-heeled Jack appeared in Bow and Old Ford, causing a great scare and frequent complaints to be made to the police and magistrates. Mr. Alsop, residing in Bearhind Lane, a lonely spot between Bow and Old Ford, and three of his daughters, made depositions,[1] with regard to him, before the Lambeth magistrates.

Miss Jane Alsop, one of the daughters, said that at a quarter to nine one night there was a violent ringing at the front door. On going to the door she saw a man in a long cloak standing on the threshold. He told her he was a policeman, and added: " For God's sake, bring me a light, for we have caught Spring-

[1] See *Annual Register*, February, 1838.

heeled Jack in the lane." Greatly excited, she ran and fetched a lighted candle and handed it to the man. The moment she did so, he threw aside the cloak that had concealed both his face and figure and fully revealed himself. What she saw petrified her. He was wearing a kind of helmet and tight-fitting white costume like an ulster. His face was hideous, his eyes resembled balls of fire, his hands had great claws, and he vomited blue and white flames. Without uttering a word he darted at her, and catching hold of her by the back of her neck he thrust her head under his arm. He then commenced tearing her dress with his claws, which seemed to her to be made of some metallic substance. She screamed and got away from him, but he ran after her, and catching hold of her again tore her neck, and arms, and hair. Fortunately, one of her sisters, hearing her screams, came running to her rescue. Her assailant then let go of her and bounded away into the darkness of the night. This story was confirmed by her rescuer, and also by Mr. Alsop. Miss Jane Alsop suffered severely from shock and from scratches on her arms and shoulders, which took a long time healing.

At Lambeth again, before the same magistrates, Mr. Scales, a highly respectable butcher of Narrow Street, Limehouse, and his sister, a girl of eighteen years of age, also made depositions. Miss Scales said that at half-past eight one evening she and her sister were returning home from a visit to their brother. While passing along Green Dragon Alley, a very lonely spot, they saw a tall figure, enveloped from head to foot in a dark cloak. He leaped towards Miss Scales, spurted blue flames from his mouth in her face, blinding her.

She fell to the ground in her terror, and there is no knowing what might have happened had not Mr. Scales, who was luckily near at hand, heard the screams of his sister, and ran to the rescue, whereupon the being in the cloak bounded away. Miss Scales was too overcome with shock to raise herself from the ground; she had to be helped up and assisted home, and for several days afterwards she was subject to violent fits. This story was corroborated by witness's brother and sister, who likewise made depositions on oath. They were able to give further details regarding the mysterious being's appearance. They stated that he was tall, thin and gentlemanly, and carried in front of him what appeared to be a small lamp or bull's eye.

The police took the matter up at once, but despite the vigorous efforts made by them to catch this Spring-heeled Jack, he invariably eluded them, and thus the mystery of his identity was never solved.

Seven years later there was a Spring-heeled Jack scare in Ealing and Hanwell. Women and children going along lonely roads at night were frightened almost out of their senses, upon seeing a figure, clad in a white gown and dark shawl, bounding over walls and hedges, and at the same time emitting dismal groans and shrieks. The local police were appealed to, with the result that this Spring-heeled Jack was soon caught. He was a Brentford butcher, named Richard Bradford, who had a mania for practical joking; however, as none of the people he had frightened appeared against him when he was brought before the Brentford magistrates, he was discharged, with a warning.

All through the fifties and sixties Spring-heeled Jack scares continued, at varying intervals and in various parts of the country, and sometimes they were proved to be due to some practical joker, as in the case of Richard Bradford; but more often the identity of Jack remained a mystery, so complete that many were of the opinion he was either some evil spirit or the devil himself.

In the seventies there were innumerable scares, some in the more remote districts of London, and some in the provinces.

Probably the biggest scare was at Aldershot, where Jack used to take a special delight in terrifying night sentries by leaping across the ground in front of them, or springing on the sentry-box when they were inside it and slapping their faces with an icy hand. Sometimes he was fired at, but whether the sentries in their terror were too unsteady to take proper aim at him or not, their shots never seemed to affect him any way. The authorities professed to think Jack was some practical joker, and laid all sorts of traps to catch him, but in this they failed, and his identity was never proved.

In October and November of the same year either the same or another Spring-heeled Jack caused a panic in the neighbourhood of Newport in Lincolnshire. This time Jack appeared in something like a sheep-skin, with a tail and prick-shaped ears. His feats were truly astonishing.[1] When pursued by a mob armed with sticks and stones, he leaped on to the roofs of cottages, ran over house-tops and jumped walls fifteen feet high. Always when on the point of being

[1] See *Illustrated Police News*, November 3, 1877.

SPRING-HEELED JACK

cornered he disappeared, to appear again soon afterwards in another part of the neighbourhood. As he was jumping on to the Newport Arch, an ancient Roman building, supposed to have been erected during the first century A.D., he was shot at by a man with a gun, with no apparent effect. A few minutes later he was fired at by someone else, with the same result; and in the end he bounded away, disappearing amid the gloom of the trees and hedges. Who or what he was was never known. Since then, so far as I have been able to ascertain, there have been no more Spring-heeled Jack scares.

A ghost that in appearance and certain of its ways resembled, in some measure, some of the Spring-heeled Jacks, was the cause of two very sad tragedies in Hammersmith.[1] In January, 1804, the inhabitants of this locality were scared at night by a tall figure in white, which used to spring out on them from behind trees and walls. It was usually to be encountered, after dusk, in very secluded spots, such as certain out-of-the-way lanes and fields and deserted brick-yards.

On one occasion, a woman was passing near Hammersmith Churchyard, about ten o'clock one moonlight night, when she saw a figure suddenly rise from behind a tombstone. It was very tall, and appeared to be clad in a winding sheet. Terrified beyond measure she attempted to run. Whereupon the ghostly being ran after her and, overtaking her, seized her in its long arms. She then fainted, and was discovered some hours later, still in an unconscious state, by some neighbours, who kindly assisted her

[1] See *The New Newgate Calendar*. Edited by Camden Pelham.

home. The shock to her system was so great—she was shortly expecting to be a mother—that she died two days later.

Not long after this tragedy, entirely owing to the ghost, an even more fatal one was narrowly avoided. The ghost, it seems, jumped out from behind a tree on to a wagon, drawn by eight horses and carrying, in addition to the driver, a man in the employ of Mr. Russel of Hammersmith, sixteen passengers. The driver was so scared that he leaped off his seat and ran away screaming, leaving the horses and passengers to look after themselves. Fortunately, the horses were soon pacified, and no accident occurred.

Accounts of these happenings spreading through the district, a downright panic ensued, no woman or child daring to venture out in the lanes or fields around Hammersmith after dusk.[1] While some believed the ghost was just a practical joker, others maintained it was the spirit of a man who had cut his throat in Hammersmith about a year previously. Parties of men who held the former view scoured the neighbourhood at night, to try and catch the supposed trickster. In this, however, they failed. There were many lonely spots around Hammersmith in those days, and when they were searching in one part for the ghost, it invariably turned up in another, frightening some poor rustic almost to death.

Among those who were bent on running the ghost to earth was a young man named Francis Smith. All along he had felt certain it was some heartless fellow belonging to the locality, who had dressed up, to frighten the poor simple country people, and he

[1] See *History of Hammersmith*, by Faulkner.

SPRING-HEELED JACK

determined to make an example of him. Armed with a gun he betook himself to Black Lion Lane, one of the spots where the ghost had recently been seen, and concealed himself there.

By and by he heard footsteps coming along the lane towards his hiding place. Peeping out, he espied a figure in white, and believing it to be the ghost he called out: " Damn you, who are you? I'll shoot you, if you don't speak." There being no reply, and the figure still advancing, Francis Smith fired.

To his horror the figure instantly fell to the ground groaning. Realizing he had actually shot a man, Smith rushed off for assistance. It was of no avail, however, for by the time a doctor arrived the man was dead. He proved to be Thomas Milwood, a bricklayer, who was returning home from work rather later than usual that night, and was wearing a new white linen jacket, the usual habiliment of his vocation.

Smith gave himself up to the authorities at once. His trial took place at the Old Bailey before Lord Chief Baron, Mr. Justice Rooke and Mr. Justice Lawrence. The defence set up was that no bad design actuated the accused in his attack upon the supposed spirit, and many witnesses were called, who proved the alarm which had been occasioned by the visits of a supposed preternatural being.

The Lord Chief Baron and Mr. Justice Lawrence expressed it as their opinion that the case proven amounted to murder; and that if a man killed another by design, without authority, but from a supposition that he ought to be killed, the offence amounted to murder. The jury attempted to bring in a verdict of manslaughter only, but the opinion of the learned judge being repeated, they returned a general verdict of guilty, and recommended the prisoner to mercy.

The Recorder, thereupon, passed sentence of death on the prisoner in the usual form; which was that he should be executed on the following Monday and his body given to the surgeons to be dissected.

The Lord Chief Baron then informed the jury that he would immediately report the case to the King, and he did so with such promptness that before seven o'clock that evening a respite during His Majesty's pleasure was sent to the Old Bailey. A few days later the prisoner received a pardon, conditionally that he was imprisoned for one year.

The case created enormous interest, the court and its environs being crowded during the trial, and news of the respite was received with great applause.

The haunting ceased after the death of Milwood, but the identity of the ghost was never established. Some were still of the opinion it was merely a bogus ghost, a local hoaxster dressed to impersonate a ghost, while others were equally positive it was a *bona-fide* phantom, the earth-bound spirit of the aforesaid suicide.

Various houses in the Brompton Road have been from time to time, by repute, haunted.[1] In 1865 crowds went nightly to that road and stood outside a certain house there, in order to try to see and hear the alleged ghostly phenomena; and, as a result, there was much disorderly conduct, which led to several people appearing in the police court.

Six years later some sensation was caused by stories of ghostly happenings in a house in the West Bromp-

[1] See *News of the World*, October, 1865.

ton Road. The tenants and servants in the house were disturbed, they said, not only by mysterious footsteps, knockings, and the ringing of bells in the night, but by a figure, enveloped in grey drapery, that used to appear in all parts of the premises. Its hands were usually clasped in front of it, and it gave all who saw it the impression that it was altogether good and in no degree evil. There was no hair on its face, but from its unusual height it was deemed to be a man. Like so many ghosts, it was shadowy and unsubstantial, and never seen save in the dark. It was discernible, owing to a luminous glow, which seemed to emanate from all over it. It never moved its head or hands, or spoke, or made any noise, excepting on one occasion, when, seemingly, it let a parcel it held fall to the ground with a thud. It moved with a gliding motion and, when stationary, gazed at people fixedly. Again, like so many ghostly figures, it usually vanished abruptly.

Beyond the nocturnal perambulations of this inoffensive apparition and the noises enumerated, nothing else of an abnormal nature appears to have happened in this house. The family alluded to here took it in 1870 and left it in 1877, moving to another house in the same neighbourhood, where, strange to say, the same phenomena occurred. But, in addition to seeing in their new quarters the same tall, shadowy figure in grey and hearing the same noises, they also experienced other phenomena, usually auditory, and much more disturbing and pronounced than those they had experienced in their former abode. Doors were now heard banging at night where no doors existed or where doors were closed; and sounds like metal trays being dashed down periodically awoke and startled everyone. Also, they heard, in certain of the rooms, noises like furniture being moved about; constant tramping up and down the stairs and about the passages, windows being opened and slammed to; loud sighing and heavy breathing; and, on one occasion, at least, a sound like a match being struck.

Christmas Day saw no immunity from the disturbances; the same figure was seen by one of the daughters of the family in the morning, standing on the staircase, and later on in the day at the foot of her bed.

After hearing some of the manifestations, one of the children, a boy, who was ill at the time, became very much worse through fright. He died two or three weeks later, and for some days prior to his death the noises were very pronounced.

The noises and the figure scared one of the other children and a housemaid very badly, too, but the generality of those who experienced the phenomena do not appear to have been in any degree adversely affected by them.

There was nothing in the history of the house, at least as far as could be ascertained, to account for the phenomena, nor could anyone discover, in either of the houses, any satisfactory explanation of the phenomena on physical grounds.

This case is strictly authentic, my authority for it being unimpeachable; and it is interesting inasmuch as it furnishes a very typical example of the really orthodox haunted house. In all such cases—and they form the majority by far—the phenomena appear to be without rhyme or reason, and as to the nature of them, beyond the fact that it is apparently superphysical, nothing can be said with any degree of finality. Indeed, superphysical phenomena are still mysteries, as purely enigmatical as life and death.

CHAPTER XII

THE HAYMARKET THEATRE, HAM HOUSE AND CRANFORD HOUSE

ONLY a year or two ago, it was reported in the Press that a certain London theatre was haunted. I cannot say which theatre it was, because I have forgotten, but interest in this reputed haunting soon fizzled out, for the simple reason that the ghost proved to be no ghost at all, but something decidedly material.

For all that, one or two of the London theatres are known to be genuinely haunted. Who has not heard, for example, of the Haymarket Theatre ghost, supposed to be Buckstone's? Rumour asserts that the phantom of this erstwhile popular lessee, who succeeded as manager, in 1853, Mr. Benjamin Webster, has often been seen in one of the boxes and other parts of the building, and I have it on good authority that the door of a certain room in the theatre not infrequently opens and shuts of its own accord, that is to say, in a most inexplicable manner.[1]

Drury Lane, also, was said at one time to be haunted, but whether a ghost has been seen there very recently or not, I cannot say.[2] Managements are not particularly communicative on the subjects of alleged hauntings—in their own theatres. Neither are the authorities who run lunatic asylums. One at least of these institutions in London is known to be haunted.

[1] See *Evening News*, January 31, 1917.   [2] See Addendum.

When there is no material inmate of its padded cell, sounds are heard proceeding from it, suggestive of "something" there trying to batter itself to death against the walls.

To revert again to the stage, a distant relative and friend of mine, the late Mr Edward Silward, who will be remembered for his extraordinary clever impersonation of a gorilla, a few years ago, at the Oxford Music Hall, once told me a remarkable experience of his on Wimbledon Common. He was crossing it, alone, one night, when suddenly a man in convict's clothes crossed the ground immediately in front of him and unaccountably vanished. Later on the same night, in exactly the same place, an actor friend of his had precisely the same experience. A man in convict's clothes suddenly appeared in front of him, and with equal suddenness inexplicably vanished. "This was the only time I ever saw what I believe to have been a ghost," Mr Silwood informed me.

I have been accompanied on several of my visits to haunted houses by actors, but as I have fully described these occasions elsewhere, I will not further allude to them here. I will merely add that I have found actors and actresses to be more interested in things superphysical than people in most other vocations of life. I think they are on the whole more spiritual and, perhaps, more inclined to be superstitious.

It was an actor who first told me that Ham House was haunted by the ghost of the notorious Duchess of Lauderdale, and those who, like myself, know this Duchess's history, will not be surprised to learn that she is still reputed to be earth-bound.

Ham House stands on low-lying ground near the

banks of the Thames, almost opposite Teddington. It was built by Sir Thomas Vavasour in 1610. The walls of some of the rooms in it are, or were up to a few years ago, hung with tapestry and other handsome draperies, having been left nearly in the same state as when the house was inhabited by Elizabeth, Countess of Dysart, afterwards Duchess of Lauderdale. She was the eldest daughter of William Murray, first Earl of Dysart. Her parents having no son, a Royal charter was obtained to enable her to succeed to the title. In 1647 she married Sir Lionel Tollemache, Bart., and if the portrait of her painted by Van Dyck,[1] probably about this time, be a true one, she must have been, then, very lovely. Sir John Reresby evidently thought so, for writing of an interview he had with her in her later years, he remarks, " She must have been a beautiful woman, the supposed mistress of Oliver Cromwell and at that time a lady of great grace." Had she not been singularly captivating, it is scarcely likely that the following contemporary lampoon would have been composed :

" *She is Besse of my heart, she was Besse of old Noll,
She was once Fleetwood's Besse, and she's now of
   Atholl.*"

In 1651 Ham House, which had passed from the hands of Sir Thomas Vavasour into those of the Earl of Holderness, and thence into the possession of William Murray, became the residence of Sir Lionel Tollemache and his lovely lady, who was later created the Countess of Dysart in her own right. Ever since

---

[1] See *The Abbeys, Castles and Ancient Halls of England and Wales*, by John Timbs.

then it has remained in the family of the Tollemaches, Earls of Dysart.

If Sir Lionel had ever expected his fair spouse to remain faithful to him, he must have been bitterly disappointed, for they were hardly married before she became steeped in " affairs." Courtiers and gay gallants flocked around her wherever she went, and there is little doubt that she encouraged and satisfied not a few of the best favoured Her carryings-on with John Maitland, Duke of Lauderdale, were too much even for the Court of those days, and the Merry Monarch's Court, in particular, as everyone knows, took a great deal of shocking.

If Sir Lionel was not aware of her goings-on, he must have been blind, but it is highly probable he knew only too well and acquiesced, from ambitious and even, perhaps, mercenary motives. Lauderdale possessed considerable political influence, and for that reason was well worth keeping in with, even if it meant sacrificing not a little self-respect.

For a while, however, after the Restoration, there was a coolness between the Countess and the Duke, due to the Countess considering the Duke was not sufficiently grateful for the service she had once rendered him. He was, in fact, one of her oldest flames, their friendship dating back to her pre-marriage days, and she was overheard once to remark to him that she only saved him from the scaffold by submitting to the familiarities of the Protector!

According to the historian Burnet, it seems pretty certain that Cromwell took a very great fancy to her, and that she met his advances more than half-way, being only too anxious to gain a hold over one so all-powerful. In the end, his affair with her scandalized his puritanical followers to such an extent that he thought it wise to limit his visits to her and conduct them with the greatest secrecy.

To revert to her quarrel with the Duke. There seems to be good reason for believing that she soon repented of it, and determining to renew her ascendancy over him and make him more than ever her slave by marrying him, she got rid of Sir Lionel. That done, she at once made advances to the Duke, with the result the latter's wife left him, in a fury, and went to live in Paris. On her death, three years later—how she died does not appear certain, but it is not unlikely her end was as premature as that of Sir Lionel and due to the same agency—the Countess speedily became a Duchess. She and the Duke were married in 1671, and it was she who, from the very first, ruled the home. Consequently they lived in the most extravagant manner, trying to outdo Royalty in the magnificence of their entertainments. Her jewellery and costumes eclipsed in cost and splendour the jewellery and costumes of any other Court lady, and probably surpassed those of any other lady in Europe.

Only too conscious of her great beauty and her power over men, she thought she could do and say anything with impunity. She had no conscience, no shame and, at the same time, no fear. Owing to her outrageous ambition and greed, she would stick at nothing to gain her own ends; and, for this reason, as well as for her arrogance, vanity and scandalous tongue, she was both hated and dreaded, dreaded to such an extent that no one, however much they hated her, dared risk incurring her animosity.

No better proof is wanting of the fear she inspired in people, generally, than the fact that she lived to a ripe old age, in times when dark deeds of all kinds were common among all classes, and people, far less unpopular than she, paid for their unpopularity with their lives. She outlived Lauderdale by many years, dying in 1698. She was succeeded in her estates and title of Dysart by her eldest son by her first husband, Lionel Tollemache, Lord Huntingtower.

Now with regard to the ghost. We need not be surprised, perhaps, with the foregoing history fresh in our minds, that it is the phantom of the beautiful but infamous old Duchess that haunts Ham House. In the still hours of the night the tapping of high heels and of a stick are sometimes heard crossing the polished oak boards of various of the rooms and ascending the beautiful old staircase. Sometimes they stop outside one room, and sometimes another, and occasionally, not content with stopping outside, the Duchess, or rather her ghost, enters. According to Mr. Hare, the little daughter of a butler at Ham House had an alarming experience with it some years ago. She was on a visit, with the kind permission of the Tollemache family, when she was awakened in the early hours of the morning by hearing a curious noise in the room.

Thinking it was a mouse or bird, she sat up, and looking in the direction from which the sounds came, saw a little old woman kneeling by the fireplace, scratching on the wall with her long, claw-like fingernails. Turning round, and seeing the child looking at her, the old woman got up, and leaning on the rail at the foot of the child's bed, stared fixedly at her. As she did so the expression on her face was so terrible that the child, screaming loudly, hid her head under the bed-clothes. Fortunately some of the household were near at hand, and came running into the room. The ghost, however, had vanished.

On recovering from her fright, the child explained what had occurred, and the family, who were informed of it the following day, were so interested that they had the panelling where the ghost was scratching removed at once, which proceeding resulted in the finding of ancient documents, proving, beyond the shadow of a doubt, that the infamous Elizabeth, Countess of Dysart, had murdered her first husband, Sir Lionel Tollemache, in order to marry the saturnine Duke of Lauderdale.

Here, then, was that comparatively rare occurrence, a ghostly visit with a purpose, but, apparently, the discovery of the tell-tale documents, although it may have relieved the mind of the aged phantom, who seems at long last to have acquired a conscience, did not terminate the hauntings, for, according to rumour, they still occur periodically.

At some little distance from Ham House is Cranford House, in the neighbourhood of Hounslow, the home of that great sportsman, the Honourable Grantley F. Berkeley. In his *Reminiscences of a Huntsman* [1] he gives the following account of a ghostly experience that once happened to him there.

"At a very early age," he says, "my brother Moreton and myself were in the habit of going out at night with the keepers, to head them, if the poachers were expected in gangs; and this fact reminds me of a

[1] See pages 7-9.

curious circumstance, attended with some degree of the supernatural, that chanced to my brother and myself at the same time.

"When a man is alone, a vision of this sort may be set down to fancy; but when two young men, in no state of alarm or nervousness, see the same thing, and make to each other a corresponding remark upon it, it is strange if something more than mere fancy or phantasy has not invited their attention.

"A gang of poachers was expected, and just before twelve at night, my brother and myself, well armed, went from the passage by the servants' hall to the kitchen, intending to leave the house the back way. I was leading, and had just opened the door, when I saw the tall figure of a woman standing on the other side of the long kitchen table, which runs the whole length of the apartment, and as the door opened, her head turned slowly to look at me. She was in the dress of a servant, even to her shawl and bonnet; the latter, rather pokewise, shading her features, as she moved noiselessly along the table, as if going towards the fireplace. The light by which I saw her arose from a steadfast red glare of embers, left in the spacious grate, and as she faced it to look at and move from me, the direct ray from the fire enabled me to remark a more than common indistinctness of feature.

"Door in hand, the instant I saw her I addressed to my brother the word, 'Look!' His reply was, 'I see her; there she goes!' He, therefore, saw what I saw, as his rejoinder proved.

"At the moment the chief feeling in my mind was fun, for I took her to be one of the maid-servants, or a friend of theirs, up long beyond the usual hour of my mother's house for rest. So I locked the kitchen door behind us, put the key in my pocket, and exclaimed, 'Come along, we will see who she is.' By the old fireplace stood the great kitchen screen, towards which she seemed so noiselessly to glide, and thither my brother and myself proceeded, dashing round either corner of it, expecting to catch her; but when we did so we met face to face, and not the vestige of a woman was to be seen. Speechless with astonishment as to where she could be gone, we searched every nook and corner, but there was no one in the kitchen but ourselves; our wonder still more increased when, on going out by the door into the scullery, we found that locked fast, and the key on the inside. The windows were too high, as well as fast, to admit of an escape by such means; and believe it or not, as you like, reader, whatever it was that had been seen by us had vanished.

"The apparition personated no one that I know, and why it appeared to us is a mystery, for neither treasure was indicated, nor warnings given; so what business the ghost was on, if ghost it was, remains a secret to this day."

Mr. Berkeley seems to think that this case of a ghost appearing without any purpose is exceptional, but I would venture to remark that more often than not ghosts do appear without any apparent purpose and perform actions for which there seems to be no object at all. They may, of course, have some reason for appearing to us and doing the things they do, and be unable, at present, to make themselves understood by us.

CHAPTER XIII

CLUB HAUNTINGS AND SOME STRANGE HAPPENINGS IN SOHO AND BLOOMSBURY

NOT a few clubs in London are known to be haunted. I have heard it said that the ghost of "Old Q" (the eccentric Duke of Queensberry) is to be encountered occasionally on the staircase and in certain of the rooms of a well-known ladies' club in Piccadilly; whilst a room in a gentlemen's club in the region of Piccadilly Circus possesses a very sinister and ill-omened corner. Person after person, after sitting in this corner, has either been taken seriously ill afterwards or met with a fatal accident. Two or three years ago, a member of the club pointed out the corner to me, and very kindly suggested I should sit in it for awhile. I politely but firmly declined.

The premises of a night club in Soho, whose existence, like the existence of many other night clubs, terminated with dramatic abruptness, were—and I believe still are—haunted in a somewhat odd manner. In reference to this haunting one of the members of the club said:

"Several of us were playing cards in the card-room one night, when we heard a thud on the floor close to the table. It was so heavy and sounded so close to us that we all started and looked round apprehensively, fearing part of the ceiling had fallen. To our surprise, however, there was nothing whatever to account for the noise. Thinking that there was something very peculiar about the acoustic properties of the place, we went on with the game, but it was not long before my partner suddenly left off playing and looked fixedly in the direction of a window that was opposite him. The rest of us then looked too, and saw an object, like an enormous cask, roll across the floor from one side of the window to the other and vanish by the wall. It was shadowy and indistinct, and moved without making the slightest noise. None of us had hitherto believed in ghosts or anything of the kind, but we were now bound to admit that what we had seen could not be accounted for, and must be attributed to some supernatural agency."

The house was old, and had, no doubt, during its long history, witnessed many tragedies, some discovered and some, perhaps, never brought to light. That the cask, whose phantom was seen by the card players, had figured in one of them is not at all unlikely.

Many stories of hauntings and other strange happenings were afloat some years ago when Shaftesbury Avenue and its vicinity gained unenviable notoriety through the undesirable female aliens living in it. Men were lured to dens of infamy by smartly-dressed women and cruelly blackmailed and robbed. It is extremely probable, too, that some of them were murdered. When the police raided the premises all sorts of devices were found, similar to those of the famous house in West Street which Jonathan Wild once inhabited. There were boards that lifted up in the floors, secret doors communicating with other rooms in the cupboards, and sliding panels in the

CLUB HAUNTINGS

walls. A stranger once inside one of these houses stood little chance, for he was entirely at the mercy of a gang of thieves hidden on the premises.

Everyone knows about "Chicago May," but she was only one of hundreds, for London then teemed with women quite as bad as she was and, very probably, even worse. To grasp this, a student of character had only to glance at the painted faces of these women, for in their eyes one saw only hardness, and in their mouths grim determination.

I recollect a story I was once told about a haunting in connection with one of these women. I had gone to the St. James's Restaurant (Jimmy's) one evening, to meet a friend, and being early for my appointment, to while away time I got into conversation with a youth from Cambridge; and it was he who told me the story I am about to narrate.

On Boat Race night he went, he said, first of all to the old Lounge in Leicester Square, and then to the Empire. It was in the days, remember, when the promenade at the Empire was at its height and one saw there some of the most beautiful women in the world, women wearing costly gowns and jewellery, in many cases supplied by some man in the background who lived on their earnings.

All this, of course, is now a thing of the long past, remembered only by those of us who are middle-aged.

Well, the Cambridge undergrad, who had, so he informed me, indulged somewhat freely in strong drink, and was, on that account, not altogether responsible for his actions or inclinations, noticed one of the women in the promenade gazing very intently at him. She was tall, and fair, and very lovely; at least, so he thought then; and being also daintily and richly clad, she looked so chic and altogether seductive that he at once succumbed and spoke to her. As a result, they had supper together at an exclusive little restaurant in Soho, and then wended their way to her flat in Shaftesbury Avenue.

About half-way up the stone staircase leading to it, a tall man, in evening clothes and without a hat, dashed past them. As he did so, for one brief second his eyes encountered those of the undergrad, and the latter saw in them an expression of such wild and intense horror that he was perfectly appalled, and turned round at once to see where the tall man went. To his amazement, however, the man had vanished. He could not possibly have got down the stairs and out of sight in so short a time, and there was no possible place of concealment near at hand. The strangeness of the whole thing so alarmed and sobered the young man that, without a word, he ran down the stairs and out into the street, his companion the while, in a voice he barely recognized, calling out lustily after him.

Greatly impressed by the incident, particularly by the awful look of horror in the face of the man who had so unaccountably disappeared, the undergraduate made inquiries about the house, and learned, on excellent authority, that it bore a very sinister reputation. He was told that the woman who inveigled him there was one of a gang of German thieves and blackmailers, that she was suspected of something even worse, and that he had acted very wisely in not entering her flat.

Concerning a ghost and thieves, there are few more extraordinary cases than this:

A well-dressed man called one day at an apartment

house in Soho and inquired about rooms. He engaged a bedroom and sitting-room, and saying that his brother had just died and was to be buried in their family vault in Westminster Abbey, he asked the landlord if he would kindly allow the body to be brought to his house, till it was time for its interment, which would take place very shortly. The stranger spoke so plausibly that, incredible though it may seem, the landlord believed him, and as he offered to pay handsomely for the accommodation he required, readily granted his request. Consequently, the stranger arrived, in due course, with the coffin, and after seeing it safely deposited in a room on the ground floor, went out, saying that he was going to make final arrangements for the conveyance of the body to Westminster and would be back in about an hour's time. However, as hour after hour passed and he did not return, the landlord grew rather uneasy. He thought it quite possible that the stranger, who had told him that he had never been to London before, had either lost his way or met with an accident; but, finally, feeling very tired he went to bed, and told the maid-servant to sit up and let the new lodger in.

The maid-servant, therefore, remained up and sat in the kitchen sewing. After a time the grandfather clock in the corner struck midnight, and ere the echo of its last sonorous stroke had died away footsteps sounded on the stone staircase outside. Wondering who it could be, but supposing it was the landlord come to inquire if the lodger had returned, the servant listened. The footsteps were soft and seemed to be produced by someone in socks or bare feet. They came straight to the kitchen, paused for a few moments outside it, and then the door slowly opened. The maid watched it with growing alarm and apprehension, and presently a white and hideous face was thrust through the aperture. The next moment a tall figure, shrouded from head to foot in a winding sheet, glided into the room and advanced towards the unfortunate servant. Hitherto she had remained in her seat, too paralysed with fear to stir, but on the figure approaching her, her faculties were at once restored. Starting up, she ran shrieking to a door in her rear, which communicated with a second staircase, leading to the upper part of the house. Up this she raced, screaming all the way, and entering a room on the top floor hid under one of the beds in it.

By this time the landlord and several other members of the household had been roused, and fearing the house was on fire they were all making for the front door, when they saw the shrouded figure coming towards them. With loud yells they instantly turned and ran upstairs again, never pausing till they had reached their respective bedrooms. They then locked and barricaded themselves in.

After a while, all being still, the landlord ventured forth, to find the lower part of the house in a state of confusion and the safe where he kept his money and other valuables broken open. Open, too, was the coffin and gone its inmate, who proved not only to be the shrouded figure, but a member of a notorious gang of thieves, the leader of which was Arthur Chambers,[1] the plausible " stranger " to London. Chambers was eventually caught and, being found guilty of innumerable serious crimes, executed.

[1] See *Mother Shipton's Miscellany*. Published 1878.

In this case, however, of a robbery engineered by Chambers, one had, perhaps, more sympathy with the robber than the robbed, the latter proving such an excellent example of the old adage, " Fools and their money are soon parted."

To revert to clubs. Many people will remember the Delphic Club in Regent Street. As several of its members declared thay had had curious experiences there, which they believed to be due to some super-physical agency, two ladies and myself decided to hold a nocturnal vigil on the premises. We selected for the occasion the night immediately prior to the removal of the club to its new premises in Jermyn Street.

During our vigil, which lasted several hours, we saw nothing of a ghostly character, but twice something odd happened.

We were sitting, in the dark, in the entrance to the club, when we heard a click, and the electric light in one of the rooms was switched on. The door of the room was wide open, so that, had there been anyone in the room, the moment the light was turned on we must have seen them; but the room was empty. After we had turned off the light, the same thing happened again. There was a click, and the room was flooded with light. Nothing further occurred, but these two incidents, especially when considered in conjunction with those stated to have been experienced there by certain other members of the club, do strike one as being, at least, strange.

What I was told happened at the Motley Club in Dean Street, Soho, was rather more definite.

The Motley Club, which was mainly for film

artists, served a useful purpose, and many regretted its abrupt demise.

One afternoon, a few weeks before its termination, a film artist, named Dickson, who was not, I believe, a member of the club, encountering a big yellow dog on the staircase, threw it a biscuit. Taking no notice of the biscuit, however, the dog walked by Dickson and descended the stairs leading to the ground floor. The following day, in precisely the same spot, Dickson again saw the dog. As before, he threw it a biscuit, and, as before, the dog passed him by without taking the slightest notice of the biscuit. Thinking this rather strange, Dickson turned round to look at the dog, but it had vanished. Much puzzled, for it was not possible for the dog to have reached the bottom of the staircase, and it could not otherwise get out of sight, Dickson resolved to visit the club at the same hour the following day. He did so, and in the same spot encountered the dog. This time he threw it a small piece of meat, and on the dog taking no notice whatever of the meat, he aimed a slight blow at the dog with his stick. The stick passed right through the dog, which at once faded away into nothingness, leaving Dickson amazed and aghast. He narrated the story to me himself one night at the club, and introduced me to another film artist, who testified to having also seen the dog. From what I gathered no one else, however, appeared to have encountered it, although one or two people told me they had sometimes experienced a very uncanny sensation when ascending or descending the staircase between the first and second floors. Ghosts of animals are by no means rare, as anyone acquainted with the lore of psychical research

CLUB HAUNTINGS

knows, so that there is nothing very remarkable in the case I have just recounted. The phantom Dickson and his brother-artist saw may very probably have been that of some dog that had once been associated with the premises; it may have lived and died there, and have revisited the spot in spirit form through the ties of affection or some other deep emotion.

Bloomsbury being ghost-ridden no less than Soho, before concluding this chapter I will once more refer to the former. One of the strangest cases of a ghost being seen in this district was contained in a letter published in the *Daily Telegraph* in 1881. The letter reads as follows:

"In the latter part of the summer of 1878, between half-past three and four a.m., I was leisurely walking home from the house of a rich friend. A middle-aged woman, apparently a nurse, was slowly following, going in the same direction. We crossed Tavistock Square together, and emerged simultaneously into Tavistock Place. The streets and squares were deserted, the morning light and calm, my health excellent, nor did I suffer from anxiety or fatigue. The following scene was now enacted: A man suddenly appeared striding up Tavistock Place, coming towards me, and going in a direction opposite to mine. When first seen, he was standing exactly in front of my door. Young and ghastly pale, he was dressed in evening clothes, evidently made by a foreign tailor. Tall and slim, he walked with long measured strides, noiselessly, without a word. A tall white hat, covered chiefly with black crepe, and an eyeglass, completed the costume of this strange form. The moonbeams falling on the corpse-like features revealed a face well known to me, that of a friend and relative.

"The sole and only other person in the street beyond myself and this being was the woman already alluded to. She stopped abruptly, as if spellbound, then rushing towards the man, she gazed intently, and with horror unmistakable, on his face, which was upturned towards the heavens and smiling ghastlily. She indulged in her strange contemplation but during very few seconds, and, with extraordinary and unexpected speed for her age and weight, she ran away with terrific shrieks and yells. This woman never have I seen or heard of since, and but for her presence I could have explained the accident, call it, say, subjection of the mental powers to the domination of physical reflex action, and the man's presence would have been termed a false impression on the retina. A week after the above event, news of this very friend's death reached me. It had occurred on the morning in question. From the family I ascertained that, according to the rites of the Greek Church and to the custom of the country he had resided in, he was buried in his evening clothes, made abroad by a foreign tailor, and, strange to say, he wore goloshes or india-rubber shoes over his boots, according also to the custom of the country he died in; these deaden completely the sound of the heaviest footsteps. I never had seen my friend wear an eyeglass. He did so, however, whilst abroad, and began the practice some months before his death. When he came to England he lived in Tavistock Place, and occupied my rooms during my absence."

This letter was signed " ARMAND LESLIE." He was a man of some distinction, having served through the

Russian-Turkish war with the Turkish army, was one of the twelve doctors sent out to Egypt at the time of a great cholera epidemic, and was chief of the medical department of General Valentine Baker's staff. He was subsequently killed at the battle of El Teb. It is not likely a man of his standing and experience would have made up the story of the ghostly happening, which one must, in consequence, conclude actually took place. It is not a pleasant idea that the spirits of those who have passed over appear sometimes as corpses, but there are many cases, such as the above, to prove that this is so. What can the Power or Powers be like who ordain such horrors!

CHAPTER XIV

THE THAMES AND KILBURN

THERE are several well-known hauntings connected with the River Thames, and anyone acquainted with the history of that river might well suppose there would be, for, in all probability, few, if any, rivers in Europe have witnessed so many tragic deaths.

A Thames tragedy comprising many deaths is narrated by Holinshed. It occurred in the reign of Edward I. A number of Jews, alarmed at the persecution of their race in London and fearing to be massacred at any moment, hired a ship, and putting all their treasure in it by stealth, embarked in it themselves. Unfortunately for them, the captain of the ship was not one of their persuasion. On the contrary, he was, apparently unknown to them, in sympathy if not in actual league with their enemies, and finding out that the Jews had secreted a vast amount of wealth on board his vessel, he resolved to have it. With this object in view, he cast anchor in such a manner that the ship was left on the sands, near Queenborough, at ebb tide.

Telling the Jews it was necessary for them all to disembark at once, in order to lighten the vessel and so get her free, he succeeded in persuading them to go on to the shore. He then got back into the vessel at once and, shoving off, left them all huddled together on the treacherous sands. As he departed, he called to them mockingly, and said if they appealed to Moses he would doubtless save their lives, as he had saved the lives of their forebears, when crossing the Red Sea.

Whether they took this advice or not tradition does not say, but the rising tide gradually bore in on them, and one and all were drowned.

According to one version of the tradition, the captain of the ship was warmly praised by King Edward I for his treacherous deed, but, according to another version, he was hanged. Be this as it may, the spot where the Jews perished was ever afterwards regarded as accursed. Even when the rest of the river flows calmly, the water there is always more or less disturbed. It is said that, at times, those passing near the spot can distinctly hear moans and groans coming from beneath the water and see a gruesome bluish-green light hovering over it.

Jews, I believe, still go to that part of the river, where a goodly number of their race were once so cruelly done to death, to try to see or hear the phenomena.

Another of the Thames hauntings, according to tradition, is associated with one of the old ferry steamboats, plying between Greenwich and Westminster. A young man who was travelling on this steamboat, one sunny summer day, noticed sitting on the deck, rather away from everyone else, a lady, whose face was hidden by a black veil. Judging by her figure and hands, which were beautifully shaped, she appeared to be quite young, and the young man was, consequently, interested in her. When the boat was within a few yards of Westminster Bridge she suddenly sprang up and, to the young man's surprise and horror, jumped overboard. In an instant he took off his coat and plunged in after her. Fortunately, he was an excellent swimmer, but though he looked around everywhere, he could see no sign of the girl. Concluding, therefore, that she had sunk, he swam back to the steamer and was assisted on board by several of the passengers and crew. Judge, however, of his astonishment, when the captain said to him, " You are the third person this week who has jumped in after that creature."

"What!" the young man ejaculated, "do you mean to tell me she was merely fooling? But what became of her? I could find no sign of her in the water."

" What becomes of her is more than I or anyone else can tell you," the captain rejoined solemnly.

The young man eyed him in amazement. " Are you inferring that she was something supernatural ? " he said at length.

The captain shrugged his shoulders. "I don't know how else to account for it," he observed ; and he then told the young man that, some time previously, a girl, who was the exact counterpart of the one he had just tried to save, had actually jumped off the steamer, in that same spot, and been drowned, and that ever since then the steamer had been periodically haunted by what he and others believed to be her apparition.

According to another tradition I have heard, and which appears to be pretty widely known and credited, the Thames, near Westminster Bridge, is haunted by a phantom boat. Two or three men, whose faces are too indistinct and shadowy to be recognizable, are aboard her, and she is seen to approach and go under the bridge, but never to appear on the other side. People have searched for her on the other side, but they have never yet been able to discover the slightest trace of her.

Most people have heard of the cavalier ghost that haunts the bank of the Thames near Ham House.[1] One summer day, in 1885, about 5.30 p.m., a lady and gentleman, whom for convenience' sake I will call Mr. and Mrs. Tait, were walking along the bank of the Thames to Twickenham, where they had ordered a boat to meet them. When about half-way between Richmond and Twickenham, Mrs. Tait drew her husband's attention to a man stealing stealthily from behind her to her left side, where he hid among some trees. As he repeated this performance several times, Mr. Tait remarked to his wife, " I wonder what that fellow is dodging about for ? He seems to be anxious to hear what we are saying. Let us get out into the open."

They then left the avenue of fine trees through which they had been advancing, and upon gaining the open beach they looked round and saw the strange man close to them. He was standing on the fringe of the avenue, and presented a very striking appearance, inasmuch as he wore a hat with a wide brim and long drooping feather, a cloak drawn round the figure and thrown over one shoulder, and high boots, turned down at the knee. He might have been a cavalier, *temp.* Charles I, and, apparently, what struck Mr. and Mrs. Tait about him most was his dignity. After gazing at him for a minute or so, something momentarily attracting their attention elsewhere, they glanced

[1] See *Sights and Shadows*, by F. G. Lee, D.D.

away from him, and when they looked in his direction again, he had gone. Upon resuming their walk, however, to their utter amazement, they saw him standing about 150 yards ahead of them.

Marvelling how he could have covered that distance in so short a time, they walked towards him, never removing their gaze from him. Then an extraordinary thing happened. Clearly defined one moment, the figure they were looking at suddenly became transparent, and gradually got fainter and fainter, till it disappeared altogether, leaving behind it nothing but empty space, and a bright open tract of land with no human object whatsoever on it. Realizing, then, that what they had seen could only have been superphysical, they were stricken with immeasurable awe, and hastened on to meet their boat, which, to their joy, they saw approaching them in the distance.

This account of the cavalier ghost is authentic; Mrs. Tait, who narrated it to Dr. Lee, being also known personally to the late Mr. F. W. H. Myers of the Psychical Research Society. The late Mr. Edward T. Bennett, a well-known Psychical Researcher, corroborated the haunting, as did Mr. R. H. Harper of Richmond, who testified to the ghost being seen by eight or ten people collectively. I have reason to believe that this haunting has not ceased entirely; it is merely getting more and more intermittent.

The interior of Hampton Court Palace, the Palace grounds, and the bank of the river that bounds them are all said to be haunted, not only by one ghost, but by several. Two of these ghosts, it is believed, haunt a gallery that has been termed " the haunted gallery " in consequence. They are the ghosts, it seems, of

THE THAMES AND KILBURN

Lady Jane Seymour and Queen Katherine Howard. Lady Jane Seymour, it will be recollected, successfully supplanted the unfortunate Anne Boleyn in the good graces of Henry VIII, and was thus, indirectly, the cause of Anne's death. Possibly it is this knowledge that weighs heavily on her conscience and gives her spirit no rest; but however that may be, wander her ghost does, not only in "the haunted gallery," but in "the silver-stick gallery," where it is seen at night, gliding noiselessly along, with a lighted taper in one of its hands.

The ghost of Queen Katherine is more harrowing. Tradition says that it was either in or near "the haunted gallery" that the final parting between her and her devilish husband took place. With sublime hypocrisy, on the day of Queen Katherine's execution, Henry went into the Palace Chapel—ostensibly to pray, but, more probably, to gloat over keenly anticipated joys with his next wife—and although told that his Royal Highness must not be disturbed at his devotion, Queen Katherine, breaking away from her guards, rushed into the chapel, to make a last appeal to him for her life. Her guards, however, following close upon her heels, dragged her out of the Royal presence, and shrieking and expostulating she was bustled out of the sacred precincts and through "the haunted gallery" to her fate. Therefore, perhaps, it is now said that her ghost rushes shrieking and screaming through "the haunted gallery," as if trying to escape from some invisible pursuers. Various people have testified either to having heard or seen Queen Katherine's ghost, among others Mrs. Cavendish Boyle and Lady Eastlake, whose apartments in the Palace were close to "the haunted gallery," but, as in so many instances of hauntings, the face of this particular phantasm was not seen by them with any degree of distinctness.

Another phantasm stated, on good authority, to haunt the Palace is that of Mrs. Penn, the foster-mother and nurse of Edward VI. Some years ago the Misses Ponsonby occupied the rooms in the Palace which Mrs. Penn had once inhabited. Every now and then they and certain of their friends, who were visiting them, heard the sound of a spinning wheel in motion, apparently close to them. As they could not account for it, they were naturally much puzzled. Subsequently, some Board of Works' officials, who were doing something to the walls of the Misses Ponsonby's rooms, discovered an unsuspected room behind one of them and in it a spinning-wheel, that showed signs of considerable usage.

One one occasion, a soldier, chancing to pass the room one day, saw the shadowy form of a woman, clad in a long, grey robe, with a hood over the head and shoulders, glide noiselessly out of it. He was so scared that he took to his heels and ran.

On another occasion, a Palace attendant was sitting one evening on a seat in the garden, waiting for the inspector to pass on his rounds, when he suddenly felt an icy hand laid on his forehead, and looking up, saw a tall lady, with very white cheeks, dressed in an old-fashioned grey costume. There was something so eerie about her that he sprang to his feet, in terror, whereupon she inexplicably vanished.

The shock to his nerves was so great that, feeling he could not run the risk of seeing the ghost, for such he believed it to be, again, he resigned his post in the Palace. It is generally believed that this phenomenon is the ghost of Mrs. Penn, though why she should haunt the Palace is not known. So far as can be ascertained she died there quite peacefully and happily. There may, of course, have been secrets in her life with which historians were not acquainted, or there may have been some secret mystery associated with her death; or, again, her haunting may simply be due to interest in and strong affection for the Palace, where she had no doubt spent some, at least, very happy days.

Apart from these three ghosts, the Palace is haunted by other strange and unaccountable demonstrations and phenomena. The servants sometimes are awakened at night by feeling icy hands laid on their foreheads and cheeks; sometimes the bed-clothes are snatched away from them, a not uncommon happening in hauntings; and sometimes they see shadowy forms of a terrifying and sinister shape. Nor are visitors to the Palace entirely exempt from the experience of unpleasant happenings.

Two ladies were talking to one another, one day, in a certain room in the Palace, which, according to repute, is haunted, when there was a terrific crash, and the whole apartment was suddenly illuminated with a strange, gruesome light.

On another occasion, either in the same room or a room adjoining it, a lady resident in the Palace saw a huge black coffin. It was on the floor, partly covered with a sable pall. Terrified, she ran and told one of the attendants, who at once went to the room and likewise saw the coffin, whereupon she, too, ran away scared.

Several of the other attendants and officials then went to the room in a body, but when they arrived, there was no sign of a coffin anywhere.

While excavating at the Palace on November 2, 1871, some workmen unearthed two human male skeletons within two feet of the surface. Medical examination proved them to have been there a very long time, possibly from 150 to 200 years. The part of the Palace in which they were found had been rebuilt by Sir C. Wren about 1690, so that it is unlikely that they were there then; had they been, they could scarcely have escaped being seen. The supposition is that they were put there some few years after that date, and lime having been found with them points, of course, to foul play. Hence, to these skeletons some of the ghostly phenomena experienced in the Palace may, perhaps, be attributed.

Kilburn is some little distance from Hampton Court, but a haunting, even stranger, perhaps, than the hauntings at the river Palace, was associated with the Priory that once stood in this district.

The origin of this Priory is believed to be as follows: In the reign of Henry I, a pious individual named Godwin, wishing to live a very secluded life, built himself a hermitage on one of the banks of the Bourne, amidst wild flowers and trees. Few spots near London could then have been more lonely or lovely. In course of time it became known as Coldburne, Coleburn, Keeleburne, and finally Kilburn.

Godwin eventually growing tired of such solitude, granted his hermitage and the adjoining fields to the abbot and monks of Westminster " as an alms for the redemption of the whole convent of brethren."

Soon after this bestowal, the abbot, with the prior, and the whole convent of Westminster, at Godwin's request, and with the consent of the Bishop of London, handed over the hermitage and its lands to three virgins, by name Emma, Griselda and Christina, who were maids of honour to Queen Matilda, wife of Henry I. The hermitage was then converted into a nunnery, and Godwin was appointed Chaplain and Warden for as long as he should live; after his death the nuns were to be given permission to choose his successor. In 1536 it was surrendered to the Royal Commissioners, and in course of time it fell into a state of decay. In its latter years it was styled Kilburn Priory, and of Kilburn Priory now absolutely nothing is left. The ghostly tradition associated with it originated thus : [1]

Sometime during the early history of the nunnery there were two brothers, Sir Gervase and Stephen de Mertoun. Stephen became enamoured of Gervase's wife, and taking advantage of Gervase's temporary absence made love to her. Being true to her husband, the lady rejected Stephen's advances with scorn, threatening to tell Gervase. This so alarmed and infuriated Stephen that he determined to murder his brother. With this object in view, he hid in a narrow lane, in St. John's Wood, close to the nunnery, and when Sir Gervase came along, all unsuspecting, he crept up behind him and stabbed him in the back.

Sir Gervase fell, mortally wounded, and seeing Stephen upbraided him with his treachery and cruelty, adding, "This stone on which I lie shall be thy deathbed." He then expired.

[1] *Abbeys, Castles and Ancient Halls of England and Wales.*

Not in the least degree abashed, Stephen, in defiance of all decency, hurried to his brother's house and tried to seduce the beautiful young widow. Failing in this he had her confined in a dungeon, for just so long, he told her, as she chose to remain obstinate. He then seized all his brother's possessions and indulged in a great orgy.

After a while, however, his conscience awoke and oppressed him to such an extent that he ordered his brother's remains to be interred in a magnificent mausoleum in Kilburn. The stones of which this mausoleum was composed were taken from the scene of the murder, and among them the one on which Sir Gervase had breathed his last. From this stone, Stephen, when he came to view the mausoleum, perceived that blood was flowing, and his horror at this sight was so great that he, straightway, went to the Bishop of London and confessed his guilt to him. Furthermore, hoping, thereby, to atone for his crime, he bequeathed all his property to the Priory of Kilburn. Soon after this, overcome with grief and remorse, he fell seriously ill and died. For many years, subsequent to his decease, however, blood flowed from the stone in the mausoleum periodically, while the scene of the murder was declared to be haunted, few daring to go near it alone after dusk.

CHAPTER XV

HIGHGATE, HAMPSTEAD AND SOUTH KENSINGTON

For many years there stood, and was standing not so very long ago—indeed, I believe it may still be there—a very old and massive red brick house in Highgate. Ivy covered its walls, which were not unworthy of a castle; rust was everywhere in evidence upon its handsome iron gates, and the paving stones of its courtyard were barely visible for moss. In its neglected garden there were curiously-fashioned yews, fountains, a statue of Pan, and a thatched summer house, all of which gave it an old-world character, reminiscent of the days of Queen Anne.

The entrance hall, with its broad, handsome staircase and gallery, was composed chiefly of black oak, and the extensive panelling to be seen in most of the rooms was of the same ancient order. No one, it seems, had lived in the house for any length of time, latterly, because it was haunted. The following story[1] which is connected with the haunting, is guaranteed to be true:

The house, many years ago, was occupied by a wealthy man, whom I will name here, for convenience' sake, Black; and one Christmas Eve his son and heir, Ralph, an abandoned young rake, who had been away two years, unexpectedly returned home, ill. He was, in fact, so seriously ill, that his grieved parents had him

[1] See *Mother Shipton's Miscellany*, published 1878.

put to bed at once, and sent for a nurse to be with him at night. The nurse in due time came and was shown into Ralph's room. As the doctor had enjoined the strictest silence, she sat down by the fire and commenced reading, pausing every now and then to look at her patient and glance round the room. Like all the principal bedrooms in the house, it was panelled throughout with black oak, and its large antique fireplace was supported by massive buttresses. In the centre of the floor was a sepulchral-looking four-poster on which Ralph lay. The only illumination in the room, apart from the fire, came from a lamp, which was on the table by the nurse's side. It was a wild night. Every now and again blasts of wind beat the snow and ivy leaves against the window panes and, by way of variation, moaned and shrieked down the old chimney.

Outside, the garden and fields beyond lay covered in a white pall, which was momentarily thickening.

Anxious to see how her patient was, the nurse presently arose, and stealing gently up to his bed looked at him. He was on his back, apparently awake. His bright blue eyes were staring fixedly at her; his under lip had fallen, showing his long white teeth that projected fearfully from his shrunken gums, and his cheeks were sunken and hollow. One bony hand lay uncovered on the bed-clothes. Not wishing to stay by his side for fear of disturbing him, the nurse returned to her seat.

About midnight, she heard him breathing very hard, and looking round saw, to her astonishment, a heavily-veiled lady sitting by his bed. She was about to get up, when the lady raised a slender gloved hand

and signed to her to be seated and silent. Thinking the stranger might be one of her patient's relatives come to visit him, the nurse obeyed, feeling at the same time considerably puzzled as to how the lady could have entered without her knowledge.

From her slim and elegant figure the lady appeared to be young, but nothing could be seen of her face, on account of the black veil. Ralph's uneasiness increased, he tossed from side to side, and from his heavy breathing appeared to be in pain. The nurse again rose, again the lady in the veil signed to her to keep her seat, and again she felt constrained to obey. Overcome with weariness, for she had travelled all day, she closed her eyes. When she opened them again, the lady in the black veil had gone.

The following night, at the same time, the same thing happened. The strange lady suddenly appeared by the bedside, and, as before, her advent was a signal for Ralph to get suddenly worse. Alarmed by his restlessness and heavy breathing, the nurse got up, and, in spite of a signal from the stranger to remain seated, ran to her patient's side. As she did so, the strange lady moved to the table, her face still turned towards Ralph, whose eyes, starting from their sockets, never left her. The nurse now seated herself by his side, and succumbing to a sudden fit of drowsiness fell asleep. When she awoke, the strange lady was no longer in the room.

Frightened and mystified, the nurse crouched over the fire till the morning. When the doctor arrived, she announced her intention of leaving, declaring the task was more than her strength and nerves could stand. The doctor begged her so earnestly to stay, however, that she finally consented, sorely against her will.

All day it snowed, and towards night a storm came on, increasing in violence the later it grew. The nurse, sitting by the fire, shivered each time the wind wailed and moaned round the house, and the ill-fitting shutters and window frames jarred and rattled. Occasionally, during a lull in the elements, she could hear the ticking of the death-watch in one of the walls and the scampering of a mouse in the worm-eaten wainscoting. As midnight grew near, Ralph became more and more restless, and the nurse more and more anxious and nervous.

The grandfather clock on the landing outside was striking midnight, when the nurse glancing apprehensively towards the bed, again saw the same strange lady seated by it, and, as before, her presence was a signal for her patient to grow worse. Presently, his breathing again so alarmed her that, disregarding the signs of the veiled lady to remain seated, she ran to the bed. This time she started back with horror. Ralph's face was horribly convulsed, his eyes, fixed on the veiled lady, were full of such terror that the nurse was appalled. She spoke to him, more, perhaps, to hear her own voice in that dreadful room than from any other motive, but he did not reply. She touched his hand: it was cold as death. Thinking he was about to die she made for the door. The veiled lady at once took her place by the patient's bedside, and bending over him thrust her face almost into his. For a few moments Ralph's gaspings and writhings were more terrible than ever. Then they suddenly ceased, and the room became ghastly still and silent. Urged by a sudden impulse, the nurse rushed at the veiled lady, who was now advancing towards her, and tore off her veil. Beneath it was no living face, but the grinning head of a skeleton. The nurse promptly fainted, and she was found still unconscious, some hours later, by the doctor and certain members of the household. Ralph was dead, with one hand across his eyes, as if to shade them from some object he dreaded to look at; the other hand gripped the counterpane.

That same morning the body of a girl, young and very beautiful, was washed ashore near Queenhithe. It had been in the water several days, and letters, in an ivory case, in one of her pockets proved that she had been on very intimate terms with Ralph, and that he had behaved very badly to her. Whether he was directly responsible for her death was not known, since it was never ascertained how she came to be in the water.

Those who were acquainted with the nurse's story were of the opinion that it was the ghost of the drowned lady that had visited the dying man, and probably it was; but, however that may be, the nurse never recovered from the shock of seeing the ghost, though she lived long enough to give a lucid account of all she had gone through on those three eventful nights.

After Ralph's death his parents left the house, and, subsequently, on account of the reputation it acquired for being badly haunted, it would never let for long, and in the end it doubtless never let at all.[1]

[1] A somewhat varied version of the story of this haunting appeared in *The New Monthly Magazine*, and was reproduced in *The Casket of Literature*, vol. ii, published in 1879.

A haunting by a somewhat similar ghost occurs in a house in Well Walk, Hampstead. My authority is a lady who once visited the house, and the story she told was as follows:

She said she had heard from her friends, who were renting the house, that it was alleged to be haunted by something that was sometimes seen on the staircase, but as none of them had ever encountered it, they did not believe that the house was haunted at all.

Well, the lady who told me this story, whom I will here call Mrs. Grey, since she did not wish her identity disclosed, for fear of trouble with her friend's landlord, went to stay in the house one wet summer, not so very long ago.

"You won't mind sleeping in the haunted room," her friend, the lady of the house, remarked, on her arrival, " all the other rooms are occupied."

"The haunted room!" Mrs. Grey ejaculated. "Why, I thought it was your staircase that was haunted."

"So it is," her friend replied; "but your room is supposed to be haunted too. I don't think you need worry though, for none of us have ever seen or heard anything unusual in it."

Mrs. Grey asserting her willingness to sleep in the room, she was forthwith conducted to it. Being very tired after a long journey from the Continent she fell asleep, almost as soon as her head touched the pillow, and did not awake till the servant rapped at her door in the morning.

The following night she was not quite so fortunate. Hardly had she got into bed, before she heard loud knockings in different parts of the room, accompanied by light, stealthy footsteps and whispering. Concluding someone was in the room, probably to try and scare her, she got up and lit a candle, but could see no one. She was about to extinguish the light and get into bed, when there was a gentle puff and the candle flame was blown out for her. This broke down her fortitude, and she ran out of the room screaming.

She spent the rest of the night on a Chesterfield, in the drawing-room, and the following day was transferred to an attic, where a bed was hastily improvised for her.

Several days later, arriving home in a veritable downpour, she was going upstairs to her room, to change her clothes, when she saw a lady in a very smart though somewhat old-fashioned blue tailormade costume ascending the stairs in front of her. The lady had, apparently, been out, for she was wearing a hat and carrying a sunshade, but strange to say neither her hat, nor dress, nor sunshade were at all wet. Wondering who the stranger could be, but supposing she was some friend of the family, Mrs. Grey followed her upstairs. On reaching the first floor, the strange lady walked quickly to the haunted room, and entering it, closed the door with a loud bang.

Mrs. Grey thought no more of the incident, but proceeded to divest herself of her wet garments.

The following day, which proved to be very hot and fine, she returned to the house, about the same hour, and again saw the lady in blue going up the staircase. This time, despite the dryness of the weather, the lady's dress and umbrella—she now carried an umbrella—appeared to be saturated. As before, she entered the haunted room, slamming the door behind her.

Considerably puzzled, and determined to solve the mystery, Mrs. Grey, without mentioning the matter to her friends, the people of the house (her reason for this is not apparent; possibly she liked doing things "on her own," or imagined her friends might think her inquisitive if she asked them who the stranger was), instead of going out the following day, remained indoors, and about the time she would have been returning, had she gone out, she repaired to the hall, whence, sure enough, she saw the same lady in blue, as before, walking upstairs. Mrs. Grey immediately ran after her, and followed her into the haunted room. The lady walked straight to the large mirror on the dressing-table and threw back the dark veil, which had hitherto screened her face. The room was full of sunlight, so that Mrs. Grey, who was close behind the lady, could see the latter's reflection in the mirror, absolutely clearly, and it was not the face of a living woman that she saw, but that of a ghastly, grinning skeleton. Mrs. Grey did not faint—she was not given that way—she simply left the room precipitately, and that very afternoon left the house. She never visited it again.

Her friends shortly afterwards vacated the premises, owing to the ghost having been at last seen by them too.

Another summer haunting takes place in a house in South Kensington. A Miss Wakefield, who had once been lady's maid in a family named Walton, took an apartment house in the above district, and had not been in it long before an alarming incident occurred.

A cousin of hers was spending the evening with her,

and as it was summer and the weather very hot, they sat in one of the unoccupied rooms, with the window open. About ten o'clock Miss Wakefield remarked, "You won't mind my leaving you for a few minutes, as I must go upstairs and see that the rooms are all right."

Her cousin replied, quite pleasantly, "Oh, dear, no." When, however, Miss Wakefield returned a few minutes later, her cousin appeared to be very upset, and observing that it was time for her to be going, hurriedly quitted the house.[1] Miss Wakefield did not see her again until some months later, when she met her in the street. She then seemed quite herself again, and as glad to see Miss Wakefield as Miss Wakefield was to see her. On Miss Wakefield asking her why it was she had not been to see her for so long, she said : "Well, as it is better, perhaps, that you should know what happened the last night I was in your house, I will tell you.

"After you left me alone in the room, I saw something so dreadful that nothing will ever persuade me to enter it again." She then informed Miss Wakefield that directly after she (Miss Wakefield) left her and went upstairs that night, a man suddenly appeared in the room. He did not enter by the door or window, but was simply there.

"He was dressed in white, with a death-like face, and a long beard."

After walking three or four times round the room, he disappeared through the wall near the fireplace.

[1] My authority (see *Ghostly Visitors*, by "Spectre Stricken") names no district, but merely says "in London." I have reason, however, for believing the house he refers to is in Courtfield Gardens, and that it is still, or was a short time ago, haunted.

Immediately afterwards, waves of something white came out from the spot where he had vanished. "It was awful to see," Miss Wakefield's cousin added. "Awful to see it. I could not cry out; I could do nothing, only sit there and watch."

Miss Wakefield then told her cousin that she would have been very surprised at hearing this, had not her servant, Jane, who had just left her, had almost the same experience. Jane, it appears, saw the same man that Miss Wakefield's cousin had seen, lying on the floor, with his arms folded on his breast, and his face and eyes looking like those of a dead person, although his eyes were wide open and staring, and she was so frightened that she had given up her situation and left the house immediately.

Some time after this meeting and conversation with her cousin, Miss Wakefield began to have alarming experiences in the house herself. She was awakened at all hours of the night by the most extraordinary noises. First of all she would hear a rushing noise, then things would, seemingly, be thrown down in the kitchen with great violence, although it was always found in the morning that nothing had been disturbed.

Jane's successor also came in for the phenomena. She was awakened one night by hearing footsteps on the stairs, and then a tremendous crash, as if numbers of trays had been dashed down on the tiled floor.

The room in which the ghost was seen was in the basement, and even in the hottest weather there was always a strange chilliness in its atmosphere.

According to a rumour in the neighbourhood, a butler had once committed suicide in the room, and for years afterwards stains, supposed to be due to his blood, were observable on the floor, near the window. Whether they are still there or ever were there I cannot say ; but that the foregoing incidents are true, I have very good reason to believe.

CHAPTER XVI

BARNES COMMON, BETHNAL GREEN AND ST. ANNE'S CHURCHYARD

QUITE recently sensational rumours of a haunting were afloat in Barnes. It was said that people crossing the Common at night saw black-robed women, suddenly and inexplicably, appear and, just as suddenly and inexplicably, disappear.

As a matter of fact, it is by no means the first time that there have been such rumours. In the spring of 1879, the finding of certain portions of the unfortunate Mrs. Thomas on Barnes Common was followed by reports that a ghost had been seen hovering around the scene of the discovery. It was described as a woman dressed like a nun; and its face, it was said, possessed one very alarming peculiarity. It lacked both eyes and eye sockets. Where the latter should have been was nothing but white and shiny flesh. When I was collecting material for my work on the Richmond murder of 1879,[1] I met several people in Barnes and Richmond who recollected hearing stories of this particular ghost. There is a reference to it in a work I have already quoted.[2] It is this:

A certain Mr. Smith (an old Oxonian) took a run up to Putney one March, in order to see the Oxford and Cambridge boat race, in which he still retained a

---

[1] Entitled *The Trial of Kate Webster* (Notable Trials Series).
[2] *Ghostly Visitors.*

very keen interest. Having dined with a friend in Hammersmith, he set off on his return journey, which led him across Barnes Common. When about half-way across it, he was overtaken by a youth named Brown,[1] whom he had met that night, at dinner, for the first time. Brown informed Smith that he was glad of a companion, as, on a former occasion, when passing the gate of the cemetery that borders the Common, he had got somewhat of a fright. He said that he suddenly saw a woman who, from her dress, appeared to be a nun, gliding along, in a curious zig-zag fashion, on the opposite side of the road. There was something so eerie and unnatural about her that he took to his heels and ran.

This was Brown's story. Well, a year later, Smith met him again, by chance, in Putney, and they renewed their former acquaintanceship. When walking together past the cemetery one day, Smith asked Brown if he had encountered any nun ghosts lately, and Brown, replying in the negative, added, " But I have something of the same ghostly nature to tell you." Some friends of his, he told Smith, lived on the outskirts of the Common, their house being in a straight line with the cemetery. Their family consisted of three: Mr. and Mrs. West, and Miss Dester, the latter's sister. Mr. West's health caused his family and friends the greatest anxiety. About the time Mr. Brown saw the woman in black outside the cemetery, Miss Dester went to the front door one evening, to have a look at the sky, before retiring to bed, according to her usual custom. To her asonishment, stand-

---

[1] The names given in this story, the truth of which is guaranteed, are fictitious.

ing in front of her, at the foot of the steps leading out of the garden, was a woman, dressed, to some extent at least, as a nun. She had her arms folded across her breast, and was staring hard at Miss Dester. Feeling frightened, for there was something curious about the woman, Miss Dester called the maid-servant, who was then removing the supper things; and the latter came at once, accompanied by the dog. As a rule the dog barked furiously at strangers, but, on this occasion, it did no such thing. It gave a glance at the woman, and then retreating behind Miss Dester, it nestled close to her and growled. As for the maid-servant, she stared wildly at the woman for a moment, and then clung to Miss Dester, who, obeying an impulse, slammed the door to. The rest of the household having retired, she did not disturb them, but went to bed as usual.

The next morning Mrs. West came down to breakfast, looking very pale and tired. She informed Miss Dester that Mr. West had had a very bad night, and that he had kept on declaring that there was a strange woman, like a nun, in one corner of the room, who never took her eyes off him. Again and again, Mrs. West tried to persuade him it was fancy, but it was of no use, he persisted in his statement that the woman was there, and that she was all the while glaring at him. He was so ill that he was obliged to remain in bed; and he never left it, for he died that day.

This was Brown's story, and he told Smith he firmly believed that the woman whom Mr. West had seen in his room was the woman Miss Dester and the maid-servant had seen, and the woman he had seen, too, zigzagging about outside the cemetery. Whether what Brown believed to be a fact in this case, was a fact, or not, one cannot, of course, say; all one can say is that in the realms of psychism no phenomenon seems to be too startling to be true. At the same time, all attempts to explain the why and wherefore of any psychic phenomenon has, in my opinion, up to the present, proved futile.

One of the most famous ghost stories of London is associated with Covent Garden. In bygone years there stood in the south-east corner of Covent Garden Market two hotels, known respectively as "Old Hummums" and "New Hummums."

The name Hummum is a corruption of the Turkish word Hamam or Humoum, a bath, and originally the hotels so named were hot-houses, that is to say houses containing hot sweating baths, or what are now styled Turkish baths. The custom of taking hot sweating baths was introduced into England several centuries ago and became, for a time, extremely fashionable (allusion to them may be seen in one of Ben Jonson's plays); but, after a while, they fell into disrepute, owing to their being frequented by bad characters of both sexes, and they were eventually suppressed. The two hot-houses in question were converted into hotels, probably at the beginning of the eighteenth century, and remained as such until they were pulled down.

The "Old Hummums" was demolished in 1881, and on its site was erected a large modern hotel, styled simply "The Hummums." I have not been able to ascertain when the "New Hummums" disappeared, but probably it was some years later. It was the "Old Hummums" that was the scene of what the illustrious Dr. Johnson described as "the best accredited ghost story that he had ever heard." No book of London ghosts would be complete without it.

When Dr. Johnson and Boswell were visiting Mrs. Thrale at Streatham one day, the following incident, recorded by Boswell, from whose account of it I will quote, took place.

"Among the numerous prints pasted on the walls of the dining-room at Streatham was Hogarth's Modern Midnight Conversation. I asked him (Johnson) what he knew of Parson Ford, who makes a conspicuous figure in the riotous group. Johnson said, ' Sir, he was my acquaintance and relation ; my mother's nephew. He had purchased a living in the country, but not simoniacally. I never saw him but in the country. I have been told he was a man of great parts ; very profligate, but I never heard he was impious.' "

Boswell goes on to tell us that he next asked Johnson if there was not a story of Ford's ghost having appeared, and Johnson replied, " Sir, it was believed. A waiter in The Hummums, in which house Ford died, had been absent for some time, and returned, not knowing that Ford was dead. Going down to the cellar, according to the story, he met him ; going down again, he met him a second time. When he came up, he asked some of the people of the house what Ford could be doing there. They told him that Ford was dead.

" The waiter took a fever, in which he lay for some time. When he recovered he said he had a message to deliver to some women from Ford ; but he was not to tell what, or to whom. He walked out ; he was followed, but somewhere about St. Paul's they lost him. He came back and said he had delivered the message, and the women exclaimed, 'Then we are all undone.'"

Continuing, Boswell says: "Dr. Pellet, who was not a credulous man, inquired into the truth of this story, and he said the evidence was irresistible."

Not relying entirely on Dr. Johnson or Dr. Pellet, however, Boswell, it seems, caused inquiries to be made at The Hummums itself, and at first the proprietors of the establishment were reluctant to say anything; but they finally admitted that the story about the waiter was true. Boswell concludes his reference to it with these remarks: "To be sure the man (*i.e.* the waiter) had a fever, and this vision may have been the beginning of it. But if the message to the women, and their behaviour upon it, were true as related, there was something supernatural. That rests upon his word, and there it remains."

A ghost story that is not so famous, though it is fairly well known, is associated with Bethnal Green.[1] Near the site of the old schoolhouse in Bethnal Green there used to be a public-house known as the "Gibraltar." For many years it was kept by John Harris, a native of Birmingham and silver-plater by trade. At first he conducted the house in a most exemplary fashion; but having made a lot of money he gradually got lax, and in the end he had to close down, the local authorities refusing to renew his licence.

The old adage that misfortunes never come singly proved very true in his case, for soon after his forced retirement from business, his wife quarrelled with him over his changed financial condition and left him.

[1] See *News from the Invisible World*. Edited by T. Ottway.

One night, soon after her departure, he was sitting by his lonely fireside, brooding over his misfortunes, which seemed almost too terrible to bear, when he suddenly heard the bell, in the now deserted bar, ring. Though rather startled, as he was alone in the house, having dismissed all his employees on the grounds that he could no longer afford to keep them, he did not stir from his seat, till the bell rang a second time. He then got up and went to the back door, thinking someone had entered that way and was indulging in a joke at his expense. The door and windows, however, were fastened. Much puzzled, he was returning to the warmth and comfort of the parlour—it was a cold winter's night—when the bell started ringing again, not so quickly as before, but more regularly, as if the hand that pulled held it for a while.

Considerably perplexed and perturbed, he armed himself with a poker, as it was the first weapon that came handy, and passed through the bar into the room beyond, where he saw a woman, dressed in a brown costume, resembling that formerly worn by Quakeresses, seated in a chair, between the two back windows. At first he was too overcome with terror and amazement to speak, for although the woman was by no means unprepossessing in appearance, there was something distinctly eerie about her, something that told him at once she did not belong to this world and which he instinctively associated with death.

Had he never done an evil thing he might have felt more courageous, but the knowledge that he had been living a thoroughly bad life made him horribly afraid and apprehensive. With a tremendous effort he summed up courage to speak.

"Who—who are you?" he stammered, clutching hold of the wall for support, for all the strength seemed to go out of his limbs, and he felt sick and faint.

"Who or what I am is not my business to relate," the strange woman replied, "but what you may hereafter become, if you do not amend your life, is my business to warn you. You have but a few years to live, make the most of them, and train up your daughter Phoebe in a good way. Be very particular whom she associates with, or she will come to a violent end. Remember her life is just now in your keeping, a short space of time will place it out of your power to avert the evil that awaits her. Your responsibility is very great. Recollect all this, John Harris, and live accordingly." She had hardly ceased speaking before she tapped the ground with a long stick on which she had been leaning, and immediately disappeared, leaving Harris paralysed with awe and amazement.

No better proof of the truth of this story, which Mr. Harris subsequently told to his friends, could be afforded than the sudden change that now came over him. From being a scoffer at religion, a heavy drinker and hard swearer, he took to going first to church, and then to chapel, and finally became a Methodist. He never touched a drop of alcohol again, and gave up using bad language. In short, he was metamorphosed from a blackguard into a really decent living person, and he remained such till his death. It was too late for him, however, to convert Phoebe. She had got mixed up with a gang of undesirables and, in the end, perished on the scaffold. In course of time the Old

Gibraltar Inn was pulled down, but up to the time of its demolition it was regarded as haunted, in consequence of what Harris was always convinced he saw there.

Another well-known ghostly incident in London is related in a work by John Taylor.[1] It occurred to Mr. Fox, the eminent member of Parliament. On one occasion, when he came to London, to attend the House of Commons, he took rooms in St. Anne's Churchyard, Westminster. He had been in too great a hurry at the time to pay any attention to the landlady or the servants, and it was not until he actually moved in with his luggage that he did more than casually glance at them. He was then struck with both the landlady and the servant who answered the door. They looked exactly like men in disguise.

Indeed, he was so unfavourably impressed with the mistress of the house, when she entered his sitting-room to know if he would like anything before he retired to bed, that he dismissed her very abruptly. Being very perturbed and apprehensive, he could not sleep for a long while, after going to bed, and when he finally did doze off, he had a horrible dream. He fancied some influence he could not resist compelled him to get out of bed and go downstairs into a dank and gloomy-looking cellar, on the damp, stone floor of which he saw the naked body of a man, covered with ghastly wounds. He awoke, sweating with terror.

The dream was so realistic that he became thoroughly alarmed, more so as he recollected his impres-

[1] See *Records of my Life*.

sions of the two women. Consequently, he got up in a panic, and dressing hastily was about to leave the house, when he encountered the landlady, fully apparelled, as if she had never gone to bed. She seemed much agitated at seeing him, and asked his reason for going out so early in the morning. Forcing himself to appear calm, for he was really terrified, he said he had to meet a friend in Bishopsgate Street and was bringing him back to breakfast. Apparently satisfied with this answer, the landlady suffered him to go out, and never in his life had he experienced such relief as when he found himself, once more, in the open.

He at once went to the house of a friend, and rousing him told him what had happened. His friend laughed heartily, assuring him it was imagination, as St. Anne's Churchyard was a very respectable neighbourhood, and hardly likely to harbour desperate criminals. He, however, agreed to accompany Mr. Fox back to the rooms. On the way to them they met a gentleman, whom they persuaded to go with them. On entering the house in St. Anne's Churchyard, they found it deserted; the landlady and servants had, apparently, decamped in a body.

The basement tallied exactly with the grim-looking place Mr. Fox had seen in his dream, and when they entered the cellar, under the pavement, there, in one corner, lay the naked body of a man, only too obviously murdered. Mr. Taylor does not say whether the murderers were caught; hence, presumably, they escaped.

In a previous chapter I described the haunting of an old house in Westminster by the ghost of a cavalier. The narrator of the case did not name the street the house was in, consequently, it might well be that the house haunted by the cavalier ghost was the same house in which Mr. Fox underwent the aforesaid very unpleasant experience.

CHAPTER XVII

ST. PAUL'S AND CRIPPLEGATE

SEVERAL strange stories and beliefs are associated with St. Paul's Cathedral. One such belief is that when a clock is heard to strike out of order, more especially if it strikes thirteen, from no apparent physical cause, it portends some grave calamity; in the case of a great city clock like Big Ben or St. Paul's, a calamity of national importance. As an example : [1]

On the morning of Thursday, the 14th of March, 1861, " the inhabitants of the metropolis were roused by repeated strokes of the new great bell of Westminster, and most persons supposed it was for a death in the Royal Family. It proved, however, to be due to some derangement of the clock, for at four and five o'clock, 10 or 12 strokes were struck instead of the proper number."

The gentleman, who communicated the fact through the medium of *Notes and Queries*, goes on to say that on mentioning this in the morning to a friend, who is deep in London antiquities, he observed that there is an opinion in the city that anything the matter with St. Paul's great bell is an omen of ill to the Royal Family ; and he added : " I hope the opinion will not extend to the Westminster bell." This was at 11 on Friday morning. " I see this morning that it was

---
[1] See *The Book of Days*, vol. i.

not till one a.m. the lamented Duchess of Kent was considered in the least danger, and, as you are aware, she expired in less than twenty-four hours."

The striking of thirteen instead of twelve by St. Paul's clock was once the means, as the following story tells, of the saving of a man's life.

John Hatfield, a private in the army in the reign of William and Mary, was tried by a court-martial on the charge of having fallen asleep when on duty upon the terrace of Windsor. He absolutely denied the charge against him, and solemnly declared (as a proof of his having been awake at the time) that he heard St. Paul's clock strike thirteen, the truth of which was much doubted by the court, because of the great distance. But, while he was under sentence of death, an affidavit was made by several persons that the clock actually did strike thirteen, instead of twelve; whereupon he received His Majesty's pardon.

This incident in Hatfield's life appeared in the *Public Advertiser*, and was contained in an account of his death, which occurred at his house in Glasshouse Yard, Aldersgate, on the 18th of June, 1770. He lived to the great age of 102. The following is an allusion to it in *A Trip to Windsor*, a poem by Timothy Scribble.

> "*The terrace walk we with surprize behold,*
> *Of which the guides have oft the story told:*
> *Hatfield, accused of sleeping on his post,*
> *Heard Paul's bell sounding, or his life had lost.*"

The story of how his life was thus saved was engraven on Hatfield's coffin.

One of the most extraordinary stories relating to

ST. PAUL'S AND CRIPPLEGATE

St. Paul's is told by Dr. Pritchard in his essay on "Somnambulism and Animal Magnetism."[1]

"A gentleman about 35 years of age, of active habits and good constitution, living in the neighbourhood of London, had complained for about five weeks of a slight headache. He was feverish, inattentive to his occupation and negligent of his family. He had been cupped, and taken some purgative medicine, when he was visited by Dr. Arnould of Camberwell. By that gentleman's advice he was sent to a private asylum, where he remained about two years. His delusions gradually subsided, and he was afterwards restored to his family."

This is Dr. Pritchard's prelude to a narration of the story that his patient, whom I will henceforth designate Mr. Deacon, when under the influence of the "delusions" from which he suffered, unfolded to Dr. Arnould. The story was this:

One afternoon in July, Mr. Deacon, feeling unsettled, went for a walk in the city and presently found himself in St. Paul's Churchyard. He was looking at some prints in the shop of Bowles & Carver, when a short, grave, elderly gentleman, in dark brown clothes, stopped beside him, and getting into conversation with him asked him if he had ever ascended St. Paul's to the ball, just below the cross. Mr. Deacon answering in the negative, the stranger proposed taking him up and showing him the magnificent view of London that was obtainable from the ball. Mr. Deacon expressing his willingness to accompany the stranger, the two dined in a neighbouring restaurant and then

[1] In the *Encyclopaedia of Medicine*. See also *Hallucinations*, by Dr. de Boismont.

made for the Cathedral. On reaching the ball they stood and gazed for some moments, in silence, at the extensive panoramic view beneath. The old gentleman then produced a mirror, the back and sides of which were decorated with symbolic figures, and placing it in the centre of the ball uttered strange cries. He left off, to ask Mr. Deacon, who was watching him with increasing apprehension, if he would like to see any of his friends who were a great distance away. Mr. Deacon, fearing to offend him if he answered in the negative, said he would like to see his father.

"Look in the mirror, then," the old man replied, and Mr. Deacon, obeying, saw in it a picture of his father, seated in an armchair, apparently fast asleep. Greatly alarmed, Mr. Deacon begged the old man to take him down into the street. The old man agreed to do so, but only on the understanding that Mr. Deacon should ever afterwards be his slave, to do whatsoever he might will. Mr. Deacon, feeling helpless to resist, acquiesced, whereupon the old man at once proceeded to escort him down the staircase to the street. On the way he pointed to a great bell, and Mr. Deacon heard sounds of laughter, anger and pain coming from it.

"That is my agent of hearing," the old man explained. "It communicates with all the other bells within the circle of hieroglyphics, by which every word spoken by those under my command is made audible to me."

The old man then conducted Mr. Deacon into the street, and went back into the building.

"Since that fatal interview," Mr. Deacon told Dr. Arnould, "the necromancer, for such I believe him to be, is continually dragging me before him in his mirror, and he not only sees me every moment of the day, but he reads all my thoughts, and I have a dreadful consciousness that no action of my life is free from his inspection, and no place can afford me security from his power."

With regard to the hieroglyphics, Mr. Deacon said the old man practised his spells by means of them on walls, walls of all kinds, and when once the symbols were there, everyone near them came under the influence of the necromancer.

"Once," Mr. Deacon remarked to Dr. Arnould, "to try and escape from his tremendous power, I walked for three days and three nights, till I fell down under a wall, exhausted by fatigue, and dropped asleep; but, on awakening, I saw the dreadful signs before mine eyes, and I felt myself as completely under his infernal spells at the end as at the beginning of my journey."

Dr. Arnould asked him what these hieroglyphics were and how he understood them, and he answered: "They are signs and symbols which you, in your ignorance of their true meaning, have taken for letters and words and read, as you have thought, 'Day and Martin's and Warren's blacking.'"

This was the gist of the story Mr. Deacon related to Dr. Arnould, and which Dr. Pritchard reproduces in his essay. Dr. de Boismont, Dr. Arnould and Dr. Pritchard believed it to be a very good case of hallucination, and, of course, it may have been, although doctors are by no means always correct in their verdicts. They thought it not improbable that Mr. Deacon's statement that he had ascended to the top of St. Paul's with a stranger was correct, but that the view he had seen from it had so impressed his exceptionally excitable mind that he had imagined the rest of his story, and, from continually dwelling on it, had come to believe it was really true. Be this as it may, other people beside Mr. Deacon have, from time to time, believed St. Paul's to be genuinely haunted.

When I was visiting St. Paul's one day, in the summer of 1899, two Americans, a lady and gentleman, came to me in a great state of excitement and declared they had just had a very curious experience.

" We were walking down that aisle," the lady said, pointing to the centre aisle, " when we both saw a great black cloud suddenly come out of the ground in front of us and ascend in the air. When about twenty feet up, it suddenly vanished."

I asked her if it were like smoke, and she said, " Oh, no. It was like nothing, nothing I have ever seen. It gave me the impression it was alive, and I was terribly frightened."

She certainly looked scared, for she was very white and trembled all over. The gentleman with her, who appeared equally alarmed, corroborated her story. They came away with me, and said they would go there again in a few days' time, when they had recovered their equanimity, to see if the same thing happened. Whether they did so or not I cannot say, for I never saw them again. Another lady told me that when resting in St. Paul's one day, she saw a woman kneeling in one of the aisles, apparently searching for something. Desirous of assisting her, she got up and was walking towards the woman, when she felt someone touch her on the shoulder. She swung round at

ST. PAUL'S AND CRIPPLEGATE

once, but there was no one in sight; and when she turned to look again at the woman, she, too, had disappeared, and not a trace of her was to be seen.

Several days later, when she was in the Cathedral about the same hour, the same thing happened. She saw the same woman kneeling in the same aisle, and as she was walking towards her, she again felt a tap on her shoulder. She glanced round immediately, but no one was there, and when she turned again the kneeling woman also had vanished. An eerie feeling then came over her, and she got out of the Cathedral as quickly as possible.

An unusual case of what some medical men might, perhaps, term hallucinations is narrated in a pamphlet [1] bearing the following title: "Strange news from the West, being sights seen in the Air Westward on Thursday last, being the 21st day of the previous March, by diverse persons of credit standing on London Bridge between 7 and 8 of the clock at night. Two great armies marching forth from two clouds, and encountering each other; but, after a sharp dispute, they suddenly vanished. Also, some remarkable sights that were seen to issue forth of a cloud that seemed like a mountain in the shape of a bull, a bear, a lion, and an elephant and castle on his back, and how they all vanished."

The author of the pamphlet says that on the 21st of March,[2] about or between 7 and 8 p.m., certain people in the city crossing London Bridge were astounded to see several clouds overhead, of the most remarkable and unusual shape. While they were looking, one of

---

[1] See *The Romance of London*, by John Timbs.
[2] He does not give the year.

the clouds suddenly assumed the shape of a cathedral with a tower in the middle of it. It then vanished. Another apparent cloud turned into a tree, spreading like an oak. Between this cloud and the first one was a big mountain, from out of which crawled a crocodile with its mouth open. It was suddenly metamorphosed into a bull; the bull into a lion; the lion into a bear, and the bear into a hog.

At the end of about fifteen minutes the mountain was divided into two shapes, each resembling an animal. One looked like an elephant with a castle on its back, and the other a lion. After a time, the elephant and castle disappeared and a number of men appeared in their stead, while the lion was converted into a horse and rider. A third cloud resembling a whale now made its appearance, and immediately afterwards a fourth cloud, like a human head or cap, with what appeared to be horns on each side of it.

Between these last two clouds there then were seen a few men, who marched to and fro and suddenly vanished, all, saving one, who continued to strut about with great dignity. Then, from close to the cloud like a head came an army, and, on the left of it, another army. The armies attacked one another with the greatest fury, and then suddenly vanished. Whilst they were fighting, a fiery flame was seen to shoot along the sky in the direction of the city. With its dying out, the visions ceased. These phenomenon are gravely reputed to have been witnessed by a number of reliable witnesses.

One wonders how the three doctors I have named would have accounted for them. If a hallucination could be experienced collectively much might be

ST. PAUL'S AND CRIPPLEGATE 217

accounted for, including, of course, the greatly discussed Indian rope trick.

The case of a ghostly dream,[1] which led to the discovery of a murder, is associated with that part of the city called Cripplegate. In the neighbourhood of Cripplegate, in the autumn of 1698, a Mr. Stockden was murdered. The motive of the crime was robbery, and the assassins escaped, without leaving any clue to their identity. Mrs. Greenwood, a neighbour of Mr. Stockden, dreamed Mr. Stockden came to her, and bidding her follow him led her to a house in Thames Street. " In that house," she thought Mr. Stockden said, " Maynard, one of the men who robbed and murdered me, lives."

She then awoke. With the dream fresh in her memory Mrs. Greenwood went the following morning to Thames Street, and identifying a house there as the one she had seen in her dream, she inquired whether a man named Maynard lived in it. She was told yes. In another dream Mrs. Greenwood again saw Mr. Stockden, who gave her a minute description of Maynard and of a certain wine-drawer. Both men were found from these descriptions and apprehended.

In a third dream Mr. Stockden again appeared to her and took her to a house in Old Street, where he said Marsh, another of his murderers, lived. She went to the street in the morning and found her dream was true. Marsh did live in that particular house. She had yet a fourth dream, in which she fancied Mr. Stockden took her over a bridge in the Borough, into a yard, where she saw a man and his wife. Mr.

[1] See *The Romance of London*, by John Timbs, and *News from the Invisible World*.

Stockden told her they were the Bevils, and that the man was also one of the gang that had murdered him. In the morning she searched for the yard, accompanied by Mr. Stockden's housekeeper. The yard proved to be the Marshalsea prison yard, and walking about in it were the man and woman Mrs. Greenwood had seen in her dream. The man was at once charged with the murder. He, Marsh, and Maynard were tried, found guilty and executed. The wine-drawer, who was a friend of Maynard, was not convicted.

The night after the execution Mr. Stockden made his final appearance in a dream to Mrs. Greenwood, and said, "Elizabeth, I thank thee; the God of Heaven reward thee for what thou hast done."

And there ends the account. Mr. Timbs merely quotes it, and leaves his readers to form their own opinion regarding it. If the Rev. Smythies, curate of St. Giles and Cripplegate, who published the story, in 1698, is to be relied on, and one can hardly imagine that he could have invented it, since he gives names and dates and localities, then it furnished a very interesting example of dreams that are brought about by some superphysical agency.

Another well-known story is also associated with Cripplegate.[1] A lady residing in Cripplegate, having lain for some time in a trance, was finally pronounced by the doctor attending her to be dead; and, in due course, she was buried.

The sexton having learned that the corpse had a valuable ring on one of its fingers determined to steal it, and, with this object in view, he went one night to the cemetery, accompanied by his wife. To an expert

---

[1] See *News from the Invisible World*.

like himself it was an easy matter to disinter the remains, and upon raising the lid of the coffin he at once caught sight of the ring. Being unable to remove it from the finger of the defunct lady by pulling, he decided to cut the finger off, and, aided by his wife, he was about to commence the job, when, suddenly, the supposed corpse sat up. The sexton and his wife then took to their heels, whilst the lady in her winding sheet, now fully recovered from her trance, stepped out of the coffin, and picking up the lanthorn the guilty pair had left behind them in their fright, quickly made for her home. After repeatedly knocking at the door, and pausing between the knocks, to listen, she finally heard the maid-servant approaching on tiptoe, after which a nervous voice inquired who was there.

"It is I, your mistress," the ex-corpse replied. "For God's sake, let me in at once. I am very cold."

Instead of opening the door, however, the maid-servant, with a loud yell of terror, ran at once to her master, to tell him that the ghost of his wife was knocking at the door. Fortunately, the gentleman in question was the possessor of strong nerves and much common sense. Discrediting the servant's story of a spirit he went to the door, and upon hearing the well-known voice of his wife, immediately let her in. Hot drinks and a warm bed prevented her from taking a serious cold, and in a short time she had fully recovered from her dreadful ordeal. Subsequently, she had, in due course, three children, and, besides, lived on to a good old age.

When she died she was buried in Cripplegate Parish Churchyard, and the story of how she had been previously rescued from the grave was inscribed, in brief, on her monument. The sexton and his wife having told someone, on the night they had fled from the cemetery, upon seeing the supposed corpse sit up, that they had seen a ghost, the lady they had unwittingly rescued from a terrible death was jokingly dubbed "The Cripplegate Ghost," a name by which she was ever afterwards known.

Whether the sexton and his wife were punished for their projected villainy the narrator of the story does not say; it may have been thought, perhaps, that owing to their scare, the two culprits had already suffered enough, and, after all, had it not been for their attempt to rob, as they thought, her dead body (the pain she must have suffered, owing to their futile efforts to remove the ring from her finger by tugging at it, undoubtedly brought her out of the trance), the lady who had been so unfortunately buried alive would very soon have succumbed to an agonizing death.

CHAPTER XVIII

THE COCK LANE GHOST

No supposed haunting in London ever created a greater sensation than the one that occurred in Cock Lane, between Newgate Street and West Smithfield, in 1760.[1] For a time it was the universal theme of conversation among the learned and illiterate alike, and in every circle of society, from the prince to the peasant.

The story may be told thus: At the beginning of the year 1760, a Mr. Kent, a stockbroker, lived in Cock Lane, in the house of a man named Parsons, who was the officiating clerk of the parish of St. Sepulchre's. Mrs. Kent had died, on giving birth to a child, the previous year, and Mr. Kent's sister-in-law, Fanny, had arrived from Norfolk to keep house for him. Presumably, they had conceived an affection for each other, for each made a will in the other's favour. Parsons, in whose house they continued living, and who was always in a state of impecuniosity or said he was, kept on borrowing from Mr. Kent; and as he refused to repay Mr. Kent, when asked by him to do so, a quarrel between the two men ensued, which resulted in Mr. Kent finding fresh quarters and instituting legal proceedings against Parsons, for the recovery of his money.

While this affair was still pending, Fanny was taken very ill with smallpox, and although, apparently, she

[1] *Chronicles of Crime.* Edited by Camden Pelham.

received every care and attention, she died and was interred in a vault under Clerkenwell Church. As has already been stated, she had made a will in Mr. Kent's favour; she had, one imagines, willed the whole of her property to him, but he had barely come into it, before it was rumoured in the neighbourhood of Cock Lane that she had met with foul play. This occurred at the beginning of 1762. It was said that the house owned by Parsons, in which Mr. Kent and Fanny had lived, was haunted by Fanny's ghost, and that Parsons' daughter, a girl of about twelve years of age, had, on several occasions, seen and conversed with this ghost, who told her that she (Fanny) had not died of the smallpox, as was currently reported, but had been poisoned by Mr. Kent.

Parsons was the principal agent in making the story of these ghostly happenings known, and he gave them as wide a publicity as possible. He declared that ever since Fanny's death (she died in 1760), ghostly knockings had been heard on the doors and walls of his house.

These statements, it seems, were believed by his neighbours and friends, who, doubtless, lost no time in imparting them to their neighbours and friends, and, consequently, the news that a house in Cock Lane was haunted soon spread, not only all over the city, but also into the suburbs. As a result, a gentleman called at the house to investigate the case, and was permitted by Parsons to do so, that is to say, he was permitted to do as much investigation as Parsons thought was discreet. He was shown by Parsons into Miss Parsons' room. The girl was sitting up in bed trembling violently. She declared she had just seen Fanny's ghost, who had again told her that she,

Fanny, had been poisoned by Mr. Kent. On leaving the room, knockings were heard in various parts of the house, and the gentleman, as gentlemen and ladies so often do on such occasions, came away mystified, afraid to doubt and yet ashamed to admit that he really believed, but with a promise to come again shortly and to bring friends.

The following day, he arrived at "the haunted house," with three clergymen and about twenty other people, including two negroes. Parsons informed them that although the ghost would never appear to anyone but his daughter, it would answer questions put to it by anyone present, and that it expressed an affirmative answer by one knock, a negative by two, and its displeasure by a kind of scratching.

The girl was then put into bed with her sister, and the bed examined by the clergymen, though why by the clergymen is not clear, since clergymen, as a rule, are far from being expert in the detection of trickery. The whole party of investigators then sat in the dark, some in the room and some just outside it. After a while, knocking was heard on the wall by the bed, and Miss Parsons declared she saw Fanny's ghost. No one else did. The following questions were gravely asked by one of the clergymen. (Mary Frazer, who had been the servant in Mr. Parsons' house, during Fanny's residence in it, and to whom it was said Fanny had been much attached, addressed the questions to the ghost; hence, presumably, her being afterwards proclaimed a medium, and the answers were given, as previously stated, by one knock for "yes" and two for "no.")

"Do you make this disturbance on account of the ill-usage you received from Mr. Kent?"

" Yes."

" Were you brought to an untimely end by poison?"

" Yes."

" How was the poison administered: in beer or in purl?"

" In purl."

" How long was that before your death?"

" About three hours."

" Can your former servant, Carrots, give any information about the poison?"

" Yes."

" Are you Kent's wife's sister?"

" Yes."

" Were you married to Kent after your sister's death?"

" No."

" Was anybody else, besides Kent, concerned in your murder?"

" No."

" Can you, if you like, appear visible to anyone?"

" Yes."

" Will you do so?"

" Yes."

" Can you get out of this house?"

" Yes."

" Is it your intention to follow this child about everywhere?"

" Yes."

" Are you pleased in being asked these questions?"

" Yes."

" Does it ease your troubled soul?"

" Yes."

(At this juncture a strange noise was heard, which someone present declared was the fluttering of wings, either spirits' or angels' wings.)

"How long before your death did you tell your servant, Carrots, that you were poisoned? An hour?"

"Yes."

(Carrots, who was present, was appealed to, but she stated positively that such was not the fact, as the deceased was quite speechless an hour before her death. This shook the faith of some of the spectators, but the examination was allowed to continue.)

"How long did Carrots live with you?"

"Three or four days."

(Carrots was again appealed to, and said that this was true.)

"If Mr. Kent is arrested, will he confess?"

"Yes."

"Would your soul be at rest if he were hanged for it?"

"Yes."

"Will he be hanged for it?"

"Yes."

"How long a time first?"

"Three years."

"How many clergymen are there in this room?"

"Three."

"How many negroes?"

"Two."

"Is this watch (held up by one of the clergymen) white?"

"No."

"Is it yellow?"

"No."

" Is it blue ? "
" No."
" Is it black ? "
" Yes." [1]
(The watch was in a black shagreen case.)
Nothing of further moment occurred at this sitting; but the news of it spreading, crowds flocked to the house, eager to see the ghost and to hear the mysterious knockings. Indeed, so great was the throng clamouring to get in, that Parsons found it expedient to charge a fee for admission, an arrangement which was, no doubt, very agreeable to him. Indeed, things had taken a turn greatly to his satisfaction, for now he not only had had his revenge on Mr. Kent, but he was in the way of making a decent bit besides.

Consequently, the ghost played its antics every night, to the great amusement of hundreds of people, and the great perplexity of an even larger number.

Among those who visited the house were Horace Walpole and Dr. Johnson. In a letter to Sir Horace Mann, Jan. 20, 1762, Walpole said :

" I am ashamed to tell you that we are again dipped into an egregious scene of folly. The reigning fashion is a ghost, a ghost that would not pass muster in the

---

[1] The code used on this occasion (subsequently referred to as a sitting), in 1762, is practically the same as that employed at modern spiritualistic séances. There is very little doubt it was the reading of or hearing about this case that inspired the Fox sisters in Hydesville, Arcadia, Wayne County, U.S.A., in 1848, to pretend their house was haunted. Any impartial person comparing the Hydesville case with that of the Cock Lane case cannot help observing a great similarity between them. In both cases a perfectly innocent man was accused of murder, but whereas the motive behind the accusation in the Cock Lane case was undoubtedly revenge, in the Hydesville case the motive would appear to have been, in the first place, merely a desire for notoriety, and afterwards, when the opportunity of making it occurred, money.

However, the lesson derived from both cases is the same, namely, that the employment of so-called mediumship may easily lead to false accusations, necessitating much persecution and great suffering.

THE COCK LANE GHOST

paltriest convent in the Apennines. It only knocks and scratches; does not pretend to appear or to speak. The clergy give it their benediction; and all the world, whether believers or infidels, go to hear it."

In another letter he writes: "I went to hear it, for it is not an apparition, but an audition.

"We set out from the opera, changed our clothes at Northumberland House, the Duke of York, Lady Northumberland, Lady Mary Coke, Lord Hertford and I, all in one hackney coach, and drove to the spot. It rained torrents; yet the lane was full of mob and the house so full we could not get in. At last they discovered it was the Duke of York, and the company squeezed themselves into one another's pockets to make room for us.

"The house, which is borrowed, and to which the ghost has adjourned, is wretchedly small and miserable. When we opened the chamber, in which were fifty people, with no light but one tallow candle at the end, we tumbled over the bed of the child to whom the ghost comes, and whom they are murdering by inches in such insufferable heat and stench.

"At the top of the room are ropes to dry clothes. I asked if we were to have rope dancing between the acts. We heard nothing. They told us (as they would at a puppet show) that it would not come that night till seven in the morning, that is when there are only prentices and old women. We stayed, however, till half an hour after one."

Unhappily for Parsons, the ghost at one of these meetings was induced by the Rev. Mr. Aldritch of Clerkenwell to promise that it would not follow Miss Parsons whithersoever she went, but would follow

Mr. Aldritch into the vault under St. John's Church, Clerkenwell, where Fanny's body was buried, and would there give a notice of its presence by a loud knock on the coffin.

The eventful night, *i.e.* February 1, arriving, Miss Parsons was taken in a hackney coach, first of all to Mr. Aldritch's house, near the church, where a large number of people, mostly society people, were assembled. Among them was Dr. Johnson.

At 10 p.m. she was put to bed, the bed-clothes being previously searched by the ladies of the party to see she had nothing secreted in them. While the gentlemen were in another room deliberating whether they should proceed in a body to the church, they were summoned into the girl's room by the ladies, who declared the ghost had come, and that they heard knocks and scratchings. The gentlemen at once went into the room.

Miss Parsons, on being asked if she saw the ghost, replied, " No, but she felt it on her back like a mouse." She was then told to put her hands out of bed, and on their being held by some of the ladies present, the ghost was asked to say if it was in the room. There was no response. The question was put several times, and with the same result. Silence. The ghost was then asked to show itself, but the result was the same. Nil. It was then asked to give a token of its presence by some sound, or by touching the hand or cheek of any lady or gentleman in the room; but again the result was nil.

The fact that when the child's hands were held no knockings or scratchings were audible, but whenever they were released in the dark knockings and scratchings were at once heard, struck everyone present as significant, and one of the clergymen went downstairs, to interrogate Mr. Parsons on the subject. He emphatically denied there was any deception, and even declared that he himself had, on one occasion, seen and conversed with the ghost. The very lenient company deciding to give the ghost another trial, the same clergyman announced in a loud voice that they were all going to the church vault, to claim a fulfilment of the ghost's promise to manifest itself there.

Accordingly, at one a.m., they proceeded to the church, and the same clergyman and another gentleman entered the vault, alone, and took up their position by the coffin. The ghost was asked to appear, but it did not; it was then asked to knock, but it did not; it was asked to scratch, but it did not; and the two came out of the vault, convinced, at last, that the whole business was a fraud practised by Parsons and his daughter. The rest of the company were not quite so hasty in their verdict. After a serious consultation it was unanimously agreed that if the ghost answered anybody at all, it would surely answer Mr. Kent, the supposed murderer. He was, accordingly, asked to go down into the vault. He went with several other people and challenged the ghost to assert in any way possible to it, that he, Mr. Kent, had poisoned Fanny. There was no response of any kind. Mr. Aldritch then spoke, and conjured the spirit to end their doubts by making some sign of its presence and by indicating the guilty person. They waited for half an hour in the vault, and there being no response of any kind, they then repaired to the house, where they had left Miss Parsons in bed, and requested her to get up and dress herself. When she had done so, she was strictly examined, but persisted in her statement that she practised no trickery, and that the ghost really appeared to her.

There are people who, if they want to believe a certain thing will believe it, no matter how forcible the arguments against it; in fact, cranks and bigots are just as numerous and rabid in these days of supposed enlightenment as they were in the so-called dark ages. Hence, many people, mostly women, upheld Miss Parsons, despite the positive evidence against her, and declared the spirit of Fanny had not manifested itself in the church vault because Mr. Kent had taken care beforehand to have Fanny's body removed. Mr. Kent, whose position was a very painful one, immediately procured competent and reliable witnesses, in whose presence the vault was entered and Fanny's coffin opened. Their depositions testifying to the body being in the coffin intact were speedily published; and, about the same time, the girl Parsons was fully found out. Being threatened by those investigating the case with Newgate, if she did not confess, she produced an apparatus on which she admitted making the supposed supernatural scratchings. She used to take it to bed with her and conceal it on her person. Her mother, she declared, was responsible for some of the knockings. Indeed, there seemed to be little doubt that the child merely acted under her parents' instructions, and, most probably, coercion.

Mr. Kent now brought an action against Mr. and Mrs. and Miss Parsons, the alleged medium, Mary Frazer, the servant, the Rev. Mr. Moor and the tradesman for conspiracy. Mr. Moor and the tradesman

THE COCK LANE GHOST

were said to be prominent patrons of the fraud. The trial took place in the Court of King's Bench, July 10, 1762, before Lord Chief Justice Mansfield. It lasted twelve hours, and resulted in all the accused being found guilty. The Rev. Mr. Moor and the tradesman, after being severely reprimanded in court, were recommended " to make some pecuniary compensation to the prosecutor for the aspersions they had been instrumental in throwing upon his character." Parsons was sentenced to stand three times in the pillory, and to be imprisoned for two years; his wife got one year, and Mary Frazer, the servant, six months, with hard labour.

The girl Parsons appears to have got off, at least I can find no record of her being punished. Very possibly her youth and the undoubted fact that she was but the tool, albeit quite likely the willing one, of her parents weighed both with judge and jury.

As a rule, crowds were not kind to people in pillories and stocks. They not infrequently pelted them with dead cats, rotten eggs and other unpleasant missiles, but on this occasion they expressed sympathy with Parsons, and not only refrained from injuring him, but got up a subscription on his behalf.

Miss Parsons grew up and married twice, dying in 1806.

Mr. J. W. Archer, visiting the vault one day for the purpose of making a drawing of it, was shocked to see coffins and human remains lying about in a terrible state of disorder; and the sexton's boy, who was with him, pointing at one of the coffins, said, "That's 'Scratching Fanny.'" The lid of this coffin being loose, Mr. Archer looked inside and saw the body of a woman. In his opinion, though how far he was competent to judge I cannot say, the body appeared to be adipocere, that is to say, in a state which he believed to be not uncommon in cases of arsenical poisoning.

In view of this statement made by Mr. Archer, and subsequently published, one wonders whether, after all, poor Fanny was poisoned. But even if Mr. Archer were right and the remains did show signs of arsenical poisoning, his testimony does not absolve the Parsons family of trickery. That they did practise fraud was proved beyond the shadow of a doubt, but it is just possible that they did honestly believe Mr. Kent to be guilty of murdering poor Fanny, and that the bogus spirit-rapping was devised and practised by them in the genuine hope that it would bring the crime home to him.

Mr. Archer's visit to the vault has therefore had a somewhat disturbing result, since, with regard to Fanny's death, it has raised questions and suggested doubts. Thanks to this visit, however, we get some idea of what poor Fanny was like. According to Mr. Archer's description, her face was oval and her features, which were all well preserved, were handsome. One imagines, therefore, that she must have been very prepossessing, as nice-looking as she was nice and amiable. Mr. Archer had no doubt that the body he saw was the body of poor Fanny, since the sexton's boy's statement was corroborated by Mr. Bird, one of the churchwardens. Mr. Archer, it seems, had asked Mr. Bird whose the body was that he had just been looking at, and Mr. Bird had told him it was the body of the woman whose ghost was said to have once haunted the house in Cock Lane.

CHAPTER XIX

STOCKWELL, WANDSWORTH COMMON, CHELSEA AND GHOSTLY CLOCKS

ABOUT ten years after the Cock Lane sensation, London was again thrilled by the report that a certain house was haunted. Near Vauxhall, in the parish of Stockwell, which was then a rather more select neighbourhood than it is now, lived an elderly lady named Mrs. Golding. Her household consisted of herself and her servant, Anne Robinson.

On the evening of Twelfth Day, 1772, Mrs. Golding was much startled at suddenly observing a most extraordinary commotion among her crockery. "Cups and saucers rattled down the chimney,[1] pots and pans were whirled down stairs, or through the windows; and hams, cheeses, and loaves of bread disported themselves upon the floor, as if the devil were in them."

Mrs. Golding, at any rate, must have come to the conclusion that the devil was in them, for she ran in a great state of agitation to her neighbours, and implored them to come at once to her house, to protect her from the devil. By no means unwilling to come to grips with his satanic majesty, Mrs. Golding's neighbours flocked to the house in numbers, and they were, probably, only too delighted at the prospect of a new subject for gossip. With the memory of the

[1] See *The New Newgate Calendar*, by Camden Pelham.

Cock Lane ghost still comparatively fresh in their minds, they did not feel particularly nervous.

Their advent at the house, however, did not put an end to the acrobatic performances of the crockery, which the neighbours, to their amazement, now witnessed. At first it was only the china that behaved thus inexplicably, but it was not long before the chairs and tables also began prancing and jumping, and things then began to look so serious that the neighbours, fearing the house itself would soon be following suit, thought it expedient to decamp. Left alone in the house with Anne, Mrs. Golding, in her terror, fell on her knees and implored the spirit to depart; but as it remained obdurate to her entreaties, and the crockery and furniture still continued to riot and racket, she repaired to the house of a kindly disposed neighbour, taking Anne with her. Soon after their arrival, the neighbour's crockery and furniture became restless, too. Plates and saucers cut mad capers on the kitchen floor, to be speedily joined by the hitherto sedate chairs and table. Finally, there was such a pandemonium and so many smashes that the neighbour thought it advisable to get rid of Mrs. Golding and Anne, before all his household goods were demolished.

Hence, back to her own house went Mrs. Golding, accompanied by Anne. Suspecting now that Anne was responsible for the disturbances, Mrs. Golding dismissed her, and forthwith all commotions in the kitchen ceased. Some time afterwards, Anne, in a fit of remorse, very unusual in servants, confessed to her new employer, the Rev. Mr. Brayfield, that she had been having a game at poor Mrs. Golding's expense.

Mr. Brayfield confided her confession to Mr. Hone, who published a detailed account of the whole affair. It appears that Anne, who seems to have been rather a prepossessing girl, as very naughty girls often are, had a lover, and being anxious to keep Mrs. Golding out of the kitchen, when her lover was about, she resolved to try to frighten her by pretending that the kitchen and the adjoining offices were haunted.

She, accordingly, placed the crockery on the shelves, in such a manner that it fell on the slightest motion and vibration, and attached strings, formed of horsehairs, to other articles, so that she could jerk them down from an adjoining room without much fear of detection. A little practice at this sort of work made her very expert; indeed, a little more practice, and she would have proved a formidable rival to many a juggler. There is very little doubt that many so-called Poltergeist hauntings and phenomena worked by mediums could be thus accounted for, and they could be so accounted for if professional magicians such as the Maskelynes were employed as investigators, instead of high-brow scientists and people who, for pecuniary reasons, wish to preserve and bolster up mediumship.

A case that savoured rather of the Poltergeist order occurred in May, 1887, in a house near Wandsworth Common.[1] Its occupants were a man and wife, a sister-in-law and one child. Soon after coming to the house, noises, such as might have been caused by the striking of a muffled sledge-hammer against brick or stone, were heard all over the house. On one occasion, the sister-in-law felt as if someone were seizing

---

[1] See *Sights and Shadows*, by F. G. Lee, D.D.

her by the shoulders from behind, and shaking her violently.

This happened in the presence of the man, who seeing her swaying to and fro, in a state of terrible agitation, put out his hand to steady her, and felt a shock through it, right up into his arm, such as might have been produced by an electrical current. So sharp and painful was the sensation that he drew back, uttering as he did so a loud cry.

Nothing was discernible to account for the phenomenon. On another occasion, the bed-clothes were snatched off one of the beds during the night, and the occupant of the bed, being aroused, saw the bed-clothes rise up from the floor and move, propelled by some invisible agency, on to the bed again. Subsequently, the disturbances became so frequent and nerve-racking that the family were obliged to vacate the premises. Five families lived there, in succession, afterwards, and all left for the same reason. The house, they declared, was badly haunted. At last, it remained untenanted, no one daring to occupy it. There was no known reason for the ghostly manifestations. What eventually happened to the house is not stated, but, very likely, sharing the fate of many other haunted houses, it was pulled down.

A haunted house, with which I am well acquainted, is situated near the Crystal Palace. As in so many cases, the disturbances in this house are periodical. Months and even years may pass without anything unusual happening, and then, suddenly, ghostly disturbances occur. One of the tenants was sitting in the drawing-room one evening, with a friend, when both of them, suddenly, saw a picture on the wall sway to and fro in the most remarkable fashion. Directly the friend got up and moved in the direction of the picture, it became still. The moment she sat down, it commenced rocking and swaying again. This went on for some minutes, and then ceased. No vehicles were passing at the time to cause any vibration in the room. Everything in the road, a very quiet turning off Gipsy Hill, was still, and there was nothing, apparently, to account for the phenomenon. On another occasion, a visitor in the house, being aroused from a siesta, one day, by the sensation that she was no longer alone in the room, upon glancing up, saw a tall, shadowy, hooded figure, in long black robes, bending over her. She was then so fearful of what might happen that she almost involuntarily shut her eyes, and when she ventured to open them again, the figure had gone.

A girl staying in the house, some years later, had a similar experience in the adjoining room. She awoke one moonlight night, to see, apparently, the same tall hooded figure, which she thought was a man in clerical robes, bending over her.

On neither occasion was the face of the figure seen. Yet another person to experience a haunting in the house was an actress, who took it for a brief period. Returning home, late one night, she was surprised to see one of the bedroom windows aglow with a light, that appeared to emanate from within.

Wondering what the light could be, she entered the house and, on approaching the room, saw a light under the door. On opening the door, however, the room was in complete darkness. She could discover no natural explanation of the phenomenon. She dreamed very vividly one night that this particular room was occupied by a very grotesque figure, and waking in a panic, she was conscious of something entering her own room and standing by her side. She got the impression, for the thing did not manifest, that it was exactly similar to the grotesque figure she had seen so vividly in her sleep.

Immediately prior to the death of a relative of the owner of the house inexplicable knockings were heard by its occupants, and servants periodically complained of heavy footsteps, which they could not account for, following them from room to room. The house, which is called in the immediate neighbourhood the " mystery house," still stands, but I do not know if its present owners have experienced any continuance of the haunting.[1]

This case affords yet another instance of what may be regarded as the most usual type of genuinely haunted house, *i.e.* the house in which phenomena periodically happen with no apparent motive, except, perhaps, to alarm, and with no apparent cause. Maybe, at some future date, they will be explicable in accordance with some at present unknown and unsuspected physical law in the spiritual world.

In Chelsea, as one may, perhaps, imagine, there are several houses said to be haunted. One is on the Embankment. For many years it was occupied by a Scottish gentleman, with a large circle of friends and acquaintances. A very curious incident happened, when I and others were having tea with him, a few years prior to his death. He and I were talking to-

---

[1] I myself can guarantee that all the incidents I have narrated in connection with this haunting actually occurred.

gether, apart from the rest of the company, when he abruptly left me, and walking to the far side of the room addressed himself to someone else. Later on he explained his conduct thus:

"When I was talking with you just now," he said, "I suddenly saw the phantom figure of a woman lying on the Chesterfield, near us. Her head was lolling helplessly on one side, and there was an ugly gash in her throat, which appeared to have been slashed from ear to ear. I was so shocked," he continued, "that I had to move, away from it and you, to the other side of the room. Did you see it?"

I told him that I had not seen the apparition that he had, but that I had seen something peculiar, though it may have been only an optical illusion. I then narrated to him what had actually occurred. I had, I said, naturally gazed after him as he left me, and while he was conversing with a lady on the far side of the room, I had seen a figure, standing behind him, that was the exact counterpart of himself.

"That is very interesting," he remarked, "because my projection, or phantom, or whatever you may like to call it, has been seen here by someone else."

He then went on to tell me that one day, when in his garden, he had looked up at the house, and had seen an exact duplicate of himself, leaning out of one of the windows, gesticulating.

A friend who was with him in the garden saw the figure, too. Another phantom seen in this house, he told me, was that of a bear. It invariably rose from the floor boards and disappeared near the fireplace.

The house, I subsequently learned, stood, according

to tradition, on ground that was once part of an estate in the possession of Anne Boleyn's father, and, in my opinion, it is not at all unlikely that as bear-baiting was much in vogue at that period, it was here practised, partly, if not wholly, to provide Anne's royal lover with an alternative pastime to courting.

If such were the case, the phantom bear would, no doubt, be the ghost of a bear that once actually lived and, probably, died on the spot where this particular haunting occurred.

A studio in the King's Road is reputed to be haunted, at times, by the ghost of a little old man, who is seen peering over the balustrade of the gallery.

Another Chelsea haunting is in Glebe Place, and of this I can speak from first-hand knowledge, that is to say, from a personal experience of it.

One summer evening my wife and I both heard sounds as of someone choking in the room adjoining ours. In the space of a few seconds, the sounds appearing to come from just outside our room, we opened our door immediately and went out on the landing; but we could see no one. However, as we stood at the head of the stairs listening, we heard the sounds, first on the staircase and then on the first floor landing, which was the one immediately below ours. The same disturbing sounds went on down the next flight of stairs and into the hall, where they finally ceased.

There was no one in the house at the time but ourselves, and no animal, so that any explanation of the phenomena, on physical grounds, seemed impossible. It transpired, upon our making inquiries, that other people had experienced inexplicable happenings in the house, but that their ghostly experiences were not the same as ours.

A house in the same street is said to be haunted by the phantom of a man on horseback; with regard to this phenomenon, however, I have not been able to obtain any reliable evidence.

One of the most unattractive ghosts I know haunts a house in Markham Square. The phantom is that of a nude woman with the face of a pig. She haunts one of the bedrooms, from time to time, and is generally seen in the act of leaning over the footrail of the bed, staring at the unfortunate occupant of it. According to my informant, an architect who once stayed in the house and saw this ghost, her limbs were well formed and her hands very beautiful.

Her head only, it seems, was abnormal, and so terribly monstrous was it that the architect refused to sleep in the room she haunted, again, and left the house, as soon as he possibly could. She appeared, he said, when the room was in absolute darkness, but could be plainly seen, owing to a light that emanated from her.

Having given a full account of this haunting in another of my works, I will merely remark before passing on, that its truth was vouched for to me.

There is a house reputed to be haunted in Wellington Square, and one in Poulton Square also: in both of them a very notorious murder was committed.

A house in Phillimore Place, recently pulled down, was haunted by an invisible ghost, that used to walk the house at night and make a sound as if it were striking a match. One wonders, if a new house springs up on the site of the old one, whether the same ghost will haunt it.

Redcliffe Square and Redcliffe Gardens both have their haunted houses, but as I have given particulars of the phenomena experienced in them elsewhere, I will not repeat them here.

To revert for a moment to the City, and to something which, although not strictly of a ghostly nature, is, nevertheless, I think, sufficiently associated with the superphysical to warrant an allusion to it here.

According to a correspondent in *Notes and Queries*,[1] there is an interesting tradition relating to the famous London stone in Cannon Street; a stone which was, and still is, perhaps, supposed, rightly or wrongly, to be under superphysical influence. It is enclosed in another stone with a circular aperture, and was the milliarium from which the Romans measured all the mileages in the kingdom.

What thrills one most with regard to it is the fact that it was once the altar of the temple of Diana, upon which the ancient British monarchs placed their hands, and at the same time took their oaths, on their accession, the rule being that until they did this they were merely kings presumptive.

Tradition avers it was originally brought by Brutus from Troy, and that it was he who laid it on its present site and ordained that it should be the altar-stone of the temple to Diana, and the actual foundation-stone and palladium of London. It was chiefly, perhaps, because it had been thus ordained London's palladium or talisman that it was always very carefully guarded and preserved, the belief that the fate of London was linked up with it (*i.e.* that so long as it remained where it was originally set, all would go well with England's

---

[1] See *Notes and Queries*, 3rd S., No. 1.

capital, but that London would be in grave danger of destruction should it ever be damaged or removed) being universally honoured and held.

Coming back to the orthodox haunting, an actor, named Robinson, whom I used to meet, occasionally, at the Old Actors' Association in Regent Street, once told me of a curious experience he and his family had in a flat that he rented in a house in Whitehead Grove, Sloane Square.

Besides hearing unaccountable sounds such as footsteps crossing the floors at all hours of the night, they would wake up suddenly to find that all the bed-clothes had been taken off them and carried some little distance away. Also, upon arriving home rather later than usual one night, they heard, to their astonishment, someone playing an old-world tune on, so it seemed to them, their piano. They went into the sitting-room, fully expecting to find someone there, but the room was empty, and the piano closed.

One evening, when alone in the flat, Mrs. Robinson heard sounds of satirical laughter just behind her. Thinking it was her husband, who had returned earlier than usual from the theatre, she turned round quickly, to speak to him, and was astounded to find no one there.

Perhaps the most remarkable of their experiences was a dual dream. Mr. and Mrs. Robinson both dreamed, the same night, that they met, on returning to the flat one day, a tall, thin, cadaverous-looking man in black, with a hare lip. He was in the act of leaving the flat, and had a yard measure in his hand.

They said to him, "Who are you? What do you want?" and he replied:

"Don't worry. I have just been measuring her, and she won't require one more than five feet long."

The man then bade them a polite good morning, and was about to pass them by, when they awoke. Struck with the singularity of the fact that they had each had precisely the same dream, they made a careful note of the occurrence.

About a month later they went on a visit to one of Mrs. Robinson's aunts. Soon after their arrival, this aunt caught a severe chill and died, and when the undertaker came to the house, to see about the coffin, Mr. and Mrs. Robinson identified him at once. Tall, thin and hare-lipped, he was the man they had both dreamed about.

He did not say, "Don't worry. I have just been measuring her, and she won't require one more than five feet long," but what his double in the dream said with regard to the coffin was nevertheless true, as Mrs. Robinson's aunt was only about four feet ten inches in height, and the coffin made for her was, consequently, well under five feet in length. Finally, the ghostly disturbances in the flat got on the Robinsons' nerves to such an extent that they left before their lease was up.

One of the strangest cases of ghostly forewarning in my experience occurred just before the Great War. Mrs. L——, an Anglo-Indian lady, living in Upper Gloucester Place, Portman Square, wrote to me about some strange happenings in her house, and asked me to call on her apropos of the same. I did so, and she told me an extraordinary story. She said one night, some years previously, she had been awakened by hearing an unusual sound. As she lay awake, wondering what it was, a clock on the landing outside began to strike. She counted twelve, but, to her surprise, the clock struck thirteen, then, after a pause, it struck again, and again, after another pause. After that there was a deep and impressive silence, which was presently broken by her husband asking her if she had heard the clock.

It struck them as so odd, that Mr. L—— made a note of it in his diary the following day. Some days later, the number of days corresponding with the strokes of the clock, when it struck for the second time, and at an hour corresponding with the clock, when it struck for the third time, Mr. L—— met with a serious accident, which ultimately led to his death. Mrs. L—— told me that various unaccountable noises had been heard in the house ever since she and her husband had been there, but she felt she must tell me about the clock, as it was the queerest of all their experiences.

Unfortunately, I did not commit her story to writing on the spot, and, consequently, when I came to narrate it in a book I subsequently published, I made some slight errors. These she reminded me of when I sat next to her, quite by accident, one night at the performance in London of "The Blue Bird."

"Do you know," she remarked to me, in between the acts, "I heard that clock strike thirteen again last night. It first of all struck thirteen, and then, after a brief pause, three. Do you think it portends anything? I have an idea it portends the death of a relative of mine, who has been ill for some time."

While she was speaking, an uncanny feeling came over me that it portended her own death. Of course,

I did not tell her so, I merely suggested that she should leave the house as soon as possible, as it obviously possessed some very sinister influence, which I could not help thinking was inimically disposed towards her, and she assured me she would.

Two days later, I read an account of her death in the *Daily Mail*. She was in a taxi with her dog and a friend, when they were run into by another taxi in Portman Square, and Mrs. L—— was killed. I do not think that anyone can fail to see that the accident in itself was remarkable. The window of the taxi furthest from Mrs. L—— had been smashed in the collision, and a piece of glass from it, missing Mrs. L——'s friend by the narrowest margin, had struck Mrs. L—— on the neck and severed an artery. That she bled to death within a few minutes is not to be wondered at, but it is surely, at least, worthy of note that in this accident, neither Mrs. L——'s friend, who sat close beside her, nor the driver, nor the dog nestling in Mrs. L——'s arms, were hurt. It was Mrs. L——, alone, who met with injury.

Among the curious and may be ghostly incidents connected with clocks is one relating to Queen Anne.

In the words of my authority,[1] Mrs. Danvers, the oldest and, probably, the most attached lady of her (Queen Anne's) household, entering the presence chamber at Kensington Palace, saw, to her surprise, her Majesty standing before the clock, gazing intently at it. Mrs. Danvers was alarmed and perplexed by the sight, as her Majesty was seldom able to move without assistance; she approached, and ascertained that it was indeed Queen Anne who stood there.

[1] Miss Strickland, the historian. See *Picturesque England*, by L. Valentine.

Venturing to interrupt the ominous silence that prevailed in the vast room, only broken by the heavy ticking of the clock, she asked whether her Majesty saw anything unusual there in the clock? The Queen answered not, yet turned her eyes at the questioner with so woeful and ghastly a regard that, as this person afterwards affirmed, she saw death in the look. Assistance was summoned by the cries of the terrified attendant, and the Queen was conveyed to her bed, from whence she never rose again.

Whether in this case there was any superphysical agency at work or not, clocks, in my opinion, do undoubtedly attract the Unknown.

CHAPTER XX

ENFIELD CHASE, SOUTH MIMMS, CHESHUNT, ETC.

SINCE Mr. Edward Walford includes "Enfield Chase and Cheshunt" in his work on *Greater London*, I will point to him, as my authority, for the inclusion of these two places in this last chapter of my book on London Ghosts.

From time to time sensational reports of ghostly occurrences in Enfield Chase and East Barnet appear in the Press. Many such appeared in 1926, and, according to these reports,[1] the ghost of Sir Geoffrey de Mandeville, the wicked Earl of Essex, who is said to have flourished, for a while, like the proverbial bay tree, in the reign of Stephen or thereabouts, and after committing all sorts of abominable crimes, to have drowned himself in the moat at Enfield Chase, walks about the Church Hill Road in the dead of night, in clanking armour, to the terror of every respectable citizen and all dogs; the latter demonstrating their horror by the most dismal howls.

Sir Geoffrey, so says rumour, is sometimes accompanied in his nocturnal peregrinations by a very beautiful phantom lady in grey, who occasionally glides about alone. Various people in East Barnet have testified to seeing her, both alone and accompanied by the phantom of Sir Geoffrey de Mandeville. The ghostly happenings in this neighbourhood, how-

[1] Vide *Daily Mirror*, *Star*, and other papers, December, 1926.

ever, are not always confined to out-of-door places. Close to the Grange Estate at East Barnet, and near some premises formerly known as "The Haunted Stables," stands a house, in which there is a cellar that is haunted, if we may believe report, by very extraordinary noises. These noises are said to resemble the low mumbling of voices and muffled thuds, the latter sounds suggesting the hauling about of heavy packages.

Here, too, by way of variety, a tinkling noise is occasionally heard, which noise appears to move round the cellar, whilst a shadowy form, too vague for description, glides about the floor. All these phenomena were vouched for at the time in the Press, and it was stated that people who ventured into the cellar to hear and see the haunting, came out of it with staring eyes and trembling limbs, vowing nothing on earth would persuade them to go there again.

That the more timid inhabitants of East Barnet were scared I know for a fact, for some of them told me so, and declared that they were too frightened to venture, alone, abroad, after dusk.

Apart from these hauntings, which break out every few years, strange stories are told of Camlet Moat, which, it will be remembered, is vividly described by Sir Walter Scott in *The Fortunes of Nigel*. Situated almost in the middle of the Chase in Trent Park, what now remains of the original moat is almost hidden from view by a thick growth of trees and bushes. Somewhere in the vicinity of this moat, according to tradition, is a deep well, paved at the bottom, in which lies the famous De Mandeville treasure. How it came to be there may be told thus: One of the De Mandevilles, being attainted for treason, feared that his life and property would be forfeited; he therefore put all his money, no inconsiderable sum, and valuables in a strong iron chest, and hid the chest in the well that he had specially prepared for it. The well was then, as now, surrounded by trees, and in one of their widespreading branches, that overhung the well, De Mandeville used to conceal himself, and watch for the arrival of his enemies. One day, when he was thus occupied, he lost his balance, and falling into the well was killed. The well and wood then became haunted by his ghost, a tall figure clad in shining black armour, and, apparently, have remained so haunted ever since. Many attempts have been made to secure the treasure, but whenever the chest has been hauled up, upon nearing the brink of the well, the cord and chain holding it has given way. This invariable mishap eventually led to the belief that Mandeville's ghost still watches over his treasure and, owing to his interference (at the critical moment), it can never be purloined.

In 1832, on the road between Enfield Chase and Barnet, a Mr. R. C. Danby was cruelly murdered by a man named Johnson, and the spot where the crime was committed is still believed to be haunted. That it is genuinely haunted would seem to be apparent from the following story, told at a "talk" I once gave on "Ghosts," at my house in St. Ives, Cornwall. The narrator of the story in question was a summer visitor at St. Ives, named Ward.

He was driving one early autumn night with his uncle, a traveller for a large firm in the city, along the Enfield and Barnet Road. The sun had sunk below the horizon, and in lieu of purple, and gold, and crimson, the usual effects of sunset, sad grey lines were streaking the already darkening sky. All around them, as they drove along (this was in pre-motor days when the road referred to was very little frequented), an utter silence reigned, a silence which they could feel, and which seemed to be merely intensified by the sharp clatter of their horse's hoofs and the low monotonous rumbling of their carriage wheels.

As the shadows of night were deepening, making the tall fir trees appear weirder and blacker every moment, a feeling of intense sadness and melancholy seemed to settle down upon everything and to add to the chilliness of the air, which was damp, too, after the recent heavy rains. Keeping to a fast trot they presently came to a part of the road which was made particularly dark and gloomy by the thick growth of trees and bushes on either side of it. Here the horse suddenly shied, all but unseating Mr. Ward, who was in the act of refilling his pipe, and then bolted. On and on it raced at such a breakneck speed that Mr. Ward was terrified, fearing that his uncle would lose control of it, and that a smash-up must come about sooner or later. However, when, in due course, they came to a clearing, and the moon, which had now risen, showed itself, between banks of slowly moving clouds, they were able to discern the cause of the animal's fright. Walking on the grass by the horse's side and keeping up easily with it, although it was going like the wind, was a tallish, bareheaded man. The moonlight falling full on his face made it appear deathly white, whilst, at the same time, it revealed a ghastly wound on one side of his head. On and on they went, rounding a bend in the road like a flash, the phantom man still keeping abreast of them; and it was not until they had covered some considerable distance that he stopped at a certain spot, close to a gate.

As soon as they had left the phantom behind, the horse slackened speed. Mr. Ward and his uncle then turned round and saw the man still standing by the gate, staring after them. They could see him very plainly in the moonlight, but, even as they looked, he gradually faded away and vanished. The following day Mr. Ward and his uncle related their experience to some friends in Barnet, and learned, for the first time, that the road upon which they had seen the apparition was well known to be haunted by the ghost of Mr. Danby.

Other ghosts that are alleged still to haunt the neighbourhood of Enfield Chase are those of Dick Turpin and the Witch of Edmonton. Mr. Mott, the grandfather of Dick Turpin, lived only a few miles from Enfield Chase and Finchley Common, both of which places witnessed some of Turpin's most daring exploits.

Mr. Mott kept "The Rose and Crown," a public-house, near the brook called "Bull Beggar's Hole" at Clay Hill, and Turpin is said to have frequently stayed there, and to have hidden, when hard pressed by the king's officers, in Camlet Moat, then a very wild and lonely spot.

According to rumour, his ghost not only haunts the moat, the nearest roads to it, and Finchley Common, but South Mimms and Hounslow, as well. Sometimes his apparition is seen, clad in three-cornered hat, riding coat and high boots, hiding, white-faced and glassy-eyed, behind a tree; and sometimes, chiefly on wild and stormy nights, it is to be encountered tearing along the high roads or across the fields on a huge black phantom horse, said to be the ghost of the renowned " Black Bess."

The Witch of Edmonton, who figures in the drama written by Ford and Dekker, was a real character. She lived near the Chase, some say in it, and, owing to gaining great notoriety for witchcraft, was ultimately burnt as a witch in 1622.

Her ghost is stated to be occasionally seen prowling about the site of the old moat and the more lonely parts of the adjoining roads. It is just a shadowy female figure in black, the figure, apparently, of a very old woman, who moves along, slowly and painfully, giving one the impression that but for her stick, upon which she leans heavily, she could not progress at all.

It has been remarked that there is no haunted house in the parish of Enfield,[1] but, according to Mr. J. Westfield,[2] there certainly was one, not so very long ago, in Enfield Chase. It was a very old house, he says, much beaten by wind and weather, standing in a very lonely spot, close to the Chase. Nearly the whole of the Chase, by the way, is now entirely enclosed, and but little of its original wildness remains. What wildness there is left is to be seen at Hadley Common, White Webbs Park, Winchmore Hill Wood and Trent Park. Formerly, it was an extensive tract of country, covered with trees, which afforded excellent cover to game, but it is now all cut up and most of it is built upon.

[1] See *Greater London*, vol. i. p. 369.
[2] See *Notes and Queries*, April 5, 1873.

Referring to the house he affirms to have been haunted, Mr. Westwood says :

"It was inhabited, when I knew it, by two elderly people, maiden sisters, with whom I had some acquaintance, and who once invited me to dine with them. I well remember my walk thither. It led me up a steep ascent of oak avenue, opening out at the top on what was called the 'ridge-road' of the Chase.

"It was the close of a splendid autumn afternoon ; through the mossy boles of the great oak I saw

> ...' *The golden autumn woodland red*
> *Athwart the smoke of burning flowers.*'

The year was dying with more than its wonted pomp, wrapping itself in its gorgeous robes, like a grander Cæsar. On reaching my destination," Mr. Westwood goes on to say, "the sun had already dipped below the horizon, and the eastern porch of the house projected a black shadow at its foot. What was there in the aspect of the pile that reminded me of the copse described by the poet?—the copse that

> ' *Was calm and cold, as it did hold*
> *Some secret, glorying.*'

I crossed the threshold with repugnance."

Mr. Westwood was now to experience phenomena which have their parallel in other cases I have referred to in this and other volumes ; they are not uncommon, but, on that account, are none the less peculiarly alarming. Having to change for dinner, he was shown at once to his bedroom, where no sooner had the servant left him than he became conscious of a strange noise close to him.

It was a curious blending of shudder and sigh that suggested infinite fear. Supposing it must be due to the wind in the chimney or a draught from the door, which was ajar, Mr. Westwood began his toilet. In a few minutes he again heard this strange mixture of shudder and sigh just behind him; and wherever he went in the room he was conscious of a presence accompanying him and emitting, so it seemed to him, every few seconds the aforesaid somewhat distressing sound. Soon it got on his nerves, and feeling frightened, he dressed hastily and left the room. The presence, however, went with him, and on the landing and the stairs he heard the sound that was so perturbing, so indicative of unlimited dread. "Surely," he said to himself, "it won't follow me into the dining-room," but he was mistaken. Neither the bright light, nor the people, nor their cheerful conversation rid him of the ghostly sound that haunted him. Every now and again he heard it close behind him, and once he felt sure that the same eerie presence, that had so persistently followed him, was sharing the same chair with him.

This very unpleasant sensation lasted all through the meal and afterwards in the drawing-room; and it was not until he had said good-night to his hostess and stepped out into the darkness of the night that he was freed from it.

When Mr. Westwood next met the two maiden ladies, he told them what had occurred, and instead of finding them incredulous, as he half-expected he should, they told him that they and other people had often heard the sound he described, and had been followed all over the house by it, in just the same manner. They could give no explanation of the phenomenon. It was always the same, just a sound, they explained, nothing ghostly was ever seen.

"Perhaps so," Mr. Westwood remarks, "but of what strange horror, not ended with life, but perpetuated in the limbo of invisible things, was that sound the exponent?"

I have already referred to South Mimms as being, no less than Enfield Chase, associated with the notorious Dick Turpin; and like Enfield Chase it not infrequently figures in the Press in connection with rumoured hauntings. Presumably it is styled South Mimms to distinguish it from its neighbour North Mimms. The word Mimms has been variously spelt in the past Mims, Mymes and Mymmes.

According to a tradition, how far true I have been unable to ascertain, a lady was murdered either in the church, dedicated to St. Giles, or in the adjoining vicarage, by Cromwell's soldiers, since which time a ghost is said to have haunted the churchyard and its immediate environments. Intermittently, that is to say, at long intervals, it is said to appear in the guise of a woman in white, but, in spite of many inquiries in South Mimms, I have not come across anyone who can say definitely that he has seen it. I have, however, met one or two people who can testify to having seen what they believed to be ghost lights, hovering over a tomb in the old churchyard. The phenomena occurred, they said, immediately after the tomb had been opened for a burial, the lights having been seen by them on several consecutive nights after the burial had taken place.

According to tradition, the ghost of Dick Turpin

haunts the old Roman Road, at a spot locally known as the Wash, and possibly the reason is not far to seek, since the famous highwayman, in his lifetime, frequented this neighbourhood more often, perhaps, than any other.

The Wash is a lonely strip of low-lying, swampy ground, with a certain eeriness about it, after dusk, which I myself have experienced ; and there is a story to the effect that not long ago a man crossing the Wash bridge saw a strange figure, something like a man but not a man, and something like an animal and yet not an animal, rise from the ground, leap high over the bridge, with a gigantic spring, and disappear in the mist-covered ground beneath. There was something so grotesque and monstrous about the figure that the man who saw it was terrified and took to his heels.

Last autumn interest in South Mimms was revived by the discovery in a field, near the village, of the body of an aged tramp. It was generally believed, and still is believed by some people, that he had been murdered, but medical testimony declared that he had died of fatty degeneration of the heart. It was subsequently rumoured that the spot where he was found was haunted by ghostly lights and the shadowy figure of a man minus his head.

This tramp is not the only person who has been found dead, in a field, at South Mimms, under mysterious circumstances. As far back as 1861 the body of a woman was discovered in a ditch, in a field, close to the village.[1] She was identified as a woman who had been missing for some months. A party of women had been at work haymaking in the field where her

[1] *News of the World*, March 10, 1861.

body was found, and she had been one of them. No one, it seems, noticed her absence at the time, and it was not until her fellow-workers had dispersed to their various homes that she was found to be missing. The whole neighbourhood was then searched, but without success, and nothing was seen or heard of her, till her remains were found in the aforesaid ditch the following March. The body being very much decomposed, the exact cause of death could not be ascertained; consequently, an open verdict was returned; but it was generally thought that she was the victim of foul play. The spot where she was found, subsequently, got the reputation for being haunted and was shunned in consequence. It would seem from these two cases that there is something in the immediate vicinity of South Mimms conducive to happenings of this nature.

Cheshunt is not very far from South Mimms and, according to Mr. W. Howitt,[1] it boasted, during his lifetime, a very notoriously haunted house. Mrs. Crowe refers to it, but does not give its exact locality. She merely places it "in the neighbourhood of the Metropolis."

Mr. Howitt, however, could have had no great difficulty in identifying it, since it seems to have been termed the "Haunted House" by those residing in its neighbourhood. I do not know whether anything now remains of this haunted house; all I can say is that it stood intact not many years ago. In appearance it was very arrestive, a long, low, rambling structure, standing in grounds, which were once very extensive. The account given by Mr. and Mrs. Charles Kean, the famous stage stars, to both Mrs. Crowe and Mr.

[1] See *History of the Supernatural*.

Howitt of what befell Mr. Chapman (Mr. Kean's brother-in-law) during his occupancy of the house, being somewhat drawn out, I will append it here, slightly abridged, but otherwise not materially altered.[1]

The Chapmans, the Keans observe, had bought the seven years' lease of the house at so low a figure that one wonders why their suspicions were not aroused, but being young they had, doubtless, had very little experience of houses. For some time after they took over the premises all went well, and they were congratulating themselves on their purchase when the totally unexpected happened. Mrs. Chapman, going into a room they had named the Oak Room, one evening, saw a girl, a complete stranger to her, leaning against the window, and gazing anxiously out, as if expecting someone to arrive. The girl was young; she had dark hair hanging loosely about her neck and shoulders, and appeared to be only partly dressed, as she was wearing a short white bodice and silk petticoat. Wondering if she were the victim of a hallucination, Mrs. Chapman closed her eyes, and when she opened them again, the strange girl had vanished. This was the first intimation that the Chapmans had that the house was haunted.

Shortly after this incident, the nursemaid, a dependable girl, when passing by the lobby that led to an enclosed courtyard, saw a hideous white face peering in at her. The owner of the face was an old woman, and she was clad in the fashion of a bygone period. The maid was so frightened that she ran at once to Mrs. Chapman, and, trembling all over, told her what had happened. Mrs. Chapman went into

[1] See *The Night Side of Nature*, by Catherine Crowe.

the courtyard, the outer gate of which was locked, and searched everywhere, but there was no trace of the old woman the nurserymaid had seen.

The next thing that happened was that the family were disturbed at night by all kinds of unaccountable noises. Sometimes they would be roused from their sleep by the sound of pumping in the courtyard (this would happen when it was ascertained that everyone was in bed), and sometimes, in the dead of night, they would hear crashes and footsteps. Also, in the daytime, once, ghostly footsteps followed a servant to the fireplace in the oak room. Naturally, thinking, at first, that they were those of a fellow-servant, the maid, whom the footsteps had followed, looked round, and upon seeing no one, was almost frightened out of her wits. These same footsteps, it seems, approached Mrs. Chapman's bedroom one night, and as they halted outside it, Mrs. Chapman, summoning up all her courage, opened the door and looked out, but no one was there, and she saw only the moonbeams and shadows. Again, when the Chapmans were seated in the drawing-room with the door shut, it frequently happened that they would hear the door handle turned and see the door open; and, although they never saw anyone enter, they always felt, on these occasions, that something did come in, and that it stood by, watching them.

One night, the servant who had been followed by the footsteps had a strange dream. She was sleeping at the time in Mrs. Chapman's room, so that she, Mrs. Chapman, should not be nervous during Mr. Chapman's temporary absence from home. To proceed: this servant, in her dream, thought she was in the oak room and that, suddenly, she saw there a girl, with long dark hair, standing opposite a dreadful-looking old hag. Both wore costumes in accordance with the fashion of more than a century ago. The old woman, after gazing intently at the girl with the long, dark hair, exclaimed, " What have you done with the child, Emily ? What have you done with the child ? " To which the girl replied, " Oh, I did not kill it. He was preserved, and grew up, and joined the —— Regiment, and went to India." Then, turning to the dreamer, she said :

" I have never spoken to mortal before ; but I will tell you all. My name is Miss Black, and this old woman is Nurse Black. Black is not her name, but we call her Black, because she has been so long in the family."

After a short pause the girl was about to go on, when the old hag came up to the dreamer, and placing a hand on her shoulder, said something that the dreamer could not catch. Moreover, the impact of the hand had produced so sharp a pain in the dreamer's shoulder that she awoke.

In the morning the servant related her dream to Mrs. Chapman, and the latter, upon realizing that the girl her servant had seen in the dream closely resembled the phantom girl she, herself, had seen in the oak room, and the old hag, the hideous woman the nursemaid had seen peering in at the lobby, came to the conclusion that the dream was no ordinary dream, but one due to some superphysical agency. Consequently, she made inquiries in the neighbourhood and learned that, about seventy or eighty years previously, a Mrs. Ravenhall and her niece, Miss Black, had lived in the house. From this Mrs. Chapman concluded that Miss Black and the phantom girl with the long, dark hair, were one and the same.

More, however, she could not discover. Some time after this affair of the dream, Mrs. Chapman again saw the ghost girl in the oak room. She was staring into one corner of it, with an agonized expression, and wringing her hands.

Mrs. Chapman had the boards of the floor in that corner of the room taken up, but nothing was found underneath them. The last phenomenon that occurred while the Chapmans were in the house seemed to have no connection with any of the other phenomena. They were preparing to quit the place, although their lease had only run for three years, when Mrs. Chapman awoke one morning to see a dark-complexioned man, in a fustian coat, with a comforter or scarf tied negligently round his neck, standing at the foot of the bed. He vanished as mysteriously and inexplicably as he had come.

A few days afterwards Mrs. Chapman asked her husband to order some coal, as their supply had almost run out. This he promised to do. In due course, apparently, the coal arrived, whereupon Mr. Chapman expressed astonishment, as he had quite forgotten to order any. This seemed very remarkable, and Mrs. Chapman asked the servants if they had given the order; but one and all denied having done so; moreover, not one of them, they affirmed, had seen the coal delivered. Mrs. Chapman, getting more and more mystified, now inquired of the person from whom they usually had coal, and he declared it had been ordered by a dark-complexioned man in a fustian jacket and red comforter. It was exactly thus, it will be remembered, that Mrs. Chapman had described the man who had appeared and mysteriously disappeared at the foot of her bed.

After this, the Chapmans were by no means sorry to leave the house. Subsequent tenants, it was ascertained, experienced similar annoyances, but they, no less than the Chapmans, were totally unable to account for them, save on the basis of the superphysical. It should be noted that the case rests on the corroborative evidence of several people, none of whom claimed to be mediumistic, or, so far as is known, had ever attended a spiritualistic séance, for which reason they were the more dependable, or, in other words, not so likely to be biassed and credulous. The case, too, as a whole, affords yet another example of what so many *bona-fide* hauntings are : just a series of phenomena, without any apparent reason, unless, maybe, it is to demonstrate to us that there really does exist a something that is quite apart from, though yet able, if it so wishes, to get in touch with our material, sometimes so painfully material, world.

Many strange tales have been told relating to old Richmond Palace, where many English monarchs lived and several died. One of the several who died there was Queen Elizabeth, concerning whose death Miss Strickland, in her interesting history, narrates the following :

" As her mortal illness drew towards a close, the superstitious fears of her simple ladies were excited almost to a mania, even to conjuring up a spectral apparition of the Queen while she was yet alive. Lady Guilford, who was then in waiting on the Queen, leaving her in an almost breathless sleep in her privy chamber, went out to take a little air, and met her Majesty, as she thought, three or four chambers off. Alarmed at the thought of being discovered in the act of leaving the royal patient alone, she hurried forward in some trepidation, in order to excuse herself, when the apparition vanished away. She returned terrified to the chamber, but there lay the Queen in the same lethargic slumber in which she left her."

Having regard to their authenticity, less reliable, perhaps, than Miss Strickland's, are many of the stories and traditions that relate to the Palace, to the old Gatehouse, and to the Mound, called Oliver's Mound, where, in 1834,[1] some workmen, when digging, found the skeletons of three people, buried about three feet beneath the surface. Passing by the Gatehouse one night a tradesman is said to have seen two men in armour fighting furiously. Amazed at the spectacle, he was standing still watching them, when a man, very richly clad in clothes of a bygone fashion, came striding up to them, dagger in hand, and stabbed one of the combatants to the heart.

As the wretched man fell without a sound to the ground, the figures all disappeared, and the tradesman found himself merely staring into space.

This story was told me many years ago by Mr. Green, an artist, who was very interested in archaeology. He said he had read it in a collection of stories about old London buildings, purporting to be true, and published about the middle of last century.

Another story he told me of the old Richmond Palace ghosts was this :

One evening a man and his son, who were engaged

[1] See *Abbeys, Castles and Ancient Halls of England and Wales.*

in repairs at the Palace, were leaving it after their day's work, to go home, when a tall, gaunt woman in black emerged from behind a tree and proceeded ahead of them. She was carrying a sack over her shoulders, with something so heavy in it that she staggered. The workman and boy were regarding her with no little curiosity, as there was something unusual in her appearance, when, to their horror, a hand suddenly emerged from a hole in the side of the sack nearest them. It was a large, coarse hand, and the thumb was missing. The mutilated state of the flesh suggested that it had been hacked or torn off. The man and boy tried to run after the woman to stop her, but their limbs refused to move any faster, and when they tried to call out, they found that they could not, that they were completely tongue-tied. In this state they were compelled to follow this strange woman, who never varied her pace and always kept the same distance ahead of them. On and on they went, right through the Palace grounds till they came to Oliver's Mound, when both the man and the boy felt a slight, though sharp, blow dealt them on the shoulder. Both turned round quickly and simultaneously to see who or what had struck them, and, to their amazement, saw no one and nothing. Facing round again, they then looked for the woman, but she was nowhere to be seen, she had vanished. A few moments later, while they were still looking around, wondering where she could have gone, they heard a series of wild, unearthly shrieks, followed by a succession of ghastly groans and gasps, that seemed to indicate, only too plainly, that someone was being done to death. The man and boy did not stop to investigate, they left the

Mound and made for home at something like a record speed.

The unearthing of the skeletons in the vicinity of the Mound had some connection, so Mr. Green and others thought, both with the phenomenon experienced by the tradesman, as he passed by the old Gatehouse, and the phenomena experienced by the man and boy as they walked through the Palace grounds, passing by the Mound, on their way home from work.

In the grounds of the Palace, too, there is a little hillock on which, it is stated, Henry VIII stood, waiting to see the signal given—a rocket sent up from the Tower of London—to apprise him that, in due compliance with his order, Anne Boleyn was beheaded. According to Mr. Green, his ghost may still be seen, occasionally, standing on the hillock, with its white bloated face, a mass of exultation, and its gaze fixed gleefully in the direction of the Tower.

ADDENDUM

To the list I have already compiled, of ghosts that have haunted, and, in some instances, still haunt the Tower of London, I must add one other, namely, the ghost of Sir Walter Raleigh. My authority for this haunting is Mr. Timbs (see his *Romance of London*), who asserts that it is in the Prison House that this ghost usually appears.

With regard to the phantom bear haunting at the Tower, according to a correspondent to *Notes and Queries* (2nd Series, No. 245), before the partial destruction of the Armouries by fire, there was a paved yard in front of the Jewel House, and, opening on to it, a gloomy doorway, leading down a flight of ghostly-looking steps to the Mint. Strange and alarming noises had been heard, repeatedly at night, on these steps, and the unfortunate sentry, whose story I have told elsewhere in this volume, heard them just before the ghost appeared to him. Mr. George Offor, who was present at the burial of the sentry, asserts that the ghost did not come up the steps, but crossed the paved yard and disappeared down the steps. Be this as it may, though I prefer Mr. Swifte's version of the occurrence, as he got it from the sentry himself, both authorities agree that the sentry died from the effects of shock, the shock he had sustained upon encountering a denizen of the Unknown.

Referring to the house in Berkeley Square, I would

remark that, according to a certain lady (a lady of title whose name my authority withholds), the police were sceptical with regard to the alleged haunting and believed that, instead of being haunted by a ghost, the house was the haunt of coiners, who carried on their illicit trade there, with such secrecy that, so far as is generally known, they were never caught.

According to a widespread story, which was in everyone's mouth in my childhood, certain owners or tenants of the house who had lived in it for some time without experiencing anything unusual in connection with it, suddenly discovered that a particular room in the house was badly haunted. The discovery came about thus :

A young army officer, the fiancé of one of the daughters of the house, was coming to stay with the family, on a visit, and at a late hour the night before his expected arrival, the whole household was startled by the screams of the housemaid, who was in the visitor's room, preparing it for his reception. On rushing into the guest's chamber, they found her, lying on the bed, in convulsions, her wide-open eyes fixed with an awful expression of terror on one corner of the room.

Restoratives not having any effect, she was conveyed at once to St. George's Hospital, where she died the following morning, without giving anyone the remotest idea of what had frightened her. All she could or would say was that she had seen something too horrible for words to describe.

Upon the arrival of the young officer at the house in Berkeley Square, that same day, the family told him what had occurred, and as the room originally

ADDENDUM

prepared for him was, they said, undoubtedly haunted, they had prepared another room for him to occupy. The visitor, however, much to everyone's concern, insisted on being allowed to sleep in the haunted room, and it was in vain that his betrothed and the rest of the family sought to turn him from his purpose. Ghosts were all tosh, he said, and he would prove it. Finally, it was agreed that he should sleep in the room, on these conditions: that when the fatal hour, midnight, arrived (when, presumably, the horror appeared, as it was at twelve o'clock, exactly, that the housemaid had screamed), he would ring the bell, once, if all was well, and twice, if help was needed.

When bedtime arrived he retired to his room, while the family, unknown to him, determined to sit up all night in the hall, in order to be on the spot, at a moment's notice, should their help be needed. As midnight approached, they listened eagerly. At last the clock on the staircase struck, and ere the echoes of the last stroke had died away, the bell in the haunted chamber rang, once, feebly. Then, after a brief interval, it gave a tremendous peal, and, a moment later, there was a loud report. Terrified to the last degree, everyone rushed upstairs to the haunted chamber, where they found the young officer, sitting bolt upright in bed, propped against the pillow, and by his side a still smoking revolver. According to one version of the story, he was dead, but according to another, he was merely in a dead faint, and, on recovery, refused to describe what he had seen, declaring that he could not, it was too dreadful.

In both versions, however, it is stated that the family left the house within a few days.

Bulwer Lytton is said to have had this house in mind when he wrote "The Haunted and the Haunters," a story which appeared in *Blackwood's Magazine*, August, 1859.

Another well-known story of this particular haunting, which gained a certain amount of credence at the time of its circulation, is to this effect:

The house being to let furnished was taken by a newly-married couple. They were still abroad, on their honeymoon, when their lease of the house commenced; and the wife's mother, upon hearing the date of their return, went to the house to see that all was in readiness for them. Feeling tired after a long journey, on the day of her arrival, she went to bed early. The servants retired at the usual time, and at midnight were awakened by an appalling scream, which, after a brief interval of silence, was repeated. Almost too terrified to move, they at last summoned up the courage to go to the room whence the appalling sounds proceeded, and there they found their future mistress's mother lying on the bed, quite dead. Moreover, the expression in her wide-open eyes was one of such undiluted horror that, panic-stricken, they fled out of the house in a body.

The house afterwards was empty for months.

Another authentic story of this haunting, briefly told, is this. A man, who was very sceptical about ghosts, having obtained permission to spend a night in the house, went there alone, or, rather, accompanied only by his dog. Both were found, in the morning, in the notorious haunted room—dead.

These are but a few of the many stories told and vouched for of the famous house in Berkeley Square,

ADDENDUM

and although one cannot guarantee those responsible for them to be entirely trustworthy, in my opinion, these stories rest, at least, upon a very substantial stratum of truth.

By some strange lapse I left out Drury Lane in my list of haunted theatres. According to a story [1] told some years ago at a charity luncheon, at Chatham, by Mr. Stanley Lupino, Drury Lane Theatre is haunted by the ghost of that great comedian Dan Leno. One night, after the show at Drury Lane, Mr. Lupino was lying on the couch in his dressing-room, intending to sleep there, as it was so late, instead of going home, when he distinctly felt someone was in the room besides himself. He then heard a noise, as if a curtain were being drawn aside, and getting up, saw a shadowy figure cross the room and disappear through the door. Greatly astonished, he asked the night watchman if he had seen anyone leave his, Mr. Lupino's room, but the night watchman had seen no one.

Back in his room, Mr. Lupino got the fright of his life. Hearing a noise beside him, he looked up from his couch, right into the white face of Dan Leno's ghost. He was so scared that he sprang up and ran, helter-skelter, out of the theatre to the Globe Hotel.

Someone who stayed in the same dressing-room, the following night, also saw poor Leno's phantasm. This person, not quite so shock-proof as Lupino, promptly fainted.

Sadler's Wells Theatre, so I have always understood, was said to be haunted by the ghost of Joe Grimaldi, and after the theatre had fallen into disuse, it was still to be seen there in one of the boxes.

---

[1] See *Reynold's Illustrated News*, October 28, 1923.

A box at Drury Lane Theatre was also long rumoured to be haunted by the ghost of the same individual. Its white, painted face, it was stated, had been seen behind the material occupants of the box; and over their shoulders it would peer at the stage, fixing its eyes, always, on one or other of the performers.

Joe Grimaldi, probably the most renowned of all the clowns that have ever performed on an English stage, was the son of a Genoese clown and dancer, who was also a dentist, such a combination of professions being surely one of the strangest on record. Grimaldi senior, known, on account of his extraordinary strength, as "Iron Legs," performed at Drury Lane when David Garrick was its manager. He was a firm believer in the superphysical, and used to visit alleged haunted houses and places, hoping that he might be so lucky as to see the ghost. It was his love of the weird that led him to invent the Skeleton Scene and the Cave of Petrifaction, in pantomime, both of which deservedly gained great popularity. He had a perpetual dread of being buried alive, and ordained in his will that after the doctor had pronounced him dead, his daughter should cut off his head, "to make sure he was not alive." We are glad to say that the daughter did not carry out her father's wishes to the letter; instead of performing the desired operation herself, she deputed someone else to do it in her presence; and that surely was as much as, if not more than, could be expected of any ordinary human.

Joe Grimaldi also appears to have been interested in things weird and ghostly, but not, perhaps, to quite the same extent. He was born in Stanhope Street,

Clare Market, December 18, 1778, and made his first appearance at Sadler's Wells before he was three years old. That his ghost should have haunted the theatre at which he made his début at this very early age, and with which he was subsequently associated for so many years, is not to be wondered at, since he must have conceived a very strong affection for it, and, as I have frequently remarked, every haunting is rooted in and traceable to a very strong emotion of some sort or another. It is more difficult to find a reason for Grimaldi's appearances, in ghostly form, at Drury Lane; indeed, I have always inclined to the belief that the ghost which occasionally manifested there was either that of Grimaldi senior or some clown of lesser note.

Apropos of the ghost stories told me by tramps whom I have met and talked with in the parks and commons at night, I would remark that those who have a real knowledge of the tramp fraternity will bear me out when I say that no class of people, as a whole, are more prone to superstition, and that those vagrants who are accustomed to tramping the country roads are the most superstitious of all. One seldom, for instance, finds a tramp sleeping in the immediate proximity of a churchyard or any house or place that is said to be haunted. Some sensation was caused in Eastry, Kent, a few years ago,[1] by a rumour generated by tramps that the vagrant ward at the local Poor Law Institution (in other words the Workhouse) was haunted. There had been a marked decrease in the number of vagrants applying for admission, and the apparent reason for this was eventually discovered.

[1] Reported at the time in the Press.

A middle-aged tramp, who was the only occupant of the vagrant ward, aroused the workhouse staff one night by his cries. On running into the ward, to see what was the matter, they discovered him sitting up in bed, trembling all over and ghastly pale. He declared he had been awakened by strange, unearthly noises in the room and had seen a ghost. He said he knew the workhouse was haunted, as tramps he had met on the road had told him so. Finding it impossible to calm him, the authorities were obliged to put him in another ward; but it took him several days to recover from his alarm.

A ghost I omitted to mention, when dealing with hauntings in greater London, is that of Lady Frederick Campbell.

In 1807 there was a fire in Coombe Bank House, Sundridge, Kent, and in it Lady Frederick Campbell perished, but whether it is for this reason or some other that she haunts, it is impossible to say. She certainly suffered a tragic and untimely death, but equally certain is it that tragic occurrences marred her life. Before her marriage to Lord Frederick Campbell, the owner of the Coombe Bank Estate, she was the widow of the notorious fourth Earl Ferrers, who was hanged at Tyburn, in 1760, for the murder of his steward; and as it was largely due to her testimony that he was convicted, he was so incensed against her that he cursed her, declaring that her end would be a much more painful one than his own. It is strange that, seemingly, this curse was fulfilled, and its being thus fulfilled makes one wonder whether it might not be owing to the curse that Lady Frederick is still earth-bound (according to repute), and still periodically haunting

ADDENDUM 275

the countryside, on and around the Coombe Bank Estate.

This concludes my list of hauntings in the present volume. It has been remarked by reviewers of some of my books that I do not explain the phenomena; but how can I? How can anyone explain phenomena that the most eminent scientists fail to explain by any known physical laws. Were I able to prove the origin of and *raison d'être* or, if you prefer it, give the correct explanation of all the genuine phenomena I have met with in my investigations of hauntings, I should surely be able to explain that seemingly insoluble mystery, the origin of Life and Creation, a mystery that is more likely than not to remain a mystery, since one can hardly imagine brains in the future being more brilliant than the brains of to-day, which it has baffled.

A certain sort of haunting, however, may, I think, be accounted for some day by physical laws, about which, at the present time, we know absolutely nothing. The haunting to which I refer is automatic, that is to say, the ghost which does the same thing, night after night, and does it in the same place, and at the same hour, without any apparent variation. Hence, it seems possible that such phenomena may be due to impressions that were once made in the ether by very strong mental and physical actions, these impressions being subsequently rendered visible and auditory by certain atmospheric conditions, at present unknown to us. Thus, I think, not only the purely mechanical actions of some ghosts but their failure to respond when we attempt to communicate with them may be accounted for. These ghosts, in fact, can no more respond to our addresses than can the shadows of trees and of other material objects, or pictures at the cinema, or televisions, which latter, if science had not taught us otherwise, might well be attributed to the supernatural.

Other species of seeming ghostly phenomena that may, at some future date, be accounted for by natural laws are projections or phantoms of the living, such for example as that of Dr. Wynn Westcott at the British Museum. Mental concentrations would seem capable of producing visualized forms, not only in the likeness of the person concentrating, but in the likeness of whatever he may be concentrating on. In some cases it would seem, not unlikely, that the phantasms seen, especially when they are seen by only one person, are not objective at all but subjective, being mere mental visions, due to telepathic communication between one forceful mind and one that is responsive; and I would like, here, to remind my readers that this faculty of concentration, which is a gift no less than second sight, is not the sole prerogative of humans; animals possess it too, for, as every student of occultism knows, hauntings by animal phenomena are just as common as those by phenomena in human shape. This theory of telepathy, as I have just remarked, may very possibly account for phenomena experienced by one person singly, and possibly —though in this case the theory would seem less feasible—it might account for phenomena experienced, simultaneously, by more than one person. If one mind is sensitive to and capable of receiving a telepathic communication, it is conceivable two or even more minds might be equally sensitive and capable of

ADDENDUM

receiving, simultaneously, such communications. On the other hand, if the phenomena are not experienced collectively, the probability of them being due to telepathic communication substantially lessens, as it is difficult in the case of only one person seeing the " ghost " to eradicate the possibility of suggestion, imagination and invention.

Apart from automatic ghosts, projections, telepathically induced phenomena and thought forms, there are other kinds of hauntings to be accounted for. Hauntings, in which the ghost performs such purely physical actions as opening and shutting doors, moving furniture and removing bed-clothes, can scarcely be explained by the theory that they are impressions in the ether, though possibly, in some instances, they might be accounted for by the theory of projection.

However, it has not yet been established on anything like a satisfactory scientific basis that mental force alone can accomplish purely physical actions; and until that has been decided, it is not possible to say, definitely, whether or not projections or phantasms of the living, which would seem to be entirely the products of intense mental concentration, can explain this type of haunting, *i.e.* the haunting characterized by physical actions. So that any theoretical explanation of this sort of haunting can only be speculative, and all we can confidently assert in discussing its origin is that it may be superphysical; but on the other hand it may not.

Another kind of haunting that defies analysis is the haunting by the Prophetic Ghost, such as the Banshee, the Drummer of Airlie, and the Gwrach y Rhibyn or Hag of the Dribble. Indeed, that these ghosts are anything but genuine ghosts, that is to say beings that exist entirely separate from this world, and entirely independent of it, is to my mind inconceivable. They are, I believe, just as much the result of Other World agency as the phenomena that appear to us in the likeness of those who have passed over, and show distinct signs of consciousness and intelligence. It may be found, perhaps, after skilled inquiry into evidence and a quite impartial sifting, that hauntings by genuine ghosts are few and far between; but no matter how many or how few they be, to those who, like myself, regard them as the surest proof of a Future Life, to know that even one exists is an untold blessing. Finally, if it ever should happen that the genuine ghost, contrary to all previous conceptions of the possible, is demonstrably proved to be subject to the natural laws of this physical world, belief in a Hereafter on our present plane will receive a crushing and even, so far as many people are concerned, conceivably a knock-out blow.

INDEX

Anne, Queen, 246
Aquarium ghost, The, 63
Argyll Rooms, The, 60

Barnes Common haunting, 199
Bear ghosts, 3, 239, 267
Bedlam ghost, 9
Bell hauntings, 210
Berkeley Square Mystery House, 26, 267
Bethnal Green ghost, 203
Bird hauntings, 133, 135
Blackfriars Bridge, 104, 121
Blackheath hauntings, 139
Bloomsbury ghost, 173
Boleyn, Anne, 5
Bridge hauntings, 120
British Museum ghosts, 47
Brompton Road haunting, 152
Brothers' Footsteps, The, 53
Bruton Street murder and haunting, 125
Buckingham Palace Road hauntings, 66
Buckstone's ghost, 156
Burton Crescent murders and hauntings, 45

Cavalier ghost, 65
Chelsea ghosts, 238
Cheshunt, 258
Chick Lane ghost, 129
Clock hauntings, 244, 246
Club hauntings, 165
Cock Lane ghost, 221
Coombe Bank, 274
Covent Garden ghost, 201
Cranford House, 162
Cripplegate crime and ghost, 217
Cumberland, Duke of, 18

de Beauclair, Madame, 15
de Mazarine, Duchesse, 15

Delphic Club, 171
Drury Lane hauntings, 156, 271

Ealing haunting, 138
Elizabeth's double, Queen, 263
Enfield Chase, 249

Fatal houses and places, 117
Field of the Brothers' Footsteps, 53

Gipsy Hill, 237
Great Coram Street murder and haunting, 46
Green Park, 23
Greyfriars ghosts, 76
Grimaldi, Joe, 271

Ham House, 157
Hampton Court Palace, 180
Haymarket Theatre, 157
Headless woman ghost, 20
Henry VIII's ghost, 266
Highbury, 108
Highgate, 187
Holland House, 116
Hospital of Star of Bethlehem haunting, 9
Hummums, The, 201
Hungerford, murderess, Alice, 77
Hyde Park ghosts, 88

Isabella's ghost, Queen, 76

Johnson's ghost story, Dr., 201

Kilburn Priory, 184

Lauderdale, Duchess of, 157
Lincoln's Inn, 69
London Bridge, 215
London Stone, 242
Lupino, Stanley, 271

Markham Square ghost, 241
Monument and its lure, The, 119
Morgans, murderesses, The, 125
Motley Club, The, 171

Newgate bell haunting, 82
Newquay ghost, 49

Old Charterhouse, 78
Oliver Cromwell and his ghost, 40, 159

Percival, Strange case of Robert, 70
Phantoms of Living, 47, 50
Piccadilly ghost, 34
Pig-face lady ghost of Chelsea, 241

Redcliffe Gardens haunting, 242
Redcliffe Square hauntings, 242
Red Lion Square haunting, 36
Rich and her double, Lady Diana, 117

Sadler's Wells, 271
St. Anne's Churchyard, 206
St. Bartholomew's in Smithfield, 79
St. James' Palace hauntings, 13
St. James' Park, Headless ghost of, 20
St. James' Street, 35

St. Paul's Cathedral, Strange 209
St. Swithin's Lane haunting, Serpentine, The, 90
Silward, Edward, 157
South Kensington, Haunted in, 194
South Mimms ghosts, 256
Spring-heeled Jack, 145
Stockwell ghosts, 235
Swifte, Lenthal, 1

Temple murders and hauntings, 72
Thames ghosts, 177
Tower of London hauntings, 1, 267
Turpin, Dick, 252

Upper Gloucester Place, 244

Wandsworth Common haunting, 235
Waterloo Bridge, 120
West Drayton Church, 137
Westminster, 65, 120
Whitehead Grove, 243
Wimbledon Common, 157
Woolwich Common, 57
Wynn Westcott, Dr. W., 47

www.ingramcontent.com/pod-product-compliance
Lightning Source LLC
Chambersburg PA
CBHW020833160426
43192CB00007B/625